HOSPITALITY SALES
and
ADVERTISING

Educational Institute Books

HOSPITALITY FOR SALE
C. DeWitt Coffman

UNIFORM SYSTEM OF ACCOUNTS AND EXPENSE
DICTIONARY FOR SMALL HOTELS, MOTELS, AND
MOTOR HOTELS
Fourth Edition

RESORT DEVELOPMENT AND MANAGEMENT
Second Edition
Chuck Y. Gee

PLANNING AND CONTROL FOR FOOD AND
BEVERAGE OPERATIONS
Third Edition
Jack D. Ninemeier

STRATEGIC MARKETING PLANNING IN THE
HOSPITALITY INDUSTRY: A BOOK OF READINGS
Edited by Robert L. Blomstrom

TRAINING FOR THE HOSPITALITY INDUSTRY
Second Edition
Lewis C. Forrest, Jr.

UNDERSTANDING HOSPITALITY LAW
Second Edition
Jack P. Jefferies

SUPERVISION IN THE HOSPITALITY INDUSTRY
Second Edition
Raphael R. Kavanaugh/Jack D. Ninemeier

SANITATION MANAGEMENT: STRATEGIES FOR
SUCCESS
Ronald F. Cichy

ENERGY AND WATER RESOURCE MANAGEMENT
Second Edition
Robert E. Aulbach

MANAGEMENT OF FOOD AND BEVERAGE
OPERATIONS
Second Edition
Jack D. Ninemeier

MANAGING FRONT OFFICE OPERATIONS
Second Edition
Charles E. Steadmon/Michael L. Kasavana

STRATEGIC HOTEL/MOTEL MARKETING
Revised Edition
Christopher W. L. Hart/David A. Troy

MANAGING SERVICE IN FOOD AND BEVERAGE
OPERATIONS
Anthony M. Rey/Ferdinand Wieland

THE LODGING AND FOOD SERVICE INDUSTRY
Second Edition
Gerald W. Lattin

SECURITY AND LOSS PREVENTION
MANAGEMENT
Raymond C. Ellis, Jr., & the Security Committee of AH&MA

HOSPITALITY INDUSTRY MANAGERIAL
ACCOUNTING
Second Edition
Raymond S. Schmidgall

PURCHASING FOR HOSPITALITY OPERATIONS
William B. Virts

THE ART AND SCIENCE OF HOSPITALITY
MANAGEMENT
Jerome J. Vallen/James R. Abbey

MANAGING COMPUTERS IN THE HOSPITALITY
INDUSTRY
Michael L. Kasavana/John J. Cahill

MANAGING HOSPITALITY ENGINEERING
SYSTEMS
Michael H. Redlin/David M. Stipanuk

UNDERSTANDING HOSPITALITY ACCOUNTING I
Second Edition
Raymond Cote

UNDERSTANDING HOSPITALITY ACCOUNTING II
Second Edition
Raymond Cote

MANAGING QUALITY SERVICES
Stephen J. Shriver

MANAGING CONVENTIONS AND GROUP
BUSINESS
Leonard H. Hoyle/David C. Dorf/Thomas J. A. Jones

HOSPITALITY SALES AND ADVERTISING
James R. Abbey

MANAGING HUMAN RESOURCES IN THE
HOSPITALITY INDUSTRY
David Wheelhouse

MANAGING HOUSEKEEPING OPERATIONS
Margaret M. Kappa/Aleta Nitschke/Patricia B. Schappert

CONVENTION SALES: A BOOK OF READINGS
Margaret Shaw

DIMENSIONS OF TOURISM
Joseph D. Fridgen

HOSPITALITY TODAY: AN INTRODUCTION
Rocco M. Angelo/Andrew N. Vladimir

MANAGING BAR AND BEVERAGE OPERATIONS
Lendal H. Kotschevar/Mary L. Tanke

POWERHOUSE CONFERENCES: ELIMINATING
AUDIENCE BOREDOM
Coleman Lee Finkel

HOSPITALITY
MANAGEMENT
LIBRARY

Sales

James R. Abbey

Disclaimer

This publication is designed to provide accurate and authoritative information in regard to the subject matter covered. It is sold with the understanding that the publisher is not engaged in rendering legal, accounting, or other professional service. If legal advice or other expert assistance is required, the services of a competent professional person should be sought.

—From the Declaration of Principles jointly adopted by the American Bar Association and a Committee of Publishers and Associations.

The author, James R. Abbey, is solely responsible for the contents of this publication. All views expressed herein are solely those of the author and do not necessarily reflect the views of the Educational Institute of the American Hotel & Motel Association (the Institute) or the American Hotel & Motel Association (AH&MA).

Nothing contained in this publication shall constitute a standard, an endorsement, or a recommendation of the Institute or AH&MA. The Institute and AH&MA disclaim any liability with respect to the use of any information, procedure, or product, or reliance thereon by any member of the hospitality industry.

©Copyright 1989
By the EDUCATIONAL INSTITUTE of the
AMERICAN HOTEL & MOTEL ASSOCIATION
1407 South Harrison Road
P.O. Box 1240
East Lansing, Michigan 48826

Printed in the United States of America
    4 5 6 7 8 9 10 93 92 91

Library of Congress Cataloging-in-Publication Data
Abbey, James R.
    Hospitality sales and advertising.

    Includes bibliographies and index.
    1. Hospitality industry—Marketing.   2. Advertising—
Hospitality industry.   I. American Hotel & Motel
Association.   Educational Institute.   II. Title.
TX911.3.M3A23 1989   647'.94'0688   89-1265
ISBN 0-86612-048-3

Editor: Jim Purvis

Contents

About the Author

Dr. James R. Abbey is a professor at the University of Nevada, Las Vegas, where he teaches hotel marketing and management. He also serves as educational consultant to the Society of Company Meeting Planners, is a co-chair of the Educational Committee of the Hotel Sales & Marketing Association International, and is a principal with University Associates, Inc., a consulting group to the hospitality industry. In addition to his academic and consulting activities, he has executive experience with clubs, restaurants, and hotels.

James R. Abbey

The author has been a guest speaker at prominent industry conferences and has won awards from the Travel Research Association of America, the National Institute of Foodservice Instructors, and the Statler Foundation. He is a graduate of Michigan State University's School of Hotel, Restaurant & Institutional Management, and holds a master's degree in finance and a Ph.D. in tourism from Utah State University.

Dr. Abbey is co-author of *The Art and Science of Hospitality Management* and *Convention Sales and Services*. In addition, he has written many articles for the hospitality industry.

Preface

The basic function of marketing, sales, advertising, and promotion is to find and retain guests so as to maintain a profitable level of business. In this age of new construction and investment, modernization, consolidation and mergers, automation, and growing competition, the name of the game in the hospitality industry is to "wear out the carpet"—that is, bring in the business.

In large hotels, there is generally a full-time, organized marketing and sales division or department; midsize properties may have a marketing and sales department or a sales office; in small properties, marketing and sales may be one of the many duties of the general manager. Regardless of the property's size, a continuous sales effort is required to obtain guests for guestrooms, dining rooms, lounges, and meeting space. Sales must never be considered the sole responsibility of a single individual; sales is an important part of every employee's job. Knowledge and application of the sales and advertising fundamentals presented in this text can benefit the reader professionally as well as help boost a hotel's profits.

Each chapter of *Hospitality Sales and Advertising* contains profiles of sales and advertising personnel from hotel firms across the country. Photographs, sample forms, and effective advertising pieces were provided by several companies whose contributions have greatly increased the educational value of the text. Each chapter also provides an outline and discussion questions to facilitate understanding.

This book is divided into four parts. Part I begins with an introduction to hospitality sales, then discusses marketing plans and examines the organization of a sales office in small, midsize, and large properties. Part II, Sales Techniques, explores personal, telephone, and internal sales, and promotion of on-site revenue centers such as restaurants, lounges, banquet facilities, and meeting rooms. In Part III—Advertising, Public Relations, and Publicity— we look at advertising media and review guidelines for writing and producing advertising that sells. Part IV, Selling to Market Segments, discusses some of the major market segments (both group and individual) and how to reach them.

In writing a textbook, an author normally starts out with a strong idea of what the book should be like. However, before the manuscript is published, there are a number of suggestions made by students, colleagues, friends, editors, and industry professionals which contribute to the author's original idea and improve the book. I particularly want to acknowledge the helpful comments and suggestions of Tom McCarthy, Paul Wise, Jim Peckrul, Michael Holt, Ed Sansovini, and my editor, Jim Purvis. To these and others not specifically mentioned, I am most grateful.

James R. Abbey
Las Vegas, Nevada

Part I

Introduction

Chapter Outline

I. Today's Hospitality Trends
  A. Computers
  B. Distribution Methods
  C. Media Planning
  D. Overbuilding
  E. Competition
  F. Guest Preferences
  G. Product Segmentation
    1. Tier Marketing
    2. Hotels Within Hotels
    3. All-Suite Hotels
  H. A Changing Industry
II. The Need for Property Marketing
III. The Marketing Mix
  A. Product-Service
  B. Place-Distribution
  C. Promotion-Communication
  D. Price-Rate
  E. Marketing Mix Decisions
IV. Management's Role in Marketing and Sales
  A. The General Manager
    1. Directing the Sales Effort
    2. Developing the Sales Staff
    3. Participating in the Sales Effort
    4. Supporting the Sales Staff
    5. Evaluating the Sales Effort
  B. The Director of Marketing
  C. The Director of Sales
V. The Importance of Sales
  A. Sales as a Career
  B. The Challenge of Hospitality Sales

1 Introduction to Hospitality Sales

In 1948, the typical hotel* (84.4% of all properties) was located in a population or trade center, had fewer than 50 rooms, and was independently owned. Only 4.7% of all properties belonged to a chain, and there were only two prominent chains—Sheraton and Hilton. Rooms were small, most had no telephone, and a few lacked a private bath. There was no standardization of product, amenities, or services. Rates averaged $3.75 per night.

Only large properties could afford to support restaurants and bars, and hotels with swimming pools were uncommon. There were a few resorts (most were located in the mountains or near lakes or an ocean), but these properties were primarily seasonal and catered to wealthy individuals rather than groups.[1]

Beginning in the 1950s, however, hotels began to change, driven by changes in the society around them:

1. *Population growth.* The population began growing significantly (at a rate of 1.35% compounded annually), especially in the South and in Mountain and Pacific regions. In addition to this growth, the population began shifting; the Sunbelt (especially Florida and Texas) and the western states (Colorado, Arizona, and California in particular) experienced a tremendous influx of people.

2. *Longer life span.* Not only did the population grow, it became older, and a significant number of new households were formed. Most of these new families relocated across the country as never before.

3. *Improved incomes.* Family incomes improved in the post-war economy, and two-income families became more prevalent. After the belt-tightening war years, families suddenly had more money to spend on travel and leisure. It wouldn't be until the 1970s, when inflation began running rampant, that this trend would be curtailed to any great extent.

4. *Increased leisure time.* Leisure time increased when the 40-hour workweek became commonplace and additional legal holidays were given to workers. Other job market factors such as part-time work

---

*Except where otherwise noted, the term "hotel" will be used generically in this text to represent all types of commercial lodging properties, including motels, motor hotels, and resorts.

Industry Profile

**Thomas T.
McCarthy, Jr., CHSE**
*Owner
Tom McCarthy
Associates*

After graduating from Villanova University, Tom McCarthy began his hotel career in 1953 as a room clerk at the Warwick Hotel in Philadelphia. Eventually he joined Hilton Hotels, where he held a variety of sales positions, including director of sales at the Capitol Hilton in Washington, D.C., before joining Marriott. McCarthy served as national sales manager, director of advertising, and vice president of advertising and public relations in his 11 years with Marriott before leaving to establish his own hotel marketing consulting firm, Tom McCarthy Associates. He co-founded the Hotel Professional Educational Series, which specializes in hotel sales and marketing training, and has served as international president of the Hotel Sales & Marketing Association International (HSMAI). He has been the sales/marketing columnist for Hotel & Resort Industry *magazine since 1981.*

❝Those who are successful in hotel sales know what it means to 'pay your dues.' They have experienced long hours, rejection, frustration, enormous work loads, difficult guests, and uphill battles with supervisors, but have found that the personal satisfaction they experience far outweighs all the negatives.

The thrill of closing the sale after competing with four or five other hotels is one of the greatest compensations for hard work I can think of. I'll never forget how excited I was when I booked my first convention at the Waldorf-Astoria—and the excitement that came with every close since.

Another compensation is the satisfaction of being a member of a winning team that takes that extra step to satisfy guests' needs. There's nothing more satisfying than having a meeting planner tell you that your efforts—and the efforts of your staff—contributed to the most successful convention in the history of their organization. And let's not forget that a hotel is an exciting place for a salesperson to work. It's a place where important events are happening; a place where interesting, and often famous, people congregate; and a place where new challenges await you every single day.

Over and above these compensations, there's the opportunity to build friendships with people from all over the world. Very few people in other businesses have the opportunity to meet so many people from so many places. Building friendships with others within the worldwide hotel community is another compensation that keeps the successful salesperson's enthusiasm high. There's no question that camaraderie with the many wonderful people in our industry, often built through active participation in organizations such as HSMAI and AH&MA, is an enriching experience.

I've been asked by many people entering hotel sales to comment on what makes a hotel salesperson successful. To name a few of the many ingredients, successful salespeople are:

- True believers in their products
- Honest, sincere, and ethical beyond reproach
- Enthusiastic even when feeling low
- Optimistic and able to spring back quickly from defeat
- Concerned about delivering more than what was promised, not just concerned about closing the sale
- Able to put themselves in the prospect's shoes and sell only what they would buy themselves
- Creative in finding ways to make the guest's experience better
- Motivated to do their most persuasive selling when the prospect says no
- Not content with the ways of the past if better ways can be found
- Aware that continuing education to improve sales skills is a career-long activity
- Willing to make an investment in time and effort to be successful

Because of intense competition, owners and operators have been forced to recognize that hotels can no longer be successful without strong selling efforts. This has created a demand for better educated, highly motivated sales executives. There's no question that opportunities for hotel sales professionals are greater now than at any time in the history of our industry. ❞

and job sharing also contributed to the increased amount of leisure time available to workers.

5. *Expanded highway system.* Construction of the interstate highway system began in earnest in 1956, and the 42,500-mile system soon became an important factor in the number of Americans traveling, both for business and leisure. Vehicle registrations grew phenomenally and Americans took to the roads in great numbers.

6. *Development of suburbs.* Not only did the interstate highway system facilitate long distance travel, it also made local travel simpler. As a result, new residential neighborhoods were established in the suburbs. These were followed by retail shopping centers, office buildings, and recreational and entertainment facilities, all of which attracted increased traffic and the need for accommodations and meeting space.

7. *Increased air travel.* Air travel also became a commonplace part of the American business and leisure scene. By the early 1980s, there were over 700 airports certified for passenger service, including 23 large hub airports (in Chicago, New York City, Los Angeles, Dallas, and so on), which were not only destinations in their own right, but also served as connection points for an increasing number of domestic and international flights. In addition, 35 medium hubs served regional areas such as the Southwest or Northeast, and 62 small hubs provided statewide connections for a growing number of business and leisure travelers.

8. *Convention center expansion.* The 1950s and 1960s ushered in a booming U.S. economy. As businesses (and business and fraternal organizations) grew, businesspeople needed facilities for conventions and meetings. Some cities already had civic centers or auditoriums that could accommodate groups, generally served by a small number of downtown hotels. But as businesses expanded into the suburbs or outgrew the limited facilities of the smaller convention centers, there was a boom in the construction of convention hotels, both in the cities and in regional and resort destinations.

But what do these factors have to do with hospitality sales and promotion? The answer is simple: everything! Changing times have had a great impact on the hospitality industry, and the industry has had to evolve tremendously to meet the new challenges posed by a changing society.

To meet the demands of road travelers in the 1950s, the industry responded with the development of a number of chain properties: Holiday Inns, Ramada Inns, Howard Johnson's, and TraveLodge were among the lodging pioneers along interstate highways. Each of these chains introduced its own standardized designs, amenities, services, and referral networks; each became easily recognizable (both in terms of service and market image) in the eyes of the traveling public.

The growth of these and other chains—coupled with developing technology—ushered in the first toll-free reservations systems in the 1960s, a decade that also introduced the first budget hotels. These "back to basics" budget properties did not come into great prominence until the 1970s, when

Exhibit 1.1 Projected Growth in All-Suite Lodging Supply

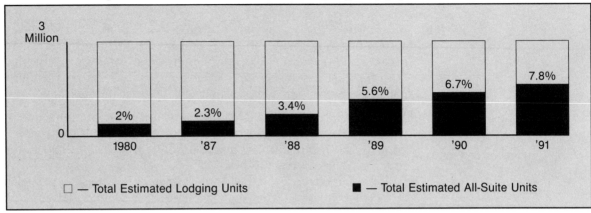

Source: Pannell Kerr Forster. Used with permission.

runaway inflation, fuel shortages, and budget cutbacks on the part of many companies resulted in an unprecedented belt-tightening among travelers.

It is interesting to note that the 1970s also introduced the traveling public to the first all-suite properties. These properties were largely ignored by travelers in the '70s, but today—over a decade after their introduction—they have become an important part of the hospitality industry. An increasing number of "extended-stay" travelers—businesspeople or vacationers who spend a week or more in the same location—prefer a suite to a conventional hotel room (see Exhibit 1.1).

The 1980s have also changed the face of the hotel industry. There are now a number of large convention hotels such as the Las Vegas Hilton, the New York Marriott Marquis, and the Hyatt Regency Maui. Even small hotels are catering to the business traveler with executive floors, business services, and fitness amenities that were virtually non-existent ten years ago. (These amenities and services will be discussed in greater detail in Chapter 15.)

But all-suite hotels and executive floors are just two of the many trends in today's rapidly changing and expanding hospitality industry, an industry that would be unrecognizable to the "mom and pop" operators of 1948.

Today's Hospitality Trends

Current and emerging economic, social, and political trends can greatly affect future demand for hospitality services, and must be identified before a property can position itself competitively in the marketplace. These trends include:

- Computers
- Distribution methods
- Media planning
- Overbuilding
- Competition
- Guest preferences
- Product segmentation

Hotels with No Guestrooms: All-Suite Hotels

All-suite hotels have taken the lodging industry by storm. While they comprise only 5% of today's market, that figure is expected to double—and continue to grow—in the early 1990s. Why the increased interest in all-suite properties? The answer is simple: profitability!

All-suite properties are currently averaging substantially higher occupancy rates than conventional hotels, and can command higher room rates for a number of reasons. First, suites are typically larger than most conventional guestrooms. While conventional guestrooms average 300 to 400 square feet, all-suite hotels generally offer combination living/working areas, separate bedrooms, and (often) kitchenettes, with a total size of 500 to 800 square feet.

Second, suites often do not provide on-premises restaurants, but rather provide a complimentary breakfast and/or cocktail hour. While these amenities generally cost between $3.50 to $4.50 per guest, the perceived value by the guest enables operators to increase room rates by $5 to $15! Limiting the scope of a food and beverage operation results in increased profits for the operator as well.

All-suite operators also benefit from the wide appeal of their properties. While many convention hotels are typically occupied at greater levels either during the week or on the weekend, all-suite properties appeal to both business travelers (who generally travel on weekdays) and leisure travelers (who are taking more frequent mini-vacations on weekends). Therefore, occupancy at all-suite properties tends to remain at steady (high) levels, rather than rising and falling as it does at many conventional hotels.

But why are all-suite properties so popular? The spacious accommodations, the home-like atmosphere, and the functional work areas (which are ideal for working and entertaining) appeal to business travelers (the largest growing segment of the hospitality market) and to those on extended stays, including leisure travelers with families. But, there is a proliferation of these properties, and confusion is rampant as to which property serves what segment—and with what product.

All-suite properties vary widely in concept and amenities offered. As mentioned, many limit their food and beverage service, while other properties, such as the Washington, D.C.-based Guest Quarters, offer restaurants and lounges similar to those found in first-class hotels. Some properties concentrate on a more traditional atrium-style mid-rise construction, while other all-suite hotels position themselves as residential-type complexes complete with green areas and recreational facilities. Some of these last, such as Residence Inns, offer amenities designed to make guests feel right at home—grocery shopping services, baby-sitting services, and so on.

With the varying concepts and services offered, it is becoming increasingly necessary for an all-suite hotel to position itself for particular target markets, and to promote its positioning so that the public will know exactly what the property has to offer. The increased proliferation of all-suite properties is expected to continue into the next decade, and competition for all-suite guests will grow more heated as more and more travelers discover the properties that have come to be called "the standard of tomorrow."

Computers

The first trend affecting the hospitality industry is the use of computers. State-of-the-art computer technology has revolutionized central reservations systems, and has provided hotels with a direct link to travel agents and airline reservations systems for virtually instantaneous verification of room arrangements.

Computers play an important role in areas as diverse as generating marketing data bases (both for current and future guests), following up on sales efforts, and sending personalized sales letters. Computer technology is also an indispensable tool for managing research information, generating monthly reports, and planning sales efforts.

Distribution Methods

Another factor that must be considered is the change in the methods of distribution of hotel rooms. Computers, of course, have played an important part in the rooms revolution—computer-generated reservations through airline systems and travel agents are increasing as trip planning becomes more complex. But new distribution technology will not be limited to third-party suppliers. Direct-to-the-consumer technology is now being developed that will permit a potential guest to purchase flight-and-room packages in the comfort of his or her home through interactive cable systems linked to home televisions. Potential guests already have direct access to property information through the use of data banks at airports and data services that can be accessed by a home computer terminal.

Media Planning

Media planning plays an important role in hospitality sales. In past decades, a general manager had few media options. He or she could advertise in the local newspaper, perhaps place an ad in one of the nation's general readership magazines, or purchase radio spots. Today, however, there is a wide variety of both print and broadcast media available. In addition to general magazines, there are now thousands of special interest magazines, trade journals, and consumer publications available. In the broadcast area, television is playing a more significant role. The hotelier has a choice of commercial television (both local and national), public television sponsorship, and a myriad of cable television options. With this wide range of media choices, audiences have become smaller, and it has become necessary to "narrowcast" advertising. Marketers must develop advertising and promotions that appeal to specific markets rather than employ national "broadcast" strategies that were once the norm.

Overbuilding

To stimulate capital investment in this country, Congress in 1981 passed the Economic Recovery Act. This law allowed for an investment tax credit of 10% as well as shorter depreciation and amortization schedules—a combination that was eagerly embraced by builders and developers who had no knowledge of hotel markets or management. Hotels were built without regard for market demands and without strong financial reserves to sustain losses during the time necessary to establish a guest base. Other properties were built at such high levels of luxury that there was little chance of making a profit.

While this disturbing trend changed with the Tax Reform Act of 1986, the industry may feel its effects for years to come. It is estimated that as much as 40% of America's total room capacity is unused each night, even with the great number of travelers today (one billion in 1986!). But it is more likely that future hotels will be built because they can be profitable, not merely because they can serve as tax shelters, and substantial new construction probably won't be necessary until 1992 or later. The glut may be further reduced by the elimination of some older properties, as well as by the growing trend to refurbish or remodel existing properties rather than construct new ones.

Exhibit 1.2 Foreign Hotel Affiliations in the United States

Hotel	Country
Four Seasons	Canada
Meridien (Air France)	France
Sofitel, Novotel, and Ibis (Accor)	France
Trusthouse Forte	England
Regent International	Asia
Nikko (Japan Air Lines)	Japan
Golden Tulip (KLM Royal Dutch Airlines)	Holland
Swissotel (Swissair and Nestlés)	Switzerland

Many foreign interests now have hotels in major cities in the United States. There are several reasons for this move to the "internationalization" of hotel chains: first, the United States is a strong market, enjoying a recent surge in visitors; second, the U.S. economy is more stable than that of most countries; and, third, foreign hotel chains see a variety of bargains in the United States, including lower construction and operating costs and relatively inexpensive land.

Competition

The changing competition is another important consideration in today's marketplace. The days of the small independent operator may be virtually over; more hotels are seeking affiliations in order to compete with the large chains, who have the budgets and the clout to command a large share of the hospitality business.

In addition to the prestige and buying power of the chains, there are other competitive factors facing today's hotelier. One is the foreign influence that is being felt today like never before. For decades, the international scene was a fertile field for U.S. hotel development, but in today's market, foreign investors are becoming heavily involved in American hospitality properties—from chains to major resorts to individual properties (see Exhibit 1.2).

These trends have had a great impact on the small or independent operator. Some independent operations can survive if they have a solid track record and can obtain the financing necessary to compete with large properties. Other independents—such as luxury resorts—can be expected to hold their own if they can depend on their guest base, while other properties have opted to join a consortium, such as Preferred Hotels Worldwide, to have more marketing clout.

Guest Preferences

The sixth trend in today's market is changing guest preferences. Today's guests are more sophisticated, more informed, and know exactly what they are looking for. These experienced travelers want value, but services and amenities are important too. In addition, most travelers are looking for the same type of experience when staying at different properties of the same chain.

While the type of hotel a guest prefers will vary depending on the reason for travel, the guest's budget, and other factors, it is interesting to note that

Exhibit 1.3   Marketing the Budget Motel

To celebrate our 25th year, here's how we're saying thanks.

Free color TV   Free local calls·

om movies   Kids free sharing parents' room

e lowest prices of any national chain.

When Motel 6 was first introduced over 25 years ago, it offered "an exceptionally clean, functionally appointed room and bath at an extremely low price." But in today's market, the product is getting a little more meat on its bare bones. While the Motel 6 rooms of 25 years ago offered little more than a bed and bath, today's properties (over 400 of them) offer color televisions and free local calls. In-room movies via a central disc player will soon be standard in all rooms.

both all-suite properties (typically upscale) and economy or limited service properties are experiencing acceptance and growth. But, even at economy properties, amenities are still expected. Guests no longer accept limited comforts. Color televisions are replacing the standard black and white sets offered for years at budget properties, free local telephone calls and continental breakfasts are offered by many properties, and in-room movies and expanded in-room work areas have been added to attract value-conscious business travelers (see Exhibit 1.3).

Because of changing guest preferences and the addition of new market segments ("yuppies," "empty nesters," and women business travelers, for example), properties have had to re-evaluate their target markets and reposition themselves to be more competitive. This has led to perhaps the most important trend in today's marketplace: product segmentation.

Product Segmentation

Product segmentation—that is, designing, building, and/or marketing hospitality properties for a specific market segment—is not entirely new. The hospitality industry has traditionally positioned itself into three broad product categories or segments: luxury, mid-price, and budget. But now there are segments within these segments, and hotels are creating "brand" images and names to distinguish their properties from competing properties (see Exhibit 1.4). Today, product segmentation has taken three basic forms:

1. Tier or niche marketing

2. Hotels within hotels

3. All-suite hotels

Tier Marketing. Tier marketing was established as properties became aware that there was an increasing number of market segments with varying preferences and budgets. Quality Inns was the first chain to adopt a multi-tiered marketing strategy, and introduced Comfort Inns (budget properties) and Quality Royale (upscale properties) to complement its mid-priced Quality Inns product. The other chains quickly followed suit, some by developing different "brand" names to attract new market segments, others by buying existing chains (as in the case of Holiday Inns, which purchased Granada Royale Hometels).

There were several reasons for this sudden diversification of hospitality properties:

- The recognition on the part of some chains that additional markets needed to be targeted in order to meet the goals of aggressive growth plans

- The need to identify the variations in facilities, price, and service between properties within a chain

- The chains' attempt to instill "brand loyalty" in their guests, a strategy that has long been used in the sale of consumer goods

- The trends toward upscale and economy properties

- The fact that many mid-priced properties were finding it difficult to compete because of their age and condition

Exhibit 1.4 Product Segmentation in the Hotel Industry

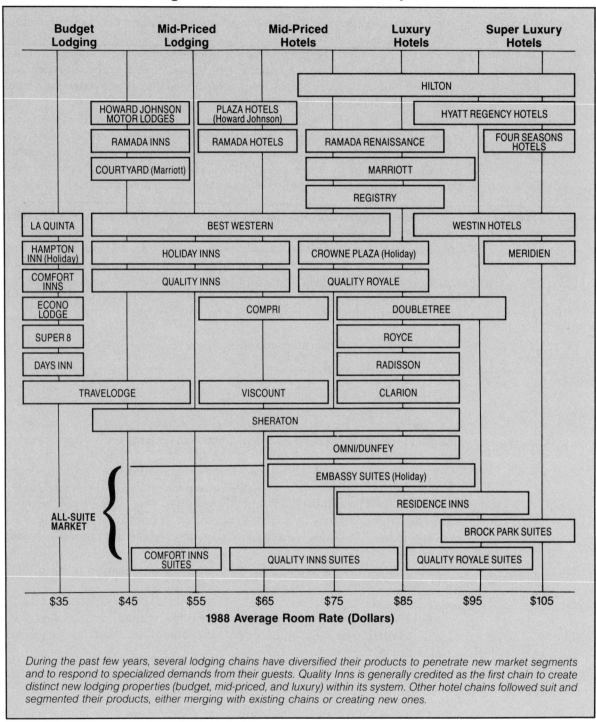

During the past few years, several lodging chains have diversified their products to penetrate new market segments and to respond to specialized demands from their guests. Quality Inns is generally credited as the first chain to create distinct new lodging properties (budget, mid-priced, and luxury) within its system. Other hotel chains followed suit and segmented their products, either merging with existing chains or creating new ones.

Source: Adapted from "An Investor's Scorecard," *Hotel and Motel Management*, April 1985, p. 1. Used with permission.

With so many hotel chains diversifying to reach as many market segments as possible, it is important that a chain make the distinctions among its properties clear. The Radisson hotel chain, for example, uses different names to distinguish its properties:

- Radisson "Plazas" are deluxe facilities featuring a minimum of 250 guestrooms and 40–50 square feet of meeting and function space per guestroom.

- Radisson "Hotels" feature a minimum of 200 guestrooms and 50–70 square feet of meeting and function space per guestroom.

- Radisson "Inns" cater to the roadside traveler, and have a minimum of 150 guestrooms and 30–40 square feet of meeting and function space per guestroom.

- Radisson "Resorts" are designed to serve incentive groups and high-class meetings with a minimum of 200 guestrooms and 45–50 square feet of meeting and function space per guestroom.

These properties are promoted differently, but are promoted (as are the properties of other chains) to generate a "brand loyalty"—in this case, a brand loyalty to Radisson properties. Brand loyalty has been used in other industries, such as the automobile industry, for years, and involves "capturing" the consumer and moving him or her up to the next product tier as wants and desires change. In the case of the automobile industry, for example, a young man might purchase a Ford Escort for his first new car, then later "graduate" to a Ford Taurus as his family grows. As his career and salary rise, he will, if he remains loyal to the Ford "brand," choose another Ford product—a Lincoln or Thunderbird—over other luxury cars.

An example of developing brand loyalty among travelers is seen in the case of the Marriott chain. Marriott currently offers the following product line:

- Fairfield Inns—an economy product

- Courtyard by Marriott—moderately priced accommodations

- Marriott Suites—accommodations that target the business traveler who requires "more than a guestroom"

- Residence Inns—all-suite properties designed for extended-stay corporate travelers

- Marriott Hotels and Resorts—full-service luxury properties marketed to upscale leisure travelers and to the convention market

The Fairfield Inn product is relatively new, and was designed to introduce new guests to the Marriott organization. According to Michael R. Ruffer, vice president and general manager, the Fairfield Inn's prime objective is to widen the chain's guest base and build brand loyalty: "Hopefully, if we have a chance to service them [economy travelers] well at a Fairfield Inn, to let them touch and feel the things that make Marriott the excellent lodging company that we are, then they will stay with us in the Marriott family."[2]

Hotels Within Hotels. Product segmentation is not limited to chains acquiring or building different types of properties, however. The "hotel within a hotel" concept has proved popular, especially with upscale guests who appreciate having a club or floor reserved exclusively for their use. Sheraton and Hilton hotels offer Tower sections, Hyatt promotes a Regency Club, and Marriott offers a Concierge level. Other properties also promote business clubs, floors, and/or services.

All-Suite Hotels. The all-suite hotel, as mentioned, has become an integral part of the hospitality industry, and appeals to value-conscious travelers who do not want to pay for extra amenities they would not use at a traditional hotel (a lounge, swimming pool, health club, and so on), as well as to travelers who enjoy the extra comfort a suite can provide during extended business or pleasure stays. To meet a variety of needs—from budget to executive tastes—all-suite hotels vary from complete resort-like properties that offer meeting facilities, restaurants, and recreational amenities for the upscale traveler to those that have trimmed the extras while still providing the comforts of home to value-oriented travelers (see Exhibit 1.5). Many all-suite hotels offer a continental or cooked-to-order breakfast as part of the room rate, and a full-service restaurant is usually located nearby for the convenience of guests.

A Changing Industry
With all of these trends affecting the demand for hospitality services, it is obvious that the typical hotel property, if there is such an entity, cannot function in the marketplace in the same way that properties of the 1940s through the 1970s functioned. In the 1980s, competition has become fierce, and it is no longer adequate to place a few advertisements, send a few salespeople out on personal calls, or rely on word-of-mouth advertising to fill guestrooms and property revenue centers. Today's challenging market requires a concentrated marketing and sales effort unheard of only a few years ago.

The Need for Property Marketing

For years, the hospitality industry focused on *selling* guestrooms and other services and facilities. In today's sophisticated marketplace, however, *marketing* has become the buzzword; properties have shifted from a strictly sales orientation to marketing in order to understand and manage the relationship they have with the client or guest.

What is the difference between marketing and sales? Marketing is basically the study and management of the exchange process. It involves those things that the property will do to select a target market and to stimulate or alter the demand for the property's services. While marketing includes sales, it also involves a number of other factors: research, action strategies, advertising, publicity, and sales promotions, as well as a means to monitor the effectiveness of the marketing program.

Sales consists of direct efforts to sell the property by personal contact, telephone, and mailings. Although we will discuss the importance of sales later in the chapter, it is important to note that the sales process has been changed considerably by new marketing concepts that focus on what

Exhibit 1.5   The All-Suite Hotel Marketplace

Company	No. Of Suites	Estimated No. Of Suites Under Construction	No. Of Hotels	No. Of Hotels Under Construction	Year 1st Hotel Opened	5-Year Development Plan Hotels/Suites	Areas Of Development Current	Future
Embassy Suites	16,400	4,750	70	18	1969[1]	200/40,000	National	National
The Residence Inn Co.	10,090	2,400	83	18	N/A	250/33,000	National	National
Aston Hotels & Resorts[2]	4,500	0	19	0	N/A	being determined	Hawaii, Calif.	West
Lexington Hotel Suites	2,200	240	13	2	N/A	30/6,000	Southwest	National
Guest Quarters	1,800	600	9	3	1972	25/5,000	Southeast	National
Park Suite Hotels	1,670	1,110	6	4	1985	40/10,000	South, West	National
Radisson Suite Hotels	1,142	200	5	1	1975	40/8,000	Midwest, West	National
Pointe Resorts	1,100	635	2	1	N/A	being determined	Ariz.	N/A
L'Ermitage	1,100	80	7	1	N/A	being determined	South Calif.	N/A
Inn Suites International	1,050	450	7	3	N/A	100/15,000	Ariz., Calif.	N/A
Potomac Hotel Group	900	200	6	1	N/A	being determined	D.C., Md., Va.	being determined
Amberley Suite Hotels	804	240	5	1	1985	15/2,600	South, Southwest	South, Southwest
Pickett Hotel Co.	670	400	4	2	1984	40/6,700	Ohio, Ga., Fla.	East of Miss.
Hawthorn Suites	500	0	6	0	1986	100/10,000	Texas. Okla.	National
Woodfin Suites	416	600	3	4	1985	25/3,750	Calif.	National
Amerisuites	400	250	3	2	N/A	being determined	Texas	South
Quality Suites	375	1,050	3	7	1985	150/19,000	Calif.	National
Royce Hotels	300	2,100	2	14	N/A	60/9,000	National	National
Comfort Suites	295	550	2	4	1985	150/19,000	Calif.	National
Doubletree Inc.	220	220	1	1	1969	30/6,600	Wash., Ark.	being determined
Hotels Luxeford	190	230	1	1	N/A	10/2,000	Minn., Texas	National
Barcelona Courts	N/A	0	1	0	N/A	being determined	N.M.	Colo., Texas
Marriott Suites	0	500	0	2	1987	30/7,500	Ga., Calif.	National
Hyatt	0	315	0	1	1987	being determined	Ill.	National
United Suites/Petite Suites	0	300	0	2	N/A	5/750	Southwest	National
Maxims	0	200	0	1	1986	being determined	Calif.	National
Clarion Suites	0	180	0	1	1987	being determined	N/A	National
TOTALS	**46,122**	**17,800**	**258**	**95**		**203,900**		

1 First Granada Royale opened in 1969. First Embassy Suite opened in 1984.
2 Formerly Hotel Corp. of the Pacific.

Source: Pannell Kerr Forster. Used with permission.

consumers want rather than on what the property has to sell. An example of this shift is the establishment of no-smoking rooms in response to requests from health-conscious guests. Because of marketing research, more properties are developing features for salespeople to sell, rather than just trying to sell existing features.

Marketing differs from sales in these key ways:

Marketing focuses on:	Sales focuses on:
Market analysis, planning, and control	Field work and desk work to sell to consumers
Long-term trends, and how to translate problems and opportunities into new products, markets, and strategies for long-term growth	Short-term considerations, such as today's products, markets, consumers, and strategies
Profit planning, such as determining the appropriate mix of business from individual market segments	Volumes and quotas, current sales, bonuses, and commissions

Marketing, then, focuses on the researching of trends and the development of successful sales techniques and efforts. Successful sales of the property depend on effective strategies, which can only be developed by focusing on market variables—the environment in general (uncontrollable or external variables), and controllable variables inherent in the property (the marketing mix).

The Marketing Mix

The term *marketing mix* is used to indicate the combining, integrating, and blending of several variables to satisfy specific consumer needs. The task of the marketing manager is to form these variables into a marketing mix that meets the needs of each consumer group or market segment targeted by the property.

What makes up the marketing mix? The most widely used model of the marketing mix is the familiar "four Ps" set forth by E. J. McCarthy in his classic *Basic Marketing*. This model can be represented by three concentric circles:

1. The innermost circle contains the focal point of the marketing effort—the *consumer*.

2. The middle circle illustrates the marketing mix of product, price, promotion, and place (the four Ps). These are termed *controllable variables*.

3. The outer circle identifies *uncontrollable variables* such as the economic environment, political and legal influences, and the cultural and social environment.

The problem with this model is that it is too restrictive for the hospitality industry, which has unique characteristics that prohibit an unadulterated application of the four Ps. This doesn't mean, however, that the hospitality industry needs a new marketing mix. The wheel has been invented; all the industry need do is add a few spokes to make it work for hospitality properties.

This wheel can be expanded, and the guest (consumer) can be put at the center of the hospitality marketing system. The guest (and there are many different types of guests in the hospitality industry) is the focus of property marketing efforts, and is termed the target market. Lodging and food service properties will likely have more than one target market—one type of guest— that they seek to attract. A resort property may have as its target markets individual leisure travelers, families, and corporate groups, for example.

The four Ps developed for the consumer goods industry have been broadened in this text to account for the unique way in which the hospitality industry operates. The *product* portion has been expanded to *product-service* because of the service orientation of hospitality properties. *Place*, the second element in the marketing mix, has been broadened to *place-distribution* to include the channels of distribution or the intermediaries who aid in the flow of the hospitality offerings to the guest. The *promotion* "P" is now *promotion-communication*, since marketing communication is different from promotion. Promotion is a one-way flow of information from the seller to the consumer. Marketing communication is a two-way exchange. Effective marketers listen to the consumer first before developing a product-service based on what they have learned the consumer wants. The last "P," *price*, has been expanded to *price-rate* since the word "price" is seldom used when discussing lodging accommodations.

Conceptually, the marketing mix might be seen as:

- Developing a product-service mix based on the wants and needs of the target market(s)

- Determining the most appropriate channels (place-distribution) or ways to reach the market(s)

- Determining promotion and communication strategies and informing markets of the property's product-service

- Establishing a price-rate mix that is competitive and will assure a fair return for fulfilling the needs of consumers

In other words, the hospitality marketing manager must have the right facilities and services (product), make them easily accessible to guests (place), with the proper amount of promotion—at the right price. This can be accomplished if the marketing manager can develop a marketing mix that will be effective in reaching his or her property's target market(s).

Product-Service

The product-service mix is considered first because without a product the industry has nothing to distribute, promote, or price. Hospitality properties offer products such as guestrooms, banquet space, and food and beverages; and services such as parking, housekeeping, and express check-in/check-out.

This product-service mix must be tailored to the needs and wants of the guests sought. A hospitality firm's offerings are based on research of who its guests are and what benefits they seek. It is important to remember that most hospitality properties serve more than one market segment, each with somewhat different needs and wants. Ramada Inns might define its market segments as families, commercial travelers, and small business meeting groups, for example. Each of these groups will seek different benefits from the property: the family might desire recreational amenities; the commercial traveler may require a secretarial service or on-site copying facilities; and the meeting group would be most interested in soundproof meeting rooms.

While the marketing and sales department cannot actually produce the physical product or render the intangible service, it is responsible for researching the guests' product-service needs and wants and then working with management to develop the property so that it meets those needs and wants. Marketing also evaluates the existing product-service mix and the property's brand name identity for possible improvements. For example, Western International Hotels recently changed its name and logo to Westin Hotels; the old name was believed to be too long, and many guests were unaware of the chain affiliation of many of the hotel's properties.

The market-oriented hospitality firm attempts to match its product and service offering to the needs and wants of its target markets, but it can face difficulty due to the fixed nature of the product. Hotel rooms and facilities are just not that versatile: a guestroom cannot become a suite, a convention center cannot be converted into a golf course, and a coffee shop cannot be transformed into a lounge without considerable effort and expense.

Service, the other element of the product-service mix, is considerably more flexible, but also poses problems for marketers desiring to meet the needs and wants of guests. It is nearly impossible to standardize hotel services. The front desk agent at night cannot duplicate exactly the service provided by the front desk agent who works the morning shift. A complicated service such as a lavish once-a-year food function featuring 12-foot-high ice sculptures and exotic menu items is impossible to create the same way each time. Some guests may be disappointed when the product-service is "not as good as last year's." This is in sharp contrast to the consistency of consumer goods. The Nautilus sit-up machine used in a gym in New York, for example, will not differ from the Nautilus sit-up machine found in a health club in California.

In addition to this challenge, providing some services may negatively affect a property's profitability. Two cases in point are telephone and room service; both generally lose money on an annual basis, but failure to provide these services could result in lost business.

Place-Distribution

Place-distribution refers to the accessibility of the product to consumers. With consumer goods, producers use distribution channels to get their product to consumers. In the hospitality industry, however, distribution is far different: instead of the product traveling to the consumer, the consumer travels to the product.

In the marketing of consumer goods, the role of intermediaries is to ensure that the product is available to the consumer when and where it is needed, and in sufficient variety and quantity. In contrast, hospitality products—clean guestrooms, a pleasant dining experience, and so on—are neither shipped nor stored. The problems of warehousing and inventory control do not arise, making distribution much simpler—and more direct—for hospitality firms.

The distribution channels available to lodging establishments can be viewed as either direct or indirect. If a hospitality firm seeks to reach potential guests with its own sales force through direct mail, telephone solicitation, personal sales calls, or media advertising, the effort is said to be direct marketing. Indirect distribution channels include intermediaries such as travel agents, tour operators, and independent hotel representatives.

Promotion-Communication

It is the task of the director of marketing to blend the most effective promotion-communication mix. Promotion is the way a hotel or restaurant communicates to target markets, and can involve advertising and direct sales techniques. Communication is different from promotion; promotion implies persuasion (something the marketer does *to* the consumer) while communication is a two-way exchange (something the marketer does *with* the consumer). Determining what the consumer wants and needs through communication is much more effective than trying to sell a product or service that is not needed.

Price-Rate

If a potential guest rejects the property and its services because of price, all of the previous efforts were wasted. Therefore, price-rate determination is one of marketing's most crucial concerns. Consumers are strongly influenced by rates and prices, and the guests a property is seeking to attract must be taken into consideration when establishing rates. Guests who stay at a budget motel, for example, have different wants, needs, and expectations from those who choose an expensive resort property.

Hotels, particularly large properties, may employ a variable rate policy to meet the needs of different market groups. A variable rate policy is characterized by charging different prices to different buyers of the same product, depending on the competitive situation and the bargaining position of the buyer.

The bargaining position of buyers (individual guests, meeting planners, and so on) will vary depending on the hotel's level of business, which can be broken down into three categories:

1. *Peak.* Also known as "in-season," this is the period when demand for a property and its services is highest and the highest prices can be charged. Peak periods vary for different types of properties. A resort, for example, may experience a peak period during the middle of the summer if it is a popular seaside destination, or in the winter if it is a popular ski resort.

2. *Valley.* This period, also known as "off-season," characterizes times when demand is lowest. Reduced rates are often offered during valley periods to attract business.

3. *Shoulder.* This period falls between a peak and a valley, and can be an excellent opportunity to build business—rooms are available and a mid to high rate can be charged. Many properties target sales and marketing efforts toward these shoulder times.

Meeting planners know they can generally negotiate better rates during valley or shoulder periods than during peak convention months, and vacationers often wait to take advantage of special reduced rates during the off-season. Commercial downtown hotels, recognizing that their peak periods occur during the week, often promote special weekend package rates to encourage business during that shoulder period.

A property's pricing policy can also affect its image. The famous Plaza Hotel in New York City always uses the phrase "20% reduction" rather than "20% discount" for their valley or shoulder period promotions. Marketers there feel that it would be contrary to the Plaza's image to discount![3]

Pricing strategies may vary, depending on the goals of the property. A new property, for example, may introduce itself at low rates in order to build guest awareness and sales volume, sacrificing some immediate profits.

Reputation can play a significant role in the pricing of hospitality products. A lodging facility may charge a higher rate for similar rooms and service because it enjoys a better reputation than its competitors. A Holiday Inn, for example, can demand a higher rate than a comparable independent property simply because of the market value travelers have placed on the chain's good reputation.

Marketing Mix Decisions

It is important to stress that a decision concerning any one of these controllable variables within the marketing mix often affects the others. While one element is frequently emphasized over another in appealing to a

Exhibit 1.6   The Interaction of the Marketing Mix

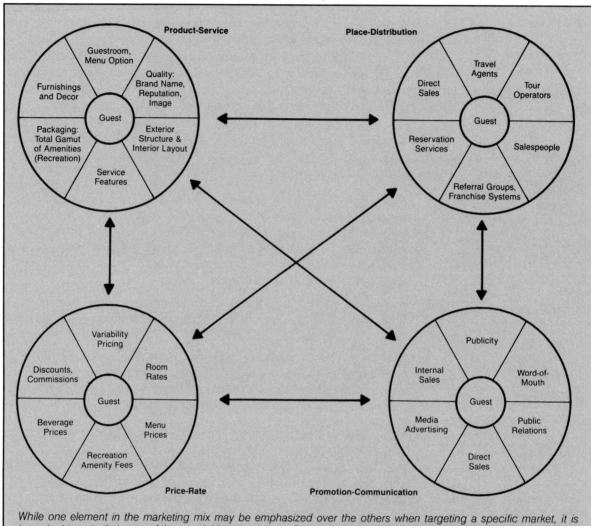

While one element in the marketing mix may be emphasized over the others when targeting a specific market, it is important to note that none of these variables stand alone. The variables are interrelated, and a decision with respect to one variable usually signals a series of decisions for the other elements of the mix.

specific target market, the elements of the marketing mix are interrelated (see Exhibit 1.6), and a decision with respect to one variable usually affects other variables of the mix.

As an example, Hyatt Corporation recently made the decision to add small luxury hotels to its holdings. After an extensive renovation, the 300-room Water Tower Hyatt House in the heart of Chicago was transformed into the Park Hyatt on Water Tower Square. In this case, Hyatt's product-service mix was altered based on research of guests' needs and wants. The interaction of the other marketing variables—price, place, and promotion—are evident, however.

But while the four Ps of the marketing mix are called controllable variables, it is important to realize that control is not absolute. For example, the lodging marketer has product limits. He or she is not free to convert conventional guestrooms to suites without substantial expense. Similarly, a property cannot raise its prices from one day to the next without some repercussions from its guests. In addition, place and promotional commitments are frequently handled on a long-term basis. An agreement with a travel agent or a contract with a tour operator must be honored to protect the property's credibility, and media contracts for print or broadcast advertising must be honored even if the market changes.

Uncontrollable variables—external environmental factors—will also affect a marketing effort. A sluggish economy cannot be controlled by a marketing staff, nor can an energy crisis, or natural disasters such as earthquakes, floods, heavy snowfalls, or other weather conditions that adversely affect travel.

Successful marketing efforts don't just happen. They must take both controllable and uncontrollable variables into consideration, and a carefully researched, planned, and managed sales effort must be developed to ensure that the property attracts guests and keeps them.

Management's Role in Marketing and Sales

The General Manager

The success or failure of a hotel's marketing and sales program starts with top management, and a marketing-oriented general manager is the key to a property's sales efforts. In small to medium-size properties, the general manager may take on the responsibilities of advertising and public relations to enable the sales manager to devote his or her time to selling. The general manager may also make personal sales calls outside the office on high priority business, and spend a half hour a day at the front desk during check-out thanking guests for their business.

The degree to which the general manager becomes involved depends on the size of the property and the sales staff, but many general managers assist the sales staff (especially with difficult or key accounts). While a general manager's involvement and duties will vary, there are five basic areas that all general managers should be concerned with:

1. Directing the sales effort
2. Developing the sales staff
3. Participating in the sales effort
4. Supporting the sales staff
5. Evaluating the sales effort

Directing the Sales Effort. The general manager is usually directly involved in the development of the marketing plan, and is often responsible for the delegation of duties to ensure that sales goals are met. It is the general manager's job to monitor the marketing plan and spot-check the function book and other sales office records to ensure that all is proceeding according to plan.

Developing the Sales Staff. The general manager should encourage the sales staff to be as productive as possible, and show an active interest in the development of salespeople and programs. The general manager may become actively involved in the actual training of the sales staff, or may closely monitor the training efforts of the sales manager or other training personnel.

Participating in the Sales Effort. A good general manager knows that sales is everybody's business, and he or she will make every effort to meet with sales managers or hotel salespeople to help close sales. The general manager may also keep up-to-date with community developments, actively participate in community groups and functions, and extend invitations to new business executives to develop business for the property. The general manager should be available to welcome guests to the property and thank them for visiting. This is particularly important in the case of key accounts—the general manager should be introduced to all key clients, especially those who have the potential for bringing in extensive group business, and make a special effort to extend a warm welcome.

Supporting the Sales Staff. Adequate information plays a large part in sales, and the general manager should see that salespeople are kept informed of the activities of the competition as well as new developments at the property. He or she should be sure that the sales office is conveniently located and staffed with enough secretarial help to free the salespeople for making sales calls. Occasional meetings with sales staff—and personal review of sales call reports and/or correspondence—demonstrate personal concern and help motivate the sales staff.

Evaluating the Sales Effort. A good general manager becomes familiar with the results generated by the sales effort, and is actively involved in analyzing the revenue produced by the sales office, the areas in which business needs to be developed, and the effectiveness of the sales staff. The general manager will also compare results with marketing plan strategies and recommend changes or revisions as necessary to meet sales goals.

The Director of Marketing

Since marketing is largely a management function, it is important that the director of marketing be capable of performing a variety of management tasks: setting objectives and policies; making decisions; organizing, selecting, and/or supervising staff; and planning, delegating, directing, and controlling the work of the sales and marketing staffs (see Exhibit 1.7).

A marketing director's job can be divided into five functions: planning, organizing, staffing, directing, and controlling. Of these, planning is probably the most important. Planning is determining what needs to be done and deciding how to meet the goals and objectives set. Without proper planning, the other functions are meaningless.

Organization is also important, as a structured approach is necessary when developing strategies or employing the staff to fullest advantage. Staffing—getting the right people into the right place at the right time—plays a key role in organization. It also involves training employees so they can reach their highest potential, and developing them for growth and additional responsibility.

Directing involves overseeing both programs and employees. Directing incorporates motivating and guiding the staff to do its job better, and requires well-developed interpersonal skills.

Exhibit 1.7 The Director of Marketing's Job in Marketing and Sales

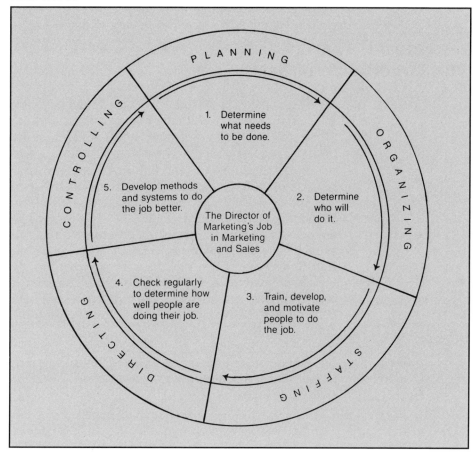

Controlling involves setting standards, measuring performance on a regular basis, and taking corrective action if needed. Looking for new opportunities—and redirecting or modifying strategies that are not working well—is an ongoing process, and requires the skills of a full-time marketing director, so many medium-size and large properties also use the services of a director of sales to motivate the sales staff and to oversee the direct sales effort.

The Director of Sales

A director of sales differs from a director of marketing, although many properties use the terms interchangeably. The two positions have entirely separate focuses: a director of marketing deals more with research and strategy and is concerned with identifying the needs and wants of consumers; a director of sales carries out marketing strategies and directs the sales staff in motivating clients to make a purchase that will benefit them (fulfilling needs and wants).

While marketing pervades everything a hotel does (from operations to advertising), sales is a more focused effort. The most important responsibility of a salesperson is to sell the product—the property and its facilities and services—that management and the marketing and sales department have created. An effective director of sales will see that the sales staff is doing just that—contacting prospective or current clients (either in person, by phone, or by letter) and selling the benefits of the property rather than wasting precious sales time on areas that belong to marketing.

The Importance of Sales

While many people have become "hung up" on the marketing function, it is important to note that both marketing and sales are vital parts of a process that will fill guestrooms and sell function and meeting room space. Both are necessary; neither works well without the other.

Putting business on the books is critical to every property's economic health and growth, and it is essential to realize that direct sales are as important today as they were before marketing efforts came to the forefront of hospitality promotion. Marketing activities such as publicity and advertising are one-way communications; in an industry that is consumer-oriented, the value of personal contact (especially in today's computer age) cannot be overstated. A prospect can pick up a newspaper and read a property's ad and remain uninvolved and uncommitted; but consider the impact of a salesperson's fifth visit to a prospect. Most prospects will be impressed by the salesperson's persistence and the fact that the salesperson really cares about landing the business.

Sales as a Career

But in today's marketing-oriented industry, is it possible to find job satisfaction and career mobility as a salesperson? There's no doubt about it. Consider these statistics:

- Hotel salespeople are young—70% are under 40 years of age; 31% are 30 or younger.

- There are an equal number of men and women in hotel sales. But a significantly higher number of entry-level salespeople are women.

- Very few hotel salespeople are involved in marketing functions; most are sufficiently challenged by the sales profession and intend to stay in sales.

- Hotel salespeople are well-educated. A vast majority (90%) have at least some college background; 57% are college graduates.

- Over 89% of hotel salespeople believe they are moving forward in their professions.

- Most hotel salespeople have been in the business from three to ten years, and most have been with their current property for two years or less.

- Of those who have worked at more than one property, over 40% have remained with the same company (changing properties rather than chains).[4]

These statistics show that sales is indeed a profession that is being taken seriously (see Exhibit 1.8). In fact, the sales profession today is vastly

Exhibit 1.8   The Sales Career Path

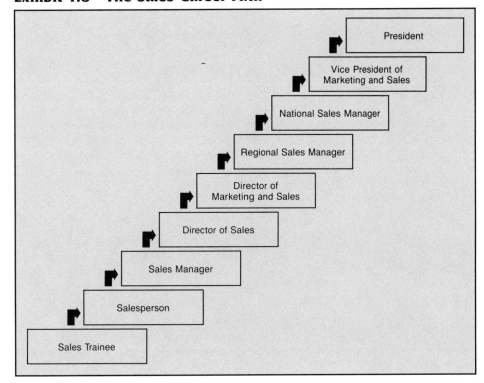

different than it was just a decade ago, both in attitude and method. Sales has become a scientifically designed function, from the way leads are generated, to the study of the psychology of buying, to the professional identification and handling of clients. Rather than being a hit-or-miss effort, sales leads are typically generated by computers relying on detailed consumer profiles or through lists scientifically developed for each property's target market(s). In addition to being trained in practical sales techniques, professional salespeople are now trained in the psychology of selling, and in both verbal and non-verbal communication. They are becoming experts in people-handling skills, such as the recognition of common personality types, and methods of dealing with each type of client.

Why all this emphasis on new techniques and sales methods? First of all, the value of a concentrated sales effort—whether a personal one-on-one sales call or an organized sales blitz—has finally been recognized. Secondly, hospitality sales has become more than a job, more than a springboard to higher or more prestigious positions. Hotel salespeople are recognized as professionals—highly trained and service-oriented members of the marketing team. And last, but certainly not least, there is the uniqueness of hospitality sales itself—the personal and professional challenge of selling an intangible rather than a tangible product.

The Challenge of Hospitality Sales   Hospitality sales differs greatly from consumer goods sales in that the hospitality salesperson is selling something—a hospitality experience—that has both tangible and intangible elements. The product offered (guestrooms, dining facilities, etc.) is tangible, but the services provided are intangible.

Guests can't take the hotel's products or services home to use or admire; when the hotel experience is over, all they have is a memory (whether pleasant or otherwise).

Hospitality salespeople have to take the following characteristics of hospitality products and services into consideration when selling potential clients on a hotel:

1. *Intangibility.* Salespeople do not sell guestrooms or banquet rooms; they sell the *use* of these rooms. Since hospitality salespeople are not selling something clients can take home with them, they must sell the *benefits* the property's products and services will provide to prospective clients. And since clients cannot see, touch, or use the hospitality experience before they buy, they must rely on what the hospitality salesperson tells them the experience at the property will be like. Therefore, the salesperson's credibility plays an important role in the sale.

2. *Perishability.* The perishability of the hospitality product presents challenges for hotel salespeople that are different from those faced by their counterparts in consumer goods. An unused guestroom, an empty restaurant seat, and an unfilled tee-off time represent business lost forever. In contrast to consumer goods, the hospitality product has no shelf life; it cannot be stockpiled or inventoried to sell later. This perishability places heavy pressure on hospitality marketing and sales executives to develop innovative pricing, promotion, and planning schedules.

3. *Inconsistency.* The service rendered by a housekeeper or a food server can vary widely from hotel to hotel—and even at the same property. This much variability is not found in consumer goods, and maintaining a consistent level of service is a challenge to all hospitality properties. Inconsistency is a special challenge to chain properties. As mentioned, clients tend to expect the same type of experience from each property in a chain, but, even with standardized training programs, employee skills and the level of service provided change from property to property. Even the same employee may provide varied levels of service from day to day.

4. *Inseparability.* Production and consumption are largely simultaneous with services. The hospitality consumer comes to the property, and services are consumed at the place and time they are created. This is totally different from the sale of such consumer goods as automobiles or appliances. In many cases, the purchase or consumption of a consumer good takes place several months after production has been completed.

While the general marketing methods advanced for consumer goods industries may be borrowed for the hospitality industry, a number of modifications must be made in order to sell the intangible hospitality product. Hospitality products are not the same as tangible goods, and the marketing and selling of rooms and services requires a different selling approach.

In this text, we will look at some of the exciting ways in which the hospitality industry has met its sales challenge. In this section (Part I), we will discuss the marketing plan—the cornerstone of sales—and examine the organization of a sales office in small, medium, and large properties.

Part II, Sales Techniques, will explore practical and effective methods of personal, telephone, and internal sales, and promotion of on-site revenue centers such as restaurants, lounges, banquet facilities, and meeting rooms.

In Part III—Advertising, Public Relations, and Publicity—we will take a look at today's changing media, and consider the new options a property has to reach mass and targeted audiences. We will also review guidelines for writing and producing advertising that sells.

Part IV, Selling to Market Segments, will discuss some of the major market segments (both group and individual) and how to reach them through an overall marketing effort and direct sales.

In today's highly competitive hospitality industry, everyone from the front desk agent to the general manager is part of the sales effort. Whether you are planning a career in sales, marketing, or management, this book will help you become a viable part of a property's sales team.

Notes

1. Laventhol & Horwath, *Hotel/Motel Development* (Washington, D.C.: The Urban Land Institute, 1984), p. 7.
2. Alan L. Dessoff, "Marketing the Economy Product," *Lodging*, June 1988, p. 24.
3. William Q. Dowling, "Marketing to the Pleasure Traveler," *Lodging*, February 1981, pp. 23–25.
4. Hotel Sales Management Association International, 1983.

Discussion Questions

1. What changes in U.S. society beginning in the 1950s had an impact on the hospitality industry?

2. What are some of today's hospitality trends?

3. What were several lodging chains that pioneered along the interstate highways?

4. What factors influenced the growth of budget hotel chains in the 1970s?

5. What impact has computer technology had on marketing lodging properties?

6. What are the reasons for the present overbuilding of lodging properties in many market areas?

7. What are several reasons for the lodging industry's move to product segmentation?

8. What is the concept of a "hotel within a hotel"?

9. What is the difference between marketing and sales?

Discussion Questions *(continued)*

10. Why must each of the four controllable variables that make up the marketing mix be carefully researched and planned to ensure a successful marketing effort?

11. What are the five management functions typically inherent to the position of director of marketing?

12. Who is the "typical" hotel salesperson?

13. How does the challenge of hospitality sales compare with that of selling consumer goods?

Chapter Outline

2 The Marketing Plan: The Cornerstone of Sales

In today's competitive hospitality market it is especially important for properties to increase their market share and profits. No business can afford to rest on its laurels, yet far too many hotel and restaurant owners fail to recognize the benefits of a structured marketing plan.[1]

As noted in Chapter 1, both marketing and sales are necessary if a property hopes to effectively compete in today's marketplace. Marketing is the foundation upon which sales are built. Without a well-developed marketing plan based on thorough research, sales efforts may be wasted. Since the marketing plan is a guide for the two primary means of selling hospitality properties—direct sales and advertising—it is necessary to understand the marketing plan's role in sales *before* delving into sales and advertising methods.

The ever-changing nature of the hospitality industry seems to lend itself to short-term sales efforts rather than long-term marketing efforts. It is probably for this reason that some properties do not take the time to develop a marketing plan. In other cases, usually at small properties, the general manager has his or her ideas in focus and doesn't feel a need to commit strategies to writing. Still other properties may enjoy high occupancy and management may feel that advance planning is not needed. Whatever the reason for the lack of a marketing plan, the obvious benefits of long-range marketing planning should not be overlooked. A marketing plan:

- Forces managers to think ahead and make better use of the property's resources

- Sets responsibilities and coordinates and unifies efforts to reach the property's sales goals

- Helps in evaluating the results of marketing and sales efforts

- Creates an awareness of problems and obstacles faced by the property

- Identifies opportunities to increase market share in some market segments and open new opportunities in previously ignored areas

- Provides a source of information for present and future reference

- Ensures that sales promotions and advertising are not wasted because of misdirected efforts

Industry Profile

Lynn O'Rourke Hayes
*Vice President for
International
Marketing
Quality Inns*

After graduation from Arizona State University, Lynn O'Rourke Hayes began a career as a business reporter. But an interview and subsequently published profile of Robert C. Hazard, Jr., who was then president of Best Western International, led to a job as manager of corporate communications for "the world's largest lodging chain."

A few years later, when Hazard and several members of his top management team were reinvigorating the Quality Inns International chain, O'Rourke was once again hired by Hazard—this time as Director of Marketing Programs. Following a year of service to Donna F. Tuttle, President Reagan's Under Secretary of Commerce for Travel and Tourism, O'Rourke returned to Quality Inns as Vice President for International Marketing. In her current position, she is responsible for marketing 106 Quality hotels franchised outside of the United States. O'Rourke is also the co-author of Crisis Management for American Hotels, *and has contributed to two additional travel-related books.*

"**A** well-researched, well-developed marketing plan is particularly important in an international environment because the management team can't be physically on the property every day to monitor market developments. In some cases, the marketing team isn't even in the same country! It's for this reason that a definite plan of action is of utmost importance to me.

A good marketing plan should take all of the factors affecting the success of your product into account. In putting the plan together, it's important to determine the goals and objectives of the entire organization. Objectives should always be in line with the philosophy of the property's leadership. But when putting the marketing plan together, it's also important to 'put on your detective hat' and find out what the successful competition is doing right—and what the unsuccessful competitor is doing wrong, so your property can avoid the same mistakes.

It's important for the property to find a vacant niche and fill it. How the property is positioned in the marketplace is critical. This area should not be taken lightly—mistakes made in this area are costly to reverse!

The marketing plan, and the creative plans and activities developed to make the marketing plan work, must be cost-effective as well. While budget guidelines are often unwelcome visitors to the marketing and sales professional, it's essential that all marketing and sales activities fit in with the economic framework of the property and its organization.

Once a cost-effective, action-oriented marketing plan is developed, it's important to *use* it. Often, many weeks are spent brainstorming, crunching the numbers, and seeking out just the right combination of thoughts, dollars, and plans—only to have the completed plan sit on the shelf collecting dust. Refer to your marketing plan! Update it. Make it a working document that helps bring you well-thought-out, long-haul success. "

A property's marketing plan should include programs to attract business to each of the property's revenue centers, with these individual programs complementing, not fighting, one another.

The Sales Committee

While the head of the marketing and sales department is ultimately responsible for the marketing plan, he or she may seek assistance and advice from other property staff members to ensure that all areas of the property are represented in the final marketing plan. A property-wide marketing team, or

Small Properties Have a Special Need for a Marketing Plan

There are several things to consider in marketing a small operation. Because many small hotels do not have a full-time or even a part-time salesperson, the owner or general manager must market the property, a task that includes market research, advertising, public relations, sales promotions, merchandising, and direct sales.

Developing a Strategy

The marketing plan for a small property should include the types of businesses and guests that must be targeted to secure additional income for the property. Once that is determined, the owner or general manager can create a strategy to develop and promote to the specific market segments that are meaningful from an occupancy and profit standpoint.

Perhaps the best way to get more business for a small property is for the owner or general manager to become involved in community activities. When top management gets involved in local activities, he or she immediately becomes known as the local hotelier. The owner or general manager develops additional business through personal exposure alone.

Marketing is Crucial

In addition to community involvement, marketing must be considered a major part of a hotel's operation. By providing the best service possible, knowing who the guests are, making guests feel at home, and providing a quality product, a small hotel will ensure repeat business.

Unfortunately, repeat business isn't enough. The owner or general manager must be willing to make sales calls in person and by phone every day. If he or she can make 15–20 personal calls and a similar number of telephone calls every week, a good amount of additional business can be generated—through the least expensive method of marketing.

The owner or general manager should plan to devote 20 to 25% of his or her time to the marketing efforts detailed above. In today's very competitive hospitality industry, a strong marketing effort—especially at the small property level—is crucial to a hotel's survival.

Source: Adapted from Howard Feiertag, "Small Properties Have a Special Need for a Marketing Plan," *Hotel & Motel Management*, October 13, 1986. Used with permission.

"sales committee," can be established to work together to create and implement marketing strategies for the entire property.

The sales committee should include at least one representative from each revenue center who is assigned planning responsibilities for that area. The committee member or "team leader" from the restaurant, for example, may be the food and beverage director. Non-revenue areas of the property can be represented on the committee as well. The director of sales may be responsible for providing input and plans relating to group business; the general manager may be assigned to gather information about specific market segments; and the public relations director may be responsible for documenting successful advertising strategies used by competitors. The sales committee can also include employees who are directly involved in day-to-day operations—front desk agents, housekeeping staff, kitchen personnel, and so on.

Once the sales committee has been established, individual marketing strategies can be developed for each revenue center. These strategies are presented to the sales committee for review and revision. The revised strategies are then incorporated into the property's overall marketing plan. Planning by the sales committee ensures that areas which might be overlooked by marketing and sales personnel are included in the marketing plan. For example, a salesperson may know basic facts about the property's restaurant, but input from the food and beverage director—perhaps the information that the head chef has served important officials or celebrities—can result in new promotional directions that otherwise would not have been considered.

Sales committees can be excellent vehicles for unified efforts to sell the entire property. The committee member responsible for a marketing strategy for his or her revenue center can often devote more time to that area than could one person from the marketing and sales department developing plans for a number of areas. And the resultant strategies, developed by committee members who have a grasp of all that is involved in their areas of expertise, are often more effective than a marketing plan developed by a director of sales who has only general knowledge of many of the property's revenue centers.

The Marketing Plan

The marketing plan should be developed for at least a three-year period, although the marketing strategies of many properties are planned only a year at a time. In most cases, one year is not long enough, because when sales objectives are limited to 12 months, salespeople tend to stay with the existing guest base rather than target new—and often more profitable—market segments that might take two or three years to develop. (Tour operators, associations, incentive groups, and many corporations are often committed well beyond one year.) Therefore, a strict adherence to a one-year planning cycle can restrict growth and long-term profits. If management is uncomfortable with a three-year plan, a compromise can be reached by setting broad goals over the three-year period and well-defined objectives and strategies for the first year of the three-year cycle.

A good marketing plan can take a number of different forms and may be developed by using any one of several techniques, but there are six key steps which must be included (see Exhibit 2.1):

1. Conducting a marketing audit
2. Selecting target markets
3. Positioning the property
4. Determining marketing objectives
5. Developing and implementing action plans
6. Monitoring and evaluating the marketing plan

This six-step process or cycle can minimize wasteful efforts. It is a systematic approach to increasing sales and developing long-term growth in the property's targeted markets.

The development of a marketing plan is a never-ending process. After one marketing plan cycle has been completed, results must be evaluated, and the process returns to the research or marketing audit portion of the marketing cycle.

Exhibit 2.1   The Marketing Plan Cycle

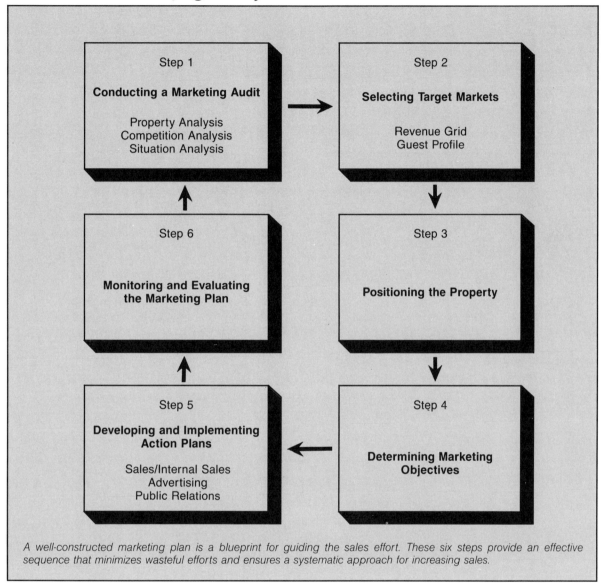

Step 1

Conducting a Marketing Audit

Property Analysis
Competition Analysis
Situation Analysis

Step 2

Selecting Target Markets

Revenue Grid
Guest Profile

Step 6

Monitoring and Evaluating the Marketing Plan

Step 3

Positioning the Property

Step 5

Developing and Implementing Action Plans

Sales/Internal Sales
Advertising
Public Relations

Step 4

Determining Marketing Objectives

A well-constructed marketing plan is a blueprint for guiding the sales effort. These six steps provide an effective sequence that minimizes wasteful efforts and ensures a systematic approach for increasing sales.

Conducting a Marketing Audit

The foundation of any marketing plan is the marketing audit—the accumulation of information regarding the property, its competition, and the marketplace. Marketing audits are a careful, systematic evaluation of the factors relating to sales potential. These audits consist of three parts: property analysis, competition analysis, and situation or marketplace analysis.

Property Analysis. A property analysis is a written, unbiased self-appraisal used to assess the strengths and weaknesses of a property (see Exhibit 2.2). More than a simple checklist, a property analysis takes into account both revenue- and non-revenue-producing areas as well as intangibles such as reputation and location.

Exhibit 2.2   Sample Property Analysis

PROPERTY ANALYSIS—CENTER CITY HOTEL

Area/Facility	Strengths/Advantages	Weaknesses/Disadvantages	Recommendations/Challenges
Exterior	a. Pool centrally located b. Ample parking space c. Covered breezeways d. Luxurious landscaping	a. Handicap parking not positioned well in all lots b. Inadequate lighting for security purposes c. Lobby located too close to highway	a. Add more handicap spaces b. Increase lighting in parking areas c. Roving security guard d. Add trees and shrubs in front of lobby area to reduce noise from highway e. Invite local police for coffee
Food and Beverage	a. Excellent food b. Live entertainment c. Ample seating space d. Coffee shop open 24 hours e. Food cost 33% f. Low employee turnover	a. No outside entrance to dining areas b. Low % of local patrons c. No room service or poolside service	a. Look into costs of adding outside entrance to dining room b. Advertising (see marketing) c. Portable bar in pool area for summer months d. Room service (see guest services)
Front Desk	a. Close to lobby and entrance b. Computerized operation c. Low employee turnover d. Near meeting rooms e. Adequate work and supply space f. Safe available for guests	a. No designated areas for check-in and check-out b. No reservations office c. PBX area too small d. Only one house phone	a. Add additional house phones b. Possible expansion of reservations and PBX
Housekeeping	a. Loyal employees, there since opening b. Guest praise of room cleanliness c. Modern equipment	a. Laundry is in bad location b. Excessive lag time	a. Schedule housekeepers to rooms in one area so walking time is kept to a minimum
Reputation	a. Friendly, clean hotel b. Courteous staff c. Moderately priced rooms	a. Positioning is as an average facility b. More individual than group business	a. Use slogan or marketing strategies to enhance image b. Involve hotel in more community support
Location	a. Near airport b. Easy access to industrial park c. Located on highway	a. Far from downtown b. No rapport with cab drivers	a. Billboard advertising on highway b. Free coffee for cab drivers
Recreational Areas	a. Heated swimming pool b. Pool area has potential for food and beverage functions c. Game room is good for family market	a. Lack of recreational areas that appeal to corporate market; no exercise rooms or jogging track	a. Promote use of pool area for receptions and F&B functions b. Explore installing exercise room and jogging track

While a checklist is the typical format used to do a property analysis, checklists don't truly evaluate the property (they are often no more than inventories). The format illustrated here provides an information base that identifies opportunities, strengths, and weaknesses that should be corrected.

First, a detailed room-by-room and facility-by-facility inspection should be made. Building exteriors, landscaping, and the property's sign should also be examined. The entire property should be carefully evaluated in terms of traffic flow, accessibility, eye appeal, and compatibility with local surroundings. Areas for change can be noted, but changes must be feasible. It would not be practical, for example, for a 20-room property to spend $50,000 remodeling the outside of its building if changes in occupancy would be minimal. Only changes with a reasonable return on the investment should be considered for the final marketing plan.

It is also important to analyze the property from a guest's perspective. In other words, management should try to see the property as guests see it. Sales staff members and the property's management should stay overnight at the property to form an impression of the property as a product. An uninvolved outsider should also be invited to spend a night or weekend at the property to provide additional input.

Competition Analysis. The objectives of a competition analysis are to discover (1) profitable guest groups being served by competitors that are not being served at your own property; (2) some competitive benefit or advantage your property enjoys that cannot be matched by major competitors; and (3) weaknesses in the marketing strategies of the competition that your property can capitalize on. This analysis should be done at least four times a year.

Before the competition can be evaluated, it is necessary to know who the property's competitors are. Simply stated, competitors are properties in the immediate area that sell to similar market segments and offer similar products and services at similar prices. Once these competitors are identified, the property's marketing and sales force can be mobilized against the competition in each market segment, and market share and fair share can be calculated (see Exhibit 2.3).

A side-by-side comparison of properties can reveal strengths, weaknesses, and important characteristics that will assist in positioning and selling the property (see Exhibit 2.4). But simply taking inventory—comparing the number of rooms, restaurants, and other facilities with those of the competition—will not get the job done. Like a property analysis, a competition analysis needs to be much more than a checklist.

A competition analysis involves walking the properties of competitors, talking with competitors' employees, and studying the advertising of competitors. For an even clearer picture, actually staying at the properties of competitors is essential. Driving through their parking lots at night on a regular basis, paying special attention to the types of cars, the states represented by their license plates, and the number of commercial vehicles; eating in their restaurants; reading rack brochures and internal literature; and conversing with their guests are excellent ways of determining differences between your property and other properties. Once these differences are determined, it is possible to set goals to "sell the differences" to each targeted market segment.

Other information needed for a competition analysis is available from a number of sources:

- Local convention and visitors' bureaus
- Chambers of commerce

Exhibit 2.3   How to Determine Market Share

In assessing competition, a worthwhile exercise is to calculate your fair share and your market share against that of the competition. The first step is to set up a table of descriptive data for competitive properties showing property size in rooms, available room nights, occupancy percentages, and the room nights sold for each.

Area Demand Analysis: Market Shares

	# of Rooms	Available Rooms*	% Occupancy	Room nights Sold	Market Share
Your Hotel	500	182,500	67	122,275	23.9%
Hotel A	350	127,750	73	93,257	18.2%
Hotel B	275	100,375	75	75,281	14.7%
Hotel C	300	109,500	75.5	82,626	16.2%
Hotel D	547	199,655	69	137,761	26.9%
Total	1,972	719,780	71%	511,200	99.9%**

*Available room nights for sale, or total rooms multiplied by 365 days per year
**Does not equal 100% due to rounding

Using this information, actual market share, which refers to the amount of room nights captured relative to the total room nights sold, can be computed for your hotel:

$$\text{Market Share} = \frac{\text{Property Room Nights Sold}}{\text{Total Market Room Nights Sold}} = \frac{122,275}{511,200} = 23.9\%$$

Fair share refers to the amount of room nights a property would sell if demand were distributed based on the number of rooms in each property. Fair share is calculated by dividing the number of rooms available in the property by the total number of rooms available in the market as a whole.

$$\text{Fair Share} = \frac{\text{Property Available Room Nights}}{\text{Total Market Available Room Nights}} = \frac{182,500}{719,780} = 25.4\%$$

In this case, your hotel is not capturing its fair share of the market since it is falling one and a half percentage points under the fair share calculated.

Market share and fair share computation are measures of success relative to competition. The absolute size of the share may or may not be important, but it is useful when measured over time to determine trends in market share and the impact of various marketing strategies.

Source: Adapted from Robert C. Mackey, "The Savvy Marketing Executive's Guide to Budgeting," *HSMAI Marketing Review*, Winter 1987/88. Used with permission.

- Local, county, and state room tax reports[2]
- Telephone yellow pages
- Hotel chain directories
- Travel guides

Making personal contact with other area hotel managers is also an effective information-gathering tool, although one must be careful not to violate the Sherman Antitrust Act.

Situation Analysis. In order to plan sales strategies, it is essential to know as much as possible about the marketplace or environment in which the property operates. A situation analysis researches the property's current position in the marketplace and reveals potential opportunities to promote the property.[3]

Exhibit 2.4 Competition Analysis

A side-by-side comparison helps to delineate differences between properties and explains why similar hotels may be performing at different occupancy and room rate levels. For example, the subject property on this chart is achieving the highest average room rate, while Hotel A is achieving the highest average occupancy in the market area yet is pulling in the lowest rate.

Using a competition analysis, the subject property's general manager determined that the occupancy and average-rate discrepancy between the subject property and Hotel A was due primarily to the different market segments the properties served. Hotel A typically secured 55% of its business from groups (meetings and conventions), while the subject property derived 65% of its occupancy from individuals (commercial travelers). The strong group orientation of the market area encompassing the properties helped explain why Hotel A was achieving higher occupancies on an annual basis. Hotel A achieved the lowest average room rate among the competition due to the discounting typically associated with booking group room nights.

A comparison of the subject property to Hotel B also produced valuable insights into the market. The analysis indicated that Hotel B was achieving occupancy levels six percentage points greater than the subject facility. The general manager's inspection revealed that Hotel B was extremely worn in appearance and in urgent need of a facelift. Moreover, both properties maintained similar meeting space, guestroom counts, and market orientation. At first, the general manager did not understand why Hotel B was performing at higher occupancy levels, but he found that Hotel B (1) charged substantially less for its rooms, and (2) derived 10% of its business from airline contracts. Airline contract business typically helps to raise a hotel's occupancy, yet is secured at severely discounted rates. In addition, Hotel B benefited from a national chain affiliation with a supporting reservation system; the subject hotel was an independent property which had to rely on its local reputation and individual marketing efforts.

COMPETITION ANALYSIS			
	Subject Property	**Hotel A**	**Hotel B**
Location	Downtown 525 Main St.	Convention Ctr. 38 North Ave.	Downtown 689 Eighth St.
Number of Available Guestrooms	350	500	375
Year the Property Opened	1968	1984	1973
Last Renovation	1982	N/A	1979
Number of Mobil Stars	4	3	3
Property Owner	Real Estate Partnership	Real Estate Investment Trust	National Hotel Company
Management Company/ Franchise Affiliation	Independent	Nationally Recognized Affiliation	Nationally Recognized Affiliation
Overall Condition of Property	Good	Excellent	Poor—Good
Largest Ballroom (sq. ft.)	5,000	16,000	4,500
Total Meeting Space (sq. ft.)	11,000	30,000	10,000
Restaurants (theme/ number of seats)	Gourmet/60 Coffee Shop/50	Gourmet/80 Specialty/75 Coffee Shop/90	Multi-Purpose/90
Lounges/Bar (theme/ number of seats)	Restaurant Bar/30 Cocktail Lounge/ 60	Lobby Lounge/40 Disco/80 Restaurant Bar/25	Disco/60
Annual Market Segmentation: Commercial Business Meeting and Convention Vacationer Airline Contract	65% 25% 10% 0%	40% 55% 5% 0%	60% 20% 10% 10%
Published Room Rates: Single Double	$ 90–$100 $100—$110	$75 $90—$100	$65–$75 $75—$85
Corporate Room Rate	$70	$70	$65
Group Room Rate	$60	$45	$55
Estimated Annual Average Occupancy	65%	75%	71%
Estimated Annual Average Room Rate	$78	$58	$63
General Comments	Gourmet restaurant has strong local following.	Guestrooms small.	In need of renovation, rooms and public space tired.

Source: Adapted from Michael Cahill, "How to Improve Your Market Position: Analyze the Competition," *Lodging*, February 1987, pp. 43-51. Used with permission.

A situation analysis consists of two parts: the *marketplace analysis* and the *occupancy and activity analysis*. The marketplace analysis identifies environmental opportunities and problems that can affect business. Changes in demographics; positive and negative happenings in the community, region, state, and nation; the cost and availability of energy; government regulation; and the cost of travel are just a few of the marketplace factors that influence occupancy and the average daily rate. The statistics for projecting environmental effects on business can be found in census data, information from industrial commissions such as the state or city division of economic development, and industry reports such as Sales and Marketing Management's *Survey of Buying Power*. Other sources of information are listed in Exhibit 2.5. The marketplace analysis checklist in Exhibit 2.6 can assist in revealing new opportunities or problems that may require attention to keep the property competitive and profitable.

The second part of a situation analysis, the occupancy and activity analysis (also called business status and trends summaries), is an analysis of the property's past, present, and potential operating statistics, and is used to track sales history patterns over a three- to five-year period. This helps to determine "soft spots"—low business periods—that most hotels have in their sales pattern. The aim of this analysis is to disclose sales areas that can be improved on, and it should be prepared for *all* the property's revenue centers. Most hotels keep guestroom statistics, but fewer track restaurant, lounge, and function space statistics such as total covers, seat turnover, average guest check, utilization of function rooms, and average size of functions. Room statistics (see Exhibit 2.7) focus on occupancy and average rate, occupancy by day of the week, geographic origin of bookings, group and individual room nights by segment and source, and the status of future group business already on the books.

The occupancy and activity analysis can be modified to fit the specific needs of a property. Perhaps a property would benefit from a geographic origin summary according to market segment. Knowing that 30% of a property's business traveler market originates in California provides more pertinent information than the general fact that 40% of total business comes from that state.

Selecting Target Markets

Although many hoteliers erroneously promote a property as though it were a single business serving one market, a hotel is actually a series of businesses that cater to a number of different market segments. The hotel's guestrooms, for example, may appeal primarily to leisure travelers on the weekends and to business travelers during the week; the property's restaurant may serve a local business clientele at lunch and hotel guests at dinner; and meeting rooms may be used primarily by local groups during the week and by convention groups from out of town on weekends.

Most consumer industries are keenly aware of the importance of selling to specific market segments, and steer clear of the broad market categories generally used in the hospitality industry. But as demographics change and guests are placed in ever-narrower market segments, the hospitality industry is targeting more segments than ever before.

It is impossible, however, to be all things to all people. Properties must realistically define their product in terms of the major market segments they can best satisfy. A property should determine the market segments for which

Exhibit 2.5 Sources of Information for Preparing a Marketplace Analysis

POPULATION AND DEMOGRAPHICS

Sales and Marketing Management
New York, NY
212/986-4800
 Ask for *Survey of Buying Power* ($65)

American Demographics Institute
Ithaca, New York
800/828-1133
 Members ($285/year dues) are allowed access to the Institute's vast statistical collection. Contact Donna Wenner.
 Statistical highlights are published in *American Demographics* ($48/year).
 Contact Michael Edmondson.

Donnelly Marketing Information Services
Stamford, CT
800/527-3647
 Current year estimates with five-year projections for population, income, and employment available by zip code and geographic areas. Report fees begin at $50.

Population Research Service
Austin, TX
512/837-0135
 1987 Annual U.S. Summary Report ($36) cites April 1987 population and growth estimates for 332 metropolitan areas as well as cities over 100,000 population.

Woods & Poole Economics Inc.
Washington, D.C.
202/332-7111
 Population statistics for 1970 to 2010 by age, race, and sex; income and employment by county, state, and metropolitan areas. Contact Sally Poole.

U.S. Bureau of Census
Population Information Division
301/763-5002

State Office of Demographics and Economic Analysis (sometimes called the Division of Research and Statistics)
 Found in the governmental pages under the state name

INCOME

Sales and Marketing Management
American Demographics Institute
Donnelly Marketing Information Services
State Office of Demographics and Economic Analysis
U.S. Bureau of Census
 Ed Welniak
 301/763-5060

State Commerce and Economic Development Department
 Division of Economic Development found (in telephone directory) in governmental pages under state name.

EMPLOYMENT

Donnelly Marketing Information Services
Woods & Poole Economics Inc. (Sally Poole)
State Office of Demographics and Economic Analysis
U.S. Bureau of Census
 Thomas Polumbo
 301/763-2825
State Commerce Department
 Division of Economic Development
U.S. Bureau of Labor Statistics
 Labor Force Statistics Division
 202/523-1944

RETAIL STATISTICS

Sales & Marketing Management
State Office of Demographics and Economic Analysis
State Commerce Department
 Division of Economic Development
Donnelly Marketing Information Services
U.S. Bureau of Census
 Ronald Piencykoski
 301/763-5294

COMMERCIAL & INDUSTRIAL ACTIVITY

State Banking Department
 See governmental pages of telephone directory under state name.
U.S. Treasury
 Controller of the Currency, listed in governmental pages under "United States"
Chamber of Commerce (Local)
State Department of Commerce

TOURISM

State Highway Department
 State Department of Transportation; Traffic and Safety Division; found in government pages under state name
Local Airport Authorities
 State Department of Transportation; Public Transportation Division; found in governmental pages under state name
Area Attractions
Area Hotels

TRANSPORTATION

State Highway Dept. (above)
Local Airport Authority (above)
Community Planning Agencies
 Regional Office of Housing and Urban Development; Community Planning and Development Division; found in governmental pages under United States

(continued)

Exhibit 2.5 *(continued)*

AREA ATTRACTIONS	POTENTIAL COMPETITION

Chamber of Commerce (local)
Convention and Visitors Bureau
	Building permits
	    Local Department of Buildings found in
	    governmental pages under County or State.
	Project Status
	    Local Department of Buildings in conjunction with
	    local banks.

SITE ADAPTABILITY	
Community Planning Agencies (above)	
MARKET SUPPLY/DEMAND	**DEMAND**
Local Hotel and Motel Association **Convention and Visitors Bureau** **Interviewing Hotels**	**U.S. Department of Commerce directories** **Local Chamber of Commerce statistics** **Hotel sales tax figures** (if available) **Monthly and yearly lodging reports** **Visitor and Convention Bureaus** **Local hotel managers**
DIRECT COMPETITION	
On-site inspections **Directories** (chain, AAA, Mobil) **Interviews with hotel managers**	

Source: Adapted from Kirby Payne, "How to Assess the Market for a Hotel," *Lodging*, November 1987, pp. 22-32. Used with permission.

it is best suited, the areas of least competition, and modifications (if any) necessary to reach its targeted market segments.

Before a property decides which segments to go after, the present guest base should first be determined. Determining the guest base and the decline or growth of a market segment can be facilitated by the use of two basic forms: a revenue grid, which details statistics and revenue for each source of business (see Exhibit 2.8); and an occupancy chart, which provides insight into the growth patterns of each market segment (see Exhibit 2.9).

Guest profiles also help identify the market segments the property is currently appealing to. For best results, guest profiles should be prepared for each revenue center—guestrooms, restaurants, lounges, banquet facilities, and any other revenue-producing service (valet, laundry, health club, and so on). This information can then be used to create a clearer picture of the types of guests that patronize each revenue-producing area of the property.

Information that should be considered in a guest profile includes: name of guest, address, and zip code; sex and age of guest; place or type of employment; place of residence; mode of transportation to property (car, airplane, bus, train); guest status (new, repeat, corporate); date and method of reservation; arrival and departure dates; length of stay; number in party; room rate paid; type of room chosen; type of guest (convention delegate, businessperson, leisure traveler, and so on); total folio charges and method of payment (cash, credit card, company billing); and salesperson making the booking if the guest is part of a group. This information will reveal:

- A breakdown of the present guest base
- The demographics of each guest (age, sex, marital status, family size, income, occupation, and so on)
- The point of origin, or the "feeder city" from which each guest arrives

Exhibit 2.6   Sample Marketplace Analysis Checklist

A.   Local Community
1.   Track trends in population and growth projections.
2.   Determine demographic profiles of locals secured through census data.
3.   Research local sports groups; social clubs; and trade, educational, professional, and political associations.
4.   List local events and attractions—historical, scenic, cultural.

B.   Local Industry
1.   Assess economic and employment trends secured from Economic Industrial Commission.
2.   Research proposed, new, and recently closed office and industrial complexes.
3.   Document details of main employers by industry type.   Information to document includes:
a.   Name and address
b.   Number of employees
c.   Independent or chain business
d.   Names of managing director and key contacts
e.   Assessment of their lodging and function needs
f.   Expansion plans

C.   Traffic Assessment
1.   Assess the location of property with respect to highways, train stations, airports, and bus stations.
2.   Determine traffic counts for highways, railroads, airports, and buses.
3.   Obtain names and addresses of decision-makers for airline and travel companies.

D.   Recreational
1.   List the amusement, recreational, and sports facilities that attract visitors from outside the community.
2.   Obtain information on source, volume, and seasonality of use.
3.   Obtain information on expansion plans, if any.

E.   Unusual Area Activities
1.   List all special events of a recurring nature that attract visitors.
2.   Obtain data on volume.

- The average length of stay and the pattern of occupancy (revealing peak, shoulder, and valley periods)
- How guests get to the property (modes of transportation)
- Sources of reservations
- Which segments of the market are most lucrative and which should be sought in future promotions

Compiling guest statistics by state, city, or zip code permits the ranking of geographic areas in terms of potential. Sales and advertising efforts can be concentrated on those zip codes with high potential.

When selecting markets, a property should keep in mind that a balanced guest mix is ideal. A full-service hotel, for example, will want to target several markets: business travelers during the week, leisure vacationers on the weekends, local food functions, convention business, and perhaps group tours during shoulder or valley periods. This mix will ensure that the

Exhibit 2.7 Sample Occupancy and Activity Chart

Room Occupancy and Average Room Rate
Four-Year Trends

	19XX/19XX		19XX/19XX		19XX/19XX		19XX/19XX	
MONTH	% OCC.	AVERAGE RM. RATE	% OCC.	AVERAGE RM. RATE	% OCC.	AVERAGE RM. RATE	% OCC.	AVERAGE RM. RATE
OCT.	77.9%	$33	72.7%	$34	71.5%	$35	71.2%	$35
NOV.	76.7	32	74.1	33	72.9	34	70.9	34
DEC.	73.1	31	70.9	32	69.7	32	70.6	33
JAN.	83.9	34	80.3	34	78.9	34	77.4	35.50
FEB.	84.3	34	81.2	33	79.9	34	79.2	35
MAR.	85.7	34	83.9	34.50	82.1	35	80.1	36
APR.	77.4	32	75.3	33	73.5	34	72.4	34
MAY	71.8	31	69.7	32	67.8	33	64.3	32
JUNE	69.8	30	66.3	31	65.5	30	61.3	21
JULY	60.3	29	58.1	30	55.5	29	54.8	29
AUG.	65.2	26	56.3	26.50	54.1	27	53.9	28
SEPT.	68.5	30	65.7	30.50	62.4	31	63.1	32
Average Total For Year	74.6%	$31.33	71.2%	$31.96	69.5%	$32.33	68.3%	$32.04

This is one of many occupancy and activity charts that may be used in a situation analysis. This analysis is basically a historical trends study. Occupancy and activity charts should be prepared and tracked for each revenue center.

property maintains a fairly steady occupancy rate regardless of changing market trends.

Positioning the Property

Every property projects a certain image in the minds of the public; this perception of a property by its guests or potential guests is known as the property's *position*. It is of utmost importance for a property to communicate its distinctive position to *each* targeted market segment.

Positioning is much more than just advertising. It is a composite of the hospitality offered by the property and the ability of management and marketers to create unique selling points based on the property's location, internal or external features, and personnel. Without positioning, it is impossible to determine what the property has to offer, where the property is going and how to get there, and how to stand out in a highly competitive arena.

There are two basic positioning choices. A property can (1) directly compare itself with the competition and strive to compete "head on" for a share of a particular market; or (2) identify a need in the marketplace and fulfill that need before the competition discovers it—that is, create a new market. Examples of this last type of positioning are the "back to the basics" budget motels of the 1960s and, more recently, all-suite properties.

Exhibit 2.8 Sample Revenue Grid

MARKET SEGMENTS	Room Nights	Average Guest per Room	% of Occ.	Average Room Rate	Room Revenue	% of Room Revenue	F&B Revenue	% of F&B Revenue	Other Revenue	% of Other Revenue	% of Repeat Business	Time of Year to Promote
Individual Traveler Business Leisure												
Group Traveler Tour Convention												
Other Airline Crews Sports Teams Government												

This chart helps to determine which market segments are most profitable. It not only shows occupancy and average rate, but also details all revenues from each market segment to help determine which guest mix is most profitable. Knowing the most profitable guest mix helps ensure that sales and advertising dollars are spent in the proper proportion to achieve or maintain the desired mix.

Developing a positioning strategy requires a great deal of creative thought. It is first necessary to identify benefits that will be most important to potential guests by knowing exactly what the property has to offer:

1. Who are we? What do we stand for?

2. How is our property different from the competition? Are there ways in which we can set ourselves apart?

3. What areas are not producing the desired revenue and/or response? Are there other areas that show a high potential for increased business?

4. Does our property have a liability that can be turned into an asset?

5. Which target market segment can be most beneficial to us?

6. Is there a way to change the use of a specific area in order to make it more profitable? Would it be more cost-effective to turn a restaurant into a cafeteria, for example? Or, would it be beneficial to remove a lounge to expand an existing restaurant?

7. Does our property have tangible or intangible advantages over competitors?

8. Does the property offer any features or services that are unique? Atrium areas, complimentary limousine service, an on-property attraction (museum, park, etc.) are examples of unique features that appeal to travelers.

The answers to these questions will greatly assist in the development of a position that will affect everything the property does and stands for. The

Exhibit 2.9   Sample Occupancy Chart

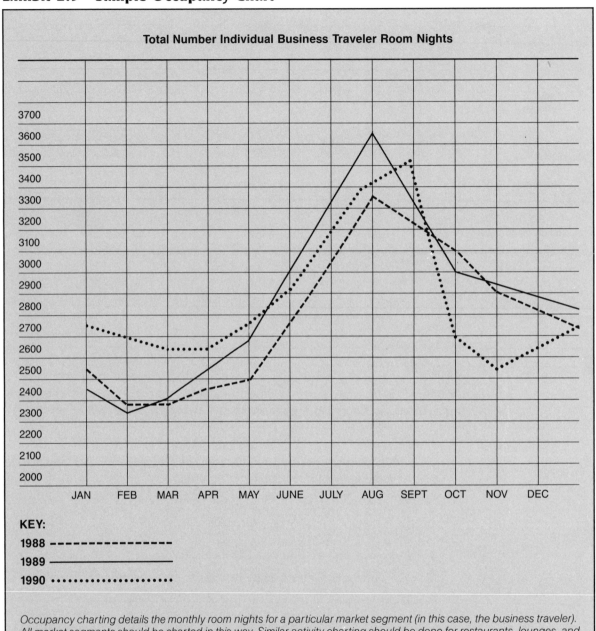

Total Number Individual Business Traveler Room Nights

KEY:

1988 – – – – – – – – – – –

1989 ————————————

1990 ••••••••••••••••••••

Occupancy charting details the monthly room nights for a particular market segment (in this case, the business traveler). All market segments should be charted in this way. Similar activity charting should be done for restaurants, lounges, and other revenue centers to facilitate assessment of market trends.

property's uniqueness can then be expressed in what is known as a "positioning statement." The positioning statement must communicate the property's advantages to its selected target markets. Of course, this statement must reflect what the property actually offers. A positioning statement such as "Friendliest service west of the Mississippi," for example, may be too general; if a guest is greeted by a discourteous employee, the guest will certainly question the property's positioning statement. On the other hand, if a property positions itself as offering "Leisure for less," and offers economy rates, recreational amenities, and a relaxing atmosphere, it has lived up to its positioning statement.

To analyze the effectiveness of a positioning statement, the following questions must be answered:

1. Do we really know who our guests are and what they are looking for?

2. How do our guests perceive our property versus our competition? How do we rate in terms of price, service, facilities, and amenities?

3. What do the competition's guests think of our property? Are they aware of what we have to offer?

The positioning statement should be targeted to a market segment of sufficient size to warrant the expenditures required to attract additional business from that segment, and the property must have the ability to meet that market segment's demands. True positioning creates an image, outlines guest benefits, and distinguishes a property from its competition.

Two Examples of Hotel Positioning. The following examples illustrate successful positioning from two extremes of the hospitality spectrum. Marriott is a hotel chain that has pursued a very successful positioning strategy over the years, while The Tides Inn represents a small independent property's approach to positioning.

Marriott Hotels. Marriott's emphasis traditionally has been on (1) positioning its name in two selected markets; (2) sticking to its guns; and (3) being single-minded in seeing that everything its hotels do or stand for reflects the positioning.

Roger Dow, vice president of marketing for Marriott Hotels and Resorts, states the company's positioning goals as follows:

1. To be the preferred lodging chain for middle- to upper-level business executives who travel *frequently* on business.

2. To be the preferred meeting site for *major* meetings and conventions.

"Frequent" is believed to mean 20–30 or more business trips a year, and "major" to mean 1,000 or more room nights.

Is the positioning successful? These two hotel markets represent over 80% of Marriott's guests!

Marriott goes the extra mile in providing product and services to its two markets. Evidence of its success is in the impressive number of awards for handling meetings and frequent business travelers; *Successful Meetings, Business Travel News, Meeting Planners International, Corporate and Incentive Travel, Sales and Marketing Management,* and *Meetings and Conventions* have recognized Marriott's excellence, and the chain has received four- and five-diamond ratings from AAA and four- and five-star listings in Mobil guides.

While Marriott positioning concentrates more on product and service than on a theme, the positioning is not without a theme—and it is a good one: "Marriott People Know How." The theme means, simply: "We have the expertise." It translates into such advertising headlines as "'Knowing How' is more than just a saying at the Marriott—it is a way of life, worldwide."

The Tides Inn. Few hotels in the world are as effectively positioned as the 106-room Tides Inn in Irvington, Virginia. Owner-operator Bob Lee Stephens, CHA, states the property's positioning as, "One of America's best small resorts," and its advertising theme as, "Quiet. Quality." In every aspect of his operation and in every ad, Stephens sticks to his positioning.

Apparently it works. Annual revenue per room exceeds $50,000, which compares favorably with such jewels of hotel operation as The Hotel duPont in Wilmington and The Pontchartrain in New Orleans.

Determining Marketing Objectives

Once the marketing audit is completed, the target market segments identified, and the positioning established, the next step in the marketing plan is to establish specific marketing objectives. Sales objectives and quotas can be developed as a result of marketing objectives. Since marketing objectives cannot be reached without sales, it is important to answer the following questions before setting specific marketing objectives:

- Which revenue centers would benefit from additional sales activity? Would offering two-for-one coupons increase restaurant business, for example? Would offering a discounted rate for families attract more business to the property? Or do such areas as the lounge, banquet facilities, room service, or recreational facilities need additional promotion to increase profits?

- When are the peak periods? the shoulders? the valleys?

- Which marketing segments can be reached, and what priority should be given to each segment?

- What can be done to ensure increased sales in each market segment?

Marketing objectives should be kept simple and should be set for each market segment, revenue center, and revenue-producing service—valet, laundry, and so on. To be effective, marketing objectives must be:

1. *In writing.* Putting objectives in writing provides concise information that can be referred to as necessary by both managers and employees. Written objectives ensure that everyone has the same information.

2. *Understandable.* Performance results will be less than desired if objectives cannot be understood by both management and staff. Objectives should be written in simple terms and adequately explained.

3. *Realistic and challenging.* Objectives must be obtainable, but they must also present some challenge to the staff. For example, an objective to maintain 100% occupancy year-round is unrealistic for many properties, but an objective to increase rooms business by 20% over the summer months is often realistic.

4. *Specific and measurable.* Objectives must clearly define the expected results, and should be as specific and measurable as possible. For example, rather than having a general objective to "raise room occupancy," the objective should be stated as follows: "To achieve an average occupancy rate of 75% (900 room nights) during June and July and maintain an average room rate of $55." Specific objectives should be:

- *Time-specific.* While the average marketing plan is developed for a minimum of three years, objectives should be broken down into annual, quarterly, monthly, weekly, or even daily objectives to make it easier to evaluate the success of marketing efforts.

- *Quantity-specific.* Detail expected sales in terms of number of room nights, number of covers, number of banquets, and so on. Expected dollar value (such as average daily rate and average guest check) might also be specified, although inflationary trends may force re-evaluation of these figures.

- *Bottom line-specific.* Since properties often experience a loss while trying to obtain business from new market segments, acceptable loss amounts (as well as desired gains) should be specified.

- *Market share-specific.* Objectives should be set for target markets that offer the highest potential to the property. In many cases, this may mean going after a larger share of an existing market rather than trying to generate business from totally new (and possibly less profitable) market segments.

As mentioned earlier in the chapter, a sales committee is perhaps the most effective way to ensure that all revenue centers are included when setting marketing objectives. Individual revenue center objectives can be reviewed by the committee to determine their feasibility, and revisions can be made as necessary before the objectives are incorporated into the property's marketing plan.

Action Plans

Once objectives have been set, action plans must be developed to reach them. There should be detailed action plans for *each* market segment and revenue center. Brainstorming by employees should be encouraged to help managers and committee members determine effective action plans.

Action plans can be as simple or as complicated as needed (see Exhibit 2.10). If the objective is to increase covers in the restaurant next month by an average of ten per evening, one action plan might be stated as follows: "Restaurant manager will contact local businesses and invite owners to drop by for a complimentary dessert with dinner." Another action plan can be created that involves a number of employees: front desk agents can suggest to registering guests that they reserve a table in the dining room for the evening. Or, switchboard operators may call guests in the early evening to offer information about the restaurant's dinner special.

Responsibility for implementing action plans should be assigned to specific individuals in each of the property's revenue centers. This accountability allows for monitoring the progress of marketing efforts. The committee

Exhibit 2.10   Sample Action Plans

I. **Market Segment—Association Meetings**

Objective: Increase room nights from 10,000 to 20,000 per year while maintaining an average rate of $74 for this segment.

Advertising Action Plans:
1. Review the files at the Convention and Visitors' Bureau and develop a list of association prospects that could meet in our area and have sleeping requirements that we can accommodate. Develop three direct mail campaigns a year for this list.
2. Place three insertions per year in *Meeting News* and *Association Management* magazines.

Direct Sales Action Plans:
1. Develop a good working relationship with the local Convention and Visitors' Bureau. Make sure it is stocked with collateral material. Invite the bureau's personnel to the hotel for cocktails and reacquaint them with the hotel.
2. Follow up all Bureau leads. Whenever possible, the site selection chairperson for an association will be invited to dinner and given a complimentary overnight stay.
3. Continue membership in local American Society of Association Executives (ASAE). Purchase a booth at the local ASAE annual meeting and trade show.

II. **Market Segment—Individual Business Traveler**

Objective: Increase total annual room sales revenue from this market segment from $1,600,000 to $1,850,000 by the end of the fourth quarter of this year.

Advertising Action Plans:
1. Contract for an attractive billboard placed permanently on the interstate which gives the name of the hotel and directions to the property. In addition, contract for billboards in prime commercial business districts of the city.
2. Send direct mail to a list of corporate travel decision-makers in the local market, developed through analysis of past reservation cards and through outside calls.

Direct Sales Action Plans:
1. A Secretary's Club will be made up of secretaries who have the potential to make reservations for their bosses and businesspersons coming into our city. As a member of our club, the secretary will receive the following:
    *   Discounted guaranteed rate on guestrooms (subject to availability)
    *   VIP treatment for their guests (quick check-in, check cashing privileges, turn-down service)
    *   Free morning newspaper for their guests
    *   Free local telephone calls for their guests
    *   A free drink ticket when used with dinner

    Two club parties will be given throughout the year, one in April to celebrate National Secretaries Day, and one at Christmas. Birthday and anniversary cards will be sent to each club member. To qualify for membership, a secretary must make reservations totaling 12 room nights per month.
2. A "Seventh Stay is Free" program will be geared to the traveling businessperson. The first time the guest stays at the hotel he or she will be given a card listing the rules and regulations of the program. Each stay thereafter, this card can be presented to the front desk agent for validation. At the completion of the seventh stay, regardless of room nights used, the guest will be entitled to one free room night. Every member of the program will be given VIP service, quick check-in, free newspapers, free local phone calls, and a free drink coupon to be used with the purchase of a dinner at the hotel restaurant.

III. **Revenue Center—Catering**

Objective: Increase annual food and beverage banquet sales revenue from $200,000 to $225,000 during this fiscal year.

Advertising Action Plan:
1. Develop special event banquets for New Year's Eve, July 4th, and Mother's Day. Promote each banquet with in-house posters prior to the event, and in local newspapers using 3 column x 5 column ads placed three times prior to the banquet.

Exhibit 2.10 *(continued)*

Direct Sales Action Plans:
1. Work with the chef and food and beverage director to develop new catering menus. Prices should be competitive with major competition.
2. Develop a personal sales and telephone sales campaign for catering clients who have the potential to rebook with the property.
3. Use the community business directory to research and compile a list of new banquet prospects, concentrating on corporate, civic, and fraternal groups.
4. Develop a wedding package that includes the reception, two hours of open bar, the cake, entertainment, and free overnight accommodations for the bridal couple. Price at $45 per person with a 100 person minimum.

---

member or "team leader" for each revenue center can be responsible for providing periodic reports of action plan results to the sales committee.

The property's entire staff should be aware of both individual revenue center and overall marketing efforts. Cooperation can make it much easier to attain marketing objectives. As in the example mentioned earlier of the action plan to increase restaurant covers, employees from several areas of the property can be involved in meeting an objective set for one revenue center. Such employee involvement is vital to the success of action plans, particularly those involving in-house promotions.

Budgeting. Action plan expenses must be figured into the marketing budget. Most marketing budgets include sales, advertising, and promotional expenses; direct mail postage and handling charges; promotional premiums; and salaries of the marketing and sales staff (see Exhibit 2.11).[4] Individual budgets should also be established for each market segment and each action plan designed to reach that market segment. As a rule of thumb, budgeting should be broken down into quarterly segments to make possible effective monitoring. The exception is media advertising, which is often budgeted on an annual basis.

Marketing budgets generally fall into four categories:

1. *Percentage of sales.* These budgets are based on the previous year's sales, and usually work best for properties that enjoy a significant base of repeat business. The budget is usually 3% to 6% of last year's sales in most cases, although this may vary depending on the size and needs of the property.

2. *Competitive parity.* This type of budget is based on what the competition is doing. A property spends according to what the competition spends, a practice which may or may not result in effective budgeting.

3. *Affordable funds.* This type of budget uses a portion of the property's profits as the basis for marketing expenditures.

4. *Zero-base.* This type of budget is based on the task method; monies are budgeted at levels to get the job done, and all expenses must be justified. This is considered the best way to budget for marketing,

Exhibit 2.11 How the Marketing Dollar Was Spent

	All Establishments	Location of Property				
		Center City	Suburban	Airport	Highway	Resort
Payroll & Related Expenses	27.2%	31.2%	26.9%	23.2%	13.0%	24.7%
Sales Expenses	9.6	11.2	8.8	10.2	3.9	12.3
Advertising Expenses						
Print	17.8	19.0	16.7	19.9	12.6	26.0
Radio & TV	4.0	2.9	2.5	4.0	3.4	3.1
Outdoor	4.8	2.3	7.9	7.4	12.3	1.3
Other	10.9	12.2	8.9	10.8	14.2	11.0
Merchandising	1.9	1.4	2.8	0.7	0.8	3.0
Public Relations	2.8	3.3	3.4	2.5	2.3	3.1
Franchise Fees	11.1	5.5	13.2	11.6	30.0	5.1
All Other Expenses	9.9	11.0	8.9	10.1	7.4	10.4
Total	**100.0%**	**100.0%**	**100.0%**	**100.0%**	**100.0%**	**100.0%**

*All amounts are means.

Source: *U.S. Lodging Industry, 1988,* Laventhol & Horwath. Used with permission.

although a number of variables—room occupancy, the business mix, gross revenues, and so on—must be taken into account when establishing a sound budget.

A great deal of attention must be given to establishing a budgeting system that works. The overall result should be a budget that provides funds for producing new business as well as allocations for maintaining the property's established business.

In most cases, it is advantageous to develop a budget form that provides instant access to information. This type of budget form can show the anticipated and actual expenditures for the previous year, and can serve as a guideline for current budget planning. The budget form shown in Exhibit 2.12 breaks the marketing plan down into specific segments, further dividing the individual segments into expenditure categories. Under "Merchandising/Inhouse Promotions," for example, the total budget allocated to that portion of the marketing plan is broken down into specific expenditures (display material, special events, free samples, and so on). This type of detail is helpful for a number of reasons:

1. *It ensures that all expenses are planned for and documented.* Using a less detailed form can mean that expenses may be overlooked. In the case of advertising, for example, it is far better to list the individual items that will be required—typesetting, printing, distribution, consulting fees, and so on—than to allocate one sum for a general advertising category. Otherwise, it is far too easy to forget to include funds for expenses that do not occur often, or forget specific products or services that are involved in the advertising process.

2. *It helps prevent arbitrary budget cuts.* When the budget is not broken down into specific expenditures, it is much more likely that

Exhibit 2.12 Sample Detailed Budget

NAME OF PROPERTY								
Marketing/Sales Methods	**Last Year**			**Next Year**				
	Actual Expenditures	Budgeted Expenditures	Variance	Budget	Allocation By Target Markets			Comments
Merchandising/ In-house Promotions								
a. Display Material	$ _____	$ _____	$ _____	$ _____	$ _____ $ _____ $ _____ $ _____ $ _____ $ _____			_____
b. Special Events	_____	_____	_____	_____	_____ _____ _____ _____ _____ _____			_____
c. Free Samples	_____	_____	_____	_____	_____ _____ _____ _____ _____ _____			_____
d. Prizes	_____	_____	_____	_____	_____ _____ _____ _____ _____ _____			_____
e. _____	_____	_____	_____	_____	_____ _____ _____ _____ _____ _____			_____
Subtotal	$ _____	$ _____	$ _____	$ _____				
Travel Trade Marketing								
a. Print Materials	$ _____	$ _____	$ _____	$ _____	_____ _____ _____ _____ _____ _____			_____
b. Trade/Travel Shows	_____	_____	_____	_____	_____ _____ _____ _____ _____ _____			_____
c. Familiarization Trips	_____	_____	_____	_____	_____ _____ _____ _____ _____ _____			_____
d. _____	_____	_____	_____	_____	_____ _____ _____ _____ _____ _____			_____
e. _____	_____	_____	_____	_____	_____ _____ _____ _____ _____ _____			_____
Subtotal	$ _____	$ _____	$ _____	$ _____				
Other Marketing Programs								
a. Marketing Seminar	$ _____	$ _____	$ _____	$ _____	_____ _____ _____ _____ _____ _____			_____
b. _____	_____	_____	_____	_____	_____ _____ _____ _____ _____ _____			_____
c. _____	_____	_____	_____	_____	_____ _____ _____ _____ _____ _____			_____
Subtotal	$ _____	$ _____	$ _____	$ _____				
TOTAL	$ _____	$ _____	$ _____	$ _____				

A budget that is broken down first into the various categories targeted in the marketing plan and then into specific expenditures in each of those categories gives a clear picture of expenditures. This form is especially helpful when planning a budget because it lists the anticipated and actual amounts expended the previous year, provides for a variance column, and breaks the current year's budget for each item into targeted market segments.

Source: *Tourism is Your Business: Marketing Management*, a promotional booklet produced by *Canadian Hotel and Restaurant Magazine* (Toronto, Canada: McLean Hunter Limited, 1986), p. 80. Used with permission.

money will be moved from one category to another without regard for the consequences. For example, if a sales manager needs more money for a blitz campaign, it may appear that funds are available from another category. This, however, may not be the case, and only a specific budget shows exactly what is needed in each area.

3. *It is a step toward increased accountability for marketing plans.* Having a detailed budget provides a means of monitoring anticipated and actual expenses for each area of the marketing plan. Actual expenditures can be measured against the results obtained from various marketing programs, and the budget can more easily be adjusted to meet changing trends. If a sales manager finds that direct mail campaigns are more effective than billboard campaigns, for example, the next budget might see more money allocated to direct mail and less to billboards.

Monitoring and Evaluating

The more carefully the marketing effort is measured, the easier it will be to plan future activities and programs for building business and profitability. While the cost-effectiveness of some public relations and sales promotions may be difficult to measure because of their inherent long-term effects, it is important to establish a monitoring system at the same time that action plans and specific promotions are developed.

Monitoring the marketing plan can be fun as well as enlightening, especially if the plan is reviewed periodically so that corrective action can be taken throughout the planning cycle (see Exhibit 2.13). Methods of monitoring the marketing plan include:

- Recording the number of room nights for each market segment. While it may seem tedious to count and code room nights by market segment, this method results in a report that facilitates the comparison of actual results with marketing plan goals.

- Charting and comparing restaurant covers before and after advertising. Evaluation should take a number of factors into consideration, including the cost of the promotion compared to the increase in profits. If profits increased by 20% but promotional costs exceeded the profits realized, the promotion should be re-evaluated.

- Surveying zip codes to determine which media are most effective in local advertising. This type of analysis is especially effective for restaurant promotions and weekend packages.

- Evaluating internal merchandising campaigns by monitoring the average expenditure by each guest prior to and throughout the promotion.

- Recording direct mail responses and telephone inquiries in a log book that indicates the specific salesperson to which each lead was assigned. Six months later, conversions (the actual bookings realized as a result of the inquiries) can be measured. This type of monitoring not only gives an indication of the effectiveness of the advertising piece, but may also provide insight into the sales strengths of the staff. If a mail campaign generated inquiries that did not convert to definite bookings, for example, the problem may lie more with the product or the sales staff than with the media.

- Couponing. The use of return mail coupons and tabulating responses to coupons distributed to guests and employees can assist in determining who is using the services and products offered by the property.

- Using specific response techniques. Using special telephone numbers or instructing respondents to ask for a specific individual can help track the effectiveness of both print and broadcast advertising.

Remember that control is an essential part of the marketing plan cycle, and that periodic evaluation should be designed into the plan from the beginning. Waiting until the end of the marketing cycle can be risky. A record should be kept each time an advertising campaign is run; any strategies that do not contribute to the bottom line can be immediately re-examined.

If action plans are effective and objectives are realized within established budget limits, corrective action need not be a part of the process. But it is a painful fact that some strategies just do not work. If hotel sales goals are not being met, the problem can often be traced to one or more of the following:

1. *Lack of responsibility.* The sales committee member or team leader for a revenue center has not assumed responsibility for seeing that schedules are met and that evaluations of results have been made.

Exhibit 2.13 Monitoring the Marketing Plan

1. Make daily comparison analyses for room sales, restaurant charges, and occupancy percentages in relation to last year's, the year-to-date, and forecasted figures.

2. Use registration card data to survey zip codes to determine which media are working well for the property's shoulder and valley periods.

3. Tabulate senior citizen discount coupons, children's fun packs, and employee paycheck coupons at the end of each week during shoulder periods to determine which segments are responding.

4. Maintain a clippings file of the property's public relations material (and that of competitors).

5. Monitor restaurant and bar sales and the comment cards received from each of these revenue centers. Offer a weekly drawing for a free meal to individuals who have filled out cards during shoulder and valley periods. Use the addresses obtained from these cards to determine where guests are coming from.

6. Keep a daily record of comment card responses. Follow up on consistent problems with employees, maintenance, and so on. Break the cards down by geographic location, income, and how respondents heard about the property.

7. Keep a weekly record of phone sales and bookings made by each salesperson. Check back with potential guests, and check the "dead files."

8. Set goals for each market segment; color code and count room nights by each market segment, and develop a monthly report that compares actual results with goals.

9. Have weekly meetings with the sales staff. Discuss the week's activities and pinpoint areas needing attention. Inform staff of upcoming events in the hotel and the surrounding area.

10. Monitor restaurant covers before and after promotions to evaluate the cost-effectiveness of the promotions.

11. Record direct mail responses. Break them down by geographic location, level of income, group or individual traveler.

12. Keep track of specials and regular items that sell well in the coffee shop. Project sales for each food server, and monitor actual sales generated against projected sales.

13. Monitor motorcoach tour packages based on information obtained from the reservations department. Each reservation taken should include the following information:
    a. package code
    b. guest zip code
    c. code for media reference
    This information should be compiled weekly and turned in to the marketing and sales department for analysis.

14. Monitor all discounts given by the rooms department in the following manner:
    a. Place a code for each discount on each folio.
    b. Compile a room count of discounts nightly. This can be done by the night auditor and can be turned in to the marketing and sales department at the end of each week.
    c. Keep records of all discounted rates requested. This information should be forwarded to the marketing and sales department on a monthly basis.

15. Evaluate internal promotions by measuring the average expenditure per guest prior to and throughout each promotion.

The specific methods listed here were used by one property to evaluate marketing and sales efforts.

2. *Lack of communication.* Salespeople or other employees are not aware of their specific part in the marketing plan.

3. *Lack of time.* Insufficient time has been allocated for making outside sales calls or directing advertising efforts in the required markets.

4. *Lack of authority.* Salespeople have not been given the authority to commit the budget to specific marketing efforts.

5. *Lack of appeal.* Guest benefits are overrated or pricing is not competitive.

6. *Lack of control.* Outside factors (the economy, an energy crisis, inclement weather) have made it necessary to lower marketing plan goals.

7. *Lack of realistic goals.* Guests have been wrongly targeted at a time when they are not planning to buy, or sales goals are simply too high.

Whatever the reason for lagging sales, it must be determined that enough time has been given for the plan to work and that corrective measures have been taken to build sales in each market segment. Objective evaluations and corrective actions may prevent costly mistakes and can lead to more effective marketing strategies in subsequent years.

Notes

1. For more information on marketing planning, see Robert L. Blomstrom, ed., *Strategic Marketing Planning in the Hospitality Industry* (East Lansing, Mich.: Educational Institute of the American Hotel & Motel Association, 1982), and Christopher W. L. Hart and David A. Troy, *Strategic Hotel/Motel Marketing*, rev. ed. (East Lansing, Mich.: Educational Institute of the American Hotel & Motel Association, 1986).

2. In some areas, it is possible to get breakdowns of occupancy tax by individual property. By knowing how much tax was collected each month, the monthly room revenue can be computed, and, by dividing this figure by the estimated average rate, the occupancy percentage can be fairly accurately determined.

3. For more information on situation analyses, see Julia Crystler, *Situation Analysis Workbook* (East Lansing, Mich.: HSMAI Foundation and the Educational Institute of the American Hotel & Motel Association, 1983).

4. For more information on preparing budgets and forecasts, see *Where the Money Goes: Expense Allocations in the Hotel Sales Office*. This 1988 study, conducted by Pannell Kerr Forster, focuses on how much marketing and sales departments spend to attract business to their properties. It also contains worksheets for use by those responsible for a hotel's marketing and sales budget. The study is available from HSMAI, 1300 L. Street, N.W., Suite 800, Washington, DC 20005.

Discussion Questions

1. The marketing plan should be developed for what time frame?
2. What are six steps in developing a marketing plan?
3. The marketing audit consists of what three analyses?
4. What are the objectives of a competition analysis?
5. What two forms are suggested for helping to determine the guest base?
6. What types of information are found in a guest profile?
7. What are two basic positioning choices?
8. What are four guidelines for marketing objectives?
9. Which type of budget is considered best for marketing?
10. What are seven reasons sales goals are not met?

Chapter Outline

I. The Marketing and Sales Division
II. Organizing a Sales Office
   A. The Sales Area
   B. Hiring Effective Salespeople
   C. Training Salespeople
      1. Property Knowledge
      2. Office Procedures
      3. Personal Expectations
      4. Salesmanship
         a. Buying motivations
         b. The personality types of buyers
      5. Training Techniques
   D. Managing Salespeople
   E. Evaluating Salespeople
   F. Compensating Salespeople
      1. Sales Incentive Programs
   G. Supplemental Sales Staff
      1. The Regional Sales Office
      2. Hotel Representatives
III. Developing the Sales Office Communication System
   A. Sales Meetings
      1. Weekly Staff Meetings
      2. Weekly Function Meetings
      3. Monthly Sales Meetings
      4. Sales Committee Meetings
      5. Annual or Semi-Annual Sales Meetings for All Employees
   B. Sales Records
      1. The Function Book
         a. Control of the function book
      2. The Guestroom Control Book
         a. Confirmations, options, and holds
   C. Filing Systems
      1. The Master Card File
      2. The Account File
      3. The Tickler File
         a. How the tickler file works
IV. Evaluating the Sales Office
V. The Automated Sales Office

3 The Sales Office

The most important part of any property's sales team is the sales office. Whether it stands alone at a small property or is part of a larger marketing and sales department or division at a medium-size or large property, a well-organized sales office staffed with enthusiastic, knowledgeable salespeople is the key to a property's sales success.

The Marketing and Sales Division

Marketing and sales divisions or departments vary according to the size, type, and budget of the property. Exhibit 3.1 shows typical organization charts for the sales personnel of a small and a medium-size property.

Exhibit 3.2 presents a sample organization chart for the marketing and sales division of a large hotel. Although the responsibilities of the division staff may vary among properties, a brief description of typical duties and responsibilities of division members follows:

Vice President or Director of Marketing and Sales—Considered the head of the sales effort at large properties, the vice president or director of marketing and sales usually serves on the executive committee of the property. Some directors of marketing and sales are actively involved in sales; others confine themselves to administering the division.

Director of Convention Service or Convention Service Manager—Hotels that have substantial convention and group meeting business will generally employ a director of convention service or convention service manager who is responsible for overseeing the servicing of group business once it has been sold. The director of convention service is available to meet with clients and sales personnel to discuss the feasibility of bookings and the specifics of meetings. He or she must work closely with all departments, coordinating the efforts of the food and beverage department, the front office, and the banquet setup crew.

Director of Advertising and Public Relations—The job of the director of advertising and public relations is to coordinate all promotional materials and establish a good public image for the property. He or she also helps select advertising media for the property.

Telemarketing Director—This member of the marketing and sales division manages the telemarketing center and works closely with the sales staff.

Industry Profile

Danielle Imming began working in the hospitality industry while attending the University of Nevada, Las Vegas. Initially she worked for a company bringing charters to Las Vegas from the East Coast, then for the Riviera Hotel as a front desk agent. She has worked as a tour and travel coordinator and director of catering/ convention services and is now Director of Sales for Bally's Resort, Las Vegas.

Danielle Imming
Director of Sales
Bally's Resort

"After graduating from college in 1980 I assumed—as we all do—that all the major companies would beat a path to my door. Wrong! Without the needed sales experience and contacts, I was not a hotly pursued candidate. Reality soon set in and I realized that the 'real world' is nothing like college.

I continued to network through the Hotel Sales & Marketing Association International, the American Marketing Association, and any other organization that could give me the contacts I needed. Finally it all fell in place, and I began my sales career at the Hacienda Hotel working in Tour and Travel Sales. Then, in 1985, I was hired as National Sales Manager for Bally's Resort. After three years with Bally's I was promoted to Director of Sales.

The role of the sales department at Bally's is vitally important. And in order to reach occupancy and revenue goals, our sales office must be organized.

Each salesperson is assigned accounts to work on and maintain. In addition, salespeople are responsible for researching and developing new accounts. This can be done through directories published by organizations or the government, attendance at trade shows, and personal sales calls. Once a sale is made, salespeople continue to interact with their clients until the function is over. This keeps the lines of communication open and, when the function concludes, the salesperson can begin the process of rebooking immediately.

Our marketing plan is our road map for sales efforts. Once a year, a plan for the next selling year is determined. We look at guest mixes and the percentage of tour/travel versus convention business we need to book on a monthly basis in order to achieve our contribution to the occupancy level. We also establish our upcoming travel schedule—from trade show and conference attendance, to personal sales trips, to our participation in special events such as the Detroit Auto Show and the AFL-CIO Executive Council Meeting.

Standard operating procedures provide a reference for our sales and catering personnel and are a great tool for training new salespeople. When procedures and policies are clearly defined in writing, communication is improved. Having the lines of communication open is very important because we all must know what others are doing in order to sell productively. Business should never be lost because someone didn't go that last step.

Sales meetings are held on a weekly basis. We normally review our books for the next two years and discuss how to fill any gaps in business that are there. All salespeople have the opportunity to discuss any tentatives they're working on as well as any problems they're having with an account. We also review any tentatives that have come up for option because it's extremely important that, if a group has cancelled, its dates be cleared ASAP.

The function book is used to control all banquet and function space. This book is the master control for us, so it must be accurate. Convention schedules are requested from clients six months prior to a convention so we can 'clean up' the space blocks and allow Catering to book local functions into space the convention client doesn't need. Soon our function book will go on computer, just like our room nights book.

Successful selling programs and a well-organized sales office go hand in hand. It's the task of the Director of Sales to coordinate all sales activities so that everyone's pulling in the same direction. An organized sales office eliminates confusion, saves time, and increases guest satisfaction while maximizing profits. **"**

It is his or her job to supervise and manage the telephone sales staff, which is responsible for developing leads, making prospecting calls, and following up on leads and previous clients.

Exhibit 3.1 Sample Organization Charts for the Sales Personnel at Small and Medium-Size Properties

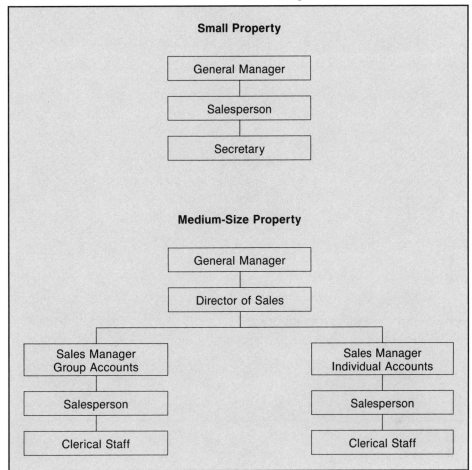

Small Property

General Manager

Salesperson

Secretary

Medium-Size Property

General Manager

Director of Sales

Sales Manager Group Accounts

Salesperson

Clerical Staff

Sales Manager Individual Accounts

Salesperson

Clerical Staff

Market Research Coordinator—Many large properties employ a marketing professional who oversees the development of information regarding the history and past performance of each account being solicited. The market research coordinator may also research current market trends, the strategies used by competing properties, and general consumer trends. This research is used in the development of sales strategies by the property.

The following positions form the heart of the marketing and sales division—the sales office.

Director of Sales—The director of sales is usually in charge of the sales office and supervises the sales office staff. In addition to administrative duties, the director of sales may also handle key accounts, assist salespeople when necessary, and prepare sales reports for top management (see Exhibit 3.3).

Sales Manager—In small properties, this position might be synonymous with the director of sales, while in larger properties, the sales manager would report to the director of sales. Sales managers usually assign territory or accounts to salespeople, monitor the progress of salespeople, and handle

Exhibit 3.2   Sample Organization Chart for a Marketing and Sales Division

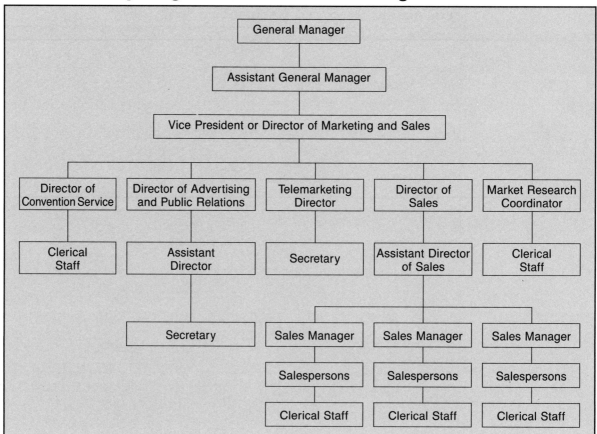

their own accounts, although specific duties will vary depending on the structure of the sales office (see Exhibit 3.4).

Assistant Director of Sales—When this position is used, the assistant director of sales serves as the chief aide to the director of sales. The assistant director of sales may manage the sales office, supervise sales staff, and handle his or her own accounts. If the sales office is headed by a sales manager, this position would be called the assistant sales manager.

Salespeople or Sales Representatives—Salespeople are the backbone of any sales organization. They are responsible for contacting, soliciting, and providing follow-up service to clients.

Although for the sake of clarity we will refer to employees in this position as "salespeople" in this text, in today's hospitality industry the title "salesperson" is seldom used. Salespeople are usually given titles such as "sales manager" to give them increased credibility. In some operations, even members of the sales office clerical staff are called "sales managers." Senior salespeople are sometimes given the title of "sales executive" or "account executive."

At small properties, a salesperson usually handles all types of business. He or she may call on meeting planners, travel agents, tour operators, and other sources of potential business. At medium, large, and convention properties, each salesperson may be given a specific assignment: individual sales

Exhibit 3.3   The Role of a Director of Sales

A director of sales is responsible for several important aspects of the sales function:

1. **Coordinating with top management.** A good director of sales works closely with the general manager and other department heads, often on a weekly basis, to ensure that all the sales needs of the property are being met.

2. **Administering a sales support system.** A good sales office needs an efficient filing system, written policies and procedures, and an effective paper flow for correspondence. It is up to the director of sales to ensure that all sales systems are operating smoothly or that needed corrections are made.

3. **Training the sales staff.** The director of sales is often responsible for initial training, but must also continue to coach and counsel the sales staff. It is up to the director of sales to identify weak areas and see that the sales staff corrects them.

4. **Setting sales targets.** A good director of sales determines specific target clients in each market segment and ensures that sales calls are tailored to meet the needs of potential clients. The director of sales also evaluates business potential and steers the sales staff to lucrative areas.

5. **Evaluating sales progress.** It is up to the director of sales to have a written sales plan with definite goals in order to measure progress.

6. **Evaluating sales procedures.** The primary job of a sales office is to sell, and all non-selling functions (sales meetings, travel time, etc.) should be analyzed to be certain they are kept to a minimum. For example, the director of sales might decide to eliminate a few non-productive sales meetings to make more time for selling.

It is also up to the director of sales to determine if he or she is communicating with both sales staff and management, and if there are any problems that need to be arbitrated. If the director of sales is competent in all of these duties, he or she will ensure that the sales office runs smoothly.

(sales to leisure or business travelers who are not traveling with a group); group sales (sales to associations or corporations in which a number of rooms and/or meeting rooms and other facilities are sold); international sales (sales to guests from foreign countries); group and/or individual sales to tour brokers, tour operators, and/or travel agents; or food and beverage sales (banquets, functions, and so on). All of these types of selling responsibilities will be discussed in subsequent chapters.

Clerical Staff—The clerical staff is responsible for maintaining sales paperwork, freeing salespeople to solicit clients. A good clerical staff is essential for the maintenance of sales reports, and may do research for salespeople. As mentioned above, the clerical staff is often included in the "sales manager" category. In many cases, the clerical staff knows as much about the property as the salespeople, and they can often generate leads or actually "sell" a client.

Organizing a Sales Office

Whether it stands alone at a small property or is included within a marketing and sales division or department at a large property, a sales office can be organized in a variety of ways, based on a number of factors:

Exhibit 3.4 Sample Job Description — Group Sales Manager

Job Title:	Group Sales Manager
Department:	Marketing and Sales
Reports To:	Director of Sales
Basic Functions:	Review the marketing strategy that will obtain maximum occupancy levels and average rate with the director of sales. Responsible for all group business within the western territory.
	Consult daily with the director of sales concerning the western territory and how it relates to the sales success of the hotel. Effective merchandising, prospecting, solicitation, and booking of business are among the areas that will be discussed.
Scope:	The group sales manager will be the primary person responsible for booking long-term group business (long-term being more than six months out).
Work Performed:	Initiate prospecting and solicitation of new accounts in the western territory; manage current accounts to maximize guestroom nights; responsible for administrative efforts necessary to perform these tasks.

Quotas for this position are:

Room nights per month:	1,200
Soft spot percentage:	20%
Phone calls per week:	
Trace/Follow-up	20
Prospecting	25
Personal calls per week:	10
New accounts per month:	10
Referrals per month:	5

The group sales manager must supply weekly, monthly, and annual reports supporting productivity standards.

Probe for client needs: rooms, suites, desired dates, day-of-week pattern, program agenda, food and beverage requirements, and degree of flexibility in each of these areas.

When available, obtain information on a group's past history; i.e., previous rooms picked up, arrival/departure pattern, and double occupancy percentage.

Review availability of clients' required dates and research any alternative dates which should be offered. The dates presented to clients should satisfy their needs while allowing the hotel to maximize occupancy and average rate.

Negotiate with clients the day or days of the week that rooms will be needed (and held), the number of rooms that will be blocked for each day of the function, and group rates (within guidelines as set by the director of sales regarding comps and function space).

Tentatively block rooms and function space in accordance with office policy.

Confirm in writing, according to office standards (via short-term contract or long-term contract and function room outline), all aspects of the meetings. Track to ensure groups receive signed contracts.

Alert all necessary departments (i.e., front office and credit) of pending tentative bookings.

Upon receiving a signed contract, process definite booking ticket, definite function room outline, and credit application.

Oversee, manage, and track the way in which reservations are made, the pick-up of group blocks, adherence to cut-off dates, and any subsequent adjustment to room blocks (positive or negative).

Periodically contact clients while in-house to be certain all is in order and going well; handle any last-minute needs as they arise.

Exhibit 3.4 *(continued)*

Conduct an exit interview with clients to determine level of satisfaction and ask for additional business.

Send letter of appreciation to clients. Letter should include actual room night consumption and should be tailored to previous exit-interview discussions.

Attend extra-curricular activities and meetings, and accept any responsibilities or projects as directed by the director of sales.

Supervision Exercised: Supervise one secretary.

Supervision Received: Primary supervision from the director of sales. Initial training, and retraining as needed, also received from the director of sales. Receive direction from the director of sales in regard to room merchandising.

Responsibility & Authority: Upon satisfactory completion of rooms merchandising and operational training, the group sales manager will have the authority to confirm dates, room blocks, and rates directly with clients.

Minimum Requirements: Bachelor's degree, preferably in business, hotel, or restaurant administration. Individual must also be professional in appearance and approach.

Experience: Minimum of two years experience in hotel sales.

Sales Competencies:
1. Ability to negotiate.
2. Ability to prioritize and manage accounts.
3. Ability to prospect.
4. Ability to judge the profitability of new business.
5. Knowledge of product.
6. Knowledge of competition.
7. Ability to make sales presentations.
8. Ability to organize and plan.
9. Ability to utilize selling skills.
10. Ability to overcome objections.
11. Ability to solve problems and make decisions.
12. Ability to write effectively.

A job description is a detailed statement about a job, including work to be performed and organizational relationships. Job descriptions aid in the hiring process by defining the specific criteria needed to fill a position effectively; note that this sample job description lists activity goals (phone calls and personal sales calls required per week), but also lists productivity goals—performance measured by the number of room nights booked per month. Job descriptions also serve as a general guideline for training personnel. It is the responsibility of the general manager and/or the head of the marketing and sales department or sales office to develop job descriptions for each sales position.

- The property's goals and objectives
- The budget available for sales
- Available outside assistance (travel agents, chain referrals, reservation systems, and so on)
- The total market potential and the number of people needed to take advantage of that potential

When organizing a sales office, it is important to detail the objectives of the sales team and select supervisory personnel to oversee the typical operations of a sales office, which include:

- Increasing property revenue through personal sales calls, telephone calls, and correspondence

- Establishing guidelines for the number of personal sales calls, telephone calls, and sales letters required from each salesperson

- Assisting the general manager with obtaining the maximum sales effort from all employees

- Holding weekly and monthly sales meetings

- Maintaining sales reports and establishing a sales filing system to ensure that all files are processed and kept up-to-date

The property's sales office must be organized so that every employee knows his or her responsibilities, authority, and accountability. Three classic organizational principles should be a part of every sales office:

1. *Unity of command.* The effectiveness of the sales office can be seriously hampered if employees have two or three bosses giving conflicting orders. By ensuring that each employee has only one boss, accountability is established.

2. *Authority commensurate with responsibility.* A sales manager who is given the responsibility to increase sales must also have the authority to secure those sales. For best results, authority should be commensurate with responsibility.

3. *Span of control.* There is a limit to the number of employees that supervisors can effectively manage. While there is no universally accepted figure, it is important that no supervisor be given more people than he or she can handle.

The sales office must be structured in such a way that business is handled profitably. This necessitates the delegation of the proper authority for the sales office to carry out its work. To function well, the head of the sales office must have full authority over all aspects of the sales office and sales promotional tools.

The Sales Area   Whether the property is large or small, the sales offices may be the first property area a potential client sees, and the importance of first impressions cannot be overstated.

Potential clients should be properly greeted by the sales secretary or receptionist. The sales area should be accessible but private—no "goldfish bowl" off the main lobby, but not stuck away in a basement or unused guestroom. (If the hotel has meeting and banquet rooms, the ideal location is adjacent to these facilities.) The furniture should be tasteful, the offices well lit and properly ventilated, and the decor uncluttered and professional. The decor should include photographs of events, guestrooms, meeting rooms, and the property's staff, as well as awards received by the property. Above all, every member of the sales office—from the sales manager to the file clerks—should be knowledgeable about the property and ready to share information about the property's benefits.

Exhibit 3.5   Sample Interview Questions for Hiring Salespeople

1. What do you like most about selling?

2. What is the greatest lesson you have learned from your sales experience?

3. How do you organize your time to maximize your sales effectiveness?

4. What would your plan be if you were asked to sell to a market segment that was new to you?

5. How do you schedule appointments?

6. How would you rate your ability to schedule appointments? Your ability in one-to-one selling?

7. How do you service and follow up an account?

8. What information is most important to collect on competitors?

9. What do salespeople need to know about their product? What is the most important thing?

10. How did you handle a difficult client objection that you have faced?

11. Can you describe a time when you didn't quit when making a difficult sale?

12. What techniques do you use for getting by intermediaries when making telephone sales calls?

13. What has been the most difficult thing for you to learn in selling?

14. What resources do you use for prospecting new leads?

15. What is your approach to closing a sale?

Each of these open-ended questions is an opportunity for the applicant to talk about him- or herself—and for the interviewer to determine sales strengths and weaknesses.

Hiring Effective Salespeople

Since effective salespeople are so important to the property's sales efforts, it is essential that a good sales staff be hired (see Exhibit 3.5).

To build an effective sales team, the sales manager should be aware of a number of characteristics common to successful salespeople:

1. *Professionalism.* Successful salespeople present a professional image. They dress well, but conservatively, and are well groomed. A successful salesperson projects honesty, reliability, and enthusiasm, and potential clients sense he or she is sincerely interested in meeting their needs.

2. *Ability to communicate.* Successful salespeople are excellent communicators, both in speaking and in writing. Their sales presentations are clear and interesting, they are able to build rapport with clients through small talk, and they can handle questions and objections calmly.

3. *Intelligence.* Successful salespeople are knowledgeable and learn very quickly. They have the ability to share their knowledge with a client, thus boosting their credibility.

4. *Ability to analyze.* Successful salespeople can objectively analyze their property's strengths and weaknesses and use their findings to

benefit potential clients. They are also adept at analyzing clients, and are able to suggest additional products or services to meet clients' needs.

5. *Motivation.* Successful salespeople have a positive mental attitude and are goal-oriented. They understand that sales is often a "numbers game," see each rejection as a step closer to closing a sale, and refuse to let failures keep them from going after additional business. They are extremely self-disciplined, and have the ability to sell in a variety of situations.

6. *Efficiency.* Successful salespeople are experts at managing their time and sales territory. They turn waiting time into sales time, and waste little effort on unproductive activities and accounts.

Since salespeople are often the first contact clients have with a property, potential salespeople should rate high in these six areas. It is important to note that salespeople are not "born salespeople," however; almost any enthusiastic, intelligent applicant, properly trained, can become a real asset to a property's sales staff.

Good salespeople can be found through word of mouth, advertising in newspapers or trade publications, employment agencies, and contacts through associations or organizations that deal with the sales profession, such as the Hotel Sales & Marketing Association International (HSMAI). They can even be found inside the property!

Training Salespeople

Once selected, salespeople (even the experienced new hires) need to be trained.[1] The initial training provided for salespeople can mean the difference between bookings and lost business, so salespeople must have a firm foundation in the following key areas.

Property Knowledge. Each new salesperson should have a complete tour of the property to become familiar with the property's staff; the facilities, services, and products offered; and the strengths and weaknesses of the property. Salespeople should also be presented with an overview of the entire operation and shown the role they play in reaching the hotel's financial objectives.

It is important that new salespeople learn about the financial status of the property. Salespeople need to understand the economics of the hotel, and should be coached regarding:

1. The property's rate structure.

2. The profit contribution of each of the hotel's revenue centers. While margins may vary from one property to another, departmental profit margins run about 75% for guestroom sales, 15% for restaurant food sales, 40% for beverage sales, and 35% for banquet revenue. Because of its high profit margin, the major source of profits lies in guestroom sales rather than the food and beverage area.

3. The present percentage of business from each market segment, and the targeted optimum business mix.

4. The property's slow business periods, so that efforts can be directed to times when business is most needed. The negative effects of booking low-rated business during peak periods, or reserving banquet or function space for local groups when that space could have been reserved for groups needing guestrooms, should be explained.

5. The targeted average rates for each market segment, and authoritative guidelines for quoting rates.

Office Procedures. Each salesperson should know the sales office routine. Sales office hours; booking policies; the function and guestroom control books; sales forms and reports; paper flow; and past, present, and future promotional material should be explained.

To avoid confusion and poor communication, it is important that each salesperson have just one boss (the unity of command principle). Each salesperson should know the chain of command in the sales office, and how he or she fits into the general sales picture. Each salesperson should also know how much of his or her work can be delegated to the sales clerical staff, and who takes the responsibility for the work delegated.

Equally important is knowledge of the office's standard operating procedures (SOPs). SOPs are written instructions explaining how recurring business activities should *always* be handled. Each property has different policies regarding expense reports, VIP and complimentary room policies, sales office room allotments, and booking procedures, so it is essential that salespeople know the guidelines and limits set by the property. SOPs should be in writing, and salespeople must be committed to studying and learning them. Written SOPs can serve as a training manual for new salespeople and a ready reference for the experienced.

Personal Expectations. Every salesperson should know exactly what is expected of him or her in terms of deadlines, sales quotas, numbers and types of sales calls (personal, telephone, and so on), correspondence, and inter-property communications. New salespeople should be given a detailed, written job description, goals—both long-term and specific short-term goals—should be outlined, and a territory or accounts assigned. A good sales manager will give a new salesperson at least one or two high-potential accounts. It is discouraging to new salespeople to get accounts that no one else wants. Success builds enthusiasm, so some "live" accounts should be given to new hires.

It is important that salespeople understand the market segments they are expected to target. If a salesperson will be working with corporate group accounts, for example, he or she will have to learn the common procedures used by corporations for booking guestrooms and meeting facilities. He or she will need to determine which corporations use a travel department for making accommodations, and which corporations have arrangements handled by a secretary or other clerical personnel.

It is vital that new salespeople learn how to recognize profitable and non-profitable accounts. Some accounts produce more business than others, and it is usually up to the individual salesperson to determine which accounts are producing—and, consequently, which accounts deserve more of the salesperson's time.

Salesmanship. While many of the attributes of successful salesmanship will be covered in detail in Chapter 4, it is important to note that instruction in the psychology of selling is part of successful sales training. More and more properties are realizing the value of training salespeople to recognize motivations for buying decisions and the types of buyers salespeople will typically encounter. The information presented in the following two sections is just an example of the many different theories, systems, principles, and hypotheses available to salespeople seeking to learn more about selling psychology.

Buying motivations. Most people purchase products and services to meet one or more of four basic needs: biological needs, social needs, self-fulfillment needs, and psychological needs.[2]

Biological needs are basic needs for food, shelter, and clothing. A hotel salesperson can appeal to a traveler's need for shelter while traveling, and to basic food needs to sell the property's food and beverage facilities.

Social needs include people's desire to belong, and their need to feel at home even in a strange city. Hotel salespeople can sell the property to individuals with strong social needs by stressing the property's friendly service, its appeal to travelers with similar interests (business travelers, families, tourist groups, and so on), and special social amenities such as complimentary "get acquainted" cocktail parties.

Self-fulfillment needs are represented by the desire to live graciously or to reward one's self for fulfilling personal goals, succeeding in business, and so on. People who are primarily motivated by this need may be more responsive to hotel salespeople who represent a property that offers status.

Psychological needs are largely undefinable, even by those who are motivated to buy as a result of these needs. Most people traveling, for example, need shelter for the night, but what makes them choose one property over similar properties? Perhaps they stayed in a Holiday Inn as a child, and staying in Holiday Inns as an adult provides a satisfying re-creation of that childhood experience. Whatever the deep-seated psychological reason, it is often difficult for a salesperson to know exactly what will appeal to a person who makes a decision based on psychological needs.

Not only do buying motivations vary, the personalities of clients also vary. Learning to recognize a client's basic personality type can greatly increase a salesperson's chances of selling to him or her.

The personality types of buyers. Like buying motivations, personalities can be divided into four basic types: the director, the socializer, the relater, and the thinker (see Exhibit 3.6).[3]

The *director* is interested in getting results quickly, and is assertive and often blunt. He or she is interested in facts and the bottom line. To successfully sell to a director, salespeople must be prepared, organized, fast-paced, and to the point. A director must be made to feel that the decision to buy is his or her own; it is best for the salesperson to present two or three options and let the director select the one most suitable to his or her needs.

The *socializer*, on the other hand, is playful and talkative. He or she enjoys the opportunity to talk about personal ideas and opinions, and is usually in no hurry to end a discussion. To successfully sell to a socializer, salespeople must be stimulating and interesting but give the socializer the chance to speak. Socializers usually respond to stories or illustrations that relate to them and their goals.

Exhibit 3.6   Four Personality Types

Source: Adapted from information developed by Jim Cathcart of Cathcart, Alessandra & Associates, Inc. Used with permission.

Like the socializer, the *relater* is a people person. Relaters tend to look upon things in terms of how they affect people and relationships. Relaters also need a lot of reassurance once the sale has been completed. To successfully sell to a relater, salespeople must be supportive and somewhat personal. They must never seem to be in a hurry to get the sale and terminate the contact. It is important that salespeople study the relater's feelings and emotional needs as well as his or her business needs.

The *thinker* is an idea person who is precise, efficient, and well-organized. Thinkers are not interested in words; they must be won through actions, and it is important that they be given solid, factual evidence to digest. To successfully sell to a thinker, salespeople must be well-prepared and have all the answers to any questions the thinker may ask. Since thinkers are task-oriented, they will get right to the point and will want the facts presented in a logical manner. In fact, logic is the key word when dealing with thinkers; they want logical solutions to problems. Documentation is essential when dealing with this personality type.

Training Techniques. Although methods of training vary from property to property, there are several common techniques that many properties use:

1. *Simulated sales calls.* These are sales calls acted out by the sales staff. A new salesperson can make a sales presentation and be critiqued by other staff members. When videotaping is used, the new salesperson can view his or her performance and make corrections as necessary.

2. *Double calling.* With double calling, a sales presentation is made by a new salesperson accompanied by the director of sales or a senior salesperson. There are drawbacks to this method, however. The new salesperson may feel nervous, resulting in a poor presentation. And it takes two people to make a call.

3. *Market segmentation drills.* New and experienced salespeople can meet to discuss market segment characteristics and the sales tactics that work best with each segment.

4. *Case study exercises.* In this training exercise, a hotel's sales staff is challenged to formulate a sales action plan for a property other than its own. It may be a competitor's property or an imaginary property. This exercise hones sales strategies that may then be applied to the staff's own property.

The success of sales training can be measured by the performance of the sales staff. At the end of training, each salesperson should be able to:

1. Explain the property's marketing plan.

2. Prepare a property fact book.

3. Conduct sales tours of the property.

4. Understand how accounts are established and approved, the property's policy on advance deposits for groups, and credit policies of the hotel as they apply to functions.

5. Research information on current and potential accounts.

6. Prepare sales correspondence.

7. Prepare for and complete sales calls.

8. Prepare sales call and booking reports and interpret monthly sales progress reports.

9. Use the sales office's filing system.

10. Analyze the financial performance of the sales office by

interpreting the income and expense items on the hotel's profit and loss statement that are directly affected by the sales office.

Giving the sales staff a firm training foundation is time well invested. The value of continuing education for the sales staff is also important. In-house seminars and industry courses such as those offered by the Educational Institute of the American Hotel & Motel Association will help ensure that a sales staff develops to its full potential.

Managing Salespeople

Managing hospitality salespeople is a specialized type of personnel management for several reasons.[4] First, in today's highly competitive market, it is often necessary for salespeople to be away from home and family for extended periods of time. Salespeople are also away from the sales office, making it difficult for them to form close ties with the rest of the property's sales team. Additionally, the business of selling has psychological effects—it is natural for a salesperson to get depressed if he or she has put on a dynamic presentation and the client doesn't buy.

A sales manager must become involved in a number of areas to ensure that sales volume goals are met or exceeded and costly personnel turnover is kept to a minimum. Sales management involves training salespeople, scheduling salespeople and assigning accounts, motivating salespeople, and supervising the efforts of the sales staff.

Training involves both the beginning and continuing instruction of salespeople in many areas. Salespeople often learn at different rates, but the sales manager should check with the sales trainer to see that expectations are being met and that minor problems are corrected before they become major ones.

Scheduling salespeople involves analyzing both the needs of the property and the strengths and weaknesses of individual salespeople. If a property targets the business traveler, for example, it is important to select a salesperson who can relate well to and is well-received by this market segment. In addition, other factors must be taken into consideration when assigning salespeople to accounts. Does the account require extensive travel? If so, is the salesperson free to travel, or would his or her family situation prohibit extensive travel? Is the salesperson more people-oriented or detail-oriented? Would he or she work better with decision-makers who are "directors," for example, rather than "relater" types? Does the salesperson have inherent time management skills, or would he or she require close supervision?

Even if the sales manager places salespeople in accounts suitable for their talents and strengths, it is still important that salespeople be motivated on a periodic basis. In most cases, money is a less effective motivator than personal recognition. It is important that salespeople be given incentives, of course, but it is often more effective to personally encourage the salesperson, especially if he or she is having an "off" period.

Supervising the efforts of the sales staff is an ongoing process, but it is often difficult to gauge efforts in selling situations. Many sales managers feel that monitoring sales quotas is enough, and a periodic review of a salesperson's weekly activity report (see Exhibit 3.7) is all the supervision given. Other sales managers more closely supervise their personnel by periodically testing them on their knowledge, including asking them to give sample presentations to ensure that their performances are up to property guidelines.

Exhibit 3.7 Sample Weekly Activity Report

Weekly Booking Activity Report

Page ____ of ____

Hotel _____

Reporting Period _____ Year _____

Name of Group	*DCT	Dates	Room Nts	Room Rates	Room Revenue	Food Covers	Bev. Covers	F&B Revenue	MTG RM Revenue	**DES.

*D-Definite
C-Cancellation
T-Tentative
**Designation
N-New Business
R-Repeat Business
U-Unsolicited Business
CW-City Wide
SO-Regional Sales Office

	Room Nights	Covers	$
Group Rm Sales			
Group Rm Cxl.			
Net Sales			
Total Food			
Total Beverage			
Total Mtg. Rm.			
F&B Cxl.			
Mtg. Rm. Cxl.			
Net Sales			
TOTAL NET SALES			

	Per Calls			Telephone Calls			Correspondence		
	WK.	MTH.	YTD	WK.	MTH.	YTD	WK.	MTH.	YTD
GM									
DDS									
DOS									
SR									
SR									
SS									
TOT									

Manager _____ Sales Director _____ Date _____

A weekly activity report is used to monitor the performance of the sales staff. This form not only tracks the number of sales calls made and other activity goals, but also details room nights booked and the dollar value of group business.
Courtesy of Quality Inns.

Their personal quotas are also reviewed on a regular basis to ensure that they are performing to the best of their ability.[5]

Evaluating Salespeople

Evaluating the hotel's salespeople plays an important part in evaluating the success of the property's total sales efforts. Evaluation usually covers personal quotas (expected number of phone calls, personal sales calls, new accounts, etc.) and the actual performance of the salesperson (a salesperson can make more than the number of calls assigned, but still bring in less business than expected). Evaluation can also cover a number of other areas. Good salesmanship is more than successful selling. It is a continual growth process that includes the salesperson's appearance and demeanor, time management and organizational skills, ability to prospect for and develop leads, ability to follow up on accounts, and attitude toward the property and selling.

To improve sales performance, evaluation systems should be established on at least a quarterly basis. Waiting for a yearly review leaves too much time for minor areas of difficulty to develop into major problems. A frequent evaluation period allows for timely feedback that can enhance the salesperson's performance. Frequent feedback also allows management to determine if suggested changes are actually being put into action.

Compensating Salespeople

Most properties pay a new salesperson a straight salary for the first six to twelve months on the job. This policy enables new salespeople to establish a client base, since most commissions are paid only after business is realized. After the prescribed salary-only period, salespeople are usually compensated on a salary plus commission basis.

There are many variables for determining the salary structure for salespeople: the geographic area, the level of experience, salaries offered by competitors, and sales quotas are a few examples.

Sales Incentive Programs. Sales incentive programs offer rewards separate from a salesperson's regular pay and commissions, and are provided to give extra recognition to good performers, reduce sales staff turnover, and build a team spirit. Incentive programs can also be used to spark competition between departments. Incentives may include cash bonuses (on top of commissions), merchandise (cars, furs, and so on), vacation trips (in the case of chain properties, sometimes to another property in the chain), or a combination of rewards. No matter what type of incentive program is developed, it must be designed to give individuals or departments a specific reward for meeting a specific objective.

One example of an incentive program is the multi-faceted program developed by The Ritz-Carlton Hotel Company. Annual sales quotas (gross room revenues booked) are established jointly by each salesperson and his or her immediate supervisor. Ritz-Carlton salespeople are eligible for a bonus of up to 15% of their annual salary for achieving 100% of their annual sales quota. Additional cash awards are given to recognize outstanding accomplishments such as reactivating lost accounts, salvaging cancellations, creating new business, or greatly exceeding set quotas. The size of these cash awards is determined by the hotel's corporate management.

Whatever the choice of incentives by a property, the main goal is to produce a motivated, productive sales staff. Properties as well as salespeople can profit from incentive programs, since such programs often result in more business.

Supplemental Sales Staff

It is often impractical or uneconomical for individual hotels to be represented nationwide by their in-house sales staff. Therefore, many properties have looked for a means to supplement their staff's sales efforts. Many chain properties are turning to regional sales offices to help them with regional, national, and even worldwide sales efforts. Sheraton, for example, operates regional offices around the globe in cities such as Brussels, London, Melbourne, Paris, Tokyo, and Toronto. Many hotels with no chain affiliation have hired hotel representatives to assist their sales teams.

The Regional Sales Office. A regional sales office usually consists of a regional director of sales, area directors of sales, senior account executives, account executives, a research director, an office manager, and a clerical staff.[6] Regional sales personnel often work in individual hotels within the region before advancing to the regional level.

A hotel chain's regional sales office may present workshops, seminars, and receptions to attract local executives desiring to learn more about the chain, and may provide news releases and feature columns for use in local newspapers. While the responsibilities of regional sales offices are typically directed toward promotions and public relations, the offices can also scout potential business and develop sales leads in a particular geographic area. For example, a regional sales office for Hilton in Chicago not only sells Hilton's Chicago hotels to people in other cities; it also sells Hilton hotels from all over the country to people within a prescribed radius of Chicago.

Regional sales offices maintain extensive records regarding business prospects in the region. The regional office's computer data banks can offer concise listings of group business; provide information on a client's needs, past meeting history, and the suitability of a property for a particular group; and serve as a central clearinghouse for public space, guestroom, date availability, and rate information for all the properties in the region.

Today, most U.S. hotel chains have regional offices in major cities such as New York, Los Angeles, and Washington, D.C., particularly if the chain serves groups. Many associations and corporations have their headquarters in these large population areas. For example, Washington, D.C., has over twenty-five regional offices to service the potential business of that city. A number of hotel chains also maintain a regional sales office at their corporate headquarters location. This allows for the close monitoring of the chain's operations, and is especially effective if corporate headquarters happens to be located in an industrial or population center or in a popular travel destination.

Hotel Representatives. Many independent properties are turning to outside hotel representatives for sales assistance. These representatives or "reps" serve as out-of-town or market-source business representatives for non-competing properties. Because hiring hotel representatives is often more economical than setting up an individual property sales outlet, hotel reps can be extremely effective for hotels that are not a part of a chain or franchise system (although hotel reps may also be used for supplemental promotion by chain properties).

Since hotels have different needs, the services provided by hotel reps can vary widely. In some cases, the rep may be hired as a field salesperson, soliciting clients who are impractical for the hotel's in-house staff to reach. A property in Florida, for example, may find it more economical to hire a hotel rep in Boston than to send its own salespeople to that city. Other hotels use large representation companies, such as Robert Warner and Loews Representation International. Services provided by these firms include consulting, market analysis, advertising, and public relations in addition to field sales.

For the most part, hotel reps usually serve as:

1. Agents for clients who want to book individual room reservations. The hotel rep may list his or her phone number in advertising targeted in a specific area by a distant property. A hotel in the Virgin Islands, for example, may target a New York City market; the property's hotel rep in New York would answer local phone calls and confirm specific reservations or answer inquiries.

2. Agents who book individual room business through business contacts. The hotel rep's contacts with travel agents, airline companies, and other sources in the area can mean business for the property.

3. Agents who provide detailed data on properties. Most hotel reps are located in major population areas where many corporate and association groups are headquartered. Hotel reps in these cities serve as a clearinghouse for information on the products and services offered by a number of hotels. Corporate and association executives make extensive use of this convenient service, which can lead to a vast amount of business at a minimal expense for a number of properties.

Since a property's hotel rep is an extension of the property's own sales and reservations offices, it is important that the property choose a rep who understands the property's marketing needs. There are several questions that need to be answered before selecting a rep:

1. Does this rep represent any major competitors?

2. Does this rep specialize in our property's target markets?

3. Can this rep provide individual attention to our property or does his or her workload preclude working closely with our sales staff?

4. Can this rep's marketing contacts and sales techniques benefit our property?

5. What is this rep's record of client satisfaction?

6. Does this rep operate adequate facilities—telephone services, field sales staff, reservation capabilities, and so on?

7. Can this rep deliver the supporting services (computerized booking, advertising, and so on) needed by our property?

8. How does this rep compare in cost with other reps who represent properties similar to our property?

9. Does the rep have offices or contacts in the cities that are likely to be our major market areas?

10. Is this rep truly interested in representing our property?

It is also important to determine how the hotel rep will fit into the property's sales organization and how the rep will be paid. Will the rep be a salaried agent of the property, or will he or she become an extra salesperson who works on a commission basis only? A hotel rep is often hired on a contract basis—paid a set fee plus a predetermined commission percentage on the volume of business that he or she directly books for the hotel. It is important with commission arrangements to set clear booking and pricing guidelines; reps should be given acceptable rate structures to ensure that they don't "give away the house" just to receive their commissions!

Once a hotel rep has been selected, it is most important that the sales staff establish a defined line of communication between the property and the rep. The rep's productivity and level of service will largely depend on input from the property.

Developing the Sales Office Communication System

For a sales office to operate at maximum efficiency, lines of communication must be established both within the sales office and with other areas of the property. Good communication ensures that all members of the property's sales team have the same information and that potential problems are kept to a minimum. In one case, for example, a salesperson once promised a corporate client that the property could accommodate the corporation's large wall displays. In the time between the initial contact with the client and the function, however, the property's meeting facilities were remodeled, and the new light-weight walls were not adequate to support the heavy display materials that were transported to the property (at considerable expense) by the client. Needless to say, this failure in communication caused considerable embarrassment—not to mention the loss of a client.

A sales office relies on various methods to communicate ideas and information, including holding meetings, keeping sales records, and establishing filing systems.

Sales Meetings   Regularly scheduled sales meetings are an essential part of a successful sales effort. To ensure maximum production and communication, the head of the sales office may want to hold brief daily meetings with salespeople to discuss daily sales calls and the next day's schedule. He or she may also schedule various other meetings, including:

- Weekly staff meetings
- Weekly function meetings
- Monthly sales meetings
- Sales committee meetings
- Annual or semi-annual sales meetings for all employees

Weekly Staff Meetings. Weekly meetings of the sales staff should be conducted by the head of the sales effort—the director of marketing and sales, the director of sales, or the sales manager (the person heading up the meeting will vary depending on the size of the property and the structure of the marketing and sales department or sales office). These meetings should include the general manager and any department heads whose departments will be discussed. Topics that may be covered in a typical weekly staff meeting are new business prospects, tentative and new bookings, conventions, client service procedures, promotions, publicity, and lost business. An open discussion and brainstorming period should be a part of weekly sales meetings to encourage a mutual exchange of ideas and information.

Weekly Function Meetings. These meetings are held with department heads to review upcoming group events. At these meetings, those departments involved in servicing groups review each group's meeting agenda, commonly called the specification sheet or meeting resume, item by item to ensure that everyone involved understands what is going to take place and to finalize any last-minute details.

Monthly Sales Meetings. These meetings are held to discuss tentative and definite bookings for the next month or quarter, review progress made in achieving sales goals, and discuss new property promotions. Monthly sales meetings are usually attended by all sales personnel.

Sales Committee Meetings. These meetings involve department heads and knowledgeable representatives from each area of the hotel. They are essentially "meetings of the minds" to ensure that every area of the property is adequately covered in the property's marketing plan. The frequency and types of meetings held by sales committees are usually determined by the head of the marketing and sales department or the general manager.

Annual or Semi-Annual Sales Meetings for All Employees. These meetings are held to discuss the marketing plan with the property's entire staff. Such meetings provide an opportunity to obtain ideas and suggestions from all employees.

The marketing plan presented to the staff can be fairly simple and abbreviated, but it should give all employees an overview of the function of the marketing and sales department and outline each employee's specific role in the plan. Sales and advertising programs should also be discussed.

Sales Records

Sales records are a vital part of a sales office's communication system. They are important in servicing accounts and generating repeat business. It is essential that salespeople familiarize themselves with sales forms, learn to complete them properly, and file them in accordance with sales office procedures. In sales offices with computers, the data from the forms is input by the clerical staff, and the information is used to produce a variety of computer-generated reports and analyses.

In most cases, the salesperson's involvement with sales records will begin with a call report, a form generated during a cold call on a prospective client (see Exhibit 3.8). The call report is then placed in the organization or individual's account file, and a notation for follow-up is placed in the tickler file. (Account and tickler files will be discussed later in the chapter.)

When a sales presentation is made, a tentative booking is usually offered if no definite booking is sold (see Exhibit 3.9). Once a definite booking has been made, the salesperson may be required to write and/or sign a contract with the client. If changes are made in the original booking information, a change sheet is required. If the meeting or convention is canceled, a lost business report must be filled out and filed with the sales manager (see Exhibit 3.10).

The Function Book. The key to successful function and banquet space control is the hotel's function book. This record shows the occupancies and vacancies of specific function and banquet rooms and facilitates the effective planning of functions.

Function books normally are divided into pages for each day of the year, with sections set aside for each meeting or function room. Information recorded in the function book includes the organization or group scheduling the space; the name, address, and telephone number of the group's contact person; the type of function; the time required for the function; the total time required for preparation, breakdown, and cleanup; the number of people

Exhibit 3.8 Sample Sales Call Report

054492

EMBASSY SUITES

Sales Call Report

Type of Call: ______ Personal

______ Telephone

______ Walk-in/Call-in

Trace Date ______ (Month) ______ (Year)

GENERAL INFORMATION

Account Name ______

Division/Department ______

Address ______

City ______ State ______ Zip ______

Telephone ( ) ______

Individual Called ______

Title ______

Other Contact(s) ______

REMARKS

SAMPLE

ACTION STEP

Potential for other Cities ______

Sales Representative ______ Hotel ______

Date of Call ______

File Copy

Welcome to the Suite Life

This form is used by salespeople to document information gathered from personal, telephone, or walk-in sales calls. The form provides for general information about the account, remarks on the needs of the group, and action steps that can be taken to sell business to the account. A notation to call the account on the date indicated on this form will be placed in the tickler file for the salesperson's future reference.

Courtesy of Embassy Suites, Inc.

expected; the type of setup(s) required; the rates quoted; the nature of the contract; and any pertinent remarks to assist property personnel in staging a

Exhibit 3.9   Sample Booking Form

METROPOLITAN BUSINESS FORMS - DALLAS, TX

LOEWS ANATOLE DALLAS CONVENTION BOOKING FORM

_____Definite   _____Tentative   _____Option

Decision Date:_____

DATE:_____

Booked By:_____

Assisted By:_____

Group

Contact

Phone

Address

City	State	Zip	Assigned To:

Convention Services:_____Catering_____

Reservations:	Comp Policy	Scope	Attendance:	Billing:
____Direct	____1 per 50	____Nat'l		____I.P.O.
____Res. Card	____Spec. Staff Rate	____State	Overflow:	____Rm/Tx To Master
____Rooming List	No.____Rate____	____Corp.		____All to Master
____Housing Bureau	Extra Comps_____	____Tour/Travel		____Catering to Master
____Cut Off Date		____Market		____Advance Deposit

Rates: Singles	Doubles	Suites	Concierge	Guest Room Block:	
				Day/Date	Room/Suites

Special Instructions:

Credit References:

Meeting Space	____Yes	____No	TOTAL ROOM NIGHTS

Meeting & Catering Requirements: EXHIBITS_____Yes_____Number_____Set Up_____Tear Down

DAY	DATE	TIME	FUNCTION	SETUP	ATTENDANCE	ROOM	RENTAL

Book Administrator_____Date Posted_____

FILE

This sample booking form, for booking firm convention dates, is one form that may be used to process sold business. In some sales offices, there may be separate forms for tentative and firm bookings as well as change forms that reflect changes to an initial booking.

Courtesy of Loews Anatole Hotel, Dallas, Texas.

successful function. Function book entries are always made in pencil because changes can occur even when a commitment seems firm.

Exhibit 3.10 Sample Lost Business Report

OPRYLAND HOTEL

Group Booking Status Change or Lost Business Report

Today's Date ______ Salesperson ______ FILE # ______

Month Day Year

☐ Group Name Change
☐ Contact Name Change
☐ Change in # of Rooms
☐ Change in dates
☐ Tentative Cancellation
☐ Def. Cancellation

Current Meeting Dates ______

New Meeting Dates ______

Organization ______

Contact ______

Address ______

______ / Phone # ______

STATUS CHANGE

YEAR	DAY													
	Date													
	Rms													

Reason for Cancelling (Tentative or Definite) ______

Where is Business going? ______

Comments ______

This form is used to document any business either cancelled or changed. In some sales offices, change forms are separate from a lost business report, and serve to note changes in the name of the group, the name of the contact person, the number of rooms reserved, and/or booking dates. A lost business report, which can also be a separate form, documents bookings which have been either tentatively or definitely cancelled. This form is used to follow up on the reason(s) for the cancellation, and is forwarded to the head of the sales office for review.

Courtesy of Opryland Hotel, Nashville, Tennessee.

Control of the function book. To prevent mismatching of entries or double bookings, a property should have only one function book maintained by only one person. In many cases, the person having control of the function book is the senior sales executive, but because sales personnel often travel frequently, the senior sales executive may designate one clerk to coordinate all entries.

When a property has a catering department, it is wise to locate it close to the sales office so that the function book can be easily shared. (Like the sales office, the catering department also does its own selling, usually soliciting local banquets and functions. This department will be discussed in greater detail in Chapter 8.)

Having a single person control the function book is essential. It is not uncommon for the sales office and the catering department to compete for the same function space. At many properties, sales office and catering department managers who want to reserve function space must submit a function book reservation sheet (see Exhibit 3.11) to the person in charge of the function book. This ensures that difficulties do not arise from a decentralized, undefined procedure of recording function arrangements.

The Guestroom Control Book. Every hotel soliciting group business should have a guestroom control book. A guestroom control book is used to monitor the number of guestrooms committed to groups. The guestroom control book should list the number of guestrooms allotted to each group and indicate whether the allotment is firm or tentative. Entries are made in pencil to facilitate making changes.

Most properties desire a mix of group, tour and travel, and individual guest business, so they establish a maximum allotment of guestrooms available to groups. This quota is usually set by the general manager and the head of the marketing and sales department, and special care must be taken to ensure that the sales staff does not exceed the prescribed allotment.

Because front desk, reservations, and sales office employees all book guestroom business, it is important that all of these personnel be aware of group allotments. The guestroom control book helps control guestroom booking activity by providing the sales office with the maximum number of guestrooms it is free to sell to groups on a given day. The remaining guestrooms (and any rooms allotted to groups that are not sold) are available for individual guests—these are the rooms that can be sold by front desk and reservations staff. Therefore, there should be constant communication between these personnel to avoid any overlapping in room sales.

The guestroom control book is kept in the sales office and is usually administered and controlled by the director of sales. In large hotels with a sizable volume of group sales, however, entries are often coordinated by a diary control clerk, so-called because the guestroom control book is called the hotel diary at some properties.

Confirmations, options, and holds. The guestroom control book is used to record all pertinent details regarding group room sales, including confirmations, options, and holds on rooms. A *confirmation* is definite group business which has been confirmed in writing and details the specific dates on which the group will be using the facilities of the hotel. An *option* is given when a group is unable to give a firm confirmation of room dates—perhaps a board meeting or approval by a superior is required. A *hold* is then placed on the rooms requested and an *option date* is set. The group must then either confirm the requested rooms by the option date or release the rooms to enable the property to solicit other clients. Reputable hoteliers will not confirm other orders for the requested rooms during the hold period. If a second group is interested in the same dates, this group may be given an option after being told about the first group's option. This puts the second group in a position to book if the first group releases the rooms on its option date.

Exhibit 3.11 Sample Function Book Reservation Sheet

US Grant HOTEL

FUNCTION BOOK RESERVATION SHEET

Group Name ______________________ Comments ______________________

Contact ______________________

Address ______________________

Phone ______________________

Dates In House ______________________

AGENDA

DAY/DATE	TIME	FUNCTION	SET-UP	# OF PEOPLE	ROOM NAME

Meeting Space Charges:

Sales Rep ______________________

Date ______________________

Option Date ______________________

Date Entered ______________________

Entered By ______________________

At many properties, sales office and catering department managers fill out reservation request forms and submit them to the one person responsible for monitoring the hotel's function space. Use of forms such as this one helps prevent double bookings.

Courtesy of US Grant Hotel, San Diego, California.

Filing Systems

For maximum efficiency in the sales office, an effective filing system is required. Up-to-date information is essential for a successful sales effort, and information must be available quickly.

There are several types of filing methods which may be used for filing client data and other necessary sales information. These methods fall into three general categories:

1. *Alphabetical filing.* Records are filed in alphabetical order by the title of the organization, firm, or association with whom the property is doing business. Many properties also file the names of contact people in alphabetical order. This system seems to be the easiest to implement and use.

2. *Key word alphabetical filing.* Client information is filed alphabetically by a general category key word that appears in the name of the client's organization; the Association of Petroleum and Oil Products would be filed under "Petroleum," for example. While this system has its advantages when a firm or organization's exact name is not known, the system may also result in accounts requiring filing under several key words. For example, perhaps the hotel serves a police fraternal organization. The account could be filed under "Police," "Fraternal," and "Law Enforcement."

3. *Numerical.* Sales files are assigned a number and a corresponding set of file cards is kept by account number, with the name of the account listed after the number. This system is often used with computers—the salesperson or sales clerk can either key in the account number or, if the account number is not known, type in the name of the account.

Once the filing method has been established, the next step is to determine the elements of the filing system. Most hotels use three separate files to record client information: the master card file, the account file, and the tickler file. Before each of these is explained in the following sections, it is important to note that these files may vary slightly from property to property.

The Master Card File. Master cards are instrumental in establishing data banks of information on the needs of clients. Each master card (usually a 5- by 8-inch index card) contains a summary of everything needed for an effective sales effort: the organization's name, the names and titles of key executives, addresses, phone numbers, month or months in which the group meets, the size of the group, where the group has met in the past, the group's decision-maker, and other pertinent data that can help to obtain and keep that account's business (see Exhibit 3.12). In many cases, a trailer card—an additional card that lists divisions or departments within the account's organization—may be filed behind the master card to serve as a source or sources of additional business.

The master card file is also a cross-reference. It can be used to see if an account file exists for a particular group without having to go to the file cabinet to look. Master card files are also used to create mailing lists and quickly obtain addresses or phone numbers for additional sales efforts or follow-ups.

Exhibit 3.12 Sample Master Card

Jan.	Feb.	Mar.	April	May	June	July	Aug.	Sept.	Oct.	Nov.	Dec.	1 to 100	100 to 250	250 to 350	350 to 500	Over 500

Convention Group *NATIONAL LIVESTOCK DEALERS ASSO.* *N-02197*

Main Contact *DAVID PRITCHARD*   Title *ASSO. MANAGER*

Address   Phone

City

Other Contacts

How is Decision Made   When

Date	City	Hotel	Attend	No. of Hotel Rms.
				Exhibits
				Functions

Master cards are often color-coded to draw attention to specific areas of consideration: geographic location, months of meetings, follow-ups required, and size of group. Some properties also arrange master cards alphabetically by market segment. For example, IBM and Xerox would be sorted alphabetically under "Corporate Business." Other properties may not separate master cards by market segment, but may use a color code system to easily identify specific market segments within the file—an association account may be flagged in blue, a government account in yellow, and so on.

Some properties keep a geographic file of master cards. These cards are organized based on the geographic location of the decision-maker. This type of file enables sales personnel to quickly identify accounts in cities to which they are traveling. Salespeople can simply pull the names of the decision-makers located in the area they are visiting and call on them during the sales trip.

The Account File. This standard-size file folder holds information needed for serving a client's basic business needs. An account file is started at the time of initial contact with a prospective client and may include programs from previous conventions or meetings the organization has held, convention bureau bulletins, and information relating to the organization that has appeared in newspapers or trade journals. Sales reports and all correspondence relating to previous efforts to secure business should also be in the file. All information in the account file should be in reverse chronological order—that is, the newest paperwork first.

Account files are usually filed alphabetically, and include past, present, and prospective groups. Like master cards, account files are often color-coded by geographic location or, more commonly, by market segment. When a color-coding system is used, the colors used for the account files should correspond to the colors used for the master cards.

When an account file is removed, a guide card detailing the name of the group, its file number, the date of removal, and the initials of the person removing the file should be left in the file drawer in place of the file. This ensures that the sales staff will have easy access to the whereabouts of the file.

The Tickler File. This file, also known as a tracer file, bring-up file, or follow-up file, is an effective aid for following up an account. A reminder note or card is filed in the tickler file by month and date; as seen in Exhibit 3.13, daily dividers are arranged chronologically for the current month. The system is used as a reminder of correspondence, telephone calls, or contacts that must be handled on a particular date.

How the tickler file works. Suppose a client has reserved space for a training meeting at the property in April. The salesperson will want to contact the client no later than February 15 to finalize meeting plans, so the salesperson would slip a note or a 3- by 5-inch index card (often called a "trace card") dated February 15th into the February tickler divider. On February 1, the notes and trace cards for February would be arranged according to date, and the reminder to contact the meeting planner would be placed into the 15th slot. This system, as long as it is updated and checked daily, works well, costs very little, and takes very little time to implement. An added bonus is that if a salesperson is transferred or leaves the property, there is a record of future contacts to be made that can be followed up by other members of the sales team.

Evaluating the Sales Office

Even established sales offices should not be regarded as permanent or unchangeable. If the head of the sales office finds that sales responsibilities are not being handled in the most efficient way possible, he or she should seek ways to improve procedures. Periodic reviews can help ensure that sales duties are handled properly. The following questions should be considered in an evaluation:

1. Does the organizational structure of the sales office make the most of the property's sales strengths?

2. Does the present structure encourage improvement, innovation, and creativity?

3. Is the sales structure compatible with the total organizational structure of the property?

4. Is authority properly delegated and understood at all levels?

5. Do all members of the sales office understand and properly carry out their duties and responsibilities?

6. Is the clerical staff performing duties that help sales personnel utilize as much of their time as possible for selling?

7. Have effective lines of communication been established within the sales office and with other departments in the hotel?

Exhibit 3.13 Sample Tickler File

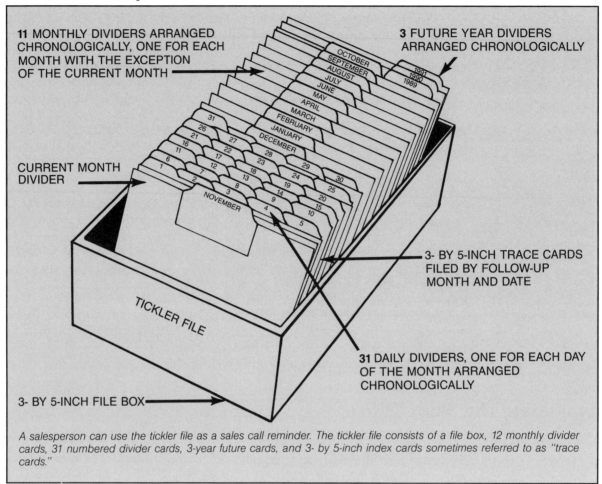

11 MONTHLY DIVIDERS ARRANGED CHRONOLOGICALLY, ONE FOR EACH MONTH WITH THE EXCEPTION OF THE CURRENT MONTH

3 FUTURE YEAR DIVIDERS ARRANGED CHRONOLOGICALLY

CURRENT MONTH DIVIDER

3- BY 5-INCH TRACE CARDS FILED BY FOLLOW-UP MONTH AND DATE

31 DAILY DIVIDERS, ONE FOR EACH DAY OF THE MONTH ARRANGED CHRONOLOGICALLY

3- BY 5-INCH FILE BOX

A salesperson can use the tickler file as a sales call reminder. The tickler file consists of a file box, 12 monthly divider cards, 31 numbered divider cards, 3-year future cards, and 3- by 5-inch index cards sometimes referred to as "trace cards."

8. Is correspondence being handled in a timely, orderly fashion?

9. Are all necessary elements for operating a successful sales office in place; i.e., a written marketing plan, employee job descriptions, standard operating procedures, an efficient filing system, a system for monitoring sales performance, a training program for new employees, and a continuing education program for veteran salespeople?

The Automated Sales Office

A typical sales office generates an incredible amount of paperwork, and a great part of each day is spent in managing the information collected through prospecting, selling, booking, and reporting. Today, at many properties much of this time-consuming and costly effort is handled with one of sales' most effective tools: computer systems (see Exhibit 3.14).[7]

While many hotels have been using computer systems for booking reservations for some time, it has only been in the last decade that sales offices

Exhibit 3.14 Manual vs. Automated Systems

Manual vs. Automated Systems

Manual	Automated
1. Account and booking information is entered on a scratch sheet.	All information is entered directly into the computer. If the account is an established one, entering the first few letters brings the name, address, contact person, and all other relevant information onto the screen. If the new booking is similar to a previous booking, the old entry can be duplicated and modified if necessary.
2. The same account and booking information is entered into the group room control log—the log is summarized manually.	The log is updated automatically; summary and forecast are calculated automatically.
3. The secretary types up group room block and function information.	The recap is automatically printed and includes all details on the group room block and the function events.
4. The same account and booking information is retyped in a confirmation letter.	Confirmation is produced automatically.
5. The same information is retyped in a contract.	Contract is produced automatically.
6. The banquet event order is typed and retyped with corrections using the same information as well as detailed menus, resource items, and comments.	Banquet event order is automatically generated by selecting menus and resources from the screen. Costs, consumption, and use at the time of the event are displayed.
7. Related follow-up correspondence is typed, referring to the same account and booking information.	Follow-up correspondence is traced and generated automatically.
8. In order to execute market research and/or telemarketing activity, a database is built by re-entering the same booking and account information.	Integrated account booking information is available for database search for marketing, telemarketing, service history, and lost business tracking.
9. Reports are created by a review of the forecast books, diaries, and booking recaps. Summary of data is entered.	Diary is automatically updated each time a booking is entered; summary and forecast are automatically calculated.
10. Salesperson booking pace and productivity reports are created through manual tabulation.	Reports are generated automatically using data in the system.
11. Tracing is done by manual entry on 3- by 5-inch cards. Traced files are delivered by secretaries to sales manager where they pile up on desks.	All activities are traced to the salesperson in accordance with a pre-developed plan. Daily trace reports remind the sales staff of such critical account and booking details as contracts due, credit checks to be done, block pick-ups, menus, and follow-up sales calls. Tentative and definite bookings are displayed and traced for follow-up. Numerous user-defined account traces and booking traces are generated for action steps.

Source: Adapted from *HSMAI Marketing Review*, Spring 1987, p. 27. Used with permission.

have been automated to provide up-to-date information to salespeople, greatly enhancing the sales effort.[8]

The benefits of automated sales office are many. Computers:

1. Allow tedious tasks to be accomplished quickly and efficiently.

2. Allow instantaneous access to sales information.

3. Facilitate personalized mailings based on the data in their memory banks.

4. Reduce the risk of human error. When specific procedures are implemented, there is less chance of information being lost or misplaced.

5. Result in decreased training costs for clerical personnel. Set procedures result in a faster training time and little deviation from standard practices.

6. Store information that can assist the sales office in directing specific sales promotions or programs to prospective clients or individual guests based on zip code, desired time periods, areas of interest, and so on.

7. Enhance communication among properties, greatly facilitating the sales effort in large hotel chains.

The proliferation of personal computers and the variety of software available from a multitude of vendors has made data processing an increasingly effective and accessible tool in hotel sales offices. A typical example of hospitality industry software programs is the Delphi system. Used by over 100 properties, the Delphi system includes programs designed specifically for the hotel industry. Among its many applications, the Delphi system has the capability to provide an "Available Dates Search" that attempts to match the needs of a prospective group with those of the hotel by providing a list of best available dates to accommodate the group (based on projected occupancy). This allows a hotel salesperson to quickly tell if a specific date is available. If an association executive calls to see if his or her meeting can be held on April 7–10, for example, a salesperson or any authorized person in the sales office can use a computer to quickly check the status of these dates, and suggest other days that the computer indicates are open if the requested days are booked.

Automated systems can be used in many day-to-day sales office operations. In Exhibit 3.15, for example, the computer provides an alternative to a master card file. The salesperson can simply call up information needed for an account, whether it be the names of contacts, specifics on follow-up calls, or remarks that can assist other members of the sales team in answering questions regarding the account in the absence of the salesperson who made the call(s). This application is also an excellent management tool: the sales manager can tell at a glance exactly how many calls were made, and the results of the calls.

Another application can be used by both the sales office and the catering department. A computerized function sheet (see Exhibit 3.16) can replace the bulky and sometimes incorrect function book, and enable any authorized salesperson or staff member to obtain accurate information without having to leave his or her department. The function book report (see Exhibit 3.17) gives an overall picture of the property's monthly activities to prevent double bookings or unsold business.

The information in the guestroom control book can easily be transferred to a concise, accurate computer report (see Exhibit 3.18). This report, too, offers instant access by any authorized staff member, and reduces the chances of human error. Every person has access to exactly the same information, and "definites" and "tentatives" are clearly defined to prevent booking errors.

Exhibit 3.15   Sample Master Account File

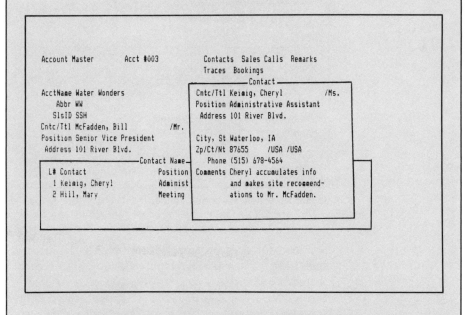

Window (or Screen) A

```
Account Master        Acct #003          Contacts  Sales Calls  Remarks
                                         Traces  Bookings

AcctName Water Wonders                     Cr Stat GOOD
    Abbr WW                              Payment DB /Approved Credit
    SlsID SSH                              Comm?
Cntc/Ttl McFadden, Bill        /Mr.         TA#
Position Senior Vice President
    Address 101 River Blvd.              Lst Call JUL24,90
                                         Lst Book DEC12,90
City, St Waterloo, IA
Zp/Ct/Nt 87655      /USA /USA
    Phone (515) 678-4564
    Telex
AcctType SC State Corporate
    Region MW Midwest                      Status A
        SIC 79 Recreation Services       Created JUL01,90 LD
       Assn 17 Recreation                Changed JUL01,90 LD
    Origin SL Solicited
    Quality G  Good
```

Window (or Screen) B

```
Account Master        Acct #003          Contacts  Sales Calls  Remarks
                                         Traces  Bookings
                                      ┌────── Contact ──────
AcctName Water Wonders                Cntc/Ttl Keimig, Cheryl        /Ms.
    Abbr WW                           Position Administrative Assistant
    SlsID SSH                             Address 101 River Blvd.
Cntc/Ttl McFadden, Bill        /Mr.
Position Senior Vice President        City, St Waterloo, IA
    Address 101 River Blvd.           Zp/Ct/Nt 87655      /USA /USA
                ┌──── Contact Name ─      Phone (515) 678-4564
  L# Contact              Position │   Comments Cheryl accumulates info
   1 Keimig, Cheryl       Administ │          and makes site recommend-
   2 Hill, Mary           Meeting  │          ations to Mr. McFadden.
                                   │
```

This computer program allows a salesperson to get detailed information on an account instantly. Window A is similar to the information recorded manually on master cards like the one in Exhibit 3.12. But by simply pushing additional keys, the salesperson can obtain detailed information on key contacts for the account (Window B). Other "windows" provide a summary of sales calls made on the account, specifics about each sales call, salesperson remarks, and specifics on tracing and following up the account.

Source: Lodgistix, Inc., Wichita, Kansas. Used with permission.

Exhibit 3.16   Sample Computerized Function Sheet

THE RIVERVIEW HOTEL
FUNCTION SHEET
44 Newmarket Road   Durham, NH 03824   603/868-1592

```
Group: Kollmorgen Corporation
Contact: David Kornfeld
  Title: Director of Conference Services        Agreement #: 17892       SPECIAL INSTRUCTIONS
Address: 3131 Campus Drive                        Acct. ID: Corp-4758
                                                                         Valet service for all attendees who arrive
     Plymouth                  MN                                        between 6:45PM and 7:00PM.

   Day: Thursday  August 13, 1988                                       VIP Basket #2 in all rooms by 5:00PM.
Function Name: Awards Banquet
Post As: Sales Meeting
Conf. Coordinator: David Kornfeld
  Date       Time        Function      Room     Setup Spec People
8/13/88  3:00PM -  3:15PM  Coffee Break  MEZZLNGE BREAK No    75
         6:00PM -  7:00PM  Coffee Break  VIKING   BAR   No   200
         7:00PM - 11:00PM  Banquet Dinner OLSO    RD10  HEAD 200
8/14/88  8:00PM -  5:00PM  Meeting       STOCKHOLM USHP  No    35       BILLING INSTRUCTIONS
                                                                  All charges expect incidentials to Master
```

```
              MENU                                  SETUP REQUIREMENTS

Banquet Dinner 1          From 7:00PM to  9:00PM    Room:  OSLO                  From 7:00PM to 11:00PM
Room: Oslo Room           Attendance   200
                                                    60" Rounds                       10
                                                    Pink tablecloths                 10
Fillet of fresh Trout marinated with Saffron  200 Serving   White napkins           200
Chilled light Chicken Veloute with Herbs      200 Serving   All wood lecturn          1
Roast Leg of Lamb in Crust, Madeira Sauce     200 Serving   Head table for 12         1
Milk Chocolate Mousse                         200 Serving   Rear screen projection    1
Coffee, Tea                                   200 Serving   12" screen                1
                                                    Hand-written name tags          200
        Price:     $38.00 per person                Flowers by Valentine Florists

                                                    Room:  STOCKHOLM   From 8:00AM to 5:00PM

                                                    VIP pen and pads                 12
                                                    Flipcharts with markers           2
                                                    Lamp Screen Pointer               1
```

```
         BEVERAGE SERVICE                        ADDITIONAL INFORMATION

Raymond Chardonnay                       1.  Allen Doyle, Executive Vice President will sign check.
  Served with Chicken Veloute  7.00 pp
                                         2.  Have photographer available through reception and dinner.
Clos de la Roche              7.50 pp
  Served with Lamb
```

```
  CUSTOMER AUTHORIZATION AND APPROVAL            GUESTROOMS
                                                 Arrival Date:  August 12, 1988
I have read both sides of this document and agree to abide by
the terms and conditions set forth by the Riverview Hotel.    Booked By:  David Sullivan
All arrangements and specifications contained herein are:     Date Booked:  February 1, 1988

_____ Approved        _____ Approved with changes as indicated.

Date:_____  Signature:_____
```

This function sheet draws together relevant booking information and important information about the account, and merges the data on one display screen.

Source: Newmarket Software Systems, Inc., Durham, New Hampshire. Used with permission.

Word processing applications enable the sales staff to use computers to personalize sales letters. High-quality personalized letters written on the property's stationery are far less likely to be considered junk mail. Computers can store mailing lists of prospective clients, previous guests, and organizations and associations. Word processing systems make short work of large mailings, providing cost-effective, targeted advertising and promotion for the property.

Market analysis is a relatively new application of computer technology, but it is growing in popularity and effectiveness. Market analysis begins with master cards or other basic information on present and potential business and sorts the information into several categories. Computer printouts can

Exhibit 3.17 Sample Function Book Report

THE RIVERVIEW HOTEL

Date Printed: October 1, 1988   Time Printed: 11:59 AM

- DELPHI - Function Space Profile   Page: 1

Report for Oct 1 1988 to Oct 31 1988

Room Name	Time Period	Sa 1	Su 2	Mo 3	Tu 4	We 5	Th 6	Fr 7	Sa 8	Su 9	Mo 10	Tu 11	We 12	Th 13	Fr 14	Sa 15	Su 16	Mo 17	Tu 18	We 19	Th 20	Fr 21	Sa 22	Su 23	Mo 24	Tu 25	We 26	Th 27	Fr 28	Sa 29	Su 30	Mo 31
WASHINTN	M	D	D	D	D				D	D						T	T	T		T												
	L	D	D													T	T	T		T												
	A	D														T	T	T		T												
	E															T	T	T		T												
ADAMS	M															DD	DD															
	L																															
	A																			DD	DD											
	E	T	T	T		T	T																									
JEFFERSN	M	D	D	D			VD	VD	VD	VD	VD	VD	VD																			
	L						VD	VD	VD	VD	VD	VD	VD																			
	A																															
	E																															
MADISON	M										T	T	T												T	T	T					
	L				VD	VD											DD	DD	DD						T	T	T					
	A				VD	VD							T	T	T		DD	DD	DD							T						
	E												T	T	T																	
MONROE	M															T	T	T														
	L															T	T	T														
	A															T	T	T														
	E															T	T	T														
JACKSON	M								D	D	D																					
	L			VD	VD	VD			D	D	D																					
	A			VD	VD	VD																										
	E																															
VAN BURN	M		T	T	T							D	D	D									T									
	L		T	T	T							D	D	D									T									
	A											D	D	D									T									
	E																															
HARRISON	M																															
	L																															
	A																															
	E																															

This report displays the status of all of a property's function rooms for a month. Each day is broken down into four periods: Morning (M); Lunchtime (L); Afternoon (A); and Evening (E); and there are four different levels of room status: Definite (D); Deposit Due (DD); Verbal Definite (VD); and Tentative (T).

detail arrival and booking dates, length of stay, rates, room type chosen (both guestrooms and conference rooms), and other information for all the property's business, helping management to plan sales strategies. (For best results, both individual and group bookings should be analyzed.) No longer does it take hours of work to determine which groups are candidates for group meetings during the property's slow periods, which zip code areas produce the highest business, or which types of rooms are most popular during a particular season of the year. As advertising costs escalate, it is particularly important to know just where to target promotional efforts, and computers can provide the information needed to make that determination in minutes.

Even the most efficiently organized office and the best computer system that money can buy cannot guarantee that the property's sales efforts will be successful, however. The key to sales success is always the property's *people*.

Exhibit 3.18   Sample Group Room Control Report

THE RIVERVIEW HOTEL

Date Printed: August 27, 1987   Time Printed: 11:41 AM

- DELPHI - Group Rooms Control Report for 1987 August   Page: 1

	1 Sun	2 Mon	3 Tue	4 Wed	5 Thu	6 Fri	28 Sat	29 Sun	30 Mon	31 Tue	Total Rooms	Total Guests	Ave Rate	Room Revenue	Decision Date	RT	SRC	Stat	Date Entered
DEFINITES for Corp.																			
D.E.C.											500	500	124.00	62,000.00	8/25/87		TRB	D	8/25/87
MASS. BAY CO											200	200	118.00	23,600.00	8/25/87		TRB	D	8/25/87
I.B.M.											90	90	125.00	11,250.00	8/25/87		TRB	D	8/25/87
COASTAL INC.											15	30	128.00	1,920.00			TRB	D	2/ 3/86
Corp.	0	0	0	0	0	0	0	0	0	0	805	820	122.69	98,770.00				D	
TENTATIVES for Corp.																			
LOTUS DEV CO			5	5	5	5					20	40	145.00	2,900.00	8/25/87		SB	T	8/25/87
CRIMSON TRVL						6					24	48	118.00	2,832.00	8/25/87		RWH	T	8/25/87
EASTERN INC.											35	70	130.00	4,550.00	8/25/87		RWH	T	8/25/87
LOTUS DEV CO											15	30	121.00	1,815.00	8/25/87		SB	T	8/25/87
INTEL CORP.											9	27	121.00	1,089.00	8/25/87		SB	T	8/25/87
EASTERN INC.											4	8	145.00	580.00	8/25/87		RWH	T	8/25/87
Corp.	0	0	5	5	5	11	0	0	0	0	107	223	128.65	13,766.00				T	
DEFINITES for Assoc.																			
TRAVEL ASSOC	25	25	25								75	75	108.00	8,100.00	9/30/87	KL		D	3/10/87
N.A.F.E.											30	60	127.00	3,810.00	8/12/87	CRW		DD	8/12/87
U.S. ASSOC.											120	240	120.00	14,400.00		TS		D	8/ 1/87
U.S. ASSOC.							7	7	7	7	63	126	112.00	7,056.00		TS		D	8/10/87
U.S. ASSOC.							5				20	20	120.00	2,400.00		TS		D	8/22/87
Assoc.	25	25	25	0	0	0	12	7	7	7	308	521	116.12	35,766.00				D	
TENTATIVES for Assoc.																			
VETS ASSOC	2	2	2								6	12	121.00	726.00	8/25/87		TRB	T	8/25/87
N.A.R.R.P.	10	10									20	40	110.00	2,200.00	8/25/87		TRB	T	8/25/87
DATA SYSTEMS			6	6	6	6					48	96	131.00	6,288.00	8/25/87		TRB	T	8/25/87
D.P.A.		10	10	10							30	60	145.00	4,350.00	8/25/87		TRB	T	8/25/87
MUTUAL ASSOC					3	3					24	48	131.00	3,144.00	8/25/87		TRB	T	8/25/87
MONT WARD CO											40	80	100.00	4,000.00	6/24/87		EP	T	6/24/87
NEWSWEEK											16	32	131.00	2,096.00	8/25/87		RWH	T	9/25/87
N.A.F.E.											36	72	127.00	4,572.00	8/12/87		CRW	T	8/12/87
INTRNTL ASSC											8	16	118.00	944.00	8/25/87		TRB	T	8/25/87
WOMENS ASSOC											4	8	110.00	440.00	8/25/87		TRB	T	8/25/87
MANUFACT ASC											48	96	127.00	6,096.00	8/25/87		RWH	T	8/25/87
N.A.T.C.O.							45				270	540	234.00	63,180.00	8/25/87		TRB	T	8/25/87
DENTAL ASSOC								2	2		4	8	110.00	440.00	8/25/87		TRB	T	8/25/87
CENTRAL ASSC									30	30	60	120	120.00	7,200.00	8/25/87		TRB	T	8/25/87
US YACHT CLB									4	4	8	16	131.00	1,048.00	8/25/87		TRB	T	8/25/87
Assoc.	12	12	18	16	19	9	45	2	36	34	622	1244	171.58	106,724.00				T	

The report illustrated here is from an automated system which can replace the guestroom control book. This report provides a concise summary of bookings for the month. The bookings are broken down into Definites (including deposit due and verbal definites) and Tentatives. Each block is listed by day, with totals for rooms, guests, average rate, and revenues. The decision date, sales source, and date entered are also given.

Source: Newmarket Software Systems, Inc., Durham, New Hampshire. Used with permission.

In the next chapter we will take a look at how the property's sales staff can effectively sell the property.

Automating the Sales Office at a Small Hotel: The Daytona Inns

Al Szemborski, a Daytona Beach hotelier with 15 years experience in innkeeping, operates two properties: the Daytona Inn at Seabreeze with 98 rooms, and the Daytona Inn Broadway with 150 rooms.

Szemborski purchased a table model IBM computer for about $15,000, and several software packages for both accounting and marketing purposes. His computer is used extensively for mailings to past guests (the computer selects and prints labels at a rate of 5,000 names and addresses in 10 to 12 hours) after a market analysis of (1) where the guests come from, and (2) in what month of the year they visit a Daytona Inn. Over 30,000 guest history records are used.

By using the computer, Szemborski found that ten states and Canada accounted for 85% of his business in the last three years. But lucrative states are not just lucrative states, period. Lucrative states are big producers during particular months of the year. Each state (or more precisely, zip code) has a visitation profile of its own. More guests come from Michigan, for example, than any other state. But virtually all Michigan guests arrive in the winter season. Therefore, advertising in Michigan is done two or three months before the winter season. (Georgia ranks second in number of guests, but all Georgia guests arrive in the summer!)

Taking advantage of his computer's capability, Szemborski can now find out how much money guests spend per day, where they come from, whether they are repeat guests, or whether they come once to see Disney World and don't constitute a good prospect for repeat business.

Notes

1. For more information on training, see Lewis C. Forrest, Jr., *Training for the Hospitality Industry* (East Lansing, Mich.: Educational Institute of the American Hotel & Motel Association, 1983).

2. Jay Diamond and Gerald Pintel, *Principles of Selling* (Englewood Cliffs, N.J.: Prentice-Hall, 1985), pp. 54–55.

3. The information in the following section was developed by Jim Cathcart of Cathcart, Alessandra & Associates, Inc., and is used with permission.

4. Some of the material in this section was adapted from Richard R. Still, Edward W. Cundiff, and Norman A. P. Govoni, *Sales Management: Decisions, Strategies, and Cases* (Englewood Cliffs, N.J.: Prentice-Hall, 1988).

5. For more information on hospitality management, see Jerome J. Vallen and James R. Abbey, *The Art and Science of Hospitality Management* (East Lansing, Mich.: Educational Institute of the American Hotel & Motel Association, 1987); John P. Daschler and Jack D. Ninemeier, *Supervision in the Hospitality Industry* (East Lansing, Mich.: Educational Institute of the American Hotel & Motel Association, 1984); and David W. Wheelhouse, *Managing Human Resources in the Hospitality Industry* (East Lansing, Mich.: Educational Institute of the American Hotel & Motel Association, forthcoming).

6. Some of the material in this section was adapted from Edward E. Eicher, "The Role of the Regional Sales Office in Hotel Sales and Marketing," *HSMAI Marketing Review*, Spring 1984, pp. 9–15.

7. For more information on computers in the hospitality industry, see Michael L. Kasavana and John J. Cahill, *Managing Computers in the Hospitality Industry* (East Lansing, Mich.: Educational Institute of the American Hotel & Motel Association, 1987).

8. For help in deciding whether or not to automate a sales office, see *Automating Hotel/Motel Sales Functions: A How-To Manual on Computerizing the Sales Department* (East Lansing, Mich.: Educational Institute of the American Hotel & Motel Association, 1986).

Discussion Questions

1. What positions are typically found in a large property's marketing and sales division?

2. What factors influence the organization of a sales office?

3. What are three classic principles of organization?

4. What are six characteristics common to successful salespeople?

5. What are SOPs?

6. Personalities can be divided into which four basic types?

7. What are several training techniques for developing new sales personnel?

8. What is the role of a regional sales office?

9. What are the functions of independent hotel sales representatives?

10. What are some of the facts recorded about an upcoming function in the function book?

11. What is an option?

12. What is contained in an account file?

13. The tickler file serves what purpose?

14. What are some of the things that should be considered when evaluating a sales office?

15. What are some of the benefits of an automated sales office?

Part II

Sales Techniques

Chapter Outline

I. Prospecting
    A. Qualifying Prospects

II. Preparing for the Presentation Sales Call
    A. Pre-Presentation Planning
        1. Property Research
           a. The property fact book
        2. Competition Research
        3. Client Research
    B. The Sales Kit

III. Projecting a Professional Image
    A. Non-Verbal Communication
        1. Appearance
        2. The Handshake
        3. Territorial Space
        4. Body Language
    B. Voice Quality
    C. Listening

IV. The Presentation Sales Call
    A. Opening the Sales Call
        1. Introduction
        2. Purpose Statement
        3. Benefit Statement
        4. Bridge Statement
    B. Getting Client Involvement
        1. Questioning
    C. The Presentation
        1. Organization
        2. Effective Speaking
        3. Visual Aids
        4. Closing the Presentation
    D. Overcoming Objections
        1. Types of Objections
    E. Closing and Following Up
        1. Following Up

V. Improving Sales Productivity
    A. Time Management
    B. Key Account Management

4 Personal Sales

This chapter discusses one of the most effective tools for selling a property and its services: the personal sales call. A personal sales call is used to build rapport with clients or potential clients and sell them the products and services offered by the property.

There are several types of personal sales calls:

1. Cold or prospect calls are usually made within a small geographic area with a minimum amount of time spent on each call. Generally, little is known about the person or organization being called on; this is strictly a fact-finding or exploratory call. The objective is not to make a sale, but to gather information so that a selling strategy can be developed and a follow-up visit made. Of course, if you run into someone really interested in doing business, you can present the property's benefits and try to make a sale.

2. Public relations or service calls are made on companies and individuals who are already clients. These calls serve to promote goodwill and your willingness to meet the future needs of the client.

3. Appointment calls are used to introduce a prospective client to the features and services offered by the property. Business may be booked or information developed so a follow-up call can be made at a future date. The person being called on is usually busy (that's the reason for requiring an appointment); therefore, as much information as possible about the prospect and his or her needs should be obtained before making the call.

4. Presentation calls usually result after several previous calls. The objective is to have the individual, committee, or group make a decision in favor of the property. It is very important that the presentation be conducted with visual aids and other support materials. If the presentation is to be made to a committee or group, you should know who the decision-makers are. You must have the confidence to make a strong sales pitch, overcome objections, and ask for the sale.

5. Inside sales calls are made to walk-ins inquiring about the property.[1]

Industry Profile

Greg Hendel
Co-owner
Best Western Host Hotel

Greg Hendel graduated from Sacramento State in 1974 with a degree in Criminology, and worked as a supervising probation officer in Palm Springs, California, for the next four years. In 1979, Hendel purchased 6% of a 160-unit property, and began a career in the hospitality industry as manager and director of sales. He now owns 50% of the Best Western Host Hotel in Palm Springs, and is currently working on the development of a 125-unit full-service property (to include meeting rooms) in northern California.

"Some people refer to sales and marketing as prospecting, but I like to think of it as detective work. The good sales and marketing person is constantly asking questions: 'Who's coming into town?' 'Who utilizes rooms of this type?' 'How can we determine additional sources for business?'

The 'leisure-overnight' type of property is perhaps the most difficult to sell. Commercial/convention and 'tour' properties can be contracted; after a meeting between the prospect and the salesperson, a signature indicating future business can be obtained. But all a leisure property can do is educate the prospect in the hopes that he or she will utilize the property when in the area. In other words, the leisure property is more likely to take any type of business it can get.

As a starting point, we utilize a daily 'manager's report' that puts each room rented into a category: AAA, Travel Agent, Special Package, et cetera. From this information, we can focus a plan of attack. For example, if we see that we're generating a good deal of travel agent business we'll focus on travel agents. The travel agent must single out the Host over 100 other properties in the area, so we want travel agents to know they are important. This month, we are sending the 'Official Desert Bookmark' to tell them we care; next month, we will send out a photograph of the entire staff, so the agent can associate a face with a call.

And we don't neglect potential business from unexpected sources. Last week, for example, a brochure crossed my desk asking for a donation to a local, non-profit educational institute. I asked myself, 'Who from that organization could use hotel rooms?' I met the director of the institute and gave him my five-minute slide presentation. He advised me that the blind students attending the institute must live in dorms, but after asking some pertinent questions I found that rooms would be needed for graduation ceremonies and a yearly golf tournament held to raise funds.

When I heard that as many as 100 golfers came from out of town, I advised the director that our property would pay the postage if the organization would mention us and allow us to include a brochure with their mailing to the golfers. His eyes lit up, as postage is one of the organization's biggest expenses. We both won!

Sales and marketing is limited only by a salesperson's imagination. One of my sayings is, 'There are no bad programs, just bad implementation and execution.' In the example above, selling was accomplished 'an inch wide and a mile deep,' and through meticulous detective work during the interview a greater amount of business was realized than a few rooms for a small graduation exercise. May all of *your* prospecting produce nuggets of new business. Good luck!**"**

This chapter looks at the components of successful face-to-face salesmanship. The chapter begins by discussing the importance of prospecting and the need for thorough preparation before making a sales call. Next it focuses on the presentation sales call, and describes how pre-presentation planning and the five basic steps of a presentation sales call can lead to bookings for the property. The final sections of the chapter discuss time and key account management.

Prospecting

In today's competitive environment, few hotels can be certain that their current client base will be adequate for the future. Prospecting for new business is essential and should be a continual part of hotel sales. Individuals and groups must constantly be cultivated to ensure that the hotel keeps pace with market trends and the competition.

Many salespeople see prospecting as a difficult, frustrating, and thankless job—after all, prospecting for new business takes time away from selling to and servicing existing accounts. Prospecting, however, serves two essential purposes: first, it increases sales by bringing in additional individual and group business; second, it brings in new guests to replace former guests who have been lost over a period of time. Prospecting is the lifeblood of sales because prospecting identifies those individuals or groups that may become the property's client base of the future.

Prospect research information is as close as the sales office files. The function books and other records from previous years are excellent sources of prospects. These records provide information on groups that have booked and not returned, the names of key contact persons, and the names of satisfied past clients.

Other sources for prospect research include:

1. *Referrals from past and present clients.* In addition to being excellent prospects for more bookings, satisfied clients can often help generate additional sales by giving the property the names of others who might be interested in the property's services. Satisfied clients may also personally recommend the property to friends and business acquaintances.

2. *Other departments within large corporations or groups that the property is currently serving.* If the property is dealing with one department within a large corporation or association, there may be a number of other departments within the organization that need hotel accommodations or services.

3. *Local organizations and companies.* Salespeople should not neglect local firms when prospecting. Business directories, Chamber of Commerce publications, and industry reports will often yield important information. A local firm, for example, may be a branch of a national organization and the potential source of a large amount of business.

4. *Front desk personnel.* Many individual guests have the potential to bring group business to the property. The front desk staff can often provide referrals that may result in additional individual or group business.

5. *Other property employees.* Many property employees belong to groups or organizations such as bowling leagues and church groups that can become potential clients. Salespeople should ask staff members for leads.

6. *The property's competitors.* A property can even get prospect leads from the competition, so knowing what competitors are doing and

who they are serving is important. These questions should be considered when researching competitors:

- Who are our top three direct competitors?

- What are the five major accounts for each competitor?

- How many room nights is each account booking and at what rates?

- What will it take (lower rates, better product-service, more promotion, etc.) to get our competitors' major accounts to use our facilities?

7. *Other sources.* Both individual and group business can be found through a number of other sources (see Exhibit 4.1). Local newspapers are a logical starting point. The local library, Chamber of Commerce, and state industrial commission or convention and visitors bureau can also furnish publications that may provide leads on both a local and national level.

Once prospect research has been done, realistic appointment goals can be set. Many hotel sales offices assign specific goals, while others create guidelines that allow salespeople to work at their own pace on prospecting calls. A specific goal might be stated: "to make ten prospect calls per week (500 per year) and to screen, follow up, and schedule appointments with qualified prospects; annual goal: 125 new accounts." To see that goals are met, salespeople should keep accurate records of prospecting efforts (see Exhibit 4.2).

Qualifying Prospects

Unfortunately, not every prospect qualifies as a potential client. Merely collecting the names of prospects does not warrant calling on each one personally. There are three basic criteria for qualifying a prospect: financial status, the need for the product or service, and the ability to purchase.

Financial status information may be obtained from national or local credit rating organizations as well as from annual reports. This information will provide an overview of the prospect's financial standing and enables a salesperson to weed out certain prospects. An organization that does a low volume of business, for example, probably cannot afford an upscale property for a business meeting or convention. Spending time on such an account would likely be a waste of time for a salesperson from an upscale property. Conversely, a large multimillion dollar corporation might only be interested in upscale accommodations for its executives and meeting attendees; a salesperson for a small budget property would probably be unable to solicit business from a corporation of that size.

Need for the product or services offered by the property can be determined by researching the prospect's previous buying record. This information can be obtained through telephone surveys, by contacting the prospect directly, or through information supplied by clients or other business contacts. Has the prospect used other facilities similar to those offered by the property? Is the prospect's company part of a chain or conglomerate that may be affiliated with other hospitality properties? Does the prospect have a need for the special services offered by the property?

The prospect's ability to purchase is based on a number of factors. Even if a prospect's company is financially secure, there may be budget limitations

Exhibit 4.1 Sources for Individual and Group Business

Companies

Potential business: Guestrooms, meeting rooms, office and holiday parties, retirement and award banquets, training schools and employee indoctrination sessions, recruiting programs, sales incentives (vacations for top-producing salespeople, and so on).

Sources: Chamber of Commerce listings, Polk's city directory (available in libraries), telephone directory yellow pages, business sections of newspapers, National Passenger Traffic Association directory, leads from clients and acquaintances, competitors' function boards (the listing of daily functions that is usually posted in the lobby or meeting area).

Contact persons: Sales managers, personnel and training directors, department or division officers or heads, traffic managers, key secretaries.

Local Clubs and Professional and Fraternal Organizations

Potential business: Guestrooms for guest speakers, regularly scheduled chapter meetings, installation of new officers (banquets), holiday parties, special project events, state and regional conventions.

Sources: Chamber of Commerce listings, telephone directory yellow pages, newspaper stories, leads from clients and acquaintances, competitors' function boards.

Contact persons: Local community professionals, fraternal organization administrators, club officers and members, key secretaries.

Hospitals, Schools, and Government Agencies

Potential business: Guestrooms, meetings and seminars, recruiting programs, parties, award banquets, training schools, conventions.

Sources: Chamber of Commerce listings; telephone directory yellow pages; government, school, and hospital directories; leads from clients and acquaintances; competitors' function boards.

Contact persons: Directors and administrators, athletic directors or team managers, department heads, military recruiting officers, key secretaries (court bailiffs and judicial secretaries, secretaries to principals, and so on), personnel and public relations managers.

Family Social Functions

Potential business: Guestrooms for out-of-town family members (for family reunions or funerals), guestrooms for out-of-town wedding guests, a honeymoon guestroom or suite, receptions, rehearsal dinners, showers.

Sources: Retail store managers, church officials, newspaper stories, leads from clients and acquaintances.

Contact persons: Family reunion organizers, retail store managers, church officials, the bride or her parents, the groom or his parents, friends or relatives of the wedding party or family.

Travel Industry Accounts

Potential business: Guestrooms (individual and corporate), guestrooms for bus tours, tour bus meal stops, familiarization seminars.

Sources: American Society of Travel Agents membership directory, National Tour Association membership directory, telephone directory yellow pages, mailing houses, newspaper stories, leads from clients and acquaintances, competitors' function boards.

Contact persons: Company presidents; national sales managers; local airline, bus, and train station managers.

Professional and Trade Associations

Potential business: Guestrooms for guest speakers or members, regularly scheduled chapter meetings, installation of new officers (banquets), holiday parties, state and regional conventions, meetings and seminars, special project events, auxiliary activities.

Sources: Chamber of Commerce listings, telephone directory yellow pages, newspaper stories, leads from clients and acquaintances, competitors' function boards.

Contact persons: Executive directors, association officers, local association members, committee chairpersons.

Exhibit 4.2   Sample Prospect Card

Prospect's Name_____
Company Name_____
Address of Prospect_____
Type of Business_____
Pertinent background information on the company and/or contact person:
_____
_____
_____
Prospect's Estimated Sales Potential in:
Room Nights_____
Dollars   _____
Facilities and/or services needed by prospect:
_____
_____
Has the prospect been qualified?   ☐ Yes   ☐ No
Action required to:
a.   Qualify the prospect_____
b.   Follow-up_____
Salesperson's Name_____
Date of Contact_____   Follow-up Date_____

for travel and business expenses, or restrictions on which hospitality properties may be chosen (the company may have a preferred list of acceptable accommodations). Other companies, although prosperous, may be "high risk" from a salesperson's point of view: payment may have to be routed through corporate offices, the company may be in the midst of a reorganization or takeover by another company, or the prospect's authority for buying may be limited. Before qualifying a prospect, therefore, it is important that salespeople do their homework in these areas.

Preparing for the Presentation Sales Call

Once a qualified prospect has been called on and has expressed an interest in the property, a presentation sales call can be made.

Although you should approach each presentation sales call with confidence, you should realize that not all presentations lead to a sale. There are three reasons within a salesperson's control why a presentation sales call fails:

1. Planning for the call was inadequate.

2. The salesperson was anxious or nervous.

3. The salesperson failed to reach the decision-maker.

All of these problems can be overcome if a salesperson thoroughly prepares for a presentation.[2] Thorough preparation results in:

1. *Increased credibility.* A prepared salesperson knows what the property has to offer, has translated property products or services into benefits, and has determined the needs of the client before attempting to make a presentation. A client will have much more confidence in a salesperson if the salesperson knows the property and how it can benefit the client.

2. *Increased confidence.* Salespeople must sell themselves as well as the property; a nervous or anxious salesperson can lose an important sale! Knowing the product, the competition, and the client increases a salesperson's self-confidence and his or her ability to influence clients.

3. *Increased probability of reaching the decision-maker.* Research gives salespeople a better chance of talking to the right person, which means a better chance of making a sale.

Pre-Presentation Planning

To be effective, pre-presentation planning should include property research, competition research, and client research.

Property Research. Salespeople must have a thorough knowledge of their property. There are two basic methods of improving property knowledge: studying a property fact book, and developing a working knowledge of all the property's departments. The facts obtained through either method should be studied, memorized, and updated when necessary.

The property fact book. The salesperson's property fact book should include pertinent information on the following:

• General property description—location, age, layout, and so on

• Guestrooms—number, types, rates, special rooms, amenities, security

• Restaurants and lounges—number, hours, menus (including room service menus), seating capacities, types of seating, entertainment, special promotions

• Meeting and banquet facilities—number of rooms, seating capacities, services offered, banquet menus, rates

• Audiovisual equipment—types of equipment offered, availability, and prices

- VIP packages—amenities and prices

- Transportation—availability and rates, with special attention to airport transportation

- Recreational facilities—types, rates, hours, lessons available, rental equipment, supervision

- Outside services—secretarial services, shopping services, and so on

- Vendors—musicians, florists, photographers, and their rates

- The community and surrounding areas—area attractions (locations, fees, hours, group rates, etc.) and community atmosphere (rural, metropolitan, suburban, and so on)

- Guests and finances—guest profiles; present guest mix; optimum guest mix; peak, valley, and shoulder periods; average daily rate from each market segment

During a presentation sales call, products and services listed in the property fact book can be presented as benefits to the client. For example, the total number of guestrooms may not be a consideration for a particular client, but he or she may be influenced by amenities, check-in/check-out times, deposit policies, the number of rooms and room types per floor, the dimensions of rooms, the number of no-smoking rooms, the number and types of recreational facilities, or other property fact book information.

Competition Research. It is necessary to know as much about competitors' properties as the home property in order to sell successfully against the competition. It is almost impossible to sell a property if you are unable to show clients how the property can serve their needs better than the competition can.

By taking a hard, objective look at competitors' properties, you can note strengths and weaknesses and emphasize your property's strengths in areas that relate to client needs. One salesperson was able to book a weekend convention after visiting a competitor's property and noting that his own property's ballroom—although approximately the same size as that of his competitor—seated 40 additional guests. Research allows salespeople to downplay those features and services in which a competitor has an advantage, and play up those areas in which their property can best serve the client (see Exhibit 4.3).

Information required for competition research may be obtained through visits to the competition, inquiries to competitors' properties, and studies of the competition's marketing plans and annual reports. In researching the competition, the important areas of the competition's sales methods, pricing strategies, promotional methods, and sales staff size and ability should not be overlooked. In addition to comparing features and services, intangibles such as the reputation, friendliness, and service standards of other properties must be considered.

Client Research. Before calling on clients, learn as much as possible about them and their organization. Information is available from a number of sources: other clients who know the client, annual reports, business

Exhibit 4.3 Sample Competition Analysis

NEEDS AND WANTS OF TARGET MARKET	CENTER CITY	OUTLAW INN	LAST RESORT	BEST HOTEL	EMPTY ARMS	COMMENT
Family Leisure Traveler						
Swimming Pool	Yes	—	Yes	—	Yes	
Children's Activities	Yes	Yes	Yes	Yes	Yes	
Recreational Facilities	Yes	Yes	—	Yes	Yes	
Game Room	Yes	—	—	—	Yes	
Double-Doubles	Yes	—	—	—	Yes	
Attractions/Tours	Yes	—	Yes	—	Yes	
Extra Towels	Yes	Yes	Yes	—	Yes	
Family-Oriented Menus	Yes	—	—	—	Yes	
Information Center	Yes	—	Yes	—	Yes	
Corporate Meetings						
Audiovisual Equipment	Yes	Yes	Yes	Yes	Yes	
Security	—	—	—	Yes	Yes	
Training Atmosphere	Yes	Yes	Yes	Yes	Yes	
Well-Lighted, Quiet Meeting Rooms	Yes	Yes	Yes	—	—	
Space on Short Lead Time	Yes	—	Yes	Yes	—	
Soundproof Meeting Rooms	Yes	—	Yes	—	Yes	
Comfortable Chairs	Yes	Yes	Yes	Yes	Yes	
Master Account Billing	Yes	—	—	—	—	
Copy Equipment	Yes	—	—	—	Yes	
Efficient Check-in and Check-out	Yes	Yes	—	Yes	—	
Association Meetings Market						
Complimentary Room Policy	Yes	—	Yes	—	Yes	
Exhibit Space	Yes	Yes	Yes	Yes	Yes	
Accessible Location	Yes	Yes	—	Yes	Yes	
Overflow Arrangements	Yes	—	—	—	Yes	
Assistance with Housing	Yes	—	—	—	Yes	
Media Coverage of Event	Yes	—	Yes	—	Yes	
Spouse Programs	Yes	Yes	Yes	—	Yes	
Overflow Activities	Yes	—	Yes	—	Yes	
Breakout Meeting Rooms	Yes	—	Yes	—	Yes	
Copy Services/Rates	Yes	Yes	Yes	Yes	Yes	
Recreation Amenities	—	—	—	Yes	Yes	
Convention Coordinator	Yes	Yes	Yes	Yes	Yes	
Sight-seeing and Recreational Activities	Yes	Yes	Yes	—	—	
Motorcoach Tour Market						
Double-Doubles	Yes	Yes	Yes	—	—	
One Large Meeting Room	Yes	—	Yes	Yes	—	
Highway Accessibility	Yes	Yes	Yes	Yes	Yes	
Confidential Rates	—	Yes	—	Yes	—	
Group Check-in and Baggage Service	Yes	—	Yes	—	Yes	
Bus Parking	Yes	—	Yes	—	Yes	
Welcome Reception	Yes	Yes	—	Yes	—	
Comp Rooms for Drivers	Yes	—	Yes	—	Yes	

A competition analysis form such as this one can reveal property strengths in relation to competitors which may be used in a sales presentation.

directories, articles, trade journals, and membership directories and lists (see Exhibit 4.4).

The information obtained during pre-presentation research allows you to custom-tailor a presentation for each client. Thorough knowledge of the property, the competition, and the client can lead to booked business.

The Sales Kit

Before making a sales call, you should prepare a well-organized and professional sales kit. Only the information pertinent to the client's particular needs should be included; too much information results in clutter and appears unprofessional.

Information basic to nearly every sales call includes a general property information sheet—a summary of what the property has to offer. A property information sheet should record the location of the property, the number and types of guestrooms, a description of the atmosphere of the hotel, parking information, number and types of restaurants, meeting room capabilities, and special amenities and features.

A meeting and banquet room information sheet may also be part of the sales kit. It should include each meeting room's seating capacity (figured for various setups) and breakfast, lunch, dinner, and break menus.

The information in the sales kit is more meaningful if it is accompanied by visual aids such as color photographs of rooms, restaurants, banquet facilities, and the exterior of the property. A map of the hotel's general vicinity which indicates transportation terminals and nearby attractions can also prove beneficial. For best results, it is a good idea to list major attractions below the map, along with the mileage from the property to the attractions.

Projecting a Professional Image

Once the pre-call research is complete, it is time to attend to personal factors which can affect the success of the sales call. Salespeople are official representatives of the property, and their appearance, attitudes, and approach to clients can mean the difference between new business and a negative response to the property.

First and foremost, never smoke, chew gum, or drink during a sales call. These activities detract from the presentation and may create a communications barrier. Other distractions or unnecessary materials (coats, umbrellas, newspapers, literature for other sales calls, and so on) should also be kept to a minimum. Leave any unnecessary items outside the office and avoid distracting motions such as shuffling papers and fumbling with visual aids.

The importance of punctuality should not be neglected; salespeople who are habitually late for appointments are wasting their time and their clients' time. They also send the message that the client is not important to the property.

Other factors in projecting a professional image include non-verbal communication, voice quality, and listening skills.

Non-Verbal Communication

According to one prominent researcher, 65% of face-to-face communication is non-verbal.[3] A presentation, no matter how well-researched, will not generate a sale if the salesperson's non-verbal communication is not

Exhibit 4.4 Sources for Client Research

National, State, and Regional Association Meetings Market

Who's Who in Association Management, published by the American Society of Association Executives, 1575 Eye St., N.W., Washington, DC 20005, sells for $80 and lists approximately 7,000 associations. A valuable reference; the names and addresses of those listed in this directory are also available for direct mail rental for properties that wish to use the names on a one-time basis rather than purchasing the book.

The Nationwide Directory of Association Meeting Planners, available from The Salesman's Guide, Inc., 1140 Broadway, New York, NY 10001, sells for $160 and lists the names and titles of over 10,000 meeting planners from 6,500 major associations. The directory also details the number of meetings held annually, the months in which the meetings are held, the approximate number of attendees, and the geographic location of the meetings. Of special interest to hotel salespeople: the type of facilities used by each group.

Corporate and Incentive Meetings Market

The Directory of Corporate Meeting Planners, available from The Salesman's Guide, Inc., 1140 Broadway, New York, NY 10001, lists the names, addresses, and phone numbers of 12,000 meeting planners. Also listed: the number of meetings held annually, months held, and locations.

Meeting Planners International Membership Directory is available to members and allied members of Meeting Planners International, 1950 Stemmons Freeway, Dallas, TX 75207. Hotel salespeople wishing to obtain a copy of this guide—the best-known source of corporate meeting planners—must join the organization with a meeting planner.

Group Tour and Travel Market

The National Tour Association Membership Directory, available from the association's headquarters, 120 Kentucky Ave., Lexington, KY 40502, lists approximately 3,000 air and motorcoach tour companies and affiliate suppliers.

The American Society of Travel Agents Membership Roster is available to allied members, and lists travel agents and suppliers. For additional information, write: 4400 MacArthur Blvd., N.W., Washington, DC 20007.

These sources are invaluable guides for the names, addresses, and phone numbers of potential group-business clients.

accepted by the client. Non-verbal communication can be divided into four general categories: appearance, the handshake, territorial space, and body language.

Appearance. A salesperson's appearance is the first thing a client notices, especially the hairstyle. For this reason, salespeople should pay close attention to their hair. A conservative hairstyle is often a major factor in closing a sale.

A salesperson's wardrobe is another important success factor. Salespeople should wear conservative clothing that projects an image of success and authority. Dark suits for men and conservative, tailored suits for women project an image of stability and credibility, setting the stage for a business-like presentation. Clothes should be clean, well-pressed, and appropriate for the region's business community.

Even the most expensive wardrobe won't erase negative impressions caused by bad grooming. Hair should be clean; makeup conservative and well-applied; fingernails neatly manicured; and perfume, colognes, or aftershaves kept to a professional level of acceptability.

The Handshake. The handshake, when done correctly, helps to establish an atmosphere of honesty and mutual respect and leads into a positive presentation. As a general rule, you should extend your hand first and maintain eye contact with the client while gripping the client's hand firmly. The handshake should be fairly brief. A long handshake may cause discomfort for a new client because it implies intimacy, but a limp "cold-fish" handshake should also be avoided—it implies unfriendliness.

Territorial Space. There are four socially acceptable distances that most people try to keep between themselves and others: public space, social space, personal space, and intimate space.[4] Since any unwelcome invasion of these spaces can make the client defensive, an understanding of territorial space is essential to successful selling.

Public space is a non-threatening area over twelve feet away from potential clients. This type of space can be used when selling to a group because a group usually feels more at ease and more willing to communicate at this distance; this much distance is not particularly helpful when making a presentation to an individual, however, as it limits his or her involvement.

Social space is an area four to twelve feet from the client, and may be an ideal beginning area for a presentation to an individual, especially if the salesperson is not acquainted with him or her. Clients often use a desk to maintain this distance.

Personal space is an area two to four feet from the client, and is often the closest a salesperson may get to a client. Depending on a person's background, even this distance may be too close, and barriers (desks, tables, and so on) may be used by some clients to protect their personal space.

When clients are comfortable with you, they may invite you into their personal space zone; this gesture shows friendliness and greatly enhances your chances of giving a successful presentation. If you are given a choice of a seat in the social space (in front of the desk) or in the personal space (beside the client on the side of the desk), you should indicate friendliness and interest by accepting the chair in the personal space. However, chairs should not be moved closer unless the client is a friend. To do so might be an unwelcome intrusion into the client's personal space, which could lessen the chance for a sale.

Intimate space is an area within two feet (arm's length) of the client and is usually reserved for close friends and loved ones. A salesperson's invasion of this space may be offensive or cause the client to feel dominated or overpowered.

Body Language. One of the most interesting parts of non-verbal communication is body language—signals sent from a person's face, arms, hands, legs, and posture. A salesperson's body language is very important to his or her presentation. The body should be erect to project confidence, the salesperson should smile to show warmth and interest in the client, and body gestures should complement, not detract from, the sales presentation.

Industry Profile

**David O'Connor,
CHSE**
*Director of Insurance
Sales
Saddlebrook*

After his graduation from Old Dominion University in Norfolk, Virginia, David O'Connor began his hotel career as a conference services manager at the Williamsburg Inn, a Five-Star hotel and conference facility in Williamsburg, Virginia. Over the years, O'Connor has advanced through various management and sales positions at Innisbrook Resort, the Key Biscayne Hotel and Villas, and the Colony Beach and Tennis Resort. He is currently employed at Saddlebrook, a Florida resort, where he is responsible for over $2.5 million in rooms sales annually. As Director of Insurance Sales, he concentrates his nationwide sales efforts on the lucrative insurance company market, but also solicits short-term corporate business from the Northeast.

"Having the opportunity to start my hotel career at a complex like Colonial Williamsburg was truly a break for me. The Williamsburg Inn was really unique; I was able to handle the details of every conceivable type of conference—from a weekend for Amway distributors and their families to the coordination of the Emperor of Japan's first stopover on his historic visit to the United States in 1976.

As conference services manager, I began with the assumption that the client was basically sold, or I would not be sitting in front of him or her. I would immediately ask questions about the group and start to form clear ideas in my mind—and sometimes in the mind of the client, I suspect—regarding just what was the purpose of the meeting. Once I had determined this, I came up with ideas on how the hotel could help the client accomplish those objectives. When I shifted from this service role to sales, however, I had to change the way I worked. I had to convince my prospects of the various wonders of the properties that I represented!

Every sales book in the world says the same thing: 'satisfy the customer's needs,' but I had to learn it the hard way. And it seemed so obvious once I realized it. I try to say practically nothing about the property until I gain the same information from the prospect that I asked for as a service manager. Essentially, the client tells me exactly what will 'sell' him or her and what will turn him or her off.

The resort I represent, Saddlebrook, fulfills so many different corporate and incentive needs that it isn't often that I can't meet the needs of the client. If my property can't meet his or her needs, however, I say so, and try to direct the prospect elsewhere. Then the client thinks of me as a friend who has been of help. **"**

Understanding body language can increase your chances of making a sale. Since non-verbal communication tends to be spontaneous and unconscious, people tend to believe the non-verbal message even if it contradicts what is being said. Therefore, it is important to make a conscious effort to display positive body language:

- Face—Maintain a pleasant expression, make direct eye contact with the client, and smile frequently.

- Arms—Keep them relaxed and uncrossed.

- Hands—Offer a firm handshake; make arm gestures with extended hands, palms open.

- Legs—Cross them in the direction of the client or leave them uncrossed.

- Posture—Lean forward to express interest or sit upright to project confidence and credibility.

You should also be alert to any negative body language sent by the client:

Caution signals include the client leaning away from you, very little eye contact, puzzled facial expressions, a neutral or questioning tone of voice, crossed or tense arms, clasped hands, fidgeting, or legs crossed and turned away from you.

Disagreement signals include the client leaning away from you, retracted shoulders, a tense face, a wrinkled brow, very little or no eye contact, arms crossed over the chest, hand motions expressing rejection or disapproval, tense or clenched hands, or legs crossed and turned away from you.

It is important to deal with negative body language as soon as it is noted. In the case of caution signals, you can depart from the planned presentation and ask questions to encourage the client to express attitudes and opinions. By carefully listening to the client, you can address the client's particular concerns, modify your presentation, and possibly re-establish rapport.

When disagreement signals are evident, it is important to *immediately* stop and adjust to the situation. Again, questions may be used to determine what is wrong, and it is quite acceptable to let the client know you are aware that something upsetting has occurred. Direct questions, such as "Have I said something that you do not agree with?" can be used to re-establish communication and lead the client back into the areas in the presentation that caused concern.

Since non-verbal communication plays such an important role in sales, salespeople should know:

1. How to recognize non-verbal signals.

2. How to interpret non-verbal signals correctly. Some signals, such as facial expressions, may not always be genuine; a client may feign interest or enthusiasm.

3. How to alter a selling strategy as needed for a particular situation. A salesperson should be able to slow, change, or even stop a presentation in order to remove communication barriers.

4. How to respond verbally as well as non-verbally to a client's body language.

Voice Quality

Every sales presentation must be clear and understandable to be effective. The human voice is a persuasive instrument when used properly, and it is vitally important that salespeople learn to use their voices as selling tools.

Salespeople should be aware of the importance of voice tone, inflection, and enunciation during a sales call. They should also remember that their purpose is to communicate: they should avoid slang and technical jargon, and should speak *slowly*. If a salesperson speaks too quickly and does not allow the client to speak, the client may feel that he or she is being subjected to a verbal barrage.

A salesperson's accent may also be a factor in giving a presentation. A New Englander may need to adapt to the slower drawl of westerners, for example. If salespeople are uncertain as to how their voice comes across to others, a tape recording of their voice may be used for analysis of strengths and weaknesses.

Listening   On the other end of the spectrum, salespeople need to know when to *stop talking*. Salespeople need to show a genuine interest in clients and their needs, and listening is an important part of building rapport. Although the average American adult has a listening efficiency of only 25%,[5] there are ways you can increase your listening efficiency—and the likelihood of making a sale.

First, when the client is speaking, face him or her and eliminate as many distractions as possible. Show the client that you are really listening by maintaining eye contact (without staring) and nodding in agreement. Appropriate facial expressions are another non-verbal way to assure the client that you are listening.

Pay careful attention to what is being said; this is not the time to be thinking about what to say when the client stops talking. It is often effective to repeat, in your own words, what has just been said as you understand it. Avoid adding content when rephrasing and refrain from agreeing or disagreeing with the client; the important thing is to communicate your understanding of what was said back to the client.

Being attentive to the client, taking notes, and not interrupting while the client is speaking can build listening skills and sales success.

The Presentation Sales Call

Regardless of the type of sales call, you must have a planned objective for the call, whether it is to establish a personal relationship with the client, invite the client to visit the property, qualify the client for potential business, or obtain a provisional or definite booking. In general, the main objective of any sales call is to get some type of commitment from the client. Having an objective in mind helps to keep you on track.[6]

The objective of a presentation sales call is to book business for the property. Once you have prepared yourself for a presentation sales call, it is time to meet with the client and follow the five steps that will help ensure success:

1. Opening the sales call

2. Getting client involvement

3. The presentation

4. Overcoming objections

5. Closing and following up

Opening the Sales Call   All sales calls begin with an opening. The opening includes an introduction and a purpose statement, benefit statement, and bridge statement.

Introduction. Introduce yourself and the property: "Good morning, Mr. Smith. I'm Terry Jones from the Red Rock Resort in Boulder, Colorado." Maintain eye contact, offer a firm handshake, and present a business card. If you have already spoken with the client, either in person or over the telephone, you may say something like "Good afternoon, Mr. Baker. It's nice to see you again" or "Hi, Jean. It's a pleasure to finally meet you after our telephone conversations." If the client seems nervous after the introduction, you may engage in some small talk to put the client at ease.

Purpose Statement. Soon after the introduction, state the purpose of the visit. Are you calling to present a new idea, service, or product? To renew a business relationship?

Benefit Statement. The next step in the opening is to present a benefit (or benefits). The benefit statement is the most important part of the opening because it gives the client a reason to listen to you.

Most clients become interested in a hotel's facilities and services only if the facilities and services can benefit them directly. Therefore, it is important that salespeople not sell a product; they must sell what the product can do for the client. In other words, they must be problem-solvers, rather than product-sellers.

Translating features and services into client benefits takes practice, but one good way to organize features-benefits information is for the salesperson to prepare a features-benefits worksheet for each targeted market segment (see Exhibit 4.5). Note that the benefits of the product or service are often intangible. What the client really buys is a feeling, a pleasure, an image. Therefore, that is what salespeople should be selling (see Exhibit 4.6).

Bridge Statement. Once you have stated property benefits, you are ready to lead into the body of the sales presentation. Bridge statements are a way of asking for permission to continue the sales call, and are usually made in the form of a question: "Would you be interested in learning how other companies such as yours have benefited from our frequent guest programs?" or "Ms. Townes, is it all right if I take a few moments to ask some questions and jot down some notes about your business to give me a better idea of how we can serve you?"

These questions ask for a response from the client. If the client is not interested in answering these questions, permission to continue has not been granted, and you can thank the client for his or her time and ask for an appointment in the future. If these questions elicit positive responses, however, you have received permission to continue, and can proceed to the next phase of the sales call: getting client involvement.

Getting Client Involvement

Step two in the sales call focuses on determining the specific needs of the client and getting him or her involved by asking questions. It is a fundamental rule that questioning precedes any sales presentation.

Getting client involvement serves several purposes. First, it helps to build the client's interest; second, it helps determine the client's needs and problems; and third, it helps determine the areas of greatest importance to the client. You should take notes during this step; these notes should later become a part of the client's account file. Questioning helps you custom-tailor the sales call. With the knowledge gained during this questioning step, you can anticipate objections and adjust the presentation accordingly.

Questioning. The use of questions helps to tie down specific areas of concern to the client. Examples of tie-down questions include: "Don't you agree?" "Does that sound fair?" "Isn't it?" "Wouldn't it?" and "Aren't you?" These can

Exhibit 4.5 Sample Features-Benefits Worksheet

Features	Benefits
1. Firm, king-size beds	A good night's sleep
2. Health club and spa	An opportunity to relax and unwind at the end of a busy day
3. Corporate rate program	Savings, value, investment
4. Electronic door locks	Safety, feeling of security
5. Quality gourmet restaurant	Impress clients
6. Express check-in/out	Save time and hassle
7. Honored guest program	Recognition
8. Frequent airport limo service	Convenience, savings
9. No-smoking rooms	Health and comfort
10. Turn-down service	Feeling of contentment, personal pleasure

This features-benefits worksheet for individual corporate travelers clearly spells out the intangible benefits of each hotel feature.

also be used throughout the presentation itself, either at the beginning or end of a sentence. For example, if a meeting planner is visiting the property, you could show him or her the ballroom and ask, "Wouldn't this room be suitable for your closing banquet?" Or, in showing the property's executive suite, you might say, "Your president would like this suite, wouldn't he?"

A salesperson needs to ask two types of questions: close-ended questions and open-ended questions. Close-ended questions generally require a specific answer and can often be answered in one or two words. "How many training meetings did you stage last year?" is a close-ended question. Open-ended questions give clients the opportunity to express their feelings and knowledge. For example, you might say, "In researching your company, I noticed that last year's attendance at your annual convention was at an all-time high. Why do you think last year's meeting was so successful?" The client's answer may give clues to what is important to the client.

Questions can also be divided into three broad categories: *fact-finding* questions determine specifics and facts; *feeling-finding* questions reveal the feelings, attitudes, and opinions of the client; *problem-solving* questions uncover the problems faced by the client and pave the way for the presentation.

Fact-finding questions are generally close-ended questions such as "How long have you been with the Builder's Association?" or "How often do you hold these meetings?" Open-ended fact-finding questions can prove more effective; by asking open-ended questions ("Could you tell me about your needs for hotels in our area?"), you can determine the information needed for an effective presentation.

To effectively sell to a client, you must accurately determine a client's feelings. This is done by asking such feeling-finding questions as "What factors are most important to you personally in deciding on a lodging site?"

Exhibit 4.6   Turning Features into Benefits

Feature	Benefit
"I'm glad you asked about our guestrooms! We have the latest in keyless lock technology;	cards for guestroom locks are simple to use and more secure than keys."
"As for the furnishings, the mattresses are firm but not rock-hard;	you're sure to enjoy a comfortable night's sleep."
"The television and lights may be operated from a remote control panel on the nightstand between the beds,	so you don't have to get out of bed to change the channel after you're comfortable."
"And each room has a desk and a love seat:	the desk gives you plenty of room to work, and the love seat is great for relaxing after a hard day."

If salespeople present only features, they leave it to the client to interpret how those features can benefit him or her. Salespeople should try to influence this interpretation by explaining the benefits that the client will receive from each feature.

Other examples of feeling-finding questions are: "What did you personally like about last year's convention?" "What do you feel made your last meeting such a success?" and "What do you think would make this year's meeting an even greater success?"

Problem-solving questions focus on the considerations which weigh most heavily on the client's mind. By beginning problem-solving questions with a statement that demonstrates the concerns of others in a specific area, you may get a more honest response: "Ms. Jones, many of our clients tell us they are concerned about delays during check-in and check-out. Do you have any concerns in that area?" The client is encouraged to reply since he or she knows others have the same concern, and you can then respond.

After you have established rapport through this questioning phase, you may use a transition statement ("Now that I understand your needs, I can show you how our property can—") to lead into step three of the presentation sales call—the presentation.

The Presentation

You should have a prepared, rehearsed sales presentation that addresses the needs of each of the major market segments the property has targeted; for example, a general sales presentation for meeting planners that relates specifically to the needs of that segment. But successful salespeople do not stop there; they custom-tailor this basic presentation to the needs of the particular meeting planner they are calling on, based on their research or questioning of the client.

There are three skills required for a successful presentation: organization, effective speaking, and intelligent use of visual aids.

Organization. Writing a presentation in advance is a good way to ensure that all important points are covered in logical order. You can then give the client an overview of the presentation ("I want to explain how our hotel will eliminate the concerns we've discussed") and present each point individually. At the end of the presentation, you can summarize the points covered. A presentation checklist containing the key elements of the opening and presentation can be a useful planning aid (see Exhibit 4.7).

Effective Speaking. The most important ingredient in effective speaking is enthusiasm. No salesperson wants to sound "canned." If you have memorized your presentation, make a special effort to put feeling and energy into your voice. Every salesperson's voice and manner should express a sincere desire to assist the client. The use of hospitality jargon should be avoided.

Since it is important to continue the client's involvement throughout the sales call, you should ask questions periodically during the presentation. This not only involves the client, but assures you that the presentation is being understood.

Besides monitoring yourself for proper voice tones, inflection, and enunciation, make sure you are not using gestures or facial expressions that could distract the client.

Visual Aids. While people recall only 25% of what they hear, they retain 50% of what they both see and hear,[7] making visual aids an important part of a sales presentation. Visual aids such as pictures, charts, and graphs also build credibility. It is seldom enough to simply state the benefits of property products or services; visual aids provide proof and increase believability.

Ideally, you should carry visual aids that have been specifically selected for each target market. It is important to note that endorsement letters, while not traditionally considered a visual aid, can be used to support a presentation. When using endorsement letters, however, consider the market segment; a training director is more likely to identify with an endorsement letter from another training director than with a letter written by a motorcoach tour organizer.

In addition to color photographs of the property, brochures, reports of favorable publicity, testimonial letters, and third party endorsements, there are a number of more sophisticated visual aids available. Examples of recent innovations include portable videotape and film equipment, multimedia presentations, and portable computer terminals. Hotel salespeople, however, should not make indiscriminate use of these high-tech visual aids. When using visual aids, the guideline should be: use the simplest and most effective method to increase believability. A well-planned presentation supplemented with endorsement letters and a presentation book that pictures past successful functions may be just as effective as a multimedia show. The important thing is that the visual aid relates to the needs of the client.

Closing the Presentation. When you have concluded the presentation, a transition phrase, which may be as simple as "Do you have any questions?" can lead to the next step of the sales call—overcoming any objections expressed by the client.

Exhibit 4.7   Sample Presentation Planning Checklist

Presentation Planning Checklist

1. Who is the client?

   Company Name_____

   Type of Business_____

   Contact Person_____

   Address_____

   Phone_____

   Receptionist's Name_____

2. Date and time of appointment_____

3. Statements of client problem and/or opportunity as related to my offering:

   _____

   _____

4. Major buying motives of the client (if known):

   _____

5. Objectives of the presentation:

Major	Minor
_____	_____
_____	_____
_____	_____

6. Important guest benefits to be stressed:

   _____

   _____

7. Evidence needed to support my claims (competitive comparisons, public relations pieces, testimonials, etc.):

   _____

   _____

8. Other information needed (color photographs of the property, list of guest references by market segment w/phone numbers, etc.):

   _____

   _____

9. Sales tools required (brochures, audiovisual equipment, samples, etc.):

   _____

   _____

10. To start the presentation, I will:

    a. Build rapport in this way:_____

    _____

    b. Capture attention, interest, and move on to the presentation in this way:_

    _____

Exhibit 4.7 *(continued)*

11. I anticipate these objections during my sales presentation:

        Objection   Response

_____   _____

_____   _____

_____   _____

12. To close the sale, I will ask for the business in this way:

_____

_____

The use of this type of form enables a salesperson to plan each phase of a sales presentation. The form provides space to list objectives, benefits to be stressed, sales aids needed, ways to overcome objections, and techniques to close the sale.

Source: Adapted from Danny N. Bellenger and Thomas N. Ingram, *Professional Selling Test and Cases* (New York: Macmillan, 1984), pp. 167–168.

Overcoming Objections

Step four of the sales call deals with those times when the client has objections to a sales presentation.[8] Objections can occur at any time (one salesperson had his business card torn up by a client before he even got started), and there is no reason to panic when an objection is raised. Some objections are a client's way of asking for more information—and some may offer an opportunity to close the sale!

Objections can be verbal or non-verbal. If a client asks a number of questions about food and beverage service, for example, it is possible that he or she has heard negative reports about the property's food and beverage operation. On a non-verbal level, clients may move back, clench their fists, become restless, glance sideways, or cross their arms when there is an objection to a suggested benefit.

Most objections should be handled immediately. The exception is an objection concerning price: if price is talked about too early, the client may think about rates throughout the presentation instead of paying attention. All other objections should be dealt with as soon as they come up, because if they are not, the client may think you are trying to avoid them and you lose credibility. Objections should be addressed with empathy and without arguing. You may need to ask questions to clarify the objection. If you feel that questions are necessary, do not interrupt the client; wait until the client has finished voicing the objection, give a sympathetic response, and restate the objection in your own words before asking questions.

The majority of sales objections are predictable, and salespeople can prepare answers to common objections well in advance of the presentation. This is one area in which pre-presentation planning really pays off: objections that are anticipated have a better chance of being dealt with successfully. Brainstorming with other salespeople about the client is an extremely effective technique for preparing answers to objections. When a number of people are involved in the creative process, a greater number of ways to handle an objection can be developed. These answers can be written down and memorized by the entire sales force to assist in handling objections adeptly.

Types of Objections. Objections fall into three basic categories:

1. Price or rate

2. Product or service

3. Lack of interest or urgency

Price or rate objections ("Your competition offers a better rate" or "My wife and I can't afford to spend that much for a wedding reception") can often be deferred to the end of the presentation, after you have had the opportunity to further detail the benefits offered for the price quoted. Price objections can also be avoided by questioning the client on other areas of concern, rather than directly answering the price question. You can say something like: "Putting price aside for a moment, what else, if anything, is of concern to you?"

Product or service objections ("Our previous experience at your property was not very good" or "Your guestrooms just don't compare with those offered at newer properties") and lack of interest or urgency objections can be handled in a number of ways. One way is to restate the objection and offer a positive response to the objection:

Salesperson:	"Mr. Stubbs, from your comments it's my understanding that you don't feel our location is suitable for your training meetings."
Client:	"That's right."
Salesperson:	"What is it about our location that concerns you?" (Because of thorough pre-presentation research, the salesperson has a good idea of what the client's objection will be.)
Client:	"I guess the biggest problem is arranging transportation for our delegates."

In this scenario, the salesperson has identified the concern of the client and can then present a benefit offered by the property that will answer that concern: complimentary bus transportation to and from the airport, bus station, and train terminal.

A salesperson can also agree with an objection but point out a compensating benefit:

Client:	"Your room rates are $10 to $15 higher than your competitor's."
Salesperson:	"Yes, our room rates are higher, but our hotel offers 24-hour transportation to the airport, a complimentary breakfast in our deluxe coffee shop, and the finest room service in the area. We also offer no-smoking rooms, and all of our rooms have special electronic locks for extra security."

Lack of interest objections can be handled by questioning the client about his or her feelings about present arrangements:

Client:	"We're happy with our present hotel."
Salesperson:	"Is it the facilities or the service you are most pleased with?" (The salesperson is already aware that the client has complained about the poor service she received at a recent award banquet.)
Client:	"Their meeting rooms and audiovisual equipment are excellent. But sometimes we have had problems with the food service."
Salesperson:	"So you need a hotel that can equal your existing hotel in meeting rooms and audiovisual assistance, but provide better food service. Ms. Stern, our property has an excellent reputation for food service, and we can meet or exceed the meeting room and audiovisual services offered by your present hotel."

When answering objections, never knock the competition or downgrade their product or services. This tactic insults the client's judgment if he or she uses the services of the competitor, and may provoke the client's natural reaction to speak up and defend his or her previous decision. It can also destroy a salesperson's credibility as an advisor.

There may be times when a salesperson is unable to overcome an objection (a meeting planner, tour wholesaler, or training director may say "no" to a sale and mean it), but in many cases, objections can be answered to the satisfaction of the client.

Closing and Following Up

Many salespeople enjoy presenting their product, but hesitate when it comes to closing. Closing is not difficult, however, when you understand some fundamental principles involved.[9]

There are two basic types of closes: test closes and major closes. Test closes try to draw a reaction from the client. For example, when a salesperson shows a client a meeting room and asks, "How do you like our meeting facilities?" he or she is hoping to get a favorable response from the client.

Test closes can be used throughout a presentation to build an "agreement staircase" that will make the major close easier. Asking questions that invite a positive response helps to get the client to say "yes" and be more receptive to the presentation. Using test closes also helps to solidify key points and lets salespeople know where they stand with the client before attempting a major close.

A major close is a question or statement that asks for the sale. The major close should elicit a commitment on the part of the client and should be attempted as soon as the client has reached a peak of excitement.

Before attempting a major close, salespeople should keep in mind that some closing situations are better than others. For example, trying to get an affirmative answer from a client who has been sitting in a cramped sales office for twenty minutes is more difficult than getting a positive response from a client who is basking in the luxury of a suite or lush atrium lobby.[10]

There are a number of major closing techniques that can be used (see Exhibit 4.8). Salespeople can determine if a client is ready for a major close by observing these clues:

Exhibit 4.8 Examples of Major Closing Techniques

Technique	Characteristic	Example
Direct Close	The salesperson asks for the business directly.	"May I reserve the space on a definite basis?"
Summing-up Close	The salesperson summarizes the benefits and then asks for the business.	"Our meeting rooms are more than adequate to accommodate your group, the rates I've quoted are within your budget, and the dates you desire are available. May I reserve the space for you?"
BIQ Close	The salesperson uses the following format: "*B*ased on_____, *I*'d like to suggest_____." *Q*uestion: "_____?"	"Based on the success that other companies in your field have had in using our meeting facilities, I'd like to suggest that we book your training seminar in our Gold Room." Question: "Does that sound good to you?"
Assumptive Close	The salesperson assumes that the sale is a sure thing.	"Shall I block 45 rooms for you?"
Alternative Choices	The salesperson suggests a choice between two positive alternatives.	"Would you prefer that your trainees be housed in our standard rooms or in the Tower section?"
Contingency	The salesperson makes an agreement based on a concession from the property.	"If we can revise the awards banquet prices to fit within your budget, then we're set?"
Trial Order	The salesperson suggests that the client try the facilities for an evaluation period.	"Why don't you book just one of your training seminars with us?"
Special Offer	The salesperson provides an added inducement.	"If you confirm next year's convention before the end of this month, we can offer this year's rates."

Source: Adapted from Tom Hopkins, *How to Master the Art of Selling* (New York: Warner Books, 1982).

1. Continual agreement throughout the presentation.

2. The client's agreement to the salesperson's response to an objection.

3. Repetition of a benefit by the client.

4. Positive non-verbal signs—the client smiles frequently or re-examines property brochures, for example.

5. The client requests further details or asks questions throughout the presentation.

After using a major close, stop talking and give the client the chance to think things over and respond. Far too many salespeople get nervous after a major close and blurt out information or otherwise distract the client from making a decision.

It is also important to refrain from doing too much talking after the sale has been made. Too much talking can actually result in the loss of the sale if you say something that brings up doubts or objections that the client had not previously considered! After the sale has been made, thank the client and leave as soon as politely possible. The one exception to this rule is when you are attempting to get the names of other potential clients.

Closing is a skill that can be learned and improved on like any other. Salespeople who are uncomfortable with closing should remember that clients *expect* salespeople to ask for the sale (see Exhibit 4.9).

Following Up. Salespeople should follow up all presentation sales calls. If a sale was not made, following up can consist of a brief thank-you letter. The letter should be accompanied by additional collateral material not given to the client at the time of the presentation and any materials specifically requested by the client, such as a copy of the property's contract, rate sheets, maps of the area, and so on.

If a sale was made, following up is even more important. Following up after a sale consists of providing excellent post-sale service. Certainly, follow-up service takes time, but it is usually easier and more cost-effective to keep a client satisfied than to replace a dissatisfied client.

Follow-up confirmation of a sale is extremely important, especially with group business. While a firm handshake and a steady look in the eye may have closed the sale with the client, most meeting or other group business also requires a signed proposal, contract, or confirmation agreement. Prompt attention to paperwork and other post-sale details reinforces the client's belief that he or she chose the right property.

Keeping the client informed between the time of the sale and the time of the meeting, convention, or other function is one of a salesperson's post-sale responsibilities. Meeting planners in particular want to be kept posted on the number (and often the types) of guestrooms actually used by members of their group(s), changes in hotel personnel, potential hotel labor problems, and any other changes that might ultimately affect their function.

During the function, you should check with the client to see that all is well. This might be done during a coffee break or meal function when the client is free. If the audiovisual equipment for a meeting is not working well, for example, you can immediately see that the problem is corrected. This personalized attention shows the client and the meeting attendees that the property is genuinely interested in the needs of the group.

After the function, a phone call or letter to determine client satisfaction is advised. Never assume that a lack of complaints means the client was satisfied; you must make sure that the client was pleased with the hotel and its service. If the response is positive, you can seek rebookings at a later date and ask the client for the names of others who would benefit from the services provided by the property.

Improving Sales Productivity

Sales is a highly competitive field, and it is important that salespeople constantly monitor their performance in a number of areas. In sales, it is not enough to give good presentations. Results are what counts, and good

Exhibit 4.9   Steps in the Selling Process

Step 1:   Opening the Sales Call
The opening consists of an introduction, a purpose statement, a benefit statement, and a bridge statement asking for permission to continue. The opening must interest the client enough so that he or she will want to hear more.

Step 2:   Getting Client Involvement
The object of this step is to build rapport and get the client to talk about problems and needs. Most sales are made or lost during this step.

Step 3:   The Presentation
This is the heart of the selling process. During this step, the salesperson explains the hotel's products and services to the client. It is impossible to over-emphasize that the salesperson must sell *benefits*, not features, and that the salesperson must serve as a problem-solver.

Step 4:   Overcoming Objections
Resistance is a normal and expected part of the sales process. When clients raise objections, they are not necessarily reacting negatively to the salesperson's proposal, but may only be seeking clarification of it. A solid objection gives direction to the sales effort—it tells the salesperson what he or she needs to do to make the sale!

Step 5:   Closing and Following Up
A successful close is the ultimate objective of the sales call. Closing is asking for the sale, and a good close is a logical finish to a good sales presentation. Following up is the crucial work to ensure client satisfaction after the sale.

The sales process is a logical series of actions that directs the client toward taking a desired action—buying the property's products and services.

---

salespeople must look at their actual productivity and search for ways to improve their performance.

In order for salespeople to measure their productivity, they must first have a written list of goals. Goals keep salespeople on track and allow them to gauge their success. By evaluating performance against these goals, areas for improvement can be noted. Time management and key account management can help salespeople reach both corporate and personal goals.

Time Management

Good time management is crucial to a successful sales career. Time management starts by knowing where time goes. Each salesperson should keep a daily log for a minimum of two weeks to determine how much time is spent on sales activities; paperwork; non-productive activities such as travel time, interruptions, waiting on the telephone, and waiting at appointments; meetings, telephone calls; and other activities (see Exhibit 4.10). Once you see where time is going, you can establish priorities—urgent, important but not urgent, and tasks to be delegated—to ensure greater production.

A salesperson's work day should be planned, with emphasis given to work items with deadlines. For best results, however, only 50% of a salesperson's time should be strictly scheduled; by leaving time for flexibility, unexpected but important tasks can be handled as necessary.

Exhibit 4.10 Sample Sales Time Record Analysis

Sales Time Record Analysis										
Salesperson_____ Day of the Week_____ Date_____										
	PROSPECTING	FACE TO FACE	FOLLOW-UP	Travel	Waiting	Paperwork	Meeting	Interruptions	Mics.	
	High Med Low	High Med Low	High Med Low							
7:00 – 7:15										
7:15 – 7:30										
7:30 – 7:45										
7:45 – 8:00										
8:00 – 8:15										
8:15 – 8:30										
8:30 – 8:45										
8:45 – 9:00										
9:00 – 9:15										
9:15 – 9:30										
9:30 – 9:45										
9:45 – 10:00										
10:00 – 10:15										
10:15 – 10:30										
3:15 –										
3:30 – 3:45										
3:45 – 4:00										
4:00 – 4:15										
4:15 – 4:30										
4:30 – 4:45										
4:45 – 5:00										
5:00 – 5:15										
5:15 – 5:30										
5:30 – 5:45										
5:45 – 6:00										
Total Time in Hours										
Percent of Total Day										

Source: William T. Brooks, *How To Do It All. . . On Time: A Time Management Workbook for Hotel Sales Executives* (Washington, D.C.: The Foundation of the Hotel Sales & Marketing Association International, 1986), p. 10.

In order to use time most effectively, time spent on routine work should be minimized. If possible, tasks should be delegated. A sales secretary can handle a routine inquiry letter, for example. If delegation is not possible, similar tasks can be grouped to save time. Salespeople who have to attend to the bulk of their own paperwork can save time by avoiding as many interruptions as possible. It may be cost-effective to provide each salesperson with a private office or have a sales secretary screen routine calls.

The saying "Time is money" is especially true for salespeople. There are a number of ways for salespeople to save time and money during everyday activities.

When on the road making personal calls, salespeople can prospect for new business by making short "cold calls" between scheduled presentations.

When making telephone calls, it is important that salespeople know exactly what they want to talk about and that they have all the information needed to answer any questions that might arise. If the office is automated, a personal computer greatly facilitates obtaining information. In non-automated offices, the salesperson should have immediate access to clients' files, property information, function book information, and so on. When the salesperson is prepared, the business portion of the call should take a minimum amount of time, allowing time for rapport-building small talk with the client.

Each salesperson should have a specific time period for accepting routine calls, and should advise clients of the best time to call; most clients are aware that salespeople are often "in the field" and will try to schedule their calls for a time when the salesperson is available. Emergency calls or client service calls, of course, should always be put through.

Personal telephone calls may be handled by a secretary or through an answering machine. Each salesperson may set aside a small block of time each day for personal calls, but family and friends should be asked not to call at the office except in an emergency.

Drop-in visitors can mean potential business, and time should be allocated for them in daily scheduling. A salesperson can discourage lengthy stays by a visitor who is "just looking" by offering him or her property brochures or pamphlets, encouraging the visitor to look them over and call back with any comments or questions, and suggesting a convenient time for an appointment. In many cases, the clerical staff can answer questions for drop-in visitors, freeing the sales staff for more productive work.

Paperwork can take up much valuable sales time, so it is important for salespeople to delegate routine paperwork to the clerical staff. Since clutter breeds confusion, each salesperson should be encouraged to generate as little paperwork as possible. This is easier in automated offices, of course. In non-automated offices, salespeople should be encouraged to refrain from writing down suggestions or ideas which can just as easily be orally expressed. It is also important for salespeople to learn to file, not pile. Each piece of paper should be handled only once—by personal action, delegation, filing, or discarding.

Travel time can be turned into productive time by using it to catch up on reading (if driving, you can listen to motivational tapes or mentally plan the work day) or correspondence (every salesperson should have access to a hand-held cassette recorder). On the road, you can save time by planning ahead, keeping a realistic schedule, and combining meetings with meals. Luncheon appointments or dinner meetings should be scheduled with high-priority clients; this is prime selling time which shouldn't be spent alone or with low-potential prospects.

Efficient time management can mean increased sales for the property. Each salesperson should be able to account for productive sales time and efforts (see Exhibit 4.11). Time management plays a major part in the second aspect of personal planning, key account management.

Key Account Management

How much time should a salesperson spend on an account? One way to determine this is to rank accounts according to their profitability. This is important because in most cases 20% of a salesperson's accounts generates 80% of the business. This prioritizing, known as key account management, provides an overview of the potential profitability and importance of each account, and helps the salesperson to allocate his or her time to those accounts with the best chance of increasing revenues and building a client base for the property.

Exhibit 4.11   Sales Time Quiz

SALES TIME QUIZ

	Yes	No			Yes	No
1. Do you always complete and forward paperwork when due?	☐	☐	14. Do you always know where your first sales call will be when you make plans the previous day?		☐	☐
2. Do you have a list of your key accounts?	☐	☐	15. Do you set objectives for occupancy rates, dollar/volume group meeting bookings, and for each client, prospect, or account?		☐	☐
3. Do you have a list of your highest priority prospects?	☐	☐				
4. Do you get enough face-to-face selling time?	☐	☐	16. Do you spend much time on non-selling activities?		☐	☐
5. Do you use your waiting time effectively?	☐	☐	17. Do you know how many calls per account it is economical to make?		☐	☐
6. Do you have a clearly defined list of objectives in writing?	☐	☐	18. Do you feel that you spend enough time on formal professional sales training?		☐	☐
7. Do you always complete what needs to be accomplished daily?	☐	☐				
8. Do you squeeze every available minute from your trade show experience?	☐	☐	19. Do you feel you are earning your full potential?		☐	☐
9. Do you have a set of weekly objectives in writing?	☐	☐	20. Do you spend adequate time prospecting?		☐	☐
10. Do you procrastinate when you must tackle difficult, demanding, or unpleasant tasks?	☐	☐				

Scoring Key

Add all **Yes** and **No** answers. Determine your score below:

17–20	**Yes**	You're an all-pro salesperson.
14–16	**Yes**	You aren't starving (yet).
11–13	**Yes**	You are heading for problems.
10 or more	**No**	You need help—NOW!

	Yes	No
11. Do you spend leisure time handling clerical duties or paperwork?	☐	☐
12. Do you know what your time is worth by the minute?	☐	☐
13. Do you have a five-year plan for your sales career?	☐	☐

Source: William T. Brooks, *How To Do It All. . . On Time: A Time Management Workbook for Hotel Sales Executives* (Washington, D.C.: The Foundation of the Hotel Sales & Marketing Association International, 1986), p. 2.

A salesperson's accounts fall into three general priority categories—high, medium, and low—whether they are established accounts or potential business sources. Priorities are determined by account rankings that reflect the account's impact, present or potential, on the property's sales:

- *Level 1.* These are new accounts with high potential, or present accounts with high potential but lower than expected profitability. These accounts should be a top priority for salespeople. (As a general rule, salespeople will make a minimum of five personal calls and five telephone calls to each of these accounts annually).

- *Level 2.* High potential accounts that are already providing an acceptable share of business. While these accounts deserve a high investment of time, they don't require the amount of personal attention needed for Level 1 accounts. (These accounts will typically be serviced with four personal calls and four telephone calls annually).

- *Level 3.* New accounts with medium potential, or present accounts that have medium potential but aren't providing an acceptable level of business. (These accounts are generally serviced with three personal calls and three telephone calls each year).

- *Level 4.* Accounts that have medium potential and are providing an acceptable level of business. (These accounts may require two personal calls and two telephone calls annually).

- *Level 5.* New or present accounts that have low potential and do not warrant a great deal of a salesperson's time. These accounts may be given token attention over the course of the year. (A salesperson may visit once annually while on a sales trip or prospecting. Or the salesperson may make a telephone call to the account after all other business has been taken care of).

How is an account's potential determined? Most information on present accounts comes from internal invoices (past performance records, advance registrations, survey sheets indicating potential booking dates, and so on), while other information on present and new accounts such as credit information and references can come from outside sources.

A typical salesperson at properties of all sizes handles 300 to 400 accounts. To rate the accounts, a salesperson should list every account on a time management spread sheet (see Exhibit 4.12). A spread sheet includes such important information as the name of the account, the name of the contact person, how often each account was called in a certain time period, how often each account is expected to be called in the future, an estimate of the account's guestroom night value, revisions of this estimate after review, and the account's priority level.

It is fairly easy to determine the amount of time that should be spent on each account in light of the spread sheet information. The number of calls must be proportionate and manageable, and will vary depending on the number of clients each salesperson serves, the property's geographic location, and other commitments the salesperson may have. A typical salesperson is usually responsible for 40 to 50 sales calls per week. These calls are normally broken down into three categories: 15 presentation calls, 15 to 20 telephone follow-ups, and 10 to 15 "cold" or prospecting calls.

After the accounts have been rated, the salesperson can discuss the ratings with the sales manager, develop a strategy for each established and potential account, and begin the exciting job of selling the property.

Exhibit 4.12 Sample Key Account Management Spread Sheet

KEY ACCOUNT MANAGEMENT SPREAD SHEET						
Name of account	Account contact(s)	How often these accounts were called on in 1989	How often we expect to call on them in 1990	Estimate of the account's room nights	Revised estimate after review	Account priority (1 through 5)

It is vital to concentrate on those accounts that are likely to produce the most significant profits. Salespeople should evaluate their accounts by completing a key account management spread sheet similar to the one shown here.

Source: Adapted from Christopher W. L. Hart and David A. Troy, *Strategic Hotel/Motel Marketing*, Rev. ed. (East Lansing, Mich.: Educational Institute of the American Hotel & Motel Association, 1986), p. 154

Notes

1. Some of the information in this list was adapted from Howard Feiertag, "Making Effective Sales Calls," *The Complete Travel Marketing Handbook* (Chicago: NTC Business Books, 1988), pp. 153–155.
2. See also *Hospitality Sales: Preparing for the Sale* (East Lansing, Mich.: Educational Institute of the American Hotel & Motel Association). Videotape.
3. Julia Crystler, "The Importance of Selling Silently," *HSMAI Marketing Review*, Winter 1985, p. 8.
4. Charles M. Futrell, *ABC's of Selling* (Homewood, Ill.: Irwin, 1985), p. 77.
5. Terry C. Smith, *Making Successful Presentations: A Self-Teaching Guide* (New York: Wiley, 1984), p. 51.

6. See also *Hospitality Sales: Making the Sales Call* (East Lansing, Mich.: Educational Institute of the American Hotel & Motel Association). Videotape.

7. Smith, p. 51.

8. See also *Hospitality Sales: Overcoming Objections* (East Lansing, Mich.: Educational Institute of the American Hotel & Motel Association). Videotape.

9. The art of closing is also explored in Tom Hopkins, *How to Master the Art of Selling* (New York: Warner Books, 1982) and *Hospitality Sales: Closing the Sale and Following Up* (East Lansing, Mich.: Educational Institute of the American Hotel & Motel Association). Videotape.

10. Adapted from Tom McCarthy, "Sales Success Starts with Closing," *Hotel and Resort Industry*, December 1986, pp. 29–30.

Discussion Questions

1. What are five types of sales calls?

2. What are some sources for prospect research?

3. What are three basic criteria for qualifying prospects?

4. What are three reasons within a salesperson's control why a presentation sales call fails?

5. To be effective, pre-presentation planning should include research into which three areas?

6. What are four general categories of non-verbal communication?

7. What should a salesperson do if he or she is given a choice of a seat in the client's social space or personal space?

8. What are the five basic steps of a presentation sales call?

9. Why should product features be converted to benefits?

10. What are the elements of a sales call opening?

11. What are three skills needed for a successful presentation?

12. What are three basic types of objections?

13. What are some of the techniques used to overcome objections?

14. When should a sale be closed?

15. What is key account management?

Chapter Outline

I. Basics for Telephone Communication
- A. Telephone Etiquette
- B. Telephone Communication Skills
- C. Listening Skills

II. Outgoing Calls
- A. Prospect and Qualifying Calls
- B. Appointment Calls
  1. Reaching the Decision-Maker
     a. Prepare an opening statement
     b. Develop respect and rapport
     c. Don't leave a message
  2. Opening the Call
  3. The Presentation
  4. Overcoming Objections
  5. Setting the Appointment
- C. Sales Calls
  1. Closing Techniques
- D. Promotional Calls
- E. Service Calls
- F. Public Relations Calls

III. Incoming Calls
- A. Reservations
- B. Responses to Advertising
- C. Inquiries

IV. Telephone Sales Operations
- A. Telephone Sales Blitzes
- B. Telemarketing Operations
  1. Telemarketing Scripts
  2. Telemarketing Programs

5 Telephone Sales

While face-to-face selling is the most effective way to sell, the telephone, if used properly, can be one of the most economical ways to find—and sell to—prospective guests and clients. Salespeople and other employees can use this sales instrument to:

- Search for sales leads
- Identify most-likely-to-buy prospects (qualify accounts)
- Make sales appointments
- Blitz a market to reach prospects and clients (this technique will be discussed later in the chapter)
- Service local accounts in an economical and timely manner
- Service geographically isolated accounts
- Assist guests in making reservations and arranging for return visits to the property
- Inform callers about higher-priced rooms and suites that would be better suited to their needs
- Sell additional services, such as room service and the hotel's restaurants, to registered guests
- Receive direct mail response inquiries (see Chapter 12 for additional information on direct mail advertising)
- Convert inquiries generated by ads (especially ads with toll-free numbers) into sales
- Secure market research data quickly
- Penetrate new markets
- Reactivate former accounts
- Increase the profitability of marginal accounts
- Announce promotional news to clients and generate business for special promotions

Since the telephone is used in so many different ways, telephone sales may be delegated to several groups of employees within a property. Incoming

Industry Profile

Thomas A. Elbe
Vice President/Sales
Nikko Hotels
International

Thomas Elbe originally had his mind set on restaurant management, but soon after enrolling in the Hotel and Restaurant Department of New York City Technical College he focused on hotel management and continued in that direction at the University of Nevada, Las Vegas. Immediately after graduation, he joined Americana Hotels in an operations position, and never considered sales as an option. But after 2½ years, an opportunity arose and he joined the sales force of the 1,850-room Americana Hotel in New York City. Elbe is now celebrating his 13th anniversary in hotel marketing and sales—including positions as Director of Sales for the Loews Hotels, Director of Convention Sales for the New York City Convention and Visitors Bureau, Regional Director of Marketing for Inter-Continental Hotels, and his present position as Vice President/Sales for Nikko Hotels International.

"Nikko Hotels is an international company with over 100 hotels on six continents, but since we're relatively new in North America it's important to our success—and future growth—to promote the Nikko name as quickly and efficiently as possible. We've found telephone sales solicitation to be an excellent way to accomplish this goal.

With broad and vast markets to cover—Nikko Hotels International has properties in New York, Chicago, San Francisco, and Mexico City on the North American continent—the telephone is valuable not only as a selling tool, but also for prospecting and qualifying potential business. While there are many sources for client lists, the information on those lists is limited, and it would be impossible to qualify each person on that list face-to-face, especially since it's estimated that personal sales call costs run as high as $250.

By using the telephone, we can relatively inexpensively and efficiently determine if a client has the potential for our product. We can virtually initiate contact with a client, qualify the business, and 'seal the deal' over the telephone. Although this type of selling isn't as personal as direct contact, it's certainly an important and cost-efficient way of doing business.

Some companies have the luxury of a telemarketing staff; others use existing staff to do the job of prospecting. Another idea which is becoming more prevalent is to cross-train or combine jobs. Essentially, this means training employees to become proficient in more than one area, thereby making them more cost efficient to the organization and broadening their scope at the same time. An excellent example of this is to use the staff of the reservations office to use the telephone to prospect and qualify for the property during down times. This is ideal for our needs, and creates a situation in which everyone wins; the hotel gets the required information and the employee benefits from personal and professional growth.

The client's first impression of a salesperson sets the tone for future relations. The appearance, approach, professionalism, and perseverance of salespeople are their most significant attributes. And we must not forget that the same is true when the telephone is used as a sales tool! The voice, the level of professionalism, and the overall approach can all be quickly evaluated over the telephone. And, to make the most effective use of the telephone, the telephone salesperson, like the direct contact salesperson, must persevere!**"**

calls for individual guest reservations may go through a front desk or reservations staff; calls promoting room service or the property's restaurant may be made by switchboard operators; sales calls may be handled by salespeople or top management. No matter how calls are delegated, both incoming and outgoing calls play an important role in a property's overall sales effort.

Large independent hotels and hotel chains may employ a telemarketing staff to research data, sell, and/or set appointments for the sales staff. Telemarketing—used solely or in combination with media advertising, direct mail, and face-to-face selling—is being increasingly used to build business, offer better service, and generate market data. In this chapter, we will discuss this new trend in marketing as well as detail the telephone's value as both a sales and public relations tool.

Basics for Telephone Communication

Many telephone calls are potential sales calls, so it is important that property employees have good communication skills. Since a friendly smile and a firm handshake can't be conveyed over the telephone, employees must use other methods—the three most important being telephone etiquette, telephone communication skills, and listening skills—to make a good impression and sell the property.

Telephone Etiquette
The lodging industry offers more than just rooms and guest services. It offers *hospitality*, and friendliness and courtesy are an important part of any interaction between a property employee and a potential guest. When using the telephone, property employees must communicate warmth and a willingness to be of service.

Telephone etiquette begins by letting the potential guest know that he or she is important to the property. One way to do this is to use phrases that will put the potential guest at ease and show the property's concern for him or her (see Exhibit 5.1). It is important that the property's representative be polite and understanding, and that the unseen guest feels that someone is concerned about what he or she has to say.

It is especially vital that salespeople use good telephone etiquette. There are a number of ways salespeople can make a good impression:

1. *Adequate preparation.* As mentioned in Chapter 4, always have pertinent information at hand before calling a client. By being prepared, you can organize your thoughts, be ready to answer questions, and avoid wasting the client's time.

2. *Adequate time.* Take steps to make sure you will not be interrupted while calling a client. An interruption can irritate a client and may result in the loss of a sale. Clients deserve a salesperson's undivided attention. Some properties even have a policy of allocating specific blocks of time during which salespeople can make calls without interruption.

3. *Direct contact.* Always dial the call personally. It can irritate a client if a secretary or receptionist places the call and the client is put on hold or asked to wait for the salesperson to come to the phone.

4. *Courtesy and respect.* Intermediaries (secretaries, receptionists, clerks, assistants, etc.) should be treated with courtesy and respect. Being arrogant or disrespectful greatly decreases chances of getting through to a prospect.

5. *Brevity.* Calls should be kept short and to the point unless the client wants to chat. When the call has been completed, let the client hang up first. Avoid giving the impression of being in a hurry, and never slam the receiver down while the client is still on the line!

Exhibit 5.1 Sample Telephone Etiquette Guidelines

THIS IS BETTER	THAN THIS
Answering the Call	
"Days Inn Reservations, Mr. Smith speaking. How may I help you?"	"Days Inn Reservations."
"Days Inn Reservations, Ms. Woods speaking. How may I help you?"	"Days Inn, can I help you?"
Making Sure	
"Would you repeat your name for me, please?"	"What name did you say? I can't hear you."
"Would you spell that for me, please?"	"What did you say? Talk a little louder."
"I'm sorry. I didn't get the name of the person."	"I can't understand what you're trying to say."
Acknowledging	
"Yes, Mr. Smith. I'll be happy to request that for you."	"O.K. I'll do what I can."
"Yes, Ms. Jones, I'd be glad to check that for you."	"All right. Let me see."
Leaving the Line	
"Would you mind waiting while I check, please?"	"Just a minute." "I'll try to find out."
Returning to the Line	
"Mr. Baker, thank you for waiting. I have that information."	"The date on that reservation was June 18."
"Ms. Woods, I'm sorry to have kept you waiting."	"Are you still waiting?"
Completing the Call	
"Thank you for calling Days Inn, Ms. Smith."	"Bye-bye." "OK." "So long." "That's OK." "All right, bye."

Courtesy of Days Inns of America, Inc.

6. *Timing.* It is important to respect the hours kept by clients. As a general rule, avoid calling during the late afternoon or early morning hours. Of course, the client's time zone should also be considered.

These simple guidelines will go a long way toward building courteous telephone habits among the sales staff. But sales and goodwill can be increased even more by understanding how to speak effectively over the telephone.

Telephone Communication Skills

It is important to check yourself often on these important communication skills:

1. *Tone of voice.* Your voice should reflect sincerity, pleasantness, confidence, and interest. It is especially important to have a verbal

"smile"—something you can achieve by smiling as you speak. Also, too many salespeople make the mistake of shouting into the receiver, especially on long distance calls. Speak into the receiver as if the client were sitting across the desk.

2. *Pitch.* A low-pitched voice is desirable. Low voices carry better and are more pleasant to the listener.[1]

3. *Inflection.* Avoid talking in a monotone. Enunciate clearly and emphasize key words; you can generate interest by the way you raise or lower your voice.

4. *Understandability.* Avoid talking with anything (gum, a cigarette, pen or pencil, etc.) in your mouth. Be careful not to talk too fast. If you talk too rapidly, words may be misunderstood, or the listener may be so fascinated by your talking speed that the message is lost.

It is a good practice for employees who use the telephone a lot, whether they be salespeople, switchboard operators, front desk agents, or top management, to check their voices on a tape recorder. Every employee should work to develop a pleasant telephone voice free of slang, jargon, and irritating habits. An enthusiastic, well-modulated voice is half of a successful telephone call.

Listening Skills   The other half of a successful telephone call is *listening* to what the prospective client or guest has to say. A salesperson in particular should be aware of several keys to good listening:

1. *Limit talking.* No one can talk and listen at the same time. The prospect should get a chance to air his or her views, and these views should be given careful attention—no interrupting or jumping to conclusions before the prospect has finished speaking. As a general rule, if the prospect does most of the talking during a telephone sales call, it is much easier to make a sale because you will know the prospect's needs and concerns.

2. *Get involved.* It is usually much easier to be enthusiastic and alert when sitting erect; leaning back and relaxing often interferes with listening. You should also try to put yourself in the prospect's place, listening for clues as to what is important to the prospect. You can learn a great deal about the prospect and his or her needs by the way things are said.

   Successful salespeople also get involved by empathizing with the caller. Phrases such as "I know how you feel" are excellent ways to build rapport and show the prospect that what he or she is saying is important.

3. *Ask questions.* Asking questions generates prospect involvement and shows that you are interested. Questions are an effective way to keep the prospect talking and gather additional information. Ask "Why is this important to you?" or "What else can you tell me about that?" and take notes as the prospect shares views and needs. These responses can be used later in a presentation to build support for the sales message.

Outgoing Calls

Outgoing telephone calls can be divided into a number of categories: prospect calls, qualifying calls, appointment calls, sales calls, promotional calls, service calls, and public relations calls. Since most salespeople use the telephone to set appointments rather than make a sale, this section will focus on appointment telephone calls.

Prospect and Qualifying Calls

The objective of prospect calls is to gather information and learn the names of decision-makers. Many calls that start out as prospect calls end up as qualifying calls. Qualifying calls determine if prospects have a need for or can afford the products and services offered by the property (see Exhibit 5.2). Qualifying calls are not sales calls, but are used to find out if an individual or company warrants an in-person sales call. This can be determined by asking several key questions:

- Does your company have a need for hotel accommodations, meeting rooms, or banquet facilities?

- How many people travel for your company? What is the destination of most company travel?

- Who decides where your traveling staff stays? What hotels are you currently using?

- Who usually makes the reservations for your traveling staff?

If a prospect seems a likely candidate for an in-person sales call, further information may be gathered by asking these questions:

- How many meetings does your company hold throughout the year? What time(s) of the year are meetings normally held and how long do meetings last?

- What types of meetings do you typically hold? What types of facilities are needed?

- How do you decide where to hold a meeting? What criteria are used for deciding on a location?

- When are location decisions made, and who makes them?

When researching information on national corporations, it is necessary to probe deeper and get the answers to these questions:

- Does the corporation have a travel department or a corporate travel directory that advises the corporation's business travelers of properties in which they are authorized to stay? Who heads the department for corporate travel?

- Who decides which properties are used? Who makes guestroom and meeting room reservations? Why are certain locations chosen?

- How many people travel for the corporation? How many guestroom nights are reserved? What department has the most travelers? Do business travelers carry corporate identification?

Exhibit 5.2   Sample Prospect Qualification Form

Prospect Qualification Form

COMPANY NAME:_____

ADDRESS:_____

CITY/STATE/ZIP:_____

PHONE:_____ CONTACT:_____

1. *Introduction*: "My name is _____, and I'm calling you on behalf of L'Ermitage Hotels located in West Hollywood/Beverly Hills. Can you tell me who handles the travel and meeting arrangements for your company?"

_____

_____

2. After locating the right contact, state the purpose of your call and ask if any of the company's business travelers stay overnight in the Los Angeles area. If so, ask "Are you familiar with our hotels?"

_____

_____

3. "Do you use an outside travel agency?"

_____

4. If so, "What is the name of the agency involved?"

_____

   OR

   "Do you use an outside travel agency? If so, may I ask which one you work with?"

_____

5. "Can you estimate how many room nights annually you reserve in the Los Angeles area?"

_____

6. "Aside from individual travel, do you hold meetings in the Los Angeles area?"_____

   "How often?"_____

7. "Would you be interested in speaking with one of our sales managers regarding our corporate rate program for your upcoming meetings?"_____

8. Thank the individual for his or her time, and state that you will follow up in an appropriate manner (via telephone or by sending brochures and a general information letter).

Forms such as this one are used to determine if corporations or firms have a need for the products or services offered by a property. Qualifying saves the property time and money by ensuring that salespeople call on promising accounts.
Courtesy of L'Ermitage Hotels, Beverly Hills, California.

- Do business travelers pay their own bills or are accommodations billed to the corporation? Do travelers pay on a per diem (by the day) basis?

- From which company properties do most business travelers originate? What is the destination of the majority of the corporation's business travelers?

The answers to these questions will give the information necessary to prepare a sales presentation.

Appointment Calls

Telephone appointment calls are used to briefly introduce a prospective client to the features and services offered by the property and ask for an appointment to meet face-to-face (see Exhibit 5.3). The object of an appointment call is to get the prospect to agree to an appointment, not to make a sale. Appointment calls save time for the salesperson and the prospect because they allow time for both to prepare for a future face-to-face sales presentation. Having an appointment also reduces the likelihood that the sales presentation will be interrupted.

Before making an appointment, you should have all necessary information available—prospect sheets, account records (if any), prices, firm and tentative booking dates (if applicable), and general property information. You should also develop an outlined presentation for each appointment call to help you remember key questions and sales points.

Like face-to-face selling, the telephone appointment call is made up of several steps:

1. Reaching the decision-maker
2. Opening the call
3. The presentation
4. Overcoming objections
5. Setting the appointment

Reaching the Decision-Maker. If a prospect call has not been made, the salesperson can learn the name of the decision-maker through an intermediary at the firm or corporation. While intermediaries can be helpful in providing the name of the decision-maker, they can also prove to be obstacles when it comes to reaching him or her. It often requires a creative approach to handle the objections and barriers that intermediaries can present (see Exhibit 5.4). There are several effective techniques that may be used to get past intermediaries.

Prepare an opening statement. The salesperson must initiate the conversation when the telephone is picked up, so it is important that he or she prepare an opening statement. Since the intermediary is paid to protect the time of the decision-maker, the salesperson should appeal to a need in order to be put through to the boss. A statement such as "The reason for my call is to let Ms. Boss know about a unique planning service now available to busy executives" will appeal to the intermediary's need to keep the boss abreast of ways to save time and money for the firm.

Develop respect and rapport. Since many decision-makers rely on their secretaries or associates to screen calls and advise them of calls worthy of reply, it is important to show respect to intermediaries. Learn the names of secretaries and receptionists and list these names in your diary of clients' telephone numbers. Calling the intermediary by name is highly effective, as is timing the call so it will not interrupt a busy schedule. (You should especially avoid making calls on Monday mornings and Friday afternoons.) Timing the call shows that you respect the time of both the intermediary and the decision-maker.

Exhibit 5.3   Sample Appointment Telephone Call Dialogue

Reaching the Decision-Maker

"Hello, my name is Dan Stern. Could you help me by giving me the name of the person who makes the convention planning decisions for your firm?"

Opening the Call

"Good morning, Ms. Merrill. My name is Dan Stern. I'm with Complete Resorts International. I'm calling to explain one of the most innovative programs in convention planning available today!"

The Presentation

"Our unique services will help you save time and money on all of your convention meeting room and banquet needs. We have recently developed a program that includes three exciting features to help you stage successful meetings: your own private operations-headquarters room adjacent to the meeting area; the use of our hotel's limousine to pick up your VIPs; and your own personal meeting aide—a fully qualified staff assistant, supplied by our hotel—to handle any last-minute problems for you!"

Setting the Appointment

"I know you will be as excited as we are about our new services that will help you stage successful meetings. When can we meet for just 30 minutes to discuss your upcoming convention for your independent distributors?

"Which day of the week would be best for you, Tuesday or Wednesday?

"What time is most convenient for you on that day, 10:00 a.m. or 2:00 p.m.?

"Great! I'll see you on Tuesday at 2:00 p.m. in your office at 1234 Goodsale Road just west of the Interstate. Thank you for your time, Ms. Merrill. I'm looking forward to meeting you in person. Have a good day!"

Note that in setting the appointment, the salesperson asked a forced-choice question which gave the prospect a choice of two alternatives (both affirmative): Tuesday or Wednesday. Other typical forced-choice questions include: "Would you prefer to meet in the morning or afternoon?" and "Is the beginning or the latter part of the week best for you?"

Don't leave a message. There may be times when a decision-maker cannot be reached. In most cases, when a salesperson is told that the decision-maker is out of town, out on a business call, or on the telephone, the intermediary is telling the truth, but you should be concerned if you are repeatedly told "He isn't available," "She's in a meeting," or "He's in conference." In these cases, you should *never* leave a message asking the decision-maker to call back; instead, ask the intermediary to suggest a time when it is more convenient to call. This technique is both polite and effective because it puts the intermediary's credibility on the line. You can call back and begin with this type of statement: "This is Ms. Jones calling from Best Resort. When I called before, you suggested that this would be a good time to reach Mr. Sullivan. Is he in, Ms. Kelly?"

Opening the Call. Once you have reached the prospect, a good opening is essential to hold the prospect's interest. Introduce yourself and state the name of the property you represent. Developing rapport is important at this early stage, and there are several techniques that can be used to make the prospect more receptive to the presentation to follow.

Exhibit 5.4   Reaching the Decision-Maker

Intermediary:	"Why do you want to know [the name of the decision-maker]?"
Salesperson:	"I'm putting together a list of people who would like to be kept abreast of some of the ways other local businesses are reducing their costs through the use of training meetings. I'm sure your manager would be interested in receiving this information."
Intermediary:	"What is the purpose of this call?"
Salesperson:	"I'm sorry, but I can only discuss that with your manager. Can you put me through to her, please?"
Intermediary:	"Is this a sales call?"
Salesperson:	"No, I'm not trying to sell anything on the phone. I'm just doing research on how area businesses are meeting their training needs. I was hoping that your manager could give me some ideas."

Handling the objections of a secretary, receptionist, or other intermediary is often necessary to determine the name of or reach the decision-maker. These questions are typical of those used to screen calls; the responses given serve as a guide to handling these objections.

First, use the prospect's name often. The prospect's name is important to him or her and, in most cases, the more it is used (without becoming overly familiar or offensive), the better the prospect will feel toward you.

Another good way to build rapport is to use a third-party endorsement. You might say: "Mr. Pritchard, a friend of yours, Jane Steward of Woodcraft, Inc., suggested that I call because she felt you would be interested in our banquet facilities." The use of third-party endorsements gives credibility to the sales message and provides a common meeting ground between prospect and salesperson.

An appointment call should be kept short, unless the prospect wants to chat or ask questions. If it is obvious that the prospect is busy or in a totally unreceptive mood, it is advisable to try to get a brief message across and offer to call back at a more convenient time. If the prospect seems interested or at least willing to listen, you can move on to the presentation.

The Presentation. During the presentation, refer to your notes, if necessary, to make sure you stay on track. Remember to sell the *benefits* of the property rather than the features.

The use of power words such as "excellent," "guaranteed," "quality," and "successful" greatly enhances a presentation and can generate prospect interest. Power words are words that have more "sales power" than others. They are dynamic, expressive, and highly descriptive words that help clients to "see" the hotel's services over the phone. Power words are an important part of a sales vocabulary, along with such personal words as "you," "me," "we," "us," and "our." Use power words often.[2]

Overcoming Objections. Be prepared to overcome objections to specific points of the presentation. It is much easier to handle objections if you have planned some answers to common objections (see Exhibit 5.5) and have backup material available that will support your claims. As with in-person selling, it is very important during an appointment telephone call to listen carefully to objections and avoid arguing with the prospect. The prospect's objections will often provide clues that will enable you to revise the presentation to meet the prospect's needs or concerns.

Setting the Appointment. Since most appointments are made or lost during the first few minutes of the telephone call, you will want to ask for the appointment early. By offering choices of a day—"Would Wednesday or Thursday be more convenient?"—you can lead the prospect into a commitment to a face-to-face sales call.

If you are unable to get the appointment during the conversation, make arrangements to call back on another day.

If an appointment is made, end the call by confirming the date, time, and location of the appointment, express thanks, and promise to follow up the conversation with additional details (property brochures, menus, etc.) and a letter confirming the date of the face-to-face meeting. Ideally, this meeting should be held at your property so you can show the prospect the property's features and facilities.

Sales Calls

Telephone sales calls may be made by a salesperson or by a telemarketer working with a sales script. Hotel chains and many large independent hotels work with specially trained telephone sales teams that call on prospects and concentrate on getting bookings or commitments by phone, rather than by in-person selling. Unlike an appointment call, the objective of a telephone sales call is to make an immediate sale, and the caller must either close during the conversation or make arrangements to call back on another day.

As in a face-to-face sales presentation, it is important that telephone salespeople sell benefits rather than features. People buy benefits, not features, and benefits must be clearly spelled out to avoid misinterpretation by the potential guest or client (see Exhibit 5.6).

Closing Techniques. There are several techniques similar to the ones discussed in Chapter 4 that can be used to close a telephone sale.

Asking for a sale can be as simple as saying, "Shall I reserve a meeting room for your district managers on Monday, July 12th?" However, this technique limits the prospect to a yes or no response, and limits the salesperson to one specific area.

A more effective technique is to *assume a sale*. Assuming a sale assumes a "yes" answer on the part of the prospect: "All right, Mrs. Grauberger, I'll confirm your group at our Lakeview Downtown Inn on the 30th of November. As I said, the rates are $42. Now let me read back the booking requirements."

Forced-choice questions limit the prospect to choosing from the alternatives presented by the salesperson, and provide the salesperson with more control than the previous two methods. Examples of forced-choice questions include: "Shall I book your tour group for Friday night or Saturday morning?" and "Would your distributors like to try our buffet when they arrive or will they be dining in our Red Lion restaurant?" Forced-choice questions make an effective close because they create a choice between positive alternatives; the salesperson is asking not *whether*, but *which*.

Exhibit 5.5   Overcoming Prospect Objections

Prospect:	"I'm not interested."
Salesperson:	"I can understand that you might not realize the values offered by our resort from just a brief explanation over the phone, Ms. Kingsbury. But didn't you tell me that you were considering an incentive package for your top salespeople? I'd like to show you in person how our resort can give you just the package you need—at a good value."
Prospect:	"I don't have time to see you now."
Salesperson:	"Mr. Smith, I realize you have a busy schedule. That's why I want to invite you to visit our hotel for a complimentary lunch or dinner. We can discuss your convention needs over a delicious meal, without taking a lot of time from your business day."
Prospect:	"Just send me a brochure."
Salesperson:	"I'd be happy to send our brochure, but I'd prefer to deliver it personally so I can answer any concerns you might have and explain how groups similar to yours have benefited from our facilities and services. Would 1:30 on Wednesday or Thursday be a good time to visit with you?"
Prospect:	"We can't afford to hold outside training seminars."
Salesperson:	"I know you are aware that sales is a highly competitive area, and that training has proven to be an effective sales tool. Our low rates make it possible for firms like yours to hold sales training seminars at a price you can afford."

Common objections should be anticipated, and responses readied, before a salesperson makes a sales call. These are typical objections that might be voiced by a prospect.

The *pause close* is uniquely effective in telephone selling because silence in a strictly audio medium is difficult for most people to tolerate. A typical pause close may be set up as follows: "Okay, Mr. Fritz. Can I go ahead and book you at the Bayside Inn in Bayport at $65?" (Pause.)

The first person to speak following the pause loses. If the salesperson speaks, the prospect is taken off the decision "hook"; if the prospect speaks, he or she must make a decision.

Closing on an objection acknowledges the prospect's objection, but counters the objection with a benefit (or benefits) and asks for the sale: "That may be true, Mr. Butler. However, the rooms will have tables, making your employees' stay more conducive to after-meeting work sessions. Shall I reserve the large meeting room or the two small ones?" or "I agree, Mr. Morton, that our property is away from the big city and its entertainment, but imagine how distraction-free this sales meeting will be! How many rooms will you be needing?"

A *series-of-minor-agreements close* summarizes the positive statements made by the prospect: "You said that our rooms are comfortable, correct? And you agreed that our location was suitable. And didn't you say that our 'Budget

Exhibit 5.6 Turning Features into Benefits

Feature		Benefit
"We have electronic door locks	SO THAT	you will enjoy a feeling of security."
"We offer 24-hour room service	SO THAT	you may enjoy a meal in the comfort of your own room."
"Every room has a desk with a telephone	SO THAT	you can take care of personal business efficiently."
"Every room features a complete package of name-brand amenities	SO THAT	you can travel light."
"We have express check-out	SO THAT	you can enjoy the convenience of a timely departure."

As mentioned in previous chapters, it is important that salespeople sell benefits, not features. To assist salespeople in thinking "benefits," the words "so that" can be used.

Meeting Plan' is just what you're looking for? Then may I set up your annual sales meeting for the 20th to the 25th?"

As you can see, there are a number of effective telephone techniques that may be used in obtaining a commitment from a prospect. Even though many telemarketing operations use a standardized telephone sales script, telemarketers as well as salespeople should become familiar with these closes.

Promotional Calls

Promotional calls can be made by salespeople, the telemarketing staff, or top management to introduce special promotions. For example, one hotel advertised in community newspapers to promote its wedding reception package. The ad requested that recently engaged couples contact the catering sales manager by dialing the "hot line" telephone number listed in the ad. The catering sales manager supplemented these incoming calls with calls to couples who had recently announced their engagements in the local newspaper. The property was able to secure 15 new accounts in one week!

Service Calls

Client satisfaction and loyalty can be developed through service calls, whether the calls are made just to keep in touch or are follow-up calls to clients after a sale has been made. Clients need to know they are important, and service calls are essential to maintaining and building business for the property. If changes are anticipated before a function, or if problems occurred during a function, a service call does far more to show concern and smooth over the situation than a letter.

Public Relations Calls

Public relations calls are made to generate goodwill. In one case, a restaurant manager made low-key telephone calls to past regulars who had not been to the restaurant for some time. The impact was immediate—the restaurant had 25 additional covers per day! Such person-to-person contact can generate additional rooms business as well. If a general manager picks up the telephone to respond to a guest's complimentary letter, it can have a great impact on the guest—he or she is more likely to feel that the property values his or her business and will want to return.

Incoming Calls

No matter what type of call is received by a hotel, it is essential that the caller have a positive first impression. When a call is answered at the hotel, the spotlight is on the person representing the property. An unfavorable impression may cost thousands of dollars in lost business.

It is both a courtesy and good business to answer the telephone *promptly*. When a call is not answered right away, the caller may become impatient and hang up; waiting time always seems longer than it is, and time is especially valuable to busy executives. Nancy Austin, co-author of *A Passion for Excellence*, explained in a speech how many callers may feel:

> During the first ring, we can hardly wait to speak to someone on the other end! But by the third ring your patient customer has already decided, 'This is it, if they don't answer the phone I'm calling the next hotel.' And by six rings, forget it! They are so thoroughly disgusted that if they are asked for a recommendation, the research shows they will *go out of their way* to disrecommend that place that didn't bother to pick up the phone. And you know why? They say, 'They didn't care.'[3]

Once the telephone receiver is picked up, the hotel's representative must be ready to talk. It is rude and unprofessional to try to carry on a conversation with a co-worker and take an incoming call at the same time. Whether the call is to the switchboard, the reservations department, or a sales office extension, the property's representative should begin the call with the name of the property, his or her name, and a courteous phrase such as: "How may I help you?"

At times it is necessary to put a caller on hold. "Hold" is not synonymous with "ignore." If a call cannot be routed or a question answered without leaving the line, the caller should be given an explanation of the delay. Instead of just saying "Please hold," the employee should say to the caller, "May I put you on hold for just a minute while I find that information for you?" If the caller is kept on the line for more than a minute, he or she should be given progress reports. The person waiting may be told, "Mr. McClendon, I'm still checking on your reservation. Do you mind waiting a little longer?" These progress reports assure the caller that he or she has not been forgotten, and may prevent the caller from getting angry or irritated. When the employee returns to the line, it helps get the caller's attention to begin with his or her name: "Mr. Sullivan, I have those figures for you now" or "Ms. Mercer, thanks so much for holding." This shows courtesy to the caller and may prevent having to repeat all or part of the information.

Incoming telephone calls that can lead to sales fall into three basic categories: reservations, responses to advertising, and inquiries.

Reservations   For years the telephone has played an important role in making reservations. Today, coupled with sophisticated computer systems, it is an even more effective sales tool. At small properties, reservations duties may be handled by a small reservations staff or the front desk agents, while at larger properties reservations may be handled by an extensive in-house staff.

More and more properties are recognizing the importance of providing training for reservations personnel. Reservations and front desk agents are given extensive information about the property, room rates, and booking procedures. They are also trained in selling techniques such as upgrading reservations and cross-selling the property's services (these techniques will be discussed in detail in the next chapter).

In addition to their own reservations personnel, many properties within hotel chains can rely on a central reservations system: a single, usually toll-free, reservations number that links each property in the chain. Some independent properties also have a central reservations system. This approach has proved so successful that many properties now operate two or more toll-free systems—one to serve the public and others for the exclusive use of corporate meeting planners or travel agents (see Exhibit 5.7).

One such system is Westin Hotels' Central Reservations Office (CRO) in Omaha, Nebraska. This system, considered one of the most sophisticated in the country, is linked to numerous airline reservations systems to better serve travel agents (travel agents account for 65% of Westin's bookings) as well as individual and corporate travelers. When a prospective guest dials the Westin toll-free number, a reservations operator asks which hotel he or she is interested in (a hotel is suggested if the caller desires that information), and the caller is given full information on the selected property (rates, availabilities, etc.) from data on the operator's computer screen. When the reservation transaction is completed, the information is transmitted to the appropriate hotel as a booking. This process takes just a few minutes, and the reservation is stored in the computer for future reference.

Since systems such as Westin's are extremely costly, it is vital to shorten "talk time." Time per call can be kept to a minimum through the use of computers (information on frequent clients, room rates and availability, and information on other properties in the chain can be instantly called up as needed) and by keeping the conversation centered on the business at hand.

Central reservations systems benefit individual properties in a chain by providing an additional source of rooms business, immediate notification of room sales, hard-copy confirmations of reservations mailed directly to guests, and a large volume of information on previous guest reservations. Ironically, the use of computer technology has also benefited properties by making possible *increased* personalization. When details of a past stay (which have been stored on the computer) are called up, it enables reservations personnel to "remember" the guest and facilitate the reservations transaction; most guests appreciate this personalized attention.

Responses to Advertising

One of the most effective advertising methods used by hoteliers today is the listing of a toll-free telephone number in print ads. Since people are more likely to respond if the call is free, this method of advertising is an excellent source of immediate reservations and business leads and can generate a large number of calls.

Toll-free calls are often handled by a telemarketing staff which tries to get either a firm commitment for a reservation or information to pass along to a hotel salesperson. It is important that these calls be answered courteously and that sufficient information is available to enable telemarketers or salespeople to answer questions and get a commitment.

Exhibit 5.7   Toll-Free Numbers for Special Markets

Inquiries   Inquiries may be generated from the recommendations of friends, acquaintances, or business associates who are familiar with the property; an article or ad in a newspaper or magazine; a radio or TV commercial; a business directory; or the telephone yellow pages. Although inquiries may generate a relatively small amount of business, the proper handling of inquiries can result in a steadily increasing contribution to the property's guest base.

Since inquiry calls often come directly to the switchboard, it is important that switchboard operators know where to place these calls. Individuals may be routed directly to a reservations agent; group accounts may be referred to the hotel's sales staff or the general manager. At small properties telephone inquiries are often handled directly at the front desk. These calls may come in while front desk personnel are especially busy registering guests. Too often, there is a tendency to treat inquiry calls lightly. However, callers with inquiries usually want a room or seek information about accommodations, and they should be given prompt attention. If front desk personnel are too busy to handle the call, the caller should be transferred to another hotel employee (a salesperson, the sales director, etc.) who can give immediate attention to the call.

Telephone Sales Operations

The telephone can be used in creative ways to boost sales. Two of the most common ways are telephone sales blitzes, which can be extremely effective for small to medium-size properties, and telemarketing, which is used primarily by large properties or properties with large sales budgets.

Telephone Sales Blitzes

Telephone sales blitzes are usually for gathering information, but they can also result in immediate sales. A telephone sales blitz is especially effective for properties that cannot afford expensive computers and other telemarketing technology; these properties are finding that the telephone can still be used in "the old-fashioned way" to generate business.

A successful telephone sales blitz begins with organization. The property's general manager or sales team usually targets a particular geographical area or market segment and develops a plan for contacting as many people as possible within a short period of time.

One advantage of a telephone sales blitz is that virtually any staff member can participate, since usually the prime objective is to gather information, not sell. And even if a blitz is designed to qualify prospects rather than gather information, reservations agents, night auditors, secretaries, and other staff members can easily be trained to use a script to ask specific questions and record the answers on a form for follow-up.

Telemarketing Operations

In today's world of skyrocketing personal-sales-call costs, telemarketing is an effective sales tool that provides person-to-person contact, immediate feedback, and the flexibility of a variety of approaches without the costs of a personal sales call. While telemarketing is often confused with general telephone sales, the two are worlds apart. Telemarketing is characterized by a systematic use of the telephone, often by a special staff of highly trained telemarketers, along with computers and other technology that provides instant access to information.

A good telemarketer can speak to up to 50 decision-makers a day.[4] Using a carefully scripted message, telemarketers can simply gather information or present a sales message and close the sale.

Telemarketing should not be taken lightly. Hotels should refrain from pulling secretaries or clerks from other departments to attempt telemarketing

These telemarketers at the Days Inns of America's telemarketing center in Atlanta use computer terminals in generating leads.

duties. A highly trained staff, dedicated to the telemarketing function only, is the most cost-effective way for a property to use this form of selling.

All potential telemarketers have good communication skills; persistence; the capability to bounce back from rejection; good organizational skills; the ability to adapt to new situations and different types of clients; and, most important, the enthusiasm, friendliness, and flexibility that result in increased sales.

Telemarketing Scripts. Telemarketers must learn to use telemarketing scripts designed to communicate effectively with prospects and either make a sale or gather information necessary to follow up on the call. A telemarketing form can be completed and given to the property's sales representatives for evaluation and possible follow-up (see Exhibit 5.8).

Most telemarketing scripts begin with an introduction that breaks the ice and explains the purpose of the call: "Good morning, I'm Mary Kelly, representing Best Rest Inns. I'm calling to ask you a few brief questions regarding your company's use of meeting rooms and accommodations for your traveling salespeople. Any information you can provide will be extremely helpful. My first question concerns the number of meetings you hold each year." This type of introduction immediately involves the respondent.

The content of a telemarketing script will, of course, depend on the

Exhibit 5.8 Sample Telemarketing Call Report

TELEPROSPECT CALL REPORT

DATE_____

ORGANIZATION_____

ADDRESS_____

_____TELEPHONE_____

KEY CONTACT_____TITLE_____

ADDITIONAL CONTACTS_____TITLE_____

_____TITLE_____

POTENTIAL		YES	NO	FREQUENCY
	GROUP			
	INDIVIDUAL			
	MEETING			
	OTHER			

HOTEL(S) CURRENTLY PATRONIZED_____

ACTION_____

TRACE_____

REMARKS_____

_____

_____

_____

_____

_____   ‒

SIGNATURE

Many telemarketers who prospect for leads use a form similar to this one to build an information base of organizations that may constitute potential business for the property.

Courtesy of L'Ermitage Hotels, Beverly Hills, California.

property's telemarketing objectives. Is the script designed to gather information only (see Exhibit 5.9)? Is it designed to generate leads for follow-up by salespeople? Does it offer a benefit or special premium in return for a booking? No matter what the objective, a telemarketing script is usually:

1. *Short.* Long surveys or presentations may irritate prospects or cause them to lose interest. It is important not to take too much of the prospect's time.

2. *Specific.* The script should be to the point. Benefits should be spelled out early.

3. *Simple.* Long words and hotel jargon should be avoided; the presentation should be readily understandable.

4. *Structured.* The script should flow from general questions to more specific or sensitive areas. For example, it is far easier to develop a rapport with a prospect if the telemarketer begins by asking general questions about the prospect and his or her type of business instead

Exhibit 5.9   Sample Telemarketing Follow-Up Survey

TELEMARKETING SURVEY

Hello_____.

This is _____ from the Sheraton Naperville Hotel. I'm calling to thank you for staying at the Sheraton Naperville. I was hoping you would assist me by answering a few questions about our hotel so we can serve you better.

1. Which of the following describes your reasons for visiting Naperville?

    Corporate Business   Training   Convention   Sales Call   Other

    If other, explain:_____

2. Did you select our hotel personally, or was the reservation made by another individual? If by another person, then who (i.e.: secretary, travel agent, other)?

3. Was this your first stay with us?   Yes   No

4. Using the following scale, how would you rate your general impression of our hotel?

    Excellent   Above Average   Average   Fair   Poor

    Comments:

5. How would you rate our registration services?

    Excellent   Above Average   Average   Fair   Poor

    Comments:

6. What was the quality of our housekeeping services?

    Excellent   Above Average   Average   Fair   Poor

    Comments:

7. Did you dine in any of our restaurants during your stay?   Yes   No

    How would you rate them?

	Excellent	Above Average	Fair	Poor	Did Not Use
Atrium Restaurant					
Banquet Service					
Beaubien Dining Room					
Cafe al Fresco					
LaSalle Drinkery					
Room Service					

    Comments:

8. Are you aware of any of the following special services we provide for our guests?

			Send Information
The Concierge Floor	Yes	No	_____
Our Video Check-Out	Yes	No	_____
The Guestroom Refreshment Bars	Yes	No	_____
The Pool and Sauna	Yes	No	_____
Our Sheraton International Club	Yes	No	_____
The Meeting and Ballroom Facilities	Yes	No	_____
Our Special Meeting Packages	Yes	No	_____

    Would you like to receive information on any of these services?

Exhibit 5.9 *(continued)*

---

9. Did you need or use information on the surrounding area?   Yes   No

   Comments:

10. Would you like the Sheraton Naperville to have any of the following services?

A Hotel Library	Yes	No
A Jogging Trail	Yes	No
Cable Television	Yes	No
Health Club Facilities	Yes	No

11. How often do you get to Naperville?

   More than once per month

   4 to 12 times per year

   1 to 3 times per year

   First visit

   What is your average length of stay?

   1, 2, 3, 4, 5, or more days

12. Would you choose the Sheraton Naperville for your next visit?   Yes   No

13. Can I make a future reservation for you at this time?   Yes   No

In appreciation for you taking the time to assist us in serving you better, we would like to send you a complimentary room upgrade or a certificate for a complimentary breakfast in our Cafe al Fresco. Which would you prefer? (Room Upgrade Breakfast)

Our records show your address as_____.

Is this correct?   Yes   No

(If incorrect, fill in correct address)_____

_____

What is the correct spelling of your name and your correct title?

_____

Thank you again for your help. We look forward to seeing you at the Sheraton Naperville again *soon* (or (*appropriate date*) if a reservation was made).

Many properties use telemarketing surveys such as this one to follow up on their guests. Information generated by the survey can be entered into a computer to determine areas of guest interest. The information can also be used to custom-tailor a letter or follow-up telephone call to the needs of the guest. Respondents to this survey receive a complimentary room upgrade or breakfast.

Courtesy of Sheraton Naperville Hotel, Naperville, Illinois.

of immediately starting off with questions about how much the prospect has paid for meeting space or accommodations.

When developing a telemarketing script, it is important to remember that the script must keep the prospect on the line long enough to gather information, get a message across, or close a sale. To do this, the script must get the prospect involved and present a benefit of interest to the prospect.

Telemarketing Programs. Since telemarketing is so important, it is essential that a telemarketing program—whether established in a large regional or district office for an entire hotel chain or headquartered at an individual property—be as disciplined as any other form of direct selling. There should be carefully developed production forms, professional training of telemarketers, continuing supervision, and tracking of results. If in-house staff is used to fill telemarketing positions, a training program should be implemented and an experienced telemarketing professional hired as either the program director or a consultant.

An example of a successful telemarketing program is the Days Inns' Automatic Telemarketing System (ATMS). This system was implemented after management considered the following telemarketing statistics:

- By the year 2000, there will be eight million telemarketing jobs.

- Telemarketing is already a $12 billion industry.

- 418 of the Fortune 500 companies are now testing telemarketing applications.

- The cost of an average out of town personal sales call is $220.

Days Inns' telemarketing operation focuses on three primary markets—the motorcoach business, group business, and the corporate market; and three secondary markets—travel agents, travel agent consortiums, and tour operators. The telemarketing program combines experienced telemarketing operators with a computer software package that includes prospect and guest tracking, an inventory of available literature and mailing materials, telemarketing representative productivity tracking, automatic telephone dialing, a program for rapid retrieval of booking information, guest booking histories, a room inventory, a directory of properties, complaint and complaint follow-up records, a program for developing effective telemarketing scripts, and marketing research functions.

In evaluating its program, Days Inns management found that 5% of telemarketing calls resulted in immediate bookings and 20% generated appointments with salespeople; 60% of the prospects contacted wanted to have further information sent in the mail; only 15% had no interest. The program was extremely cost-effective. In the first year of the program's operation, six telemarketing representatives were responsible for over $3 million in bookings.[5]

In addition to sales calls, telemarketers can utilize the ATMS for market research. Telemarketing surveys are used by Days Inns to monitor the needs of prospects. Survey results are entered into the computer system and the resulting profiles make it far easier for Days Inns to meet the needs of its clients and guests.

Any successful telemarketing program depends on a detailed marketing plan and a great degree of professionalism, but this tool provides an efficient answer to today's needs for pinpointing prospects, selling to serious buyers, and keeping in touch with regular clients and guests.

Notes

1. From a speech by Bruce J. Orr, AT&T National Market Manager for the lodging industry, at AH&MA's 1985 annual convention in Las Vegas, Nevada.

2. A helpful resource for building a "power word" sales vocabulary is Richard Bayan, *Words That Sell.* The book is available from Caddylak Systems, 60 Shames Drive, West Berry, NY 11590.

3. From a speech given at AH&MA's 1987 annual convention in San Francisco, California.

4. Robert A. Meyer, "Understanding Telemarketing for Hotels," *The Cornell Hotel and Restaurant Administration Quarterly,* August 1987, p. 26.

5. From a speech given by John Russell at the 1985 Hotel Sales & Marketing Association International's midyear workshop in Nashville, Tennessee.

Discussion Questions

1. Why is telephone etiquette important?

2. What are three keys to good listening?

3. Outgoing telephone calls can be divided into which categories?

4. What is the objective of a prospect call?

5. What are the five steps of a telephone appointment call?

6. What are three techniques that can be used to get by intermediaries?

7. What is the main difference between an telephone appointment call and a telephone sales call?

8. What closing techniques can be used to get a commitment when making a telephone sales call?

9. How can a caller be put on hold in a courteous manner?

10. What are three types of incoming calls that can lead to sales?

11. What are some of the telemarketing statistics that caused Days Inns' management to establish a telemarketing program?

Chapter Outline

I. What Are Internal Sales?
II. The Role of the General Manager in Internal Sales
    A. Hiring Sales-Oriented Employees
    B. Training Employees
    C. Motivating Employees
III. The Role of Employees in Internal Sales
    A. Knowing the Property
    B. Knowing the Area
    C. Interacting with Guests
        1. Using Names
    D. Sales Skills
        1. Upgrading
            a. Top down
            b. Rate-category alternatives
            c. Bottom up
        2. Suggestive Selling
        3. Cross-Selling
    E. Applying Sales Skills
        1. Switchboard
        2. Reservations
        3. Front Desk
        4. Food and Beverage
        5. Service Personnel
    F. Employee Incentive Programs
IV. Internal Merchandising
    A. Guest-Contact Areas
        1. The Lobby
        2. Guestrooms
        3. Elevator Floor Landings
        4. Elevators
        5. Restaurants and Lounges
        6. Barber and Beauty Shops
        7. Reservations or Convention Desk
        8. Cashier's Desk
    B. Back-of-the-House Areas
V. Special Services and In-House Promotions
    A. Special Services
    B. In-House Promotions

6 Internal Sales

As mentioned in previous chapters, selling the property is everyone's business. Every employee, from the general manager to the front desk agent to the food server to the bellperson, makes an impression on the property's guests—an impression that can either leave guests looking forward to their next visit or send them packing in a hurry, never to return. In this chapter, we will discuss the vital area of internal sales, focusing on upgrading, suggestive selling, cross-selling, merchandising, and promotional techniques, and explore how employees in every department can generate additional sales and repeat business for the property.

What Are Internal Sales?

Internal sales can be defined as specific sales activities engaged in by various employees of the property in conjunction with a program of internal merchandising to promote additional sales and guest satisfaction. The main objective of internal sales is to increase sales by promoting effective guest-employee relationships. Management can encourage these vital relationships in three ways:

1. Provide an environment conducive to good guest-employee relations

2. Instill a sense of pride (both in the property and in the value of their respective positions) in employees

3. Provide employees with training that encourages them to become more helpful to guests

The sales impetus must start with top management and filter down to employees. It is up to management to support and encourage employees in internal sales efforts, and to provide internal sales training, product training, and motivational programs. An enthusiastic management team can produce an entire staff that sells with enthusiasm.

There is a tremendous profit potential for internal sales, because in-house sales efforts are directed toward a captive audience. When selling to in-house guests, sales costs are minimal. Each additional dollar spent results in nearly pure bottom-line income. If every hotel guest could be induced to

Industry Profile

Mary Jean Bublitz started her hospitality career as a food server in her parents' restaurant while she was a high school student. Since that time, she has worked as a front desk agent, night auditor, bookkeeper, salesperson, maintenance person, and housekeeper—training that came out of necessity after she and her husband purchased a 20-room motel,

Mary Jean Bublitz, CHA
Co-owner
Quality Inn

then a 42-room motel, and, finally, their present 96-room franchised Quality Inn in Flagstaff, Arizona. In 1980, she was invited to serve on the Convention and Meetings Committee of the International Operators Council (IOC), an organization of Quality Inns International licensees, and is presently serving her seventh year on the IOC Operations and Standards Committee. Bublitz earned her CHA certification in 1983, and is currently involved in the opening of a 102-unit all-suite hotel which is franchised as .a Quality Suites property.

"The real joy of innkeeping is the challenge of promoting hospitality at its finest. Pleasing the hotel guest builds repeat business. I like comparing a hotel guest to a delicate crystal ball which will break and be ruined unless it is handled with tender care at all times. Every person choosing our hotel deserves the finest product we can provide, at the fairest charge possible; this can be accomplished by pricing our services competitively and by providing a friendly, well-trained staff of professionals who perform their jobs correctly.

My husband and I are involved in creating each job description and performance standard. We try to personally motivate our employees and train by good example. We treat employees as family members and have them participate in business decisions. And we emphasize that all employees should have two job titles on their name tags: General Manager/Sales Director; Guest Service Attendant/Salesperson; Maintenance/Salesperson; Room Attendant/Salesperson, and so on. This formula produces excellent results and is an exciting challenge to new staff people.

The best place to learn about the operation is still the front desk. It is still possible to learn more—and keep improving the bottom line—if I spend time at the front desk daily and listen to the guests' requests and comments. The non-smokers rooms idea evolved this way. Guests said, 'We like your hotel. The rooms are immaculately cleaned and properly maintained, but wouldn't it be nice if you could get rid of those stale smoke smells!' My husband and I, being non-smokers, understood their comments since we had that same problem staying in hotel rooms. We decided we could do something about this, and began a non-smokers rooms program at our Flagstaff property. In June of 1984 I suggested the non-smokers rooms idea at an IOC board meeting. The IOC and Quality Inns International decided immediately to adopt the program chain-wide, and mandated a minimum of 10% Non-Smokers Rooms. That figure is now up to 15%.

We had introduced these rooms at the Flagstaff Quality Inn in 1980, and had kept a constant 100% occupancy in Non-Smokers Rooms. In 1987, we set aside 25% of our rooms for non-smokers, and continue to enjoy the same occupancy rate! These statistics emphasize the importance of my crystal ball theory, an internal sales method that can work for any property that is willing to provide courteous, friendly service—and listen to its guests. **"**

spend just $2 more per day, the additional sales for a 200-room property running an 80% occupancy (and an average per-room occupancy of 1.5 persons) would be $175,200 per year![1]

In order to be effective, in-house sales efforts must be continual. A one-month program is usually effective for only one month. Ideally, an internal sales program is tied to the marketing plan, is designed for the *whole* hotel (not just one department), and is a systematic *yearly* plan rather than a one-shot blitz effort. Internal sales, like external sales, should be planned for and directed to high-priority market segments and given special emphasis during periods when business is most needed.

The Role of the General Manager in Internal Sales

The attitude and direction of the general manager will greatly influence the success of an internal sales program. If the general manager is not sales-oriented, it is unlikely that the hotel staff will want to sell. A good general manager recognizes the value of guest satisfaction and sets goals to attain guest goodwill—and repeat business—by using effective internal merchandising and developing sales-oriented employees.

While internal merchandising will be discussed in greater detail later in the chapter, at this point it is important to note that a good internal merchandising program doesn't just happen; it is the result of planning, coordination, and careful evaluation of results. For maximum return, the general manager should see to it that an internal merchandising committee is made up of representatives from each area who have an interest in promoting facilities and services, and that *one person* is given the responsibility for coordinating internal merchandising efforts (it is advisable to select a creative person). He or she not only should assist in training employees in sales techniques, but also should supervise the production, placement, and storage of posters, displays, and other internal merchandising items.

To develop a sales-oriented staff, the general manager must:

1. Hire sales-oriented employees

2. Train employees in sales techniques

3. Motivate employees to sell

Hiring Sales-Oriented Employees

Sales-oriented employees can greatly increase in-house sales. The personnel or human resources department at large properties, or the general manager at smaller properties, should develop sales-oriented job descriptions and be able to recognize sales-oriented applicants. When new employees realize that selling is a part of their job description and that selling is the lifeblood of the property, they will be more willing to learn sales techniques.

Training Employees

Training employees in sales techniques is necessary for effective internal selling by employees. Once an employee has a thorough knowledge of the property and the benefits the property offers to guests, it is a matter of learning the types of selling required for the position (upgrading, suggestive selling, cross-selling, etc.) and learning to recognize verbal and non-verbal clues from guests. These clues include tone of voice and body language (discussed in Chapter 4); employees as well as salespeople should be well versed in how to "read" others. This knowledge will enable employees to better sell to a receptive guest, and help them know when *not* to approach a guest (perhaps the guest is angry, wants privacy, and so on).[2]

Motivating Employees

As mentioned earlier, the general manager plays a vital role in motivating employees to sell. He or she can begin with convincing the employees that they can, indeed, become effective salespeople. Armed with this confidence—and management encouragement—employees can put their skills to work to earn more money for the property. Many properties also offer incentive programs to employees to encourage sales. These programs may be similar to those offered to hotel salespeople, or may be interdepartmental, inter-property, or special promotional contests.

When the general manager sets a good example, encourages others to sell, and oversees and evaluates the success of the internal merchandising program and employee training, the property's internal sales efforts can result in an improved guest perception of the property and increased sales.

The Role of Employees in Internal Sales

For employees to become an effective part of an internal sales effort, it is essential that they be made aware of the importance of selling. Involving employees is very important; using their ideas and suggestions in creating sales targets and action plans helps to motivate them.

Many employees make hundreds, even thousands, of guest contacts weekly, so it is important that all employees be trained in the following areas:

- Knowing the property
- Knowing the area
- Interacting with guests
- Sales skills

Knowing the Property

Knowledge of the property's facilities and services is essential for internal sales. If employees do not know what the property has to offer, they cannot promote its features and services. As part of the orientation process after being hired, every employee should be given a complete tour of the property, with an emphasis on the employee's particular area of service. All employees should learn an abbreviated form of the hotel fact sheet. Employees should also know about special promotional packages, special events, and other property happenings.

To sell effectively, hotel employees must sample the product. Food servers should taste *every item* on the menu so they can make a specific, personal recommendation if asked by a guest. Front desk agents will do a much better job of upselling if they have actually slept in the property's suites. It costs little to have employees stay at the hotel (employees can become "guests" on a slow Sunday night, for example), but the benefits of such stays can be great.

Knowing the Area

Employee knowledge of the general area surrounding the property can be helpful in two ways: employees can encourage guests to extend their stays by suggesting attractions in the area; employees can build rapport with guests by being versed in local current events, local television programming, and other things of interest to guests. Supervisors should encourage employees to keep abreast of area attractions (including hours, prices, and special events) and local developments that might interest guests.

Industry Profile

Chad A. Martin, CHSE
Regional Director of Sales
Howard Johnson Division, Prime Motor Inns, Inc.

Chad Martin says that he was fortunate to have been brought up around hoteliers, and that "this business has never not been fun." He held positions from pot washer to bellperson to outside salesperson for a hotel chain before joining the Ploss Hotel Group of 17 hotels on the Eastern seaboard. He was given an opportunity to add to his sales knowledge when Peter Ploss, the chain's president, sent him to Cornell University. His next position was with Mid-State Management, which was owned by Senator John Glenn and Henry Landworth, "the innkeeper to the astronauts." Landworth was responsible for increasing Martin's knowledge of making hotels profitable, an education that was invaluable in Martin's next position, at the 824-room Court of Flags resort in Orlando, Florida. After six years there, Martin joined the Howard Johnson Division of Prime Motor Inns, Inc. In his capacity as regional director of sales, he works with a variety of salespeople, from property directors of sales to district sales managers who represent more than one property in the Southeast region.

"**P**robably the most overlooked area in the hotel business is the people who work in hotels: the housekeepers, engineers, bellpersons, front desk agents, and night auditors. How much time is really spent with these people: talking to them, telling them how important it is to have a smile on their faces, and that it's the person visiting the property—the guest—that's literally paying their checks?

In many cases, especially at small properties, the first person that guests see is the front desk agent. But now, in this age of automation, most of the time a guest will walk in and see only the top of the agent's head as he or she looks down at the computer, punches in information, and mumbles, 'How do you want to pay for this?' or

'How long will you be staying with us?' The guest doesn't even see the agent's face—or smile! We've got to get back to the fact that we are in the hospitality business; we've got to make front desk agents aware that they are in the sales business. The agents have to look up and say, 'Good day, ma'am. How are you doing?' The guest should be made welcome, made to feel comfortable, made to feel that the hotel is a 'fun' place to be!

This doesn't just happen. We must teach internal sales consistently, and we must spend the time to continually re-emphasize internal sales programs. I used to make it a point to go down to the housekeepers' office with a couple dozen donuts and talk with housekeepers. I wanted those housekeepers to remember that when they saw me walking across the hotel with a client it was their job to smile and say 'Good day, Mr. Martin,' and look at the client and say, 'Good day, sir.' In other words, the housekeepers had to be trained not only to clean rooms properly, but to give the guest a smile, a greeting.

I always tell the story about the dishwashers at the properties. Many meeting planners and association executives want to see a property's kitchen; they want to know that it's clean, that their food is going to come out hot, and that they won't have to worry about having any problems from the kitchen. First impressions, in this case, can make or break business, so I always made it a point to speak to the dishwashers. I wanted to be sure they knew my name, and that when I walked through the door with a client they would smile and nod at me and say, 'Chad, how are you doing?' And they would greet the client with the same courtesy and friendliness!

The reason people stay at our hotels—and especially the reason that they stay again at a particular hotel they've visited—is that they've been treated properly. They've been given good service, and they've been 'sold.' Internal sales is one of the most valuable tools we have. I believe that internal sales will bring guests back—and that's the name of our business. "

Interacting with Guests
Positive interaction with guests is crucial to making a good impression and generating repeat business.[3] Each employee is a representative of the property, and should be trained in the areas of proper appearance, courtesy, and personal habits (food servers should be taught that it is not acceptable to

touch their hair or mouths while serving guests, and so on). Every employee should be reminded that each guest is valued and important to the property. And each employee should know that a friendly smile and a willingness to assist are vital in building rapport with guests. It is especially important to make guests feel welcome, that they are more than just room numbers. Employees should anticipate the needs of guests, learn details of previous visits if applicable, and call guests by name whenever possible.

Using Names. Calling guests by name is one of the keys to repeat business. Remembering guests' names shows a special caring—a respect for guests as individuals. In today's automated world, people appreciate recognition more than ever before, and there are a number of ways employees can learn and use names:

1. A list of names can be prepared to match room numbers. This list can be distributed to all the property's revenue centers, so that when a guest displays a key, the employee can match the room number to the guest's name and immediately begin calling the guest by name. In the lounge, for example, guests often place their keys on the table or bar. A server can note the room number, check it against his or her master list, and return with the drink—and a personal greeting: "Here's your manhattan, Ms. Clark."

2. New computerized telephone systems automatically display the room number and the guest's name on a monitor whenever a guest calls the switchboard from his or her guestroom. The operator can greet the guest by name: "Good afternoon, Mr. Herndon. What can I do for you?"

3. Before a guest registers with the hotel, the bellperson or porter can look for names on luggage tags.

4. The front desk agent gets guests' names upon receiving the completed registration forms. He or she can begin calling guests by name, and may ask the bellperson to "Show Mr. and Mrs. Lewis to Suite 201, please." The bellperson can then begin calling guests by name also.

5. In restaurants, the host can greet the guest by name if the guest has a reservation, and pass the guest's name along to the food server.

6. Switchboard operators can use names when making wake-up calls. A cheery, "Good morning, Ms. Ricker. It's 7:00 a.m. Would you like room service to bring you a fresh pot of coffee and a danish?" is much more hospitable than "It's 7:00."

7. Any time guests use credit cards, there is an opportunity to learn—and use—names. Local patrons of the restaurant or lounge can be recognized in this way, or by simply asking them their names and welcoming them back to the property.

Name recognition works both ways. Not only do most guests appreciate the recognition accorded them by the property's staff, they also like to see a familiar face and greet staff members by name. Employee name tags are an excellent way to make guests feel at home and build rapport between employees and guests. Many properties use name tags displaying the employee's name and home state. These can be excellent conversation starters: "You're from Michigan? I went to school there—at MSU!"

Sales Skills   Sales skills help employees make the most of sales opportunities in their particular areas of guest contact. There are several techniques that can be used to ensure that selling begins at the property's front door. Three of the most effective are upgrading or upselling, suggestive selling, and cross-selling.

Upgrading. Upgrading reservations is an effective way to increase revenues, but very few front desk or reservations staffs are trained to use upgrading techniques.[4] Although most hotels have several room types and prices, there is often no prescribed formula for selling rooms; employees simply quote a price and make no attempt to sell additional services or amenities.

One reason for management's reluctance to tell employees to try to sell rooms with higher rates is that they fear guests may be offended or feel pressured. A "shopping" caller, however, may be unaware of varying rates and amenities, and may appreciate the property's efforts to place him or her in a room that meets specific needs. Meeting specific needs is an important part of upgrading, and employees must be trained to listen to the caller, anticipate wants, and make suggestions for an appropriate accommodation.

Front desk or reservations agents should be trained to recognize when and how to upgrade a guest's request, and to attempt to sell high-priced rooms first, selling lower-priced rooms only if the higher rates are unacceptable. Upgrading can be accomplished without pressuring a guest by using one of three methods:

- Top down
- Rate-category alternatives
- Bottom up

Top down. This technique is used to encourage guests to reserve middle- and high-rate rooms. It begins with the front desk or reservations agent enthusiastically recommending the highest rate available. The guest may either accept or reject the recommendation. In the latter case, the agent moves down to the next price level and enthusiastically discusses the merits of this accommodation. The guest perceives the lower rate as a compromise on the part of the agent, and may be much more open to accepting this recommendation. If the rate quoted is still unacceptable, the agent would drop to the next-highest rate, continuing this process until the guest is satisfied with the price quoted.

Rate-category alternatives. This technique offers an easy and effective way to sell middle-rate rooms to guests who might otherwise choose a lower standard rate. The front desk or reservations agent provides the guest with a choice of three or more rate category alternatives, and puts no pressure on the guest. The guest will, in most cases, attempt to avoid extremes: choosing the lowest rate could cause him or her to feel cheap, while choosing the highest rate might make the guest feel that he or she is being extravagant.

Under these circumstances the logical decision would be to choose the middle rate.

Bottom up. This technique is used when a guest has already made a reservation or has requested a low-priced room. During the registration process, the front desk or reservations agent can suggest extra amenities or the merits of a more expensive room: "For only $10 more, you can enjoy a room with a view of the ocean," or "For an extra $25, you can have a deluxe room and two complimentary continental breakfasts." The higher rate must appear to be an attempt by the agent to enhance the guest's stay at only a small increase over charges anticipated by the guest.

It is much easier to show—and sell—the differences in rooms by using photographs. An effective sales tool for front desk personnel is a loose-leaf notebook of 8- by 10-inch color photos of the different types of guestrooms offered by the hotel. Simply telling a guest about an ocean-view room is not as effective as showing the room—and the view—in a photo.

No matter what method is used to upgrade a reservation, the guest should *never* feel that he or she is being pressured; sales pressure has no place in the hospitality industry. Rather, internal sales should be aimed at giving the guest the opportunity to purchase additional products and services or to "trade up" from those already purchased. To do this, it is important to convey that the guest is not just buying a room, but a "home away from home," and that his or her needs—and a pleasant stay—are important to the property. By combining upselling techniques with a knowledge of the needs of guests, front desk employees can sell a pleasurable experience to guests while increasing revenues.

Upgrading can also be used in the food and beverage department. If a guest has ordered à la carte items, for example, it is acceptable for the food server to suggest a complete dinner for just a small additional cost.

Suggestive Selling. Suggestive selling is the practice of influencing a guest's purchase decision through the use of sales phrases.[5] Almost any employee can use this sales technique in most areas of the property. Suggestive selling may be used in all of a property's food and beverage outlets, for example. A host may inform guests of the special of the day after greeting them; a food server may suggest a cocktail before dinner, an appetizer, the special of the day, or a dessert; a bartender may suggest a specialty drink at a discount price. The power of suggestion is also a good way to introduce new menu items, promote low-overhead food items, and increase the server's tip base.

Food servers can follow these guidelines for suggestive selling:

1. Avoid asking questions that require a yes or no answer; it is far more effective to give the guest a choice. For example, ask: "Which of the desserts would you like from our dessert cart?" rather than "Would you like dessert?" If the guest orders a steak, ask: "Would you like a red or a rosé wine with your steak?" rather than "Would you like a glass of wine with dinner?"

2. Suggest in specific terms. Don't just suggest an appetizer, suggest a specific item such as fried zucchini, shrimp cocktail, or escargot. For even more effectiveness, paint a "word picture" in the guest's mind. It is far more effective to approach a guest with: "Our catch of the

day is rainbow trout stuffed with a delightful mixture of shrimp and fresh crabmeat, lightly floured and sautéed in butter, and garnished with fresh lemon and parsley," than with, "Our catch of the day is stuffed trout."

Suggestive selling is only as effective as the verbal communication between the employee and the guest. Employees must be knowledgeable about the product or service and learn the art of making a sales approach. An employee must be enthusiastic, considerate, and aware of how the sale will benefit the guest for a sales approach to work (see Exhibit 6.1).

Suggestive selling can also be used in other revenue centers at the property. The health club attendant may suggest a relaxing massage after a workout; the front desk agent can suggest a return visit during a special promotional period; the golf pro can suggest a new set of clubs from the pro shop after a private lesson.

Cross-Selling. Cross-selling in advertising is simply using media in one area of the property to promote a different area of the property: a tent card in a restaurant may advertise another specialty restaurant or a sale in the pro shop, a poster at the front desk can promote the health facilities and spa, the matches in the gourmet room may advertise the property's lounge.

Registration and reservation confirmation forms also offer opportunities to cross-sell. A hotel might use its registration forms to tell guests about on-site restaurants, lounges, and other revenue centers. A reservation confirmation can remind guests to bring workout clothes so they can use the hotel's health facilities.

Employees can also cross-sell: employees working at one facility can suggest that a guest take advantage of other facilities and services offered at the property. Employee cross-selling can begin at the front desk when the front desk agent recommends the property's coffee shop, restaurant, or lounge. To assist front desk employees in promoting the property's restaurants, a special display might be posted within sight of the front desk, and copies of the restaurants' menus could be available for guests to examine. A sincere invitation to visit the property's facilities—along with display advertising or other aids to enhance the employees' presentation—can greatly increase business and make guests feel welcome.

Cross-selling is everyone's business. Every employee must be thoroughly knowledgeable about all aspects of the property's operations before this technique can be fully effective. All employees, not just the food servers, should know the hours, specialties, dress requirements, and atmosphere of each of the property's restaurants. If a bellperson recommends the property's seafood restaurant, for example, it is not enough to mention the restaurant's name. What feature of the restaurant would make it worth the guest's visit? The food? A special buffet? The atmosphere? The low prices?

Employees should also be aware of special promotions (two-for-one coupons, discounts, weekend packages), pool and/or health club hours and services, live entertainment offered (if the property offers live entertainment, employees can be invited to hear the entertainment in order to offer a personal endorsement), and special services (valet, laundry, child care or baby-sitting services, secretarial assistance, complimentary transportation, and so on).

Exhibit 6.1   Sample Sales Phrases

Situation	Suggested Sales Phrases
Front Desk	
Early Morning Check-ins	"Our valet service can have your suit pressed and returned to your room within an hour while you freshen up."
Early Evening Check-ins	"Do you enjoy Spanish music? We are featuring Carlos, one of the finest Spanish pianists in the country, in our La Mancha lounge."
	"Have you seen the exciting Hawaiian revue in our main showroom? It's almost like being on the Islands!"
	"If you'd like to have a refreshing drink to help you unwind, our Baron's Pub is located in the east wing near the coffee shop. Besides offering the best drinks in town, the Pub features continuous entertainment from 7:00 p.m. to midnight."
Late Evening Check-ins	"Our excellent room service is still available. Here's the phone number, sir."
Checking Out	"Would you like me to make your return reservation for you now?"
	"Your next stop is Orlando, and our chain has another hotel there. Would you like me to confirm a reservation for you?"
Restaurants	
After taking the order for an entrée	"Would you care for a manhattan or a martini while you wait for your order?"
	"We have just received a new shipment of 1952 French champagne. Shall I bring you a bottle, or would you prefer to see our regular wine list?"
After the main course	"Would you like a B&B or a Drambuie to finish your meal?"
	"Would you care to try our new after-dinner coffee? We add a dash of brandy and top it off with whipped cream. Of course, we also offer Irish coffee."
Lounges	
While handing guests a drink list	"Exotic drinks are a house specialty. Perhaps you would like to try a Scorpion, one of our most popular drinks."
In hot weather	"Would you like a nice, cool Tom Collins or would you prefer to try one of our refreshing fruit drinks?"
In cold weather	"Our bartender makes the best hot Tom and Jerry available anywhere. Would you care for one to warm yourself up?"
Room Service	
After delivering a meal	"Have you tried our Captain's Table restaurant yet? Tomorrow night they will be featuring a special seafood buffet that I'm sure you'd enjoy."
When coming to clear	"Don't forget that we're available 24 hours a day. If there's anything else you'll need, you can reach us at extension XX."
Valet Parking	
Before parking the car	"Welcome to Complete Resorts. If you like Hawaiian cuisine, you'll love our Lanai Buffet. It's on the second floor above the pool area."
When delivering the car	"I hope you enjoyed your stay. Don't forget that we'll be having a special Western Barbecue next week. I'm looking forward to seeing you then."

Every guest contact presents an opportunity to sell additional features and services. Sales-oriented employees that use key sales phrases can greatly increase a property's profitability and build guest goodwill.

Applying Sales Skills
Most guest-employee contacts are potential sales situations. It is important, then, that all employees learn about all the property's revenue centers and develop effective sales approaches. To ensure that this is done, employees may participate in role-playing and periodic testing; employee sales skills can be evaluated and changed as necessary during these training sessions (and information kept current) to ensure that each guest-employee encounter will be a productive one.

What follows is a list of property areas and personnel that are particularly important to internal sales.

Switchboard. The switchboard operator is often the first contact that a prospective guest has with a property, so it is important that switchboard operators answer calls in a pleasant manner which conveys a sense of welcome. Since the switchboard serves as an indicator of the property's efficiency as well as hospitality, calls should be answered promptly and transferred to the proper department without delay.

The switchboard operator can also direct guests to the property's revenue centers. A call from the operator in the late afternoon can recommend the hotel's dining room or room service. Since guests have to eat somewhere, this is often just what it takes to keep them at the property. Operators can also make suggestions for restaurants or room service when they make wake-up calls.

Reservations. Since the basic function of the reservations department is to turn a prospect into a guest, the reservations staff must be well-trained in sales, public relations, and guest service.[6] A reservations agent must be pleasant and informed, and aware of upgrading and suggestive selling techniques that can increase the number of room nights at higher-than-standard rates.

While it is important that the reservations staff have a guest-oriented approach, equally important is a knowledge of room types, prices, special rates, and hotel packages. Staff members should have a complete knowledge of the property and an understanding of what determines the differences in price among the hotel's guestrooms. An ocean-view room, for example, may cost more than a comparable room on the other side of the hotel; the same guestroom may double in price during the "season." By following a policy of selling from the top down if the inquiry is from a new guest, or using a rate-category or bottom up approach if a reservation has already been made, reservations agents can increase revenues while providing service to the guest.

When potential guests telephone for a room after the house is full, reservations agents should offer alternatives in an attempt to not lose business. For example, the reservations department might adopt a waiting list system. The reservations agent can tell the caller: "I'm sorry, Mr. Jackson, we currently have no rooms available, but we often have last-minute cancellations. If you will give me your name and phone number, I'll call you immediately when a room opens up." If the reservations department is too busy to make call-backs, the agent might assign the guest a reference number and suggest that he or she call again after the 6:00 p.m. cut-off for holding reservations.

Suggesting that the caller change his or her arrival date is a selling technique that is seldom used, but could prove of immense value. While this certainly won't work with all guests, many business and leisure travelers will change their plans to stay in their "first choice" hotel. The reservations agent can make this option attractive by making a statement such as: "Ms. Stewart, we are presently booked to capacity and have several names on a waiting list for Wednesday, November 30. But if you could change your travel plans, we have several attractive suites available on Thursday, December 1."

Front Desk. Interacting with front desk employees is often the guest's first *personal* impression of the property, and it is here that hospitality begins.[7] Each guest should be greeted with a warm smile and a sincere, friendly welcome, *not* a curt, "Do you have a reservation?" A repeat guest should be greeted by name and with a warm, "Welcome back." And, from this point on, guests have *names*, they are not just room numbers.

The check-in function should be handled efficiently, with a minimum of waiting by guests. To encourage guest loyalty, guests should be made to feel far more important than a computer screen or a few sheets of paper. Paperwork unrelated to registering the guest should be put aside until registration is completed. Additional help should be called if "traffic" backs up.

Front desk personnel often have the opportunity to upgrade existing reservations. A low-key approach is best: "Since you made your reservation, two better rooms have opened up; one with a mountain view for $48, the other with a beautiful ocean view of Diamond Head for $52. Would you be interested in moving to one of these rooms?" Such an approach may increase room revenues and guest goodwill. The guest is being sold a better experience, not just a more expensive room.

This is also a good time to mention special coupons or discount offers and suggest hotel facilities and services. The front desk agent can ask if the guest would like a wake-up call, and use this opportunity to make sales suggestions: "Fine, Ms. Smith. We'll wake you up at 7:00 a.m. Would you like room service to deliver our breakfast special of hot coffee, a cheese omelet, and freshly squeezed orange juice at 7:15?"

Another approach would be to inform the guest: "Mr. Jones, we have one of the best seafood restaurants in the city right here in the hotel, but it is generally very busy. I can arrange a reservation for you and Mrs. Jones now if you'd like, however. Would you like me to reserve a table for you for our early-bird buffet or for our regular dining hours?"

Too often hotel guests are unaware of what the property has to offer. Suggesting a light snack in the coffee shop, a relaxing swim or whirlpool in the health club, valet service, or room service—even if the guest declines—increases guest awareness, which may generate additional sales at a later time.

Food and Beverage. Good service, which includes a friendly attitude and a timely delivery of the food or drink ordered, is the key to guest satisfaction and sales success in the food and beverage department.[8] In addition to increasing sales, good service ensures that the guest has a favorable experience and will want to return to the restaurant, coffee shop, or lounge, or continue to order room service.

Food servers who share with guests their knowledge of the food, its ingredients, and preparation time (as well as the specialties of other property restaurants) add to guest involvement in the property, which can add to profits. A good sales approach by the server results in his or her having to spend less time answering questions (avoiding guest irritation) and more efficient service as well.

Food and beverage service offers practically unlimited opportunities to make use of suggestive selling techniques. It is imperative that food servers offer suggestions that deliciously describe an item: "Have you tried our award-winning cheesecake, topped with fresh strawberries and a dollop of whipped cream?" is much more effective than "Would you care for anything else?" A food server can give the guest a choice of two or more items and state why the guest should choose one of them. For example, "Would you like a shrimp cocktail to start or would you prefer our freshly made onion soup? The shrimp were just received this morning and are absolutely fresh, and the onion soup is excellent—the chef prides himself on having the best onion soup in the city." Suggestive selling benefits guests, food servers, and the property alike as it can lead to increased guest satisfaction, increased tips for the servers, and increased revenues.

Cross-selling can also be used by food servers. Room service personnel can suggest the dinner special in the main dining room or a special breakfast buffet for busy business travelers. A food server in the gourmet restaurant can ask guests if they have tried the "traveler's lunch" in the coffee shop. These soft-sell techniques are excellent methods of raising revenues, exposing guests to facilities they might not have tried (and might later recommend to friends), and encouraging satisfying guest experiences.

Service Personnel. Service personnel fall into two basic categories: guest-contact employees and back-of-the-house employees. A great deal of guest interaction is usual for the valet parking staff, door attendants, bell staff, and housekeepers, while guest contact is not as pronounced with maintenance crews and back office personnel.

Service employees with a great deal of guest contact have excellent opportunities for suggestive selling. If the hotel is an airport property, the hotel's limo drivers can sell the hotel's facilities and the local area as they drive guests from the airport to the property. A valet parker can welcome guests and ask if they have tried a particular property restaurant. A bellperson can promote the property's restaurants, lounges, laundry and valet services, and other amenities as guests are being shown to their rooms. The bellperson might suggest: "Ms. Kent, we have one of the finest steak restaurants in town. If you'd like, I could reserve a table for you." As guests leave, the door attendant or valet parker can suggest coming back for a promotional event or special hotel package.

In all of these guest contacts, it is important that the service staff be sincerely friendly without being pushy. Guests should feel that suggestions are made to improve their present stay or future contacts with the property.

While employees who have less guest contact may be limited in their selling capacities, they "sell" the hotel by their appearance, attitude, and attention to small details. A friendly greeting from a pool attendant and the cheerful attitude of the maintenance crew can help make the guest's stay a memorable one.[9]

Employee Incentive Programs

Employee incentive programs can be an effective means of motivating employees and tracking sales results. Management may establish an incentive program for front desk or reservations agents who upgrade reservations (see Exhibit 6.2), or may provide a bonus to split among the front desk staff for

Exhibit 6.2 Sample Reservations Incentive Program

Schedule of Bonuses

Upgrade Bonuses

$10 Upgrade to Poolside	.$1.00 per night
Upgrade to Bi-level or Fallback Rate	.$3.00 per night
Upgrade to Bi-level or Rack Rate Suite	.$5.00 per night

Booking Bonuses

Reservation booked under Rack Rate	.$ .50 per night
Reservation booked at Rack Rate	.$1.00 per night
Reservation booked at Poolside Rate	.$1.50 per night
Reservation booked at Suite Fallback Rate	.$3.00 per night
Reservation booked at Suite Rack Rate	.$5.00 per night

This is a very liberal bonus program with lots of opportunities to increase your monthly take home pay by $50, $100, or even $200. Every time you upgrade or book a guest, just take a copy of the reservation with the appropriate information, and put the copy in your folder, located in the count room.

The person who converts the most room nights during the quarter will be eligible for a grand prize (to be determined) at the end of the year.

This is an excerpt from an incentive program developed by a Best Western property. Reservations agents are given bonuses for room conversions and upgrades monthly, and a grand prize is awarded at the end of the year.

Source: From a speech by Robert A. Rauch, CHA, at Best Western's annual convention in Las Vegas, 1985.

every night occupancy reaches a predetermined target. In the property's restaurants, management may promote contests to reward suggestive selling and give bonuses for most desserts sold, or largest percentage of sales increase per restaurant. Other incentive programs may include a cross-selling contest with prizes and bonuses to employees or departments sending the most guests to a specific restaurant. The bellperson who sells more laundry or dry cleaning services than average and the telephone operator who makes breakfast sales with morning wake-up calls can also be rewarded.

Incentive programs must include methods of tracking results. A discount coupon which bears the name of the food server who has recommended the lounge, a business card or coupon from the bartender that the guest can give to the host of the specialty dining room, a special two-for-one invitation to the lounge show from the bellperson—all three examples provide a means of tracking the effectiveness of both the promotion and the employee.

When developing any incentive program, it is important that management realize that while incentives in the form of cash, merchandise, or trips are often used to motivate employees, recognition is as important as the reward for many workers. In the example of the bartender above, he was enthusiastic because he was distributing cards with his name on them; he began receiving recognition from his guests. And certainly one of the best forms of praise and commendation is public recognition. Honoring top-producing employees with photographs and plaques that are prominently displayed, writing up success stories in the property's newsletter, and even singling out employees as being outstanding among their peers at a special ceremony or awards dinner can mean more to some employees than monetary rewards.

Incentive programs, while not essential to an internal sales plan, provide an additional impetus, a way to get the entire staff involved in the selling process. A sales-oriented, motivated staff with proper training can be most effective in increasing property revenues while maintaining positive guest-employee relationships.

Internal Merchandising

Internal merchandising is the use of guest service directories in guestrooms, tent cards on restaurant tables, lobby display cards (see Exhibit 6.3), elevator cards or posters, bulletin boards, and other promotional items to promote the property's facilities and services.

Technology also plays a part in internal merchandising. The Hilton chain is one of several hospitality organizations that utilize a "video magazine." Video magazines may be shown in either the hotel's lobby (guests can watch the presentation on special monitors set up near comfortable chairs) or in guestrooms through the use of an in-house channel. The Hilton's one-hour video showcases the facilities and services of the host hotel as well as detailing the history and sights of the host city. The Hilton's video magazine changes monthly and is slightly different for each property, but each video provides traveling tips; features geared toward the business traveler; and, most important, information on other hotels in the chain, with a suggestive selling message to book into one of these properties.

Internal merchandising is an important sales avenue which should be carefully planned and controlled. All internal merchandising posters and print materials should be *professionally* done, and should be changed regularly. (There are few things less appealing than stained or torn tent cards or guestroom directories.) As a general rule, there should be attractive, persuasive internal merchandising media in each area of guest contact.

Guest-Contact Areas

The Lobby. Posters displayed in the lobby should promote *all* of the property's food service outlets and other property features. Lobby posters should have sales appeal and be placed in high traffic locations. Posters on walls and columns where they can be illuminated are eye-catching. Many properties find that the use of transparencies—slide-like posters illuminated from behind—is especially effective.

Guestrooms. Essential information should be located in one attractive room directory whenever possible; the usual practice of cluttering a room with tent cards, folders, notices, and fliers does little to promote readership. Room directories should be attractive and small enough to be carried (directories make excellent promotional pieces). Most important, room directories should not only list services offered, but also include *complete* information, including telephone extensions.

In addition to the directory, the property may opt for a simple message placed on the television set or on the nightstand. One effective technique is the use of a message like the following, signed by the chef:

Exhibit 6.3   Sample Lobby Display Cards

SATURDAY NIGHTS BELONG TO YOU.

Enjoy dinner and dancing—to live entertainment and under the stars—in Old New York's most romantic setting.

Join us on Saturday nights from 6-11 PM for an elegant 4-course dinner. Just $25.50 per person. Reservations recommended. Second Floor Plaza Level.

the **Greenhouse**
RESTAURANT and WINE BAR

OUR SUNDAY BRUNCH BUBBLES OVER.

Start Sunday in a very special way, with Vista's Champagne Brunch, served in the stunning atrium setting of the Greenhouse Restaurant.

Enjoy an array of elegantly prepared hot and cold dishes, served buffet style and accompanied by champagne and live music. Reservations recommended.

the **Greenhouse**
RESTAURANT and WINE BAR
Second Floor Plaza Level

CATCH OUR SEAFOOD ON FRIDAY NIGHTS.

The Greenhouse proudly reintroduces our popular Seafood Buffet on Friday Nights from 6-11 PM.

Hook onto everything from Snow Crab Legs and Poached Shrimp to the Catch of the Day. Dine and Dance under the stars, to live entertainment. Just $25.50 per person. Reservations recommended. Second Floor Plaza Level.

the **Greenhouse**
RESTAURANT and WINE BAR

Targeted for in-house guests, these display cards promise a lively setting for singles to meet on Friday nights, a romantic and elegant atmosphere on Saturdays, and an elegant Sunday brunch with live entertainment.

My specialty tonight is beef Wellington. Please call 9049 to reserve a table.

Chef Lambert

A sales technique used in guestrooms by the Grand Hyatt in New York is extremely effective. The management of that hotel designed a unique room service menu that is, for all intents and purposes, a picture book. The menu, which is left open on the guest's desk, features a photograph of the finished dish on one side of the page and a description of the dish and its ingredients on the other. Door hanger menus (completed by the guest and picked up at 2:00 a.m.) also serve to merchandise room service.

Elevator Floor Landings. Many guests walk out of a hotel to breakfast in an outside restaurant simply because they do not know breakfasts are served in hotels. Attractive signs in a glass-framed cabinet located next to the elevator call button can feature the property's restaurants, bars, and lounges, and the services and hours of each. The elevator area can also be used to promote inter-hotel reservations, valet or laundry services, entertainment offerings, and special upcoming packages such as a family discount package, a ski weekend package, and so on.

One of the most effective restaurant display posters used near elevators is found in the Marriott Southeast in Denver. When the guest pushes the call button on the elevator, a display case on the wall next to the call button lights up. Almost without exception, guests are immediately drawn to reading the restaurant poster in the display case as they wait for the elevator to arrive.

Elevators. Many properties make use of framed posters within elevators to advertise their restaurants. It is curious that some posters are positioned in the rear of the elevator, since most guests face forward or look upward when riding. A sign in the rear gets a momentary glance—if the car is empty!

Attractive posters on the sides of the elevator may be printed on both sides and should be rotated to reflect the meal(s) being served during a particular time period. To make the cards more appealing and persuasive, they should feature a mouth-watering photograph rather than just copy.

Restaurants and Lounges. Restaurant promotion can begin at the restaurant's entrance with an attractive poster announcing the day's specials. Inside the restaurant, well-designed menus can serve as promotional pieces, and tent cards (one per table is ideal) can promote specialty dishes or other restaurants on the property.

Lounges can be promoted through matchbooks, tent cards, attractive drink or snack menus, and souvenir items. For lounges with entertainment, a souvenir program or an autographed photograph of the performer mounted in a folder embossed with the property's logo makes an effective promotional tool.

Barber and Beauty Shops. Hotels with barber and/or beauty shops can sell the captive audience in these shops on the property's restaurants, bars, lounges, special facilities, and reservations services through the use of posters mounted in strategic locations.

Reservations or Convention Desk. Properties with a reservations or convention desk can have fliers, brochures, and other promotional material readily available in attractive displays. Local attractions might also be promoted to encourage longer stays by guests.

Cashier's Desk. Many properties provide inter-hotel reservations information and/or souvenir items (key chains, postcards, etc.) at the cashier's desk to encourage repeat or new business. Many properties offer souvenir items such as shoehorns, key chains, and garment bags, but neglect to imprint the property's telephone number on them. *All* giveaway items should be imprinted with the hotel's name, address, and telephone number to make it easy for the departed guest to call the property to make return reservations. It is surprising how many people can picture a great hotel or a pleasant restaurant experience in their minds, but can't remember the name of the property after a short period of time.

Back-of-the-House Areas

Posters and bulletin boards in back-of-the-house areas that detail current sales promotions, selling suggestions, and incentive programs can stimulate employee selling and remind employees that they can powerfully influence a guest's decision to return to the property.

Special Services and In-House Promotions

Special Services

Another effective way to sell the hotel to guests is to offer special services that will make their stays enjoyable and productive. Because of the large size of the business traveler market, many hotels are offering "business centers"—24-hour offices with personal computers, photocopiers, telefacsimile or fax services, electronic mail capabilities, and secretarial services. Other properties may promote food and beverage service targeted at business travelers: continental or buffet breakfasts, designated business lunch hours to quickly and efficiently serve busy executives, and combination meeting/dining rooms.

To attract families, properties may offer supervised play activities, package tours to local attractions, in-house baby-sitting services, special children's menus, and amenities such as cribs, high chairs, and play equipment.

Limousine service or transportation to and from airports, shopping centers, and area attractions are also services used to promote a property and give guests a positive experience. Other special touches—free coffee, free newspapers, in-room closed circuit television, complimentary samples of local produce (apples, raisins, nuts, etc.) or products (wines, chocolates, and so on), and fresh flowers also play an important part in creating an atmosphere that will make a guest feel welcome and generate repeat business and referrals.

In-House Promotions

Many properties sponsor in-house promotions—special two-for-one coupons, contests and drawings, and special events—that make a stay more enjoyable and generate additional revenue.

One example of an internal promotion is a secretaries' club—a program that involves the secretaries of corporate guests in a number of planned

The Omni Shoreham in Washington, D.C., developed a month-long food festival with a Paris theme to attract guests and locals to its charming Monique Cafe et Brasserie. The festival was publicized in-house with posters throughout the hotel and at the cafe's entrance.

activities. By guaranteeing corporate room rates, providing an exclusive telephone number and/or a direct contact person at the hotel, and ensuring VIP treatment for guests referred by these secretaries, a solid corporate business base can be built and maintained. To keep secretaries motivated, properties may offer health club privileges (or discounts), complimentary or discounted meals and/or drinks at food and beverage outlets, annual lunches or

Exhibit 6.4   Promotional Idea Bank

Rooms

Suite & Surf Package—Includes a three-day, two-night stay in a spacious suite, a welcoming bottle of champagne, complimentary breakfasts, a voucher for beach equipment rental, and the use of a heated pool and spa.

Bed & Breakfast for the Business Traveler—Includes room accommodations and a choice of a continental breakfast or a "serve yourself" breakfast bar.

Christmas Package Tours—Includes deluxe accommodations, tours of historic homes decorated for the holidays, complimentary wine and cheese on the tour, and a special Christmas party.

Festival Events—Features a special promotional package around a local festival—a harvest festival, the anniversary of the date the local community was founded, a "Rodeo Day," and so on—or a special event created by the hotel: "Chocolate Lover's Festival," "Wine Tasting Festival," and so on. Guests receive room accommodations, participate in festival activities, and are given a special souvenir.

Romance or Anniversary Package—Includes deluxe accommodations; welcoming champagne; and special amenities such as French perfume, breakfast in bed, whirlpool baths or hot tubs, and so on.

Food and Beverage Outlets

A Day with the Chef—Guests have the opportunity to watch the chef in action, ask questions, and taste the results. As an incentive, discount coupons or a complimentary meal ticket may be included.

Wall of Fame—Reward frequent lounge guests with their own pewter mug. Engrave the mugs with the guests' names, display them prominently on a shelf along the wall, and explain to other guests that they can have their own mug after, for example, 30 days of patronage over a 12-week period, or after bringing a certain number of guests to the lounge.

Monday Night Football—Attract guests and local visitors with a giant TV screen, free snacks, and complimentary drink tickets to backers of the winning team.

Suntan Contests or Amateur Nights—Contests and audience participation events are an excellent way to attract hotel guests and patrons from the local community. Invite guests or local celebrities to act as judges, and offer property amenities—free dinners, weekend packages, and so on—as prizes.

Cruising the Swimming Pool—Sell drinks and snacks through the use of a portable bar brought around to each poolside guest, or have food servers clad in swimming suits or Hawaiian dress provide tray service from a tropical poolside bar and snack stand.

The opportunities for promotion are almost limitless, and there are thousands of good ideas that can be used to generate additional business.

receptions, annual gifts (roses, chocolates, a free weekend getaway, etc.), and other amenities to secretaries participating in the program.

Other promotions geared to encourage repeat business may include frequent traveler programs—a point system that rewards guests who accumulate a certain number of points with gifts and/or room nights; promotional giveaways—all guests in the hotel are given a gift, but must fill out a redemption coupon to receive it (these coupons provide information that can help generate repeat business); and special packages for frequent guests or a specific target market.

The property's food and beverage outlets can benefit from in-house promotions such as two-for-one specials, discount coupons, special activities and contests, and "get acquainted" teas or cocktail hours.

The number of ways to promote to guests that are already registered (or guests that frequently return and already have a favorable impression of the property) are practically unlimited (see Exhibit 6.4). By developing creative approaches, fun-filled activities, and awarding appropriate gifts or prizes, the property can greatly increase its base of business and leave its guests eagerly looking forward to the property's next special promotion.

Notes

1. 200 guestrooms $\times$ 80% = 160 rooms rented $\times$ 1.5 persons per room = 240 guests per day $\times$ 365 days per year = 87,600 guests $\times$ $2 additional expenditure each = $175,200 per year.

2. For tips on how to handle angry guests, see *Front Office: Handling Guest Complaints* (East Lansing, Mich.: Educational Institute of the American Hotel & Motel Association). Videotape.

3. Examples of positive employee-guest interaction are shown in *Guest Service: Putting the Guest First* (East Lansing, Mich.: Educational Institute of the American Hotel & Motel Association). Videotape.

4. Information on upgrading reservations is provided in *Front Office: Upselling and Suggestive Selling* (East Lansing, Mich.: Educational Institute of the American Hotel & Motel Association). Videotape.

5. Suggestive selling techniques are discussed in *Front Office: Guest Relations* (East Lansing, Mich.: Educational Institute of the American Hotel & Motel Association). Videotape.

6. For more information on selling reservations, see *Selling Out: A How-To Manual on Reservations Management* (East Lansing, Mich.: Educational Institute of the American Hotel & Motel Association, 1985).

7. For a more detailed discussion of front desk procedures, see Charles E. Steadmon and Michael L. Kasavana, *Managing Front Office Operations*, 2nd ed. (East Lansing, Mich.: Educational Institute of the American Hotel & Motel Association, 1988).

8. Information on providing good food and beverage service is provided in *Professional Dining Room Service* (East Lansing, Mich.: Educational Institute of the American Hotel & Motel Association), a two-videotape set; and *Food & Beverage Suggestive Selling* (East Lansing, Mich.: Educational Institute of the American Hotel & Motel Association). Videotape.

9. For suggestions on how to get all employees involved in guest service, see *Guest Service: Building a Professional Team* (East Lansing, Mich.: Educational Institute of the American Hotel & Motel Association). Videotape.

Discussion Questions

1. What is the role of the general manager in internal sales?

2. What is the three-part process for developing a sales-oriented hotel staff?

3. What are several ways employees can learn and use guests' names?

4. What are three internal sales skills?

Discussion Questions *(continued)*

5. What are three techniques for upgrading reservations? Distinguish among the three and suggest when each should be used.

6. What two suggestive selling guidelines should be observed by food servers?

7. What is cross-selling?

8. How do employee incentive programs provide additional impetus to internal sales?

9. What are some examples of internal merchandising?

10. Add to the promotional idea bank in Exhibit 6.4. What outstanding internal promotions have you seen at hotels?

Chapter Outline

I. Positioning Restaurants and Lounges
   A. Positioning Research
      1. Guest Profile Research
         a. Personal conversation or observation
         b. Special promotions
         c. Guest surveys
      2. Situation Analysis
      3. Competition Analysis
      4. Current Trend Research

II. Merchandising Food and Beverages
   A. Creating Menus That Sell
      1. Image
      2. Price
         a. Determining prices
      3. Message
      4. Design
      5. Supplemental Menus
   B. Other F&B Merchandising Methods
      1. Product Packaging
      2. Added-Value-Alternatives
      3. Point-of-Purchase Materials
      4. Suggestive Selling
      5. Special Promotional Items

III. Promoting Restaurants and Lounges
   A. Types of Promotions
      1. Personal Promotions
      2. In-house Promotions
      3. Outside Promotions

IV. Building Repeat Business
   A. The Importance of Employees
      1. Recognition
      2. Recommendations
      3. Reassurance
   B. Guest Follow-up

7 Restaurant and Lounge Sales

There was a time in the not too distant past when hotel managers considered in-house restaurants to be a necessary evil. Today, however, hotel restaurants are being promoted and patronized more than ever before. Hotel restaurants have become "in" places that attract patrons from the surrounding community as well as in-house guests.

In this chapter, we will examine trends that are causing hoteliers to take a fresh look at the former stepchild of the hospitality industry. We will see how proper merchandising, creative promotion, and staff involvement can generate even more revenue from these increasingly popular facilities. (Because much of the following information can apply to both restaurants and lounges, unless otherwise noted the word "restaurant" will be used in this chapter to represent lounges as well.)

Positioning Restaurants and Lounges

Since hotel restaurants may have to co-exist with other in-house food and beverage outlets (as well as room service and banquet service at some properties) and compete with local free-standing restaurants, the positioning of each restaurant becomes extremely important. For many years, hotel restaurants projected a tired, ordinary image. They existed as a token gesture to guests of the property, a boring alternative to eating out or eating alone in a guestroom.

Today's hotel restaurants range from the bright and cheery to the intimate and elegant; from coffee shops to lavishly decorated gourmet rooms. Despite improvements in hotel restaurants, a recent survey revealed that most hotel guests usually prefer to eat in an outside establishment.[1] With dramatic changes taking place, why aren't more guests discovering and frequenting hotel restaurants more often?

The answer is found in positioning. Many guests don't feel that a hotel restaurant or lounge is as good as a free-standing restaurant or night spot. This view presents a challenge to hoteliers. Their food and beverage outlets must be positioned (in terms of physical location, atmosphere, and prices) to compete with free-standing eateries and lounges despite this negative view (see Exhibit 7.1).

Combating the negative physical positioning of a property restaurant (or restaurants) can be a fairly simple matter. To make the restaurant more

Industry Profile

Bruce MacKenzie worked for six years with Sky Chefs in airline terminal food service before joining Atlas Hotels and working in several food and beverage positions. In 1983, he was promoted to his present position as Director—Food & Beverage at the 1,000-room Town & Country Hotel. This hotel features five restaurants and lounges, and banquet facilities for 3,000 people. MacKenzie currently supervises a management staff of 32 managers and chefs and an employee staff of approximately 350.

Bruce MacKenzie
Director—
Food & Beverage
Town & Country
Hotel

"San Diego is a changing market. In the past four years, seven major hotels have opened and another five are expected within two years. In order to be competitive and remain profitable, we've been forced to make major changes in our approach to selling food and beverage. In addition, our hotel sales staff must increasingly use our food and beverage facilities to differentiate the Town & Country from the new competition.

In past years, Atlas Hotels had the philosophy that all food and beverage advertising should be aimed at local residents; hotel guests were considered a captive audience. As we improved our marketing analysis, however, we began to see a trend in hotel guests; they were going off-property more often to eat. With over 125,000 guests staying at Town & Country each year, we decided to shift our emphasis.

We began changing our strategy by placing 'mini menu' handouts from each restaurant in display racks. We also started handing out a brochure at check-in. This brochure provides food and beverage outlet descriptions and directions to supplement the photos of the outlets in elevators, the lobby, and the room directory. The in-house TV channel advertises the restaurants and lounges, and bellpersons describe them as guests are escorted to their rooms.

Once in the restaurants and lounges, our guests are constantly exposed to visual promotions. At Cafe Potpourri, the bakery case welcomes the guest with trays of fresh cakes, pies, cookies, and giant muffins. Bonacci's Pizza & Pasta uses an extensive Italian soup and salad bar to provide the first impressions. And the hotel's original restaurant, The Gourmet Room, offers guests a variety of items to view—from the morning's juice and fruit cart, to the Winery of the Month display, to the refrigerated dessert cart.

After being seated, guests are presented menus which are checked daily by the hostess for stains and tears. A good impression is important, and, as the guests look at the spotless menus, they see a professionally designed layout with the proper-size printing. Through item placement, the guests' eyes are drawn to the items we most want to sell. Item descriptions are simple and interesting, with a focus on accuracy.

When the server arrives at the table, the merchandising is continued. 'I'd like to suggest this evening's special—the Medallions of Tenderloin with Pink Peppercorn Sauce. It's one of my favorites, and it's perfect with the cabernet sauvignon from our Winery of the Month program.'

Is this merchandising and internal advertising important? If we can entice only one of every two hotel guests to use one of our outlets one additional time during his or her stay, we will realize an increase of approximately $950,000 in food sales each year! If our merchandising convinces only one of three current patrons to spend just $1 more on a juice or dessert, we can realize an increase of an additional $375,000 each year! That's an increase of $1,325,000 per year, just for making sure that our current hotel guests are completely aware of the varied facilities offered by the hotel.

While local residents will certainly remain an important market for the Town & Country, our primary target will continue to be the hotel's guests."

accessible to non-guests, many properties now provide an outside entrance so that local patrons can enter the restaurant without going through the hotel

Exhibit 7.1   Building the Image of Hotel Restaurants

This eye-catching promotion, featuring a wooden spoon attached to a brochure, was placed in guestrooms at The Summit Hotel in Hartford, Connecticut, to promote the property's restaurant, Gabriel's. This campaign is typical of those that try to upgrade the image of hotel restaurants in the minds of guests. The brochure was designed to convince guests that Gabriel's offered better food and service than what a guest would expect to find at a hotel restaurant. It also stressed the convenience factor. There was no need to drive or take a cab to find superior food; the restaurant was just an elevator ride away.

Courtesy of The Summit Hotel, Hartford, Connecticut.

lobby. These restaurants are often promoted as separate entities—dining or entertainment choices that just happen to be located in a hotel.

Creating a unique restaurant atmosphere can be more difficult. Years ago, property restaurants were usually built just as a convenience for in-house guests, and were often poorly designed and underrated in terms of potential profitability. Most of these restaurants have not done well, and must be repositioned to attract both in-house guests and local patrons.

For some properties, repositioning may mean dividing a large restaurant into smaller, more intimate rooms, or "theme" rooms. For other properties, repositioning may require other creative approaches—restaurant lighting can be varied and "props" (a portable salad bar, greenery, etc.) can be used to produce different atmospheres for different meals.

An important part of repositioning an ineffective food and beverage outlet is to find out who makes up the property's guest base, why they are dining out, and what would appeal to these guests—and attract additional guests. The best way to accomplish this is with thorough research.

Restaurant Positioning:
The Case of the Johnny Appleseed Restaurant

"A motel restaurant can be a tremendous drain on time, energy, and financial resources. If you don't have the expertise, don't get into the restaurant business—you'll be courting a financial disaster. What's more, if your restaurant's a mess, they'll stop lodging with you."

This is the opinion of Peter Watts, owner of an 88-room Best Western Motel and the adjacent (and enormously profitable) Johnny Appleseed Restaurant in Fredericksburg, Virginia. The restaurant provides a higher gross and a better return than his thriving motel, chalking up a volume of over $850,000 a year.

How?

First, Watts cites "certain basics." A prime location, right off busy Interstate 95, a key route to Florida. A unique name (it's now registered) that's "family-oriented and has a wholesome appeal—people love apples." And a "simple, inviting building" that won't deter those who associate frilly architecture with high prices. If there is any doubt about the nature of the place, a 14-foot replica of Johnny Appleseed near the entrance is enough to reassure the wary. "Hi, I'm Johnny Appleseed," says the replica when a visitor pushes a button, "and I'm so glad you're here. You'll love our apple fritters." It's actually the recorded voice of Peter Watts, who frequently assumes the Appleseed role—in complete costume—for promotional and goodwill appearances.

Inside, a rustic setting—provided by wood paneling, folksy art, and other homey effects—lends a casual, comfortable atmosphere. Long-gowned waitresses attend guests in private booths and free-standing tables.

For every breakfast and dinner patron, there's a free apple fritter, and for every lunch guest a free helping of popcorn. Service is virtually round-the-clock to help ensure maximum return on the facilities: hours are 6:00 a.m. to 10:00 p.m. daily.

Watts also places enormous emphasis on the quality of his staff. "Hiring the best people is the single most important thing the property owner can do to assure top efficiency and maximum profits. All other factors are secondary. You've got to have excellent people in managerial positions."

Source: Adapted from *Lodging* magazine. Used with permission.

Positioning Research

Positioning research falls into four basic areas:

1. Guest profile research

2. Situation analysis

3. Competition analysis

4. Current trend research

All of these areas figure into the restaurant's positioning. Therefore, positioning research should become an ongoing part of the operation of the restaurant. *Differences* between the restaurant and its competitors as well as the restaurant's benefits must be promoted. The restaurant's atmosphere, decor, theme, and menu must appeal to targeted market segments and present an image consistent with the property's overall market position.

Lounge Positioning:
The Case of the St. Regis Sheraton

Managers at the St. Regis Sheraton in New York City were faced with the problem of revitalizing the hotel's dining room and lounge business and creating a new image for the hotel.

"The well-known entertainers who used to perform in our Maisonette lounge priced themselves out of our reach over the last few years," said Guenter H. Richter, vice president and managing director of the St. Regis Sheraton. "The unknown entertainers or middle-of-the-road performers didn't draw customers," he continued, "so we were forced to close the lounge."

"Furthermore, the King Cole dining room, as it was designed originally, was meant to be strictly a restaurant serving breakfast, lunch, and dinner," Richter said. While breakfast and lunch business was satisfactory, the King Cole room—like many city hotel dining rooms—died at night.

Clearly, a new positioning strategy was needed to attract guests in the evening. An extensive renovation was undertaken. The Maisonette room was converted into an elaborately designed lounge called Astor's, and the King Cole room was completely redesigned and redecorated.

Next, Richter set about developing a budget and a marketing strategy for pumping new life into the two rooms. He engaged an entertainment director, Jerry Kravat, to assist in determining the clientele to target. Kravat said, "We analyzed the market profile, the activity of competitive hotels, and what we thought would be appropriate for this well-respected landmark hotel."

Concept and Strategy for the King Cole Room

The concept developed for the King Cole room was to produce a cabaret show—"A Salute to Famous Composers and Producers." Examples included: "Rhapsody in Gershwin"; "From Rodgers and Hart with Love"; and "Thank Heaven for Lerner and Loewe." Many of the performers booked for these shows had appeared in the original Broadway musicals but were not top stars.

Kravat put together the producers and writers necessary to create the shows and negotiated the contracts with most of the cast. Richter then took the following four steps:

1. Retained a public relations firm that had excellent contacts in theatrical and musical circles, especially with critics and columnists.

2. Developed advertising and promotional pieces and guest reply cards that were directed at the hotel's target audience—in-house guests and upscale local residents and visitors to Manhattan.

3. Reworked the dinner menu to offer an à la carte menu to dinner guests and a supper menu to late-show guests. A cover charge of $7.50 in midweek and $10 on weekends was added to dinner guests' checks ($10 midweek and $12.50 on weekends was charged for guests who did not have dinner).

4. Established a reservations system, using the hotel's own reservations system as well as Ticketron and Chargit (outside, independent reservations systems).

The results have been outstanding, both for the room and the hotel's overall business. Business has increased dramatically in midweek, and on weekends it is not unusual to see lines all the way into the lobby of people waiting to get in for the first or second shows.

(continued)

Concept and Strategy for Astor's Lounge

At the same time that the entertainment strategy for the King Cole room was being planned, a completely different but compatible strategy was being planned for the lounge downstairs, Astor's. Richter decided to position Astor's for the local business community for early evening business, with piano entertainment from 5:30 to 8:30 and complimentary hors d'oeuvres and a two-for-one cocktail hour.

From 8:30 to 9:30 Astor's picks up some of the pre-show crowd before they go into the King Cole, and from 9:00 p.m. to 1:00 a.m. (2:00 a.m. on weekends) the lounge offers live entertainment and dancing.

In order to draw a good local crowd into Astor's, some of the stars who had appeared in previous King Cole shows were encouraged to visit Astor's as guests of the hotel. This created a strong following in the Broadway theatrical community.

It was decided not to have a cover or minimum charge in the lounge, in order to get more pre- and post-show guests. Promotional material used the lines "Rendezvous at Manhattan's hottest new bar. Right out of New York's golden slipper days."

The entertainment concepts and marketing of the King Cole room and Astor's have helped to build a new image for the St. Regis Sheraton. It has increased the hotel's rooms business at the same time that it has significantly increased evening activity in its two public rooms.

"No hotel has done what the St. Regis has done," commented Jerry Kravat. "They looked at the marketing of entertainment as a long-term commitment that would eventually benefit all departments in the hotel."

Source: Adapted from *Lodging* magazine. Used with permission.

Guest Profile Research. Research into a guest's age, sex, type (new or repeat), and employment can be important in restaurant positioning. If a restaurant manager finds that he or she is catering to predominantly businesspeople at lunch and hotel guests in the evening, for example, it makes it easier to design menus that will appeal to each group.

Information for guest profiles can be more difficult to obtain in restaurants than at the front desk. If the restaurant patron is a guest of the hotel and charges his or her meal to the room, the patron's room number can be noted and information can be obtained at the front desk from the patron's registration form. In cases where a great deal of business consists of walk-in guests (whether local or traveling), there are a number of ways in which information can be obtained.

Personal conversation or observation. The host or food server can get information by conversing with the guest, or by observing details such as an out-of-town driver's license used as identification when cashing a check, or a briefcase or business conversation that identifies the guest as a businessperson, and so on.

Special promotions. If the restaurant caters to a business trade, it can run a free-meal promotion and request the business cards of patrons as entry forms. One or more of the cards can be drawn on specified dates, and the winners given a complimentary meal. This type of promotion yields names, occupations, and telephone numbers, and is extremely cost-effective.

Guest surveys. Questionnaires or evaluation forms can be excellent sources of information that may assist in menu planning and the planning of promotions for certain target markets. Questionnaires vary in content. A property targeting business lunch guests, for example, can use a questionnaire that asks questions relating to favorite food selections, speed of service, and other amenities that would make the restaurant more attractive to the business community. Or, a questionnaire can focus on food preparation (such as the trend from fried foods to broiled and steamed items), service (whether guests prefer buffets or table service), or general demographics (to get an accurate breakdown of market segments currently using the restaurant).

To encourage filling out questionnaires or other survey forms, a server can draw attention to the form and tell the guest that he or she will receive a bonus gift or discount coupon if the form is filled out and presented when making payment. The restaurant can also provide conveniences to make filling out the form easier. This can include a complimentary pen, or providing an envelope for the completed survey. A guest who has received less-than-perfect food and/or service may feel intimidated when turning in an unflattering survey to his or her food server; an envelope ensures anonymity and may be the key to greater response. Still other food and beverage outlets provide stamped, self-addressed survey cards or questionnaires that may be filled out and returned at the diner's convenience.

Completed guest surveys can assist the restaurant staff in serving present markets and give clues as to markets being missed. They can also aid management in making pricing decisions.

Situation Analysis. Situation (or current business) analysis can be used to identify market segments. If a situation analysis shows that most of the property's lunch guests are businesswomen, for example, the property can appeal to that market segment with an eye-catching salad bar and specially priced small lunch portions for light eaters.

The singles market is a rapidly growing segment at many properties. Properties with a large singles clientele have developed a number of innovative ideas to profit from this lucrative market. One idea is the "Friendship Table." Friendship tables are designed to provide single diners with company and conversation if that is desired (see Exhibit 7.2). While this idea has long been used on cruise ships, it is relatively new to the hospitality industry and has become a popular addition in many restaurants.

The senior citizens market may be important in a restaurant's positioning, especially if the restaurant is located in a hotel that is a favorite destination of seniors. Many hotel restaurants are now offering to seniors special menus, small portions, and discounts on purchases.

Situation analysis also entails a look at statistics. Nearly all hotels make use of room occupancy statistics, but fewer have access to restaurant occupancy data such as total covers and table turnover ratios per meal. Covers should be tracked by the meal as well as by the day and month to determine the patterns of spending, menu choices, and restaurant usage highs and lows. Comparing covers sold against seating capacity often reveals usage as low as 30% of capacity. The information gained by studying this statistical data can prove invaluable in scheduling staff, targeting areas for sales emphasis, and tailoring service to the needs of guests.

Exhibit 7.2   The "Friendship Table"

Thoughts on Friendship
The old familiar friend warms the heart.
The new and intimate friend nourishes the soul.
DEIDRE LAIKEN

My Best Friend
My best friend is not the one I talk to the most or the one who makes me laugh all the time.
My best friend is not the one who is with me constantly . . . does not call me on the phone everyday.
My best friend is not the one who flatters me or gives me fine presents.
My best friend is not the one who always agrees with me or the one who slaps me on the back when I win.
My best friend is the one who can see my hurt from across the room and say with his or her eyes, "I understand."

You may not have the answers to all the questions I ask, but at least you listen to the thoughts I express. I can't say in words how much this means to me. So, I'll try and show in the things that I do, how grateful I am to know you.

It is easy to make the mistake of assuming that the person talking to us wants our advice. And too often we rush to tell other people what we think or what they ought to do, when what they really want from us as a friend is just that we hear and be with them to give them strength.

Friendship Table™ is . . .
Not just a seating place in an eating place — it's a MEETING place.
A good place to lift spirits when you're lonely and hungry.
An alternative to eating in the park with the birds or in front of the TV.

What does Friendship Table™ mean to you? Please write to us about your experiences or send us any suggestions you may have. If we use your ideas or stories in an upcoming issue, we'll send you a free gift. Write to: Leons, c/o The Friendly Exchange, 135 Somerset Street, North Plainfield, NJ 07060

We can never replace a friend.

When a man is fortunate enough to have several, he finds they are all different.

No one has a double in friendship.

Shiller

WELCOME TO FRIENDSHIP TABLE™
where good food and service are accompanied by friendship.

The best way to enjoy Friendship Table™ is to participate. So look around. Introduce yourself. And get acquainted.

Do You Know What Xenaphobia is?
ACCORDING TO Webster's Dictionary Xenaphobia is the fear or hatred of strangers or aliens. Earl Nightengale in his "Insight" program defines Xenaphobia as the fear of meeting strangers. He says this fear may have been derived from our caveman origins, in which every stranger was an enemy. When we put aside this fear, Nightengale comments, "We may meet the man, the woman, or couple who will bring new richness and fulfillment to our lives, and we to theirs". If we can recognize and learn to control our Xenaphobia we may lead a life of excitement and discovery.

Recipe for a Friendship Table™
INGREDIENTS
A) Two or more people
B) Pleasant Introductions
C) Good Conversation
D) Delicious Food
E) Good Drink

DIRECTIONS
A) Combine two or more people
B) Sprinkle lightly with Introductions. Include your name, your city and state and your occupation.
C) Mix together with questions and comments from other diners, such as; "I was born in Seattle, too. Isn't it a lovely city?",
D) Add in conversation on current events, weather, travels and experiences. Stir in other topics, if desired.
E) Blend in a fine meal.
F) Serve with warm feelings
G) Makes two or more new friendships.

Friendship tables are relatively new to hotel restaurants but are rapidly gaining in popularity with singles, senior citizens, and business travelers who prefer not to dine alone. A newsletter such as this one can provide conversation starters.
Courtesy of Leon's Restaurant Services, North Plainfield, New Jersey.

Competition Analysis. While in-house research is extremely necessary, it is equally important to be aware of what the competition is doing. Areas that should be studied include the competition's:

- Menu items and prices
- Facilities and services
- Mix (source and volume) of business
- Extra amenities—parking facilities, special menus or discount clubs for seniors, and so on
- Promotional efforts

Analysis of the competition should be used as it is in the rooms division—to determine property strengths and weaknesses and develop ways to differentiate the property's facilities from those of the competition. While forms are useful for this task (the competition analysis forms in Chapter 2 can be modified for restaurant use), it is far more effective to actually *experience* what the competition has to offer. Restaurant staff should visit competitors at a variety of times (breakfast, lunch, and dinner; traditionally slow periods; and peak times) to get a complete picture of service and atmosphere.

Current Trend Research. Food and beverage managers should also look to current food trends and eating habits. Over the past several years, the trend has been away from heavy meals to lighter, healthier fare (salads, fresh fruits and vegetables, lean meats and fish, and so on). While some restaurants have gotten left behind by changing trends and have suffered financially, hotel restaurants can avoid this problem by supplementing traditional menu selections with trendy specialties. Menus can be changed each night to alleviate "menu boredom" for long-term guests, dining "adventures" (a sushi bar, a "select your own lobster" seafood buffet, meals prepared table-side, etc.) can be introduced, and special menus can be created for dieters and the health-conscious.

Merchandising Food and Beverages

Food and beverages can be merchandised by special packaging and pricing, promotional materials such as posters and table tent cards, and suggestive selling by food servers. But perhaps the most important merchandising tool is the restaurant's menu. A good menu, through the types of items offered and the presentation of those items, can enhance the image and increase the profits of any food and beverage operation.

Creating Menus That Sell

A menu must reflect the restaurant's positioning or image, provide information, and serve as a suggestive selling tool. While this may seem like a monumental challenge, it is actually quite easy when food and beverage management follows a menu development cycle which includes image, price, message, and design.

Image. The menu development cycle begins with the restaurant's positioning or image. What image does the restaurant create? What type of ambience or atmosphere does it have? When people visit the restaurant, do they expect a romantic atmosphere or a casual dining experience? In other words, the restaurant's image refers to how the restaurant is perceived by its patrons, and the restaurant's menu must live up to their expectations (see Exhibit 7.3).

Since a restaurant's image is determined in part by the type of clientele the restaurant is attracting (or hopes to attract), it is important to determine whether patrons are coming from inside or outside the property (or a mixture of both), and what market segments the restaurant serves. Does the restaurant cater primarily to the health-conscious? Do business travelers, who usually prefer rapid service during their lunch hours, make up the largest number of patrons? Or does the restaurant serve a great number of families and therefore need a more varied menu?

Price. Price information is a critical menu consideration. What prices do guests expect to pay for menu items? Will items be priced individually (à la carte) or as full meals? Will prices appear at all? Pricing strategy must be determined long before the menu is designed, and must correspond to the restaurant's positioning.

Exhibit 7.3 Sample Restaurant Menu—Beef Barron

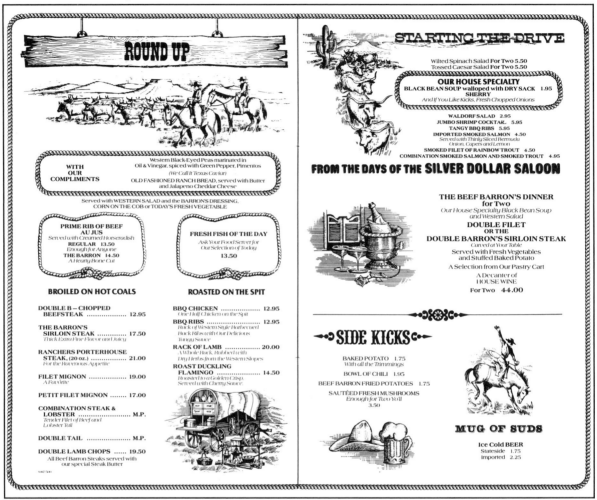

Menus should be designed to reflect the character or image of the restaurant. The headings in this menu from the Beef Barron are reminiscent of the Old West ("Starting the Drive" for salads, "Side Kicks" for side orders, and so on). Important dishes are encircled by lariats, and line drawings reinforce the Western theme.

Courtesy of Hilton Hotels Corporation.

Determining prices. Unlike free-standing restaurants, which operate with established overheads, hotel restaurants often share facilities (kitchens, storerooms, etc.) with other arms of the food and beverage department, making it difficult to determine operating costs or to properly price menu items. For this reason, hotel restaurants price menu selections primarily on a cost-of-merchandise basis. Since cost-of-merchandise can vary significantly, it is impractical to use a general percentage for all items. Lobster, for example, has a much higher cost percentage than coffee and soft drinks. Common guidelines are a markup of 30% on food, 17% to 22% on bar drinks, and 33% to 50% on wines. Labor costs for certain items (oysters must be shucked, for example) should also be considered.

In addition, hotel restaurants face the problem of changing market conditions, including fluctuating wholesale prices for merchandise and alterations in what the competition is offering and charging. Menu prices in most establishments must be monitored constantly and adjusted for seasonal and competitive changes.

The following factors should be studied in order to properly price menu items for hotel restaurants:

1. *Type of operation.* Is the hotel restaurant a coffee shop, a multipurpose dining room, or an elegant supper room? Does the restaurant offer a varied menu or are selections fairly consistent? Offering a consistent menu may keep costs down, but if the restaurant caters primarily to hotel guests who stay for an extended period of time it may be more cost-effective to offer a varied menu that could keep extended-stay guests interested in on-property food facilities.

2. *Guest perception.* How do guests perceive the restaurant? Do they expect to pay high prices for superior service and menu selections, or do they see the restaurant as a casual dining room and expect to pay lower prices?

3. *Competition.* How many restaurants are nearby, and how do their prices compare with the hotel restaurant's? How does their food, service, and atmosphere compare? When a patron has a special occasion for dining out, does he or she have only a few acceptable restaurants to choose from or are there many high-quality restaurants in the vicinity? The more limited the alternatives to the hotel restaurant, the more flexibility the restaurant has to adjust prices. Most patrons are relatively tolerant of price adjustments if they feel they are getting value for their money, or if they realize that changing market conditions are responsible, at least in part, for higher menu prices.

Message. The menu's message—the kind of information it contains—is an important part of a menu's appeal. Will the menu be a simple listing of the foods and beverages offered, or will it have more appeal if it presents the size of the item, the cooking method, the main ingredients, and methods of service? In addition to describing menu selections, will the menu be used to provide information such as restaurant hours, methods of payment, special dietary information, and cross-selling messages for other property facilities? A restaurant with historic significance may opt for menus featuring background stories; a "fun" restaurant (a restaurant that features zany decor or that involves guests in sing-alongs, for example) may feature offbeat information.

The copy written for the menu should be clear and concise. Food and beverage selections can include a description of the ingredients, method of preparation ("deep fried in vegetable oil," "flame-broiled to order," or "steamed to perfection"), and garnishes offered. What is included with each selection must be distinctly spelled out ("includes choice of soup or salad, vegetable of the day, and dinner rolls"). Describing each selection with vivid and tempting words can increase sales.

When writing menu copy or checking menu copy written by a menu specialist or advertising agency, it is important that the restaurant's image not be tarnished by the use of sexist language, negative restrictions ("Your credit card

Exhibit 7.4   Sample Basic Menu Layouts

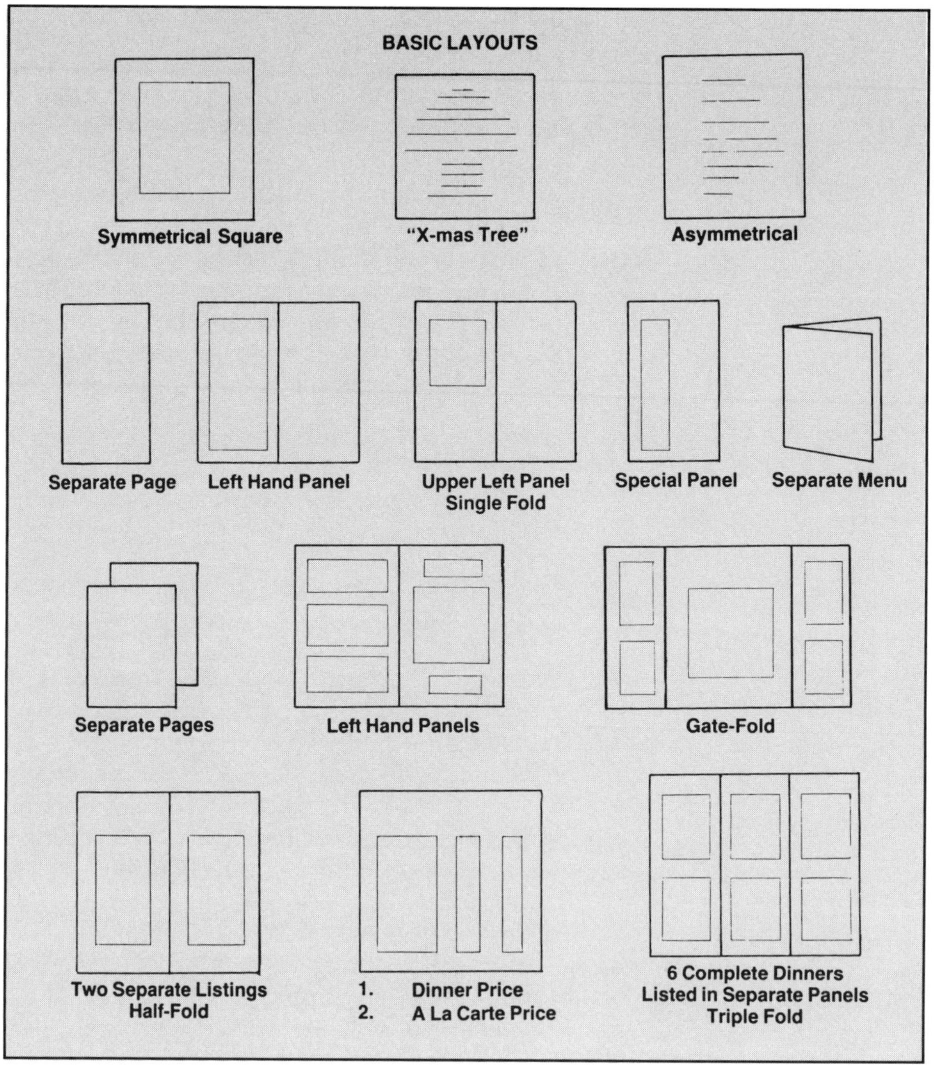

BASIC LAYOUTS

Symmetrical Square   "X-mas Tree"   Asymmetrical

Separate Page   Left Hand Panel   Upper Left Panel Single Fold   Special Panel   Separate Menu

Separate Pages   Left Hand Panels   Gate-Fold

Two Separate Listings Half-Fold

1.   Dinner Price
2.   A La Carte Price

6 Complete Dinners Listed in Separate Panels Triple Fold

welcomed here" is far more diplomatic than "Positively no personal checks"), or poorly designed promotions. One of the most common errors—and a striking example of poor taste—is the lumping together of a senior citizens' menu and a menu for children: "For those under 12 and over 65."

Design. The message, however positive and potentially effective, is only part of the presentation. An attractive design will enhance the copy and draw guests to featured items and specials (see Exhibit 7.4). There are many styles of menus, from a simple blackboard on the wall to parchment paper tied with gold cord, and the factors previously mentioned (image, price, and message) will play an important role in determining the menu's design (see Exhibit 7.5). A restaurant with contemporary positioning and an emphasis on fresh foods, for example, may select a menu enhanced by color photography. A family restaurant or a coffee shop that caters to a variety of tastes may prefer using a menu divided into categories: a breakfast section, a light-lunch

**Exhibit 7.5 Sample Restaurant Menu—
Healthy Habit**

Courtesy of JP Hotels.

section, a "hearty fare" section, a dessert section, a "for the youngsters" section, and so on.

Good menus, no matter what the format, share the following design characteristics:

1. *Effective use of space.* The menu must be clean and uncluttered. Wide borders, space between selections, and large type are effective ways to increase the menu's readability.

2. *Effective layout.* The most popular items, or those that the restaurant wants to promote, should be placed at the head of a list, boxed, featured graphically, or otherwise set apart. If a two-page menu is used, the right page gets the most attention; with three-panel menus, the middle panel should be used for special promotion.

3. *Eye appeal.* Menus must have eye appeal. The choice of paper, type style, and artwork is important. It should be remembered that the color of ink and paper affects readability. Dark ink on light-colored paper is best, especially if lighting in the restaurant is dim.

Supplemental Menus. In addition to its regular menu, a restaurant may provide supplemental menus such as drink menus and wine lists (see Exhibit 7.6), children's menus, and dessert menus. Children's menus are often designed as colorful take-home items, and may feature games or stories to keep children occupied while waiting for the meal. Dessert menus are an effective addition to the regular menu; by the time the meal is over, guests may have forgotten which desserts are available.

Clip-ons are used to avoid expensive reprinting when restaurants supplement the regular menu with daily specials, theme meals, or special menu items in season. If a restaurant plans to use clip-ons, appropriate space should be allotted in the menu's design. Perhaps a blank inside flap or a blank space in the center of the menu can be set aside so the clip-on does not obscure other entrées.

Other F&B Merchandising Methods

In addition to using menus that sell, restaurants can use other merchandising methods to increase sales. Other forms of merchandising include:

- Product packaging

- Added-value alternatives

- Point-of-purchase materials

- Suggestive selling

- Special promotional items

Product Packaging. Product packaging relies on an appeal to the senses to sell. This is not limited to eye appeal; the aroma of freshly baked bread wafting through the restaurant or the sound of sizzling platters also invites sales. But product packaging—both table setting and the garnishing of the food or beverage—usually involves producing a special *visual* impact which can turn something ordinary into a special delight.

Product packaging can begin at the restaurant's entrance—a display of wines, a tempting dessert cart, or an attractive display of fresh produce are all effective sales tools. A display of fresh produce not only whets the appetite but also conveys the message that the restaurant uses only the freshest ingredients. This message can be carried throughout the restaurant through salad bars and table decor.

Exhibit 7.6   Sample Wine List

primavera wine list

Bin No.	Sparkling	
210	Asti Spumante, Cinzano	36.00
211	Asti Spumante, Martini & Rossi	36.00
215	Il Grigio Brut, E. Collavini	25.00
216	Prosecco Di Congeliano, Santa Margherita	35.00

Bin No.	Bianco	
138	Montecarlo, Fattoria Michi, 1982/83	20.00
139	Cortese Di Gavi, Granduca, 1985	25.00
531	Cortese Di Gavi, Pio Cesare, 1985	35.00
532	Gavi Principessa, Villa Banfi, 1983	32.00
140	Pinot Grigio, S. Margherita, 1984	30.00
533	Frascati Superiore, Gotto D'Oro, 1983	20.00
141	Soave Classico, Santa Sofia, 1984/85	20.00
544	Soave Classico Superiore, Mirafiore, 1984/85	20.00
545	Est! Est!! Est!!!, Antinori, 1983/85	20.00
142	Verdicchio, Fazi Battaglia, 1984/85	20.00
546	Corvo Bianco, Della Salparuta, 1984/85	22.00
547	Torre Di Giano, Lungarotti, 1983/84	24.00
548	Chardonnay, Santa Margherita, 1985/86	22.00
549	Luna Del Feldi, Santa Margherita, 1984/85	40.00

Bin No.	Rosso	
143	Chianti Classico, Nozzole, 1981/82	25.00
146	Chianti Classico Riserva "Ducale," Gold Label, Ruffino, 1980/81	50.00
147	Chianti Classico, Riserva, Castello di Ama, 1982	28.00
561	Chianti Classico Riserva, Castello di Gabbiano, 1979	20.00
562	Chianti Riserva "Marchese," Antinori, 1980/81	40.00
144	Brunello di Montalcino, Il Poggone, 1979	70.00
564	Brunello di Montalcino, Biondi-Santi, 1978	140.00
145	Barolo, Riserva, Pio Cesare, 1979	60.00
148	Rubesco, Riserva, Lungarotti, 1975	50.00
565	Barbaresco, "Costa Russi," Angelo Gaja, 1979	125.00
566	Inferno, Nino Negri, 1979	20.00
568	Gattinara, Antoniolo, 1979	30.00
569	Amarone, Bertani, 1978	55.00
571	Valpolicella, Sergo Aligheri, 1983	25.00
570	Catullo, Bertani, 1983	25.00

Sales tax will be added to retail price on all taxable items

Wine lists are often as simple as the one reproduced here, which lists the wines by name, vintner, vintage, and price (the number to the left is the bin number, provided to assist guests in ordering). Other wine lists may detail characteristics of the wine (sweet, sparkling, robust, etc.) and provide suggestions for wines to accompany food selections.

Product packaging can inspire promotions that generate additional business. One restaurant featured an apple promotion that included theme posters, recipe brochures, bushel basket displays of apples, special menu items such as baked apples and apple bread, and a free apple with each deli soup and sandwich lunch.

Many food and drink items can be made special through product packaging. Colorful garnishes of fresh fruits or vegetables give a feeling of quality and abundance and can make even simple food and beverage items more salable. A bowl of dry cereal, for example, becomes a more memorable breakfast when served with a choice of colorful fruits (bowls of bananas, strawberries, raisins, and so on). A simple salad can become a work of art when enhanced with skewers of fresh fruits and/or vegetables.

Unusual presentations can also be used for eye-appeal. A hollowed-out avocado can become a unique bowl for homemade guacamole, a pineapple half may showcase a special chicken curry or salad, and an impressive tortilla bowl can hold a taco salad. Drinks, too, whether alcoholic or non-alcoholic, can generate impulse sales when presented in unique ways. An unusual glass; the addition of attractive garnishes, whether as simple as a few grapes placed in a glass of wine or as elaborate as artistically arranged skewered fruit in frosted glasses; and the use of specialty items (tiny umbrellas, unusual stirrers, or even a clay parrot or sombrero attached to a wooden skewer) can generate interest and sales.

Novelty service-ware might also increase food sales. Eggs served in cast-iron skillets, bread warm from the oven and offered on miniature bread-boards, and soups brought to the table in small covered kettles are all examples of creative merchandising that sells.

Creativity is equally important in how the food is offered to guests. When every restaurant in town is serving prime rib, for example, why should a guest choose the hotel's? One answer might be the hotel's unique way of serving the meal. Perhaps the ribs are rolled to each table on a serving cart and the guest chooses his or her cut and watches it being sliced to order. Or, rather than making a salad in the kitchen, dousing it with salad dressing, and setting it unceremoniously on the table, a food server can prepare the salad at the guest's table, spinning the salad and sprinkling dressing over it as it spins. In either case, the difference is *entertainment value*, and dining becomes more than satisfying hunger. It becomes an experience to be enjoyed.

Sales can be increased by presenting a spectacular dessert early in the evening. A complimentary dish such as bananas flambé can be presented to one table of guests (the guests can be told they have been chosen to receive the dessert for any number of reasons), and sales of that item are almost guaranteed to increase as other guests are impressed by the flaming presentations. The ways that creative product packaging can be used to boost sales are almost endless.

Added-Value Alternatives. Not all guests are influenced by showmanship, however; there will always be guests who are most interested in getting value for their money. That's when added-value alternatives play a key role in merchandising restaurant selections. The principle behind added-value alternatives is simple—the guest is given an opportunity to purchase the greatest value among several alternatives. The ways in which to offer greater value are limited only by the imagination of the restaurant manager.

One way to provide value alternatives is to offer various sizes of items, whether the item is a cup of coffee or a fine steak. Salad items can be sold on different-size plates; steak can be sold by the ounce to appeal to those with small appetites. When large sizes are offered, it is important to note that although the cost-of-merchandise percentage rises, the contribution margin or profit per guest also rises.

Another option that will appeal to value-conscious guests is offering price alternatives—the choice of full meals or à la carte entrées, for example. Other examples of price alternatives are salad bars priced both with and without a dinner entrée, pie offered with or without ice cream, and drinks offered with or without appetizers. In order for this method to be effective, guests must see real value—an alternative that appeals to their lifestyle. Guests who never eat ice cream on their pie, for example, will appreciate not having to pay a higher price.

Prices also figure into another way to provide added-value alternatives: package pricing. This technique is often used in restaurants, and involves including a number of items in one selection; the price of the items, of course, would be higher if purchased separately. Examples of this type of alternative include offering a glass of wine with dinner; a sandwich served with a choice of soup or salad and beverage; a dinner entrée that comes complete with a choice of salad, vegetables, breads, and dessert; and so on.

Point-of-Purchase Materials. Sometimes guests are not influenced by either product packaging or value factors, and must be coached into making selections. Point-of-purchase merchandising can be used to promote specialty or high-profit items to best advantage. Merchandising at the point of purchase makes extensive use of display advertising such as posters, tent cards on tables (see Exhibit 7.7), and additional graphic reinforcement such as strategically placed salad bars, displays of wines, and dessert carts. Although point-of-purchase methods vary, the method used must draw attention to the featured product.

Some properties also use tabletop selling—for example, a bottle of wine labeled with a tag identifying it as the "wine of the month," or complimentary samples of appetizers or entrées that the restaurant is promoting. When using tabletop selling, the restaurant must make it clear whether the item is complimentary or for sale. If a bottle of wine is for purchase only, it must be clearly identified as such and guests must not feel obligated to buy. If a fruit basket contains complimentary fruit and is not on the table strictly for decoration or for sale, a simple banner ("With our compliments") can clear up any confusion and make guests feel more at home.

Point-of-purchase merchandising can lead undecided guests into making impulse decisions but, like menus, it has a limitation: it is a one-way communications medium. There is still a missing ingredient: people.

Suggestive Selling. Food servers and other restaurant personnel play an important part in merchandising food and beverages. As discussed in Chapter 6, one of their most effective merchandising tools is suggestive selling.

Suggestive selling can begin from the moment a guest is seated. The food server can suggest a cocktail from the bar or a special appetizer to begin the meal. A group can be offered an appetizer sampler plate, and the food server can suggest several appetizers that can be ordered by various members of the group and shared. Entrées may be suggested or upgraded with a few suggestive-selling phrases, and after the meal the food server can suggest a choice of desserts rather than just asking if anyone would like dessert. The chances of sales success can be enhanced with the use of an attractive dessert cart.

Suggestive selling can also be used in a lounge. The bartender or cocktail server can suggest appetizers or specialty drinks: "We have a terrific new tropical drink that I know you'd enjoy. It's made with a blend of fresh pineapple juice and orange juice with our quality rum, and is served in a tall, frosted glass."[2]

Suggestive selling responsibilities should be a part of a food or cocktail server's job description. These employees should be taught proper suggestive selling techniques and be shown that suggestive selling is a vital part of *serving* the guest.

Special Promotional Items. Some restaurants use special promotional items such as recipe cards, postcards depicting drinks, and souvenir menus. (If a menu is expensive to produce, a smaller-scale souvenir version can be designed to take home.) If the property is part of a chain, special promotional items may be available through corporate headquarters. They can also be specially designed by an advertising agency, freelance artist, or menu specialist. If outside sources are used, however, it is important that the food and

Exhibit 7.7 Sample Point-of-Purchase Display

Some point-of-purchase displays are as elaborate as this six-panel, full-color tent card promoting exotic drinks. Point-of-purchase materials are used to encourage impulse sales.

Courtesy of Flamingo Hilton and Tower, Las Vegas, Nevada.

beverage manager approve the final design and ensure that the copy and design accurately reflect the positioning of the property.

Promoting Restaurants and Lounges

While word-of-mouth advertising lends exceptional credibility to a restaurant, it is usually not enough to properly promote the facility. Even if a restaurant has a popular menu, a good atmosphere, and an excellent, service-oriented staff, it won't be profitable if no one (or only a small group of loyal patrons) knows it's there. The restaurant must be *promoted* in order to attract patrons and make a profit.

Types of Promotions

There are three basic ways to promote a hotel restaurant:

1. Personal promotions

2. In-house promotions

3. Outside promotions

Dessert trays are often used by food servers to enhance their suggestive selling presentation.

Personal Promotions. Personal promotions include sales calls (both telephone and in-person) and sales letters to introduce prospective guests to the restaurant. Restaurant sales calls differ very little from sales calls made for rooms or banquet business. Whether the sales call is made by the restaurant manager or a member of the food service or sales staff, it should follow the basic presentation sales call format: an opening, getting prospect involvement, the presentation, overcoming objections, and closing the sale. Since these steps were covered in Chapter 4 it is not necessary to repeat them in detail here, but restaurant representatives should thoroughly familiarize themselves with these steps before attempting to make telephone or in-person sales calls.

Sales letters are another important phase of personal promotion, and may be used either as an introductory or follow-up tool to supplement telephone or in-person sales calls. Sales letters should be tailored to individual needs—a restaurant manager should not send the same letter to a business group and a bride!

In-house Promotions. In-house promotions range from coupons and contests to drawings and special events. In-house promotions have already been discussed in Chapter 6, but the ideas presented in that chapter represent only a small number of the possibilities for promoting restaurants in-house. The types of in-house promotions a restaurant engages in depends on the size, type, and staff of the restaurant as well as its typical markets and target markets. Promotions must be consistent with the positioning of the facility, and present a good reason for guests to patronize it. Creative promotions not only generate additional business, but also help to build guest goodwill and word-of-mouth advertising.

No matter what type of in-house promotion is used, it must be developed in a systematic fashion. A restaurant should:

1. *Analyze business patterns.* Records should be analyzed by volume and profit in as many different ways as possible to determine areas that need promoting. Liquor versus food sales, lunch versus dinner volumes, and business by days of the week can be analyzed, for example.

2. *Identify profitable current business.* The direction of promotions will often depend on which areas are already most profitable; perhaps the gourmet restaurant is enjoying extensive local patronage or the coffee shop is attracting a large crowd for its Friday night "clambake." Can profitable areas be expanded? Are potentially profitable areas being promoted to best advantage?

3. *Identify the audience.* What target market segments will the promotion be reaching? What types of promotions will appeal to the targeted segments?

4. *Set objectives.* Once the areas of greatest opportunity have been identified, specific objectives should be set, whether in terms of dollar volume, percentages, or number of covers or items sold.

5. *Evaluate promotion techniques.* A promotion may lend itself to publicity, paid advertising, internal merchandising, personal selling, or combinations of these techniques. Each of these techniques should be evaluated for possible use before actually creating a promotion.

6. *Determine an offer.* What types of items might be offered in a successful promotion? Prizes? Free meals? Discounts? Special dishes?

7. *Develop a budget.* The costs of the suggested promotion should be considered: printing costs, advertising costs, costs of incentive gifts for staff members involved in the promotion, costs of special offers, and so on. If not enough money is available to meet these needs, the promotion may need to be trimmed to ensure effectiveness. A well-done small promotion is usually more effective than a poorly financed, half-hearted large one.

8. *Monitor the promotion.* An ineffective promotion can be dropped quickly if provisions are made to monitor results on a timely basis. If a restaurant is offering a half-price dinner special, for example, it is important to know the number of specials ordered, the number of regular dinners ordered, and the cost per person of the promotion.

9. *Involve the staff.* While this item has been listed last, it is certainly not least. An enthusiastic staff can make an in-house promotion

more successful than can paid advertising, and at a substantially lower cost. But the staff must be totally familiar with and sold on the promotion, especially if it involves special costumes or extra effort on the part of the staff.

In-house promotions that are cost-effective, build enthusiasm among the staff, and provide a benefit to guests (whether value or excitement) greatly enhance the image of the property as a friendly, comfortable place to eat and be entertained, and can help to overcome the stereotype of the boring hotel restaurant or dreary lounge.

Outside Promotions. Outside promotions fall into two general categories: paid advertising and supplemental promotion.

Most restaurants, whether they are hotel outlets or free-standing facilities, make extensive use of a number of forms of paid advertising—both print (newspaper, magazine, direct mail, and so on) and broadcast (radio and even television in some cases). Paid advertising offers the advantage of controlling the message to the consumer, and will be discussed in detail in Part III, but Exhibit 7.8 provides examples of the types of creative advertising that can be used to promote a restaurant to both new and repeat guests.

Supplemental promotion includes the use of sales materials—discount coupons, fliers, offers of giveaways, and so on—and free publicity. Publicity can play an important part in public awareness of a restaurant, and opportunities to receive free publicity are almost everywhere. Local newspapers may eagerly snap up news of restaurant expansions, special promotions and offers to local patrons, and feature stories about employees or special recipes. (The benefits of publicity will be discussed further in Chapter 14.)

Building Repeat Business

Repeat business is a significant factor in the success of hotel restaurants. Therefore, it is important to cultivate guest loyalty.

The Importance of Employees

It should be remembered that people are not just buying a meal or a few drinks; they are buying a social experience as well. And social experiences mean people. Food and beverage employees can help make dining or relaxing over a drink a pleasurable occasion. Well-trained employees dedicated to serving guests can make the difference between a highly successful operation and empty seats.[3]

A good manager will make sure that his or her staff not only serves guests but makes friends of them as well. Managers should start with employees with personality, employees who are truly interested in each guest and eager to give guests the three free "gifts" that can make each visit memorable and build guest loyalty: recognition, recommendations, and reassurance.

Recognition. Recognition of guests, as mentioned in Chapter 6, is one of the most effective tools for building guest goodwill and repeat business. Almost everyone likes to hear his or her name and feel valued.

Name recognition should begin as soon as a guest walks in. This important part of guest relations can take a number of forms. In some restaurants,

Exhibit 7.8   Examples of Restaurant Advertising

Every Sunday We Bayou Brunch.

Every Sunday at the White Water Cafe, you can get a taste of New Orleans and Mardi Gras. There's a Dixieland band to get your toes tapping. And Cajun treats like blackened red fish, fried catfish, jambalaya and 25 other selections to make your taste buds tingle.

Fact is, it's probably the most deelish $14.95 brunch you ever slid past your ever lovin' choppers. But to get a sample for yourself, you need to call 344-7000 for reservations right now.

Or else this Sunday's food'n'fun might slip Bayou.

white water CAFE

Make A Splash!

Omni Richmond Hotel in Shockoe Slip, 100 South 12th Street, 804-344-7000

An Event That May Be More Than You Can Stomach.

If you had a great time at our Oktoberfest and you're hungry for more, this is for you. From March 20 through April 30, we're turning the Omni into Little Italy, with mountains of pasta and rivers of wine and more at our incredible buffet. Only $5.95 for youngsters, $10.95 for adults.

From 4-7 p.m. Monday-Friday, there'll be free Antipasto at the Lobby Bar. And on the weekends, there'll be great food, Italian music and much more.

You don't have to be Italian to come. Just hungry.

Italianfest at

OMNI ✦ INTERNATIONAL HOTEL

777 Waterside Drive. For reservations call 622-2868.

guests are greeted personally by the manager. If this is not feasible, a host can make guests feel welcome and introduce them to their food server, or give the food server the names of the guests before he or she waits on them. Food servers should use the guests' names often while greeting and serving them.

Recommendations. Recommendations are another part of the server's job which can help build repeat business. Good recommendations depend on both food and service knowledge. Servers should be fully informed about each item on the menu and should be ready to respond to guests when asked for suggestions. Far too many servers are inadequate in this area. They answer questions about what's good on the menu with an evasive "Everything," and, if pressed about a personal preference, reply, "It's all good. I like everything."

These replies do not help the guest or increase the size of the check, so it is important that each food server know the ingredients in each dish, the method of preparation, and the approximate preparation time. In addition, each menu item should be taste-tested to enable the food server to answer questions about the dish's flavor, spiciness, consistency, and so on. For even better results, the restaurant's staff should be encouraged to occasionally eat at the establishments of competitors. If the server has had a personal experience, he or she can honestly tell the patron what the difference is between the French onion soup offered by another restaurant and the French onion soup served in the hotel's restaurant.

When food servers have this extensive knowledge, it is far easier for them to assist the restaurant's guests in making selections, which helps build guest trust and loyalty.

Reassurance. Reassuring guests means making them feel at home. Food servers can use conversation and personal observation to "tailor" their service to each guest. A leisurely diner, for example, has time to talk to the server and taste-test different foods, linger over a meal that takes time to prepare, and enjoy a dessert. A businessperson, on the other hand, may want to place his or her order immediately and may prefer foods that can be prepared quickly. A group of guests engaged in an animated discussion may not want to be disturbed. In this case, the food server should simply take the order and interrupt as seldom as possible.

Food servers should be sensitive to the special needs of certain guests. Diners eating alone, for example, may feel conspicuous, or families dining with small children may feel uncomfortable if the children become restless or cranky. In these cases, the food server can become a public relations ambassador by meeting the unique needs of these guests.

If a lone diner apologetically says, "There's just one today," for example, the host or food server can project a friendly image, be sure that the lone diner is not seated in an out-of-the-way location, and check back to make sure that everything is all right. Some restaurants offer a daily newspaper to guests dining alone, or (as previously mentioned) offer to seat them at a "Friendship Table" for company and conversation. Providing these special touches can prove to be enormously profitable for the restaurant. Lone diners that are treated well are more likely to become repeat guests and may bring their friends to the restaurant as well.

In the case of a family dining situation, the food server can be friendly and attentive, and assure the family that the children are welcome. It is helpful for the food server to take the order promptly and, if possible, offer a light complimentary snack to the children to help prevent restlessness. Most children are satisfied when given a cracker, a piece of fresh fruit, or some type of "finger food" to occupy them while they wait for the meal. A little extra personal attention helps keep children (and parents) content.

Food servers can make all guests feel at home by engaging them in conversation, truthfully answering questions, and involving them in the restaurant by sharing "trade secrets," providing useful information on preparation techniques, and soliciting feedback about the food or service. This usually enhances a guest's restaurant experience, and provides an excellent reason for the guest to return to "his" or "her" restaurant.

Exhibit 7.9   Sample Calendar of Events

S Sheraton **Buffalo Airport** Walden Avenue at I-90 (Exit 52E) (716) 681-2400			**Lounge** **August 1987** *Join us for Happy Hour!* Mon. - Thurs. 4:30 to 7:00 pm – Friday Night 4:30 to 10:00 pm (Each Friday we give away a FREE WEEKEND FOR TWO!!)			*Coming in* *September!!* Complete **renovation** and **expansion of** The **Gazebo Bar**
SUNDAY	MONDAY	TUESDAY	WEDNESDAY	THURSDAY	FRIDAY	SATURDAY
Be Our Corporate Salute! *Schedule your office cocktail party for 15 or more people and we will provide hot and cold hors d'oeuvres and reduced drink price. All you have to do is come! We do the rest! Have your own section of our plush lounge. See Manager for details.*			**EVERY WEDNESDAY IS** 5 **BUFFALO'S BEST OLDIE'S NITE**	*Coming Soon . . .* 6 Watch For Our All New And Expanded **GAZEBO BAR** Join us after work Monday thru Friday for *Happy Hour*	**JOIN US** 7 **FOR** **50's & 60's** **FRIDAY** **HAPPY HOUR** **EVERY**	1 **SPEND YOUR WEEKENDS AT OUR GAZEBO BAR**
2 Two Large-Screen T.V.'s for your favorite sports or movies	3 ***Beat The Heat!*** Try Our Large Assortment of Ice Cream Specialty Drinks	4 **Buffalo Special Beef On Week**	**FEATURING MUSIC** 12 **AND DANCING**	13 *Cool Down* with an Ice Cream Drink	**FRIDAY** 14 **FROM** **5:30 - 7:30 pm** **COMPLI-** **MENTARY**	**Open** 15 **Friday** And Saturday Till Midnight Sundays Until 5:00
9 *Try Our Lavish* **Sunday Brunch!**	10	11 *Bring a group of 10 or more to Happy Hour and receive a complimentary bottle of champagne*	**FROM THE 50's, 60's AND 70's** 19	20 **Buffalo Special Chicken Wings**	**CHICKEN** 21 **WINGS** **ALONG** **WITH** **PRIZES,** **GIVEAWAYS,**	22 Dance the night away every Wednesday Friday and Saturday
16 **Buffalo's Best** ***Oldie's Night*** Every Wednesday $1.00 Drafts	17 *Get Ready For* **Monday Night Football!**	18 *Complimentary hors d'oeuvres Monday - Friday*	**CONTESTS, GIVE-AWAYS AND PRIZES INCLUDING DINNER,** 26 **BRUNCH, & WEEKENDS FOR TWO**	27	**AND** 28 **DANCE** **CONTESTS** **YOU WON'T** **WANT TO MISS**	29 **Monday Night Football Party** *Every Monday Starting Sept. 14th*
23	24	25 **Visit Our TROPICAL GAZEBO BAR**				
30	31					

Calendars of events can be simple or elaborate, and may be printed in newspapers, distributed to local businesses, placed in guestrooms and on posters throughout the property, or used in a follow-up mailing to previous guests.

Courtesy of Sheraton Buffalo Airport Hotel, Buffalo, New York.

Guest Follow-Up

One of the easiest and most inexpensive ways to build guest goodwill and loyalty is with a follow-up telephone call. Telephone numbers can be obtained from the reservations book or a guest survey card provided at each table. The call should be kept brief, but should express the fact that the guest is valued by the restaurant. Asking if everything was satisfactory can give guests an opportunity to express themselves and can provide the caller with the opportunity to handle complaints and obtain information to help serve guests better.

Personal notes or mailings are another way to provide guest follow-up. Notes may be sent after a telephone call or may be used to thank a guest for completing a guest survey. General mailings can also announce special promotions, new menu items, or upcoming events (see Exhibit 7.9).

One way to follow up is to offer guests incentives to return, such as free meals after they have purchased a required number of dinners, prizes (food or merchandise) to frequent guests through drawings or special contests, and discounts on rooms or other property facilities for regular patrons.

Another creative way to reward frequent guests is the use of special programs such as the Fine Dining Club offered by the Stouffer Hotel

Company in conjunction with American Express. The Fine Dining Club gives gold paper medallions to diners who use their American Express cards to pay for dinner entrées. After accumulating 20 medallions, the club member is entitled to a "Free Spirit Weekend"; 60 medallions earn an "Anniversary Weekend" that features a deluxe suite for two nights, complimentary meals, and champagne.

Other properties make use of display items to recognize frequent visitors. Lounges, as mentioned in Chapter 6, may provide engraved mugs to regular patrons. Restaurants may even name a dish after a patron who has suggested the item or who is a frequent consumer of the selection.

Making sure guests are satisfied through guest follow-up is one of the most effective ways to build a loyal guest base and promote the restaurant. Satisfied guests are repeat guests and excellent sources of word-of-mouth advertising.

Notes

1. *Lodging Hospitality*, October 1987, p. 32.
2. Serving alcoholic beverages properly is the subject of *Serving Alcohol with Care* (East Lansing, Mich.: Educational Institute of the American Hotel & Motel Association). Videotape.
3. The importance of food and beverage employees is discussed in Anthony M. Rey and Ferdinand Wieland, *Managing Service in Food and Beverage Operations* (East Lansing, Mich.: Educational Institute of the American Hotel & Motel Association, 1985).

Discussion Questions

1. What are four basic areas of positioning research?
2. In what ways can information be obtained for developing guest profiles for a restaurant?
3. What areas should be considered when assessing a restaurant's competition?
4. The "Friendship Table" appeals to what market segment?
5. How have eating habits and food preferences changed in recent years?
6. What are four elements of the menu development cycle?
7. What are some examples of product packaging used in restaurants?
8. What is package pricing?
9. What are three basic ways to promote a property restaurant?
10. What are nine steps for developing in-house restaurant promotions?
11. What are the three "gifts" that can make each restaurant visit memorable for guests?

Chapter Outline

I. The Catering Department
    A. Catering Department Personnel
    B. The Marketing Plan
        1. Analyzing the Competition
        2. Identifying Key Catering Markets
        3. Setting Goals
        4. Developing Action Plans
        5. Evaluating Results

II. Catering Sales
    A. Developing Leads
        1. In-Person Soliciting
        2. Telephone Soliciting
        3. Sales Letters
        4. Responses to Inquiries
            a. Written inquiries
            b. Telephone inquiries
            c. In-person inquiries
    B. Selling to Clients
        1. Catering Sales Procedures
    C. Planning the Function
        1. Menus
            a. Client preferences
            b. Food costs
            c. Labor costs
        2. Beverage Plans
            a. Cash bar
            b. Host bar
            c. Charge by the hour
        3. Finalizing Arrangements
    D. Managing the Function
    E. Following Up Accounts

III. Other Food and Beverage Sales
    A. Creative Coffee Breaks
    B. Cocktail Parties
    C. Special Functions

IV. Meeting Room Sales
    A. Types of Meeting Rooms
    B. Meeting Room Setups
    C. Meeting Room Furniture
        1. Chairs
        2. Tables
        3. Platforms
    D. Booking Meeting Rooms
        1. Release Dates
    E. Managing Meetings

8 Banquet and Meeting Room Sales

The catering department of a hotel can produce additional, often high, revenues and generate positive guest relations through well-run functions. Successful banquets can contribute greatly to the overall profitability of the hotel. The profit margin on sales for banquets often runs 35%, as opposed to 15% for hotel restaurants. There are several reasons for this difference:

1. Banquet sales volume often exceeds restaurant volume at a large hotel—in some cases two to one.

2. Banquets allow flexibility in pricing. Prime rib priced at $18 on the restaurant menu may bring $30 on the banquet menu. (Part of this increase is due to the cost of erecting and tearing down the banquet setup.)

3. Food costs are lower due to volume preparation. Also, no large inventory is needed for a banquet kitchen to function, since ordering can be done as needed.

4. Beverage costs can be controlled through pricing flexibility and volume purchasing.

5. Labor costs are lower. Since banquet servers can be supplemented by part-time employees on an as-needed basis, the regular banquet serving staff can be kept small. The cost of restaurant employees, in contrast, is largely fixed: restaurants operate on a continuous basis, and a regular staff must be maintained even during slow periods.

In this chapter, we will take a look at the dynamics of a successful catering operation—its staffing, responsibilities, and role in relation to overall sales—and learn how banquet and meeting room business contributes to a property's overall image and profitability. The chapter is divided into two parts. The first part will focus on the catering department. This department provides services for functions such as banquets, parties, and other business or social functions involving food and beverage. The second part will discuss the sale of meeting rooms, which, unlike banquet business, is most often handled directly by the hotel's sales office.

Industry Profile

Gus Moser
Director of Catering
The Las Vegas Hilton

Gus Moser began his career at the Las Vegas Hilton at the age of 16. During his 16 years with the property he has advanced through ten different positions in six departments. He has held management positions within the steward, room service, convention setup, and banquet departments, and currently serves as the Director of Catering for the world's largest resort and convention hotel. In this capacity, Moser oversees more than 225,000 square feet of convention, banquet, and trade show space, and directly supervises a managerial staff that consists of two catering managers, two banquet managers, three convention setup managers, and a stage and sound department manager. This staff is responsible for the direction of over 350 food servers, 40 bartenders, 60 convention setup porters, 16 stage and sound technicians, and a full office staff.

"Availability, creativity, and personal service will bring you the repeat business that every hotel strives for. The meeting planner of today is a sophisticated traveler who is continually encouraging his or her staff to surpass a previous year's convention program. The most difficult challenge for a catering director is to continually upgrade and be personally creative with a convention that's booked on an annual basis.

A catering director needs the human relations skills to make all clients comfortable with assigned rooms, but, at the same time, he or she must continue to upgrade menus, contribute to the uniqueness of each event, and create an occasion which will be long remembered. A catering career is diverse, with clients booking everything from early morning breakfasts and sales meetings to late evening receptions. And there's the ever-increasing market for special events, which range from boxing matches to concerts.

A catering director must be able to adjust to different clients from appointment to appointment—switch from the hard-driving sell required for a meeting planner or a training director, for example, to the gentler approach necessary for a nervous bride-to-be. The client that genuinely trusts the catering director and his or her staff will generate much-needed repeat business.

The Las Vegas Hilton may house as many as six separate, independent conventions occupying function space during the same time period. Well-organized office files prevent the catering director's nightmare—a double booking. If careful attention is paid to the initial meeting, pre-planning, setup, and eventual execution of service, however, the catering director derives the complete satisfaction of a job well done. **"**

The Catering Department

Most catering departments have two basic responsibilities:

1. To sell food and beverage functions to businesses and individuals in the local community

2. To service in-house convention and group functions sold by the property's sales office

To plan and manage functions, catering department personnel must possess extensive knowledge of sales, service, the use of facilities and function space, food production, menu planning, and cost control.

The size and organizational structure of the catering department (see Exhibit 8.1) depends on a number of factors:

Exhibit 8.1 Sample Catering Department Organization Charts

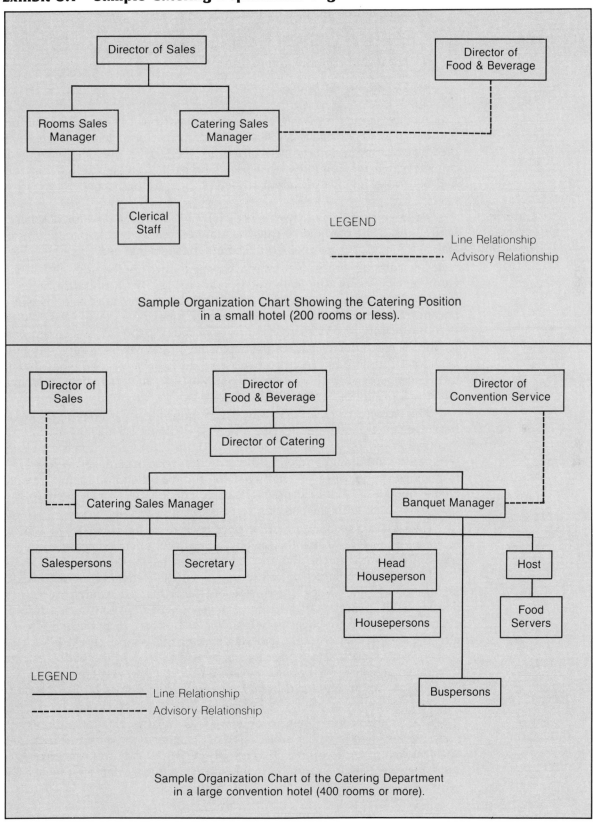

Sample Organization Chart Showing the Catering Position
in a small hotel (200 rooms or less).

Sample Organization Chart of the Catering Department
in a large convention hotel (400 rooms or more).

- Size of property and amount of function space available
- Types of catering to be handled
- The property's business mix
- Local and regional competition
- Departmental budgets

At most large properties, the catering department is an arm of the food and beverage department, while at smaller properties catering is often handled by a salesperson in the sales office. To be effective, this salesperson must be given extensive training in all aspects of the function business; selling food and beverages involves different strategies than selling rooms.

Catering Department Personnel

At large properties, catering is usually headed by a director of catering who supervises a banquet or catering manager, catering salespeople, clerical staff, and service personnel (food servers, buspersons, and so on).

The *catering director's* primary responsibilities are the sales and administrative aspects of the catering operation; as the hospitality industry becomes increasingly competitive, the catering director's sales responsibilities become more crucial. Today's catering director may give a great deal of attention to soliciting or servicing accounts. The catering director is also responsible for the cost-effectiveness of the department, and works closely with hotel personnel (purchasing agents, chefs, and the marketing and sales department) to ensure that the catering operation falls within budget guidelines while still providing service to clients (see Exhibit 8.2).

The *banquet* or *catering manager* is responsible for overseeing food and beverage functions and supervising service personnel, and may be directly involved in setting up function rooms. At large convention hotels, however, setup duties are often handled by a convention service manager, whose job is to manage the logistics of functions: the room preparation, setup, maintenance, and so on. Banquet managers also schedule personnel, prepare payrolls, and work with the catering director on special functions.

Catering salespeople are often employed by large properties to actively solicit business not brought in as part of conventions or meetings, such as weddings, Rotary luncheons, and similar local business. These salespeople should also be available to follow up on written, telephone, and walk-in inquiries. Catering salespeople must know the proper procedures to follow to develop leads, process paperwork for an account, and follow up the account after a function. Knowledge of what type of business to book and when is also important. For example, catering salespeople should avoid booking a social function such as a bridge tournament luncheon in the ballroom on a weekday. Such a booking could prevent booking a four-day corporate meeting with rooms business and breakfast, lunch, and dinner business each of the four days.

The catering department may employ a *clerical staff* to maintain the paperwork generated by the solicitation of business, handle routine inquiries, and follow up on accounts. In large properties, a catering secretary may assist the catering director with administrative duties or manage the catering office.

Exhibit 8.2 Sample Job Description for a Catering Director

Catering Director

1. *Basic Function*:
   To service all phases of group meeting/banquet functions; coordinate these activities on a daily basis; assist clients in program planning and menu selection; solicit local group catering business.

2. *General Responsibility*:
   To maintain the services and reputation of Doubletree and act as a management representative to group clients.

3. *Specific Responsibilities*:
   a. To maintain the function book. Coordinate the booking of all meeting space with the sales office.
   b. To solicit local food and beverage functions.
   c. To coordinate with all group meeting/banquet planners their specific group requirements with the services and facilities offered.
   d. To confirm all details relative to group functions with meeting/banquet planners.
   e. To distribute to the necessary hotel departments detailed information relative to group activities.
   f. To supervise and coordinate all phases of catering, hiring, and training programs.
   g. To assist the banquet manager in supervising and coordinating meeting/banquet setups and service.
   h. To assist in menu planning, preparation, and pricing.
   i. To assist in referrals to the sales department and in booking group activities.
   j. To set up and maintain catering files.
   k. To be responsive to group requests/needs while in the hotel.
   l. To work toward achieving Annual Plan figures relating to the catering department (revenues, labor percentages, average checks, covers, etc.)
   m. To handle all scheduling and coverage for the servicing of catering functions.

4. *Organizational Relationship and Authority*:
   Is directly responsible and accountable to the food and beverage manager. Responsible for coordination with catering service personnel, the kitchen, and accounting.

While a catering director's duties may vary depending on the size and organizational structure of the property, successful catering directors are fully aware of the value of involvement with the local community, sales letters, telephone solicitation, and in-person visits to develop and keep local and convention business.

Courtesy of Doubletree Hotels.

Service personnel serve food and beverages, set up function rooms as required, and maintain banquet areas and equipment. Service personnel include hosts, food servers, buspersons, and maintenance or setup crews.

It is important to note that all of the employees mentioned above are involved in sales, whether they are actually selling banquets, servicing existing accounts, or simply projecting a friendly and hospitable image as they serve guests. This sales orientation is extremely important, especially since banquet sales at some properties represent 40% to 45% of the total revenue generated by the food and beverage department. It is vital that members of the catering department see themselves and the department as important parts of the property's overall marketing and sales efforts.

The Marketing Plan
The catering department should have its own marketing plan which supports the property's overall marketing plan. The catering department's plan should include:

1. Analyzing the competition
2. Identifying key catering markets
3. Setting goals
4. Developing action plans and defining the roles of staff members in these action plans
5. Evaluating results

Analyzing the Competition. An analysis of the competition is needed to determine the catering department's strengths and weaknesses in relation to competitors. Factors to consider include the location of the competitor, size of the function space available, aesthetic quality of function rooms, availability of equipment (podiums, audiovisual equipment, portable dance floors, and so on), and the competitor's reputation. The use of a banquet competition and pricing comparison sheet can greatly facilitate this effort and provide invaluable information for positioning the property's facilities (see Exhibit 8.3).

Identifying Key Catering Markets. Once the department's strengths have been determined and weaknesses corrected, key catering markets must be identified. There are three types of local business that can prove profitable: business from local corporate sources, business from civic and academic sources, and social business (see Exhibit 8.4). Local corporate business might include sales meetings, conventions, lecture-format breakfasts or dinners, and other meetings requiring the use of food and beverage service. Civic and academic business can include fund-raising banquets, conventions, annual parties, and special project events such as a property-based telethon or beauty pageant for such groups as the Jaycees. Social business includes weddings, parties, family reunions, and similar events.

Setting Goals. After identifying potential sources of local business, the sales goals of the department can be set. When setting these goals, it is important to focus sales efforts on valley and shoulder periods. This is only possible when accurate information on function room usage is available.

Useful function room statistics to monitor include:

- Function room occupancy by meal period
- Types of functions
- Use of guestrooms by function groups
- Popularity of individual banquet menu items
- Sales revenue per square foot of function space
- Average banquet check by type of function
- Pattern of unused times and days
- Average number of persons by type of function

Exhibit 8.3 Sample Banquet Competition and Pricing Comparison Sheet

Prepared by _____ Date _____

BANQUET COMPETITION AND PRICING COMPARISON

HOTEL NAME	YOUR HOTEL HERE	HOTEL A	HOTEL B	INN C	HOTEL D
LOCATION Address and Phone Number:	(xxx) xxx-xxxx	(xxx) xxx-xxxx	(xxx) xxx-xxxx	(xxx) xxx-xxxx	(xxx) xxx-xxxx
BANQUET SPACE	# of Rooms/sq ft.	# of Rooms/sq ft.	# of Rooms/sq ft.	# of Rooms/sq ft.	# of Rooms/sq ft.
Ballroom	1-7,050	1-5,500	1-4,000	1-15,000 1-4,578 blrm	1-2,178 1-3,608
Board Rooms	3-608		11-350 each	5	1-276
Meeting rooms	2-304		2-1,200 each	6	10-5,779
Prefunction	1-1,218			1-3,044	
Other			a lot of pre-function space!	Theater	

PRICING	B	L	D	B	L	D	B	L	D	B	L	D	B	L	D
Lowest pkg	7.50	7.95	13.50	5.59	6.95	11.75	5.50	7.50	13.50	7.25	8.25	12.75	5.95	7.25	9.95
Highest pkg	11.50	12.75	22.00	8.95	9.95	16.00	8.50	12.95	25.00	13.50	14.25	23.75	8.95	10.95	18.95
Est Avg Ck	9.50	10.35	17.75	7.45	8.45	13.88	7.00	10.23	19.25	10.25	11.25	18.25	7.45	9.10	14.45

BEVERAGE	HOST	CASH	HOST	CASH	HOST	CASH	HOST	CASH	HOST	CASH
House Brands	2.25	2.50	2.00		2.25	2.00	2.25	2.50	Bottle only $48–$60 per bottle	2.00
Call Brands	2.50	2.75	2.25		2.50	2.25				2.50
Premium Brands	2.75	3.00	Bottle avail.				2.50	2.75		
Beer/Wine	1.75	2.00	1.50/1.75		1.75	1.75	1.75	2.25		1.75
							13.50 beer	2.75 beer		
							bottle	wine		

PERCEIVED POSITIONING	Highly social, Corporate rooms	Corporate 16% gratuity	Corporate 16% gratuity	group/convention some social	corporate/airport
PERSON CONTACTED AND TITLE		Linda Smith DOS	Don Marcos DOS	Mary Giesling SALES MANAGER	Ed Fisher SALES MANAGER

B = Breakfast   L = Lunch   D = Dinner

A banquet competition and pricing comparison sheet can be used to compare the property's positioning to that of competitors, and to record information that may be used to differentiate the property's catering services.

Function room statistics can be revealing. Chris Carey, the catering director of the St. Regis Sheraton in New York, found that while the hotel's function rooms seemed very busy during certain times of the year, the hotel often booked only one function per day per function room. Keeping track of function room business can disclose valley and shoulder periods and help the department sell and schedule banquet business when it is most needed.

Developing Action Plans. After sales goals have been set, action plans to reach those goals can be implemented. If a property has set a goal to increase wedding business by 65% over a specific three-month period, strategies might include the development of wedding brochures and planners; promotion of special wedding packages; attendance at local bridal fairs; and soliciting leads from local jewelers, photographers, and bridal boutique owners.

Action plans will vary depending on a number of factors: goals set, target markets, budget available for promotion, and so on. Action plans may range from the simple to the elaborate. An action plan at one property may be to make 15 sales calls per week on local businesses to increase public awareness, while another property in the same city may stage a spectacular event for the same purpose.

Exhibit 8.4 Sources of Local Business

Local Corporate Business

Sources: Chambers of Commerce, yellow pages, business section of the newspaper, trade journals, property staff members, competition's reader boards, referrals, past accounts.

Contacts: Sales managers, personnel directors, department or division officers or heads, key secretaries.

Types of events: Sales meetings (coffee breaks, lunches, receptions); conventions (coffee breaks, breakfasts, lunches, dinners, receptions); trade displays and exhibits (refreshment breaks); seminars and demonstrations (meals and refreshment breaks); retirement dinners; office and holiday parties; incentive vacations (meals included).

Civic and Academic Business

Sources: Chamber of Commerce listings; club directories; yellow pages; society, local news, and sports sections of local newspapers; competition's reader boards; referrals; past accounts.

Contacts: Organization officers, committee chairpersons, officers of alumni associations, social chairpersons of sororities or fraternities, coaches, key secretaries.

Types of events: Banquets; conventions (meals and refreshment breaks); annual parties; special project events (refreshments, beverage sales); class reunions (meals and refreshments); dances (refreshments, beverage sales); receptions.

Social Business

Sources: Society section of local newspaper; bridal fairs; mailing lists; personal contacts in related areas (jewelers, photographers, and so on); competition's reader boards; referrals; past accounts.

Contacts: Church secretaries, direct contact with the prospective client.

Types of events: Weddings (luncheons and teas, bridal showers, bachelor and bachelorette parties, rehearsal dinners, receptions); parties (holiday, anniversary, birthday, cocktail); family reunions (banquets, receptions); bar and bas mitzvahs; church-related functions (lunches, receptions).

These sources can be used to build catering sales. Since most competitors have access to the same sources, however, it pays to be creative. One successful catering manager, for example, visits local funeral directors twice a year, bringing wine, cigars, or other appropriate gifts along with information cards offering special rates for group dinners. His approach is rewarded by business from out-of-town families who are unfamiliar with area eating places.

Evaluating Results. Evaluating the results of sales and promotional efforts can reveal successful strategies and areas needing improvement or new action plans. Action plans should be monitored on a monthly or quarterly basis. An "action calendar" is an effective way to keep track of activities and results. This calendar maps out sales, advertising, and public relations activities month by month. It allows the marketing and sales team to identify the time of year to approach each market. It also enables the sales manager to spread

---

Action Plans:
New Year's Eve in Vienna

Action plans may involve publicity. Money spent on publicity can generate wide interest—and future bookings—as evidenced by the success of one promotion sponsored by the Hyatt Regency Grand Cypress in Orlando, Florida.

This special event, a "New Year's Eve in Vienna," is a black-tie extravaganza that transforms the property's ballroom into a "European palace" and the property's grounds into a "winter wonderland." Sixty tons of snow are imported for the event, and guests are transported to the "Viennese ball" in horse-drawn carriages. The evening includes a five-course Austrian dinner served by food servers attired in traditional Austrian costume, and entertainment by members of the Florida Symphony Orchestra.

Creative promotions such as this one can be supplemented by strategically placed advertisements in local newspapers and in publications read by prospective guests in key feeder cities.

---

the workload and assign salespeople to specific solicitation dates. Periodic meetings of the catering sales staff will help ensure that goals and objectives are met for each market segment targeted.

Catering Sales

There are a number of different strategies used to sell food and beverages. While the majority of catering sales result from conventions and meetings sold by the property's sales office, catering department salespeople in midsize to large properties are responsible for selling to local meeting planners and other local clients (in conjunction with sales office staff). In this section we will look at the strategies used by catering department salespeople to increase food and beverage sales.

Developing Leads   A major factor in the success of catering department sales efforts is the development of leads that will supplement banquet sales generated through the sales office. There are four basic ways to generate function sales:

- In-person soliciting
- Telephone soliciting
- Sales letters
- Responses to inquiries

In-Person Soliciting. Personal selling involves contacting the owners of businesses frequented by members of a targeted market segment. The catering director may call on public relations firms to attract business from cultural organizations, for example. Or, as mentioned previously, the catering director or a catering department salesperson may call on the owners of jewelry stores, bridal boutiques, or photography studios for wedding business

---

Action Plans:
Theme Parties

Property banquet sales can be boosted with a little creativity. The Hyatt hotel chain, a leader in developing creative banquets, has developed several innovative approaches to boost banquet sales.

Theme-design sets have been introduced at the Hyatt Regency Cambridge across the river from Boston, Massachusetts. Three designs are available—Oriental, Mediterranean, and Caribbean—for a rental cost of $500 each. Meals to match these themes are available.

Theme parties are the specialty of the Hyatt Regency Maui in Hawaii. One of the favorite themes is a M*A*S*H Bash that features an elaborate set including an officer's club, a mess tent, an infirmary, and an operating room flanked by an assortment of jeeps, machine gun trolleys, and ambulances. The guests are issued dog tags and fatigues or surgical gowns and are hustled through a chow line featuring beef goulash, Yankee pot roast, fried chicken, and beans. Alcoholic beverages are available from IV tubes, a USO show is presented, and the highlight of the evening is the arrival of a helicopter flying in the "wounded" for treatment!

Additional parties offered by the Hyatt Regency Maui include a Great Gatsby Garden Party, a Shogun party, and a '50s party. Other Hyatt properties offer innovative parties such as the Chicago street party, an original creation of the Chicago Hyatt. The Chicago street party features a re-created Southside playground complete with a basketball court, break dancers, and music videos.

Any property regardless of size can come up with innovative ideas that will be popular with guests and employees alike, but it takes a team effort for a theme party to be successful. The chef must create a menu that will complement the theme, the beverage manager must plan drink specialties and novel ways to serve drinks, and the banquet manager must develop a setting—complete with props—that will be cost-effective as well as add to the atmosphere of the party.

---

referrals. Photographers are an excellent source of information regarding family reunions, wedding anniversaries, and other family social activities.

Property tours can be used in conjunction with an outside solicitation program to promote the property to local corporate sources and civic organizations whose members can provide future business (Rotary Club, Kiwanis, Chambers of Commerce, and so on).

Telephone Soliciting. Telephone soliciting is another excellent way to develop leads. Selling over the phone involves far less time than in-person visits. If the catering director has hired a sales-oriented staff, it can make most of these calls, freeing the catering director for other duties.

Sales Letters. Sales letters are another effective way to build business. Sales letters can be categorized as form letters or personalized letters. Form letters are most commonly used by the sales office to solicit out-of-town convention and meetings business, while the catering department usually writes personalized letters to solicit local business. Writing a personalized letter does not mean the property cannot use a format that is easily modified; today's word processing capabilities make it easy to "personalize" a letter by changing names, adding a date, or mentioning facts gained through stories in the press or other sources.

A sales letter should be targeted toward the prospective client; the requirements of a meeting planner will be far different from those of a wedding party, and letters should be prepared accordingly. But, no matter what target market is selected, the letter should attract the prospect's *attention*, create an *interest* in and then a *desire* for the product, and give the prospect a means to take *action* (a telephone number, invitation to stop by for a visit, and so on). This is known as the AIDA formula, discussed in greater detail in Chapter 12.

Responses to Inquiries. No matter what type of inquiry is received, it is important to determine pertinent information about the client, his or her organization (if applicable), and function needs *before* trying to make a sale. Inquiries are made in writing, by telephone, or in person.

Written inquiries. A written inquiry from a prospective client should not be answered in writing! A telephone call will reach the client (who has probably written to a number of properties) much faster.

Another reason for replying by phone is that letters from prospective clients are rarely specific. Few letters include the client's exact specifications. Will the function be formal or informal? What is the budget limit for the function? Does the potential client expect special services or setups? By talking to the client over the phone, the catering director or salesperson can determine exact needs, give details about function rooms and banquet menus, and negotiate terms. If a written communication is needed (a letter or proposal to be submitted to a board, for example), it can then be tailored to address specific needs and concerns.

Telephone inquiries. Telephone inquiries from clients must be handled quickly and efficiently in order to ensure that business is not lost. A potential client who is put on hold—or transferred from one department to the next— will usually try another property. To avoid this problem, the catering director can leave instructions with the switchboard that all calls should be put through to him or her without delay, and without asking the caller what he or she is calling about. While this may be somewhat inconvenient at times, it is important to remember that one of the primary responsibilities of the catering director is to generate business—he or she must be available.

If it is impossible for the catering director to be available at all times, catering salespeople can handle banquet inquiries. At the very least, the clerical staff can be trained to take routine information (name of caller, type of function desired, preferred date, etc.) and assure the caller that the catering director will return the call as soon as possible.

In order for inquiry calls to be handled efficiently, the function book and other information should be readily available (sample menus, room capacities, price lists, and so on). In addition, catering department salespeople must have the ability to obtain enough pertinent information over the phone from a prospective client to accurately quote prices, suggest serving styles, and book the request.

In-person inquiries. In-person inquiries should also be handled efficiently and hospitably. When someone drops in unexpectedly and inquires about function space, the following steps should be taken:

1. A member of the staff (the front desk staff if the person is asked to wait in the lobby, the catering staff if the person is shown to the catering department) should welcome the prospective client and offer him or her a seat.

2. The client's name should be taken and given to the catering director or a catering salesperson immediately. If there is going to be a wait (which many clients will expect due to the nature of walk-in calls), the client should be advised of the approximate time he or she will be seen.

3. The client should be offered coffee or tea and some reading material. The reading material should relate to the catering department—a photo album of previous functions, scrapbooks containing publicity features and photographs, brochures or information sheets, sample menus, etc. This type of material may answer some of the client's questions or give him or her a better idea of what is available.

Selling to Clients

The key to successful selling is putting yourself in the client's place. It is important to determine what area is most important to the client—menus, price, theme, and so on—and focus the sales presentation on that area. For example, a client who is staging a regional dinner and wants to impress company officials may be more concerned with the menu and the type of service than with the cost. The catering director could meet the needs of the client—and increase banquet revenues—by suggesting three different levels of service:

"Mr. Johnson, our property offers three different types of functions—each featuring a superb sit-down meal. The difference is in the level of service. Our standard service is one server for every 20 persons, our first-class service provides one server for every 15 persons, and our regency or premiere service offers the ultimate in personal attention by providing one server for every ten persons."

Since the client in the example above has already expressed an interest in impressing company officials, chances are he will choose the regency service. This forced-choice suggestive selling can be used for all inquiries, whether the client's concern is primarily for upgraded or budget service. Given alternatives, the client will often "trade up," especially if alternatives are presented in the right way—that is, as answers to specific needs or concerns.

Another way to sell function space is to offer a tour of the facilities, preferably when the ballroom or an appropriate function room is set up. It is far easier for the client to picture a successful event if he or she has seen the facilities, decorations, and table service that will be used.

Experienced hoteliers report that less than 5% of catering sales are made on the first contact. Catering department salespeople will need to follow through with additional contacts to ensure that business is booked. Since new business is so difficult to book, catering departments rely heavily on past business—clients who know the product and are satisfied. In many catering departments, sales efforts are focused more on these repeat clients than on developing new business, but, whatever the business mix, it is important to develop an efficient filing and trace system to service catering accounts.

Catering Sales Procedures. As with group guestroom sales, all catering inquiries should be recorded using a catering inquiry form, whether the inquiry is from a new client or a previous one (see Exhibit 8.5). The top part of the form lists the name of the organization, the address, the telephone number, and the name of the contact person. There is usually a space to record the type of function, the date and time of the proposed function, and the number of people expected to attend. The middle portion of the form is used to determine the action to be taken: Does the client want additional information? Is he or she asking for a definite date? On the bottom of the form is a section that specifies the materials to be sent to the client (menus, additional information sheets, a confirmation letter, and so on).

Before taking action on a request or inquiry, it is necessary to check the function book to determine if space is available (see Exhibit 8.6). Since the function book is generally kept in the sales office, it is wise to have the catering department and sales office in close proximity. If the date of the function is tentative, the booking can be entered in pencil and an alternate date may also be penciled in. Information entered includes:

- Name and telephone number of the individual responsible for the function

- Name and type of function

- Hours of function

- Number of persons expected to attend

- Status (tentative or definite)

- Initials of the sales representative who made the booking

- Initials of the person making the entry in the function book and the date entered

- Type of setup(s) required and rates quoted

- Estimated time for setup, breakdown, and cleanup

In addition, any other hotel space used (hospitality suites, the pool area, etc.) should be noted. Many properties have separate function sheets for each public room in addition to the overall function book to ensure optimum use of all function space.

After the inquiry has been noted and the function tentatively or definitely placed in the function book, a file is created for the client. This file includes all information pertinent to the account: details of telephone calls, written inquiries and return correspondence, contracts, etc. And, as in group guestroom sales, a trace system should be established to facilitate additional contacts.

The tickler or trace file, as we learned in Chapter 3, divides the current year into monthly segments, with daily divisions for the current month. A tickler file is useful in catering sales since it may take four or five contacts with a new account to close a sale, and because existing accounts are the backbone of catering sales.

Past accounts, as we have noted, are fertile fields for future business, and files from previous functions should be updated periodically. To facilitate this process, files can be separated into "repeat" and "non-repeat"

Exhibit 8.5 Sample Catering Inquiry Form

RMI

EXAMPLE

TIME: _____2:35 P.M._____   SALES MANAGER: _____SS_____

DATE: _____3/9/xx_____

CATERING INQUIRY

ORGANIZATION: _____Carter/Hale Wedding_____

ADDRESS: _1414 E. 14th St., Anywhere_   STATE: _____AZ_____   ZIP: _____81414_____

NAME: _Mrs. Andrew Hale_   PHONE: _____262-2626_____

TITLE: _Mother of the Bride_

BUSINESS POTENTIAL

TYPE OF FUNCTION: _____Wedding Reception_____   TIME: __7 p.m.-12:30__

NO. OF PERSONS: ___175___ DATE: ___8/22/xx___

ALTERNATIVE DATE: _____None_____

GUEST ROOMS: _____5_____   ROOM RATE: _____(current rack)_____

Have you ever used the Ramada Anywhere?   No, but

Where are/were functions held? _____Neighbor had her reception here last year._____

ACTION: _____X_____   TENTATIVE BOOKING

_____   DEFINITE BOOKING

_____   FUTURE BUSINESS

MENU ACTION:

    TO BE MAILED: YES _X_ NO ___   MENU _____Wedding package_____

    OTHER: _____

FOLLOW-UP BY: _____3/18_____   HOLD SPACE UNTIL: _____4/9_____

REPORT ON FOLLOW-UP - LOST DUE TO (check one):

    SPACE RELEASE POLICY _____

    PRICE _____   NO SPACE _____   SPACE NOT SATISFACTORY

                                                        (reason below)

    OTHER _____

    NO EXPLANATION GIVEN _____

CHECK LIST

ENCLOSURES REQUIRED FOR LETTER(S) CHECKED OFF:

BUSINESS CARD	X
CATERING MENU BROCHURE	X
MENU PRICE LIST ONLY	
LETTER	X
CREDIT APPLICATION	
RACK BROCHURE	
AIRPORT TRANSPORTATION BROCHURE	
A/V SHEET	
WEDDING INFORMATION	X

Catering Administration Manual

This type of form can be used for all kinds of inquiries—written, telephone, or in-person—and serves as an information base for the client's file. Note that the form makes provision for potential business (tentative booking, definite booking, and future business) and provides a space for following up the account.

categories; the non-repeat files (weddings, companies that have gone out of business, etc.) should be placed in a "dead" file, but the repeat files should be organized into the tracing system for periodic action.

Exhibit 8.6 Sample Function Book

ROOM	A.M.		P.M.	
IMPERIAL	Organization		Organization	
	Function		Function	
	Time	Number	Time	Number
	Tentative	Confirmed	Tentative	Confirmed
	Engager		Engager	
	Booked By	Type Set Up	Booked By	Type Set Up
SALON ROOM	Organization		Organization	
	Function		Function	
	Time	Number	Time	Number
	Tentative	Confirmed	Tentative	Confirmed
	Engager		Engager	
	Booked By	Type Set Up	Booked By	Type Set Up
BOARDROOM	Organization		Organization	
	Function		Function	
	Time	Number	Time	Number
	Tentative	Confirmed	Tentative	Confirmed
	Engager		Engager	
	Booked By	Type Set Up	Booked By	Type Set Up
CONVENTION REGISTRATION OFFICE	Organization		Organization	
	Function		Function	
	Time	Number	Time	Number
	Tentative	Confirmed	Tentative	Confirmed
	Engager		Engager	
	Booked By	Type Set Up	Booked By	Type Set Up
THEATRE OF PERFORMING ARTS	Organization		Organization	
	Function		Function	
	Time	Number	Time	Number
	Tentative	Confirmed	Tentative	Confirmed
	Engager		Engager	
	Booked By	Type Set Up	Booked By	Type Set Up
TOWER-CAMELOT POOL	Organization		Organization	
	Function		Function	
	Time	Number	Time	Number
	Tentative	Confirmed	Tentative	Confirmed
	Engager		Engager	
	Booked By	Type Set Up	Booked By	Type Set Up

The function book must be kept up-to-date to ensure that maximum use is gotten from function rooms. When a date is requested, a member of the catering department checks the function book for the day and time requested. If the inquiry date is open, an entry (either a tentative, a hold, or a definite commitment) is made in the function book for the date and time requested. In addition to the time the room will be in use, each entry includes the name of the organization requesting the room, the name of the contact person, the type of function, and the salesperson's name. When confirming or denying that function space is available, it is vitally important to check the times that the space is booked. A small function can often be booked between other functions.

Most past accounts should be approached several months prior to their previously scheduled function date. Many companies, associations, and clubs stage banquet functions at the same time each year, making it easier to set up a trace file for these accounts. The catering director or a catering salesperson can call the past account's contact person, tell the client that the catering department is preparing a schedule of events, and ask if the client would like to rebook.

If the client responds negatively, it is important to find out why the account has been lost. If a specific reason is given, the catering department staff can look into the problem. After a week or so a representative from the catering department can send a letter thanking the client for his or her suggestions and informing him or her of steps taken to remedy the situation. The following week, a personal call should be made. At that time, the catering department representative can again thank the client for his or her suggestions and invite the client to take a firsthand look at the improvements that have been made. If the client is still adamant about using another property, the account can be filed and followed up in another year or two.

Whatever the type of account—new or repeat business—no inquiry should be dropped without final resolution. If business is lost, a lost business report should be filed; if business is canceled, the tentative entry should be removed from the function book, and a lost business report filed; if business is booked, a definite status should be entered in the function book, a confirmation letter sent to the client, and further arrangements made.

Planning the Function

After a date has been confirmed, the catering director or salesperson must work with the client to plan the function. Most properties use a banquet/catering checklist to ensure that all requirements are met for both meeting and food and beverage functions (see Exhibit 8.7). This checklist can be used for telephone and in-person contacts, and will help build client confidence in the department's thoroughness as well as provide instructions for the proper management of the function.

It is important that the client know just what is available: a dinner, for example, may be sit-down or buffet-style, formal or informal, set with round banquet tables (called "rounds") or rectangular tables. The number of people expected, the theme or atmosphere desired, and the client's budget will all play a part in the final decision.

Catering directors or salespeople who put themselves in the client's place can make use of suggestive selling to both increase revenues and ensure a successful function. A meeting planner, for example, may be worried that a luncheon won't finish on time; a buffet or a simple menu can be suggested so that the meal can be eaten quickly. Coffee breaks a couple of hours before the luncheon or serving the dessert at an afternoon break are other time-saving suggestions that can (1) help build the meeting planner's confidence that the meeting will be successful, and (2) increase sales of profitable food items as well.

Menus. Providing banquet menus that are cost-effective yet appropriate for the function is an important responsibility of the catering director. At some properties this is handled by the food and beverage director, although the catering director, working with the client, has the option of creating custom menus.

The catering director should try to sell banquet menus that can be prepared at different stations throughout the kitchen. A menu featuring cold hors d'oeuvres, cold salads, and deli plates puts the burden of preparation on one station; a combination of hot and cold hors d'oeuvres, a cold salad, and a conventional meal would spread the preparation out. For this reason as well as others, the catering director should try to sell banquet menus that have already been developed whenever possible. A variety of tempting menus can be created (see Exhibit 8.8). With pre-developed menus, costs are already known, while custom meals may require extra staff and costly ingredients. If a custom menu is requested, however, the catering director should consult with the chef for suggestions to keep costs as low as possible. A food cost chart may also be helpful when customizing menus.

Exhibit 8.7   Sample Banquet/Catering Checklist

```
┌─ RMI
│                        BANQUET/CATERING CHECKLIST
│
│  I.  MEETING                              _____ PA System (other than existing
│                                                 hotel system)
│      1. Time:_____           _____ Type _____
│      2. Location: _____           _____ Size _____
│      3. Expected Attendance: _____    _____ Video Recorder/Player
│      4. Set Up:                                  _____ Type/Player-Recorder
│         _____ Classroom                                (circle one or both)
│         _____ Theatre                            _____ 3/4" VTR - Price
│         _____ U-Shape                            _____ 1/2" BETA - Price
│         _____ Hollow Square                      _____ 1/2" VHS - Price
│         _____ Other _____            _____ Other
│         _____    _____ Monitor(s)
│                                                  _____ Size
│      5. Speaker Requirements:                    _____ Color _____
│         _____ Headtable                                _____ Price _____
│               _____ Size                   _____ Advent Screen _____
│               _____ #Ppl                         _____ Size _____
│               _____ Draping                            _____ Price _____
│               _____ Other _____          _____ Other_____
│         _____     _____
│         _____ Tabletop Podium
│         _____ Standing Podium              7. Registration Requirements:
│         _____ Risers                       - _____ Time _____
│         _____ Other _____        _____ Set Up:
│         _____            _____ Draped Table(s)
│      6. Audio Visual Requirements:                 _____ Chair(s)
│         _____ Hotel Provide                        _____ Telephone
│         _____ Client Provide                       _____ Message Board
│         _____ Delivery Time                        _____ Wastebasket
│         _____ Set Up Time                          _____ Signage
│         _____ Screen(s)                            _____ Other
│               Size _____        8. Coffee Break Requirements:
│               Price _____              _____ Times _____
│         _____ Projector(s)                         _____
│               _____ 16MM - Price                   _____
│               _____ 35MM - Price                   _____
│               _____ Lens Size - Price              _____ #Ppl
│               _____ Overhead Projector - Price     _____ Location _____
│               _____ Acetate Roll - Price    9. Breakout(s)
│               _____ Grease Pencils - Price         _____ Time _____
│               _____ Other                          _____ #Ppl
│         _____ Other                                _____ Location _____
│         _____ Microphones - _____ Stands           _____ Set Up _____
│                            _____ Table             _____ Audio Visual Requirements
│                            _____ Floor             _____
│               _____ Lavalier - Price              10. Meeting Room Charge _____
│               _____ Handheld - Price              11. Shipments_____
│               _____ Other
│               _____ Mixer - Price                 12. Security _____
│         _____ Flip Chart - Price                  13. Reader Board Posting Policy:
│               (includes 2 markers and 1 pad)       _____
│                                                    _____
│
│
└─ Catering Administration Manual
```

This form is designed to aid the catering director or salesperson in determining specific client needs. This form can be used when dealing with the client face-to-face or over the telephone, and can be customized to include pertinent details for individual properties.

In order to keep food costs down yet still offer attractive menu selections, the following factors must be considered:

Exhibit 8.8   Sample Creative Banquet Menu

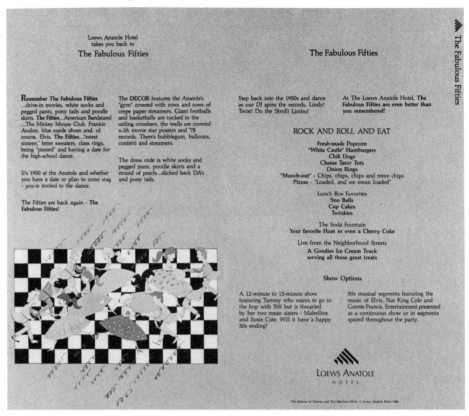

A banquet menu doesn't have to be ordinary. This banquet menu from the Loews Anatole features a taste of "The Fabulous Fifties." While this may be considered a "theme" menu, it is just as easy to develop a creative banquet menu around regional specialties or tastes.

Courtesy of Loews Anatole, Dallas, Texas.

- Client preferences
- Food costs
- Labor costs

Client preferences. Knowing the regional food preferences of an area and having access to local foods can help keep costs low while providing palate-pleasing menu selections. It is also important to keep the client's preferences or background in mind. When serving Jewish groups, it is necessary to know about kosher laws and how they apply to menu planning and other aspects of food and beverage operations. Some senior citizens may have difficulty with a menu that features steaks, corn on the cob, and other difficult-to-chew food. And health-conscious groups may not want to indulge in rich desserts.

Food costs. When developing banquet menus, it is essential to choose foods that retain good flavor, texture, and appearance even when produced in volume. Food items that are inexpensive but can still be sold at a good retail price (chicken, vegetables in season, etc.) should be included in banquet menus.

Labor costs. Labor costs fall into two categories: food preparation costs and food service costs.

Food preparation costs can vary greatly. A filet mignon and a beef Wellington entrée may require the same amount of beef, but the latter dish requires extensive preparation time. It takes one person to put prime rib in the oven, set the temperature, and take the cooked meat out, while an elaborate chicken dish may require the skills of three chefs or assistants. Food preparation costs must be taken into account in all areas: appetizers (melons must be cut and seeded while tomato juice is only poured); entrées (a chicken dish may keep costs down, but a simple beef dish may produce extra revenues); and desserts (fancy cakes require much more labor than a simple dessert like ice cream).

Food service costs vary depending on the type of service requested:

The most common form of banquet service is *plate service*. Plate service requires a large kitchen and serving staff for a short service time. The food is plated in the kitchen. Cold food may be plated ahead of time and stored in large roll-in refrigerators or in five-tiered carts called Queen Marys. Hot food must be plated at the moment of service, and is sometimes served from a number of stations set up in the kitchen.

With *Russian service,* food is served from platters or other large dishes, and sufficient food for one table is placed on each platter. One food server serves the meat and sauce while another serves the potato and vegetables, so a large labor force is needed.

Buffet service is suitable for all types of meals and all types of functions— from informal breakfasts to formal dinners served in silver chafing dishes. Hot and cold foods are attractively displayed, and guests walk up and help themselves. Service personnel may be required to assist—carvers at dinner meals, omelet-makers at breakfast buffets, and so on—but labor costs are reasonably low.

Pre-set service is sometimes used for lunch meetings or for other occasions when time is short. The first course (a cold soup, salad, or appetizer) is set on the table before guests sit down; in some cases, the dessert may also be pre-set. While this type of service may be necessary at times, pre-set food is rarely as attractive as food that is set in courses during the meal.

Receptions or cocktail parties typically feature *butler-style service.* Hors d'oeuvres are placed on platters and circulated among the guests by servers.

A combination of service styles is often used for wedding receptions or corporate dinners. Many wedding receptions feature a buffet of appetizers and then a sit-down dinner. Another common combination is having the first course and dessert served by servers, with a main-dish buffet.

Seating arrangements may affect service style and prices and should be determined before plans are finalized. The typical seating arrangements for a banquet function feature either rounds (tables five feet in diameter are most commonly used) or eight-foot rectangular tables. Other factors that will influence the choice of service style include:

- Size of room and tables
- Type of function
- Number of people attending

Beverage Plans. In addition to food, alcoholic beverages are a part of many functions. Properties may use one or a combination of the following popular beverage plans to provide alcoholic beverages.

Cash bar. At a cash bar, guests pay cash to the bartender who prepares their drinks. Sometimes a ticket system is used at a cash bar for control purposes. With this system, guests pay a cashier for their drink and are given a ticket to present to the bartender. The food and beverage manager generally sets drink prices, which can be the same as or different from normal selling prices. Frequently, management will reduce drink prices from the normal lounge rates in order to attract beverage business.

Host bar. With a host bar, guests do not pay for drinks; rather, the host is charged, either by the drink or by the bottle. If by the drink, bartenders and/or cashiers must keep track of every drink served. This can be done by using tickets, ringing drinks up on a register, or keeping a tally sheet. If the host is charged by the bottle, the cost of every bottle consumed or opened is assessed to the host.

Charge by the hour. This plan involves establishing a fixed beverage fee per guest per hour. Obviously, arriving at an accurate estimate of the number of drinks guests will consume in an hour is extremely important. While an estimate that will apply to all groups is not easy to make (a health- or weight-conscious group will probably consume less alcohol than a fraternity, for example), a rule of thumb used by some major food and beverage departments is three drinks per person during the first hour, two the second, and one and a half the third. The number of drinks per person must be multiplied by an established drink charge to arrive at the hourly drink charge per person. As managers use the hourly charge system, they will obtain their own specific information that will assist them in setting hourly charges for future events.

Finalizing Arrangements. Once the menu, beverage plan, and other arrangements have been set, the catering director or salesperson must complete a banquet event order (BEO), also called a banquet function sheet or banquet prospectus. This sheet acts as a final contract for the client and serves as a work order for the catering department. The form includes the time and place of the function, physical arrangements of the function room, menu (foods are listed in the sequence in which they will be served), prices quoted for the menu items, beverage requirements, special requests, service notes (number of staff, special costumes, and so on), personnel required (servers, cashiers, checkroom personnel, and so on), tax and gratuity, payment arrangements, and guarantee clause.

A guarantee clause requires groups booking food functions to give the hotel a count of the expected attendance prior to the function (usually 48 hours in advance). This count is the minimum expected or "guaranteed" attendance; the group is charged for their guaranteed number even if actual attendance falls below the guarantee. Most hotels will agree to set tables for a percentage above the number guaranteed in order to accommodate additional guests. Many properties set for an additional 10%, others hold to 5%. The guarantee clause is important because it helps to control labor and food costs.

Managing the Function

As noted earlier in the chapter, the banquet manager is primarily responsible for the management of the actual function, and supervises room arrangement, service personnel, and service procedures (see Exhibit 8.9). It is his or her job to see that the instructions on the function sheet are followed and that food is prepared and served at the designated time.

The banquet manager should make sure the function room is set up as far in advance as possible, and that extra or "dummy" tables for up to 10% over the guarantee are set up (if the number of expected guests exceeds the guarantee, time will be saved if tables are pre-set). A bulletin board in the service area outside the function room also helps to facilitate pre-function preparations. The bulletin board should list the name of the group, the time the function-room doors should be opened, the names of food servers and other service personnel needed, the menu that will be served, what items can be pre-set (if any), service assignments, and special notations (wait to clear tables until after the speaker has finished a presentation, dancing is scheduled between the dinner and dessert courses, and so on).

Just prior to the function, the banquet manager should check to be sure that the dessert is ready to serve, the appetizers or "starters" (fruit cups, etc.) are chilled and ready to serve, and that tables are properly set. He or she should also check with the chef to ensure that food preparation is proceeding on schedule, and advise the chef of any last-minute changes in the number of guests.

During the function, the banquet manager should be present to see that everything is going smoothly, that the order of service is followed properly (see Exhibit 8.10), and (in some cases) to present the bill to the client and thank him or her for the opportunity to serve the group. Thanking the client is the first step in following through on the account.

Following Up Accounts

Follow-up service is an important step in building a base of repeat clients. Immediately following the function, a thank-you letter and an evaluation form should be sent to the client. A notation should be made in the tickler file and a follow-up note sent if the evaluation is not received within a specified length of time. While it is not a replacement for having checked on the success of the function in person, an evaluation form is an important source of feedback, both on the positive and negative aspects of service (see Exhibit 8.11). Any negative information can be used to correct flaws in service or avoid a similar problem with other clients, while positive comments can be a source of encouragement for catering department employees.

If problems occurred, adjustments in charges may have to be made; at the very least, a letter of apology is in order. The client should be given a reason to try the property again and recommend the property to business associates and acquaintances.

Other Food and Beverage Sales

While banquets are important sales, there are a number of other food and beverage functions that can increase catering department revenues. The following list suggests a few of the opportunities a creative catering director has to serve guests, create repeat business, and increase sales.

Exhibit 8.9   Sample Job Description for a Banquet Manager

Banquet Manager

1. Supervises and directs all catering food and beverage functions.
2. Supervises all banquet service personnel. May also supervise setup and maintenance staff if not supervised by a convention service manager.
3. Schedules service personnel for food and/or beverage functions.
4. Supervises room setups and implementation of special instructions from the catering office.
5. Prepares payroll and maintains records for service personnel.
6. Inspects catering facilities and equipment as required.
7. Works with the catering director to implement innovative services and/or to make changes in policies and procedures.

Unlike the catering director, whose job is primarily administrative and sales-oriented, the banquet manager is responsible for the actual management of functions scheduled by the catering department. Although a banquet manager's duties will vary depending on the size and organizational structure of a property, this excerpt from a sample job description gives an example of typical responsibilities.

Creative Coffee Breaks

Meeting planners may forgo lunch or dinner breaks and opt instead for coffee breaks. The catering department can build business by offering a selection of creative coffee break items rather than the usual Danish and coffee. The property can charge more for unique selections while building client goodwill.

One alternative to the typical coffee break is a theme coffee break. Examples include a New York Deli coffee break—vegetable juice, lox and bagels, cream cheese, jellies, and cream sodas; and a Mexican coffee break—exotic fruits and juices, Mexican pastries, and so on. Coffee breaks can also feature unusual house specialties—hot spiced cider, a variety of breads, dried fruit and assorted nuts, and so on.

Cocktail Parties

Cocktail parties are an excellent way to generate revenues at a low cost. Most cocktail parties involve a host or cash bar and simple hot and/or cold hors d'oeuvres. Such parties require little in the way of setup time (many cocktail party settings require only a few chairs around the room). When taking orders for cocktail parties, the catering director should determine the purpose of the party, budget limits, and method of pouring drinks (measured or as requested).

Special Functions

There may be occasions when special promotional packages are offered by the hotel's sales office for weddings, family reunions, and so on, and the catering director acts as a consultant for the client. While events such as weddings may not lead to immediate repeat business, a well-staged event may result in extensive word-of-mouth advertising. When planning a wedding, for example, the catering director should offer options as part of the package: tuxedo rental services, limousine services, special dressing rooms for the bride and the wedding party, photography services, a complimentary honeymoon suite, and so on.

Exhibit 8.10   Sample Order of Service

1. The head table is always served first, no matter what type of service is ordered.

2. The appetizer should be placed on the table just before or as guests are seated. Appetizer dishes should be cleared away before salads are served if the party is small; for larger parties, service is faster if the salad is placed on the left side of the plate immediately after placing the appetizer.

3. All appetizer dishes, bar glasses, empty salad bowls, and salad dressings should be removed before serving the entree. If cracker baskets were placed with the salad course, they should now be replaced with bread baskets.

4. The entree should be served, more water poured, and the beverage served.

5. Coffee can be served throughout the entire course of the meal.

6. Entree dishes should be cleared from the table and water glasses filled.

7. Before serving dessert, all items not needed should be removed from the table. A dessert utensil, coffee spoon, glass of water, and beverage cup or glass should be the only items on the table when dessert is served.

8. The dessert should be served.

9. Dessert dishes should be removed, and additional coffee and/or water poured.

10. Ashtrays should be kept clean throughout the meal.

This is a typical order of service followed in serving a banquet. This order may vary in certain circumstances—the dessert may be served following a speaker's presentation, and so on—but service should always be handled as efficiently and quietly as possible.

Other special functions may include requests for special kosher service or requests for menus to meet dietary restrictions. When preparing for these types of functions, the catering director and kitchen staff must pay close attention to special requirements for purchasing and preparing foods.

Meeting Room Sales

Meeting rooms are usually sold by salespeople in the hotel's sales office who sell group guestroom business to corporations and associations, although at some large properties a separate convention department may solicit meetings and convention business. However meeting room sales are handled, it is important to understand the dollar value of meeting room space, and to keep these points in mind:

1. The amount of revenue that can be generated relates directly to the amount of space available. By arranging for the most effective use of meeting room space—for example, meetings following meetings in the same room rather than a banquet function following a meeting—costs can be kept down and more space can be sold.

2. Selling the least desirable space first increases maximum space usage. If the least desirable space is sold, it is far easier to sell the desirable space at a later date. If the desirable space doesn't sell, the previously booked meetings can be moved into the prime space.

Exhibit 8.11 Sample Evaluation Form

RAMADA® — SERVICE CRITIQUE —

Group Name: _____ Date of Function: _____

Type of Function: _____

	Excellent	Good	Fair	Poor	Comments
REGISTRATION					
EMPLOYEES' ATTITUDES					
Banquet Staff					
Sales & Catering Staff					
Restaurant Staff					
Front Desk Staff					
Telephone Operators					
Bell Staff					
Housekeeping Staff					
RESTAURANT					
Food & Beverage Quality					
Food & Beverage Service					
LOUNGE					
Beverage Quality					
Beverage Service					
BANQUET FUNCTION					
Room Appearance					
Food & Beverage Quality					
Food & Beverage Service					
MEETING ROOM FUNCTION					
Room Appearance					
Equipment					
Lighting					
Temperature					
Reaction of your guests					

ADDITIONAL COMMENTS: _____

_____

_____

_____

A thank-you letter and an evaluation form should be mailed to the client as soon as possible after the function. An evaluation form helps the catering department determine the quality of service provided, uncover any unsatisfactory areas, resolve any difficulties, and compliment the staff on a job well done.

Courtesy of Ramada, Inc.

3. "Holds" that reserve space for all day or all evening should be questioned; few meeting planners need rooms for an entire day or evening, and a few hours of "dead" time can be used for another meeting.

4. Selling activity should be targeted to times when business is slow. Meeting rooms will practically sell themselves during peak periods, so selling activity should be aimed at valley and shoulder periods.

At large properties, a convention service manager may set policies on selling meeting rooms, while at a smaller property the sales director or manager may deal with this aspect. In either case, it is important to note that meeting rooms were often provided free of charge in the past if a banquet was involved; today, however, there is a trend to charge for meeting rooms even if the group uses banquet facilities. This makes it even more important to provide clients with the services they require.

Types of Meeting Rooms

Meeting rooms fall into three basic categories:

1. Exhibit halls

2. Ballrooms for large meetings and/or banquets

3. Conference meeting rooms

The type of room used will depend on a variety of factors: the type of meeting, the number of people expected to attend, the size and layout of the room, and special requirements (audiovisual equipment, access to freight elevators, and so on). A meeting planner may also be interested in such room features as ceiling height, the location of electrical outlets, proximity to elevators, the location of exits, the number of doors and windows, and the presence of pillars or other obstructions.

Meeting Room Setups

There are various meeting room setups that can make the best use of space while still meeting the client's needs (see Exhibit 8.12):

1. Theater (also known as cinema or auditorium) style—Chairs are set up in rows (with aisles) facing the head table, stage, or speaker's podium.

2. Senate style—Same as a theater setup, except chairs are placed in a semi-circle rather than in rows.

3. "V" shape—Same as a theater setup except that chairs are placed in a "V" (the base of the "V" begins at the center aisle).

4. "U" shape—Tables are set up in the shape of a block-letter "U"; chairs are placed outside the closed end and on both sides of each leg. This setup is also known as a horseshoe setup.

5. "T" shape—Tables are set up in the shape of a block-letter "T" and chairs are placed around the outside.

6. Hollow square style—A series of tables is placed in a square with a hollow middle; chairs are placed around the outside.

7. Schoolroom—This is perhaps the most common setup. Tables are lined up in rows (one behind the other) on each side of an aisle. There are usually three to four chairs to a table (depending on table size), and all tables and chairs face the head table, stage, or speaker's podium. This is sometimes called a classroom setup.

Exhibit 8.12 Sample Meeting Room Setups

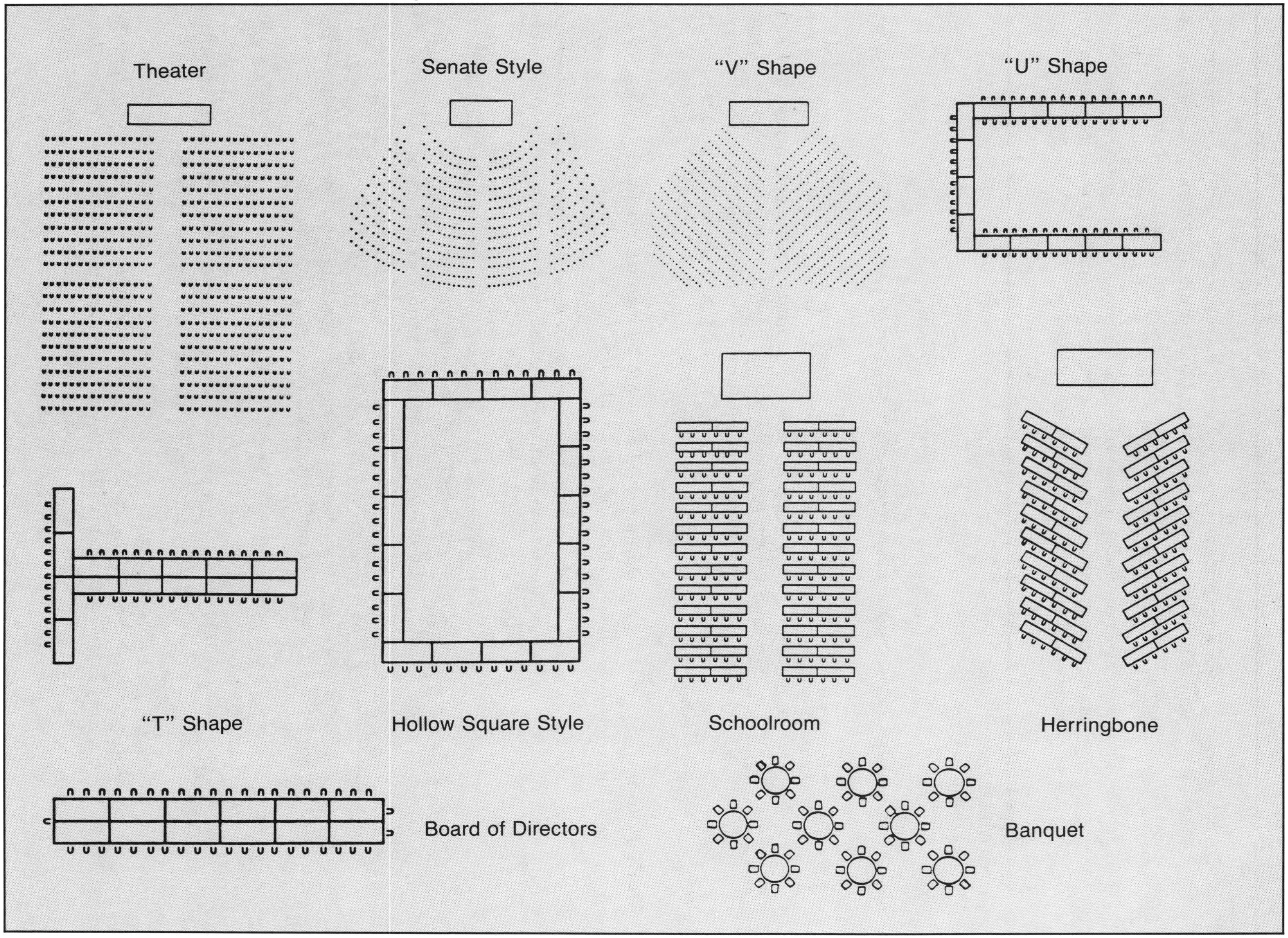

"U" Shape

"V" Shape

Senate Style

Theater

Herringbone

Schoolroom

Hollow Square Style

"T" Shape

Banquet

Board of Directors

Source: Adapted from Convention Liaison Council, *The Convention Liaison Council Manual*, 4th ed. (Washington, D.C., 1985), pp. 40–41. Reprinted with permission.

8. Herringbone—This setup is similar to a schoolroom setup except that tables and chairs are arranged in a "V."

9. Board of directors—This is a popular arrangement for small meetings. It calls for a single column of double tables with seating all the way around.

10. Banquet—Rounds are used most often for food functions. As mentioned, the most popular round is a five-foot table which seats eight to ten people. An eight-foot rectangular table may also be used, set in a "U" shape setup, "T" shape setup, or other setup that accommodates the needs of the group.

The type of setup used will affect the capacity of a meeting room, so it is essential that salespeople be knowledgeable about room capacities under all possible configurations. Most properties provide detailed scale drawings of each meeting room which include physical characteristics and room capacities (see Exhibit 8.13). Simple formulas for determining room capacities for three common setups are given below:

1. Theater—With this setup, a room's square footage should be divided by six. For example, if a room is 20- by 30-feet (a total of 600 square feet), the seating capacity would be 100 persons.

2. Schoolroom—A room's square footage is divided by eight with this setup. Total seating capacity may vary, however, if wide traffic aisles, exhibit space, or additional furniture is requested. In these cases, one square foot (or more, if a large exhibit area will be used) should be added per person—in other words, square footage would be divided by nine or more.

3. Banquet—With this setup, a room's square footage should be divided by ten, whether the setup calls for rounds or rectangular tables. The resultant figure gives *maximum* seating capacity; in many cases, however, more room is desired per guest. This is especially true in the case of formal dinners, when additional place setting pieces and courses are required. For formal dinners, two square feet should be added per person—in other words, square footage should be divided by twelve.

Meeting room capacities are extremely important to meeting planners, and salespeople should be aware that the equipment required by a group often affects the room size and setup needed. Typical equipment offered by properties includes audiovisual equipment (microphones of various types, a PA system, overhead or slide projectors, and so on), speakers' equipment (flip chart stands, easels, blackboards), and accessory equipment such as portable stages and podiums.

Meeting Room Furniture   The choice of meeting room furniture is important to most meeting planners, and the types of furniture chosen will affect a room's capacity. While meeting room furniture can vary a great deal, there are certain types and sizes that are frequently offered by properties.

Exhibit 8.13 Sample Meeting Room Plans

CARAVAN EXHIBIT HALL

School Room Style Seating	Approx. 450
Theatre Style Seating	Approx. 800
Banquet Style Seating	Approx. 650

MONACO ROOM

School Room Style Seating	Approx. 250
Theatre Style Seating	Approx. 500
Banquet Style Seating	Approx. 300

Fluorescent Ceiling Lights
220 110 Outlets
Exit Lights
Electric Floor Outlets
Recessed Ceiling Lights
Wall Bracket Light Outlets
Telephone
Air Wall Room Dividers
Ceiling Speakers
Plumbing Outlets
Duplex Recp't. Outlets
Portable Transformers Available
Ample Stage Lighting
Rheostat Lighting
Movable Spotlights in Ceiling for Displays
Closed Circuit T-V Facilities Beside Telephone Jacks

Ceiling Height of Caravan Exhibit Hall — 13 Ft.
Ceiling Height of Monaco Room — 12 Ft.

HALL 8

REGISTRATION DESKS

SULTAN'S TABLE RESTAURANT

KITCHEN AREA

AMPLIFIER & SOUND EQPT STORAGE

DRES G RM

DROP

MOVIE SCREEN

STAGE

BAR

FREIGHT ENTRANCE & LOADING AREA

10 X 12 ft.

MONACO ROOM 41' x 102' Approx. 4182 Sq. Ft.

HALL

CARAVAN EXHIBIT HALL 48' X 184' Approx. 8,832 Sq Ft

Meeting room plans showing such details as exits, electrical outlets, telephone jacks, lighting, door openings, and ceiling heights are often requested by experienced meeting planners, and are an aid in making a sales presentation. Note that this drawing also presents the room's capacities for schoolroom, theater, and banquet seating.

Chairs. Most chairs used for meetings are 18 inches wide by 18 inches deep by 17 inches high. Stackable armchairs are slightly larger—usually 20 by 20 by 17 inches. Most folding chairs are smaller, and not as comfortable as upholstered chairs; folding chairs are generally used for last-minute overflow accommodations.

Tables. A standard table has a height of 30 inches and a width of either 30 or 18 inches. When seating is required on both sides of the table, the 30-inch-wide table is used. In common schoolroom setups, in which people sit on only one side of the table, the 18-inch width is sufficient. The 30-inch-wide rectangular table is used most frequently for head table seating, even though people are seated on a single side, and is also used for displays and exhibits. The 30-inch-wide table is the most versatile of all tables available, as it comes in four-, six-, and eight-foot lengths, making it easy to create a variety of total lengths by combining tables of different lengths.

Rounds are used for meeting sessions as well as many food functions, and are most often available in four-, five-, and six-foot diameters. For the most comfortable seating, the four-foot table can accommodate four to six people; a five-foot table, eight to ten people; a six-foot table, ten to twelve people.

Platforms. Folding platforms are often used to elevate the speaker's podium and the head table at banquets. The usual heights are six, eight, twelve, sixteen, and thirty-two inches; lengths fall into the four-, six-, and eight-foot range, and widths vary from four to six feet.

Booking Meeting Rooms

Once arrangements have been finalized, the salesperson can fill out a function book space request form detailing the client's meeting room needs. In some cases, space is placed on a tentative "hold" basis. It is important that a hold period does not extend beyond the time when the space can be sold if the commitment is not firmed up. To avoid this, an appropriate release date should be set.

Release Dates. When a large group such as a convention buys out the vast majority of the hotel's guestrooms, the group's request to hold all meeting rooms seems reasonable. But, in this case as well as in the cases of smaller groups, a release date should be set in the contract. The reason for this is simple: many groups estimate requirements for meeting space a year or more prior to the actual event, based on a rough outline of the convention program. As the convention draws nearer, extensive changes may be made. By setting a release date (usually 60 or 90 days prior to the event), meeting rooms can be released if they are not needed. This permits the hotel to sell this space to other groups—and illustrates the importance of having just one function book under one person's control.

In many instances, another group can be given a tentative booking if, as in the example above, a group seems to have reserved more space than it will need. If the tentative booking cannot be filled because it turns out the first group does indeed need all the space it reserved, the second group must be notified and a lost business report filled out.

Managing Meetings

While policies for managing meetings will vary from property to property, there are certain requirements that are followed almost universally. First, the rooms are set up well in advance if possible. This allows for any last-minute changes. Setup teams vary depending on a property's size; small properties may use house attendants, medium-size properties may rely on crews supervised by the banquet manager, and large convention properties may have special setup crews.

Most properties provide general meeting room accessories. These include draped head tables, ashtrays, and pitchers of ice water with glasses. If the meeting is scheduled to run more than two hours, setup personnel or food servers usually refresh the room by removing dirty or wet linens, straightening chairs, cleaning ashtrays, refilling water pitchers, and replacing glasses with clean ones.

Setup crews may also be involved in setting up exhibit booths or display areas. Many properties offer partitions that can be used to divide a room into smaller rooms or be opened to provide display or ballroom space. This option offers flexibility, and is popular with training directors who wish to divide meeting attendees into small groups after a general training session. Partitions also benefit the property by making possible better space control.

Putting a meeting of 20 persons in a room built for 100, for example, wastes space and cuts into profits; with the use of partitions, the room can be divided to accommodate several small groups at a time.

After a meeting, follow-up should be taken care of promptly—a thank-you letter and an evaluation form sent and traced. Providing hassle-free meeting space and personalized service can help ensure repeat and referral business and keep the meetings business profitable.

Discussion Questions

1. Why is the profit margin for banquets often greater than the profit margin for a hotel's restaurant?

2. What are two basic responsibilities of most catering departments?

3. What are the catering director's primary responsibilities?

4. What five steps should be included in a catering department's marketing plan?

5. Why should function room occupancy and activity statistics be tracked?

6. What are four basic ways to generate function sales?

7. The catering department usually writes what type of sales letter?

8. What steps should be taken with in-person inquiries?

9. What is the most common form of banquet service?

10. What are three popular beverage plans?

11. What is a guarantee clause?

12. What are some of the responsibilities of the banquet manager in managing a function?

13. Who usually sells meeting rooms?

14. Why should the least desirable meeting room space be sold first if possible?

15. What are some common meeting room setups?

INTRODUCTION: *Although a color ad is more expensive than a similar black and white ad, color ads and collateral materials are much more likely to attract attention. Color gives an ordinary ad "stopping power." A new property, or an existing property trying to penetrate a new market, would be wise to consider color when planning advertising strategy.*

In this section, we will look at some colorful alternatives to black and white advertising. Many of these ads have won awards in the Hotel Sales & Marketing Association International's annual advertising competition, and all are representative of the hospitality industry's growing awareness of the need to communicate effectively in today's highly competitive marketplace.

ABOVE: **Sandals – A Colorful Difference.** *This ad for Sandals is shown in black and white in Exhibit 17.1. Even a quick glance will show the enhanced appeal of the property's facilities when presented in color.*

LEFT: **Healthy Habit – Mouth-Watering Color.** *Like ads, menus are much more attractive in full color. This menu cover appears in black and white in Exhibit 7.5, and the difference in appeal is readily apparent. Whether foods are represented by artwork (as in this example) or in full-color photographs, diners are greatly influenced by colorful menu presentations.*

RIGHT: **The Peabody—Capitalizing on a "Ducky" Image.** *This ad campaign features the ducks that have been thoroughly incorporated into The Peabody's image as a grand hotel.*

ABOVE: **The Stanhope—The Fine Art of Advertising.** *The Stanhope in New York City is located directly across the street from The Metropolitan Museum of Art, the source for the painting used in the ad.*

RIGHT: **St. Andrews Country Club—"Tennis, Anyone?"** *The generous use of white space enhances this ad's appeal.*

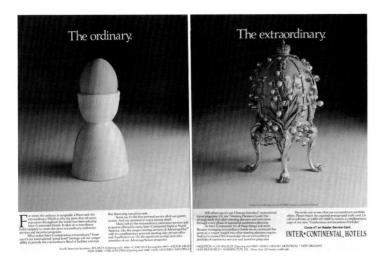

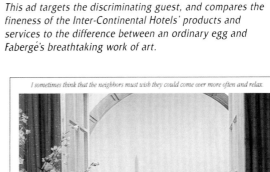

LEFT: **Inter-Continental Hotels – Eggs-traordinary Elegance.**
This ad targets the discriminating guest, and compares the fineness of the Inter-Continental Hotels' products and services to the difference between an ordinary egg and Fabergé's breathtaking work of art.

ABOVE: **The Hay-Adams Hotel – A Capitol Neighborhood.**
While color and ambience play an important part in this ad, this property also has the advantage of a historic location across from the White House.

LEFT: **The Portman – Picture-Perfect Weekends.** *This elegant ad, promoting weekend getaway packages, was designed to introduce and position The Portman as San Francisco's ultimate luxury hotel.*

"At Marriott, breakfast arrives in your room on time. Or it's on us."

"That's right. You enjoy a delicious, wholesome breakfast when you want it....or we eat the cost. *Guaranteed.*

How do we do it? Simple. Just order from our *Guaranteed Breakfast Menu* at any participating Marriott Hotel or Resort. Check off your order and the 15-minute time period during which you'd like to have breakfast. Then hang the menu on your doorknob before you go to sleep.

The next morning, as sure as the sun rises, you'll enjoy a piping-hot room service breakfast delivered within the 15-minute time period you selected.

We guarantee it.

Room service breakfast when you want it. Guaranteed reservations. Quick check-ins and check-outs. Superb accommodations. Marriott's high standard of service. All add up to an enjoyable, hassle-free stay.

After all, I have to make sure we do things right. It's my name over the door."

Bill Marriott

President, Marriott Corporation

800-228-9290

Marriott
HOTELS • RESORTS

ABOVE: **Marriott Hotels – A Self-Testimonial.** *This type of ad, which usually features the CEO, president, or general manager of a chain or property, is called a "self-testimonial," and is used by a number of properties.*

RIGHT: **Bonaventure Hotel & Spa – A Celebrity Testimonial.** *This is a striking example of an ad in which a recognized celebrity speaks on behalf of a property and its services.*

"Bonaventure is truly the ultimate spa." Linda Evans

If you believe that health, fitness and beauty are one and the same, experience Bonaventure: world class spa, 2 championship golf courses, 23 tennis courts, riding, swimming, racquetball, jogging, elegant accommodations, gourmet cuisine.

BONAVENTURE®
HOTEL & SPA

250 Racquet Club Road, Ft. Lauderdale, FL 33326   800-327-8090   In FL 800-432-3063   ® Bonaventure Hotel & Spa

RIGHT: **Embassy Suites – A Unique "Spokes-Cat."** *Embassy Suites chose an unusual celebrity to promote "The Suite Life." Garfield not only put people in a good mood, he also offered flexibility, since cartoon characters adapt readily from print ads to TV commercials.*

BOTTOM: **The Anchorage Seafood Restaurant—"Seafood and Service Worthy of a Standing Ovation."** *When the standing ovation comes from a colorful lobster, it becomes a real eye-catcher.*

LEFT: **United Nations Plaza Hotel—Here Comes the Sun.** *In addition to its vibrant colors, this ad's shape attracts attention.*

CENTER: **Longboat Key Club—Extraordinary Color.** *Subtle pastel colors help position this resort as an upscale property.*

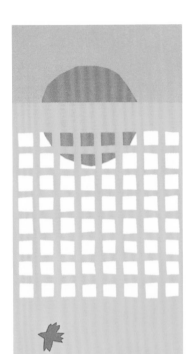

An Extraordinary Resort
Should Be Everything You've Heard.

Listen to what they're saying about Longboat Key Club and you'll hear some extraordinary things. Like the fact that we offer golf on two championship courses overlooking the Gulf of Mexico and Sarasota Bay. You'll learn about our tennis on 30 Har-Tru courts. And everything they say about the award-winning dining and exceptional service is true. But what really makes this such a memorable experience is the enticing combination of Four Diamonds, Four Stars and miles of dazzling white beach on a tropical island enclave. That's Longboat Key Club. For information and reservations, call **800-237-8821.** In Florida, **800-282-0113.** Or write 301 Gulf of Mexico Drive, Longboat Key, Florida 34228, 813-383-8821.

ENTER THE REALM OF THE EXTRAORDINARY   LONGBOAT·KEY·CLUB
An Arvida Resort Community

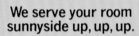

We serve your room sunnyside up, up, up.

Beginning on the 28th floor and moving up, each elegant room opens on a dazzling view of the city. Discover the small, stylish hotel where international travelers swim and play tennis high in the sky.

Weekend packages available.

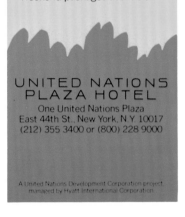

UNITED NATIONS
PLAZA HOTEL
One United Nations Plaza
East 44th St., New York, N.Y. 10017
(212) 355 3400 or (800) 228 9000

A United Nations Development Corporation project,
managed by Hyatt International Corporation.

Seafood and service worthy
of a standing ovation.

the Anchorage
Seafood Restaurant
I-35 North at Industrial Blvd. • Minneapolis, MN 55413
For reservations, (612) 379-4444 • Next to the Minneapolis Hilton

EASILY THE MOST MAGNIFICENT RESORT BUILT IN AMERICA IN THE PAST CENTURY AND A HALF.

Spacious rooms and luxurious suites. Wood-burning fireplaces and private balconies. Elegant restaurants and comfortable lounges. All, reminders of the era that so eloquently gave birth to The Sagamore.

Today, this magnificently-restored Victorian masterpiece welcomes guests with more luxury and activity than ever before. Six dining choices with moods from formal to casual. A sophisti-cated nightclub for entertainment and dancing. Year round, a variety of sports including tennis, racquet-ball, swimming, hiking, fishing, skiing, riding, and more. And an immaculately-groomed 18-hole championship golf course, designed by Donald Ross, nestled in our mountain hillside.

A complete spa offers exercise, sauna, plunge pools and massage. And just a half hour away is Saratoga, home of the famous race track and the renowned Performing Arts Center.

Luxurious amenities and modern convenience. The ambi-ance, architecture and hospitality of another era. The rolling green mountains of the Adirondacks and a sparkling blue freshwater lake.

Together at The Sagamore. A landmark in luxury since 1883.

THE SAGAMORE

AN OMNI CLASSIC RESORT & CONFERENCE CENTER
ON LAKE GEORGE, AT BOLTON LANDING, NEW YORK 12814

For reservations see your travel planner, call 518-644-9400 or 800-THE-OMNI.

into the new Kingsmill Conference Center, you will immediately
quality. The welcoming lobby is handsomely designed for efficient
level combines privacy and security with maximum versatility.
appointed with adjacent break-out space. Numerous lounges and
ption areas, a penthouse cocktail lounge and choice of three res-
offer refreshing options for relaxation and private dining. Most
soundproofing, adjustable lighting, 8-hour chairs, individual
al capabilities are all precisely as they should be to enhance

milarly beyond compare. From the Conference Coordinator
ails, to the Conference Concierge in constant attendance just
Kingsmill personnel exceptionally flexible, accommodating
conference.

CREATED FOR THE PEOPLE WHO DEMAND QUALITY.

THE KINGSMILL RESORT AND CONFERENCE CENTER
Williamsburg, Virginia

ABOVE: **The Kingsmill Resort and Conference Center.** *These colorful collateral materials were developed after extensive research to determine the priorities of meeting planners. The property received over 200 responses from its first month's direct mailing effort.*

RIGHT: **Saddlebrook—"Our Meeting Book is Great, But You Should See the Movie!"** *This colorful ad, which is targeted to meeting planners, is unusual in that it promotes another ad for the property—a video brochure.*

OPPOSITE: **The Sagamore—A Picture of Magnificence.** *This colorful consumer ad is targeted to the upscale pleasure traveler and features nature's own beauty as well as the created beauty of this restored Victorian resort on New York's Lake George. While the copy promotes the "rolling green mountains of the Adirondacks and a sparkling blue freshwater lake," the photograph of the resort is the ad's primary selling point. This ad is also an excellent example of reversed copy.*

Our Meeting Book is Great, but You Should See the Movie!

Call Convention Sales for Our New Meeting Brochure and Videotape.

(813) 973-1111

Saddlebrook

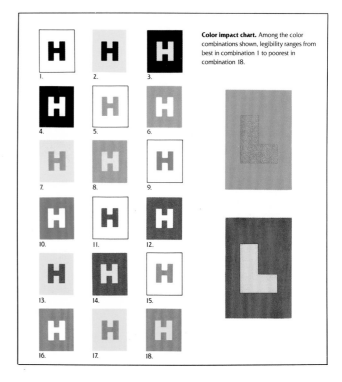

BELOW: **Outdoor Advertising – Colorful Combinations.** *This color chart lists eighteen commonly used color combinations. Color combinations should show contrast in hue and value; yellow and purple, for example, attract more interest than green and blue.*

Color impact chart. Among the color combinations shown, legibility ranges from best in combination 1 to poorest in combination 18.

ABOVE: **The Grove Park Inn and Country Club – Colorful *Innsights* to Build Business.** *A well-designed newsletter is an excellent way to build business through direct mail. These newsletters feature full-color photographs, news of special packages and promotions, and other items of interest to past and present guests.*

BELOW: **Outdoor Advertising – Promoting Hotels and Casinos, Las Vegas-Style.** *With dozens of hotels competing for tourist dollars, outdoor advertising in Las Vegas has to be unique. The California Hotel & Casino captures attention with its three dimensional tree that moves in the desert breeze.*

Part III

Advertising, Public Relations, and Publicity

Chapter Outline

I. Why Advertise?
   A. To Whom Does a Property Advertise?
   B. Advertising Goals
   C. Advertising at Small Properties
II. Types of Advertising
   A. Outdoor Advertising
   B. Displays
   C. Collateral Materials
   D. Print Advertising
      1. Newspapers
      2. Magazines
      3. Directories
   E. Direct Mail Advertising
   F. Broadcast Advertising
      1. Radio
      2. Television
      3. Video
III. Developing an Advertising Plan
   A. Deciding Where to Advertise
   B. Advertising Strategies
      1. Differentiation
      2. Segmentation
      3. Combination
      4. Frequency
      5. Consistency
   C. Budgeting for Effective Advertising
IV. Advertising Agencies

9 A Guide to Effective Advertising

There are basically two methods of reaching potential guests and clients: direct selling and advertising. While direct selling is the backbone of hospitality sales, you should recognize the importance of advertising as a supplement to sales efforts. Advertising can assist you by creating an awareness of the property *before* you make a sales call. Property advertising can produce a positive image of the hotel in the potential client's mind, and can generate interest in special services and promotions as well.

Because advertising is becoming more widely used in the hospitality industry, and because today many salespeople assist in making advertising decisions, it is important that you have an understanding of the various types of advertising available, their advantages and disadvantages, and how advertising decisions are made. In this chapter we will discuss what makes advertising such an important sales tool. In subsequent chapters we will look at the nuts and bolts of many types of advertising—from billboards and brochures to radio and television spots—and see how each can enhance the sales effort.

Why Advertise?

There are several reasons for advertising:

1. *Advertising reaches a vast audience.* Advertising—especially print and broadcast advertising—can reach thousands of potential guests and clients. Even advertising that is not targeted to a mass audience (brochures for meeting planners, for example) is seen by hundreds of people who may be sources for sales or sales leads.

2. *Advertising is relatively inexpensive.* While printing, column space, and airtime costs are not cheap, the cost per reader or listener can be quite low. When figuring advertising costs, however, it is important to weigh one major disadvantage: not every reader or listener will be interested in the property's message.

3. *Advertising can create a direct response.* Coupons, reply cards, and telephone numbers can be included in advertising to elicit responses. Invitations to call in or write for a reservation or more information

Industry Profile

G. Douglas Hall
*Vice President
Corporate
Communications
Four Seasons Hotels*

Douglas Hall began his business career with a Canadian advertising agency. After achieving the position of vice president there, he joined the Toronto office of Young & Rubicam, a multinational advertising firm. Hall was responsible for directing the advertising of such clients as General Foods, the Whitehall Laboratories division of American Home Products, Metropolitan Life, and Thomas J. Lipton (he spearheaded the successful introduction of Lipton Cup-A-Soup to the Canadian consumer) before acquiring Four Seasons Hotels as a client. Hall, who had no previous hospitality-industry experience, directed the development of the advertising that was ultimately to position Four Seasons Hotels as the leading luxury hotel group in North America. With this advertising Hall won the coveted Adrian Award, the Hotel Sales & Marketing Association International's highest honor for excellence in hotel advertising. It also brought him a job offer from his client, and today he serves as Four Seasons Hotels' Vice President—Corporate Communications.

"**O**f course I believe in advertising. But the key is to use it properly. I'm a firm believer in research. It doesn't always have to involve a large, expensive consumer study; research is often just listening. Listen to your hotel guests, listen to your competitors, listen to the people who report to you. I get some of my best ideas from listening to others.

While I knew nothing about operating a hotel, I had used hotels for years, and my packaged-goods background had disciplined me to be consumer-directed; that's the basis of all marketing. Tell your customers about the benefits they'll enjoy, not just the features you offer. And don't let the fact that thousands of people will see your advertisement deter you from speaking directly to the customer as if you were selling face-to-face. Good advertising copy talks to one person: your ideal prospect.

Selecting the media in which your advertising will appear depends on your target markets and where they live. Start with a plan based on your budget. I'm a great believer in the rifle versus the shotgun approach. It isn't wise to scatter your advertising all over; you'll have so few exposures to any one target segment that you'll make no impression. It's far better to pick a few publications that reach the customers you've targeted and advertise in them with sufficient frequency to ensure that customers see and remember your ad.

If you're selecting an advertising agency, think of it as a potential partner in marketing. Share all the information you have about your hotel, your customers, and the times when you need business—and the times you don't. Your long-term success is the agency's success!

There's an expression in the advertising business: clients get the advertising they deserve and good clients get good advertising. Good clients aren't pushovers. They're tough, but fair; demanding, but realistic in their demands. Your agency often understands your customers and how to reach them better than you do; your agency can also be the source of good marketing and operational ideas. "

get the reader or listener involved in the property and can open doors to future sales.

4. *Advertising demonstrates a property's competitiveness.* Because other properties advertise, it gives the reader or listener an opportunity to compare benefits and features. A property that can present superior benefits or answers to a reader or listener's needs can gain a competitive edge.

Advertising is an invaluable tool that can target those areas or audiences that have not yet been reached and offer additional information to those who already have a favorable impression of the property.

To Whom Does a Property Advertise?

The property's marketing plan, especially the first three steps (conducting a marketing audit, selecting target markets, and positioning the property), lays the groundwork for determining the type of advertising the property will use and the target audiences for the advertising effort. It is far better to concentrate advertising on a targeted audience than to spread it out to general audiences that may not have a need for the property's products or services.

Before the first ad is designed or the first script written, management must address the following questions to obtain a clear picture of the market(s) that would be most suitable for a property's advertising:

1. *What is management's perception of the property?* Does management see the property's products and services as luxurious or geared to middle-income travelers? What are the prime sources of income for the property? Business travelers? Leisure travelers? Group business? Does management have the statistics to back up these perceptions?

2. *What is the marketplace's perception of the property?* Questionnaires and telephone surveys are excellent sources of information about the public's view of a property. In one instance, for example, a Chicago luxury hotel found that respondents thought the hotel was a private club or that it catered to "high-society dowagers." After discovering the public's perception, the hotel was able to alter its advertising to promote its convention facilities and luxury services for businesspeople.

   In another instance, the Hyatt hotel chain positioned itself as a top-of-the-market chain, and reflected this positioning in its "A Touch of Hyatt" ads. Research two years later indicated that the positioning intimidated some buyers, causing them to think that Hyatt hotels were too ritzy for them. As a result of the research, a new ad campaign was developed to position the chain as a service and value-oriented property. Public reaction, and sales, improved (see Exhibit 9.1).[1]

3. *What is the property's positioning statement?* The property's positioning statement has a significant impact on the types and content of advertising and who the property will advertise to. The positioning statement is an important part of the property's marketing plan, and must be consistent with what the property has to offer. The positioning statement can be used in advertising to reinforce the property's message.

4. *Who are the property's target audiences?* Management has to take a hard look at target audiences in light of the property's positioning statement. Audiences with the maximum potential to respond must be selected for advertising efforts. If a property determines that 65% of its business comes from corporate groups, advertising dollars should be spent accordingly.

Advertising Goals

Although advertising can take many forms, it is used to accomplish the following goals:

Exhibit 9.1   The Importance of Positioning

This ad is an example of Hyatt's campaign to position itself as a service and value-oriented property.

1. Attract potential guests' attention and create product awareness.

2. Create an interest in potential guests' minds. This is not the same as creating product awareness; potential guests must become interested enough to want additional information.

3. Turn potential guests' interest into a desire to experience the property for themselves.

4. Generate action on the part of potential guests. This is especially important in the case of hospitality properties, which sell intangibles. Consumers have the opportunity to inspect tangible products before they make a purchase; they can see for themselves whether or not the product will be suitable for their needs. When buying an intangible product, however, they must base their decision on someone else's word; they are literally buying promises that their experience will be a good one. A hotel's advertising must show potential guests the benefits available from the hotel and sufficiently motivate them to respond to the message.

Advertising at Small Properties

Many general managers or directors of sales at small properties feel that advertising goals can be achieved without the assistance of outside sources, but, all too often, this just isn't the case. Effective advertising requires education and experience that few property managers can claim.

For best results, small properties should involve professionals at some point to ensure that advertising dollars are not wasted. For some properties, this may mean retaining a free-lance advertising specialist to assist with special promotions or specific advertising materials such as brochures or posters. Other small properties may benefit from retaining a small advertising agency that would welcome the property's account and work hard to produce results.

Whether a property chooses to contract a free-lance advertising professional, hire a small agency, or employ the services of an agency with branches in several cities, the property should be knowledgeable about the different types of advertising and the advantages and disadvantages of each in order to work well with advertising professionals.

Types of Advertising

There are several types of advertising commonly used in the hospitality industry—outdoor advertising, displays, collateral materials, print advertising, direct mail advertising, and broadcast advertising. Each type has strengths that can be capitalized on for generating name recognition, selling property features and services, or opening up new markets, but each also has limitations that must be considered before an advertising plan for the property is developed.

Outdoor Advertising

Outdoor advertising includes the property's sign and off-property billboards located along streets and highways. Billboards have the advantage of heightening awareness and recognition of the property, have a great deal of flexibility, and can attract impulse travelers. Disadvantages include the limited message that can be conveyed, the cost of production and maintenance, and the difficulty of measuring a billboard's effectiveness.

Displays

Displays include advertising materials such as transit cards and posters off the property in such places as buses and taxis, transportation terminals,

Advertising a Small Property

Michael Handlery, CHA, general manager of the 93-room Handlery Motor Inn in downtown San Francisco (half a block from Union Square), emphasizes amenities in his advertising. The three most popular, according to guest comment cards, are (1) free valet parking; (2) coffee makers in guestrooms; and (3) in-room food service. Other property features that find their way into advertising copy include: sauna, heated pool, in-room movies, remote control TV, electric shoe polishers, sun lamps, free morning newspaper, and special soap.

Handlery researches guest folios to find out where business comes from, then buys magazine advertising to reach the zip codes he wishes to target. *Time* magazine is a favorite medium—in regional editions, that is. He also advertises in regional editions of *Newsweek* and *TV Guide*, as well as, occasionally, the *Wall Street Journal*. Advertising in national magazines gives the message credibility, in Handlery's experience, and doesn't cost all that much if you can buy coverage for target markets only.

The following are four components in Michael Handlery's advertising program, with hints about how he rates each in effectiveness.

1. *Reciprocal Advertising.* Handlery uses reciprocal advertising with radio stations, concentrating on the Los Angeles/San Diego area and central California. Response: very good. And this advertising is inexpensive. Fewer than 50% of the room nights "traded" are used by the radio stations.

2. *Premiums.* Handlery, advertising in publications such as the *Los Angeles Times*, has offered special guestroom rates ($69.95 single or double with children free) plus gifts—a Parker pen/calculator set, for example—to guests during slow periods. Response: not worth it, considering the costs.

3. *Special Discount Rates.* Special discount rates during slack periods without a premium have been somewhat more cost-effective. But good recordkeeping is required to ensure that guests don't use the discounts when (1) business isn't needed, or (2) guests would be in the hotel with or without discount offers.

4. *Magazine, Directory, and Radio Advertising.* In addition to advertising in regional editions of the magazines mentioned earlier, Handlery advertises in regionally based travel publications such as *Sunset* and *Travel Age West*. Also used are national travel directories such as *Hotel & Travel Index* and *OAG TRAVEL PLANNER Hotel & Motel RedBook*.

   All radio and printed advertising is directed at zip code areas that represent lucrative present markets. Response to total advertising: good.

and trade shows. This type of advertising is especially effective at airports and trade shows: at airports, deplaning passengers may make last-minute lodging decisions, while visitors to many trade shows (such as shows for travel agents or tour operators) are already in the market for lodging industry products and services. Displays do have disadvantages, however. For example, many people arriving at transportation terminals have already made a lodging decision. And the cost of producing quality, eye-catching displays is high when you consider their limited (and often uninterested) audience.

Collateral Materials

Collateral materials include brochures, posters, fliers, tent cards, and specialty items designed to promote the property's products and services (see Exhibit 9.2). Collateral materials can be used as in-house and off-property promotional tools. Unlike newspaper and magazine ads, which are usually designed for a mass audience, special collateral materials can be designed for smaller, more specific groups such as travel agents, tour operators, and in-house guests.

Key chains, shoehorns, and other specialty items which show the property's name (and, if possible, address and telephone number) are also considered collateral materials. Specialty items offer name recognition and a reminder of the guest's experience at the property. They also make excellent promotional pieces for travel agents, tour organizers, and meeting planners. A complimentary wall or desk calendar, for example, can keep the property's name in front of a meeting planner. One Holiday Inn that sought to book more honeymooners designed a special apothecary jar for travel agents. Imprinted with the words "Honeymoon Kisses" and the property's name, the jar was filled with chocolate kisses and hard candy and distributed to travel agents at trade shows or delivered to their offices to serve as a decorative desk item—and a reminder to book newlyweds into the hotel.

There are disadvantages to specialty item advertising, however. In most cases, the small size of specialty items makes printing a long message impossible. Other disadvantages include the lengthy time required for production and delivery of the items, the difficulty in measuring results generated through the use of specialty items, and the poor distribution rate (many items are thrown in drawers or kept by guests rather than being passed on to other potential guests).

Print Advertising

Print advertising media include newspapers, magazines, and directories.

Newspapers. Newspapers are used by the hospitality industry more than any other medium, and with good reason (see Exhibit 9.3). Newspapers are:

1. *Widely read.* Since newspapers are widely read, they are an ideal medium to reach the local community and can be a good source of word-of-mouth advertising. Special interest and ethnic newspapers can be used to open or penetrate markets.

2. *Targetable.* Newspapers offer a variety of sections which can be used to target specific readers. In addition to the Sunday travel magazine or section (the most effective place for selling leisure travel), there are business sections in which to promote meeting facilities and corporate services, society pages to promote function space, and food and entertainment sections to promote the property's restaurants and lounges.

3. *Flexible.* Newspapers offer a choice of ad sizes and the opportunity to place last-minute ads that promote newly created packages or special offers.

4. *Inexpensive.* Last, but certainly not least, is the advantage of low advertising rates. Low rates permit frequent ad placement, which can generate name recognition. In addition, many local newspapers

Exhibit 9.2   Sample Collateral Material

This poster was used by the Red Lion for in-house promotion.

offer special local advertiser rates or bulk rates, enabling a property to place more ads for less money.

With all these advantages, it may seem that newspapers are the perfect advertising medium. But there are drawbacks. Few people actually read the entire newspaper, so ads must be carefully placed. Newspapers can be cluttered with advertisements, causing some ads to get lost or be negated by placement next to undesirable advertising. Newspapers, for the most part,

Exhibit 9.3   Sample Newspaper Ad

This newspaper ad won the top award for single entry newspaper advertising at the 31st Annual HSMAI Advertising Awards Competition. The ad was complemented by direct mail advertising (see Exhibit 9.5) promoting weekend getaway packages.
Courtesy of The Ritz-Carlton, Boston, Massachusetts.

are thrown away, not saved—a disadvantage when even a great advertisement is usually forgotten after a day or two. Newspapers have a reputation for poor production quality: the paper stock is coarse, and color does not reproduce as well as in magazines or other publications. In fact, most newspapers rarely use color, and so are a less exciting medium visually.

Magazines. Magazines have the advantage of more readers per copy than newspapers. Most magazines are audited by an independent firm, and their publishers can provide a statement that gives information on circulation (broken down by paid subscriptions, number of copies available at newsstands, circulation of regional editions, and so on), subscription rates, advertising rates, and other information (see Exhibit 9.4). This data can prove invaluable for properties. Knowing that subscription rates are fairly expensive, for example, enables the property to target upscale consumers who can afford to purchase expensive magazines; knowing the number of paid subscriptions versus newsstand copies can help a property determine whether the magazine is going to a specific audience or is being read by the public in general.

Magazines can provide a sophisticated, exciting format for promoting a property. Magazine advertising offers:

1.   *A specific audience.* Since most magazines are targeted to a specific readership, the property has a better chance of reaching its target audience.

Exhibit 9.4 Sample Publisher's Statement

VERIFIED AUDIT CIRCULATION

13366 BEACH AVENUE, MARINA DEL REY, CALIFORNIA 90291-9990 • 213 306-1577

19___

MAGAZINE
PUBLISHER'S STATEMENT

___6___ MONTH PERIOD

ENDING _6/30/_ ___

1. HOTEL & TRAVEL INDEX
   NAME OF PUBLICATION

2. One Park Avenue   New York   New York 10016
   ADDRESS   CITY   STATE

3. Ziff-Davis Publishing Co. Inc.
   PUBLISHING COMPANY   ADDRESS   CITY   STATE

4. 1937   5. Quarterly   6. (212) 555-5625
   ESTABLISHED   FREQUENCY   TELEPHONE

7. **FIELD SERVED:**

   HOTEL & TRAVEL INDEX serves owners, presidents, partners, managers, sales
   and other executives of retail travel agencies and wholesale tour companies,
   corporate travel managers and other corporate executives and departments
   requiring travel information: airlines, railroads, steamships, and other
   transportation companies; hotel reservations departments; hotel and motel
   representatives and other travel related services.

8. **AUDIT OF CIRCULATION**

	PAID	CONTROLLED	TOTALS
Individual (subscriptions or controlled)	45,617		45,617
Group (paid only)		X X X X	
Association (paid only)		X X X X	
Single copy sales (paid only)		X X X X	
Bulk (paid or controlled)			

TOTAL AVERAGE (QUALIFIED) CIRCULATION PER ISSUE .

| 45,617 | | 45,617 |

TOTAL AVERAGE (NON-QUALIFIED) CIRCULATION PER ISSUE (advertisers, agencies, file, samples, etc.) . .   5,048

TOTAL AVERAGE COPIES PRINTED PER ISSUE.   50,665

9.

   Verification of Accuracy of Circulation List and Receivership will be determined
   in the Annual Field Verification and Market Research being conducted presently
   on the SPRING 19__ issue and which will be made a part of the Annual Audit
   Report.

Publisher's statements provide a circulation breakdown to help a property's marketing and sales staff determine if the publication will reach targeted market segments. The publisher's statement presented here also provides a circulation audit. Circulation audits, usually performed by a third party, are much more reliable than individual publication research, and break down circulation by qualified (paid) circulation and non-qualified circulation (free issues that are sent to advertisers, used as sample copies, and so on). While only the first page of the statement is shown, other pages provide invaluable information about the publication's distribution.

Source: *Hotel & Travel Index.*

2. *Longer life.* Magazines, unlike newspapers, are generally read more than once, and are often shared.

3. *Credibility*. Properties benefit from the image of the magazine in the minds of readers.

4. *Quality and readability*. Most magazines make extensive use of quality color production that can be visually appealing to readers. In addition, readers are usually reading material that is of interest to them, and are generally more likely to be receptive to high-quality advertisements in magazines.

There are disadvantages to magazine advertising, however. Cost-effectiveness can be lessened through duplication of readership if a property advertises in more than one specialty or trade magazine. The national nature of most magazines means that much of the circulation paid for is wasted if the property's markets are limited geographically. Since magazines come out less often than newspapers, the property's ad is seen less often. There is much less control over positioning in a magazine than in a newspaper. Magazine readers are not necessarily looking for travel/hotel information as they are when reading through the travel section of the local newspaper.

Two production factors also create disadvantages: the higher cost of production and the long lead time which restricts last-minute advertisements. The use of color, photographs or illustrations, and special artwork or graphic effects greatly increases the cost of magazine advertising, yet the property's ad may be placed next to a competitor's and be overlooked. This fact, coupled with the average 45- to 60-day lead time needed by magazines, may play a part in a property's magazine advertising decisions.

Directories. Hotel and motel headings in the telephone directory yellow pages are referred to over 124 million times a year by people actively seeking information about a particular property or service. But while 86% of people "shopping" for a property through the yellow pages follow up with a phone call, letter, or visit, the high cost of this type of advertising may be prohibitive for some properties.[2]

Business directories for the hospitality industry fall into two categories: hotel directories which list hospitality products and services, and trade directories that are targeted toward travel intermediaries such as travel agents, tour operators, and meeting planners. Business directory advertising reaches a consumer actively seeking hospitality products and services, and is designed to give readers enough information to recommend the property or make a booking.

Direct Mail Advertising

This print medium goes directly to the property's target audience, something that cannot be guaranteed by any other medium (see Exhibit 9.5). Despite the advantage of being able to mail a long illustrated message, the cost of direct mail to a small target audience can be quite reasonable. Direct mail pieces, especially letters, fliers, and simple newsletters, can be relatively inexpensive to prepare even if color is used. They are also trackable. Pieces may be coded or sent with reply coupons that ensure measurability.

Although direct mail may be produced professionally, many people still think of direct mail pieces as junk mail. Some people, in fact, are annoyed by direct mail advertising and may have a negative impression of a property that engages in it. In addition to this "waste" factor, direct mail can become costly if it is used to blitz large target markets.

Exhibit 9.5   Sample Direct Mail Package

WEEKENDS AT
THE RITZ-CARLTON.

A WARMER VIEW
OF WINTER.

AS WINTER GROWS NEAR, AND YOUR
THOUGHTS TURN TO GOING SOMEPLACE WARM,
MAY I SUGGEST PERHAPS THE WARMEST
PLACE IN NEW ENGLAND:
THE RITZ-CARLTON.

As General Manager of The Hotel, I would like to
invite you to share in some very special weekends we have
planned for our guests. Romantic weekends by the fire.
Weekends of fantasy and enchantment. Even a weekend
of social savvy for children.

Where could you find a more personal holiday gift, or
a more well-deserved reward for yourself than overlooking
The Public Garden? The Ritz-Carlton.

Please call soon for reservations or return the enclosed
reservations card. The Hotel Staff looks forward to your
visit. And we all wish you a most joyous holiday season.

Sincerely,

Sigi Brauer
General Manager

P.S. If you wish to present a Weekend to someone as a gift,
please reserve as soon as possible so we may send a per-
alized Gift Certificate in time for the holidays

This direct mail package, which included a cover letter, direct mail piece, reservations/order form, and reply envelope, was used in conjunction with The Ritz-Carlton's newspaper advertising (see Exhibit 9.3) to promote winter weekend packages to upscale potential guests throughout New England and New York.

Courtesy of The Ritz-Carlton, Boston, Massachusetts.

Broadcast Advertising   Broadcast media include radio, television, and video. For many years, this advertising avenue was overlooked by hoteliers for two reasons: cost and unfamiliarity. The cost factor included both the production of broadcast ads (especially for television) and the nature of the media itself. Unlike print advertising, broadcast advertising is not a form of advertising that can be kept and referred to. Therefore, to be remembered, the property's broadcast message has to be repeated frequently, often over several stations—which greatly escalates costs. Many hoteliers more accustomed to using the familiar print advertising methods hesitated to make a commitment of time and money to broadcast advertisements.

This is changing in today's highly competitive industry. Many hoteliers are turning to broadcast media to reach a nation on the go, and radio, television, and video advertising is becoming more popular.

Radio. Radio's greatest advertising strength is that it is heard by over 83% of the public daily. Nearly everyone in America owns a radio. Most American households average three radios, making radio one of the greatest saturation mediums available to the hospitality industry.[3]

Radio has many advantages:

1. It costs less to reach potential guests (on a cost-per-person basis) through radio advertising than through newspaper advertising.

2. The relatively low cost of radio advertising allows for frequent advertising and image-building in the community.

3. Radio can be targeted to specific audiences and is an extremely flexible medium.

4. Radio is one of the most effective media in regard to instant recognition and retention of a slogan or message.

5. Radio can be used to reach a variety of audiences in time periods when these audiences are listening.

Radio also has several disadvantages. There are many radio stations and it is easy for a property's message to get lost or become confused with other messages. There is no visual image to back up a radio ad; unlike print ads, radio ads cannot be saved and referred to at a later time. And, because of the widespread listening audience, radio messages must be broadcast over several different stations at frequent intervals for maximum effect.

Television. Through television, a property can give a total, "living" picture of the image it wishes to project. Since the message is both seen and heard, it is more likely to be retained by a segment of television's vast viewing audience.

While television is today's most popular saturation medium, many hoteliers forgo television advertising due to several disadvantages. First, there is the high cost of airtime and production. Unlike radio, which usually includes a bank of background music and announcers in the price of the advertisement, television costs are quoted for airtime only; the production of television advertisements can add thousands of dollars to the price quoted. And, despite the high cost of a television commercial, it is impossible to accurately target the audience. While commercials can be aired in specific time slots, there is no guarantee that the message will reach the targeted audience.

Video. Since we are living in the television age, it is not surprising that many hotels now have videotapes to help sell their property. Many lodging properties use video brochures in addition to their printed brochures when soliciting travel agents and meeting planners. A video brochure is a short (usually four- to six-minute) presentation of the property's features and services. Some properties also have video "magazines," longer videos shown on television monitors in high traffic areas at the property such as the front desk. And some properties are finding that a videotaped interview with a satisfied client is a great sales tool.

Developing an Advertising Plan

Because of the media clutter that exists today, careful attention must be given to both the purpose of advertising and the means that will most effectively communicate a property's message. An advertising plan should be developed that will enable the property to reach its selected target markets within a predetermined CPM (cost per thousand)—the cost of reaching 1,000 households or individuals. Once each target market or market segment has been categorized according to its need for advertising, the property must determine which advertising media will reach each target market, the best advertising strategies to pursue, and how much money will be needed to adequately advertise to each market (see Exhibit 9.6).

Deciding Where to Advertise

The media in which a property advertises will depend on the media's ability to reach the property's target audience(s). It may be far less costly for a property to place an ad in a local newspaper, but who will read the ad? Will it be read by locals who have limited needs for guestrooms instead of the meeting planners that the property hopes to attract? In this case, it would be far more cost-effective to place an ad in a trade journal or business directory, or develop a direct mail program for meeting planners.

In many cases, print and broadcast media can provide information on their readers and audiences which can assist a property in selecting media. Broadcasters can provide "reach and frequency" computer printouts that list the demographics of listeners. Most print media are able to provide detailed statistics regarding readership such as the publisher's statement shown in Exhibit 9.4. The property can also study publications to determine who is already advertising in them. A firsthand look at consumer and trade magazines, for example, can give invaluable insights into their quality, content, and readership. Is the content such that the property's advertising would benefit from the publication's credibility, or is the publication a poorly produced, controversial vehicle that would detract from the property's advertising?

Before deciding where to advertise, a number of questions should be asked. Which advertising media:

- Reach the largest number of potential guests at the lowest cost per guest?
- Can deliver an adequate selling message?
- Sell the property rather than merely identify or announce it?
- Can repeat the property's message on a frequent basis?
- Are flexible enough for special promotions?

Exhibit 9.6   Sample Advertising Worksheet

ADVERTISING WORKSHEET

Property: Ritz-Carlton   Date: September 1
Address: Newberry Street   Telephone: 555-1564
               Boston, MA   General Manager_____
                                                          Director of Sales_____

A.	Primary Objective	To sell 200 more weekend room nights in December, January, and February.
B.	Target Audience (Business people, families, diners, honeymooners)	Visitors traveling by car within three hours driving time; couples over 45 years old who no longer have to worry about babysitters or leaving their children. Primarily two income families desiring to get away with other couples.
C.	Unique Selling Points	Good value—offers several package alternatives including room, breakfast, and three course dinner. Stress "weekend package" as an ideal gift.
D.	Specify details to be included (prices, hotel facilities, location, nearby attractions)	Importance of spending time together. Complete attention, pampering. Relax in whirlpool, sauna, and exercise room. Complimentary breakfast in your room. Chilled bottle of Ritz-Carlton champagne awaiting arrival. Late check-out time on Sunday. Boston's only Five Diamond Hotel. Private Manager's Weekend Reception. Theatre district just steps away—Boston Pops Concerts. Historical attractions: Beacon Hill, Bunker Hill, The Tea Party Ship, Old North Church, Waterfront Marketplace, Charles River.
E.	Suggested Publications or stations (newspapers—local or urban area, radio, magazines, direct mail)	Suggested publications—local newspapers in urban areas within a radius of 200 miles. Advertisements should appear in the holiday/travel or amusement section of the newspapers. Place weekend break brochure in the envelope with confirmation slip to every business person booking a Thursday night stay. Message: "Why not spend a weekend break with friends." Direct mail to past guests in key geographic areas: Boston, New York, New England.
F.	Dates Advertising is to appear and frequency	Advertisements to appear once weekly beginning last week of December through end of February. Direct mail piece to be sent last week of November.
G.	Direct Response Required	[X] YES [ ] NO
H.	Any Other Information	Direct response—telephone number and address for reservations. Coupon for weekend brochure request.

An advertising worksheet makes it easier to develop ads and other promotional material by stating the objective, targeting the audience, and listing unique selling points of each promotion. This worksheet was used by The Ritz-Carlton for its winter weekend campaign (see Exhibits 9.3 and 9.5).

- Cover the property's targeted marketing areas or audiences?
- Offer the least "waste" coverage?
- Best fit the property in terms of image and prestige?
- Fall within the advertising budget?
- Are affordable without sacrificing other important media coverage?

When considering the last two questions, the property should take a look at three money-saving advertising resources: advertising agencies, reciprocal advertising, and cooperative advertising.

Advertising agencies offer expertise and experience in placing advertisements where they will be most effective. The low agency fee (often 15%) is usually paid by the media in which the advertisements are placed, saving even more advertising dollars for the property. (Advertising agencies will be discussed in more detail later in the chapter.)

Reciprocal advertising, also called "due bill" or "trade-out" advertising, is the exchange of hotel rooms (and sometimes food and beverages) for outdoor, newspaper, magazine, radio, and/or television advertising (see Exhibit 9.7). Reciprocal advertising can be especially effective for properties with limited advertising budgets. Properties can control how many unsold rooms can be used and when. A property may receive an additional return on its trade-out because participants in a reciprocal agreement often spend money in the property's other revenue centers. A radio station manager, for example, who is given use of the property's health club may stay for lunch, or a newspaper executive given a free room for the weekend may buy meals and drinks at the hotel. There is an added benefit to reciprocal advertising—the endorsements of publishers, advertising executives, and broadcasters are influential and their recommendation of the property to their peers and friends can prove invaluable.

Cooperative advertising involves advertising in conjunction with another advertiser. Cooperative advertising may involve advertising with a dissimilar business—for example, hotels teaming up with an airline or a car rental agency (see Exhibit 9.8); with a similar business (see Exhibit 9.9); or in conjunction with a local, regional, or state advertising campaign.

There are many advantages to cooperative advertising: the costs of advertising are shared, identification with another prestigious product or firm may increase sales, and co-op advertising is available in a number of media.

Cooperative advertising also has disadvantages. In the case of the three competing properties in Exhibit 9.9, advertising costs may be shared equally by the three properties but they may not receive equal patronage. Some advertising partnerships may prove inflexible in terms of meeting each other's needs. Lastly, cooperative advertising agreements may have conditions that are less than ideal for one or more of the participating advertisers. Perhaps the contract limits the advertising to a specific medium, or the property must limit its message to specified areas—the property can promote its convention capabilities but not its weekend packages, for example.

Advertising Strategies

An important part of any advertising plan is deciding on advertising strategies. The three strategic options most commonly used are differentiation, segmentation, and a combination of the two.

Differentiation. Differentiation emphasizes how the property is different from its competitors. In order to be effective, there must be meaningful differences—differences that are readily identifiable to potential guests. In using differentiation, however, properties should steer clear of a disturbing trend that has clouded hotel advertising in recent years: ads that boost the

Getting the Most from Reciprocal Advertising

There are a number of guidelines that should be followed in order to receive the most from reciprocal or "recip" advertising:

1. Try to set up the exchange on a one-to-one basis; i.e., an equal dollar-for-dollar trade based on each party's retail price. You may have to give $1.50 in value for each $1 received in a high-quality print medium exchange, but generally one-to-one is the rule. Radio airtime can usually be negotiated at a more favorable exchange rate than television airtime or print ad space.

2. When possible, exclude your peak periods of occupancy in the exchange. The idea of barter is to work off "unsold" room nights, so be sure your recip contract eliminates periods when you'd normally be doing full rack-rate business.

3. Consider making your recip arrangement good for *group* business only rather than individual room nights. You will have more control over what inventory is being used at what time. Most media are willing to go along with the group concept since they have sales meetings, rallies, and staff seminars in which bulk space can be used.

4. Try to trade whatever costs you *least*—rooms instead of food and beverage, tennis or golf lessons, rental equipment, etc.

5. Consider a 50–50 deal, in which each recip dollar spent at your property is matched by a cash dollar. Thus, half the bill is paid in a media exchange, the other half in cash. This kind of arrangement can be negotiated when the media outlet needs you more than you need it.

6. Make sure the recipients (media personnel) of your recip program can't sell your "credits" to other people. Your trade should be limited to specific personnel (station manager, sales director, key executives, publisher, etc.), and they alone should be eligible to use your facilities.

There are three accounting methods for exchanges:

1. You can issue a "script" certificate which, when redeemed, entitles the bearer to use your services; e.g., one night's accommodations or a credit line of $100.

2. A special credit card can be issued with a ceiling set at the amount of the reciprocal agreement.

3. Monthly statements can be exchanged showing credits used and balances remaining.

Whatever method you use, seek the simplest format which protects you against credit abuses and does not require excessive time to administer.

Source: Adapted from Howard A. Heinsius, "Reciprocal Advertising: Marketing Tool for the Eighties!" *Resort Management*, March 1982.

image of one property while knocking the competition. Far too many properties are making use of advertising claims that either directly or indirectly derogate other hotels or destinations, a technique that may discredit the industry as a whole.

Exhibit 9.7   Reciprocal Advertising

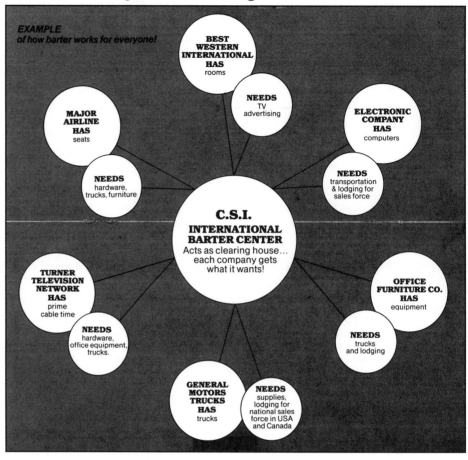

Many properties deal directly with the media to place reciprocal advertising, while others, including Best Western International properties, use a central clearinghouse to trade for advertising and other needs.

Courtesy of Best Western International, Inc.

Headlines such as "Don't Book Your Convention into a Tourist Trap" or "Some Resorts Resort to Anything" do little to promote either a particular property or the industry in general, and should be avoided if a property (as well as the industry) wants to establish credibility. Classic ads that feature positive positioning statements, a unique selling position such as an island location or guestrooms decorated with antiques or fine art, or themes that cast no aspersions on the competition are more effective in the long run.

Segmentation. A segmentation strategy can also be used to advertise the property. The basic premise of this advertising approach is that a target market can be carved up into several smaller segments. The business traveler market, for example, can be segmented into women business travelers, businesspeople who travel on extended trips, meeting planners who book business for large groups, teams of business travelers rather than individual business travelers, and so on. Once a segment has been identified, advertising can be developed to appeal specifically to it. Advertising that attracts a

Exhibit 9.8   Sample Cooperative Advertising for Dissimilar Businesses

In this example of cooperative advertising, Southwest Airlines and the Westin hotel chain have teamed up to present a promotional package. In this type of advertisement, the costs are shared by both advertisers, and both benefit from the prestige and following of the other.

woman business traveler would be totally different from advertising for a meeting planner, for example.

A property should carefully assess each market to determine if a segmentation strategy would be more successful than a general advertising effort to the entire market. If the property is already attracting a large number of women business travelers, for example, it may not be necessary to advertise to this segment of the business traveler market; advertising dollars may be better spent on general business traveler advertising or on a segment

Exhibit 9.9   Sample Cooperative Advertising for Similar Businesses

Located within the heart of San Antonio's economic center, we can offer you a convenient convention.

It's not often that competitors call a truce, but we've done just that for you. With our combined forces we can supply your convention with over 500 rooms, meeting facilities up to 1,000, 5 restaurants, 3 swimming pools and 3 cocktail lounges. All within minutes from San Antonio International Airport. Our location also puts our triple treat in the middle of San Antonio's economic hub. There's all kinds of shopping available from giant malls to tiny one-of-a-kind boutiques. Plus banks, major office buildings and national corporate headquarters within easy reach. So take advantage of a convenient location and the services and facilities of not one, but three fine hotels.

In this example of cooperative advertising, three hotels have produced a brochure to attract convention and large-meetings business. The three properties, all located within minutes of the airport, together offer what one individual property could not; all will benefit from overflow guests from any one of the other properties.

Courtesy of La Mansión del Norte, San Antonio, Texas.

of the business traveler market that is not staying at the property in acceptable numbers.

Combination. This strategy combines differentiation and segmentation. A specific market segment is selected to advertise to, and an attempt is made to differentiate the property from other properties by offering unique benefits which will be of interest to the selected segment. This strategy can work well for small properties, since small properties don't always have the wide range of products and services offered by larger properties or chain properties. A small property can focus on one of its assets (a rustic location, for example) and then advertise to a market segment that will be attracted to that asset. Market segments interested in a rustic location might include families, businesspeople who want to relax, and so on. This strategy can also work for any size property that has been rehabilitated or repositioned; the advertising strategy would focus on a particular aspect of the property (its restoration to its original condition, for example).

No matter what strategy is used, advertising must cut through the media clutter and promote the property in a creative, memorable, and cost-effective way. Two characteristics, frequency and consistency, are a part of all successful advertising strategies.

Frequency. It generally takes a number of exposures of a print ad or radio or television commercial to familiarize potential guests with the property's name or image and prompt them to respond. The frequency of a property's advertising will depend on the urgency of the property's message. A specific event or promotion, for example, will require a number of messages, placed within a relatively short period of time, to get the attention of the public. Advertising dollars for general promotion of the property can be concentrated during certain periods of the year when business is most needed, rather than being spent over an entire year.

Consistency. A property's advertising is far more effective if it has a consistent look and, in the case of broadcast media, a consistent sound. It is generally easier to recognize something than to remember it, and a property that positions its print ad elements (headline, illustration, body copy, pricing, logo, etc.) in the same order and uses ads of the same size will be recognized more often than a property that tries a different look with each of its print ads. When broadcast media are used, time frames, jingles or other sound effects, the announcer, and the message should be similar for easier recognition.[4]

Budgeting for Effective Advertising

Perhaps the most crucial part of an advertising plan is the budget. First it is important to note that advertising expenses are only a portion of the total budget for marketing and sales. While 3% to 6% of a property's revenues may be allocated to cover the total cost of the marketing and sales department, only about one-third of this amount will be spent on advertising (see Exhibit 9.10). The remainder of the monies allocated will be spent on salaries, office expenses, and other expenditures that supplement the sales effort, such as fees for reference materials, memberships in trade organizations, and so on.

Before a property can establish a workable advertising budget, management should be aware of a number of variables that will affect the kind of advertising budget that will be used by the property:

1. *The type of property.* The size of a property and the types of services and facilities it offers will greatly affect the amount of money necessary to effectively advertise the property. Typically, it costs far less to advertise a standard highway property than a luxury resort (see Exhibit 9.11).

Exhibit 9.10   Advertising Expenditures

	% OF MARKETING AND SALES BUDGET		
	MEAN	**LOW**	**HIGH**
TOTAL ADVERTISING EXPENSE	32.6	29.0	37.1
Print Media	12.9	9.6	18.9
Radio & TV	4.6	3.5	6.0
Outdoor	4.3	1.7	9.5
Other	10.8	10.3	14.9

Some of these figures are medians and do not necessarily add to the totals shown.

As a general rule, hotels spend an average of 3% to 6% of total revenues on marketing and sales. Of this amount, approximately one-third is spent on advertising. This table provides a breakdown of how typical properties might allocate their advertising dollars among the various advertising options available.

Source: Adapted from Laventhol & Horwath, *U.S. Lodging Industry—1986* (Philadelphia: Laventhol & Horwath, 1986).

2. *The competition.* A property's advertising budget will be greatly affected by the competition. Although an advertising budget should not be established simply to match funds being spent by competitors, the level of the competition's advertising activity helps determine how much of an advertising effort will be needed by the property to receive a fair market share in the area.

3. *The property's marketing objectives.* The advertising budget should be tied directly to the property's marketing plan. If the property wants to expand its facilities or target markets, management may invest more in advertising. If the property enjoys a comfortable guest base and is generating a steadily increasing flow of new guests, management may want to concentrate efforts on direct mail or in-house promotions, usually far less expensive than broadcast or national print advertising.

4. *Target markets.* The number and sizes of a property's target markets will affect the amount of advertising needed to reach potential guests. A hotelier who is targeting a regional market will spend less than one who is attempting to attract guests from across the country.

5. *Cooperative advertising opportunities.* As mentioned earlier, this type of advertising enables advertisers to share costs and stretch advertising budgets. In some cases, a property may tie into a community or state plan that promotes an entire area and its services. A case in point is the successful "I Love New York" campaign.

These variables will need to be considered before the advertising budget is developed. Like the general marketing and sales budget, the advertising

Exhibit 9.11   Advertising Expenditures by Type of Hotel

TYPE OF HOTEL	AVERAGE AMOUNT SPENT PER ROOM PER YEAR				
	Total	Print	Radio/TV	Outdoor	Other
City Center	$417	$187	$67	$23	$140
Airport	392	111	51	58	172
Suburban	361	115	48	62	136
Highway	266	77	28	76	85
Resort	593	302	96	22	173

Source: Laventhol & Horwath, *U.S. Lodging Industry—1986* (Philadelphia: Laventhol & Horwath, 1986).

budget requires the setting of objectives. Good planning ensures that advertising dollars are not thrown away in haphazard fashion. To get the most from advertising dollars, management should:

1. *Make sure the advertising budget conforms to the property's marketing plan.* The property's marketing plan details the property's overall marketing goals and objectives, and should be the basis of the advertising budget. If one of the property's marketing goals is to increase weekend business by 45%, for example, more advertising dollars should be spent on newspaper and magazine advertising than on in-house brochures.

2. *Target profitable market segments.* Some market segments bring more dollars into the property than others, and additional expenditures may be more cost-effective in the long run. Costly ads in consumer magazines that reach a small proportion of the property's guests may be a poor substitute for a series of ads, a direct mail campaign, or a distribution of promotional items that targets travel agents, meeting planners, and other travel intermediaries who can bring a great many guests to the property.

3. *Promote benefits.* No matter what a property decides to promote—its most profitable services; special values (weekend packages, corporate rates, and so on); special services such as VIP limousines; or the property's location—in advertising, as in sales, the property should promote its *benefits* rather than its features.

4. *Decide when to advertise.* Advertising costs are most effective when spread out into "campaigns." An advertising campaign is a series of messages on a given theme developed to reach an audience when it is most receptive to the property and what it has to offer. Preparing advertising budgets requires breaking down specific advertising campaigns and individual promotions into quarterly phases for best results.

5. *Research the budget options available.* As discussed in Chapter 2, there are a number of methods that can be used to develop a budget: percentage of sales, competitive parity, affordable funds, and zero-base. Each of these should be studied to determine which will work for the property.

No matter what budget method is used, it should be reviewed periodically. Advertising results should be analyzed on an ad-by-ad or campaign-by-campaign basis, and adjustments should be made immediately. An ad campaign's contribution to the bottom line will help determine whether shifts in strategies or media used by the property are necessary.

Advertising Agencies

Since developing an overall advertising plan or creating a single ad campaign within a workable budget can be a complicated process, many properties opt for professional assistance from advertising agencies. Advertising agencies can be extremely helpful in making media decisions that keep costs low. In addition, an agency will be expert in determining which media can showcase the property's message most effectively.[5]

Before a property selects an advertising agency, it is important that it first understand its own needs. Does the property need to create a new image? Are new ideas needed to reach present markets or to cultivate new target audiences? Is additional technical expertise required to develop effective, creative advertising?

Once its needs have been identified, a property can prepare a list of suitable agencies and begin the task of selecting one. A general questionnaire could help the property in the sorting-out process (see Exhibit 9.12). During its preliminary investigation, a property should ask for:

1. The full name of the agency and its address and telephone number.

2. The names and titles of key agency personnel and the nature of the agency's nearest office. Is it a branch? If so, where is the agency's headquarters?

3. The length of time the agency has been in business and financial information (annual reports, financial statements, an accounting of gross billings, and so on).

4. The percentage of media billings for:
   a. Newspapers
   b. Magazines
   c. Directories
   d. Radio
   e. TV
   f. Outdoor advertising
   g. Other types of advertising (collateral materials, direct mail, and so on).

5. The number of full-time employees who work at the agency. Is the agency large enough to meet special needs and yet small enough that the property will not get lost in the shuffle? Has the staff had extensive experience in the hospitality industry?

6. The number of clients the agency currently serves. Are there any accounts that might present a conflict of interest? What is the typical size of an account? Can the agency provide a list of several of its accounts for reference purposes?

Exhibit 9.12 Sample Advertising Agency Questionnaire

Background, Management Business Philosophy

1. When was your agency established? Is it part of a larger organization? If so, what is the name of the senior company and what degree of control does it exercise over your operations?

2. Please provide the names and titles of your principal officers and a brief résumé of each.

3. Do you or your organization handle advertising for any hospitality industry facility at the present time? If yes, please list the degree of involvement.

Personnel

1. Please submit an organizational chart of your agency showing its various departments and functions.

2. Provide the names of the people who would work on our account, including creative staff. Please submit a brief résumé of each and describe their talents.

Agency Size and Growth

1. What has been the growth rate in the past 5 years in terms of:
   (a) how many accounts do you currently service that are in excess of $200,000 gross billings yearly?
   (b) percentage change since previous year?
   (c) sources of billings, i.e., percentage from old accounts and percentage from new accounts?

2. Please list your accounts according to:
   (a) the year account was acquired.
   (b) national or regional assignments.
   (c) which office handles these accounts?

3. Where is your main office located? Where are branch offices located?

4. Indicate, by percentage, the degree of emphasis you place on the various services carried out by your agency with your current accounts.

5. In the past year, how were your billings distributed in dollars and percentages among the following:

Dollars	**Percentages**	
_____	_____	Newspaper
_____	_____	Consumer magazines
_____	_____	Radio advertising
_____	_____	TV advertising
_____	_____	Outdoor advertising
_____	_____	Other

Public Relations

1. What services in the area of public relations have you provided for your clients?

2. Do you have specific staff who handle these activities? If so, please provide a brief background on the key people.

Sales Promotion

1. Do you have a specific department or personnel to handle sales promotions?

2. What types of sales promotions have you prepared for your clients?

Marketing and Research Services

1. What ability does your agency have to plan and conduct target market surveys and other advertising research? Who are the key people in the research department and what are their backgrounds?

2. Describe the techniques of "advertising effectiveness research" that you have found to have been the most useful.

(continued)

Exhibit 9.12 *(continued)*

Compensation and Service Structure

1. What compensation structure would you prefer?

2. Please provide a copy of your agency-client contract with any changes or modifications you would suggest for our account.

3. Please provide a sample of contact reports and any other reports that you would provide to us on a regular basis.

---

7. The media the agency is advertising in. Can the agency provide a list of the media it has used (radio and television stations, newspapers, and so on), the contact persons at each media office, and statistics relating to media effectiveness?

8. Samples of advertising and collateral materials that have been used successfully in hospitality industry or other related-industry campaigns.

Based on the information gained from the preliminary investigation, a tentative determination of acceptable agencies can be made. A selection committee composed of key property staff (the general manager, the director of marketing and sales, the sales director, the rooms manager, and so on) should visit each of these agencies rather than having agency representatives come to the property. This serves two purposes. First, it involves property employees in choosing an agency, which will help commit them to maintaining a successful relationship with the agency after the selection. Second, it provides the opportunity to observe how the agency conducts business, the type of staff employed by the agency, and the agency's creative processes.

Although the first meeting with an agency should be kept informal, it is important. The following topics should be discussed as part of the visit:

1. Who specifically would work on the property's account if the agency were selected? Does that person have hotel/restaurant experience?

2. How willing is the agency to cooperate with the property in the things most important to the property: research, direct mail advertising, in-house promotions, and so on?

3. Is the agency willing to stick to the property's budget? Is the agency experienced in reciprocal or cooperative advertising?

4. How would the agency be compensated? Will the agency work for a fee, a commission, or a combination of both? Has the agency spelled out its rate schedule clearly and accurately? Are services and their costs covered individually?

Once the field has been narrowed to two or three agencies by this process, a formal meeting should be scheduled at the property with each agency. This meeting would include the presentation of the agency's final advertising proposal, and a sample presentation of what the agency would do for the property. A property should not expect this sample presentation to include speculative advertising promotions; it is unfair to ask for such without compensating the agency. Instead, the sample presentation should detail the types of advertising that the agency thinks will work best for the property, and include suggestions for brochures, direct mail promotions (if applicable), and other types of materials that the agency thinks should be used to promote the property. In many cases, this presentation is supplemented by examples of the agency's advertising that was developed for other properties, services, or products.

At this time, it is important to clear up any loose ends: how the agency would handle emergency situations, who would cover the account if the property's agency representative was transferred or left the firm, and how communication will be maintained between the property and the agency.

In an ideal situation, the advertising agency a property chooses to work with becomes part of the property's sales team—familiar with the marketing plan, aware of the property's positioning statement, and willing to work with the property to ensure that the property's image is presented as effectively and economically as possible.

Notes

1. Mel Hosansky, "Hyatt Slows Growth, Marketing Chief Says," *Meetings and Conventions Magazine*, May 1984, p. 52.
2. "The Effective Yellow Pages Ad," *Lodging Hospitality*, July 1979, p. 37.
3. Bess Ritter, "Radio Advertising," *Restaurant Hospitality*, November 1982, p. 105.
4. William Q. Dowling, "Getting the Most From Your Marketing," *Lodging Hospitality*, July 1987, p. 34.
5. Some of the material in this section was adapted from Tom McCarthy, "Selecting an Advertising Agency," *Hotel and Resort Industry*, October 1984, p. 36.

Discussion Questions

1. Why do hospitality properties need to advertise?

2. What are four advertising goals?

3. What are the advantages and disadvantages of using each of the following print media?

   a. Newspapers
   b. Magazines
   c. Direct Mail

4. What are the strengths and weaknesses of radio and television advertising?

5. What are some advantages of using cooperative advertising?

6. What are three strategic advertising options discussed in the chapter?

Discussion Questions *(continued)*

7. What two characteristics are a part of all advertising strategies?

8. What variables may affect the size and structure of the advertising budget?

9. What are some questions a hotel should ask during its preliminary investigation of an advertising agency?

Chapter Outline

I. Outdoor Advertising
    A. Property Signs
        1. Reader Boards
    B. Billboards
        1. Location
        2. Size
        3. Design
        4. Copy
        5. Maintenance
        6. Contracts

II. Displays
    A. Transit
    B. Trade Show
    C. General

III. Collateral Materials
    A. Fliers
    B. Tent Cards
    C. Brochures
        1. Design
            a. Match the brochure to the property
            b. Heighten the property's image with photos
            c. Use photos to sell
        2. Copy
    D. Specialty Items

IV. Conclusion

10 Outdoor Advertising, Displays, and Collateral Materials

In today's highly competitive market, outdoor advertising, displays, and collateral materials are an important part of the sales efforts of properties of all sizes.

Outdoor advertising is a catchall term that includes a property's sign, billboards, and other methods used outdoors to put the property's name and image before the public. This type of advertising is especially well-suited to motels because motels rely on passing motorists for a great deal of their business.

Displays are used primarily indoors to attract guests to the property. In this chapter, we will take a look at several options for using this type of advertising, including displays in transportation terminals and at trade shows, conventions, and other gatherings.

Collateral materials cover a wide spectrum of advertising pieces—from rack brochures to intriguing specialty items. Nearly every property uses collateral materials to support the efforts of its sales force.

Outdoor Advertising

Although posters may sometimes be used for outdoor advertising, in this section we will focus on the two most common means of advertising a property outdoors: property signs and billboards.

Property Signs A familiar property sign featuring the logo of a well-known chain often is a welcome sight to an undecided tourist in an unfamiliar area (see Exhibit 10.1). In addition to identifying and calling attention to the property, a property's sign can advertise the property's restaurant, lounge, function facilities, and other revenue centers. It can also be an effective public relations tool when used to welcome groups or promote a community charity campaign.

It is important to note, however, that many properties have very little input into their property sign, especially if they are part of a chain or have a franchise agreement which requires standard signs. Some lodging chains, such as Best Western International, Quality Inns, and Holiday Corporation, offer their members a choice of several standard property signs. But even these chains closely monitor property signs to ensure that members conform

Industry Profile

Donna Hicks was introduced to the hospitality industry when she worked as a wedding consultant. She served as director of sales at three diverse properties for over nine years. In addition to service at Inn on the Park and the Sheraton Inn and Conference Center in Madison, Wisconsin, and the Karakahl Inn in Mt. Horeb, Wisconsin, Hicks has actively participated in the Wisconsin Society of Association Executives, Meeting Planners International, Toastmasters International, the American Marketing Association, the Sales & Marketing Association International, Downtown Madison, Inc., and the Greater Madison Convention and Visitors Bureau. With a partner, Hicks recently founded Effective Hotel & Motel Management. She is looking forward to putting her expertise in communications, advertising, and sales to work for a number of clients.

**Donna D. Hicks,
CHA, CHSE**
*Co-Owner
Effective Hotel &
Motel Management*

"Is a billboard right for your property? The answer depends on your marketing objectives and the audience you plan on targeting with your message.

Special attention must be paid to billboard copy. Magazine and newspaper advertising has the advantage of being studied, while billboards are often seen with a fleeting glance. Billboard copy must be instructive but easily readable—and the audience should always be considered.

The cost of billboards will generally be related to the location and the number of people that pass that location on a daily basis. The higher the traffic count, the higher the cost. Lengths of outdoor contracts will also be a factor in determining monthly cost. Generally, a contract that can be negotiated for three to five years is more economical. However, the contract should allow for yearly review and include an 'escape clause' that protects against detours.

Billboards can offer imagery that's appealing and eye-catching. Brilliant colors are available for billboards, but it's important to consider changing climate conditions when choosing a billboard's background color. A white background would not be ideal for a billboard located in an area that has snow on the ground several months of the year.

The overall effectiveness of billboard advertising is difficult to measure. One method of monitoring is 'TAB,' the Traffic Audit Bureau, an impartial monitoring organization supported by advertising agencies and billboard companies. TAB verifies the number of billboards in a given market and their impact in that market.

Billboard advertising can be effective as directional or informational sales tools, as in the case of the two Madison hotels that I worked with. The billboards we had for the Sheraton were located on the interstate and featured Sheraton's logo, the exit number, the number of miles to the property, and directions. A second directional billboard was located after the interstate exit and gave final directions to the Sheraton. Our target audiences were tourists and corporate travelers.

Billboards utilized by the Karakahl Inn had to be more descriptive. Our logo was familiar only to locals and past guests, so the billboards had to convey the size of the property and its amenities. The Karakahl Inn was bypassed recently when a new highway was built around the village of Mt. Horeb. Since our directional highway billboards were not yet complete, our tourist traffic dropped significantly. But when the billboards were completed, tourist traffic increased just as significantly.

Billboard advertising can be effective. It offers an advertising message all day long, every day of the year. As with any type of advertising, creativity is important. An advertising image must command attention, and a good billboard must be properly placed after being properly created to be an effective advertising tool for your property.**"**

to graphic requirements and design specifications. Uniformity in property signs establishes consistency and brand identification throughout the country and, in some cases, throughout the world.

Independent properties are most likely to create their own property

Exhibit 10.1 Holiday Inn's Changing Image

Holiday Inn's "Great Sign," which featured a giant neon arrow (left), was originally designed to generate business from passersby on America's highways but, during the 1970s and 1980s, the chain became more popular with business travelers and a change of image was necessary. An updated version of the sign (right) was designed. It cost 34% less than the Great Sign, used subdued backlighting (cutting energy costs by two-thirds), and was preferred by a consumer panel by a three-to-one margin. In addition to providing an updated image, the sign also reduced maintenance costs by 55%. Note the reader boards on both signs.

signs. It is important that these signs fit into their respective property's overall marketing strategy. To develop the most effective property sign, managers of independent properties should consider the following factors (most of these factors should also be considered with billboard advertising):

- What is the purpose or purposes of the sign? Will the sign only promote name recognition, or will it also advertise the property's revenue centers or provide other information such as the time or temperature?

- A property sign's audience is most often in a moving vehicle, and the greater the letter height, the sooner the audience can read the message. Certain color combinations also make reading easier.

- To be most effective, the property sign should complement the hotel's design and image. The sign's layout should be clean and uncluttered, and the sign itself should be attractive, well-maintained, and illuminated whenever possible. Signs can be electric, engraved, subsurface, movable, and so on.

- A sign's design and complexity will affect the engineering needed to erect it. Before selecting a sign, one must consider climate, the structural strength of the proposed sign, maintenance, and local zoning codes.

- Since a property sign is a long-term investment, care should be taken to select a manufacturer that will provide a quality product at a reasonable price. The property should also take into account the time needed to manufacture the sign, especially if the sign is to be used for a grand opening or is scheduled to be unveiled at a special promotional event.

- Installation must comply with safety standards and codes, and should be accomplished at a time least inconvenient for the property's guests. Property management should check with the manufacturer or the firm actually doing the installing to determine installation time and costs.

- Some properties have the option of leasing a sign rather than purchasing it, and may choose this option for the tax benefits and the maintenance contract included in the lease agreement. If a sign is purchased outright, the property must take the cost of regular maintenance into consideration.

Reader Boards. Some property signs feature a reader board—an area on the sign set aside for temporary messages.[1] Reader boards on property signs are an important part of a day-to-day promotional program. They are often a small hotel's most-read advertising. Properties large and small should take reader boards seriously. Messages should be changed frequently—every three days is not too often—and messages kept brief. To passersby, the outside sign indicates the quality of the inside operation, so the sign should be kept neat. Use reader boards to promote:

- Special rates or packages

- Special facilities or services: waterbeds, suites, saunas, continental breakfasts

- Community activities (this is a real opportunity to build community goodwill and create a favorable image for the property)

- Whatever features or benefits separate your property from the competition

Reader boards can be creative or humorous too. Some examples from Super 8 reader boards include:

- BUY AND RAVE AT WHAT YOU SAVE

- HANDS UP! THIS IS A STEAL!

- OUR GUESTS ARE WISE; DON'T BE OTHERWISE

- WE WATCH OUR Ps AND Qs: PRICES AND QUALITY
- LAND HERE FOR DOWN TO EARTH PRICES
- THIS IS WHERE YOU COME IN
- TEED OFF ON YOUR DRIVE? PUTT IN HERE
- LUXURY FOR LESS
- SUPER 8—FOR THE BEST SURPRISE OF YOUR TRIP

For small properties which often can't afford the expense of large billboards, a catchy reader board is one way to attract interest.

Billboards   There are several differences between property signs and billboards. One of the most obvious is that a property's sign is on property grounds, while billboard advertising is placed away from the property at strategic locations on well-traveled streets and highways. A good billboard location can mean the difference between increased sales and wasted advertising dollars.

Location. Before selecting a location—whether it be alongside a highway or a city street—a drive past the billboard should be made. This drive can disclose pertinent information on a billboard's potential. Factors to look for include the number of other billboards in the immediate vicinity, visibility (the closest distance at which the billboard becomes visible and then readable while traffic is moving at the maximum legal speed), and variable conditions such as tree foliage which might obscure the billboard at various times of the year. Another important factor to consider is highway construction. The highway department should be contacted to determine if any construction is scheduled near the billboard's location in the immediate future. A detour can mean drastically reduced readership for the billboard.

Before deciding on a highway billboard, it is important for city properties to determine which highways leading into the city are used more by traveling motorists than local commuters. Special in-city billboards featuring property restaurants, lounges, and facilities may be designed to attract the latter group.

The number of a property's billboards will help determine their location on a highway. As a general rule, a property's billboards should be placed no less than two miles and no more than ten miles apart, although this will vary depending on the size of the billboards, their proximity to the property, and the number of competing signs in the area.

Highway billboards can be complemented by in-city billboards that give directions to the property (see Exhibit 10.2). In-city billboards can also be used in key feeder cities and, as mentioned, to attract local patrons to the property.

Size. The optimum size for a billboard is usually based in part on the number of other billboards a property has on a given highway or street. For example, if a property is using only two or three billboards, they should be fairly large (14 by 48 feet). If a property is using a number of billboards (see Exhibit 10.3), the first two or three can be large, while the remaining billboards can be smaller in size.

Exhibit 10.2   Sample Directional Billboard

RESERVATIONS   800-325-3535   CALL TOLL FREE

This directional billboard will be illuminated, since about 30% of a billboard's annual audience will pass the billboard between sunset and dawn. The billboard will have more visual impact at night (when the property is trying to attract business) than during the daylight hours.

Courtesy of the Sheraton Corporation.

Design. After the location of the billboard, its design is the most important selling factor. Today's designs offer a wide array of choices.

The most common billboards fall into two general categories: posters and painted displays. Poster billboards have their designs printed on several paper panels of a standard size that are then affixed to the face of the billboard.

Painted displays are usually more expensive, and fall into two subdivisions: walls and bulletins. Painted walls are usually used only in cities, and consist of designs and/or copy painted directly on a wall rented by the property. Painted bulletins are usually painted in sections and then transported to the billboard site for assembly. Most painted bulletins are illuminated for best effect. They must be repainted several times each year to keep them looking attractive.

Whatever their type, billboards should be simple, readable, and designed to be read quickly from left to right. Colors should be bright and contrasting; lettering, simple and bold (see Exhibit 10.4). Fancy type styles, though appropriate in other advertising, do not work well on a billboard since they are often unreadable at traveling speeds. The type style should complement the billboard's overall design and be large enough to make an impression.

There are several design elements that can make a billboard more interesting. One is the use of cutouts. Cutouts can take many forms, but the most popular is an illustration that extends beyond the billboard itself. In addition to making the billboard more interesting, cutouts make billboards seem larger.

Another popular design, often used by resorts, is a billboard with a panel at the bottom that allows for easy copy changes. The bottom panel is used to advertise coming events, entertainment, or specialty restaurants on a rotating basis.

Exhibit 10.3   Sample Series of Billboards

In this series of billboards from Harrah's in Reno, Nevada, questions featuring the benefits offered by the hotel/casino are asked, and a final billboard proclaims: "Harrah's. Who else?"
Courtesy of Donrey Outdoor Advertising, Las Vegas, Nevada.

Lighting should be considered when designing a billboard. If a billboard is not illuminated, the property may want to have the property's name and one or two selling points treated with reflective material so that these elements can be read at night.

Painted Display Cost Guidelines

Here are the most important things you need to know before you sign a contract:

1. *Period of Purchase.* Normally, painted bulletins or painted signs or walls are bought for a minimum term of one year to a maximum of three (occasionally, five) years at a guaranteed rate, and payment is rendered on a monthly basis.

2. *Discounts.* Discounts are frequently offered for purchases extending for more than one year—most commonly, 5% for two years and 10% for three years.

3. *Cancellation Privileges.* Standard practice is that one-year contracts are non-cancelable, while second and third years may be canceled upon 60 days' notice prior to each anniversary of the initial completion date. If this notice is not given by the advertiser, the contract is not cancelable until the next anniversary date. The contract should clearly specify cost penalties for such cancelation.

4. *Initial Completion Date.* This is the day on which the sign is first completely painted and fully serviceable. This date establishes the effective date of the contract as well as any subsequent anniversary dates and the monthly billing dates.

5. *Painting.* A minimum of two complete paintings per year should be included in the monthly space charge. Under normal circumstances, the sign should be painted approximately every six months to keep the display in a bright and attractive condition, unless the sign faces within approximately 60° of true north, in which case it may be possible to get by with only one painting per year. Between paintings, the seller is obligated to maintain the painted surface in good repair without additional charge.

6. *Illumination.* The sign should be fully lit between 6:00 a.m. and sunrise, and between sunset and midnight. A cash credit of 25% of the daily cost is normally extended for any day on which illumination is not provided.

7. *Embellishments and Extensions.* Any requested special effects in the form of structural additions or embellishments to the face, top, bottom, or sides of the sign such as cut-out letters, neon effects, time/temperature modules, etc. will be charged for. These are normally billed on a one-time basis for fabrication and installation, and are the property of the advertiser. Frequently, a charge for monthly maintenance may be added.

Negotiating

Obviously, it helps if there are several sign companies operating in your area, since competition tends to keep prices down and produce wider availability. It also affords a chance to check on comparative pricing and invite competitive bidding.

Pricing of a sign is generally determined by several factors other than simply its basic cost to the operator:

1. Size of the sign's audience.
2. Size of the sign.
3. Visibility and impressiveness of the sign.
4. Exclusivity—how many other signs there are covering the same general area.

Item 1—the audience—is usually the most important single factor in the price. A painted bulletin ranging in size from 14 by 48 feet to 20 by 60 feet with a satisfactory approach should normally cost no more than about $1 to $2 for each thousand people who see it.

You can compute this cost yourself if you secure a vehicular traffic count for the primary approach artery (or arteries, if the sign can be clearly seen from more than one street). Take the traffic count, which is the number of cars passing the sign during a specified period of time—usually, a day—and multiply it by .83 if it is a two-way count on a two-way artery or 1.66 if it is on a one-way street (these figures are industry standards developed by the Outdoor Institute Association). Take that total and convert it to a monthly figure (by multiplying the daily count by 30, for instance). Next, divide the monthly figure by 1,000, and then divide that result into the monthly cost of the sign to get a cost-per-thousand-viewers figure. Here is an example:

Sign cost: $1,800 per month

Daily two-way traffic count: 200,000

$200,000 \times .83 = 166,000$ viewers per day

$166,000$ viewers per day $\times$ 30 days $= 4,980,000$ viewers per month

$$\frac{4,980,000}{1,000} = 4,980$$

$$\frac{\$1,800}{4,980} = \$.36 \text{ per 1,000 viewers}$$

Once you have arrived at an acceptable price, go ahead and contract for it, keeping in mind the relevant items above.

Source: Adapted from Sheraton Worldwide Advertising Manual, 1984, pp. 12–13. Courtesy of Sheraton Hotels.

Many hotel chains have design and logo specifications for billboards that must be adhered to by individual properties, although properties often have a choice as to billboard size. Chain requirements may include the shape of the billboard, colors, and a standardized logo. Individual properties can often "personalize" the sign with property information.

Copy. The key to successful billboard copy is to keep it brief. A billboard should convey one main idea: the most exciting and persuasive message will not work if it is too long to be read by passengers in a moving vehicle. Advertising experts suggest that copy be five to ten words long, seven being the number of words most often suggested.

Since most billboards feature artwork which conveys an immediate impression, copy can be kept simple. An illustration showing the size of a property is far more effective than using copy such as "150 rooms." Also, copy should not be wasted on advising travelers of services that they expect a property to have (air-conditioning, television, attractive rooms, and so on).

Billboard copy can be approached from a number of angles. It can notify travelers of the number of miles to the property, list amenities offered by the property, describe one special feature, or state the property's slogan.

Exhibit 10.4   Hilton's 3-D Billboards

The prestigious image of the Hilton chain is preserved in creative billboards which feature motion and three-dimensional images. This "Pot o' Gold" billboard is enhanced through the use of "gold coins" that rotate on the display area.

Courtesy of Donrey Outdoor Advertising, Las Vegas, Nevada.

A slogan is especially effective if the property is part of a chain with name and value recognition.

Maintenance. No matter what type of billboard is used, it is important that it be maintained on a regular basis. Peeling or cracked paint, rips in the design, or other damage can detract from a property's message and create a poor impression of the property. When contracting for a billboard, the property should determine maintenance responsibilities. Many contractors of painted billboards offer two or three repaintings as part of their service. Proper maintenance helps ensure that the property's billboards create the impression for which they were designed.

Contracts. To offer properties the best value for their billboard advertising dollars, some outdoor advertising companies offer a rotary plan that ensures that the property's message is seen in a number of areas. Most rotary plans operate on a six- or twelve-month basis; on a six-month plan, for example, the billboard advertisement is rotated on a fixed timetable (it may be every thirty days) to allow the message to be seen in six different areas. Many hotels and restaurants use a rotary plan to give the impression that they are advertising "all over town."

Other properties with larger advertising budgets may opt for other types of contract plans that offer a fixed location. Some outdoor advertising companies offer a "trial plan" to enable a property to test the effectiveness of an outdoor advertising campaign. A trial plan may range from three to six months or be available on a seasonal basis.

Displays

Like billboards, displays are designed for use off the property's grounds in high-traffic locations for maximum effectiveness. Unlike billboards, displays are used mainly indoors and, because they are less costly, are changed more frequently.

Displays can be used for several purposes: transit advertising (advertising in or on buses, taxicabs, and, in some cities, the subway), trade show advertising (promotion of the property at conventions and trade shows), and general advertising (transportation terminal advertising, periodic displays at tourist attractions, local Chambers of Commerce, and so on).

Transit

Transit advertising (see Exhibit 10.5) falls into two separate categories: transit or inside cards and outside posters. Transit advertising has several important advantages:

1. *Low cost*. Transit cards offer excellent color reproduction at a relatively low cost. The advertiser pays only for the production of the transit card (design, typesetting, printing, etc.) and for the rental of the transit space. Rental fees for this space are usually quite low compared to the cost of advertising in newspapers or using billboards. Operators of transit systems realize their profits from the fares of users of the system. Renting space to advertisers is extra income, and reasonable fees are usually charged to attract as many advertisers as possible.

2. *High readership*. Many riders read transit advertising to relieve boredom; surveys show that readership of transit card advertising is high. This is an effective medium with which to reach urban consumers, middle-to-lower income groups, and tourists.

3. *Frequency*. People who take the same routes day after day are exposed to the transit card message on a regular basis. They can become guests or excellent word-of-mouth advertisers.

There are also some disadvantages to using transit advertising: it is not a prestigious medium; it is not targeted to a specific audience; and, if there are numerous cards on a bus or if someone tries to read a poster as a bus or taxi goes by, the property's message may get garbled or be missed entirely. Still, a carefully planned, attention-getting message can make transit advertising worthwhile.

When planning transit advertising, it is important to remember that it can appear in two different locations—inside a bus or outside a bus or taxi. Inside transit advertising is read by a captive audience and can contain more copy than a typical billboard. In addition, pads of coupons can be attached to a transit card at a small additional charge. These coupons enable the reader to take action on the property's offer. Outside transit advertising, however, must be designed to be read quickly, and artwork may play a more important role.

Trade Show

Trade shows are another avenue for displays. Trade shows are held for a variety of industries, trades, and professionals, including such travel-oriented professionals as travel agents, tour group operators, and meeting planners. A hotel may also wish to advertise at a trade show or convention that caters to a

Exhibit 10.5   Sample Outside Transit Advertising

Transit advertising space on taxicabs is generally sold on weekly or monthly contracts. Hotel advertisers must supply the advertising cards at their own expense.

targeted market segment such as medical doctors, construction companies, the computer industry, and so on.

Trade show advertising usually includes display posters, collateral materials, and personal selling. Display posters are used to attract delegates to a property's booth, and may picture property amenities in detail.

General   General display advertising usually includes color posters of the property and its features, or posters describing special property promotions such as a Hawaiian week or a special two-for-one room rate. A poster can vary in size from the large 9- by 20-foot size to one-half to one-eighth that size. The size, of course, will vary depending on the intended use of the poster and the location. Some transportation terminals, for example, have fixed spaces for display posters; the display posters have to be made to fit into the frame or mounting panel available.

Collateral Materials

Virtually all hotels use collateral materials in one form or another. Collateral materials include printed items (fliers, tent cards, brochures, and so on), and specialty items (matchbooks, shoehorns, key chains, and other giveaways). Collateral materials serve two useful purposes: first, they get the property's name in front of a great number of people; second, they can serve as "silent salespeople"—aids to supplement the message of the property's sales staff.

Collateral materials are usually given away either by salespeople or through other means such as in-house promotions, leaving the items in guestrooms, handing items to departing guests, and so on. Even though they are often given away, the value of collateral materials should not be taken lightly. Collateral materials are generally targeted specifically to a market segment desired by the property, and usually cost far less than mass-media advertising in terms of cost per inquiry and the number of inquiries converted to sales.

In this section, we will take a look at various examples of collateral materials and discover what makes them such effective sales tools. We will learn how to make the most of printed material such as fliers, tent cards, and brochures, and see what types of specialty items can keep the property's name and message in the minds of prospects and guests.

Fliers

The simplest printed collateral items are fliers (see Exhibit 10.6). Fliers can be used as envelope stuffers, general direct mail pieces, or inexpensive promotional material. They can also be effective property fact sheets, especially when printed with photographs of the property, and may serve as an alternative to the rack brochure. Fliers are especially useful to promote special events or packages, since they can be quickly produced and usually cost much less than a brochure.

In order for a flier to be effective, it must be attractive. The copy, if possible, should be prepared by a writer who has seen the property or the products it is offering, and should contain the following elements:

1. *A headline.* The attention-grabber.

2. *Headings.* Headings feature key points and break up copy for easier reading.

3. *Body copy.* The selling message. The copy should include prices if the property is offering a special package or promotion. The type should be large enough to be easily read.

4. *Art or photographs.* Artwork and photographs add interest to fliers. Photographs must be clear and sharp for good reproduction, and should almost always be captioned.

5. *Logo and signature.* The property's logo lends credibility to the flier, and the signature (the property's name, address, and telephone number) provides information a reader needs to contact the property.

Tent Cards

Tent cards may be simple three-fold cards or elaborate fold-together pieces that advertise restaurant specials, dessert menus, or other products and services offered by the property (see Exhibit 10.7). Tent cards advertising the restaurant may be placed in guestrooms as a suggestive selling tool, while tent cards featuring dessert specials or exotic drinks may be placed on restaurant or lounge tables.

Tent cards may be printed in one or two colors or, as is usually done, as full-color pieces. Tent card copy should be brief. A tempting dessert photograph will do far more than copy to sell desserts.

Exhibit 10.6   Sample Flier

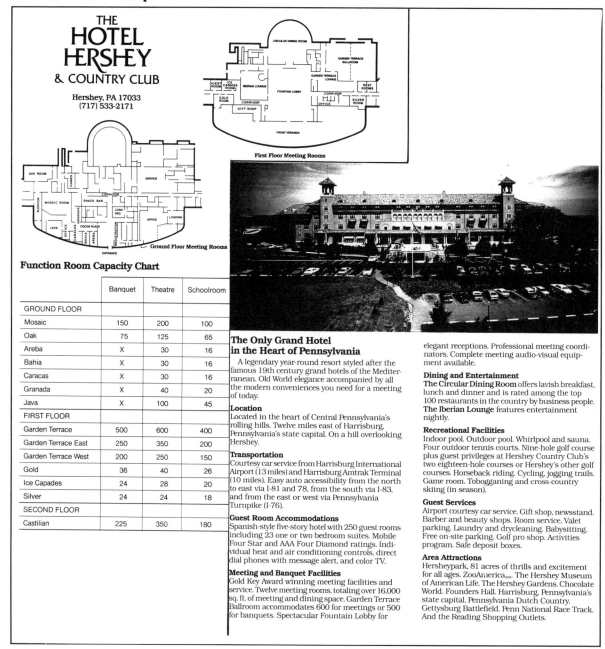

Function Room Capacity Chart

	Banquet	Theatre	Schoolroom
GROUND FLOOR			
Mosaic	150	200	100
Oak	75	125	65
Areba	X	30	16
Bahia	X	30	16
Caracas	X	30	16
Granada	X	40	20
Java	X	100	45
FIRST FLOOR			
Garden Terrace	500	600	400
Garden Terrace East	250	350	200
Garden Terrace West	200	250	150
Gold	36	40	26
Ice Capades	24	28	20
Silver	24	24	18
SECOND FLOOR			
Castilian	225	350	180

The Only Grand Hotel in the Heart of Pennsylvania

A legendary year-round resort styled after the famous 19th century grand hotels of the Mediterranean. Old World elegance accompanied by all the modern conveniences you need for a meeting of today.

Location
Located in the heart of Central Pennsylvania's rolling hills. Twelve miles east of Harrisburg, Pennsylvania's state capital. On a hill overlooking Hershey.

Transportation
Courtesy car service from Harrisburg International Airport (13 miles) and Harrisburg Amtrak Terminal (10 miles). Easy auto accessibility from the north to east via I-81 and 78, from the south via I-83, and from the east or west via Pennsylvania Turnpike (I-76).

Guest Room Accommodations
Spanish-style five-story hotel with 250 guest rooms including 23 one or two bedroom suites. Mobile Four Star and AAA Four Diamond ratings. Individual heat and air conditioning controls, direct dial phones with message alert, and color TV.

Meeting and Banquet Facilities
Gold Key Award winning meeting facilities and service. Twelve meeting rooms, totaling over 16,000 sq. ft. of meeting and dining space. Garden Terrace Ballroom accommodates 600 for meetings or 500 for banquets. Spectacular Fountain Lobby for

elegant receptions. Professional meeting coordinators. Complete meeting audio-visual equipment available.

Dining and Entertainment
The Circular Dining Room offers lavish breakfast, lunch and dinner and is rated among the top 100 restaurants in the country by business people. The Iberian Lounge features entertainment nightly.

Recreational Facilities
Indoor pool. Outdoor pool. Whirlpool and sauna. Four outdoor tennis courts. Nine-hole golf course plus guest privileges at Hershey Country Club's two eighteen-hole courses or Hershey's other golf courses. Horseback riding. Cycling, jogging trails. Game room. Tobogganing and cross-country skiing (in season).

Guest Services
Airport courtesy car service. Gift shop, newsstand. Barber and beauty shops. Room service. Valet parking. Laundry and drycleaning. Babysitting. Free on-site parking. Golf pro shop. Activities program. Safe deposit boxes.

Area Attractions
Hersheypark, 81 acres of thrills and excitement for all ages. ZooAmerica_sm. The Hershey Museum of American Life. The Hershey Gardens. Chocolate World. Founders Hall. Harrisburg, Pennsylvania's state capital. Pennsylvania Dutch Country. Gettysburg Battlefield. Penn National Race Track. And the Reading Shopping Outlets.

A flier that serves as a property fact sheet can be an effective sales tool. This property fact sheet for The Hotel Hershey & Country Club features a full-color photograph and a description of the property's features and amenities on the front. The back shows function room layouts and room capacity information.

Courtesy of The Hotel Hershey & Country Club, Hershey, Pennsylvania.

Many hotel chains offer tent cards or a combination package of tent cards and posters through corporate advertising departments. Individual properties can also design their own tent cards.

Exhibit 10.7   Sample Tent Card

Tent cards can promote desserts, beverages, or property specialties. They may also be used as cross-selling tools to promote various property facilities. For example, tent cards may be placed in guestrooms to promote the property's restaurant or lounge.

Courtesy of Days Inns of America, Inc.

Brochures

Brochures are probably the most important collateral items and must be designed and written properly to be effective. When developing a brochure, a property should:

1. *Set objectives.* What is this brochure meant to accomplish? Is the objective to attract banquet business or increase weekend occupancy? Will the brochure be directed to new guests or previous guests?

2. *Target the audience.* If the property is attempting to reach a number of audiences, it cannot do so with one brochure; trying to talk to everyone with one brochure is usually a waste of money. A brochure for business travelers is of little value to a family group; a brochure for convention planners has little meaning for a retired couple looking for a leisure vacation (see Exhibit 10.8). In cases in which a property wishes to reach several market segments, using several four-panel brochures is usually more effective than trying to cram everything about the property into a general eight-panel brochure.

Exhibit 10.8 Sample Targeted Brochures

For best results, brochures should be targeted for individual market segments. Each of these Days Inns brochures was developed for a specific market: businesspeople, sports teams, government workers, educators, and senior citizens. Each has the advantage of addressing the specific needs of a group rather than attempting to "sell it all" in one general brochure.
Courtesy of Days Inns of America, Inc.

3. *List benefits.* Benefits should be listed for each target audience based on its needs. Each brochure must answer the question, "Why should I (the businessperson, the family member, the convention delegate, and so on) stay at this hotel?"

The amount of information and number of photographs or other artwork will determine the final length of a brochure. Brochures usually consist of four, six, or eight panels, although special brochures with additional panels or reply cards may be designed.

No matter what type of brochure is designed and written, the property should never skimp on quality. It is far better to print a two-color brochure on quality paper than a four-color brochure on cheap paper that gives an image of shabbiness. If the property has done its job—created a brochure that lets readers know what the property can do for them—it should not then insult readers with a poorly produced piece.

Design. When creating or reviewing a brochure's design, property managers or salespeople should keep in mind the following guidelines.

Match the brochure to the property. The brochure should reflect the personality of the property. It is the personality of the brochure that will distinguish it and the property from the competition (see Exhibit 10.9). If the property is a luxury hotel, a cheaply printed brochure would not convey the proper impression. A luxury hotel should use quality paper, distinctive type, and special touches such as embossing, foiling, or top-notch photography. In short, the brochure should exude elegance.

On the other hand, if the brochure is designed for a leisure resort, the personality of the brochure should be casual. If the property is a dude ranch, for example, paper and artwork with a western look can add to the brochure's appeal. If a resort is family-oriented, a brochure that features photographs of family "fun in the sun" is an effective sales aid. A brochure designed for families would not be written to appeal to a guest's need for status as in the case of a brochure for a luxury property; instead, the copy would be more informal, focusing on what the property has to offer in terms of leisure options, scenery, and so on.

Heighten the property's image with photos. Photographs must be chosen with an eye toward embellishing the property's image. The property may be known for a garden setting, for example; words would not portray the garden's beauty as well as a photograph or two would. If a property is famous for unusual architecture, detailed close-ups of special architectural features may entice readers.

Showing special features is not enough, however. Photographs without people can appear cold and lifeless; photographs work best when they include people enjoying the property's amenities. When preparing brochures for specific target markets, it is important to show people that the particular brochure's readers can relate to. While professional models are often used, the models should reflect the brochure's target audience—families for a family-oriented brochure, businesspeople for a business-traveler brochure, and so on.

Use photos to sell. Properties can use photos to promote tempting food specials; ski slopes, beaches, or parks; recreational facilities such as the property's golf course or tennis courts; beautiful scenery; or other property attractions. The property's biggest attraction should be featured in the largest photograph. If all photos are the same size, nothing stands out as being particularly significant.

Copy. The following are guidelines for writing or reviewing brochure copy:

1. *Position the property.* Every property should develop a short (ten words or less) positioning statement that can be used in all of its advertising. The positioning statement may represent a key benefit or a property philosophy, but it should be easy to understand and remember.

2. *Put the property's name and location on the cover.* If the property is located near a major city or recreational area, this information, along with the property's name, can be turned into an eye-catching

Exhibit 10.9   Sample Rack Brochure

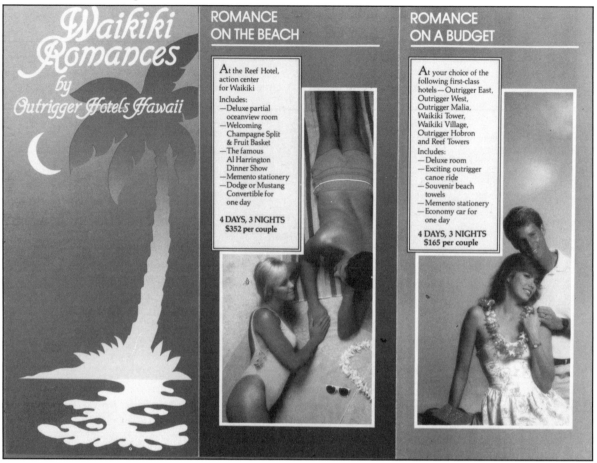

Although most rack brochures contain the same basic elements, designs differ to reflect the image and atmosphere of a property. This brochure reflects Outrigger's romantic location and features special packages for romantic weekend getaways. (Only three panels of the six-panel brochure are shown.)

headline. At the very least, the property's name should appear at the bottom of the cover.

3. *Use headings to highlight key facts.* Headings draw the reader to the property's key features. Even if the copy isn't read, the reader can still see the main points.

4. *Highlight the property's most popular features and benefits.* Each brochure should highlight features and benefits that will appeal to the brochure's targeted market segment. This can be done in a number of ways, including giving more copy space to these features, setting copy in a different type style or size of type, and positioning the copy where it is most likely to be read (an advertising professional can make recommendations for optimum positioning). Special graphics can also highlight copy: copy can be placed in a box, enhanced with designs such as stars or bold lines, or be accompanied by catchy illustrations or photographs.

5. *Build credibility.* The property should back up claims and make use of testimonials for additional credibility. The property can develop a testimonial file by sending previous guests a token gift along with a survey card; the responses may provide hundreds of good quotes that can be used in brochure (and other) advertising.

6. *Tell the whole story.* Pack as much information as possible into each brochure.

7. *Urge the reader to take action.* Include invitations throughout the brochure to visit, call, or write. Then make it easy for the reader to do so by providing a reply card or a toll-free number.

These elements can be incorporated into any brochure, whether it is designed by an in-house staff, an advertising agency, or a chain property's corporate advertising staff. Many chain properties provide generic brochures that can be personalized with photographs or copy from an individual property.

Some brochures have different copy requirements than general rack brochures. In the case of a convention brochure, for example, detailed information is more important than fancy photography or scenes of leisure activities (see Exhibit 10.10). A convention brochure, in addition to listing the property's name, address, and telephone number, will usually include the following information: references from previous convention groups; guestroom information such as room block policy, reservations policy, list of rates, and registration information; dining room information (names, types, and capacity); meeting room information (names, capacity for different types of functions, audiovisual equipment available); exhibit space (dimensions, scaled drawings, floor load, ceiling height); banquet and beverage service (capacities, types, and so on); special services and facilities (electronic mail, convention service personnel, contract photographers); transportation (distance to the airport or other travel terminals, parking facilities, tour facilities); auxiliary activities (spouse entertainment, and so on); and billing procedures.

Specialty Items   Specialty items are economical sales tools which can be remarkably effective. Surveys have shown that the recall factor with specialty items averages over 70%, especially in cases where the users of specialty items see the items every day.[2]

A specialty item can be used as a promotion in itself or in conjunction with other property promotions. Even a small property can afford high-use specialty items such as ballpoint pens and key chains, while other, higher-priced items like coffee mugs, calendars, and T-shirts can be purchased by properties with larger advertising budgets.

Since many specialty items are small, the property should develop a message that is brief. In many cases, just the property's name, address, and telephone number appear on specialty items.

Sometimes specialty items are designed around a unique theme. For example, for the grand opening of the High Q Hotel in Orlando, Florida, a "First International Aerial Exposition Competition of the World" campaign was developed. Over six hundred businesspeople in the Orlando area were mailed parts of a balsa airplane. Wings for the planes were issued at the hotel's grand opening. Each of the participants was given a stylized name

Exhibit 10.10 Sample Convention Brochure

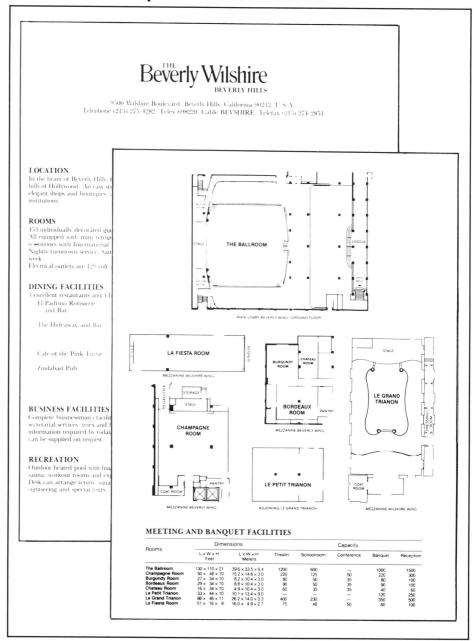

Unlike rack brochures, convention brochures must provide detailed function room and banquet information for meeting planners. This sample convention brochure lists the property's location and general amenities on the second page, room layouts and capacities on the third. Other convention brochures may rely more heavily on photographs of function facilities.

Courtesy of The Beverly Wilshire, Beverly Hills, California.

badge and escorted to the twenty-first floor to launch his or her plane toward a painted target in the parking lot. Winners were awarded special prizes. All participants were given a coffee cup imprinted with the hotel's name.

The coffee cups awarded by the High Q could be used on a daily basis and were a reminder of a fun experience at the hotel. Other specialty items

Exhibit 10.11   Sample Chain Specialty Items

W. Tennis Balls The same **Dunlop** ®Championship tennis balls that are used in most major pro and amateur tournaments. Suitable for all types of courts. 3 Balls Per Can. **Minimum Order: 4 Cans**

X. Golf Balls Blue Maxfli ®golf balls have been a favorite of country club business and professional golfers for over a generation. Super high energy cores give extra distance to every stroke and the exterior is covered by a tough-to-cut cover. 3 Balls Per Sleeve. **Minimum Order: 4 Sleeves**

Y. Days Inn Sewing Kit 6 colors of thread, a needle, buttons, and a safety pin to handle most mending emergencies. This is one room give-away your customers will surely use! **Minimum Order: 50**

Z. Luggage Tag Executive tag with plastic strap holds a business or identification card (included). Makes a wonderful complimentary convention or conference gift. **Minimum Order: 50 Tags**

AA. Days Inn Emery Boards An inexpensive way to welcome your guests. Each board has a fine and a coarse side for neat manicuring. **Minimum Order: 100**

BB. Hand Lotion What a soft sell — Soothing Balm Argenta lotion in a **Days Inn** Logo bottle. Each once bottle holds 85 applications. **Minimum Order: 50**

CC. Survival Kit All life's little necessities in one neat kit! Includes: moist towelette, antiseptic, aspirin, antacid, adhesive bandage, and a HELP decal. **Minimum Order: 50**

DD. Plastic Coasters They hold any size glass, bottle, mug or cup — while protecting room furnishings! America's top-selling line of coasters. White Only. **Minimum Order: 50**

EE. Stadium Cup Employees and guests will enjoy this sturdy plastic cup for all their cold beverages. Holds a full 12 oz. Yellow or White. **Minimum Order: 50**

FF. Days Inn Coffee Mug Toast **Days Inn** round the clock with this mug that looks like ceramic but is ultra chip proof, break resistant plastic for both hot and cold beverages. Microwave and top rack dishwasher safe. Black Only. **Minimum Order: 12**

Properties belonging to a chain often have the option of ordering specialty items from a catalog prepared especially for the chain. This page from the 1987 Days Inns catalog shows a variety of items—from emery boards to tennis balls—that can be used as inexpensive promotional giveaways.

Courtesy of Days Inns of America, Inc.

that can be used daily include ashtrays, lighters, pens, and calendars. Unique or especially attractive specialty items, such as unusual ceramic or brass souvenirs, are more likely to be displayed rather than being thrown in a drawer and forgotten.

Another example of an unusual specialty item campaign is the placement of dictionaries in the rooms of the luxury Stanford Court Hotel on Nob Hill in San Francisco. This campaign is the result of an article by *New York Times* columnist William Safire, who wrote how nice it would be if hotels provided dictionaries. The president of Stanford Court, James A. Nassikas, is a fan of Safire's and decided to do just that. Since early 1987, a copy of Webster's *New World Dictionary* has been placed in guestrooms alongside the familiar Gideon Bible. Although the dictionaries are not take-home items, they receive favorable guest response, and the hotel receives nationwide publicity for the "good words" placed in each room.

To ensure getting the most from specialty items, a property may wish to consult an advertising agency, or contact corporate headquarters if the property is part of a chain. Many chains offer specialty-item catalogs that feature everything from playing cards to clocks (see Exhibit 10.11). Items available from chain sources are more effective if they are imprinted with a toll-free reservations number.

Conclusion

The advertising discussed in this chapter ranges from gigantic billboards to matchbook covers. For this advertising to be effective, it must be carefully designed and coordinated to reflect the property's personality and make the property stand out in a crowd of competitors. Outdoor advertising, displays, and collateral materials—even in today's world of broadcast and high-tech advertising—still play a vital part in the successful marketing of a property.

Notes

1. Much of the material in this section was adapted from *Lodging* magazine. Used with permission.
2. "Specialty Advertising: Economical, On Target," Special to *Hotel and Motel Management*, April 10, 1981, p. 1.

Discussion Questions

1. What factors should be considered by an independent property before it contracts for a property sign?
2. What should be considered when scouting a billboard's location?
3. Advertising experts suggest that billboard copy be limited to how many words?
4. What are three types of display advertising?
5. What are two categories of transit display advertising?
6. What are the advantages of transit display advertising?
7. What are examples of collateral materials?

Discussion Questions *(continued)*

8. What factors should be considered when developing a brochure?

9. What key elements should be included in brochure copy?

10. What kinds of information are required in a convention brochure?

11. Why should a message designed for a specialty item be brief?

Chapter Outline

I. Newspaper Advertising
   A. Selecting Newspapers
   B. Placing Ads
   C. Positioning Ads
   D. Determining Ad Size
   E. Newspaper Production
   F. Designing Ads
   G. Writing Ads
      1. Headline
      2. Copy
   H. Evaluating Ads
   I. Advertorials

II. Magazine Advertising
   A. Types of Magazines
      1. Consumer Magazines
      2. Trade Magazines
   B. Creating a Statement with Photography
   C. Creating Effective Ad Copy

III. Directory Advertising
   A. Telephone Directories
   B. Business Directories

IV. Measuring the Effectiveness of Print Advertising

V. Conclusion

11 Print Advertising

Print media, newspapers and magazines in particular, are some of the most effective means of reaching potential guests and clients. Each day, millions of Americans pick up newspapers and magazines in search of information and entertainment. A well-placed advertisement can generate thousands of room nights for a property.

Print advertising can greatly assist you by making potential clients aware of your property prior to being contacted. If potential clients already know about the property, it makes the job of selling easier. In this chapter, we will look at newspapers and magazines and how to make the most of these sales avenues. We will also discuss directory advertising and ways to measure the effectiveness of print advertising.

Newspaper Advertising

Newspapers are an excellent medium for selling hospitality products and services. Read by over 80% of American adults daily,[1] newspapers are considered an authoritative source of information, a source that is turned to when people seek information on vacation or business travel. Newspapers are also an effective medium for selling perishable hotel space on short notice. If room reservations, banquet bookings, or restaurant sales are less than projected, a newspaper ad can stimulate last-minute business.

There are problems with newspapers, however. Most people don't read the entire newspaper, which means large portions may be skipped. In addition to this drawback, there is the problem of "clutter"—a large number of ads placed on a page. If a reader is thinking of taking a resort vacation, he or she will probably look at all of the resort ads, no matter how many are on the travel pages. But if the reader is not interested in a resort vacation at the time the property's ad appears, the ad may not even be glanced at. Every ad must fight to get attention. An advertiser has to be aware of the variety of factors that promote consumer buying, has to know how to write and position an ad that will generate sales, and has to set newspaper advertising goals. Newspapers are generally used to achieve three basic goals:

1. *Building awareness of the property.* While newspapers may have a disadvantage when it comes to targeting certain market segments,

Industry Profile

Neil W. Ostergren, CHSE
Vice President Marketing Services Wyndham Hotels

Neil Ostergren has been in the hotel industry since 1960. He held sales, marketing, and operations positions with Roger Smith Hotels, Hilton International, and Americana Hotels before assuming his present responsibilities as Vice President—Marketing Services for Wyndham Hotels. Long active with the Hotel Sales & Marketing Association International, Ostergren served as president of HSMAI in 1987 and is now chairman of the HSMAI Foundation. He has also served as a marketing consultant, and is a regular contributor to industry publications. A Certified Hotel Sales Executive, Ostergren has received a number of awards, including the Albert E. Koehl Award for significant contributions to hotel advertising and Murdoch Magazines' Hotel Marketing Executive of the Year.

"Throughout my career in the hospitality industry, it's been my belief that both consumer and trade advertising is of great importance in reaching marketing plan objectives. Well-developed and properly targeted advertising is probably the most efficient sales component in any business, hotels included. Advertising is essential because it's the best way to create awareness, make product information available, and influence the consumer's buying decision. This is particularly true in print advertising.

Before any advertising decisions can be made, research is the mandatory first step. Only by knowing about the demographics and psychographics of consumers can a proper print advertising program be developed. Research must be continual so that advertising adjustments can be made when market changes occur.

Trade advertising to travel agents, meeting planners, and tour wholesalers should be looked at as a strategy designed and developed to support direct sales. In most cases, the ads alone will not sell anything. But good trade advertising, with the right message in the right media for the right target audience, can play a very influential role in persuading travel intermediaries to learn more about the property.

Consumer advertising in newspapers and magazines is somewhat different. Consumer ads should have less copy than most trade ads, but should clearly tell the reader what's being offered. Consumer ad copy can be about a package with a special price and a list of included features; it might be about the property itself, its location and its amenities; or, it might describe a guest benefit offered by the hotel. Consumer advertising should also be more visually attractive than a trade ad need be.

Marketing is nothing more than moving a product from concept to consumption. Well-planned advertising is important to the success of a lodging property, but advertising is not a science—it's very subjective. And hoteliers should keep in mind that advertising is just one part of the total promotion mix. **"**

they can be effective in building a broad base of public awareness. Taxi drivers, for example, may not be potential guests, but they can exert a positive influence on those who are if they become familiar with a particular property through newspaper ads.

2. *Building rooms business.* Newspapers are an effective medium for filling guestrooms on short notice. A simple newspaper ad can be prepared in hours, and can normally be scheduled on short notice (one to three days is the norm). If room sales are down, a timely newspaper ad placed in the major metropolitan newspapers of the property's key feeder cities could stimulate needed business.

3. *Building restaurant, lounge, and function business.* This advertising differs somewhat from advertising used to build awareness of the

property or to attract guestroom business. For the most part, restaurant, lounge, and function business advertising is done in the entertainment sections of local newspapers.

Before selecting a newspaper and designing and writing an ad, the property must know exactly *whom* it is trying to attract and *what* it wants to offer each targeted market segment (see Exhibit 11.1). Will the ad be designed to stimulate weekday or weekend business? Will the ad be addressed to business travelers or to families looking for a vacation destination? Are there special packages or rates that the property wishes to promote? These considerations will help determine the placement, size, design, and content of the ad.

Selecting Newspapers

There are three important factors to consider when selecting the newspapers that will best reach the property's targeted markets:

1. *Readership.* While total circulation is one factor to consider, it may not be the most important reason to advertise in a particular newspaper. To evaluate a newspaper ad's potential effectiveness, a newspaper's readership should be broken down into demographic groups if possible. A large newspaper that serves a general audience of 1,000,000 people may not generate as much business as a special interest newspaper with a circulation of 10,000 that serves a targeted market segment.

2. *Content.* The newspaper's content plays a part in successful advertising. Does it provide special sections, Sunday magazines, travel guides, and so on? Does it publish suburban or regional editions? Many large newspapers have regularly scheduled special interest sections for particular days—a special sports section on Mondays, business sections on Thursdays, weekend sections on Fridays, and travel sections on Sundays are some examples. These, in effect, are publications within publications, and may be of particular interest to a property's targeted markets.

3. *Advertising rates.* Advertising rates are usually designed to stimulate advertising by certain advertisers and limit advertising by others. This is accomplished by setting different rates for local, national, retail, classified, and, often, hotel and restaurant advertisers. Newspapers also vary rates for advertising supplements and special pages or sections (see Exhibit 11.2). Cooperative advertising is also available in some newspapers.

These factors should be considered before selecting a newspaper. Once a newspaper has been selected, the advertiser must decide on where in the newspaper an ad should be placed. Deciding where the ad should be placed may seem premature, since the ad does not exist at this point in the process. However, an ad's design and copy are affected by the ad's placement, its position on the page, and its size. Therefore, placement, positioning, and size decisions should be made before design work is begun or copy written.

Placing Ads

The placement of a property's ad will often mean the difference between whether the ad is read or ignored. For maximum effectiveness, ads should be placed where they are most likely to be read by the target audience.

Exhibit 11.1   Sample Targeted Newspaper Advertising

Our weekday rates get better with age.

$43*

SENIORS
MID-WEEK SPECIAL

If you're 50 or older, you can get this low rate on a mid-week vacation in the heart of historic New England. The Sheraton Sturbridge gives you a great room, a full country breakfast, two tickets to Old Sturbridge Village (it's right across the street), and free use of the health club, indoor swimming pool and tennis courts. You'll also have plenty of places to shop, including antique shops, factory outlets and more. Call 1-800-325-3535 (in MA, dial 1-617-347-7393).

Sheraton Sturbridge Resort
The hospitality people of ITT

U.S. 20, opposite Old Sturbridge Village, 366 Main St., Sturbridge, MA

For the same low price, Host Farm Resort gives people 50 and over a great way to discover Amish Country. The rate includes your room, two tickets to an Amish Country tour and free use of the health spa, indoor swimming pool and outdoor tennis courts. There's also an 18-hole PGA golf course and outdoor tennis. And Host Farm's right down the road from historic Gettysburg and all kinds of factory outlets, too. For details, call 1-800-233-0121 (in PA, dial 717-299-5500).

Host Farm Resort
The most complete family resort in Pennsylvania Dutch Country.
2300 Lincoln Highway East, Lancaster, PA 17602

Per person, per night, 2 night minimum. Sunday through Thursday, by reservation only. Taxes not included.

This ad, published in regional senior-citizen publications, was designed to increase mid-week business by promoting a special weekday senior citizen's package. Note that this ad is a cooperative ad.

The placement of an ad will depend on the type of traveler or local patron the property wishes to reach and the sections available in the newspaper. To reach leisure travelers, for example, a Sunday travel section is the best choice; if the paper has no Sunday travel section, however, alternatives such as local news or family sections have to suffice. Business travelers will be more likely to see ads placed in the business section or in the paper's first news section. Ads for "escape weekends" (see Exhibit 11.3) may be placed in the entertainment or media sections, or in the sports section if the escape weekend features sports facilities such as golf, tennis, or horseback riding.

When it comes to selling restaurants (see Exhibit 11.4) or function space, ads usually should not be placed in the Sunday travel section. Many newspapers offer a "Restaurant Guide" to assist locals and out-of-town visitors in choosing restaurants. Since many people go to restaurants before or after attending a special event such as a concert, sports event, or movie, restaurant ads can be effective if placed in the newspaper's entertainment section, or in the sports section if the property is promoting a post-game buffet or pre-game dinner special.

Exhibit 11.2 Sample Rate Card

R.O.P. GENERAL RATES

A. OPEN

BLACK & WHITE RATES PER INCH

Daily $35.00
Sunday $36.60

BULK CONTRACT RATES WITHIN ONE YEAR

	Daily	Sunday
126`	$34.30	$35.87
250`	$33.95	$35.50
500`	$33.60	$35.14

In the event Advertiser fails to fulfill contract, a rate adjustment will be made to nearest contract rate actually earned or to the open rate.

B. REPEAT RATES

A 30% discount will be given for the second insertion of an identical ad run within a 6-day period. Discount is calculated on second run. Copy and ad size to be same. Subject to earned contract rate.

C. SPECIAL POSITION CHARGES

35% premium in addition to space charge - available daily & Sunday.

D. SPECIAL ADVERTISING RATES

	Daily	Sunday
Political Advertising (per column inch)	$35.00	$36.60

`Requires cash with space reservation

COLOR RATES - R.O.P.

Use Black & White inch print rate plus the following applicable flat costs for daily or Sunday.
Black plus 1 color $650.00
Black plus 2 or 3 colors .. $950.00 (min. size 31½ `)

Most rate cards list several rates based on an advertisement's size, position, color(s) used, and frequency. Newspapers usually quote different rates to national and local advertisers; frequently the local rate is lower. The basic unit of space quoted for local advertising is usually the column inch, an area one column wide by one inch deep. National advertising costs are quoted in standard advertising units (SAU).

It should be noted that dinner sales are much easier to promote than luncheon business. Traditionally, dinner is an "experience," and patrons are willing to travel for exotic foods or atmosphere, while lunches are usually eaten in close proximity to the home or office. Businesspeople looking for a prestigious lunch setting for entertaining clients may be reached by an ad in the business section or in the first news section.

Exhibit 11.3   Sample Ad for Weekend Business

A ROOM WITH A WOO

ROMANTIC WEEKENDS FROM $59.50* We've got everything to put you in the mood. Four-course candlelight dinner in our rooftop Squared Circle Restaurant, with your first cocktails on the house. Free Sunday breakfast. Even free use of our Jacuzzi to warm you up, and our huge indoor pool when you need cooling off. Call (413) 781-0900 or 1-800-HOLIDAY for reservations.

Holiday Inn®
SPRINGFIELD

711 Dwight Street, Springfield, Massachusetts 01104

*Price per person, per night based on double occupancy. Subject to availability.

This ad for an escape weekend might be positioned in the newspaper's business section (to attract weary executives), the first news section (where it is most likely to be read by readers who do not read the entire newspaper), or in the entertainment or radio and television sections. Other ads offering different products or services would be positioned according to the product or service offered and the target market.

The first news section is also an effective place to advertise special holiday promotions of both rooms and restaurants since this section is the most

Exhibit 11.4 Sample Restaurant Ads

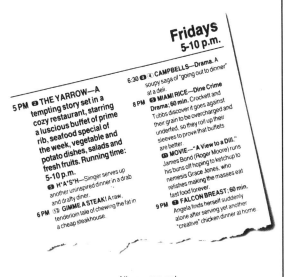

These ads for The Yarrow Resort Hotel & Conference Center offer both continuity and variety. The ads are the same size and the ad elements are positioned in the same sequence (headline, illustration, body copy, pricing, and signature). In addition, the same typefaces are used for the headlines, headings, and text, giving the ads a similar appearance. The consistent use of white space gives these ads an uncluttered look and "protects" them from adjacent ads.

widely read section of the newspaper. The first news section is also an excellent place to advertise function rooms to businesses (the business section is another good choice). Function rooms for social events can be advertised in the society pages or family sections.

Positioning Ads

Once the newspaper section has been selected, the ad must be positioned on a page. There are several preferred positions, such as insertion of the ad at the top of the page alongside reading matter. This position is called *full position*, and may cost the advertiser more money in some cities, but the ad will be seen by more people than an ad placed next to other advertisements or "buried" at the bottom of the page. Most advertisers also try to avoid the "gutter"—the inside portion of the paper where the two pages meet—in favor of an outside position next to reading matter.[2]

Another important positioning consideration is which day of the week to run an ad. The best day(s) of the week to run an ad will vary depending on what the property has to offer. The Sunday travel pages are considered the best option for promoting leisure travel. In determining other key days, the property should take the paper's general makeup into consideration: Which days are typically light news days? What days are given over to supermarket food ads? Which sections have the most readership, and on which day(s) of the week? On what days are supplementary sections published?

By determining the answers to these questions, the property can get a general idea of the best days to advertise. If a paper publishes a prestigious business section on Monday, for example, this would provide good positioning for the sale of business services or function space.

Determining
Ad Size

The next step in creating newspaper advertising is determining ad size. As mentioned earlier, newspapers often are cluttered with ads promoting similar products or services on the same page or in the same section. Therefore it is often a large ad that will stand out in the crowd.

But is bigger always better? The answer depends on the ad's objective. In some cases a series of small ads placed frequently will do more for promotion and name recognition than an occasional large ad. The choice of a restaurant or night spot, for example, is often a last-minute decision, and most properties find that a series of small daily ads generates the most business. Two exceptions to this rule are (1) the promotion of special restaurant weekend events, which may be advertised with larger ads on Fridays, and (2) holiday meal promotions, which should be published the week prior to the holiday to allow time for reservations.

Some advertisers recommend using a large, even full-page, ad to build a property's image and promote name recognition. Many hospitality industry professionals think that large ads attract more readership than small ads, and that these additional readers are generally people who are not present users of the property. A large, eye-catching advertisement has stopping power and may indeed grab the attention of the public, but it is important to remember that newspapers are not usually saved. Unless a person takes immediate action—or saves the ad—the property's message is usually quickly forgotten.

In the final analysis, the decision on ad size must be based on a property's objectives and its media budget. To keep its name before the public, a property with a limited budget may use a series of small ads placed over the course of several months.

Choosing the size of an advertisement or a series of advertisements is often difficult; unfortunately, newspapers add to this dilemma because the number of columns per page varies among newspapers. Newspapers can be printed with five, six, eight, or even nine columns. The number of columns per page will affect the width of each column and the number of lines it will take to print an ad. Copy that is 100 lines long in one newspaper might be 150 lines in another, for example. Advertisers often have to create two or more different-size advertisements to fit the different space offered by competing newspapers.

Newspaper advertising is usually offered by the column inch, an area one column wide by one inch deep. National advertising is quoted in terms of standard advertising units (SAU), which have 14 lines to an inch and are one column wide. To figure a rate, advertisers must multiply the number of inches deep an ad would run, times the number of columns wide, times the cost per inch. For example, if an ad that is five inches deep and two columns wide costs $5 per column inch at a particular newspaper, the cost is 5 × 2 × $5 = $50.

When figuring costs for ad sizes, it is important to remember that ads at most newspapers shrink somewhat due to the mechanical process used to make plates for printing the ad. Shrinkage normally runs around 2%, making it necessary to either prepare a slightly oversize ad or reconcile billing charges to ensure that the property is billed for the lines actually used.[3]

A property should select a specific ad size and shape and use it repeatedly. Rapid newspaper reading often precludes study of a property's ad copy, but name recognition can be generated if a reader's eye is drawn to the familiar size and shape of a frequently published ad.

Newspaper Production

Before an ad is designed or written, a few things should be known about the mechanics of newspaper production. Newspaper production is worlds apart from the slick production capabilities offered by magazines. The high-speed presses used by newspapers can distort images and type; the paper stock is coarse; color reproduction capabilities are mediocre at best; and production techniques limit the use of eye-catching graphics and condensed type.

When planning newspaper advertising, stick to simple techniques. Use line drawings instead of photographs unless the photographs are extremely clear and the ad is large. Special techniques such as reversed copy, in which the letters are white on a black background, should be used only occasionally. Condensed type should be avoided, especially in small ads.

Spot color—the use of one color (other than black) to enhance an advertisement—helps the ad stand out and generates significantly more reader response. The use of full color printing, or ROP (run-of-the-paper) color, often produces less than desirable results because, as mentioned, high-speed newspaper presses may distort.

Newspaper representatives can assist in determining the production problems that may be inherent in a suggested ad, but properties should limit a newspaper staff's involvement with their advertising to that kind of problem-solving. Many newspapers offer "pub-set" advertisements—ads designed, written, and typeset by the newspaper's staff. At first glance, pub-set may seem an attractive, economical alternative to the high costs of in-house or advertising agency ad development. While costs may be lower, most pub-set ads are lower in quality and far less effective than a carefully planned ad developed by the property, its free-lance advertising personnel, or its advertising agency.

Designing Ads

Many advertisers find it better to design an ad before writing the copy for it. A distinctive design helps create an image for the property. Since the repeated use of a basic ad design can ultimately result in an ad's instant recognition by readers, once a satisfactory design is developed the property should be willing to use it for some time, departing from it only for special promotions.

The design process includes ad size and shape (discussed earlier) and graphic elements, including the property's logo, line drawings, and the use of white space (see Exhibit 11.5). White space is an important layout element in print advertising since the average newspaper or magazine page is so "heavy" with type. Generous use of white space tends to separate or "protect" an ad from other ads on the page, increase the ad's readability, and make the headline and illustrations stand out.

As a rule, photographs only work well with large newspaper ads, so most newspaper ads should be designed around an eye-catching line drawing or headline instead of a photograph. Line drawings or photographs (if used) should show people in action around the product or enjoying the facility. The use of an action or leisure image can be far more effective than copy in prompting readers to respond. Pictures can also eliminate the need for a large amount of copy to tell the property's story.

Whether or not readers will read an ad depends in large part on the design. A catchy headline will not compensate for poor eye appeal, so the design should:

- *Be simple, but "flow."* The typeface selected should be bold and clear, and artwork—borders, logos, and so on—must reproduce well.

- *Use artwork and/or photographs.* Artwork and photographs can either break up the copy at strategic points or lead the reader's eye to additional copy.

- *Have captions under all photos.* While a picture is worth a thousand words, adding a few more words underneath it can prevent misconceptions and add information without cluttering the ad.

- *Identify the property.* The property's logo, preferably placed at the end of the ad as a signature, adds to credibility and name recognition.

- *Be appealing.* A poorly designed, unattractive ad will cast a negative shadow on the property, no matter how much the property has to offer.

A simple factor such as the choice of type can make a vast difference in readership of and response to an ad, so it is important that design be given careful consideration before one word of copy is written.

Writing Ads

The chances that a newspaper ad will be read are increased when ad copy includes:

1. A dominant attention-getter. This is usually a provocative headline, although it can be a catchy illustration (normally line drawings in small or medium-size ads, photographs in large ads).

2. Attention-getting claims or buyer benefits.

3. Specific offers such as special packages, benefits, low costs, and so on.

Exhibit 11.5 Effective Newspaper Design Elements

This ad for the Ocala Hilton is an excellent example of a newspaper ad that successfully uses the basic principles of newspaper ad design. While the ad is fairly simple, it is striking in design, the type is large enough to read, and the copy is reduced to essentials. A good newspaper ad has an eye-catching headline or illustration (this ad has both), and makes good use of white space. The graphics used here increase the ad's image of sophistication.

4. Believable offers—benefits and claims backed up by facts, statistics, or testimonials.

Headline. The first consideration in writing a newspaper ad is to create an attention-getting headline. For best results, the ad's headline should offer a benefit, include news or information, lead into the body copy, and evoke a positive response.

While it is extremely difficult to get all of these elements into one short headline, for maximum effect as many as possible should be included. This can be accomplished not only by the words used but by a typeface that attracts readers and prompts them to read the rest of the ad.

Copy. Once the headline has captured the reader's attention, the ad's copy must give him or her a reason to respond to the ad. What does this property have to offer to me? When are special offers or promotions in effect? Why should I respond to this ad?

Many different styles of newspaper advertising have been used by hospitality properties. Advertising copy can be serious, sophisticated, cute, innovative, or even instructional. The use of one or more of these styles is determined in part by the target audience and what the property has to offer to its markets.

As a general rule, advertising copy should be brief and factual. Benefits should be offered *early*. Contrary to popular belief, the name of the property often is not the most important feature of a successful ad. If the property or restaurant has name recognition, that may give credibility to the message, but if what the property or restaurant offers will generate more reader response, that is what should be featured in the copy.

In brief, effective copy should:

1. *Follow up on the headline.*

2. *Offer benefits early.*

3. *Be limited to one or two ideas.* Too much copy overwhelms readers and can cause confusion.

4. *Contain all necessary information.* The name, address, and phone number of the property should always be included. A small map that pinpoints the property's location may also be effective. A toll-free number, if applicable, or a special offer can increase reader response. Prices should almost always be mentioned. Providing price information attracts only those buyers that can afford the room, meal, or package described in the ad and keeps down the number of telephone inquiries that result when price is not mentioned.

5. *Ask for the sale.* The copy should give reasons for the reader to buy, then ask him or her to respond.

Evaluating Ads

After an ad has been designed and written, it should be carefully checked to be sure the message is coming across as the property intended. If the answer to "Will it sell?" is "Probably not," the reasons must be determined and the ad redone. Some common reasons a newspaper ad doesn't sell include:

1. *An ineffective headline.* Headlines should grab the attention of readers and make them want to know more.

2. *Inappropriate copy length.* Copy length is a key factor in readability. Consider placing short ads in a newspaper's morning edition, when most people are more likely to be in a hurry, and long ads in

the afternoon or evening editions. If long copy is required to get the message across, it should be broken up with headings or artwork.

3. *Meaningless benefits.* Whether benefits are included in the headline or in the copy, they must be meaningful to the ad's targeted market(s).

4. *Meaningless photographs or illustrations.* All photographs should be relevant and captioned. Even if the reader doesn't read the entire ad, he or she may respond to an enticing photograph. Illustrations should complement the copy, not overpower it or draw attention away from it.

5. *Incorrect style.* The copy should flow in a logical, interesting order, be free of ambiguities, and offer enjoyable reading. Hotel jargon, technical terms, and difficult-to-read copy can turn readers off. The style of illustrations and other graphic elements such as borders must also be correct.

6. *Passivity.* The copy should involve readers. Verbs should be active, not passive. Readers can be asked questions, or asked to imagine themselves in a particular situation.

7. *Lack of credibility.* Too many claims, promises, and extravagant descriptions can leave readers wary and unresponsive. Claims, limited to one or two, should be backed up by testimonials or statistics. Even if the property has a lot to offer, it is usually better to present no more than one or two benefits in each ad.

8. *Lack of urgency or immediacy.* The ad should urge immediate action and tell the reader what to do. A promotional package should be accompanied by a telephone number or reply coupon to encourage quick action. Readers should be urged to "call today," "mail coupon now," or "call our toll-free number for complete information."

In addition to these considerations, how does the ad make people feel? Is it attractive and inviting? Is the copy enhanced by the use of white space and eye-catching artwork? Does the ad project the image the property intends? If all these questions can be answered "yes," the property has probably developed a good ad and should be willing to stick with it for an extended length of time. While modifications can be made from time to time, a well-placed, frequently appearing, recognizable ad is the key to success in newspaper advertising.

Advertorials   Before leaving newspapers, it is important to look at another form of advertising: the advertorial. An advertorial is a combination of an advertisement and an editorial statement. Written by a property's general manager, the banquet manager, the publicity director, or another member of the property's management team, an advertorial can enhance the property's credibility or promote the property's products and services. Advertorials are usually printed in a different typeface than the non-advertising copy on the page, and are distinguished further by the phrase "Advertisement" or "Paid Advertisement" at the top or bottom of the copy. An advertorial is usually enclosed in a box.

Advertorials have several advantages. An advertorial looks more like an article or an editorial than a conventional ad, so many readers will pay closer attention to the copy. An advertorial, since it often makes no use of graphics or illustrations, can present more information to the reader.

Before opting to use an advertorial in newspapers, however, the property's advertising staff should weigh the advertorial's potential effectiveness against the impact of its regularly placed newspaper advertising. In many cases, it is wiser to use advertorial advertising in magazines, since magazines are typically saved and read by people reading for enjoyment as well as for information (see Exhibit 11.6). Newspaper readers tend to be less inclined to read long ad copy, especially if they are in a hurry.

Magazine Advertising

Magazines are another effective means of reaching potential business and leisure travelers. Magazine advertising offers the following benefits over newspaper advertising:

1. *Specific readership.* Most magazines are targeted to specific audiences or interest groups. Whether the property's target market is the business traveler, family travelers, honeymooners, golfers, travel agents, or retirees, there is a publication available to reach that particular market.

2. *Longer life.* Magazines have a longer reading life than newspapers.

3. *Wider scope.* Since most magazines are national in scope, a magazine ad may be seen by more people.

4. *Quality of production.* Unlike newspapers, most magazines offer slick, high-tech production capabilities. Full-color photographs, multi-page spreads, and special effects (pop up pages, fold-out sections, and so on) are commonly used in magazines.

When considering using magazine advertising, remember that there are disadvantages: long lead time precludes promotion of last-minute or short-term packages or services; magazine ad costs are significantly higher than newspaper ad costs (when considering this medium, inquire into discount rates for frequency); and, because of the national nature of this medium, advertising dollars are wasted if a property's markets are limited geographically. But magazines can provide an excellent avenue for hospitality advertising if the property knows whom it is targeting, what it is offering the target market, and whether a consumer or trade publication would bring the most return.

Other things to consider when using magazine advertising:

1. Readership does not increase proportionately with ad size. In magazine advertising, the message and position within the publication are more significant factors.[4]

2. While there is no advantage in using either a right or left page in a magazine, there is a distinct benefit to using the back cover: back

Exhibit 11.6 Sample Advertorial

(ADVERTISEMENT)

Las Vegas casino tests a radical slot machine; If it doesn't pay off, it gives back your money

LAS VEGAS—Lady Luck Casino Hotel has installed a bank of slot machines that can't win a penny for the house. They actually lose money.

The machines either give players a payoff up to $1,000.00, or give back the money the customer put in.

In the first few months of testing, 59 players hit $1,000.00 jackpots on the radical "Can't Lose" machines. The casino says "thousands" have hit smaller payoffs of $2.00, $5.00, $10.00, $20.00, $50.00, $100.00 and $500.00.

"Most dollar slot machines are set to hold 3% to 10% for the house," said Alain Uboldi, Lady Luck General Manager. "These new machines do the opposite. They're set to pay back 20% to 30% to the customer—or give back his money."

Each out-of-state customer with Lady Luck's "Best Casino Fun Book in Las Vegas" gets a pull on one of the special machines. And four times a day the casino holds drawings and lets the win-

ners play for three minutes each.

"People were skeptical at first," said Uboldi. "They didn't believe we would give back their money on a losing pull. It was tough to convince some people they were risking nothing."

The machines are located in the casino's "Welcome Center." Besides the free pull, the casino presents players with their photos, free drinks, a free long distance call and a shrimp cocktail for 25 cents.

Lady Luck's unusual offers are part of a strategy to introduce a new 16-story highrise called the "Luxury Tower," and two new restaurants.

"We took a look at Las Vegas fun books and found they all had one thing in common—they weren't fun," said Uboldi. The casino then produced its new "Best Fun Book in Las Vegas" as a satire, but Uboldi says the response has been "positively overwhelming."

The book is written in campy prose

that brags about the hotel's "ferociously delicious" $2.49 buffet, offers a tongue-in-cheek "$8.00 for $10.00" slot tokens sale and admits the casino "must be crazy" for guaranteeing that a player's first card in blackjack will be an ace.

As a zany final touch, the casino rigged its parking payment machine to pay a $25.00 jackpot to every 2,000th user.

The "Best Fun Book in Las Vegas" is free to out-of-state residents, 21 years or older. Uboldi advises readers of in-flight magazines to "just tear out this page and bring it to our Welcome Center to get the book." Lady Luck is at 3rd & Ogden, downtown Las Vegas.

For a complimentary copy of the book by mail, send this story to "Best Casino Fun Book in Las Vegas", Lady Luck Casino/Hotel, P.O. Box 1060, Las Vegas, NV, 89125.

Or call free, 800-634-6580. ■

AMWE

Advertorials differ from typical newspaper and magazine ads in that they appear to be feature stories or editorials. This advertorial reads like a feature story, but note the word "Advertisement" at the top to distinguish it from editorial and feature material which appeared on the same page.

Courtesy of the Lady Luck Casino/Hotel, Las Vegas, Nevada.

covers pull 65% more readers than the middle section of a publication.[5]

3. Tall-column ads attract more attention than square ads, and tend to pull better. Horizontal ads don't grab the reader's attention as effectively as vertical ads.[6]

4. Every ad should be a complete sales message, and provide an incentive and a means for reader response.

5. As in newspaper advertising, an ad format that is repeated helps to create name and product recognition. Many magazines are published monthly; therefore, in most magazines the property's ad appears only twelve times a year. For this reason, ads should not be changed too often, especially if they are effective. Research shows that ads must generally run four to seven times to register with readers and stimulate recall.[7] As an added benefit, increased frequency gets better advertising rates.

6. Advertisements should be developed to fit the character of the magazine; an ad for a consumer magazine may be far different from an ad created for a trade publication.

If there are a number of magazines directed toward a targeted market segment, the property should not use every publication, especially if mass

Exhibit 11.7   Sample Consumer Publications

General Interest	Business-Oriented
Atlantic	*Business Week*
Better Homes and Gardens	*Dun's Review*
Harpers Bazaar	*Forbes*
McLeans	*Fortune*
New Yorker	*Inc.*
Saturday Review	*Nation's Business*
Southern Living	*Venture*
Sunset	
Town and Country	**Travel**
Vogue	*Holiday*
	Signature
Special Interest	*Travel and Leisure*
Brides	*Travel/Holiday*
Field and Stream	
Golf	**Outdoor Life**
Golf Digest	*Ski*
Gourmet	*Skiing*
Mature Outlook	*Tennis*
Modern Bride	
Modern Maturity	

These consumer publications are excellent for promoting hospitality products and services. When considering advertising in consumer publications, it is important to remember that publication schedules may differ—some magazines are published monthly, others weekly, and so on. The variety of magazines may seem tempting, but most properties should target a maximum of two or three publications and repeat ads rather than place one ad in a number of publications.

coverage would be at the expense of frequency or ad size. If ads are placed in too many similar magazines, there may be considerable duplication of readership. The best strategy may be to utilize two or three publications which are considered the best in the field, or can reach the most readers.

Study several publications aimed at specific target audiences before making a selection. Which one is most likely to enhance the property's image? Which one offers an attractive format that would complement what the property has to offer? Which publication offers the production capabilities required by the property (full-color, pull-out pages, reader response section, and so on)?

Types of Magazines

Magazines can be divided into two general categories: consumer magazines and trade magazines.

Consumer Magazines. Consumer magazines are excellent vehicles for reaching the individual business or leisure traveler (see Exhibit 11.7). Consumer magazines fall into two broad categories: general interest magazines such as *The New Yorker, Sunset,* and *Better Homes and Gardens*; and special interest magazines such as *Car and Driver* and *Personal Computing.*

One of the advantages of consumer magazines is their format. Most use highly sophisticated production techniques, and contain colorful, attractive ads that can capture the attention of readers. Consumer ads must be catchy, because most readers do not pick up a magazine for the express purpose of reading an ad about a vacation spot, for example. It is for this reason that hospitality ads in consumer magazines are typically lush and inviting, with

Exhibit 11.8 Sample Consumer Ad

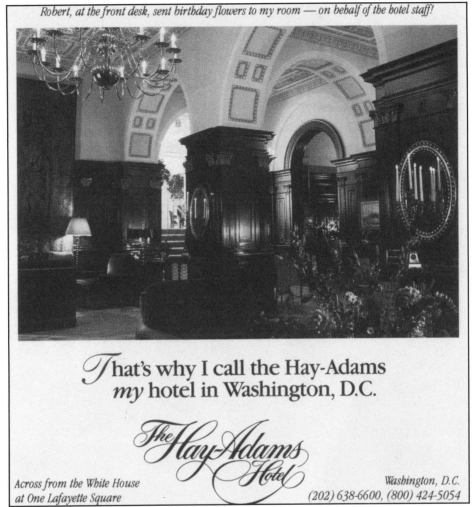

Robert, at the front desk, sent birthday flowers to my room — on behalf of the hotel staff!

$\mathcal{T}$hat's why I call the Hay-Adams
my hotel in Washington, D.C.

The Hay-Adams Hotel

Across from the White House
at One Lafayette Square

Washington, D.C.
(202) 638-6600, (800) 424-5054

This award-winning ad from the Hay-Adams Hotel in Washington, D.C., expresses elegance and personal service.

extensive use of photographs depicting leisure activities, sumptuous foods, or elegant facilities (see Exhibit 11.8).

Many consumer magazines have a reader response card section or reply cards inserted in the magazine, making it easy for readers to respond to ads. Names taken from the reply cards that are mailed in can become the foundation of a mailing list for special promotions.

For many properties, the cost of advertising in a national consumer magazine is prohibitive. Some national magazines offer special regional or city editions that reach specific target areas or market segments. Many medium-to-large properties have found advertising in regional editions of national magazines to be a cost-effective way to reach key target markets.

Trade Magazines. Trade magazines are specialized publications that appeal to people in specific industries or professions. Examples of trade magazines that would be useful to the hospitality industry include *Travel Weekly*, *Successful*

Exhibit 11.9 Sample Trade Magazines

Users	Magazines
Travel agents, wholesalers, corporate travel managers, tour operators, special-interest-group organizers, airline executives, cruise-ship executives, tourist-board executives, hotel representatives, rental car executives	*ASTA Travel News* *Business Travel News* *Corporate Travel* *Corporate Travel Agent* *Courier* *Destination* *Hotel & Travel Index* *Jax Fax* *OAG TRAVEL PLANNER Hotel & Motel RedBook* *Official Airline Guide* *Official Hotel and Resort Guide* *Pacific Travel News* *Travel Age Network* *Travel Agent* *Travel Trade* *Travel Weekly*
Corporate meeting planners	*Medical Meetings* *Meetings & Conventions* *Meeting News* *Official Meetings and Facilities Guide* *Physicians' Travel & Meeting Guide* *Successful Meetings*
Association and society executives	*Association & Society Manager* *The Association Executive* *Association Management* *Best's Insurance Convention Guide* *Insurance Conference Planner*
Incentive operators	*Corporate & Incentive Travel* *Corporation Meetings & Incentives* *Directory of Incentive Travel* *Incentive Marketing* *Incentive Travel* *Incentive World*
Training and development managers	*Training* *Training & Development Journal*
Corporate administrators and sales executives	*Sales & Marketing Management*

Trade publications and journals can be used to reach travel agents, incentive operators, motorcoach tour operators, corporate meeting planners, and administrators and executives in a variety of professions and trades. This is just a partial list of trade publications available to target specific market segments.

Source: Peter Warren and Neil W. Ostergren, "Trade Advertising: A Crucial Element in Hotel Marketing," *The Cornell Hotel and Restaurant Administration Quarterly*, May 1986, p. 62.

Meetings, and *Incentive Travel.* These publications are targeted to travel intermediaries such as travel agents, tour operators, and meeting planners. There are a number of other specialized trade magazines that target other businesses and professions (see Exhibit 11.9). These magazines are excellent opportunities to introduce the property's services to businesspeople who make their own travel decisions.

Exhibit 11.10   Sample Trade Magazine Ad

When it came right down to it, Bob Talley didn't care about our space.

Bob Talley, Manager, Association Services Division

"I could have gotten that anywhere. What I needed was experience."

Everyone who knows the business knows that the Sheraton Washington is one of the largest meeting and convention hotels on the east coast. 1,500 guest rooms and suites. 60,000 square feet of meeting and banquet space, including 34,000 square feet of ballroom area and 26,000 square feet of breakout meeting space. 95,000 square feet of permanent exhibit space. But that's *not* the main reason why Bob Talley's clients like the American Federation for Clinical Research meet here. No. They come to the Sheraton Washington because they're guaranteed something they can't find just anywhere. Experience.

"The people are what sold me. And the people are what keep me coming back."

You can tell the world that you've hosted every major group imaginable. *But,* if they don't come back, you've got nothing but an empty claim.

At the Sheraton Washington, they come back alright. Major associations. Fortune 500 companies. But not because of our 72-foot permanent registration desk. Or the ten separate loading docks we offer for easy access to our exhibit hall. No, they're coming back for one simple reason. Our people.

That's the way it should be. And that's why the first thing we do is assign every group their own personal meeting coordinator. One person who oversees everything. One person to call if you have a question. A request. Or even a problem.

"A convention is a big investment. I wanted mine well-protected."

A comfort level. That's exactly what we offer at the Sheraton Washington. A convention services staff whose experience combined, totals over 100 years. A staff of 1,000 who cater to large groups, day in, day out, year after year. And a hotel that's dedicated to only one thing. Successful meetings.

So, let's face it. You probably already know we've got the space. The amenities. Like seven different restaurants and lounges. Two huge outdoor pools. Even a Metro subway stop right on our grounds. But when all is said and done, the reason you should hold your meeting or convention at the Sheraton Washington should be what Bob Talley's was. Simply put, because we do what we do *so well.*

For more information, call John Hyland, Director of Marketing at (202)328-2000.

Sheraton Washington Hotel

SHERATON HOTELS, INNS & RESORTS WORLDWIDE

Circle #110 on Reader Service Card

Trade advertisements must promote business-oriented benefits such as profit, efficiency, or service. The credibility of this ad is enhanced by the photograph of a meeting planner and the quotes throughout the ad.

Trade magazine advertising differs from consumer magazine advertising in that it usually contains more copy and fewer photographs (see Exhibit 11.10). Since business and group decision-makers are more interested in facts than fantasy, trade ads generally provide more complete information. While a property may attract leisure travelers with promises of a fun and relaxing stay, business and group travelers are usually more interested in how the property can save them time or money while providing necessary services.

Exhibit 11.11   Sample Cost-Effective Photograph

Photo sessions should be set up to photograph property features in both color and black-and-white. This photograph from The Willard Inter-Continental in Washington, D.C., was shot in black-and-white for newspaper advertising and in color for full-color brochures, magazine ads, and posters. Its general nature makes it ideal for repeat use.

Courtesy of The Willard Inter-Continental, Washington, D.C.

**Creating a
Statement with
Photography**

Consumer and trade magazines can provide excellent photograph reproduction. Since so many magazine advertisers take advantage of this capability in their ads, the use of photographs in magazine ads is essential to get attention for the property's message. Color photographs are much more effective than black-and-white photographs, but are more expensive to reproduce.

Even properties with a limited advertising budget can use photographs if they plan carefully. It is often possible to schedule one photo session that will cover all the print advertising needs of a property. Shots of the property's exterior, grounds, recreational amenities, restaurants, lobby, guestrooms, and special features can be taken at the same photo session and used as needed for all types of advertising (see Exhibit 11.11). When scheduling a photo session, it is best to ask the photographer to bring both color and black-and-white film.

Whether color or black-and-white, all photographs should be:

- *Sharp.* The sharper the image, the better a photograph will reproduce. This is especially important for color photographs.

- *Simple.* While photos employing special effects are sometimes used in ads, clear, simple photographs usually work best. Small groups of three or four people can be included in each shot to add interest.

- *Relevant.* Photographs that depict rooms, restaurants, or the property's lobby do not belong with ad copy that describes the property's recreational amenities. Conversely, a campaign promising a romantic, secluded hideaway loses credibility if the property's ads feature airplanes flying overhead, shots of a nearby metropolis, or crowd scenes.

- *Consistent with the property's image.* The property's image may be expressed by photographs portraying a romantic, casual, outdoor, or sophisticated image. Photographs are also an excellent way to express such intangibles as impeccable service or a relaxing stay. Is the promise of a good night's sleep better conveyed by a sentence or a photograph of a guest deep in slumber?

If a property decides to have photographs taken of its buildings or grounds, there are certain considerations. First, there should be a plan—a carefully developed photographer's schedule that will make the most of the property's features and services. Copies of the schedule should be delivered to department heads and, at large properties, shop owners and concessionaires. Second, all care should be taken to ensure the photographs project the desired image. Props must be selected, models chosen, settings prepared. Third, legalities should be addressed. The photographer's contract must be signed and model release forms obtained (every staff member or professional model who appears in a photograph must sign a release form). Last, but certainly not least, the shoot should be orchestrated to create as little inconvenience as possible. Guests should be notified in advance of the project; a luggage cart can be provided to help move camera equipment; and additional personnel should be available to provide assistance.

Creating Effective Ad Copy

Magazine advertising, like newspaper advertising, is not designed to entertain, it is designed to sell. While photographs or artwork can grab a reader's attention, good copy is needed to convince readers that they would benefit from patronizing the property. The following guidelines, very similar to newspaper ad guidelines, should be kept in mind when writing magazine copy:

- *Use an effective headline.* More people read headlines than copy, and a good headline is essential to get the property's message or intent across. Many properties include their name in the headline to build credibility and reader interest.

- *Be specific.* Provide enough specific, factual information in the ad to permit readers to build accurate images in their minds of what a stay at the property or an experience at the restaurant or lounge would be like. Ads in trade magazines and business directories may contain special information such as booking policies, commission rates for travel agents, and so on.

- *Keep it simple.* Stick to a minimum number of points. An ad for a leisure traveler shouldn't contain information about a property's meeting rooms or function space.

- *Caption every photograph.* After the headline, photo captions are the second most-read item in an ad.[8] Captions should be lively and interesting.

- *Include prices.* Include the price of guestrooms, special promotional packages, or other products and services offered in the ad. While some advertisers argue this point, including prices saves time for both the property and consumers.

- *Stick to a campaign that gets results.* This is perhaps the most important guideline of all. Repetition of an ad that gets results can mean more results; don't make changes just for the sake of change. The advertisement will always be new to some readers.

Directory Advertising

Another effective avenue for reaching the buying public is directory advertising. While the list of directories grows yearly, directories can be divided into two basic categories: telephone directories (yellow pages advertising) and business directories.

Telephone Directories

The yellow pages section of the telephone directory is a popular advertising medium. As mentioned in Chapter 9, Americans turn to the hotel and motel headings in telephone directories more than 124 million times a year, and 86% of those times the inquiry is followed up by a phone call, letter, or visit.[9] In other words, yellow pages users are ready to buy, and a yellow pages ad can mean increased revenue for a property (see Exhibit 11.12).

When considering yellow pages advertising, a property must determine whether to place one large ad under the hotel and motel listing or a series of smaller ads under various categories such as restaurants, entertainment, resorts, and so on. If the budget allows for both types of ads to be placed, the property's small ads can refer readers to its large ad.

The property's name is very important in yellow pages advertising, since many yellow pages users already have a property in mind when they open the phone book. If the property is part of a chain, the chain's name or logo should be prominent in the ad.

If a property does not have great name recognition outside the local area, its name can be relegated to a lesser position (smaller type, bottom of the ad, and so on), while the benefits, products, and services of the property can be highlighted. As in most advertising, the target market will determine what features and services a property emphasizes, regardless of whether the property is part of a chain or is an independent property.

Exhibit 11.12   Sample Yellow Pages Ad

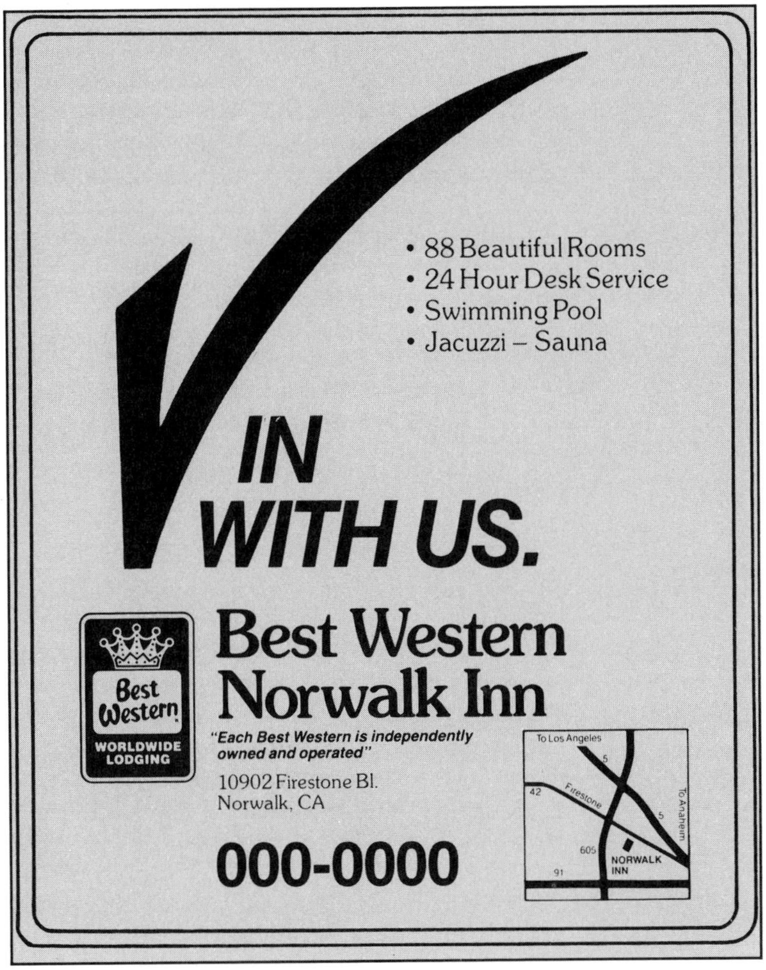

This Best Western yellow pages ad has elements that can attract a potential buyer—an eye-catching graphic, a listing of the property's key features, and a map showing the property's general location.

Courtesy of Best Western International, Inc.

It is important to give travelers an idea of the property's location, landmarks close to the property, and proximity to freeways and transportation terminals. The property can also advertise "Only five minutes from the airport," "Walking distance to Disneyland," and so on.

In an age when many properties are offering similar amenities, a listing of special features and services (in-room movies, waterbeds, baby-sitting service, and so on) can make the property stand out from the competition. The ad should give readers as many reasons to visit the property as possible: AAA approval, Mobil rating, awards, etc.

When evaluating a yellow pages ad, several questions should be asked. Does the ad attract the reader? Does the artwork make the ad stand out on the page, or does the ad fade into the background? Many chain properties have the advantage of pre-designed or "shell" ads—all the property has to do is insert its location and unique features (see Exhibit 11.13). Small independent properties may choose to use the graphic arts services offered by yellow pages representatives. These representatives can help with graphics, typefaces, and even copy writing.

For best results, an ad should be placed in the yellow pages of key target market areas and distant feeder cities as well as the property's own city. Ads should also be placed in the yellow pages of nearby cities, since travelers are often willing to go a little farther for additional amenities and services.

Business Directories

Along with trade publications, business directories have become a popular tool to reach travel agents, group tour planners, and corporate meeting planners. To get the most from business directory advertising, a property should determine:

- Its key sources of business—transient, corporate, family, group, conventions, retirees, small meetings
- Its key feeder cities and markets
- Which business directories corporate planners or other target audiences use
- Which directories are being used by competitors

There are a number of general business directories for the hospitality and travel industries. Some of the major ones are: *Hotel & Travel Index*, *ABC Worldwide Hotel Guide*, *OAG TRAVEL PLANNER Hotel & Motel RedBook*, and *Official Meeting Facilities Guide*. These directories are produced as resource materials for various groups such as travel agents and meeting planners. The areas of the world each directory covers can vary. The *Hotel & Travel Index*, for example, is most widely distributed in North America, while the *ABC Worldwide Hotel Guide* covers markets in the United Kingdom, Germany, France, and the Asia/Pacific region. Most directories include the property's location and reservation information, rates, facilities, services, amenities, commission payment policy, billing information, and information on the local area and attractions.

In addition to advertising in hotel industry directories, a property can advertise in business directories published for other industries and trades. One of the best of these is the American Society of Travel Agents (ASTA) membership directory. Travel agents are responsible for over 70% of the bookings at some properties. Among other important directories to target are directories of meeting planners, executives, and key business and industry leaders. Advertisements in these directories will not follow the format of general consumer ads: as noted previously, travel agents, meeting planners, and executives want the facts.

Measuring the Effectiveness of Print Advertising

In order for print advertising to be cost-effective, ads must be read. To determine if ads are being read, ads must be tested and their effectiveness measured. There are several methods of accomplishing this important phase of print advertising:

1. *Sales measurement.* This method is a comparison of the gross dollar volume generated before and after an advertising promotion. This

Exhibit 11.13   Sample Chain "Shell" Ad

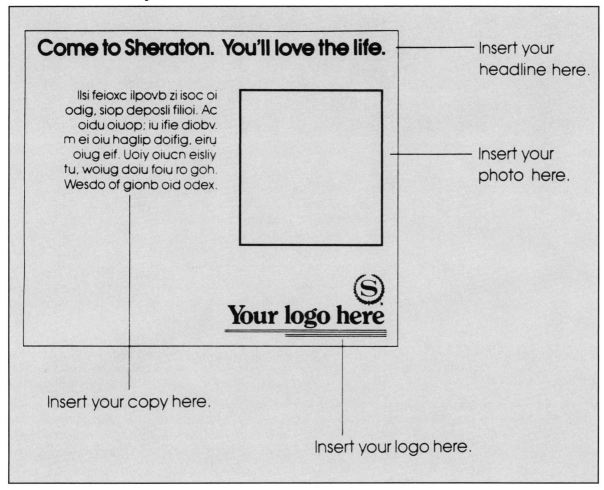

Some hotel chains provide individual properties with guidelines for creating successful ads. In addition to a shell ad, the chain provides suggested borders, typefaces, and headlines. The property can then insert its own copy and photographs to "personalize" its ad.

Courtesy of the Sheraton Corporation.

method, however, is not always accurate, especially if the property is advertising in a number of publications, or if sales have been affected by other factors (bad weather, economic conditions, a good internal sales program, and so on).

2. *Sales analysis.* This method divides sales by geographic area, and involves looking at the relationship between the amount of advertising in an area and the response from that area. In order for this method to be effective, guest history records must be available.

3. *Inquiry measurement.* Telephone numbers, post office boxes, or contact persons can be assigned to particular ads to determine which publications are pulling. For example, if the same ad is being run at the same time in more than one newspaper or magazine, responses from Dallas can be directed to Ms. Smith; responses from

Los Angeles can go to Mr. Jones; and so on. Inquiries, however, are not a measurement of sales. It is important to know how many inquiries are actually converted to sales.

4. *Communication impact.* This last method involves testing the public's awareness of and attitude toward the property before and after an advertising campaign. Professional testing services are often used to assist in this effort. Communication impact may only provide an indication of potential market response.

Conclusion

While print advertising can be a valuable selling tool, it can also be complicated and confusing. The large number of marketing arenas (newspapers, consumer and trade magazines, and directories are just the most commonly used print media), technical elements (type styles, photography, and so on), and market segments that read print media can make the task of designing effective print advertising a difficult one. But there is help.

As mentioned previously, chain properties can often take advantage of pre-designed corporate advertising that can be personalized for each individual property. This service saves considerably on the high cost of design, and provides guidelines for effective print advertisements.

Many properties depend on the expertise of a skilled advertising team, whether in-house or a contracted agency. In today's competitive market, this approach is often the most cost-effective, because chances are less that the property's advertising will be lost in a sea of similar, bland ads.

Small properties can make use of independent free-lance artists and writers, or small advertising agencies. After a successful ad has been developed, it can be used in a number of publications for maximum cost-effectiveness.

For the best results in print advertising, it is important that all properties, large or small, keep abreast of the latest developments in the field. Ads of competitors should be studied. Books on the technical aspects of advertising can be read, and assistance can be requested from organizations that serve the hospitality industry such as the American Hotel & Motel Association and the Hotel Sales & Marketing Association International.[10] By studying trends, determining key newspaper and magazine markets (especially those publications with local and regional editions), and developing advertising for targeted market segments, a property can create print advertising that reaches thousands of potential guests, generates increased profits—and makes the sales job easier.

Notes

1. Howard A. Heinsius, "Newspaper Advertising in the '80s," *Resort Management*, April 1981, p. 14.
2. Courtland L. Bovee and William F. Arens, *Contemporary Advertising* (Irwin: Homewood, Ill., 1982), p. 508.
3. Bob Stein, "Newspaper Advertising for Impact," *Contemporary Hotel Advertising* (Margate, N.J.: Hotel Sales & Marketing Association International, 1974), p. 43.

4. Heinsius, "How to Select Advertising Media More Effectively," *Lodging*, May 1977, pp. 33–35.

5. Heinsius, "How to Select Advertising Media," pp. 33–35.

6. Heinsius, "How to Select Advertising Media," pp. 33–35.

7. "Developing Advertising that Works," a lecture by Peter Yesawich, president of Robinson, Yesawich, and Pepperdine (a marketing, public relations, and advertising firm). Lecture given to students at the University of Nevada, Las Vegas, Fall 1983.

8. John D. Rose and Donald K. Rose, "Resort Marketing," *Resort Management*, December 1979, p. 9.

9. "The Effective Yellow Pages Ad," *Lodging Hospitality*, July 1979, p. 37.

10. *The Art of Hotel and Travel Advertising* (Margate, N.J.: The Hotel Sales & Marketing Association International) is an attractive, four-color book illustrating award-winning collateral materials and print, brochure, and direct mail advertising.

Discussion Questions

1. Newspapers are generally used to achieve what three basic goals?

2. What factors should be considered in selecting a newspaper?

3. Where is a newspaper's "gutter" located?

4. What is spot color?

5. How can advertisers "protect" or separate their ads from other newspaper ads?

6. Should a property's name always be featured in a newspaper ad?

7. What are some common reasons why a newspaper ad doesn't sell?

8. What is an advertorial?

9. What are some advantages of magazine advertising over newspaper advertising?

10. How does trade magazine advertising differ from consumer magazine advertising?

11. What are some criteria for an effective photograph?

12. What guidelines should be followed for preparing effective magazine ad copy?

13. Why should a property advertise in the yellow pages?

14. What are four methods of measuring the effectiveness of print advertising?

Chapter Outline

I. Developing a Direct Mail Campaign
- A. Guest Profiles
- B. Types of Direct Mail Campaigns
  - 1. Series Mailings
  - 2. Single Mailings
  - 3. Timing Direct Mail

II. Mailing Lists
- A. Commercial
- B. General
- C. House

III. Direct Mail Pieces
- A. Types of Direct Mail Pieces
  - 1. Letters
    - a. Design
    - b. Format
    - c. Copy
  - 2. Newsletters
  - 3. Collateral Materials
  - 4. Specially Designed Direct Mail Pieces
- B. Guidelines for Direct Mail Pieces
  - 1. The AIDA Formula
  - 2. The Five Ps
- C. Posting Direct Mail Pieces

IV. Measuring the Cost-Effectiveness of Direct Mail Campaigns
- A. Campaign Costs
- B. Reader Response

V. Conclusion

12 Direct Mail Advertising

Just ten years ago, direct mail advertising represented a 15% share of total advertising expenditures; today that figure is over 30%.[1] More and more properties are discovering that direct mail advertising sent to selected potential guests can be one of the most effective means of advertising used in an advertising campaign. Direct mail has several advantages. Direct mail is:

- *Controllable.* Direct mail is often called a "rifle" medium in contrast with other methods of advertising which employ a "shotgun" approach. Rather than a hit-or-miss effort, direct mail is sent directly to prospects with the most potential. As one hotel sales manager put it: "I go fishing with my advertising, but I catch fish with my direct mail."

- *Personal.* A direct mail piece, unlike newspaper, magazine, and broadcast advertising, is directed to a specific individual. The recipient is more apt to feel that he or she is important to the property.

- *Conspicuous.* A direct mail piece is not lost in the media clutter of ads in a newspaper or magazine.

- *Flexible.* Direct mail offers flexibility in the types of pieces available, the timing of a mailing, and the types of mailings.

- *Designed for prospect involvement and action.* Unlike what can happen when ads are broadcast over radio or TV, recipients do not miss key points of the message while they rush to get a pencil to jot down a name or telephone number. All the information needed is contained in a single, convenient form, and reply cards and toll-free telephone numbers make responding easy.

- *Easily cost-controlled.* Direct mail pieces are limited only by postal regulations and the property's budget. Expenses can be minimized by limiting mailings to qualified prospects or cutting the size of a direct mail piece. Also, to save money, parts of the direct mail promotion (a cover letter, for example) can be prepared by the property's staff rather than by an agency or contracted graphic arts studio.

- *Easily tested and measured.* The ability to accurately and quickly determine the success or failure of a direct mail effort is a great advantage and the biggest difference between direct mail and other

Industry Profile

Jim Mastrangelo began his career in the hospitality industry in 1962, when he worked at a banquet hall. Since that time he has received 2- and 4-year degrees in Hotel and Restaurant Administration. During his career, Mastrangelo has had the opportunity to work for various types of hotels which differed in size (400-room corporate properties to 1,800-room convention hotels) and client mix. He is currently Director of Sales of Ramada's New York Worldwide Sales office, a position that entails promoting Ramada properties throughout the world to accounts within the Northeast region.

**Jim Mastrangelo,
CHA, CHSE**
*Director of Sales
Ramada, Inc.*

❝I've always been a strong believer in direct mail advertising. Direct mail advertising plays a very important part in the overall success of a hotel's marketing program. It's an excellent balance to outside sales calls and telephone solicitation. It presents your product to a client without the expense of a personal sales call. In addition, you're able to solicit many clients at one time—often many more clients than you'd be able to solicit individually—through direct mail.

A direct mail campaign can either be very successful or a complete disaster. All too often direct mail programs have little thought behind them. But direct mail should be as carefully thought out as any other marketing or sales activity. Above all, there should be a central message or theme. Conveying one message successfully is much better than trying to clutter the communication with three or four thoughts, all of which are usually weakly presented.

Each direct mail campaign should be part of your overall marketing plan. If during a particular time of year you know you can expect a drop-off in business, for example, you can develop a direct mail campaign to bring in additional business.

Such a campaign may involve offering free breakfasts to all business travelers, for example.

The promotional piece you develop for your direct mail campaign is as important as the message. It's critical that this piece include some form of response mechanism—a coupon so the client can request additional information, or a phone number for booking a meeting or making a reservation. To further stimulate inquiries, your campaign could offer a gift for each response.

The mailing list is another critical part of a direct mail campaign. You can develop a mailing list from your own hotel's sales department and catering department account files and reservations forms, or names can be purchased from outside sources. Before purchasing an outside list, it's very important to be sure it contains the names of potential buyers of your product. Many lists contain names of people who have absolutely nothing to do with making hotel travel arrangements or booking meetings. If you're soliciting meetings, the best source of potential clients are past clients.

Another type of mailing list that may prove profitable is a list of residents within neighboring communities. This list can be used in a direct mail campaign designed to generate weekend business. Before choosing this option, remember that a direct mail campaign can be costly. You should compare the revenue you expect to generate to the cost of the program. In many cases, an advertisement in a local paper can develop more weekend business at a lower cost.

With direct mail, a property can remain in contact with its clients—and generate new business. But, as with any successful marketing activity, direct mail campaigns must be carefully thought out, directed to a specific target market, developed around a strong theme or central message, and backed up by the capability to 'make good' on claims. If your direct mail campaign meets these criteria, it could be one of the most profitable parts of your hotel's sales program. ❞

advertising methods. Direct mail pieces can easily be coded to track prospect response. A simple comparison of the number of names on a mailing list to the number and types of responses from that list also offers an effective measurement.

With all of these advantages, it is difficult to imagine why every property isn't using direct mail advertising. While the advantages clearly outweigh the disadvantages, certain disadvantages must be considered when developing a direct mail campaign or incorporating direct mail into the property's overall advertising plan:

- *Mailing lists can be expensive or may become ineffective quickly.* Unless a property uses the names of previous guests exclusively, it must purchase mailing lists, and costs can be prohibitive. Also, direct mail experts estimate that 15% to 30% of the names and/or addresses on mailing lists change annually. This necessitates the evaluation, updating, and purging of lists on a regular basis.

- *Direct mail takes extensive planning and production time.* While direct mail pieces can be as simple as a letter or series of letters, many direct mail campaigns include four-color brochures, specially designed folders, or other collateral materials that require extensive production. Add to this the time involved in (1) preparing mailing lists if the lists are compiled in-house, or sorting through purchased mailing lists if the mailing is to go to a specific market group; (2) processing bulk mailings (folding, stuffing, addressing, sorting, mailing); and (3) responding to and recording inquiries, and costs can become prohibitive.

- *Direct mail may be viewed as junk mail.* A segment of the public views direct mail advertising as junk mail and may develop a negative image of a property that sends direct mail pieces. If a direct mail piece is relevant and attractive, it may dispel this image.

Developing a Direct Mail Campaign

Before a direct mail campaign is developed, a property should analyze its markets and determine what features and benefits are most important to its present and potential guests. One way to do this is to develop guest profiles. Guest profiles can be used to create relevant direct mail advertising materials and develop a list of potential direct mail recipients.

Guest Profiles   Accurate profile information can be obtained in a number of ways. The property can analyze data on previous guests. Guest registration forms, questionnaires, and even personal interviews can yield invaluable information on guests and what is most important to them.

The property can also send questionnaires to potential guests in selected target markets. If a property is planning the addition of a convention facility, for example, it may send a questionnaire to meeting planners, group tour operators, or decision-makers in national or local associations. This type of questionnaire could provide input into the types of services required by the targeted market segment. It could also introduce the property and its facilities to the targeted market segment and provide a list of potential guests for the new facility. A future direct mail campaign could take questionnaire responses into consideration—a "you asked for it, you got it" approach.

A guest profile should include the guest's:

- Age (or age group)

- Sex

- Occupation

- Income

- Education

- Place of residence

- Source(s) of travel information (travel magazines, newspapers, travel agents, word-of-mouth, and so on)

- Reason(s) for travel decisions (influence of travel agents, friends, business associates; corporate policies; last-minute choice; and so on)

- Time(s) most likely to travel (season of the year, specific holidays, and so on)

- Number and length of previous stays

If a property finds that its average guest is a businessman who typically stays three days during the week, for example, the property can mail out invitations for an extended weekend stay at a special rate; or, a businessperson's newsletter can be mailed monthly to business guests to keep them informed about special discounts, upcoming promotions, and other items of interest about the property.

Types of Direct Mail Campaigns

In addition to the direct mail pieces used (direct mail pieces will be discussed later in the chapter), there are two key elements to a direct mail campaign: (1) the type of campaign—whether it will be a series of mailings or a single mailing; and (2) the timing of the mailing of each piece.

The following factors help determine whether a campaign will be a series of mailings or a single mailing:

1. The purpose of the mailing. Is the mailing designed to introduce new products, services, and/or facilities? Complement a current media campaign? Attract group business? Solicit inquiries? Solicit rooms or food business?

2. The target markets to be solicited, and the potential return from each.

3. The property's budget for direct mail.

Series Mailings. A campaign that involves a series of mailings has the advantage of keeping the property's name before the prospect: as most salespeople know, it is rare that a sale is made on the first call. A series of mailings can address a variety of prospect needs, since each package in the series can offer one or two new benefits. In addition, a variety of direct mail pieces can be used in a series of mailings—postcards, full-color fliers or self-mailers, or even specialty items. This variety helps keep readers involved and looking forward to the next mailing.

When using a series of mailings, a thematic approach is especially important. The pieces *must* "tie in" and be mailed on a timely basis to encourage consumer recognition and involvement.

Single Mailings. A single mailing is handled differently. To avoid overwhelming the prospect, a single mailing is usually limited to one or two benefits, but the property should say all it has to say and ask for an immediate response. A single direct mail piece may take a number of forms—a letter, postcard, flier, or a combination of these in one package. Timing—the best time to mail the piece—becomes especially important with a single mailing.

Timing Direct Mail. The best timing for a direct mail piece varies with the type of piece being mailed, the lead time before a special promotion, the geographic locations of recipients, and other factors such as the mailing schedule of the local post office.

Whether the piece is a single mailing or part of a series of promotional pieces, a property should avoid peak mailing periods when mail is likely to be delayed. These peak periods include the Christmas season, the period immediately preceding the deadline for income taxes, and special holidays such as Mother's Day, Valentine's Day, Father's Day, and so on. Direct mail pieces should also be timed to avoid periods when big bills are due (Christmas bills usually begin arriving shortly after January 1, and income taxes must be paid by April 15).

The intended recipients will also make a difference in when a piece should arrive. Sales letters to businesspeople, for example, should be timed to arrive on Tuesdays, Wednesdays, or Thursdays to avoid the Monday rush and the Friday cleanup of business for the week. When mailing to a home, a piece should be timed to arrive on a Thursday or a Friday so the family can discuss the property's offer over the weekend. For a weekend promotion, however, an arrival on the Monday or Tuesday preceding the weekend in question would be best (see Exhibit 12.1).

Appropriate direct mail pieces can be mailed at specific times of the year to target groups or individuals who are likely to want a relaxing vacation around that time—CPAs after the tax season, ministers after the Easter or Christmas seasons, families during school vacations, etc.

Mailing Lists

Mailing lists are the heart of any direct mail campaign. Mailing lists fall into three basic categories: commercial lists, general lists, and house lists (see Exhibit 12.2).

Commercial

Commercial mailing lists are usually rented for a one-time mailing rather than purchased. Often, a property does not even see a rental list; the mailing is sent to the list owner's offices for labeling and distribution. If a hotel buys a commercial list, the hotel has complete control over it and can use it as many times as needed; that particular list cannot be sold to any other property.

Before purchasing a list, it is wise to test a portion of it. If a commercial list offers 150,000 names, for example, a property should buy perhaps 5,000

Exhibit 12.1   Direct Mail Brochure for Weekend Business

BED & BREAKFAST
W E E K E N D

Just the other day you said, "We're a sad case. If I get to work after 8 am, I feel guilty. And your only constant companion is that briefcase." Well, the Vista's got a simple question for you. Isn't it time the two of you spent some *real* time together?

Then it's time for our Bed & Breakfast Weekend.

Your weekend includes an American breakfast in the Greenhouse Restaurant, or room service. Full use of the pool, sauna and fitness center, parking privileges, late check-out and much, much more. The real plus of this weekend is that it allows the two of you to spend some time together—to do what you want—or to do nothing at all. $69 per person, per night, double occupancy. For reservations call (212) 938-1990.

SUITE & LOVELY
W E E K E N D

How long has it been since you've felt the excitement of "young love?" Or, rekindled a flame that was starting to dim? If you answered either question with "It's been so long, I don't remember," then it's time for a Suite & Lovely Weekend.

Your weekend includes either a duplex or one-bedroom suite—making the weekend ideal for honeymooners and other loving couples. Complimentary champagne, American breakfast in the Greenhouse Restaurant, or in your room. Full use of the pool, sauna and fitness center—and more. Best of all—you can get the Suite & Lovely "Weekend" *any* day of the week. $149.00 per person, per night, double occupancy. For reservations call (212) 938-1990.

Courtesy of Vista International Hotel, New York, New York.

names. If the test mailing works well, the property can try an additional 10,000 names and continue to purchase if responses warrant the additional expense.

Lists are available with the names of people in particular professions, owners of certain makes of cars, and subscribers to various magazines. Costs vary depending on the type of list requested. Rates usually run from $40 to $100 per thousand names.

Some mailing list firms specialize in creating general lists of past and potential users of hospitality products and services. Names are often obtained from surveys, or by purchasing mailing lists from properties. This method of acquiring a list may seem to be the simplest and most cost-effective, but these lists fail to take a number of points into consideration.

First, guest mixes differ from property to property. While a city property's ideal mix may be 80% business travelers and 20% leisure travelers, a

Exhibit 12.2   Mailing Lists

Commercial Lists

Sources: Magazine subscription lists; clipping bureaus (firms that search magazines and newspapers for items of specific interest to the hospitality industry; there is a fee for this service, but the leads that are provided are specifically targeted for the individual property and/or chain); membership lists of groups and associations (Meeting Planners International, the American Society of Association Executives, etc.). Commercial lists are available through a wide variety of services, including the Standard Rate and Data service, which lists over 25,000 direct mail lists. Lists can also be rented or purchased through association boards and commercial list brokers.

Advantages: Names targeted for specific markets; continually updated lists.

Disadvantages: Cost; possible duplication of names; use of same lists by competing properties.

General Lists

Sources: U.S. Government directories and specialized publications; city and state directories; industry trade directories; credit rating books (Dun & Bradstreet, Standard & Poor, and so on); local and national telephone directories.

Advantages: Low or no cost; a large number of names at one time; availability of names from selected markets.

Disadvantages: These lists are untested and will result in a "hit or miss" effort; lists are often outdated—business and government executives often change positions; an extensive amount of time and research will be needed to cull out unwanted names.

House Lists

Sources: Guest registration cards, surveys, responses to advertising, leads from the property's sales staff, referrals from guests and employees.

Advantages: Low cost; greater percentage of responses than from any other list.

Disadvantages: It takes time to develop a good house list; someone must frequently update the list.

---

resort may prefer to cater to a strictly leisure trade; small properties along state highways would be more interested in individual leisure travelers than would properties with facilities for large groups. Since not all hospitality properties are the same, the names on a general list might not reflect market segments that the property is trying to attract.

Second, general commercial lists do not provide a customer preference breakdown. Although a general list may give the names of people who have stayed in hotels more than six times in one year, for example, it does not provide customer preferences. Does the guest prefer an upscale downtown hotel over an airport property? If so, an airport property would be wasting money on both the list and the expense of mailing. While more specific general lists are available, they may prove to be too costly for a small property or a property with a number of market segments that it wishes to target.

When shopping for a commercial list, the following factors should be considered:

- Does the list contain the desired market segments?
- How were the names obtained? Direct mail responses? Research?
- When was the list last updated?
- Who has tested this list?
- Who is using the list?
- What are projections for future names?
- What types of selections are available? Is the list broken down by zip code, age, income, occupation, job title, and so on?
- What is the cost for selections? Are separate charges incurred for the use of a particular selection criteria (zip code, occupation, income, and so on)?
- What percentage of deliverability is guaranteed? Older lists will have more non-deliverable addresses; newer lists should offer up to 95% deliverability.

Many properties use list brokers to purchase commercial lists for selected target markets. If a property decides to use the services of a broker, it is important that the list broker chosen work closely with the property throughout the entire direct mail process. He or she should have a thorough understanding of the property's needs.

General

General lists are usually obtained in two ways: through business directories or through the membership rosters of associations.

Business directories can provide good lists of key decision-makers. If the property is seeking convention business, for example, a publication such as the *Directory of Corporate Meeting Planners* can prove invaluable. Other publications, such as the *Encyclopedia of Associations*, can also provide the names of group decision-makers. (See Exhibit 4.4 for a list of additional directories containing the names of group planners.)

Another excellent tool for creating a list is the membership roster of associations to which the property's sales staff belongs. Many hotel salespeople are members or associate members of associations relating to the hospitality industry, such as Meeting Planners International (MPI), the Society of Corporate Meeting Planners (SCMP), the American Society of Travel Agents (ASTA), the National Tour Association (NTA), and the American Society of Association Executives (ASAE).

House

House lists are prepared by the property itself, usually from information gathered from registration cards. House lists can also be compiled from responses to surveys, responses to advertisements, leads from the property's sales staff, referrals from the property's guests, and names supplied by the property's employees.

House lists are the most effective of all lists available. Many properties have received up to a 30% response using house lists, as opposed to an average 2% response obtained from a "cold" mailing to names purchased from a commercial list broker. One disadvantage of house lists is that they usually take time to develop.

Once the type of campaign has been determined and mailing lists developed or purchased, the property's staff can begin the process of creating successful direct mail pieces.

Direct Mail Pieces

Direct mail pieces represent the property, so it is important that they be creative but relevant, consistent with the property's image.

Before developing a direct mail piece, the following questions should be considered:

- What does the property want to accomplish with the piece?

- Who is the target audience?

- What type of piece will convey the property's message most effectively?

- How much money is available to develop the piece?

- How many pieces will be needed? Will the mailing be a single mailing or a series of mailings?

- How long will it take to complete the pieces needed?

To address these concerns, a brainstorming session might be held with the property's marketing and sales staff, and with the ad agency if one is employed by the property. The study of successful past campaigns can also provide good ideas.

Types of Direct Mail Pieces   Types of direct mail pieces include letters, newsletters, collateral materials, and specially designed direct mail pieces.

Letters. By far the most common and simplest direct mail pieces are letters (see Exhibit 12.3). Letters have several advantages:

- They are simple to prepare.

- They can be used for a variety of purposes—announcements of packages, products, and/or services; follow ups; introductions to collateral materials sent in the mailing; and so on.

- They can be personalized to involve the reader with the property.

- They can invite immediate action.

- They are relatively inexpensive to produce and mail.

A letter must give the reader a reason to read it and respond. Personalization is often used today to try to ensure that the letter doesn't end up in the wastebasket unread. Personalization may be as simple as addressing the letter to a specific person and using that person's name throughout the letter, or as complex as mentioning details of past stays (obtained from the guest history card) or other personal information (hobbies, preferences for specific locales, etc.) that has been obtained through referrals, surveys, and so on.

Exhibit 12.3   Sample Direct Mail Letter

The
STANFORD COURT

EXECUTIVE OFFICES

Dear Mrs. Smith:

I would like you to send me your husband.

I promise to return him intact, extravagantly well fed and
cared for, and a very happy man.

I work for the brand new STANFORD COURT HOTEL here in San
Francisco. It's my job to convince Very Important People
to try us just once, the next time they're in San Francisco.

And it occurred to me that the quickest way to convince your
Very Important Husband is to convince his Very Important Wife,
namely you, that the STANFORD COURT is perfect for him.

To do that, I've come up with the attached questionnaire.
Please look it over. When you finish it, you might be surprised
to find out how much more it's taught you about your husband.

And when you've finished, if you're convinced that he'll like us,
please let him know. And suggest that he try us, just once.

Ninety-nine times out of a hundred, he'll come home so pleased
with himself for having "discovered" a beautiful new San Francisco
experience, he'll bring you back with him to share the joys on his
next trip.

And in all the questionnaire results I've ever tabulated, I've
never seen anyone turn down a trip to San Francisco.

Sincerely,

Gail Jones

Gail Jones
Sales Representative

GJ/sd

NOB HILL · SAN FRANCISCO · CALIFORNIA 94108 · 415-989-3500

Letters are the most common form of direct mail. They can be used alone, as a cover accompanying brochures or other collateral items, or to introduce a guest survey.
Courtesy of Stanford Court, San Francisco, California.

Computers make it possible to produce personalized letters efficiently, quickly, and economically. But the property's efforts should not stop there. Letters to important guests or clients, especially meeting planners who can bring in thousands of dollars of business, should be *hand-signed*, as time-consuming as it might be. It is surprising how many people examine a signature to see if it is real or printed.

To further increase the chances that letters will be read, letters and envelopes should be of high quality stock, and a dateline should be included to prompt a quick response.[2] Datelines tend to personalize a letter and give a sense of urgency. Mail with postage stamps will generally command more attention than metered mail. Properties mailing in large quantities, of course, may have to opt for metered mail in the interest of saving time and labor, but many properties find the more personal look achieved by using postage stamps worth the extra time and effort.

Design. The design of direct mail letters (as well as other direct mail pieces) will depend in part on the design and type of the property's other advertising. Direct mail is far more effective if the targeted audience can identify it with other advertising—newspaper ads, radio spots, and so on. This kind of "thematic" approach lends credibility as well as name recognition.

There are a number of factors to consider when designing a direct mail letter:

1. *Stationery size.* While a smaller size might offer eye appeal, it is far more practical to use the standard 8½- by 11-inch stationery or the slightly smaller 7¼- by 10½-inch monarch style. The property's letterhead may take up considerable space on smaller-size stationery, limiting the length of the message or necessitating the use of two or more sheets of paper.

2. *Stock color and finish.* Standard white stationery is effective and conservative, and is used primarily for corresponding with groups and businesses. For individuals, a neutrally colored paper stock (buff, tan, gray, etc.) is acceptable (neutral stocks convey a conservative, businesslike image), particularly if the color fits into the property's overall advertising image. Regular bond finishes are normally used for all colors.

3. *Letterheads.* A one-color letterhead is most commonly used, and the same color can usually be used for both white and colored stocks. The letterhead should include the property's name, street address, and telephone number; a logo is also an effective eye-catcher. If desired, the property's slogan or the name of a contact person or the general manager may be included as part of the letterhead.

4. *Envelopes.* Most properties use standard business-letter envelopes that can accommodate 8½- by 11-inch stationery and a rack-size brochure. The property's name, address, and logo or slogan should appear in the upper left corner of the envelope. Envelope and stock colors should match—white envelopes with white stock, and so on.

An attractive envelope will help ensure that the letter is opened, but this is only half the battle. The format and content of the letter will determine whether it is read and acted on or tossed in the wastebasket.

How to Write an Effective Sales Letter

Think before you write. Many people start writing before they know what they really want to say. That's always a mistake. An important factor in business writing—indeed, in any kind of writing—is advance thinking. Before you write a word, ask yourself these questions:

1. What am I trying to convey? How can I express what I want to say most effectively?
2. Who is my reader? Think in terms of one person, even if you're writing a letter that will ultimately be addressed to 100 persons. Firmly visualize that person in your mind.
3. How can I make this letter truly readable? Imagine that the intended recipient has just walked into your office and is sitting across the desk from you. Write to him or her as you would talk to him or her in person.

The best way to become proficient in writing is by observing certain rules—and practicing. Here are six steps to get you started:

1. Jot down notes in advance on what you want to cover in your writing. Decide which is the most important point and *put it up front*.
2. Express your thoughts clearly and concisely. Avoid redundant expressions and long, involved sentences. Use personal words—such pronouns as I, my, ours, theirs (as you would in talking to the person).
3. Use concrete words that involve seeing, tasting, touching, feeling, and hearing. For example, avoid abstract terms such as "recreational activity" in favor of concrete words that can be visualized such as "tennis, golf, swimming." Don't say "meeting facilities" if you can truthfully say "12 meeting rooms on the mezzanine."
4. Keep your reader's vocabulary in mind. Not everybody knows what a "familiarization tour" is. Anybody would respond to "Visit us as our guest and see our facilities for yourself." Avoid trite expressions and slang.
5. Use live words that convey action. For example, "Our staff will prepare the dinner" is better than "The dinner will be prepared by our staff." Keep it active, not passive.
6. Place the person doing the action—the doer—before the verb. For example, "The manager invites you to use the pool" is better than "Guests are invited to use the pool."

Source: Adapted from Robert D. Lilien, "How to Write a Better Letter," *Lodging*, August 1982, pp. 55–59.

Format. An attractive format can make a letter more inviting. The block letter format is used most often, but there are a number of variations that can be used effectively. Unusual formats can be used as a sales gimmick as long as they are tied to a specific promotion or market segment. For the most part, business executives prefer a conservative format rather than a gimmick. The typeface used should be in keeping with the format and content of the letter. Conservative type is more suitable for standard business letters, while script type can be used for "personal" invitations.

Copy. While people may open attractive letters, few make buying decisions without having a good reason.

Meeting the needs of the reader is of utmost importance, and the first paragraph should do just that. Many business letters start out with the same trite phrases; these letters often don't get read. Readers should not have to read half the letter before they know what the property is expressing or offering. Direct mail letters must be informative and interesting, complete but not repetitious.

The body of the letter should be written in clear, concise statements that inform the reader of property benefits. Long sentences, fancy words, and industry jargon should be avoided. The letter should get the reader involved. Avoid beginning sentences with "I" or "we"; begin sentences with phrases such as "As you can see," "Knowing how you feel about," and so on. Emphasizing "you" focuses on the reader and his or her personal interests. "You can enjoy a workout or a tennis game no matter what the weather" is far more involving than saying, "We have a complete indoor gym and tennis courts."

Letters should also contain a reason or reasons for the prospect to respond, and a means to do so. In addition to a toll-free telephone number, a reply card, postcard, coupon, or certificate can be included with the letter.

Letters are effective only if they are read. A professional presentation, interesting copy, and reader involvement will ensure that the property gets the most from the letters in its direct mail campaign.

Newsletters. Newsletters are often used to solicit business for a property (see Exhibit 12.4). While some properties limit the use of their newsletter to public relations campaigns, this sales tool also can be used to entice potential guests, travel agents, and meeting planners to purchase the property's products and services. Like letters, newsletters can be fairly inexpensive to mail and are excellent sources of information about the property.

When using newsletters as direct mail pieces, keep the following in mind:

1. *Appearance.* While white paper is adequate, colored paper attracts more attention. Artwork should be kept simple, photographs (if used) should be sharp and clear, and the type should be easily readable. Since readers' eyes can only take in so much copy at a time, most newsletters should be set in two columns. Copy that extends across an entire page tends to be hard to read.[3]

2. *Layout.* The reader should be led from one article to the next through the use of bold headlines or enticing artwork. Copy should be concise and to the point, with no unnecessary duplications or trite material that might give a negative impression. White space should be used skillfully to make the newsletter more attractive and readable.

3. *Identification.* The property's logo, name, address, and telephone number should appear on every page of the newsletter. This information can be prominently displayed in a box, or at the bottom of each page, or can appear somewhere in the copy on each page. This repetition makes it easier for the reader to respond to attractive promotions or packages.

While newsletters may cost more than letters to produce and mail, they have the advantages of a longer reading life (many are passed on to friends and acquaintances) and more room for illustrations. The problem of timing may also be solved with newsletters. Most newsletters are produced on a regular basis, and seasonal special editions can be included to coincide with peak buying times.

Exhibit 12.4   Sample Newsletter

Newsletters are rapidly becoming one of the most popular forms of direct mail. This newsletter, highlighting the grand opening of Marriott's Orlando World Center, was mailed to 10,000 meeting planners across the country.

Courtesy of Marriott's Orlando World Center, Orlando, Florida.

Collateral Materials. Whether used separately, in conjunction with letters, or enclosed in bills or business correspondence, collateral materials play an important role in direct mail (see Exhibit 12.5).

Some collateral materials such as fliers are inexpensive to produce and can be used most effectively in a general mailing or as envelope stuffers in routine correspondence to previous guests. Other collateral materials such as

Exhibit 12.5   Sample Postcard

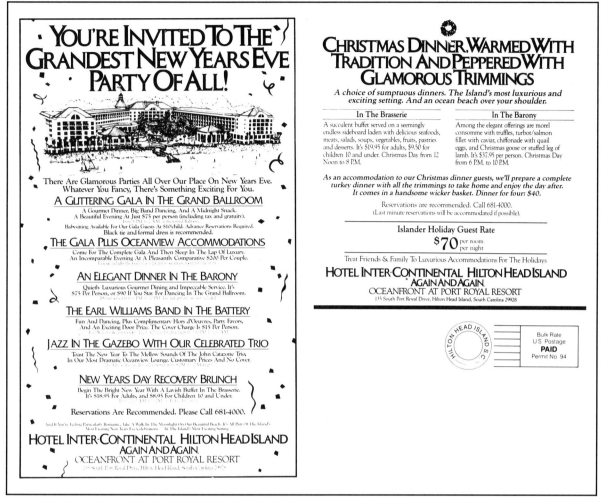

Postcards can be inexpensive and effective direct mail pieces. This postcard promotes holiday specials.

Courtesy of Inter-Continental Hilton Head at Port Royal, Hilton Head, South Carolina.

brochures are often expensive to produce and should not be sent out as a general mailing. It is far more cost-effective to save four-color materials for responding to inquiries.

The Denver Inn used collateral materials creatively in a direct mail campaign that featured a teddy bear theme. For the first mailing, travel agents were sent a colorful direct mail piece with a tiny teddy bear attached. Responding travel agents were sent a second mailing which included a small teddy bear wearing a Denver Inn banner with the property's toll-free reservations number printed on it.

Specially Designed Direct Mail Pieces. Specially designed direct mail pieces are often used in direct mail campaigns. There are a number of formats or styles that can be used. One of the most popular is the four-page letterhead: a personally typed letter on the first page with three pages of illustrations or descriptive materials following. Another widely used form is a full-color postcard with a reservation reply card attached. Still other properties use a self-mailer: a specially printed piece that advertises a special promotion or the property itself. A self-mailer saves a property both time and money—there is no need for the piece to be inserted into an envelope and the mailer can be sent third-class.

Guidelines for Direct Mail Pieces

The following guidelines can be used when creating all types of direct mail pieces.

The AIDA Formula. For best results, many properties use the AIDA formula: *A*-ttention, *I*-nterest, *D*-esire, and *A*-ction.

1. *Attention.* Before a direct mail piece can be effective, it must first get the reader's attention, whether that attention is gained through an intriguing teaser on the envelope, a clever caption or drawing on the mailing piece, or the copy itself. The main point of the property's message should be presented at the beginning of the piece. It is estimated that group travel planners, for example, receive at least 75 different promotional pieces each week;[4] to get read rather than discarded, direct mail pieces must capture attention immediately.

2. *Interest.* Once the reader's attention has been captured, it is important to offer the reader the promise of a reward. In other words, his or her interest must be kept through offering an answer to the question, "What's in this for me?"

3. *Desire.* If the prospect's interest has been maintained, he or she may then begin to desire to experience what the property has to offer. But doubts may still exist ("Can anything be this good?" "Is there a catch?"). Additional creative copy can both dispel these doubts and enhance the reader's desire.

4. *Action.* Just because readers have a desire to respond does not mean they will; the property's message should *ask* for action. If a reply card is enclosed, a postscript may suggest: "Interested? Mail the convenient, postage-paid reply card today!" Or, the copy may note the property's toll-free reservations number.

In order for the AIDA formula to work, the emphasis should be on the consumer; he or she will respond far more favorably when the piece is directed to meeting personal wants and needs. Secondary attention should be placed on considerations such as availability and price. An exception is when the direct mail piece is designed for travel agents—then availability and price become more important.

The Five Ps. Another approach to developing a direct mail piece can be called the Five Ps. No matter what type of direct mail piece is being designed, with this approach the message should first form a *picture* in the prospect's mind. The prospect should get involved in what the direct mail piece has to offer.

The second part of the message should offer a *promise* and show how the property can fulfill that promise. This portion of the message should clearly define products and services that can make the promise a reality.

Features and benefits should be carefully spelled out. A property should never assume that everyone knows what it stands for and what services it offers.

Next, the message should *prove* what the property is claiming is true. Testimonials, endorsements, success stories, and statistics can be used to support the property's claims.

The fourth part of the message should provide a *push*—tell the prospect exactly what the property wishes him or her to do: fill out a reply card, call a toll-free number, or answer a questionnaire. Because it is so important, the push should be included in the last paragraph or part of a message, and may also be included in the first part. The push should be specific and directly relate to what the direct mail piece has to offer.

The final—and sometimes most important—part of the direct mail piece is a simple *postscript*. When most people read a direct mail piece, they first glance at the letterhead (which should always be included at the top of each piece); their next glance is to the bottom of the letter, to the signature and the P.S. (if there is one).[5] An interesting postscript can generate reader involvement.

Posting Direct Mail Pieces

There are three basic ways to send direct mail advertising:

1. *First class*—Personal letters and postcards.
2. *Third class single piece*—Booklets, brochures, catalogs.
3. *Third class bulk*—newsletters or other pieces mailed in quantity.

Third class bulk is the most inexpensive way to mail, although it takes longer than first class mail. As of January, 1989, properties using bulk mail were required to pay an annual fee of $50 for the privilege, in addition to $50 for a mailing permit. Permits are issued for an indefinite period, provided the property mails under the permit at least once during a twelve-month period.

There are certain restrictions which may limit the use of third class bulk mail:

- The mailing must consist of a minimum of 200 pieces, or the total weight of the mailing must be 50 pounds.
- The pieces must be identical in size and weight.
- The address of each piece must include a zip code.
- Pieces must be presorted and bundled or sacked according to zip code.
- The pieces must be separately addressed to different persons and must carry postage permit imprints, meter stamps, or pre-cancelled stamps.
- The mailing must be deposited at the post office which issued the bulk mailing permit, or at a location designated by the postmaster.

These restrictions and additional steps make third class bulk mailings a little more work than first class mailings, but many properties find the savings worth the extra effort. At the current rate, direct mail pieces can be bulk mailed for almost half the cost of first class mail for the first 250,000 pieces mailed in one year.

Measuring the Cost-Effectiveness of Direct Mail Campaigns

The cost-effectiveness of a direct mail campaign can be measured by comparing campaign costs with the level of reader response.

Campaign
Costs

To address the first consideration, let's look at the classic four-part direct mail package—a mailing envelope, a letter, a brochure or other piece of collateral material, and a reply form. In developing this direct mail package, there are a number of costs involved:

- Material costs: paper, envelopes, collateral materials or specialty items used as collateral materials

- Production costs: ad agency or free-lance personnel costs (if used); typesetting, artwork and/or photographs; printing costs

- Labor costs: costs of compiling the mailing list if it is created in-house; costs of inserting, sorting, stapling, and so on; costs of recordkeeping (responses, updating lists, etc.)

- Other costs: mailing list fees, postage

Many properties employ mailing services or lettershops to reduce labor costs and save time. The mailing list and the components of the direct mail package are delivered to the mailing service, which stuffs the envelopes, sorts the mail, and meters and mails the finished pieces. Using a mailing service is often more cost-effective than hiring additional office staff or burdening the property's regular staff with a large mailing.

Reader
Response

The success of any direct mail campaign is measured primarily by reader response (see Exhibit 12.6).

To measure reader response, a response code or number should be printed on direct mail pieces. If a piece is being sent to the Midwest, the South, and the Northeast, for example, each of these areas can be coded with a particular number that allows for tabulating the responses. In the case of pieces that invite response via a toll-free number, a particular operator's name or number can be used for tabulation—respondents in the Midwest could ask for Operator 1, for example. Responses can be tabulated to determine which list is most effective, which market segment is responding most favorably to the promotion, and which areas seem most profitable for follow-up promotions.

A test mailing is sometimes used to measure reader response. With a test mailing, a property mails inexpensive pieces to targeted audiences—audiences defined by occupation or geographic location, for example. The response to this test mailing gives a property an idea of the number of responses it can expect from a regular mailing. A property can send out more expensive direct mail pieces to a particularly responsive market segment or geographic location.

Exhibit 12.6   Computing Direct Mail Costs

This formula is used to determine the costs *per piece* of a direct mail effort. While the $8 figure calculated in this example may seem high, it is important to remember that this cost is a *front-end cost* only. "Front-end cost" refers to the cost per response from the initial mailing. Over a period of time, the respondents to the initial mailing will likely respond to additional offers. Therefore, the property will make money on the *back-end*—the subsequent responses—in addition to having acquired each respondent for a house list (an additional savings on the back-end; the property no longer has to purchase these respondents' names).

Typical Costs Per Direct Mail Piece

LIST	$.065
COMPUTER	.005
LABEL	.005
LETTER	.025
BROCHURE	.040
RESPONSE DEVICE	.020
ENVELOPE	.020
LETTERSHOP	.020
POSTAGE	.120
TOTAL	**$.320**

$$\text{Cost per response} = \frac{\text{Cost per piece} \times \text{number of pieces mailed}}{\text{Number of responses}}$$

Assuming the cost per piece is $.32, and that 2,500 pieces were mailed and generated a response rate of 4%, the cost per response would be calculated as follows:

$$\frac{\$.32 \times 2,500 \text{ pieces}}{100 \text{ responses}} = \$8$$

It is also possible to measure the potential of two similar package promotions by split-testing a direct mail list. A split test assigns every other name from the mailing list to one promotion, the remaining names to the other. Whichever promotion draws the most responses is the better package, and the one that will be used in future mailings.

The audience that receives the mailing influences cost-effectiveness in terms of sales per direct mail piece. A property may send out 2,500 letters to individuals and 2,500 letters to travel agents and group meeting planners, for example, and even though the initial cost of production and mailing is the same, the resulting sales may vary greatly. It is likely that more business will be generated by the travel agents and the meeting planners, so their mailing will probably be more cost-effective. While this fact may lead a property to send out more direct mail pieces to sources of group business, a property's desired guest mix also has to be considered. A property may need to continue sending direct mail pieces to individual potential guests in order to maintain its desired guest mix.

When monitoring responses, it is important to remember that it may require six to eight mailings before the public is ready to buy. In other words, a property should not rely on one campaign. This does not mean that every

Some Important Direct Mail Do's and Don'ts

DO

- Keep in mind that direct mail is a pinpoint or "rifle" medium that is most effective when used on specific markets.
- Compile or purchase mailing lists with utmost care. The mailing list is the single most important element of the mailing.
- Keep lists up-to-date. Lists deteriorate at a rate of 20% or more a year. "Dead" names cost you money.
- Insist on quality production and careful attention to details. The impression readers get from your mailing is the impression they get of your hotel. Make sure that first impression says "I care."
- Spell names right. A person's name is his or her most important possession.
- Use the reader's name whenever possible; direct mail is the only medium in which you can.
- Follow up inquiries fast. Be sure information requested is furnished.
- Make your copy interesting and persuasive, of course. But most of all make it sincere and believable. Promise only what you can deliver—and *deliver what you promise*.
- Tell readers exactly what you want them to do. Ask for the sale.
- Be consistent. Repeat your important sales points often.

DON'T

- Try to say too many things in one mailing. Make one important point clearly and completely in any one mailing.
- Forget to plan and prepare for follow-up of leads that may be developed. Make sure literature and employees are available in sufficient numbers.
- Go after stale names. Any name inactive for three or more years is of questionable value.
- Quit after one or two mailings. Good salesmanship and good advertising require patience.
- Tire of a good theme or program before your readers do. They pay a little less attention to your promotion than you do. Only *results* can tell you when a good idea is wearing thin.
- Make it hard for your readers to reach you. See that your address and phone number appear on every major element of your mailing.
- Mail duplicate pieces to the same person. Duplicates cost money for printing and postage and create an impression of management carelessness and disinterest.
- Try to "do it yourself." Direct mail is a complex medium. A qualified consultant helps you two ways—by maximizing results and minimizing production and postage costs.

Source: Adapted from John J. Patafio, "Direct Mail—A Personal Medium for a Personal Business," *Contemporary Hotel Advertising* (Margate, N.J.: Hotel Sales & Marketing Association International, 1974), p. 35.

campaign has to be a series campaign; as mentioned previously, single mailings can be used to announce special events or services, and may also be sent to coincide with major holidays and other times when specific major market segments may be planning their vacations.

To make the most of direct mail responses, inquiries should be answered at once. Many direct mail pieces are offers of additional information; the key to an actual sale is the prompt mailing of the material requested. The cost of additional office help to accomplish this should be figured into the direct mail budget. Before initiating a direct mail program, the property should detail exactly how leads will be followed up, particularly if requests will be coming in from widely dispersed geographic areas. It may make more sense to rotate the distribution of mail by geographic area, allowing adequate response time for inquiries to come in from one area before distributing direct mail pieces to another.

Conclusion

Direct mail, when properly planned, managed, and followed up, can be an excellent source of future referrals, rooms and facilities business, and repeat business. By using a good mailing list, designing attractive direct mail pieces, offering appropriate benefits to each targeted market segment, and promptly following up on responses, a property can build an excellent guest base at a relatively low cost.

Notes

1. "Direct Mailing," a presentation to the HSMAI Annual Conference in Atlanta on November 23, 1987, given by George Lynaugh, Executive Vice President, McCann Direct Inc.
2. *Direct Mail and Local Media Advertising Guide*, prepared by TWA, p. 22.
3. *Direct Mail and Local Media Advertising Guide*, p. 37.
4. Todd Englander, "What's in the Mail," *Meetings and Conventions*, June 1987, pp. 31–33.
5. Helen Recknagel, "Direct Mail Promotion," *Cornell Hotel and Restaurant Administration Quarterly*, August 1975, p. 47.

Discussion Questions

1. What are the advantages of direct mail advertising?
2. What drawbacks must be considered before incorporating direct mail into a property's overall advertising plan?
3. What information should a guest profile contain?
4. What are some of the factors that help determine whether the direct mail campaign will be a series of mailings or a single mailing?
5. What are three basic categories of mailing lists? Which list is most effective?
6. What factors should be considered before purchasing a commercial mailing list?
7. What are some questions that should be considered before developing a direct mail piece?
8. What are some advantages of direct mail letters?

Discussion Questions (*continued*)

9. What is the AIDA formula?

10. What are six criteria that must be met for a mailing to qualify for the third-class bulk rate?

11. What costs are involved in developing a typical direct mail package?

Chapter Outline

I. Radio Advertising
   A. Selecting Radio Stations
   B. Developing Radio Ads
      1. Types of Radio Ads
   C. Radio Ad Costs
      1. Buying Radio Airtime
   D. Measuring the Effectiveness of Radio Ads
II. Television Advertising
   A. Selecting TV Stations
   B. Developing TV Ads
      1. Types of TV Ads
   C. TV Ad Costs
      1. Buying TV Airtime
   D. Measuring the Effectiveness of TV Ads
III. Video Advertising
   A. Video Brochures
   B. Video Magazines

13 Broadcast Advertising

Until the twentieth century, advertising was limited largely to the printed word. Today, however, through radio, television, and video advertising, a property has many exciting alternatives available to get its message to thousands, even millions, of potential guests at one time. Properties can use radio and television in conjunction with newspaper and magazine ads to reach more than 80% of the nation's population.[1]

Radio Advertising

Radio is an excellent saturation medium. That is, radio is a medium that allows a property to repeat its message with considerable frequency to reach a large number of people. Best of all, radio is a selective medium. Unlike commercial television, which is programmed for a mass audience, radio stations generally appeal to a more focused audience. There are rock, top-40, country, classical, all-talk, all-news, and ethnic music stations. Before a property plans a radio strategy, it is important to know the demographics of a station's audience, and the best times to advertise a particular message.

To reach the teen audience, top-40 and rock stations offer the most exposure. Many properties overlook this important market, but teenagers are generally an affluent group and are excellent prospects for restaurant and special local promotion advertising. In addition, teenagers often influence the family's choice of vacation spots, so this market may well be worth the advertising dollars spent.

To reach people in the 18 to 30 age bracket, progressive rock, soft rock, adult contemporary, and golden-oldie stations are effective avenues. Most people in this age group either work or go to school, so the best times to reach them are drive times (6:00 to 10:00 a.m. and 3:00 to 7:00 p.m.), in the evening after 7:30 p.m., and on weekends after 10:00 p.m.[2]

If the target audience is families, messages can be offered on golden-oldie, adult contemporary, country, all-talk, and all-news stations. Surveys have shown that radio stations reach their largest family audiences between 6:00 a.m. and 7:00 p.m. on weekends.[3] A large audience of upscale families and working women can also be reached between 7:00 p.m. and midnight.[4]

Industry Profile

Michael J. Dimond
*Senior Vice
President—Marketing
Caesars Palace*

Michael Dimond held a number of positions within the Hyatt Hotels Corporation from 1962–1973, including serving as national sales manager for the chain's New York City properties during his final three years with the firm. He has also served as the national sales director for Doral Hotels of Florida, and was vice president of marketing for the Opryland Hotel from 1975–1985. In 1983 Dimond was named chairman of the corporate marketing committee for Opryland USA, Inc. He later served as vice president for the Boca Raton Hotel and Club and as general manager of Saddlebrook Resort (both located in Florida) before assuming his duties as Senior Vice President—Marketing for the 1,600-room Caesars Palace in Las Vegas. Dimond is an active member of many industry organizations, and has served as vice president of external affairs for Meeting Planners International and as the first vice president of the Hotel Sales & Marketing Association International. Dimond has also won a number of awards, including Salesman of the Year (Insurance Conference Planners), Supplier of the Year (Meeting Planners International), 1984 Marketing Executive of the Year (HSMAI), and recognition as one of the nation's 25 top travel executives in 1984 (Business Travel News).

❝Television delivers a message immediately to large numbers of people. Although areas of programming such as sports or special-interest subject matter allow television to be targeted to fairly narrow groups, most television programming is designed to appeal to the largest possible audience.

Frequency is important if the TV ad's message is to be thoroughly understood and remembered. Cost will depend on the length of the commercial.

The primary unit of commercial length is 30 seconds, although 10-, 15-, and 60-second lengths are also common. A 60-second spot generally costs twice as much as a 30-second spot; however, a 10-second spot is 50–60% of the cost of a 30-second spot, and a 15-second spot is about 75% the cost of a 30-second commercial.

Television requires a fairly lengthy lead time in terms of commercial production. Commercial production and purchase of time must be planned well in advance to assure the ad's exposure during programming that will best contribute to a property's image.

One of the best uses of television is to purchase time during programs whose content ties in with the property or its message. A special program on Las Vegas, for example, would be an excellent vehicle for a Las Vegas property's commercial. Or, long-term sponsorship of a local sports team can stimulate community goodwill and provide local identification for a property.

Radio is used more for frequency than for high reach. You must buy time at a lot of radio stations in order to reach a mass audience, since radio offers such a wide variety of stations. But radio is useful when the property wishes to closely target a particular audience segment. Radio is also used to announce special events or promotions as they arise, or to boost sales on an as-needed basis.

Production of radio spots can be quick and inexpensive. In fact, an advertiser can choose to have copy read live by a station announcer and avoid expensive production costs. The most common length for radio commercials is 60 seconds, although 30-second spots are available at 80%— or more—of the 60-second costs. Rarely are radio spots under 30 seconds. The rates for radio commercials are highly negotiable and are based on a combination of audience size, ratings, and supply and demand. ❞

Selecting Radio Stations   There are several factors to consider when selecting the radio station or stations that will best get the property's message across to the property's targeted audiences. Demographics, costs, a station's image, and special promotions offered by radio stations to attract advertisers will all play a part in the selection process.

Almost all radio stations offer demographic information on their listening audiences, but before making a final selection, a property's marketing and sales staff, advertising staff, or ad agency representative should listen to each station. Important factors to note are the number and frequency of ads. Are there ads from competitors? Are ads lumped together or are they spread out over each hour? How many ads does the station run on an average day? A property's message might easily get lost if ads are run too frequently, or if a competitor can afford to advertise more often during a certain time period.

Before deciding on a station, it is important to determine:

1. *Reach.* How many households are reached by the station? What are the demographics of the audience in specific time periods? Early morning audiences may not be the same as late evening audiences, for example.

2. *Frequency.* How often will a property's message be aired? Will it be aired during the target market's prime listening time?

3. *Cost per thousand (CPM).* How much will it cost the property to reach 1,000 listeners?

4. *Target market group(s).* Does the station reach the specific audience or audiences targeted by the property? If not, is there another station that does? If the target market is spread out over a large area, how cost-effective would it be to split advertising between two or more stations?

The decision-maker for selecting radio stations varies from property to property. At small properties the general manager may be ultimately responsible for choosing a radio station or stations. At midsize properties, this decision may fall to the marketing director, who may request recommendations from the property's advertising staff or ad agency. In the case of large properties, recommendations are usually given by ad agencies, and the final decision may be made by the marketing director or by another designated member of the property's management team, such as the director of advertising.

Selecting a radio station can be confusing, but there is a way to make the selection process easier and at the same time promote the property to the stations that will be advertising its products and services: a "Radio Day."

The concept of a Radio Day is simple. Each radio station is contacted by phone and follow-up letter and asked to come to the property for a 30-minute presentation of what the station has to offer. Each station is told which target markets the property wishes to reach, and asked to bring a sample tape of typical programming, information on marketing strategies, and demographic data.

At the conclusion of the presentations, all of the station managers or salespeople can be invited to a complimentary reception or buffet. The station representatives may be told the date of the final decision at that time.

Selecting radio stations in this way prevents executive wear and tear, and gives the property's marketing or advertising staff an opportunity to review all pertinent data in a relatively short time. It is also an excellent way to develop rapport with the local media.

Developing Radio Ads   Once a station has been selected, the next step is to decide how to best present what the property wants to promote.

For the most part, a radio ad should keep to one general idea. Ads should be tailored to specific market segments. Background music, sound effects, and method of announcing are very important. Some properties opt for a local disc jockey or celebrity to announce the ad. This technique can give the ad credibility, especially when the announcer has a large following. But no matter what the property's choice, it is important to create an ad that will stand out from the rest (see Exhibit 13.1).

Since a radio ad can only be heard—leaving behind nothing for the listener to use as a reference should he or she have a question—the message must leave a memorable impact. Products and services should be mentioned often to become memorable.

A typical radio ad includes:

1. *An attention grabber.* It is essential to reach listeners immediately, before they switch to another station. This can be done with sounds or music as well as copy.

2. *A message.* An ad's message should focus on one idea only and should be clear and direct; unnecessary information should not be included. The property's name should be mentioned early and often. Once name awareness has been built, the ad should stretch the listener's imagination: word pictures, references to current events, imaginative sound effects, and music can all add to the impact of the message. Listeners should be given reasons to call or visit rather than overwhelmed with a barrage of property facts.

3. *A call to action.* Radio is an excellent tool for building urgency, and the property should not neglect to ask for the sale. The ad should urge the listener to "Call for reservations now," "Drop by for a visit today," or "Call our toll-free reservations line." The property's name should be repeated at the end of the ad to give listeners who tuned in late an opportunity to respond.

After radio copy has been written, it is not enough to read it; it must be *listened to* in order to judge its impact on radio listeners. The ad should be judged in terms of clarity and interest, and for compatibility with the station's format or programming. Properties can get help in this area from the radio station itself. Most radio stations can provide background music, sound effects, and technical assistance (most of these services are offered as part of the ad price). If the property is part of a chain, the property may use special "donut" ads that have been prepared by corporate offices (see Exhibit 13.2). Donut ads are either 30- or 60-second prerecorded ads (usually music and a voice-over) that leave room for individual property messages. The prerecorded tapes are taken to the radio station along with individual property copy for final production.

Types of Radio Ads. There are several types of radio ads that can be used by a property:

1. *Straight announcement.* This type of ad simply lists the benefits of the product offered and asks the listener to act. In most cases, little or no background music is used. Straight announcements can work

Exhibit 13.1 Sample Successful Radio Advertising

SAWGRASS Radio :60	
(office sounds in background)	
WOMAN #1:	Stella, you notice anything weird about Mr. Hastings?
STELLA:	Ahhh, you mean like wearing sunglasses in the office?
WOMAN #1:	Well, ya.
STELLA:	Mmmm, mmm.
WOMAN #1:	And look at his feet.
STELLA:	He's wearing golf shoes.
WOMAN #1:	Right.
STELLA:	Uh!
WOMAN #1:	You know at the coffee area, he asked me if he could play through.
STELLA:	Oh, well, listen, I caught him at his desk, hanging ten, yelling
BOTH WOMEN:	Surf's up!
WOMAN #1:	I know, I heard that.
STELLA:	Mmmm, mmm.
WOMAN #1:	Well, at least he's still wearing a tie.
STELLA:	Ya, but with a tennis outfit?
ANNOUNCER:	People all over Jacksonville are driving themselves to distraction. A beautiful distraction. Sawgrass. With our Commuter Vacation Package, you can go from desk to dunes in 30 minutes or less. Stay in the Sawgrass Resort Village, play golf, tennis or just relax on the beach after work and be back in the office the next day. Give your family a week or weekend at Sawgrass, complete with supervised programs for the children. Call 285-2261 and say you want to drive yourself to distraction. No one at work will know you're on vacation, unless you get carried away.
(office sounds in background)	
WOMAN #1:	Stella, what's he doing in the secretarial pool?
STELLA:	I don't know. Look's like a half gainer.
(springboard)	
STELLA:	Stand back.
(splash)	

PIER 66 Radio :60	
TOM:	Boy, it's good to be home again. I wonder who called? *SFX: (Click, rewind phone message machine)*
RAY:	*(telephone voice, beep)* Tom. It's Ray. I'm going to spend the weekend at Pier 66. Meet me there. They've got this great Get Aquainted Summer Deal. Just 25 bucks a day if we share the room.
JONI:	*(second message; SFX/Beep)* Tom, this is Joni, Sally's friend. Meet me at the Pier Top Lounge at Pier 66 Friday night. Bye.
RAY:	*(third message; SFX/Beep)* Tom, Ray again. Sunday night. Where have you been?! You missed a great weekend at Pier 66. I met this terrific gal named Joni.
DON PARDO:	*(SFX soap opera music)* Will Ray find out about Tom and Joni? Will Joni find out about Tom and Ray? Find out at Fort Lauderdale's Pier 66 Hotel and Marina, the 22-acre island resort on the Intracoastal. They'll be talking about it around the pool, on the courts, in the jacuzzis, at the restaurants and high above it all in the revolving Pier Top Lounge. Make your reservations now. Call 525-6666. So long for now from Pier 66.

These radio spots were winners in a recent advertising competition. Note that both ads use an attention grabbing statement, both use a humorous approach to keep the listener's attention, and both give the listener an opportunity to act on the property's offer.

Source: *The Art of Hotel & Travel Advertising, A Look at the Past—A Guide to the Future* (Washington, D.C.: Hotel Sales & Marketing Association International, 1987), pp. 53–54.

well for a property, but the copy must be interesting to attract and keep the listener's attention.

2. *Musical.* Musical ads rely heavily on jingles or a musical background to promote a product or service. There are several ways that music can be used. In some ads, the entire message is sung. In others, jingles are interspersed throughout the message—the ad may begin and close with a jingle, for example. Still other ads use background music that the advertiser hopes listeners will begin to associate with the product. A classic example is Coca Cola's use of "I'd Like to Teach the World to Sing" in many of its ads in the early seventies. Many people who hear the song associate it with Coca Cola.

3. *Slice of life or problem solution.* This is an ad in which characters discuss a problem and propose the product as the solution. While

Exhibit 13.2   Sample Donut Ad

Sample 60 sec."Come to Sheraton" w/36 sec. donut

SINGERS:
(MUSIC/VOCAL --
approx. 15.5
seconds)

When you plan a trip you know
Excitement's in the air
Any place in the world you go
You want it all right there.

SAMPLE
LOCAL ANNCR:
(Music under)

(Approx. 36 sec.)

Come to Sheraton you'll love the life
Next time you're going to New York for business,
bring your family and stay through the weekend!
Taste a Sheraton holiday in the Big Apple! The
Sheraton Centre is right in the heart of the city,
so it's perfect for business and a great family
weekend! Here's our Big Apple weekend
package—3 days and 2 nights of wining, dining
and entertainment. A Continental breakfast every
morning ... delicious prime rib accompanied by
fine wine for dinner and an evening of
entertainment and dancing. Just call the
Sheraton Centre at 581-1000 or ask your
travel agent.

SINGERS:
(MUSIC UP)

· Come to Sheraton you'll love the life
You'll love the life at Sheraton.

LEGAL REQUIREMENTS/RESTRICTIONS

As part of Sheraton's agreement concerning the use of this recording, we are legally required to quote the following:

"This commercial has been produced under the provisions of AFTRA National Code of Fair Practice for Transcription for broadcasting purposes, and its use is governed thereby. Accordingly, the dealer (Sheraton Manager) is granted a limited license to use this commercial only as a local program or commercial on local non-interconnected stations."

Please note that this commercial is not cleared for use in all countries. Currently, this Radio Donut is for use in the United States and Canada only.

This donut ad, from the Sheraton Corporation, provides a music/vocal background with a 36-second gap for individual property information. Note legal information at the bottom of the suggested ad copy.

Courtesy of the Sheraton Corporation.

these ads can be either factual or humorous, they must quickly present the problem—a dilemma over which restaurant the family should choose, for example—and quickly propose the solution: "At XYZ Hotel, there's a restaurant for every taste under one roof."

4. *Personality.* Personality ads rely on the talents of the announcer chosen to promote the product (see Exhibit 13.3). In many cases, a local celebrity is used, or the ad is presented by a local disc jockey or talk show host. In some cases, the property may hire a

Exhibit 13.3   Sample Personality Radio Ad

ANNOUNCER:	Hi, Tom Bodet for Motel 6 with some relief for the business traveler or anyone on the road trying like the dickens to make a buck. Well, money doesn't grow on trees and I'm probably not the first person who's told you that but maybe I can help anyway.
	Why not stay at Motel 6 and save some of that money? 'Cause for around 22 bucks, the lowest price of any national chain, you'll get a clean, comfortable room, free TV, movies, local calls, and long distance ones without a motel service charge.
	No, we don't have a swinging disco or a mood lounge with maroon leather chairs and an aquarium where you can entertain your clients, but that's O.K. I got a better idea. Take the money you save and meet that client in town. Besides, they probably know all the best places to go anyway. Let them tell you what they know best and you do what's best for business.
	Call 505–891–6161 for reservations at Motel 6. I'm Tom Bodet for Motel 6. . . and we'll leave the light on for you.

While Tom Bodet's name may not be a household word, his folksy messages and delivery have made Motel 6's radio ads memorable. Bodet is just an "average guy" whose ads with their "We'll leave the light on for you" tag line have pulled the chain out of a five-year slump and catapulted the radio spokesperson to national prominence.

Courtesy of Motel 6 and the Richards Group (an advertising agency).

professional actor or a prominent figure to lend credibility to the property's product. This can be especially effective if the personality has influence over the target audience.

Radio Ad Costs

There are a number of factors that will affect radio ad costs. First, the property has to decide whether the ad will be live or taped for presentation. A live ad usually requires less work—the script and background music or special sound effects (if any) are brought to the station and the only costs incurred are for airtime (unless a celebrity has been hired to read the script) and the script.

In the case of a taped or recorded ad, costs of production have to be considered. Since many hospitality professionals are not completely familiar with broadcast media, it is often necessary to hire an agency to develop the ad. This process involves writing the script (costs may be lower if there is someone on the property's staff who can write an effective message), casting an announcer or an entire cast for the production, finding background music (this may entail acquiring taped music or hiring musicians and/or singers), and recording the ad several times. In most cases, the music, sound effects, and vocals are recorded separately and mixed on a final master tape. This master tape is then duplicated (the duplicate tapes are called "dubs") and sent to the radio station(s) for broadcast.

Buying Radio Airtime. While prices vary from station to station, and even at the same station (discounts during slow periods, and so on), there are several basic ways to buy radio airtime:

1. *A "fixed position" spot.* The property's message is run in a specific time slot every day over the contract period. Since this method prevents the station from selling additional spots in that time period, it is usually the most expensive way to buy radio time.

2. *A weekly plan.* Weekly plans usually consist of ten to forty spots per week, and can be set up in a number of ways:

   a. *Total Audience Plan (TAP).* The broadcast day is divided into four basic time periods: morning drive time (6:00 to 10:00 a.m.), daytime (10:00 a.m. to 3:00 p.m.), evening drive time (3:00 to 7:00 p.m.), and nighttime (7:00 p.m. to 6:00 a.m.). A TAP spreads announcements throughout this broadcast day. This plan ensures that the message is heard in each time period, but it is important to note that it may be heard by a different audience, and not just the target audience, at different hours of the day.

   b. *Morning-Afternoon-Night Plan (MAN).* Announcements must be aired in parts of each broadcast day as specified by the station.

   c. *Run-of-Station Plan (ROS).* Announcements are aired in different time slots as time is available. This is one of the least costly plans.

   d. *Best Time Available (BTA).* Like the ROS plan, the times for the property's announcements are chosen by the station and costs are fairly low. The difference between BTA and ROS is that a BTA spot may be run at the same time each day, while an ROS ad is aired in a variety of time slots.

3. *A monthly plan.* Monthly plans charge a flat rate for a fixed number of ads no matter what time slot is selected.

4. *Bulk or annual rates.* This method of purchase is often the cheapest way to purchase radio time. If the property runs 250 or more ads a year, a contract can be signed in advance to ensure the lowest possible rate.

5. *Co-op.* Like cooperative print advertising, co-op radio advertising involves two or more businesses that advertise together. All parties share in the cost of the ad, and all may benefit from the prestige and following of the other advertiser(s).

6. *Radio sponsorship.* This is another good way to build on someone else's prestige and following, but in this case, a property is associated with a radio program or personality. The property pays for a certain amount of airtime and receives mention throughout the program ("This program is sponsored by ABC Resort").

7. *Reciprocal advertising.* As mentioned in Chapter 9, reciprocal advertising is a method of bartering for reduced advertising fees. The property exchanges rooms, meals, and/or services for all or part of the advertising bill. This method can be extremely cost-effective for the property, especially when rooms are designated for use during slow business periods.

Before leaving the subject of time and costs, it is important to mention that the cost of a radio ad will also depend on the length of the ad. Most radio ads fall into the 30- or 60-second category, although some stations may sell shorter or longer ads. In most cases, 60-second ads do not cost twice as much as 30-second ads and may be the better value. Sometimes 30- and 60-second ads sell for the same price! It pays to shop around for the best radio buys.

Measuring the Effectiveness of Radio Ads

The final test of a radio ad is its effectiveness. There are several ways to measure the success of a radio ad:

- Listener participation promotions

- Premium offers

- Survey cards

- Monitoring sales before and after a radio promotion

Listener participation promotions involve offering a special product or discount in return for action on the part of the listener. An excellent example of this type of monitoring is the radio coupon. Some years ago, selected McDonald's franchises ran an advertising promotion that encouraged listeners to make their own dollar-bill-size coupon and bring it to the nearest McDonald's for a free soft drink with the purchase of a Big Mac. The response was phenomenal—thousands of coupons poured in, sales increased 15% to 17% at all participating outlets, and the promotion saved the corporation thousands of dollars in printing costs.

Radio coupons can also be effective for the hotel industry, and can be used to promote special room packages, restaurants, lounges, and special events. To ensure greater measurability, listeners can be asked to write the call letters of the radio station on each coupon.

Premium offers are similar to radio coupons in that they invite listeners to take advantage of a giveaway when they mention the ad or the call letters of a particular station. In many cases, restaurants offer a free glass of wine or a complimentary dessert. If the property or restaurant advertises on more than one station, the premium advertised at each station can be different in order to help measure listener response.

Survey cards can also be used to measure a radio ad's impact. Front desk agents or restaurant hosts can ask guests how they heard about the property or a special offer. If radio is the answer, call letters can be entered on the card to determine which radio station is reaching which markets most effectively.

Monitoring sales before and after a radio promotion is another way of measuring radio effectiveness, although it may be less accurate than direct monitoring. A property restaurant may experience an increase in sales after a radio promotion, for example, but the promotion might not be the only factor: increased suggestive selling by food servers may have played a part in the increased sales.

Whatever the method used to measure results, hospitality advertisers should remember that name recognition takes time and that promotions should be given a chance to work. Canceling all radio advertising simply because sales have not increased dramatically may be a mistake; often, a great deal of repetition is required before a significant impression is made on radio listeners. If a particular radio promotion has not paid off after a reasonable length of time, however, the advertising staff should consider changing it. Radio is a flexible medium that lends itself to a variety of approaches— perhaps a contest, or a series of ads focusing on trivia questions or famous facts would spark interest.

Used properly, radio can give a property the reach, frequency, selectivity, and efficiency available in no other medium. And radio, a part of almost everyone's daily life, can often get the property's message across at a fraction of the cost of print and other broadcast media.

Television Advertising

Like radio, television is a saturation medium. Millions of people watch local, national, or cable television every day. Television offers the advantage of appealing to the eye as well as the ear. The audience can see and hear the message and become familiar with the property long before they visit it.

With these advantages, it would seem that properties would be extremely interested in making television a part of their overall advertising plan. However, commercial television has a number of drawbacks that greatly limits the use of this medium:

1. *General audience.* Because of high viewership levels, it is difficult to target specific market segments. As a general rule, people with above-average income and education (often the market that a property wishes to target) watch less television, although more higher income families are watching cable television.[5]

2. *Decreasing viewership.* With the advent of cable television, commercial television's viewing share has dropped to under 80% of the total market.[6]

3. *High costs.* Although it is relatively easy to buy local and national coverage, television costs can be extremely high. In addition to airtime fees, production costs for TV ads have risen dramatically.

Selecting TV Stations

Before selecting TV stations, a property must decide whether to advertise nationally as well as locally. Some target audiences may be effectively reached through local advertising alone, while other target audiences may require the use of national advertising. In the long run it may be more cost-effective for a property to advertise in distant key feeder cities or nationally, even though initial costs may be higher.

To select the station or stations most likely to give the property the most exposure to its target markets, the property has to look at the available stations and compare audience coverage. Like radio, television stations take periodic surveys of their audiences and pay close attention to their total number of viewers and the ratings of specific programs. These factors are also important when selecting a time slot, especially if the television station uses viewing measurement services (Arbitron, Nielsen, etc.) that provide a detailed, accurate survey of the viewing habits and demographics of the station's audience.

Television Measuring Systems

There are two primary measuring systems used to determine television viewing habits: The A. C. Nielsen Company's A. C. Nielsen Station Index (NSI) and the Arbitron Company (ARB). The Nielsen Station Index uses a method known as *designated market areas* (DMA), while Arbitron, the company that introduced this method of measuring, uses *areas of dominant influence* (ADI). In both of these surveys, geographic areas are broken down into counties or cities, and the public's viewing habits are monitored to give a rating for local television viewership.

The Nielsen ratings are derived from Audimeters, complex electronic instruments attached to the television sets of 1,200 scientifically selected households. The Audimeter reports time of day the set was used, total amount of set usage, and station tuning; the information is relayed to a central computer where it is analyzed.

The Arbitron system uses diaries in which families record television viewing habits for each set in the home. The diaries are analyzed to determine stations watched, programs watched, time periods of viewing, and demographics of the viewers. Arbitron uses electronic meters in New York, Chicago, Los Angeles, and San Francisco.

No matter what method is used, the data is used to determine a number of viewing statistics:

TVHH (TV households)—the number of households that own television sets (over 98% of the households in the United States have at least one television set). This statistic is used to gain a sense of the market.

HUT (Households using television)—This statistic refers to the number of households with television sets actually in use at a given time. If there are 2,000 television sets in a small town and 1,000 are turned on, the HUT figure would be 50%.

Program ratings—The program rating is figured by dividing the number of people actually tuned in to a television program by the number of television households in the test area:

$$\text{Rating} = \frac{\text{Number tuned to specific station}}{\text{TVHH}}$$

Share of audience—This statistic is calculated by determining how many HUT homes are viewing a specific program. A program watched by 500 viewers in an area that has 1,000 HUTs will garner a share of 50%.

Total audience—the total number of homes reached by a program (even if a portion of those homes watched only a part of the program).

Commercial television is watched primarily by middle- or lower-income families, although television specials or popular programs can attract a greater—and more affluent—audience.[7] As mentioned previously, commercial television also has the drawback of being viewed by a general audience. It is extremely difficult to determine the demographics of general viewership, and advertising dollars can be wasted. On the positive side, however, local advertising for general products or services can usually be purchased for a moderate sum, especially if the airtime purchased is not during prime time. Of course, if prime time is not purchased, you must consider: Is the property sacrificing audience for the sake of spending a few less dollars?

Properties wishing to attract a more affluent audience are turning more and more to cable television. Cable television can reach specific target segments through special stations such as CNN and ESPN. Another advantage of cable television is that cable subscribers watch more hours of television than do watchers of commercial television.

The number and type of announcements aired also plays a part in station selection. Many stations suffer from media clutter—too many announcements run back-to-back during commercial breaks or between programs. The frequency of advertising and the type of advertising can make the difference between a property's expensive ad being effective or being tuned out.

Certainly an important factor in selecting a station relates to costs. Costs may vary widely depending on the station, time slot, and time of the year. Like radio, television offers co-op advertising to help cut costs, and it is another medium that lends itself well to reciprocal advertising. Television stations give prime consideration to an advertiser who is willing to pay cash for airtime (as do radio stations), but reciprocal advertising can play a role in negotiating final terms.

Developing TV Ads

As with any other form of advertising, it is important for the property to develop a TV ad that will attract the attention of the audience. A creative approach is essential. If attention and interest are not captured during the first few seconds of the ad, viewers may either change the channel or head for the kitchen.

A successful television ad should:

1. *Grab the viewer's attention.* The viewer should immediately be given an incentive to watch and listen. This can be done through the use of interesting visual images or creative audio approaches such as unusual speech (accents, rapid talking, and so on), playing a jingle, etc.

2. *Be visual.* In television, the picture should tell the story—many viewers will remember more of what they see than what they hear. Since the message should be told visually, a storyboard is often used to judge a proposed ad. A storyboard is a panel or series of panels with small rough sketches depicting in order the important scenes of an ad. To help anticipate audience reaction, planners should look at the storyboard sketches and determine if the whole story is given in the visual images.

3. *Be uncomplicated.* Television thrives on simplicity. An ad should be built around one frame, called a "key visual," that tells the whole story simply and directly. A simple "name-claim-demonstration" format has proven to be the most effective; if more time is available, the key point should be repeated rather than additional points added. A storyboard can help show if an ad is too complicated. Television screens are not movie screens, and crowded, fast-moving ads can confuse viewers.

4. *Have an identity all its own.* Each ad should have its own personality, one that reflects favorably on the products and services offered. The tone or image of the ad should give viewers an idea of what to expect when they visit the property. Once that image has been established, it should be a part of all future TV advertising.

5. *Avoid wordiness.* A 30-second ad gives the advertiser approximately 60 words or less to get the message across, so it is essential that the verbal message be clear, concise, and convincing. An ad should use the simplest, most memorable words and avoid cliches, flowery adjectives, and ambiguous statements.

6. *Create name recognition.* The ad must register the name of the property in the viewer's mind, whether this is done by words, visuals, or, ideally, a combination of both. For maximum effect, a combination of spoken words, visual images (perhaps the property's sign or logo), and a superimposed graphic of the property's name can be used during the message.

Types of TV Ads. There are several general types of television ads:

1. *Straight announcement.* This is the oldest type of TV ad. It can be effective if the announcer is convincing and the script is well written. A straight announcement ad is also relatively inexpensive, since it consists simply of an announcer giving a message as a slide or film is shown. Few ads of this type are made today. Some are seen on late-night TV.

2. *Demonstration.* In demonstration ads, products or services may be shown in use, competing with another product or service, or in before-and-after situations. A property may use this type of ad to show a first-class chef in action, for example. Demonstrations should relate to a viewer's needs.

3. *Testimonial.* Most people are more influenced by a TV ad that features a third-party endorsement than by a property saying something good about itself. Satisfied guests can be excellent testimonial spokespersons, as can local or national celebrities.

4. *Slice of life or problem solution.* While ads that try to portray a real-life situation may be less believable for consumer products (do people really spend their days admiring their reflections in a waxed floor?), slice of life ads can be highly effective for the hospitality industry. The key to success is to show believable situations and people: a family checking in, receiving a warm welcome, and taking a relaxing dip in the pool after a hard day on the road, for example. But creating believability requires professional talent.

5. *Lifestyle.* This type of ad, which can also be highly effective for the hospitality industry, focuses on the consumers of a product or service. For example, a lifestyle ad would show the "beautiful people" enjoying dinner at the property's restaurant or relaxing around the pool. The emphasis would be on the type of clientele the property wishes to attract rather than on product benefits.

6. *Animated.* The use of cartoons, puppets, or animated demonstrations is an effective way to capture interest, especially if a property's message is complex. The entire ad can be animated, or animation can be used to accentuate specific parts of a more conventional ad. Production costs for this type of advertising are often prohibitive.

TV Ad Costs

Before deciding on the type of ad that the property wants to present, the following costs should be considered:

1. *Preproduction.* All work done prior to the actual filming: casting, arranging for locations, hiring a production company, props, costumes, etc.

2. *Production.* The actual filming or videotaping. This includes equipment, lighting, salaries for actors and crew, etc.

3. *Postproduction.* The work done following the filming or taping of the ad: editing, processing, recording sound effects, mixing the audio and video, and duplicating the final film or tapes.

When considering costs, the property should find out what assistance is offered by the television station. Many stations, especially on the local level, offer production facilities at relatively low rates, usually charging only the amount required to cover costs incurred by the station. The station may recommend a local production company that will work within the property's budget—and may even work on a reciprocal or due-bill basis.

Buying TV Airtime. There are basically three ways for a property to buy advertising time on commercial television stations: sponsorships, participations, and spot announcements.

Sponsorship means that an advertiser presents a program as the sole advertiser or in cooperation with other advertisers. Sponsorships are usually quite expensive, and sole sponsorship is usually limited to television specials and sporting events. Hallmark, for example, sponsors the "Hallmark Hall of Fame."

Most television advertising is sold on a *participating* basis. With participations, several advertisers purchase 30- to 60-second spots within a specific program. For example, several different advertisers can purchase advertising in a situation comedy that is aired nationally on a weekly basis. Under a participation arrangement, an advertiser can choose several options: to advertise on the program once, to advertise on a regular basis (once a week, once every two weeks, and so on), or to advertise on a sporadic basis—when the property is having a special promotion, for example.

Properties that do not choose to sponsor or participate in a program or programs can also purchase *spot announcements* on both local stations and the networks. Spot announcements are usually grouped together in "clusters" and run between programs, and are far less expensive than the other two options. The most common length for spot announcements is 30 seconds, although they may also be sold in 10-, 20-, and 60-second segments.[8]

Time of day is also a factor when purchasing television time. An ad scheduled for the early morning, for example, will be far cheaper than an ad scheduled during TV's prime time—7:30 p.m. to 11:00 p.m. But the property should not automatically opt for the lowest rate. Is its target audience watching during the non-prime-time hours?

Measuring the Effectiveness of TV Ads

Television advertising is expensive. Properties using it should develop a plan for measuring its effectiveness. When airtime is purchased, a contract is drawn up listing the dates, times, and programs on which the ads will appear; this contract also details the length of the ads, the rate per ad, and the total amount of ad time purchased. After the contract has been completed—that is, the ads have been aired—the station returns a form to the client that states when the spots were run. This form, called an affidavit of performance, is the client's guarantee that he or she got what was paid for.

Comparing the information on the contract and the affidavit to the number of viewer responses can help a property determine how much money was spent per viewer response and whether television advertising is cost-effective for the property. Many of the techniques used to measure listener response to radio ads can be used to measure viewer response to TV ads: monitoring sales before and after television promotions, using survey cards, and using premium or discount offers.

Video Advertising

In addition to radio and television, a great many properties are taking advantage of a relatively new form of broadcast advertising: video brochures and magazines (see Exhibit 13.4). Video can be used both in-house and off-property, and has the advantages of being relatively inexpensive and versatile.

Video Brochures

One of the most effective uses of today's new video technology is property video brochures. A video brochure, unlike a printed brochure, has the advantage of not just telling prospective guests about the property but of actually showing the property, often at various times of the year. The sound, color, and action characteristics of video brochures have made them an extremely effective sales tool when selling to travel agents, group tour organizers, and central reservations systems agents who might not have the opportunity to visit the property in person. Videos can be used in face-to-face presentations or they can be mailed out as supplements to printed brochures and other collateral materials.

A video can assist travel intermediaries in choosing a particular property in a number of ways. A video can show:

1. *Property facilities at their best.* While site visits can be disastrous if a banquet or meeting room has recently been used and is in a state of disarray, a video can show each dining facility, banquet room, and meeting room in its most attractive state.

2. *A variety of setups.* Prospects can see exactly what the different types of setups look like in the property's banquet and meeting rooms. A meeting room, for example, can be shown with a theater setup, a V-shape setup, a schoolroom setup, and so on—all on the same tape.

3. *Seasonal attractions.* If a meeting is planned for the spring, a site visit might take place in the fall; a video could give the meeting planner the opportunity to see the hotel's gardens in bloom. A summer visitor might not be aware of the winter sports opportunities nearby; a video could show the property's facilities year-round and generate business in other seasons.

Exhibit 13.4   Sample Video Brochure Transcript

OUTRIGGER HOTELS Video 5:00
(Hawaii Five-O theme music and under)

JAMES
MCARTHUR: Book 'em Dano. That's how we usually end-
ed our shows on Hawaii Five-O. Book 'em.
And that's probably how you'd like to end
any story in your business too. Let's book
'em. I'm Jim McArthur, and this is Waikiki.
We filmed a lot of shows right here. And in
the last few years there's this tall, good
lookin' guy with a moustache who's filmed
quite a few more. Those shows have helped
to give Waikiki its image as the world's most
exciting and varied beach resort. But it's not
just an image. It's the truth.

(ukulele music and under)

There is literally something here for
everyone, from anywhere, something for
every taste.
For every appetite.
For every age.
For every station in life.
For every level of fitness.
For every level of curiosity.
For every level of intelligence.
For every demand for pleasure and
entertainment.
For every sense of excitement.

Waikiki. There's something here to appeal to
any, and every client that comes to your
desk. But this very diversity, this sweeping
appeal, does give you a problem. Many
different kinds of people want to come to
Waikiki. How can you be absolutely confi-
dent, that your client with a twenty-two
dollar a day room budget, and your client
with a two hundred dollar a day room
budget, will both come back from Waikiki
happy. The answer is when you book 'em,
book an Outrigger. Outrigger is by far the

largest hotel chain in Waikiki offering you and
your clients 18 hotels to celebrate the sun.

(piano music background and under)

The accommodations range from clean and
reasonable.
To luxuriously elegant.
From family convenience.
To indulgent opulence.
With a broad selection of banquet and conven-
tion facilities.
No other host in Waikiki can produce such a
range of price and luxury.
Yet, it is just not the number or the accommoda-
tion that sets Outrigger Hotels Hawaii apart.

These are two of Outrigger senior vice presidents
on a regular walking tour. It's policy that senior
management at Outrigger personally visit every
one of their hotels several times a week. Senior
management of any national chain couldn't begin
to make such a claim.

While's it's the largest hotel chain in Waikiki,
Outrigger is still a family headed group. The
pride they share in their enterprise is infectious.
It doesn't matter at which hotel an Outrigger
employee works, or what the rates are, or
whether the hotel is economical or prestigious,
the services your clients have paid for at any
Outrigger will be excellent. In fact, most Outrigger employees can move from one property to
another, and back, and not miss a beat. Thank
you Karena.

Outrigger likes to say that its service ranges from
excellent to excellent. So when your clients want
Waikiki, and nearly all of them do sometime,
give them the confidence of being with Waikiki's
largest chain and the genuine warmth you get
only in a family hotel. Book 'em in an Outrigger.
Aloha.

(Wrap · Hawaii Five-O theme music up)

The winner in a recent advertising competition in the video category, this video brochure for Outrigger Hotels Hawaii features a "Hawaii Five-O" theme. The brochure was developed for travel agents and ran five minutes.

Source: *The Art of Hotel & Travel Advertising, A Look at the Past—A Guide to the Future* (Washington, D.C.: Hotel Sales & Marketing Association International, 1987), pp. 71–72.

4. *Remodeling or expansion.* A video may eliminate the necessity for a meeting planner or travel agent to make an additional site visit, if the site was selected before a remodeling or major renovation. The video can also serve as a reminder of property amenities and services.

Video brochures can also help salespeople sell convention services to meeting planners. In many cases, it is impossible for meeting planners to visit every suggested site, and a video brochure can be an effective substitute. A video brochure also indicates to meeting planners that a property is serious about the meetings business.

The optimum length of a video brochure is four to six minutes. This allows adequate time to present the property without losing the viewer's interest. Since time is short, it is important to present the property's best points. This means the property should plan the video brochure before asking for ideas and advice on the video's actual production.

To ensure the best video brochure possible, the property should consult with video experts, especially firms that specialize in hotel videos. While these firms might be somewhat more expensive than a general video production company, a hotel specialist will have more experience in putting hotel videos together without causing undue inconvenience to property employees and guests during the filming process.

As video becomes more and more common, there will be few properties that do not make use of this dynamic sales tool. In fact, some experts predict that soon hotels that do not have at least one video brochure will be as rare as a property that does not have a printed brochure today.

Video Magazines

Video magazines, unlike video brochures, are primarily designed for in-house viewing. While a few video magazine presentations may be found at airports or other transportation terminals, most properties show video magazines at the property over in-room TV or lobby TV screens. A typical video magazine takes a guest on a tour of the property's facilities, promotes the various restaurant and entertainment offerings, and provides information on reservation services, special upcoming packages, and other promotions. Some video magazines, like those produced by the Hilton chain, feature tours of local attractions, general travel tips, and promotions of other properties within the chain in addition to specific property information.

Like video brochures, video magazines are perhaps best produced in association with a hotel video specialist, or, if the property is a chain property, through the chain's corporate headquarters.

An interesting, lively video magazine that changes monthly (as does the Hilton's) is an excellent sales tool that can help make guests feel at home and promote additional sales by showing the various services offered at the property. The use of video in this manner continues to grow, and video magazines will no doubt play an important role in the future advertising plans of many hotels.

Notes

1. Howard A. Heinsius, "How to Select Advertising Media More Effectively," *Lodging*, May 1977, pp. 33–35.
2. Harry A. Egbert, "Radio Advertising for Hotels," *The Cornell Hotel and Restaurant Administration Quarterly*, May 1980, pp. 31–36.
3. Egbert, "Radio Advertising for Hotels," pp. 31–36.
4. Egbert, "Radio Advertising for Hotels," pp. 31–36.
5. *Nielsen Report on Television 1980*, A.C. Nielsen, Chicago, 1980, pp. 1–9.
6. Nielsen, *Television 1980*, pp. 1–9.
7. Nielsen, *Television 1980*, pp. 1–9.
8. Courtland L. Bovee and William F. Arens, *Contemporary Advertising* (Irwin: Homewood, Ill., 1982), p. 561.

Discussion Questions

1. Which is a more selective medium, radio or television? Why?

2. What types of radio stations would be effective in reaching people in the 18 to 30 age bracket?

3. What factors should a hospitality firm consider before making a final decision on whether to advertise on a particular radio station?

4. What is a "Radio Day?"

5. What are four types of radio ads?

6. What are basic ways to buy radio airtime?

7. What is the difference between an ROS plan and a BTA plan?

8. How can a radio ad's effectiveness be measured?

9. What are the advantages and disadvantages of commercial TV advertising?

10. What factors should a property weigh before selecting a particular television station?

11. What are some elements of a successful television ad?

12. What are several general types of television ads?

13. What are the advantages of a video brochure?

Chapter Outline

I. Public Relations
    A. The Public Relations Plan
    B. Selecting a PR Staff
    C. Contracting for Outside PR Services
    D. Measuring PR Performance
II. Publicity
    A. Publicity Planning
    B. Developing Promotional Materials
        1. News Releases
            a. How to write a news release
        2. Press Kits
    C. Travel Writers
        1. Qualifying Travel Writers
        2. How to Maximize a Travel Writer's Visit
III. Press Relations
    A. News Media Interests
    B. Personal Interviews
        1. TV Interviews
    C. News Conferences
    D. Sensitive Subjects
    E. If a Story Contains Errors

14 Public Relations and Publicity

While advertising is a powerful sales tool, especially since the content and timing of the message can be controlled, advertising alone is not always enough to keep the property's name before the public. But advertising coupled with public relations and publicity can form a powerful partnership to reach the property's target audiences.

In this chapter, we will take a look at public relations, publicity, and press relations. We will see how public relations and publicity can enhance a property's image, and why good press relations are important to a property's public relations program.

Public Relations

In today's hospitality industry, the term *public relations* is often bandied about, but there are varying opinions on just what it means. While there may be many definitions of public relations, most hoteliers agree that a public relations program supplements sales efforts and is necessary for a property to compete in today's marketplace.

We will define public relations as the process of communicating favorable information about the property to the public in order to create a positive impression. Public relations is much more than merely getting a property's name in the paper or on the TV screen; the purpose of public relations is to create a good image, a positive aura, a favorable public perception of the property.

Public relations is everybody's business; it is not the exclusive domain of the general manager or public relations director. Public relations starts with the guest's first contact with the property—the switchboard operator who answers a call, or the front desk agent who welcomes an arriving guest. From the moment a guest or potential guest becomes involved with the property, the property is involved in public relations.

Public relations starts at the property itself, but it is probably most useful in the "outside world." News releases, news conferences, special events, and community service are some of the ways a property seeks to communicate favorable information about itself to the "outside world" of the local community, current and potential guests, and other properties and professionals throughout the industry. Ideally, public relations can result in

Industry Profile

Anne S. Burnburg
Sales Manager
Maxim's de Paris Suite Hotel

Anne Burnburg began her career in the hotel business in 1972 and has worked in a variety of operations and sales positions. After advancing through operations to positions as assistant manager and general manager, Burnburg feels she has a better perspective for her current job as a sales manager. In addition to this challenging position, she serves on the curriculum committee for the Hospitality Program at the College of the Desert in Palm Springs, California, and has served as president of her local Hotel Sales & Marketing Association International chapter for two years.

"Publicity is of major importance in any marketing plan. You must begin with a clear idea of who your targeted markets are. The motivations and needs of the targeted markets must be understood before embarking on any course of action in publicity. Without this knowledge, it's possible to do more harm than good. Once an image has been created in the minds of buyers, it's very difficult to change it.

Going for any activity that will generate publicity can be a mistake if that activity does not reinforce the property's desired image. This sounds like an obvious point; however, it's often overlooked by those in a hurry to get all the 'free advertising' they can.

Sales for Maxim's is very much intertwined with positioning in the marketplace. Our property offers an upscale and unique alternative to the traditional properties found in the desert; however, transmitting this image to prospects has been very challenging. A large part of the hotel's success is due to the successful publicity campaign launched prior to the opening of the hotel and continued over the past two years.

Pre-opening publicity stressed Maxim's image as a first-class, European-style property in a desert setting. 'Opulent' and 'elegant' were key words in descriptions, and the tie-in to French design was emphasized—as well as the amount of money being spent and the exotic origin of many of the materials used in the construction and decor of the property. To reinforce this opulent image, the Grand Opening was a very lavish and star-studded event. Consequently, it was picked up by a variety of television programs, including 'Lifestyles of the Rich and Famous.'

Since that time, there have been shifts in competition, markets, and emphasis. However, because of the strong image created in the minds of buyers from the start, it's been simpler to perpetuate our upscale image. Publicity, then, can be one of the strongest and least expensive sales tools if it's properly carried out. Our various publicity campaigns have certainly made selling easier. If enough time and thought is given to publicity, the benefits may be enjoyed for a long time.**"**

favorable media attention for the property, attention that can be much more effective than advertising because the favorable message is coming from a source other than the property itself.

The Public Relations Plan

For any public relations effort to be successful, it must start with objectives and a plan of action. A good public relations plan does not simply seek publicity for publicity's sake. Just because a hotel was mentioned numerous times by various media throughout a given year does not mean the property's public relations efforts were successful. To be effective, a public relations plan should be integrated into the overall marketing plan, targeted toward important market segments, and timed to reduce occupancy soft spots. When public relations efforts are aimed at solving particular marketing problems and meeting particular marketing objectives, the results are far greater than those obtained through unorganized publicity seeking.

Four Examples of Creative Public Relations

Sheraton Washington Hotel

When medical meeting planners attended a joint conference on medical conventions at the Sheraton Washington Hotel, the hotel took the name "Sheraton Memorial," transformed its lobby into a hospital reception area, and had its front desk employees wear hospital uniforms. Wheelchairs carried VIPs to their rooms. As a result of this promotion, the hotel booked two medical conventions good for 9,000 room nights!

Halloran House in New York City

Public relations can be used to stimulate inquiries about a hotel. The Halloran House, a deluxe hotel, prepared a pocket street guide to New York City as a service to travelers. Copies of the guide were sent to travel editors across the country, with a news release offering the guide free to anyone who sent a self-addressed, stamped envelope to the hotel. The hotel received thousands of inquiries from travelers as a result of the articles written about the guide. Along with the guide, the hotel sent a general information brochure and a brochure promoting the hotel's special weekend package.

New Orleans Hilton

The New Orleans Hilton already had a public relations program for cab drivers that included furnishing drivers with free coffee or lemonade according to the season, but the hotel wanted to do something more.

That "something more" turned out to be a special folder, containing a two-week calendar headed "Coming Attractions at the New Orleans Hilton." The calendar lists conventions coming in, the name and size of each group, the date of major arrivals and departures, and which evenings groups have no in-house functions. The folder also contains a letter from the general manager that compliments the drivers on their service. The hotel's door attendants hand out the folders to cab drivers; new calendars are distributed on a biweekly basis.

The response has been excellent—drivers from all over the city pull up to get one. The result has been that on mornings of major departures, cabs line the surrounding streets and there are no more 20-minute waits for the Hilton's departing guests!

The Greenbrier

The Greenbrier in White Sulphur Springs, West Virginia, has maintained a culinary training program since 1957. The hotel, which usually experienced a period of low occupancy around the time of the commencement exercises of the chef trainees, developed an annual Gourmet Weekend package to boost business.

The publicity campaign for each year's Gourmet Weekend includes (1) a news release to food and travel editors in The Greenbrier's major market areas; (2) stories about graduating chefs sent to their hometown newspapers; (3) invitations to a select group of food, travel, and trade press editors for a weekend visit; and (4) press invitations to a Gold Service dinner.

The cost of these campaigns is approximately $25,000, but the return on the investment, in addition to 200 additional guests for the weekend, has included feature stories in the *Washington Post* (circulation 702,000), the *Chicago Daily News* (circulation 328,581), several national travel magazines, and in daily newspapers in virtually every major market from which The Greenbrier draws patronage.

A written public relations plan can allow for a review of objectives, eliminate wasted time and money, ensure better (or at least measurable) results, and involve all of the property's key people in a concentrated effort. A public relations plan should be kept simple. It should integrate six major factors:

1. *Goals.* Goals should be specific. The more defined goals are, the more effective the public relations plan is likely to be. A typical goal might be: "Submit three press releases to local media during the first quarter of the year. These press releases will highlight our guest-room renovations, and will be aimed at the individual business traveler market."

   The time and effort proposed for each targeted market segment should be in direct relationship to the importance of that segment. It may be helpful to assign priorities and allocate funds to each market segment in relation to its potential return.

2. *Audience.* The best public relations plan will do little for a property if it is not reaching the people in the best position to buy the products or services offered. The public relations plan should target specific markets or promote specific revenue centers as set forth in the marketing plan.

3. *Media.* Once market segments have been selected, it is vital that the public relations plan identify the media that can best reach those segments.

4. *Message.* Once a medium has been selected, the public relations staff can begin developing ideas for feature stories or news spots, keeping in mind that these ideas must appeal to the medium and its audience. The staff should look at the property through the eyes of the specific medium (a TV station, for example) to determine what information would appeal to that medium and its audience while accomplishing the property's goals.

5. *Special projects.* Ways in which the property can create news through special projects or community service can then be developed (see Exhibit 14.1). Seminars, workshops, and special functions that are worthy of news stories can be held. These projects should be integrated into the marketing plan and, ideally, should be scheduled to take place during the property's slow periods.

6. *Measuring results.* Results of public relations strategies should be checked often. The property can monitor how many stories are submitted to the local media and how much print space or broadcast airtime is given by medium outlets, for example. By measuring results, a property can see which medium is more effective and which media outlets are not as interested in using public relations releases.

Selecting a PR Staff

A public relations plan is only as good as the staff that implements it (see Exhibit 14.2). No matter what the duties, or what size the property, it is best that a *professional* public relations person or staff be employed or contracted. Small properties may rely on one person and/or an outside agency; larger properties may engage a staff with diverse capabilities and/or work with an outside agency.

Exhibit 14.1   Sample Community Service Event

Quality International's
Clarion for Kids

Clarion Hotel
& Conference Center
Lansing

CLARION'S FOR KIDS SAFETY CARNIVAL

WHAT: Safety Carnival for Children and their Parents

WHEN: Thursday, May 26, 1988, from 4:00 pm - 7:00 pm

WHY: Clarion's for Kids Safety Program

WHERE: Clarion Hotel & Conference Center, 6820 S Cedar Street, Lansing

Your child will have an opportunity to start the summer off right with some basic lessons in safety. The Clarion Hotel and Conference Center is sponsoring a "Safety Carnival" as part of the CLARION'S FOR KIDS Safety Program, on Thursday, May 26, 1988, from 4:00 pm - 7:00 pm.

The children will learn all about "Summer Safety" from a Pediatric Nurse from Ingham Medical Hospital; "Poison Safety" from St. Lawrence Hospital; "Electrical Safety" from the Board of Water and Light; "Bike Safety" from Denny's Schwinn Bike Shop; and "Burn Care" from watching a puppet show "Kids on the Block", presented by the Burn Care Center of Sparrow Hospital. The children will also be able to tour an ambulance from Lansing Mercy Ambulance. There will be balloons, "Pluggie" the Walking Fire Hydrant, and "McGruff the Crime Dog" Puppet Show, and "Whistles the Clown" and Company from Circus Clown Alley.

The Lansing School District is conducting field trips to the Safety Carnival during the day and a special Open House will be held from 4:00 pm - 7:00 pm for those children and parents who did not attend through the schools.

Admission is free.

Properties can develop a good community image by offering community service events, such as the Clarion Hotel & Conference Center's safety carnival. Other types of community involvement may include sponsorship of telethons, walk-a-thons, and other fund-raising events; offering property facilities free of charge to charitable organizations; and participation of staff members in community organizations.

Courtesy of Clarion Hotel & Conference Center, Lansing, Michigan.

An in-house public relations staff may have many responsibilities: developing local promotions, contacting the media with news releases, writing promotional literature, sending thank-you notes to past guests, and so on. Since maintaining good relations with the media is important, there may be a staff member that meets with at least one member of the media each week. Another staff member may write a weekly column for a local publication.

Exhibit 14.2 Typical Duties of a Director of Public Relations

1. Develop, implement, promote, and publicize programs and/or special events designed to attract and meet the needs of markets targeted by the marketing and sales department.

2. Publicize special rates and packages to markets through story placement, direct mail, brochures, flier distribution, etc.

3. Package special events to build awareness of the hotel and its facilities in order to bring potential guests into the hotel.

4. Create and develop sales aids to be used by the property's sales team, such as slide presentations, photographs of the property and various events it has hosted, and scripts that can be used by telemarketers and other members of the property's sales force. Scripts may also be developed for other property employees such as front desk agents and food servers.

5. Compile and update direct mail lists for all special interest groups to sell special packages, events, and weekend rates.

6. Assist major meeting planner clients in press contacts; place stories for key convention groups.

7. Develop, implement, promote, and publicize programs and/or special events to increase food and beverage and catering sales and gain maximum publicity for the hotel.

8. Formulate plans and a strategy for a promotional calendar of events.

9. Maximize press relations by:

   • Seeking story placement in local and national media

   • Soliciting media coverage for all special events and programs

   • Generating publicity for new facilities, entertainment, services, and functions of the hotel through news releases, memos, and story solicitation of the news media

   • Initiating and placing hotel and/or hotel personnel stories in local media that will add to the awareness and prestige of the hotel

   • Placing photos of officers or meeting planners of important groups, along with key hotel personnel, in places where other meeting planners may see them, such as insurance, banking, electronics, and manufacturing publications

   • Acting as a liaison between the hotel and the press to answer all media inquiries

10. Assist with the property's newsletters, whether they are written in-house or by an advertising agency.

11. Administer the department by:

   • Developing long-range plans and goals for public relations

   • Preparing monthly reports of activities

   • Supervising subordinates

Source: Adapted from Chad A. Martin, "Public Relations: It Works For You," *HSMAI Marketing Review*, Fall 1986, p. 20.

In those cases where it is impractical to hire an in-house public relations staff, or at those properties where public relations duties are new or overwhelming, a public relations agency may be the answer.

**Contracting for
Outside PR
Services**

Before hiring a public relations agency, there are several factors to consider which are very similar to those considered when hiring an ad agency (see Chapter 9):

1. *Location.* Is the agency headquartered in the property's locale? Is the local office a branch office? If so, where is corporate headquarters?

2. *Longevity.* How long has the agency been in business? What is its track record with clients?

3. *Effectiveness.* How can the agency benefit the property locally? Do the agency's representatives know local media representatives? What is the agency's working relationship with the local media? Does the agency employ writers, researchers, and media-contact specialists?

4. *Experience.* Does the agency specialize in the travel industry or related industries? In areas that relate to the property's markets? Specialization can save start-up costs and time.

5. *Fees.* How does the agency charge for its time? Is the agency working for the property on a fixed retainer, or will the property be charged on an hourly or daily rate? Or does the agency expect a minimum fixed guarantee, billing the property for any extra hours of personnel time?

6. *Other factors.* Does the agency represent clients that would present a possible conflict of interest?

A property should request a proposal outlining how the agency would support the property's marketing objectives (see Exhibit 14.3). Proposals enable the property to weed out agencies with unsatisfactory plans or exorbitant rates.

It is also important that management meet with the agency representative who would be assigned to the property. Since a good working relationship between the property's staff and the representative is essential, there are several questions that should be answered before making a final decision. The potential representative should be asked:

1. How long have you been with the agency? How long have you been in your present position?

2. What other accounts do you handle? If you were transferred or if one of your other clients had an emergency requiring your services for several days, who would handle our account?

3. If we had an emergency, how much time could you devote to our account? Could you focus your energies on our account for several days?

4. What are the names of some of your other clients? May we ask them for references?

Once a public relations agency has been selected, the property should work closely with it. An employee can be appointed to keep the agency representative posted on happenings at the property. For closer contact (and

Exhibit 14.3 Agency Proposal Checklist

> Before deciding on a public relations agency, a property should ask for a detailed proposal. A good proposal should include:
>
> 1. An outline of an overall public relations plan for your property.
>
> 2. Examples of specific story ideas, promotions, special events, and media-oriented activities that will be created for your property under a three-month, six-month, or one-year contract.
>
> 3. The amount of time the agency will spend on your account every month.
>
> 4. Names of media contacts who will be approached on your behalf.
>
> 5. A meetings schedule. A good agency will request frequent meetings with the property for input and review.
>
> 6. A specific review period. A good agency will want to review its work and its relationship with you, usually after three months.
>
> 7. The agency's fee schedule. Always compare fees with similar agencies to make sure fees are competitive.

Source: Adapted from Tom McCarthy, "Selecting Your Public Relations Agency," *Hotel and Resort Industry*, May 1985, p. 26.

better results), the representative should be invited to sit in on important staff meetings, treated as a member of the marketing and sales team, and expected to provide monthly or quarterly reports on the results of the agency's efforts.

The agency representative should review the property's marketing plan so he or she can allocate time and effort to the market segments and time periods that are priorities to the property. The representative should make sure hotel personnel are the first to know about any public relations activities planned for the hotel. A notified staff is not necessarily an informed staff, however. The staff needs to know more than just when an event will take place. It should know the purpose behind a particular public relations event in order to help promote and sell the hotel.

Measuring PR Performance

Whether public relations efforts come from an outside agency or an in-house staff, every public relations plan should include a periodic audit. It is important to measure the results of the public relations plan against the goals that were set. The plan should be monitored at least every six months (at shorter intervals during the plan's initial implementation) to determine progress.

Measuring the impact of public relations is extremely difficult. Public relations cannot be measured in terms of how many sales leads or room nights are generated. While responses to advertisements and direct mail pieces can be tracked, it is difficult to determine how many guests checked into the hotel because they read a glowing article in a national magazine or a favorable story in a newspaper, although the staff can be instructed to ask guests how they decided to stay at the property.

Public relations has to be measured in terms of media space and "value equivalencies." Measuring media space in print media can be as simple as keeping a log of publications that articles have appeared in, the date of publication, the number of column inches featuring the property, and the circulation of the publication (see Exhibit 14.4). While this type of measurement does not help track reservations or sales, it is a good indicator of the amount of recognition and awareness (and, one hopes, goodwill) that public relations is generating.

The second measurement, value equivalency, is a means of measuring the dollar value of the publicity received by the property. Value equivalency is determined by auditing the exact amount of space or airtime given to a property over a specified period of time, and determining the value of the exposure in terms of what it would have cost to purchase the space or airtime for advertising purposes. For example, if a property gets a full-page editorial in a travel magazine that charges $8,400 for a page of advertising space, the equivalent value would be $8,400. It should be noted, however, that this figure represents a *conservative* estimate of value; the actual value includes credibility that is priceless.

Since free space or airtime may be worth many times the equivalent advertising space or airtime, it is essential that the property's management evaluate public relations efforts often, and review and revise plans and strategies to maximize their return.

Publicity

Publicity is one of the most effective promotional tools available to the hospitality industry, yet few properties include publicity in their marketing plans. But publicity—the media's gratuitous mention of the property, its staff, and special property events—can reach thousands of potential guests at little cost to the property.

Publicity should not be confused with advertising. With advertising, a hotel buys media space or time and controls the message; with publicity, the media provide the space or time, and the media—not the property—control the message. This "drawback" is the real strength of publicity. With advertising the property extols its own virtues, but when the property, through successful public relations efforts, receives favorable publicity, someone else is praising the property—which results in greater believability.

Publicity, while it is not advertising, *supports* advertising. The public may respond much more readily to advertising messages after reading of the property's community involvement; special programs such as safety fairs, bike rodeos, and business seminars; and contributions of cash or services to charities, scholarship funds, or other community organizations.

Publicity can be unplanned. A celebrity might stay at the property and talk about his or her stay during an interview; this could be good publicity even though it was unplanned. A restaurant reviewer might give the property's restaurant a bad review; a property might counteract this bad publicity by making adjustments in its menu or service and inviting the reviewer to return.

Other unplanned publicity includes natural disasters, labor disputes, mishaps at the property, and so on. In 1978, for example, heavy flooding was reported in the area of Phoenix, Arizona. While this flooding did not affect resorts in nearby Scottsdale, extensive media coverage gave the impression that everything was under water, and the resorts had to convince soon-to-arrive vacationers and other guests that the resorts were still operating. The

Exhibit 14.4   Measuring Public Relations

Publication	Story and Reporter	Day, Month, Year	Column Inches	# of Photos	Circ.
The Washington Post	"Personalities" Chuck Conconi	Tuesday September 30	4.00		728,857
Business Review Vienna, VA	"Design Elements Seen Aiding Willard Office Building Success"	Monday September 29	1.50		17,000
Swimming Pool Age & Spa Merchandiser Atlanta, GA	"Accommodations in Nation's Capital Range From Economical to Luxurious"	October	7.00		15,000
New York Air Skylines	"Metropolitan D.C." Karen R. Heuman	October	1.00		400,000
The Washington Post	"Personalities" Chuck Conconi	Wednesday October 1	4.00		728,857
The Daily News Newport, RI	No Title	Thursday October 9	1.50		16,450
The Examiner Chronicle San Francisco, CA	"Dining at the Willard Recalls the Best of Washington's Past" Paul Lasley & Elizabeth Harryman	Sunday October 19	22.00		711,560
San Diego Union	"Commercial Real Estate Outlook Poor"	Sunday October 19	3.00		391,100
Madison Avenue Magazine	"Menus and Venues" Vanessa Duchesne	November	2.75		32,000

While it is difficult to put a dollar figure on the value of public relations, properties can measure the amount of publicity generated with the aid of charts such as this one used by The Willard Inter-Continental in Washington, D.C.

Courtesy of The Willard Inter-Continental, Washington, D.C.

Wigwam, for example, called everyone with a reservation, while Marriott's Camelback Inn sent Mailgrams. In other emergencies—a fire at a property, for example—more extreme measures are needed to counteract unfavorable publicity; these measures will be discussed later in the chapter.

Publicity can fulfill a variety of marketing needs, but publicity can also backfire. The difference between successful and unsuccessful publicity programs is *planning*.

Publicity Planning

Publicity is most valuable when it communicates a favorable message to people with whom the property wishes to communicate. A well-developed plan can lead to favorable publicity, which can attract new business, remind previous guests about the property, and build community goodwill.

The plan begins with knowing what the property has to offer. This includes becoming aware of everything there is to know about the property—its history, facilities, services, staff, and marketing and sales goals. There is a wealth of stories under a property's roof—an exciting marketing concept, an upcoming event sponsored by the property, and employees who have excelled in a certain field (see Exhibit 14.5). Many media representatives recognize that hotels are full of interesting stories and people. Unique staff members, upwardly mobile management personnel, and VIP guests may generate reams of publicity for the property.

Once the staff compiles a background or inventory of what the property has to offer, the next step is to get to know the media. What are the most

Exhibit 14.5 Publicity Opportunities

- Celebrities who visit the property (and agree to publicity).
- Appointments of key personnel.
- Humorous events at the property.
- Public service activities.
- Special events. This is one of the most productive areas for publicity. Some examples include:

    The Detroit Plaza gave a reception for the city's cab drivers. They were lavishly entertained and given bumper stickers which read "I love Detroit," a handbook with detailed information about the city, and various buttons and badges.

    The Olympic Hotel in Seattle brought the "Big Bands" back for an old-fashioned Friday afternoon tea dance. People came in droves and the dance received tremendous publicity.

    To kick off the local yachting season, the general manager of The Bayshore in Vancouver, B.C., posed with the Yacht Club commodore waist-deep in the hotel swimming pool as they launched a miniature boat. It was a very funny picture that got coverage across the entire continent.

- Interviews with celebrities, visiting corporate executives, or general managers from other properties.
- Receipt of community awards.
- The opening of another property in the chain.
- Anniversary celebrations for the property or chain.
- Speeches. Often, talks to civic groups by hotel employees make news, especially if they have a strong local flavor.

Source: Adapted from Ron LaRue, "How to Develop and Implement a Public Relations Program for Hotels and Motels," *Lodging*, June 1978, p. 18.

appropriate media outlets for the property's publicity? Who are the journalists, columnists, and broadcasters who can assist in getting the property's message across? What materials must be developed in order to facilitate the publicity process?

Developing Promotional Materials

One way to interest the media in the property is to distribute promotional materials that will make a journalist's job easier should he or she choose to write about the property. Promotional pamphlets and brochures are excellent examples of materials that provide useful background information. Previous articles are also effective because they show the property has been newsworthy and provide background on what has already been done in print.

Newsletters can bring news of the property, its staff, and its services to the attention of the media as well as the public. As mentioned in Chapter 12, newsletters range from typewritten copy on property letterhead to slick full-color presentations. No matter what the treatment, the important point is getting the newsletter into the right hands so it can generate favorable publicity about the property and its employees. Although not specifically prepared for them, newsletters may be sent directly to print and broadcast journalists.

Promotional materials especially prepared for the media include news releases and press kits.

News Releases. A news release is a news story about a special event, celebrity guest, new promotional program, or other interesting item that is sent to the news media in hopes that it will generate an article, interview, or photograph (see Exhibit 14.6).

Before writing a news release, the marketing and sales department or the property's public relations specialist or staff must know the media and their needs. What may seem newsworthy to the owner of a property may be of little interest to a busy television producer, for example. The challenge is to "create" news that is really news, not just a publicity stunt.

If a particular story seems most appropriate for a newspaper, the public relations staff should check with a local newspaper to find out which department (food, entertainment, travel, business) may be interested in the story. If there is sufficient time, the staff may write a letter about the story to the department's editor. Ideas, clippings, statistics, and photographs that would enhance the story might be included with the letter to help the editor decide on the story's value.

While it is best to send a specific story to only one media outlet, there are times when news of a general nature can be written up in a general news release and sent out to many media outlets. This enables each outlet to determine the release's value—and allows each to develop its own individual story. General news releases may be sent out when a property books a new act in the lounge, plans new restaurants or meeting facilities, redecorates or expands, implements new energy conservation programs, or participates in community service events (see Exhibit 14.7).

How to write a news release. Releases should be double-spaced on a "News Release" form or on paper with the property letterhead. Many properties use a specially printed news release form that includes the words "News" or "News Release" on the top of the paper. White stock is usually used to facilitate the copying of news releases. A release date (the date on or after which the story can be published or "released") should be given unless it is the same as the dateline. The name and phone number of the property's media contact person should be included.

Start the news release about a third of the way down the first page (this leaves room for an editor's headline), and begin with a paragraph detailing the who, what, when, where, why, and how of the article. The release should be accurate and complete, with names spelled correctly. The release should also be brief and factual; avoid opinions or editorials. Direct quotes of the general manager or other authorities may enhance the impact of the release.

Properties must realize that whether or not their news release or special event is reported in the media will depend on its merit. A property should not pressure an editor or broadcaster for space or airtime just because it buys advertising.

Press Kits. Somewhat similar to the sales kits discussed in Chapter 3, press kits are designed to give journalists background material about a property. Since media personnel may receive hundreds of press kits each year, it is important that a property's press kit make a positive first impression. All materials should be attractively presented in a sturdy folder that features the name, logo, address, and telephone number of the property. All materials within the folder should be clearly marked in case the folder is dropped or mishandled.

Exhibit 14.6 News Release Do's and Don'ts

DO

- Write clearly in plain language, using short sentences and paragraphs.
- Be brief. Rarely should a story be longer than 500 words (about two pages).
- Give your news release a professional appearance. Always show the name and address of a person to contact for more information.
- Respect media deadlines. Learn radio, TV, and print media deadlines and allow as much lead time as possible when submitting material.
- Establish a reputation for honesty. If you do not have the answer to a question, tell the media representative. Credibility is basic to good press relationships.

DON'T

- Request or expect news space simply because your property or chain is an advertiser.
- Expect writers or broadcasters to report only the good news about your property and its personnel. Their job is reporting all the news—good, bad, or neutral. Don't expect your friends in the media to play down a negative story.
- Try to manage the news. Let the editor decide if your story merits space or time.
- Assume you know what media representatives want. Instead, make it a point to find out how you can be helpful.
- Ask to review a reporter's story or notes. If you believe a reporter is misinformed, discuss it.

Travel Writers

Another way a property can encourage publicity at a reasonable cost is to invite travel writers to the property. Travel writers write about modes of transportation, hotel accommodations, and business and vacation destinations.

Qualifying Travel Writers. Because travel writers vary in their styles, abilities, and markets, it is wise to develop guidelines to ensure that any travel writers given discounts to stay at the property are qualified journalists. (Discounts normally apply to room costs, exclusive of food and beverage and incidental expenses.) While there are relatively few writers who take vacations at a property's expense, making sure travel writers are qualified will ensure that the writers entertained by the property have the expertise to make the most of their visits.

Travel writers fall into two basic groups: staff writers and free-lance writers. Staff writers work for specific publications, and assignments are often arranged through an editorial staff. Free-lance writers are harder to qualify. Many belong to professional organizations such as the Society of American Travel Writers as either active or associate members.[1] Some free-lancers dislike group memberships, however, and the property must rely on the writer's reputation for qualification purposes.

If the property is part of a large chain, a call to the corporate public relations department can facilitate the qualification process; most corporate offices keep request logs (a list of writers requesting to visit a property),

Exhibit 14.7   Sample News Release

SUGAR RAY IN TRAINING
PAGE TWO

To accommodate the boxer's training needs, a section of the hotel's main ballroom has been set up as a workout center. In it are a boxing ring; a dance floor for rope jumping; heavy and speed punching bags; an exercise table and mirrored walls for shadow boxing. Leonard also runs every morning on the hotel's Atlantic Ocean beach.

roundings are beautiful, and the people of Hilton Head ly needs," Leonard said. "I'm looking forward to a good rd work and preparation for this fight."

to take a break from his rigorous training routine he'll ental Hilton Head is one of the country's most complete el can enjoy three PGA championship golf courses, 16 ee major playing surfaces), full gym and fitness center, eautiful Atlantic Ocean.

1985, the award-winning Hotel Inter-Continental Hilton sic seaside resort reminiscent of the grand hotels that entury. It has 416 rooms and 47 suites, most with ocean d on 24 acres at the Port Royal Resort, and has become ing and business groups as well as for individual travelers s of everyday life.

Sugar Ray Leonard at the property adds that extra spice the competition," explained Wicky.

\#   \#   \#

HOTEL INTER•CONTINENTAL HILTON HEAD

Contacts:
Debi Poole/Lynn Baker
Hotel Inter-Continental Hilton Head
803/681-4000

FOR IMMEDIATE RELEASE

SUGAR RAY LEONARD SETS UP TRAINING BASE AT

THE HOTEL INTER-CONTINENTAL HILTON HEAD;

MOST SESSIONS OPEN TO THE PUBLIC

HILTON HEAD ISLAND, SC, January 29 - - Sugar Ray Leonard, the former welterweight and junior middleweight champion of the world who makes his ring comeback April 6 against world middleweight champion Marvelous Marvin Hagler, has set up his training camp headquarters at the **Hotel Inter-Continental Hilton Head.** Leonard will train at the hotel until March 15 when he leaves for Las Vegas, site of the Hagler encounter.

All of Leonard's weekday training sessions, which begin at noon, are open to the public, free of charge.

"We're very excited about having Sugar Ray Leonard stay and train here," said Tom Wicky, the hotel's general manager. "We'll certainly go out of our way to make his stay a pleasant one, and we realize the importance of his visit as he prepares for the fight. Having Sugar Ray here is a real feather in our caps."

Ray and a party of 18 will stay at the hotel throughout the two-month training period. Included in the party are his manager and trainer, as well as several sparring partners and aides. The Leonard party will occupy 10 rooms, with Leonard housed in a VIP suite. Cicero Leonard, the fighter's father, will stay in a room adjacent to the boxer. He will prepare most of the fighter's meals in a special satellite kitchen.

- more -

Courtesy of Inter-Continental Hilton Head at Port Royal, Hilton Head, South Carolina.

clippings, or media directories. Independent properties can also refer to media directories. If questions arise, it is permissible to verify a writer's assignment by contacting the publication he or she is writing for. As a last resort, clippings or tear sheets of previous work may be requested from the writer.

How to Maximize a Travel Writer's Visit. Although travel writers are guests of the property, they are also critics obligated to present an impartial view of their stay. There are several things a property can do, however, to create a favorable impression and enhance a travel writer's visit:

1. *Be prepared.* Preparation is essential to a positive experience for the travel writer. Both the writer and the property should know what to

Press Kit Materials

Letter of Introduction

A letter of introduction simply explains that the press kit contains promotional materials and gives permission to use them. A letter of introduction should be typed on property letterhead and should include the name and telephone number of the property's media contact person.

Summary Sheet

A summary sheet lists what is contained in the press kit, enabling the recipient to tell at a glance exactly what materials he or she has received.

Property Fact Sheet(s)

Fact sheets are written in a non-narrative style and include information about the general design and appearance of the property; guest services; food and beverage outlets; parking facilities; safety features; and names of key property personnel.

Basic Property News Release

This news release is a short, general article (usually no more than 500 words) in narrative form about the property. Written on a news release form or hotel letterhead, this two-page (maximum) article highlights the range of special facilities and services available at the property (including weekend and other promotional packages); unique features of the property (unusual architecture, murals, fountains, and so on); and other basic information about the property that may be of interest.

Photographs of the Property

Exterior views of the property from a number of angles, and interior photographs of guestrooms, dining facilities, and special services should be included in the press kit. All photographs should be black and white and no smaller than 5- by 7-inches. The sharper the image, the better the photograph will reproduce, so hiring a professional photographer is often a good investment.

All photographs should be identified by a title or caption that is written or typed on a separate sheet of paper and then attached to the photo. At no time should a title or caption be written directly onto the back of a photograph as this may cause damage.

For best results, photographs should include small groups of people in unposed, natural situations. A release must be obtained from each person pictured. This release need not be included in the press kit, but should be kept on file at the property in case the photograph is published.

Biographies and Photographs of Key Property Personnel

A brief biographical sketch detailing the experience and expertise of key property personnel may result in a feature story. Profiles should be kept short (one page is usually sufficient), factual, and interesting. A biography's appeal is enhanced by a sharp black and white photo of the subject.

News Clippings

Several previously printed articles, if available, should also be included in a press kit. These stories may lead to additional stories (perhaps with a different slant), and let members of the media know that the property has been considered newsworthy in the past.

Advertising Materials

Full-color brochures, pamphlets, fliers, and other promotional materials provide additional information and appeal.

expect during the visit. What is the writer's itinerary? What will be provided on a complimentary basis? What does the property expect in the way of publicity?

2. *Don't overtax the writer.* The needs of the writer should be taken into account. Specially scheduled events and appointments should not cut excessively into the writer's time. A travel writer needs the opportunity to see the property through the eyes of a *guest*.

3. *Don't overdo.* When conducting tours of guestrooms or facilities, show only one in each category. It is also important to entertain travel writers when the property's schedule is relatively free. Combining a writer's visit with property openings or social events may leave little time to discuss the project at hand, and can leave the writer with a bad impression of management if he or she is ignored.

4. *Follow up.* It is generally a bad idea to load down the travel writer with materials as he or she is leaving, so press kits or other informational materials should be sent to the travel writer following the visit if they were not sent in advance of the trip. After the visit, a short note expressing the hope that the writer enjoyed his or her stay is appropriate. A few weeks after the visit, the writer's editor may be called to get an idea of the coverage the property will receive. After reviewing the finished article, another letter of thanks should be sent to the writer, even if the story contains negative elements. After all, public relations includes enhancing the property's image with everyone, even an unhappy travel writer.

Press Relations

It is easier to establish or maintain an effective public relations program if a property enjoys a good relationship with the press.[2] A property's chances of receiving positive publicity are enhanced if it can build an image as a place that makes it easy for reporters to do their work.

Never underestimate the power of the press. A few well-placed stories can propel an unknown property into the public eye as nothing else can; even established properties can benefit from—or be damaged by—the press's "third party" credibility. Therefore a good relationship with the media is vitally important.

News Media Interests

To develop good media relations and get the most from media coverage, there are several factors that must be considered. First and foremost, the property public relations person or staff must understand media interests. Just as property employees must sell the benefits of the property to guests, newspapers and magazines must generate reader interest and increase circulation; radio and TV stations must appeal to their audiences and increase ratings. Publishing or airing interesting features or news stories is one way the news media seek to appeal to audiences.

Good public relations staffs are aware of the elements required for a good news story. They are also aware of the problems faced by the media. Excellent press relations can be maintained by following a few simple guidelines:

1. *Prepare news releases properly.* A news release should be well thought out, written in the particular medium's typical style, and double-spaced to allow for editorial revisions. A who, what, when, where, why, and how paragraph should be included.

2. *Avoid duplication.* With the exception of general news releases (news of expansions, new entertainment offerings, and so on), properties should resist the temptation to submit the same story to a number of media outlets. Instead, the property should write the story from a number of angles. If a well-known performer is staying at the property, for example, the property can send out stories relating to the performer's past career, other performers who have stayed at the property, the history of the suite in which the performer is staying, and so on. In this way, the property can offer a measure of exclusivity, without seeming to show favoritism to one or two media outlets.

3. *Be honest.* If questions arise, the property's staff should be candid and straightforward. Inquiries should be dealt with quickly.

4. *Respect deadlines.* Deadline pressure is a fact of life for most news media representatives, and a prompt response to a question may mean the difference between a story that is "killed" and one that influences thousands of potential guests (see Exhibit 14.8). News releases and conferences should be timed with deadlines in mind.

It is important to get to know the local media. The property's public relations coordinator should make an effort to establish and maintain contact with radio and television reporters and program producers; he or she should also contact local newspaper offices and obtain a list of columnists and reporters who may be interested in material the property has to offer. Food, travel, and business editors at newspapers and local magazines should be cultivated. The property's public relations staff should get to know newspaper and magazine editors and their needs, perhaps by inviting them to the property.

By developing good relations with news media personnel, unfavorable publicity concerning the property might be played down at a future time.

Personal Interviews
There may be times when a journalist asks a hotel manager or other hotel employee for a personal interview. It is almost always a good idea to comply with interview requests, whether they come from print or broadcast journalists. If an interview is refused, a reporter may try to piece together a story from outside, often uninformed, sources, or the reporter may ignore the property at a future time. Interviews can generate good exposure for the property and serve as a powerful public relations tool.

If you have an idea of the general purpose or direction of the interview, study pertinent information and develop answers to questions that may be raised. Avoid giving off-the-record information or taking potshots at competitors. Above all, be honest; a "no comment" response projects a negative image. It is usually best to answer questions briefly, but it is permissible to volunteer information that will help clarify the topic.

Keep in mind that the journalist is running the interview, and that clearance of the article or broadcast material that results is seldom offered. Most reporters will use a tape recorder to ensure accuracy, especially in cases

Exhibit 14.8   Media Deadlines

Morning newspapers	3 p.m. to break the following day. Reach the editor the morning before.
Afternoon newspapers	9 a.m. that day. Reach the editor the day before.
Sunday newspapers	Wednesday (some sections 1–2 weeks ahead).
Sunday magazines	4 weeks in advance.
News magazines Weekly newspapers (based on Thursday publication date)	Monday. (Stories are written or rewritten Tuesday; printing and delivery take place Wednesday.)
Monthly trade magazines	Either the 1st or 15th of the month preceding cover date.
National monthly magazines (e.g., *National Review*, *Vogue*, *Atlantic*)	Either the 1st or 15th of the month preceding cover date. However, these magazines generally work on a three-month lead time (so, in April, they're working on the July issue).
Television news	2 p.m. that day for 6 o'clock edition. Most TV news conferences take place at 10 a.m.
Television features, talk shows	Book 2–5 weeks ahead of time (except in the case of big celebrities). Differs for each show, so check with the producer.
Radio news	Anytime. All-news stations are a particularly good bet.
Radio talk	Roughly 2 weeks ahead but, again, it varies from show to show. Check with producers.

A property must adhere to media deadlines in order to receive timely coverage of property news and features. This exhibit gives general guidelines for various print and broadcast media.

where the material is of a complex or technical nature. In the majority of cases, a story or broadcast based on an interview will be correct and unbiased.

TV Interviews. A TV interview is slightly different from a print or radio interview in that the public will have a visual image of the property and/or its personnel. Obviously, appearance is important. If you are asked to give a TV interview, it is essential that you look and feel your best. Conservative clothes work best for television; stark white and bold patterns should be avoided. Flashy jewelry should also be avoided. You should project an image of credibility and stability.

What is said during a TV interview is also important, of course, especially if the broadcast is live. Being well-prepared is a must. You must be absolutely certain of the information you are giving. If asked a loaded question, deal with your objection first before answering the question. It is not necessary for you to pretend to be an expert in areas outside the hospitality field. In areas where you have no expertise, admit that fact or give an opinion and label it as such.

It is especially important for you to stay alert during a TV interview. You should follow the interviewer's instructions regarding the cameras and always assume the cameras are on until the interviewer says the interview is over.

Although a television experience can cause some nervousness or anxiety, you can learn to enjoy time before the cameras. TV interviews can be exciting opportunities to promote the property to a large, potentially profitable audience.

News Conferences

There may be times when a news release or an interview with one member of the media is not adequate. Perhaps the property has experienced a labor dispute or a disaster, and it is important that the facts be presented to all of the media to avoid speculation or misrepresentation. If there is sufficient cause for a news conference, these guidelines will help to increase its effectiveness:

1. *Schedule appropriately.* Except when the time of a news conference is dictated by a disaster or emergency, try to select a day and time convenient to the schedules of the news media. Most television and newspaper staffs need sufficient lead time to prepare stories or edit film, so an early morning news conference (9:00 to 10:00 a.m.) is usually best.

2. *Be prepared.* Special press kits relating to the presentation should be available. The speaker(s) should be adequately prepared— background or fact sheets should be studied, and answers to possible questions rehearsed.

3. *Keep the conference brief and to the point.* Presentations should be limited to around fifteen minutes and be followed by a question and answer session.

4. *Be aware of media requirements.* Make sure that the room the news conference is held in (whether on or off the property) is adequate in terms of space for the reporters and their equipment. If the news conference will be televised, there must be adequate electrical wiring and outlets, sufficient room for television equipment, and easy access. Also, do not use white backdrops or table covers. Make it easy on the press by displaying the property's logo on the lectern or conference table, and by providing biographies of the principals involved (the property's general manager, safety engineer, and so on).

5. *Maintain good press relations.* Be sure there is adequate parking and that someone from the property greets press members. If time permits, provide coffee and/or refreshments.

6. *Provide press kits to media members who were unable to attend the conference.* This should be done the same day, if possible, and immediately after the conference in emergency situations.

Sensitive Subjects

Bad news about the hotel may create lasting memories and negatively affect the property's image well after the disaster, labor dispute, or financial crisis is over. It is important, therefore, for a property to develop a public relations strategy to handle emergencies or other situations that can generate bad news. Proper planning can limit potentially negative publicity and reinforce a positive public image.

One of the most important elements in handling sensitive subjects is the naming of one spokesperson. This helps minimize conflicting reports and misrepresentations of facts. The entire staff should be aware of this policy and refer any questions from the media to a spokesperson who is fully briefed on the situation and measures being taken to rectify it.

In most sensitive situations, information should be given to the media at a scheduled news conference so that each medium receives the same information at the same time. The spokesperson can then answer questions and describe positive actions being taken by the property. This often results in a more sympathetic press.

The press may raise difficult questions, including how or why the problem or accident occurred, the name(s) of the person(s) involved, and estimates of damage. The spokesperson should never reply to these questions with a "No comment," but should provide a reason if he or she is unable to answer the question with specifics. It may be illegal to answer questions, especially when next-of-kin must be notified or in cases where only an insurance company can make an assessment of damages. The spokesperson can truthfully say that he or she cannot speculate on the cause of a disaster—the cause will be revealed after an investigation by the proper authorities.

The important part of crisis public relations begins long before there is an emergency. Managers and employees must be aware of property policy and their roles in dealing with the media. By following a well-directed comprehensive plan, the positive aspects of a property's press relations can combat any negative feelings the press and public may have toward the property because of the crisis.

If a Story Contains Errors

There may be times—no matter how good press relations have been—when a newspaper or magazine article, radio spot, or television report is slanted or contains misleading or incorrect information. In some cases, the property's image may be such that the negative story will not affect business and it is best to let the story die. In other cases, however, the negative publicity may be damaging and the error must be dealt with.

The best way to deal with an error is to contact the writer or broadcaster responsible and discuss it. Never appear to be trying to manage the news, but do present the property's case—backed up by facts—in a friendly, professional manner. If the journalist does not offer a satisfactory solution, the next step is to contact the editor or station manager and ask for a correction, retraction, or apology. Most media representatives are as anxious as hotel managers to maintain good public relations, and will generally cooperate by offering rebuttal time or an additional story to correct errors.

It is extremely important in these cases, no matter what the outcome, to avoid discussing the error with other media representatives or to attempt to discredit the offending journalist. It is important to maintain a good public image and build a reputation for fairness with the press.

Notes

1. The Society of American Travel Writers membership directory is available from the Society of American Travel Writers, 1120 Connecticut Ave., N.W., Suite 940, Washington, DC 20036.
2. How to establish or maintain good press relations is discussed in *Protect Your Image: Effective Media Relations for the Lodging Industry* (East Lansing, Mich.: Educational Institute of the American Hotel & Motel Association, 1987).

Discussion Questions

1. What is public relations?
2. What are six factors to consider before developing a public relations plan?
3. What factors should be considered when hiring a public relations agency?
4. What are two ways public relations efforts can be measured?
5. How does publicity differ from advertising?
6. What are two examples of promotional materials especially prepared for the media?
7. What should be included in a press kit?
8. What can a hotel do to maximize a travel writer's visit?
9. What guidelines should be followed to maintain good press relations?
10. What guidelines should be followed if a news conference is required?
11. What is the best course of action if a story contains errors?

Part IV

Selling to Market Segments

Chapter Outline

I. Business Travelers
  A. Frequent Business Travelers
    1. No-Frills Travelers
    2. Cost-Plus Travelers
    3. Extroverted-Affluent Travelers
  B. Women Business Travelers
  C. Types of Stays
    1. Overnight
    2. Extended
    3. Relocation
    4. Vacation
II. Meeting the Needs of Business Travelers
  A. Executive or Business Floors
  B. Business Services
  C. Special Amenities
  D. Frequent Traveler Programs
  E. All-Suite Properties
III. Reaching Business Travelers
IV. Conclusion

15 Selling to Business Travelers

The business traveler market is the fastest growing market in the hospitality industry today, accounting for over half of all hotel room revenues.[1] That figure continues to escalate each year as more business travelers—and the increasing number of business trips—continue to affect the hospitality industry. In this chapter we will discuss different types of business travelers and how properties are meeting their needs.

Business Travelers

While statistics on this market vary from year to year (and from source to source), a recent survey of the U.S. business traveler market reported that:

- 92% of all business travelers spent at least one night away from home on their most recent trip;

- 73% stayed in hotels or motels;

- the average length of stay was 4.3 nights; and

- more than half paid $50 or more per night for their accommodations; 11% paid $100 or more per night.[2]

These statistics explain why more and more properties are developing special amenities and services to attract business travelers.

Of all the different types of travelers, business travelers are perhaps the most knowledgeable and sophisticated, and they have definite preferences regarding the selection of a hotel:

1. *A convenient location.* Approximately 78% of all business travelers rated this factor as the prime reason for choosing a hotel.

2. *Clean, comfortable rooms.* This factor came in second (67%), and was in all probability influenced by the growing number of women travelers, who rate cleanliness high on their list of priorities. Several years ago, cleanliness was low on the list of selection factors—although it has remained consistent as a primary factor in whether someone *returns* to a hotel.

Industry Profile

Karen Roberts began her hotel career in 1974 as a reservations agent with Commonwealth Holiday Inns in Toronto, Canada. After mastering front office procedures and working as a front office manager, Roberts directed her energies toward marketing and sales. In 1978 she joined Loews Hotels and worked successfully as a director of sales for a resort hotel, a metropolitan property, and a regional sales office over a period of nine years. Roberts is currently pre-opening The Ritz-Carlton in Phoenix, Arizona, as Director of Marketing and Sales.

Karen Roberts
Director of Marketing and Sales
The Ritz-Carlton

"The business traveler market should be given importance second to none. According to a survey of business travelers, 33 million Americans—nearly one-fifth of the adult population—took a business trip of 100 miles or more in the past 12 months. Each property must find ways to influence the buying decisions of these business travelers. Of course, there are a number of effective ways—including advertising, direct mail, and corporate rate programs.

To make the most of advertising, start by identifying those publications which specifically target the property's audience. Research demographics, look at competitors' advertising, and talk with other advertisers to determine what results they're getting.

Direct mail is perhaps most effective if it's directed to corporate traffic managers or travel agents. It's been my experience that direct mail sent to purchased lists is far less likely to build business. When targeting corporate traffic managers or travel agents, however, it's important to keep pieces short and simple. These people are deluged with hundreds of direct mail pieces daily, so your direct mail piece must be interesting, readable, and *consistent*. If you mail to the same people on a regular basis, they'll eventually consider your property.

Since most hotels offer corporate rate programs, the most effective way to make yours known is to deal directly with corporate traffic managers or company purchasing agents. In addition to special rates, you may want to include incentives such as a secretarial program. These programs—along with special attention from the property's salespeople—have proven to be very effective in this marketplace.

Regardless of the type of property you represent, identify the source of your business before attempting to sell anything. In many cases, up to 75% of a property's business may come from within a 100-mile radius. If this is the case, a direct mail effort and local advertising is the most viable avenue. If your city is serviced by a number of airlines, you can research the cities that feed in a large number of visitors and concentrate advertising efforts in those locales.

Marketing a property to business travelers is one of the most challenging opportunities available in sales. With the increasing number of business travelers—and the growing number of women in this segment—selling to business travelers will offer even greater challenges and rewards in the years ahead. **"**

3. *Room rates.* Over 55% of all business travelers cited room rates as a factor in hotel selection, although this priority is likely to change as a new influx of upwardly mobile, more affluent travelers enters the business traveler market.

4. *Recommendations of friends and colleagues.* Over 87% of business travelers make their own decisions regarding accommodations, and many (35%) base their decisions on the recommendations of colleagues or friends rather than on the recommendations of travel agents (11%); 22% make a choice based on corporate or company policy.

5. *Previous experience with the property.* Previous experience with a property or a chain figured as a selection factor with 33% of the business travelers surveyed. The respondents favored chain properties for their consistency and predictability; 41% cited chains as having better service and 16% preferred chains for ease in making reservations.

6. *Facilities.* Meeting facilities influenced 33% of the respondents, while restaurants and food service were important to 22%. Restaurants and food service tend to be more important to business travelers who travel frequently, especially to women business travelers. Women business travelers were more likely to select hotels on the basis of extended-hour or 24-hour room service.

7. *Frequent traveler programs.* Although many properties place a great significance on these programs, this factor played a part in selection decisions for only 2% of those surveyed. Prospective guests were often much more concerned with the availability of services and amenities than with saving money through frequent traveler programs.[3]

Business travelers can be divided into two general categories: occasional business travelers and frequent business travelers. Frequent business travelers are responsible for approximately 50% of all business generated by business travelers and are more easily targeted than occasional business travelers. Many of the programs and services developed for frequent business travelers can also be utilized by occasional business travelers. Therefore, in this chapter we will focus on frequent business travelers and learn how properties are tailoring amenities and developing unique marketing strategies to reach this lucrative segment of the business traveler market.

Frequent Business Travelers

Frequent business travelers spend an average of 21 nights a year away from home on business and use hotels or motels 76% of the time. They are typically employed in managerial, sales, or professional positions, are well-educated (67% hold four-year college degrees), and affluent (67% earn over $35,000 per year, while 44% earn more than $50,000 annually).[4] While this group is largely male, an increasing number of women are becoming frequent business travelers, a statistic that should lead to increased revenues because women are traditionally higher users of in-house food and beverage services than are their male counterparts.

Several independent surveys have been taken to help hotels design services for frequent business travelers. A recent MasterCard survey,[5] for example, asked the question, "Assuming that the primary considerations of location, room price, and cleanliness were comparable, what other factors are most important in making a lodging selection?" The following factors are accompanied by the percentage of frequent business travelers who found them important:

- Restaurant on premises (32%)
- Quality service (22%)
- Room appointments (14%)

- Sports and recreational facilities (14%)
- Ambience (11%)
- Entertainment on premises (10%)
- Prior knowledge (10%)
- Safety and security (3%)

The survey further revealed that there are three distinct groups of frequent business travelers: no-frills travelers, cost-plus travelers, and extroverted-affluent travelers. By studying the requirements of each of these groups, a property can create or revise amenities and services to attract one or all of them.

No-Frills Travelers. The largest group in the MasterCard survey (36%), no-frills travelers, is made up largely of middle- to upper-management men and women primarily interested in a clean, comfortable, and quiet room at a fair price. No-frills travelers have little interest in hotel-sponsored social events. In fact, the businesspeople in this group are almost hermit-like in their business travels. They are not as interested as the other two groups in meeting people, staying where they are known, staying at a fashionable hotel, or partying.

Although these travelers have higher budgets than cost-plus travelers, no-frills travelers are likely to stay at budget properties. Properties without facilities such as swimming pools, saunas, tennis courts, and putting greens, and properties that do not offer large bars or organized social activities have an excellent opportunity to attract this group. No-frills travelers were the only group to express a definite preference for a particular property atmosphere, and properties wishing to meet the needs of this group must convey a sense of peace and quiet—the atmosphere most desired by no-frills travelers. Peace and quiet is a quality these guests are willing to pay for.

Cost-Plus Travelers. This is the next largest group of frequent business travelers (34%). Like no-frills travelers, these travelers are extremely cost-conscious, often to the point where they forgo convenience in favor of a lower room rate. Although cost-plus travelers—typically salespeople and middle-management executives—are often on strict expense accounts, many pride themselves on their ability to find bargains, and look for amenities at no-frills prices.

Cost-plus travelers are more interested in being sociable than no-frills travelers. The hours of a restaurant, the availability of hospitality suites or lounges at which to meet peers, and other no-cost amenities are important to cost-plus travelers.

Cost-plus travelers are generally more loyal or brand-oriented guests than the other two groups. Cost-plus travelers are more apt to belong to a frequent traveler program—both because of the value offered, and because of their loyalty to a property. Although cost-plus travelers are more likely to stay in a mid-price property on an interstate highway than in a first-class downtown hotel, they can be attracted to other properties if the price is right.

Extroverted-Affluent Travelers. This group, which made up 30% of the frequent business travelers in the MasterCard survey, holds the promise of generating higher sales per room than either of the other two groups. Extroverted-affluent travelers are typically young, affluent, and either self-employed, top-level executives, or members of a well-respected profession. They demand the best in amenities and service.

Extroverted-affluent travelers are not concerned with saving money (either on business or pleasure trips), and demand properties that are fashionable. More than the other two groups, this group puts a high priority on amenities. Recreation facilities, bars featuring live entertainment, and restaurants featuring the best in decor and cuisine are important to extroverted-affluent travelers, and the expense involved is less important than having a good time. In fact, this group is more likely to add vacation time to a business stay.

While the travelers in this group make their own decisions when selecting a property, they are more likely to be influenced by the suggestions of friends and colleagues than any other group. This group is also more likely to use the services of a travel agent or a corporate travel manager for actually booking the reservation.

Women Business Travelers

Women are an important segment of the business traveler market. This segment is growing at a phenomenal rate: only 1% of business travelers were women in 1970; today, 35% of business travelers are women, and this figure is expected to top 50% by the year 2000.[6] Women already constitute 50% of business meeting attendees and 51% of all meeting planners; therefore, properties should take a close look at the wants and needs of these travelers.

Although businesswomen express many of the same preferences (location, rates, etc.) when making a hotel selection as their male counterparts, they appreciate different things when they travel than do men business travelers. Two out of three women mentioned cleanliness and attractiveness of hotels as reasons for booking, while only half of the men cited this factor as a selection criteria, for example.[7]

Since women tend to be more loyal repeat guests than men, it is especially important that a property provide the features most important to women travelers:

1. *Security.* Women tend to be far more security-conscious than men. Most women consider door chains, dead bolt locks, and door "viewports" or "peepholes" essential guestroom features. Many women prefer hotels with a single entrance close to the front desk, and an atrium atmosphere, where all rooms open into a central, well-lighted area. Women also prefer hotels that feature an inside restaurant, room service, and a well-lit lobby. Valet parking or a well-lit parking garage are other security essentials.

   A property can add to a woman's feeling of security by following security procedures in place for all guests, such as making sure front desk agents, restaurant staff, and valet parkers do not call out room numbers; refusing to give out room numbers to callers or visitors; and instructing bell staff to leave the room door open and check the room before leaving the guest. Of course, proper guestroom key control is a must.[8]

2. *Comfort and service.* Women are especially appreciative of clean, attractive, well-lit rooms and friendly, courteous service. Amenities such as full-length mirrors and skirt hangers are popular with women (see Exhibit 15.1).

Women are more influenced by good service than men are; an unsatisfactory experience in this area will irritate women business travelers and make them less likely to return. Hotel staff should be trained to treat women courteously and in a businesslike manner. Women tend to react negatively to overly familiar terms such as "honey" and "dear."

3. *Convenience.* Most businesswomen prefer to have a small space set aside for work or small meetings. This is one reason that suites are finding increased popularity with women—the bed is in a separate room away from the entertaining area. When suites are not available, foldaway beds are sometimes used, although these meet with mixed reactions. At the very least, a woman business traveler should have a desk with a telephone and good lighting.

4. *Facilities.* Because women tend to stay on the property more than men do, special facilities such as swimming pools and fitness facilities are attractive to them. As mentioned in Chapter 7, many women prefer light or low-calorie meals, so property restaurants should offer selections for light eaters.

For the most part, women do not like discrimination—either for or against them—and simply want to be treated equally. Since they take more mini-vacations than businessmen, typically spend 25% more in restaurants than men do, and often entertain associates while at the property, it is important that properties provide the security, comfort, and service that will appeal to this loyal market segment (see Exhibit 15.2).

Types of Stays

Business travelers, no matter what type or gender, generate the following types of stays:

- Overnight stays
- Extended stays
- Relocation stays
- Vacation stays

Overnight. Overnight stays are probably the most common, and may include food and beverage sales as well as guestroom business. Quick check-in and check-out; clean, comfortable rooms; and easy access to quick food service are the keys to attracting overnight business guests.

Extended. Extended stays may be a combination of a business trip and a vacation, a longer stay for a conference or study program, or a sales trip. Business travelers on extended stays typically require more amenities and services than do overnight travelers. Extended-stay business travelers look for on-site restaurants, entertainment, recreational facilities, and business

Exhibit 15.1 Amenities for Women Business Travelers

Amenity	Percent Requesting the Amenity
Skirt and Suit Hangers	87%
Iron and Ironing Board	63%
Shampoo and Conditioners	53%
Hair Dryer	47%
Moisturizing Soap	44%
Curling Irons	25%
Cosmetics	7%

While women business travelers cite the same general preferences for selecting a hotel (location, cleanliness) as their male counterparts, they have different requirements for amenities. This survey lists the amenities most requested by women business travelers, and can serve as a guide to properties wishing to attract this growing market segment. Other preferences of women travelers include: good lighting, large vanity areas, closets high enough to accommodate floor-length dresses, and clotheslines over the tub in the guestroom bath.

Source: "Hotel Security Concerns Women Business Travelers," *USA Today*, 18 June 1984.

services. Extra amenities such as suites, in-room bars, and kitchenettes may offer added appeal to this market segment.[9]

Relocation. Relocation stays are becoming increasingly important to hospitality properties, particularly all-suite hotels. Many of these properties provide additional services to guests such as city tours and baby-sitting services.

Vacation. Vacation stays are often an offshoot of business travel either at the end of a business trip or at a later time (either alone or with family members). In most cases, vacationers will require recreational facilities or easy access to recreational opportunities in the immediate vicinity.

Meeting the Needs of Business Travelers

Properties are meeting the needs of business travelers in a number of unique ways, including the introduction of women-only floors, executive or business floors, business services, special amenities, frequent traveler programs, and all-suite properties. Most of these services have met with wide approval, especially the concept of executive or business floors. An exception is the women-only floor; over 90% of women travelers prefer not to be segregated.[10]

Executive or Business Floors

Executive or business floors are designed to provide a secure, comfortable environment in which to meet peers, conduct business, or relax after a busy day. Compri Hotels, for example, offers Compri Clubs—5,000-square-foot facilities that include lounging areas, intimate bars, libraries stocked with books and periodicals, work desks complete with credit-card

Exhibit 15.2   Selling to Women Business Travelers

THE TRAVELING WOMAN . . .

THE TRAVELING WOMAN'S BILL OF RIGHTS

These are among a few of Ramada's policies that make a woman's trip problem-free. They are the heart of Ramada's employee training program designed to meet the specific needs of traveling women.

1. You have the right to a room that fits your needs for security or convenience to facilities.

2. You have the right to expect that your room number will be handled in a most confidential manner.

3. You have the right to have a bellperson check your room for security, and to make sure that all towels and amenities are in full supply.

4. You have the right to a good table in the dining area where you are assured privacy, yet aren't singled out as being alone.

5. You have the right to refuse cocktails sent gratis — and your server or bartender should not serve you an unrequested drink, or pass a note to you.

6. When arriving alone by car at a hotel without valet parking, you have the right to have a bellperson drive with you to the parking area, or meet you there, and accompany you back to the hotel with your luggage.

7. You have a right not to be addressed in a casual or familiar manner by employees.

8. And like any guest, you have the right to be treated with courtesy and to receive prompt, attentive service.

WHAT MAKES RAMADA SPECIAL TO WOMEN TRAVELERS

Ramada inaugurated its Traveling Woman Program and spearheaded the movement in the hospitality industry to provide women travelers with the utmost in security and comfort.

Ramada has set the industry standard in providing courteous, conscientious, and efficient service to traveling women by responding to their unique needs and the problems they encounter. By undertaking an extensive employee training program throughout the country, every member of the hotel staff is trained to respond to the problems and discourtesies encountered by women travelers. Ramada has instituted property-level improvements and provides room amenities to accommodate the particular needs of women travelers such as installation of skirt hangers, increased lighting, and added security measures.

Today, Ramada is leading the industry by addressing the more sophisticated needs of the woman traveler, who now represents a full 37% of the business traveling public. As a traveling woman, you will feel more comfortable at Ramada, whether you're traveling with business associates or alone, because Ramada understands your needs.

Ramada took the lead in addressing the needs of women business travelers several years ago with its Traveling Woman Program. The chain developed an extensive training program to teach employees to be sensitive to the needs of women travelers, and, like many other chains, continues to sell to women travelers through its frequent traveler program, the Ramada Business Card Program.

Courtesy of Ramada, Inc.

telephones, and large-screen televisions. Some executive floors are set apart strictly for the use of affluent guests and executives. The Club Floor at the Biltmore Hotel in Los Angeles offers a library, television center, game room, billiard room, and bar.

Executive floor guestrooms are designed for an increasing number of executive travelers who want special amenities such as special soaps and shampoos, terry bathrobes, turn-down service, and complimentary chocolates.

Executive floors require special promotion. Hotels are turning to direct mail, press releases and other forms of publicity, and advertisements in airline magazines and such newspapers as the *Wall Street Journal* to reach upscale business travelers. Word-of-mouth advertising and personal calls on corporations have also generated business for these special floors. Properties hope these floors will help change the image of businesspeople from harried travelers to pampered executives relaxing in facilities as comfortable and secure as their own home.

Business Services

Business services are becoming important to—and expected by—business travelers. Secretarial services, copying machines, telex and cable services, computer terminals, and electronic mail are just some of the business services now offered by properties for the convenience of business guests. At many properties, for example, a business traveler can call the secretarial service, dictate over the phone, and have his or her materials delivered the following day.

Special Amenities

Some special guestroom amenities for businesspeople have already been mentioned. For both overnight and extended-stay business guests, many properties are also featuring work areas in rooms (some complete with personal computer hook-ups or special writing desks), and executive check-in/check-out programs, some of which are available via computer or through an in-room television screen. Other special amenities include complimentary copies of the *Wall Street Journal* or other daily papers, cable television featuring news and business stations, and even telephones and televisions in bathrooms to enable busy executives to keep up with the daily news while getting ready for the day.

Frequent Traveler Programs

The growing number of business travelers has also prompted the development of frequent traveler programs which offer discounts, premiums, and hotel services to corporations or guests booking a specified number of room nights. The Holiday Inns' Priority Club, Hyatt Hotels' Gold Passport, Marriott Hotels' Honored Guest, Ramada's Business Card, and Sheraton's International Club are all examples of these programs. Properties should carefully weigh the expense against the results before heavily promoting a program, however. As mentioned earlier, only 2% of business travelers in a recent survey said a frequent traveler program was important when deciding on a hotel.[11] Location, cleanliness, and rates remain the key factors in hotel selection.

All-Suite Properties

All-suite properties also play an important role in serving business travelers. These properties are ideal for businesspeople who are relocating. Residence Inn, for example, caters to businesspeople who stay seven or more nights, and offers monthly as well as daily rates to guests. Guests staying at Hawthorn Suites enjoy a living area, full kitchen, and separate bedroom. Hawthorn Suites also offers free breakfast buffets and hospitality hours, grocery shopping services, free daily newspapers, and outdoor recreational amenities.

Residence Inn has identified four areas of importance to today's transferees and their families:

Business Services: Going that Extra Mile

If you're a guest of the Chicago Hilton & Towers and want to dictate a letter or memo, you can go to your room phone any time of the day or night, dial 6500, and reach the hotel's Business Center. An operator comes on the line and tells you how to proceed with dictation (it's easy—you start talking).

To get a replay of your last sentence, you touch 3; to get a replay of the entire message, you touch 7. If you need the dictation by early morning, you call the concierge and make arrangements. Otherwise, you'll get it by 10:00 or 11:00 a.m.

If you leave the hotel and recall a business memo you forgot to write, you can telephone the hotel, ask for the Business Center, and then ask to be put on transcription service. You can start dictation immediately. Cost is $17 setup charge (for the length of your stay) and $6.50 a page for transcription.

The best is yet to come. You can request the hotel's executive messenger service by dialing 4040. The responding voice agrees to send a representative from the hotel's Business Center to your room promptly. The representative tapes your answering message ("This is John Smith. I can't come to the phone right now, but if you'll leave your name—"), and the tape is hooked up to your telephone line to provide an answering service. (The idea originated with a telephone operator as a way to relieve the switchboard.) You then get a beeper to take with you when you go out. Wherever you are, the beeper alerts you when you get a message. You can then call the hotel, ask for your room, access your tape with the beeper, and get your message. You can play the tape again when you return to your room or even take it home. Cost is $20 for the setup, or less than $7 a day for the average stay of three days.

Source: Adapted from "The Chicago Hilton & Towers: Marketing for the Right Mix," *Lodging*, July/August 1986, p. 68.

1. *A home-like atmosphere.* A home-like atmosphere is important to 58% of this market segment. To address this need, Residence Inn properties are designed as a "neighborhood" of two-story, residential-style buildings.

2. *Residential-style housing.* Buildings that look residential are important to 36% of this segment. Residence Inn meets this need by offering both single-story studio and two-story townhouses surrounded by landscaping and recreational facilities.

3. *Price.* Of those surveyed, 32% listed price as an important consideration. Residence Inn's suites are priced competitively with hotels, and offer a sliding rate scale based on the length of stay.

4. *Reduced relocation stress.* Residence Inns meets this need by offering grocery shopping services, arranging for baby-sitters, and providing orientation activities.[12]

Reaching Business Travelers

Business travelers are relatively easy to locate. Some, in fact, might be vacationers staying at the property who will be traveling on business sometime during the year. But in today's competitive market, it is not enough to rely on repeat guests or word-of-mouth referrals to reach business travelers. The property must actively solicit specific business traveler market segments.

Business traveler business—meals, functions, and rooms—can be obtained from corporations in the immediate vicinity of the property. Local corporations are often the sources of national business from traveling salespeople or state, regional, and national meetings. These corporations can be identified through a number of sources:

- Office building locator boards
- Chamber of Commerce listings
- Competitors' function boards
- Local newspaper articles
- State and regional publicity materials

Business travelers throughout the nation may be targeted by obtaining the names of corporations and decision-makers through:

- Business publications and directories
- Travel publications
- State industrial commissions
- Mailing list brokers
- National trade conventions

Potential business leads obtained through these sources should first be screened to determine market potential before any costly sales efforts are initiated. This screening may be done in the form of a direct mail questionnaire or a telemarketing survey, and a computer can be used to categorize responses.

As in all sales efforts, a direct approach will probably be the most effective for reaching potential business guests, and sales letters, telephone calls, and even personal sales calls may be employed. Some properties locate a potentially profitable area and use a sales blitz to saturate the market and obtain business. A sales blitz can be effective if it is properly planned and monitored, and if collateral materials, follow-up information, and personal contact supplement the blitz.

In addition to contacting business travelers directly, properties can reach business travelers through a variety of other sources:

- Corporate travel managers
- Secretaries' clubs
- Travel agents
- Tour operators (group leisure travelers might have an occasion to revisit the property on company business)
- Real estate agents and relocation services
- Hotel representatives in key cities

Corporate travel managers often plan travel for company executives and are excellent sources of referral business. Many corporate travel managers are members of a professional organization such as the National Passenger Traffic Association (NPTA). This association serves the travel managers of over 400 corporations and business organizations and may prove to be an excellent source of business leads. Hotels may join the NPTA as allied members.

Secretaries' clubs are another effective way to reach business travelers and build repeat business (see Exhibit 15.3). Secretaries' clubs are primarily social organizations. A property may offer annual parties, familiarization tours, the use of recreational facilities, and other rewards or incentives to secretaries who refer guests to the property. The Sheraton Meridian's Inn-Siders Club, for example, offers discounted food and drink tickets, the use of recreational facilities, and quarterly prizes to secretaries with the most bookings.

Travel agents and tour operators will be discussed in later chapters. Real estate agents and relocation services may be the source of leads regarding people in the local community who will be vacating a home, or people moving to the community who need a place to stay temporarily. Hotel representatives, discussed in Chapter 3, may serve to build both new and repeat business.

Properties can also target business travelers through advertising, promotion at trade shows, and public relations and publicity.

Advertising can take a number of forms, depending on the business traveler segment the property is targeting.

Print advertising can be especially effective, as long as ads are designed to show benefits and amenities that will attract the targeted segment: no-frills approaches for the no-frills traveler, elegance and impeccable service for the extroverted-affluent traveler, and cleanliness and security for the woman business traveler. Ads can be placed in local newspapers, regional newspapers of targeted cities, business and trade magazines, and travel and in-flight magazines.

Billboards can be used to attract business travelers on the road, while direct mail promotions can be used to promote to specific market segments. Radio and television spots can also be used to reach business travelers. Radio is most effective during the early morning and late afternoon drive times and on all-news stations.

Trade shows can be excellent opportunities to promote a hotel's facilities and services. Since trade shows are most often used to reach association and corporate meeting planners, this strategy will be discussed in Chapter 18.

Public relations and publicity are also excellent ways to reach the business community. A property can get business press for expansions, promotions within various departments, and announcements of special business plans or amenities.

Public relations efforts can include sponsoring a business seminar, donating money for business scholarships, or organizing a "Career Day" at which representatives from a variety of businesses meet with students. The business community can also be cultivated with special "Business Appreciation Days," receptions or tours, and special discount rates for food and beverages or health club facilities and other recreational amenities.

Exhibit 15.3 Secretaries' Clubs

Lori White presenting diamond cocktail ring to lucky winner, Faith Glover (Meridian Insurance).

Bonus Points!!

Important Announcement!!

Inn-Siders start booking your functions at the Sheraton Meridian! You can earn bonus points on functions you book and hold with us between now and December 31, 1987. Here's how it works—we'll give you one bonus point for every $100 spent in Food & Beverage. So, if your company is planning a luncheon or dinner between now and the end of the year—call us and start earning those bonus points.

We Have A Winner!

April 23rd marked our 2nd Inn-Siders' party and it was fun, filling (lots of food and drink), and profitable for some of you lucky winners out there! We gave out **more** L.S. Ayres gift certificates (you can never have enough of those!), some dinners at our restaurant, the Ramsgate, and our quarterly prize, the diamond cocktail ring. Our lucky winner for this quarter was Faith Glover from Meridian Insurance. Unfortunately, Faith could not be at the party that evening - she was finishing up last minute details for her wedding occurring that weekend. Nevertheless, when Faith found out the good news she was one happy woman! And deserving too! Thanks for your business Faith, we are proud to have you as our diamond ring winner!

Who will be the next? We will find out August 12.

We Are Saving Pan Am Space For You

August will be a busy month for Indianapolis, and because of all the out of town visitors coming into our city for the Pan Am Games, hotel space will be limited. We don't want our corporate travelers to be stuck without a place to stay. So we have reserved a block of rooms just for them! There is no need to worry. While the excitement of the Pan Am Games overwhelms the city we will still have room for those who are going about business as usual!!

We Want You to Know Us!

We want you to be familiar with the hotel that you are booking rooms or meetings in. If you would like a tour of our facilities, please contact me. I or another sales manager will be happy to set up a time convenient for you to come look us over!

Get those Inn-Siders' candy jars ready.......We will be around soon to fill them up with goodies!!

We Have a New Gift Shop

Our Gift Shop is open and its NEW! Still in the same location (lobby level), our Gift Shop is under new management. It provides everything our guest may need, want, or forgotten at home! The Gift Shop even has a wide variety of cards for every occasion, along with a large selection of Pan Am items and Indianapolis memorabilia. Open from 8 am - 8 pm, 7 days a week, the Sheraton Meridian Gift Shop provides our guests with their every need!

Membership in secretaries' clubs is offered to secretaries and other personnel who make reservations for company VIPs, guests, and employees needing hotel accommodations. Newsletters such as this one keep members informed of special events at the property, membership functions, and incentive awards available to club members.

Courtesy of Sheraton Meridian, Indianapolis, Indiana.

Conclusion

Business travelers spend over $66 billion each year for transportation, accommodations, and meals.[13] It is no wonder that many hospitality properties are developing special programs and services to appeal to this market, especially the frequent business traveler segment. Executive or business floors, business services, special amenities such as executive check-in/check-out programs, frequent traveler programs, and all-suite properties are just some of the new facilities and services that have changed the nature of the hospitality industry. Most hoteliers feel that the change has benefited properties and business guests alike.

Notes

1. Laventhol & Horwath, *U.S. Lodging Industry—1987* (Philadelphia: Laventhol & Horwath, 1987), p. 17.

2. These statistics are a part of the 1985–1986 Survey of Business Travelers conducted by *Travel Weekly* and the U.S. Travel Data Center.

3. The statistics in this section are a part of the 1985–1986 Survey of Business Travelers conducted by *Travel Weekly* and the U.S. Travel Data Center.

4. MasterCard International Frequent Business Traveler Study. Prepared by MasterCard International, New York, NY 10106. Sample size: 344 telephone respondents.

5. MasterCard International Frequent Business Traveler Study.

6. "The Woman Traveler: A Special Report," *Lodging Hospitality*, December 1985, p. 32.

7. This statement and some of the other material in this section on women business travelers was adapted from "The Woman Traveler: A Special Report," *Lodging Hospitality*, and Joan Moulsdale, "What Do Women Business Travelers Want?" *HSMAI Marketing Review*, Winter 1985.

8. Appropriate security measures to safeguard guests and their property are discussed in Raymond C. Ellis, Jr., and the Security Committee of AH&MA, *Security and Loss Prevention Management* (East Lansing, Mich.: Educational Institute of the American Hotel & Motel Association, 1986). *Security: Key Control and Guest Privacy* (East Lansing, Mich.: Educational Institute of the American Hotel & Motel Association) is one of a series of four videotapes that discuss hotel security issues.

9. The needs of business travelers staying at properties for conventions or meetings are discussed in Leonard H. Hoyle, David C. Dorf, and Thomas J. A. Jones, *Managing Conventions and Group Business* (East Lansing, Mich.: Educational Institute of the American Hotel & Motel Association, 1989).

10. Jane Maas, "Women Travelers: Selling the Market," *The Cornell Hotel and Restaurant Administration Quarterly*, August 1986, p. 4.

11. 1985–1986 Survey of Business Travelers conducted by *Travel Weekly* and the U.S. Travel Data Center.

12. The statistics in this list were gathered from Residence Inns' sales literature for prospective franchisers.

13. Laurie Berger, "New Breed of Hotel Specialist Works Directly with Companies," *Corporate Travel*, April 1988, p. 1.

Discussion Questions

1. What do business travelers cite as the prime reason for choosing a hotel?

2. How many nights during the year does the average frequent business traveler spend away from home on business?

3. The study on frequent travelers discussed in the chapter revealed what three distinct groups of frequent business travelers?

4. Which group of frequent business travelers expressed a definite preference for a particular property atmosphere?

5. Which group of frequent business travelers holds the promise of generating higher sales per room than either of the other groups?

6. Women made up what percentage of business travelers in 1970? What is that percentage today?

7. What are some security measures hotels can follow to meet the security needs of women business travelers?

8. How are hotels meeting the needs of business travelers?

9. What sources may be used for locating local and national business travelers?

Chapter Outline

   I. Individual Leisure Travelers
       A. Families
           1. Meeting the Needs of Family Travelers
               a. Special services
               b. Weekend packages
               c. Advance-purchase discounts
           2. Finding Family Travelers
           3. Reaching Family Travelers
       B. Mature Travelers
           1. Meeting the Needs of Mature Travelers
           2. Finding Mature Travelers
           3. Reaching Mature Travelers
       C. Others
           1. Business/Leisure Travelers
           2. Single Leisure Travelers
  II. Group Leisure Travelers
       A. Tour Intermediaries
       B. Types of Tours
           1. Motorcoach Tours
                a. Meeting the needs of motorcoach travelers
               b. Finding motorcoach tour brokers
               c. Reaching motorcoach tour brokers
           2. Airline Tours
           3. Amtrak Tours
           4. Property Package Tours
 III. Conclusion

16 Selling to Leisure Travelers

In addition to selling to business travelers, properties can increase room occupancies and food and beverage sales by attracting leisure travelers. Over 65% of all Americans take an annual vacation; Americans spend some $73 billion on leisure travel each year![1] The leisure traveler market can be divided into two segments: individual leisure travelers and group leisure travelers. In this chapter we will take a look at the needs of each of these segments and show where each segment can be found. We will see how properties are reaching leisure travelers through advertising, direct mail, travel intermediaries, and other avenues. Finally, we will discuss how properties are meeting the needs of leisure travelers through discounts, unique marketing methods, and special packages and programs.

Individual Leisure Travelers

Individual leisure travelers can be defined as non-business guests who are traveling independently rather than with a group on a pre-arranged tour. They can be divided into three general categories:

1. Families
2. Mature travelers (senior citizens)
3. Others

Families   Families can be defined as married couples and married couples with children. The latter may travel with or without their children. Families take mini-vacations (weekend trips and other stays of less than a week) and extended-stay vacations. Families are also excellent sources of functions business for such family occasions as reunions, birthday and anniversary dinners, and so on.

Families—especially those with children—are generally value-conscious, but most families perceive vacation travel as costing less than the actual expenditure. They realize that if they stayed at home they would still have to eat, pay utility bills, drive the car, and pay other out-of-pocket expenses.

Many married couples without children are also cost-conscious, but they tend to place more emphasis on quality. They can afford to spend a little

Industry Profile

Ann C. Seidl
*Account Services
Director
Alaska West Associates*

Ann Seidl graduated from the University of Nevada, Las Vegas, in 1981 with a B.S. degree in Hotel Administration, but she started her career in the hospitality industry two years earlier by working as a front office clerk at the Best Western Barratt Inn in Anchorage, Alaska. Seidl advanced to marketing and served as an administrative assistant before moving to the Sheffield Hotel in Anchorage as a front office manager. She later purchased Midnight Sun Tours, a tour wholesale corporation that targeted groups and leisure travelers. She is now Account Services Director for Alaska West Associates, an Anchorage-based advertising, marketing, and public relations firm that specializes in hotel and restaurant accounts.

❝The key to selling successfully to the leisure traveler is *service*. Leisure travelers want to feel welcome in your environment, and know that you want them to enjoy themselves and have a good time. They also want to be treated with respect.

Service starts with a contact, either phone or personal. Service continues with making reservations, checking the client in, assisting the guest once he or she is at the property, and recommending a good restaurant that you personally frequent. Going that extra step with service is what will be remembered by the leisure traveler after the bags are unpacked at home and the photos have been put away. Without good service, you can kiss the dollars of the leisure traveler good-bye—along with any word-of-mouth advertising.

Remember that your largest expense is the money you don't make. Leisure travelers have the time and money to enjoy what you have to offer; don't make them work for it! Be ready for any request, anytime. It all adds up to a satisfied guest. ❞

more on a vacation, since in many cases both the husband and wife work. Married couples without children do not always travel alone; they often travel with other couples.

While in the past husbands were usually the decision-makers for families, today women make almost 90% of vacation travel decisions.[2] This new trend is important because women and men generally look for different things; many women like romantic vacations and new destinations or experiences, while men tend to stick with the familiar.

Meeting the Needs of Family Travelers. Families will usually shop around when looking for lodging. They tend to prefer resort properties or properties that are near a number of attractions. Properties seeking to appeal to families can offer special rates (no charge for children staying with their parents, for example), low-cost recreational amenities (swimming pools and arcade games rank highest in popularity), and kitchenettes (to enable the family to save money on meals). Other conveniences attractive to families include ice and soft drink machines, parking close to the guestroom, and laundry facilities.

Other ways properties are meeting the needs of families include special services, weekend packages, and advance-purchase discounts.

Special services. Services can make a difference in a family's decision to visit or return to a property. Many properties provide families with free cribs, extra towels, and information of interest to parents, such as the names and telephone numbers of local pediatricians. Items for children in the gift shop, children's menus, and discount coupons for meals and attractions are other special services properties may provide.

Some properties provide recreational facilities designed specifically for children. The Westin Hotel in Winnipeg, for example, offers a weekend child-care center equipped with furniture and play equipment for children between the ages of two and eleven. The center is staffed by professionals and has proven to be a business-builder for the property.

Hilton Hotels offers youth programs at the Las Vegas Hilton and Flamingo Hilton and Tower in Las Vegas, the Anaheim Hilton in California, the Hilton at Walt Disney World Village, and the Fontainebleau Hilton in Miami Beach. Activities range from breakfast with Mickey, Goofy, and Donald to pool and playground activities, movies, and arts and crafts. At both of the Las Vegas properties and at the Walt Disney World Village property, Hilton offers Youth Hotel dormitories for naps and overnight stays.

Weekend packages. Families, while sources of business for extended stays, are also taking more weekend trips, usually within 200 to 300 miles of their home. This can be explained by the growing number of two-income families who have more discretionary income but less time. Properties are taking advantage of this trend by creating special weekend packages offering quality accommodations and access to a wide range of facilities and recreational amenities.

Weekend packages can be action-packed or relaxing, budget or luxury. The Stouffer Hotel Company, for example, offers weekend "Breakations," special packages which range in price from $49 per night per couple to $279 per night, depending on the type of package chosen. A number of other creative approaches have been taken by properties to attract families and other weekend travelers.

Theme weekend packages range from food or event-related festivals to elaborate murder mystery weekends (see Exhibit 16.1). Hyatt has had great success with its Hyattfest Weekends, packages designed around such themes as wine tastings and ice cream festivals. Hyattfest Weekends include accommodations, participation in festival events, and discounts on meals and recreational amenities. Murder mystery weekends involve the guest in a dramatized "murder." After the murder, guests are divided into groups that receive clues about the motive for the killing, the murder weapon, and the killer's identity. Clues may be on restaurant menus or in conversations with the mystery's cast members. At the end of the weekend, guests gather to determine who has correctly solved the mystery. This type of package includes accommodations, meals, and the fun of playing detective.

Sports weekend packages are popular with guests who desire an active weekend. The Woodlands Inn, located 27 miles north of downtown Houston, is a good example of how a suburban property with appropriate recreational facilities can attract city-dwellers. The Inn's "King of Aces" sports package features unlimited golf on the property's renowned golf courses, breakfast, a seasonal gift, and use of tennis facilities and the health and fitness center.

Shopping weekend packages can be used by downtown hotels to boost weekend business. In many cases, properties provide transportation or gift certificates to leading department stores or shopping malls, in addition to discounting guestroom or restaurant charges. This type of weekend may also be combined with theater tickets or tickets to other special events—all for one inclusive price.

Exhibit 16.1   Murder Mystery Weekends

Date	Location
January 13th/14th	BLOSSOMS, Chester.
February 3rd/4th	BEECH HILL, Windermere
March 2nd/3rd	ROYAL ALBION, Brighton
March 9th/10th	NEW CLIFTON, Blackpool
March 16th/17th	PRINCE OF WALES, Southport
May 25th/26th	PRINCE OF WALES, Southport
June 29th/30th	PRINCE OF WALES, Southport
July 13th/14th	IMPERIAL, Blackpool
August 3rd/4th	IMPERIAL, Blackpool
August 17th/18th	GOLF HOTEL, Woodhall Spa
September 7th/8th	PRINCE OF WALES, Southport
October 5th/6th	PRINCE OF WALES, Southport
October 26th/27th	ROYAL ALBION, Brighton
November 2nd/3rd	ROYAL ALBION, Brighton
November 9th/10th	PRINCE OF WALES, Southport
November 16th/17th	CAIRN, Harrogate
December 7th/8th	NEW CLIFTON, Blackpool

Other Murder Weekends for Private Parties can be arranged. For any further information contact:

Prince of Wales Hotels,
72 King St., Southport,
England. PR8 1LG.
Tel: (0704) 37700

To attract weekend guests, some properties offer murder mystery weekends. For one inclusive price, guests receive accommodations, meals, and the opportunity to play detective after a dramatized "murder." This concept, which is extremely popular in Britain, is also gaining in popularity in the United States.

Courtesy of Prince of Wales Hotels, Southport, England.

Escape weekend packages can vary greatly in price and scope. Often properties simply discount guestrooms and offer the use of the property's recreational facilities (swimming pool, health club, golf course, and so on) for the cost of the room (see Exhibit 16.2). Other escape packages may include special amenities such as breakfast in bed, champagne, and gourmet meals. Whether simple or luxurious, an escape weekend package must be perceived as a real value and targeted to audiences within a reasonable distance from home. Some properties have pushed back check-out time to 4:00 p.m. to allow for a more leisurely departure day.

Exhibit 16.2   Sample Escape Weekend Package

OUR SECRET TO A MEMORABLE THANKSGIVING IS IN THE DRESSING.

Warm Up To Our Thanksgiving Package, From $87.50 Per Night.*
Avoid the blustery weather and Aunt Jane's jellied salad this Thanksgiving. Start a new and elegant tradition at The Boca Raton Hotel and Club. We offer Five Stars, Five Diamonds and one dazzling experience on the Gold Coast.

Our special Thanksgiving rates include accommodations, breakfast and dinner daily, unlimited golf greens fees and tennis and lots of festivities. All for $87.50 per person, per night, based on double occupancy. Write P.O. Box 225, Boca Raton, FL 33429, see your travel agent or call toll free 800-327-0101.

And feast your senses at the most tasteful resort in all the world.

The Boca Raton Hotel and Club
QUITE SIMPLY THE BEST*

This weekend package, which invites prospective guests to escape "blustery weather and Aunt Jane's jellied salad," includes meals and recreational amenities.

Courtesy of The Boca Raton Hotel and Club, Boca Raton, Florida.

A property's target markets, facilities, and in-house amenities, as well as local attractions, will greatly shape the nature and success of packages offered. If a property has an 18-hole golf course, for example, a golf package is a logical choice. But if a hotel across town also has a golf course, the property's golf package should offer something more, either in terms of value or extra amenities.

Advance-purchase discounts. The family or budget traveler's interest in value has led to a new trend in the hospitality industry: discounts based on advance purchase of rooms. Ramada, for example, offers a discount of 30% off rack rates when travelers book 30 days in advance, while Holiday Corporation's discount rate program, "Great Rates," offers discounts of 20% to 40% at its Holiday Inn and Crowne Plaza properties. These programs are patterned after "Super Saver" airline fares, and certain restrictions may apply (and will vary from chain to chain). For example, Great Rates cannot be used in conjunction with any other discount, must be guaranteed by credit card, and must be made at least one week (but not more than four months) in advance; any cancellation made within 72 hours of the arrival date results in a $25 fee.

Advance-purchase discounts, which are also offered by Hyatt, Marriott, and Days Inns of America, are aimed at families, leisure travelers on a fixed budget, and value-conscious travelers who often make airline reservations in advance to save money. While most of these programs are available at any time during the week, Hyatt's program is specifically targeted to the weekend market.

Finding Family Travelers. It is generally more difficult to obtain the names of individual leisure travel prospects than it is to find group leisure travelers, but families can be contacted through lists of names from mailing list brokers, from membership lists of family-oriented organizations such as the YMCA and YWCA, and from referrals, direct mail questionnaires, and previous guest registrations. The most effective way to contact this market may be through travel agents (travel agents will be discussed in Chapter 17).

Reaching Family Travelers. Family leisure travelers can be reached through a number of means: direct mail; advertising in newspapers, magazines, and travel guides; collateral materials; radio and television advertising; and public relations efforts.

Direct mail can be especially effective if a member of the family has already visited the property on business or on vacation. He or she will appreciate the opportunity to return to the property for a special promotion at a special rate. Direct mail can appeal to first-time visitors as well, especially if the direct mail effort follows a recent promotion or publicity-generating event at the property.

Advertising in newspapers, magazines, and travel guides can also get the word out to family leisure travelers. When advertising to families, however, it is important to remember two things. First, most families are not just seeking a hotel; they are seeking a "vacation experience," whether the trip is for the weekend or for an extended period of time. Advertising must communicate the type of experience the family desires, whether it be an active-leisure experience or a quiet getaway. Second, many families make impulsive vacation decisions. While some families may plan their vacations for a year or more, many families decide on the spur-of-the-moment to take mini-vacations or weekend trips. This makes advertising in newspapers especially important because frequent newspaper advertising keeps the public informed of special packages and events that may stimulate impulse getaways.

Magazine advertising can reach a vast audience. Since many family decisions about vacations are made by women, advertising should be placed in general interest magazines and in magazines especially for women. Ads can also be placed in special interest magazines such as golf magazines and other publications that relate to property facilities.

Travel guide advertising can also be an effective way to reach family travelers. Many families seek the recommendations of sources such as AAA and Mobil travel guides. Along with providing locator maps, these guides list a property's accommodations and services, but do not offer a property the opportunity to advertise special promotions.

Collateral materials designed for families may be placed at bus, train, and airline ticket counters, at car rental counters, and at Chambers of Commerce in key feeder cities. These materials can also be distributed through direct mail packages, travel agents, or organizations that cater to families.

Radio and television advertising is used by many properties to reach family leisure travelers. While television is usually too costly for the average small to midsize property, these properties can use radio to announce family promotions.

Hotels can also reach family leisure travelers through public relations efforts. A special family-oriented weekend such as a tennis clinic can generate favorable publicity, both in terms of press coverage and word-of-mouth advertising. In addition, a property can offer special rates that might interest the news media. Offering adjoining rooms for a single price or rolling back to 1950s prices in conjunction with a '50s promotion may make newsworthy copy that generates family leisure business.

Mature Travelers

Mature travelers are a growing—and highly profitable—part of the leisure traveler market. Statistics show that one out of every five Americans is over the age of 54; this age-group accounts for nearly one-third of all hotel business.[3] The average household income for Americans between the ages of 50 to 65 is almost $30,000, nearly 20% higher than the national average. Senior citizens control nearly half—an estimated $150 billion—of the nation's discretionary income (see Exhibit 16.3).

Our nation's older population is healthier and more active than ever before; according to the American Association of Retired Persons (AARP) and the U.S. Travel Data Center, mature travelers account for:

- 30% of all travel

- 30% of air trips

- 32% of nights spent in hotels and motels

- 72% of trips in recreational vehicles

- 44% of adult passports issued

Mature travelers are especially important to the lodging industry, since many older Americans have the time and money to travel more often, stay longer, and, if retired, more easily travel any time of the year. Mature travelers are also frequent users of in-house restaurants, and can be extremely loyal, generating both repeat business and word-of-mouth advertising.

Meeting the Needs of Mature Travelers. Like family leisure travelers, many mature travelers are value-conscious. Many properties are now offering clubs or other programs that provide special rates or services to mature travelers.

Days Inns of America's September Days Club offers travelers aged 50 or above a 10% discount on room rates, gift items, pharmaceuticals, and dining at nearly 300 properties across the country. In addition to these discounts, the $10 annual membership fee also entitles mature travelers to discounts on rental cars and on travel by bus, airplane, and cruise ship.

Hilton Hotels' LXV (65) Club offers unlimited lodging for two for $999 per year. This fee entitles the member to share a room with another person (who does not have to be over 65) at over 215 hotels and inns in 42 states. Members cannot exceed five nights per trip or 15 nights per year to any one destination area, cannot stay within 100 miles of home, and can only get rooms on a "space available" basis for such special events as the Kentucky Derby and the Super Bowl.

Omni Hotels offers a special program for AARP members that includes 50% off room rates any night of the week (based on space availability) in 23 luxury hotels nationwide. A complimentary continental breakfast is

Exhibit 16.3   The Mature Market

Distribution of
U.S. Discretionary Income

Total Discretionary Income = 100%

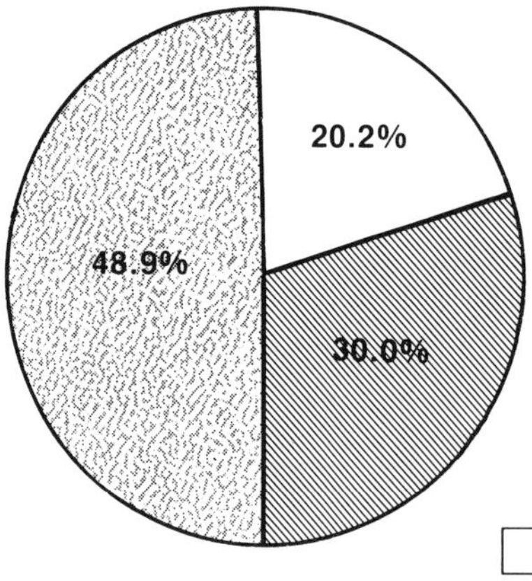

Year	Population 65 or older	% of total population
1985	28.6 million	12.0%
1990	31.1 million	12.7%
2000	35.0 million	13.0%
2015	44.8 million	15.4%
2030	64.6 million	21.2%

20.2%

48.9%

30.0%

☐ under 35

▨ 35-50

▨ 50 and over

That portion of the U.S. population that is 65 or older is expected to dramatically increase in the coming years. What does this mean to the hospitality industry? The mature market already controls nearly half of the discretionary income in the United States, and with the number of senior citizens with more money and more leisure time increasing, the hospitality industry is in an excellent position to capture more of this discretionary income in the future. Mature travelers can be more flexible about when they travel than can families, making mature travelers an excellent potential source of business for the off-season.

Source: U.S. Census Bureau projections, and "Midlife and Beyond: The $800 Billion Over-Fifty Market," Consumer Research Center.

provided to the guest and the guest's registered companion, and a 15% discount is offered on food and non-alcoholic beverages at Omni Hotel restaurants. To qualify for these benefits, guests only have to show their AARP membership card at check-in.

Other properties offering discounts or special services to mature travelers include Hampton Inns (Lifestyle 50 program), Sheraton (Retired Persons Plan), Marriott (Leisure Life Program), TraveLodge (Golden Guest Program), Quality Inns (Prime Time), and Ramada (Best Years). Age limitations and membership fees, if any, vary somewhat in each of these programs.

While many mature travelers are value-conscious, they also insist on quality and service. Clean, comfortable rooms and public areas are important to them. Many of these travelers prefer rooms with two beds, and look for well-lit public rooms for conversation and card playing. Mature travelers are also interested in safety and security, and generally prefer guestrooms on the ground floor or near elevators, smoke detectors in guestrooms, and light-colored carpets (especially on stairs).

Mature travelers are also influenced by personal attention. A property's staff can build guest loyalty if it takes the time to talk to and listen to older guests and meet their specialized needs. One of these needs is personalized service in the dining room, and, since older guests tend to dine early, it is usually possible for restaurant staff to provide this extra personal attention.

Other opportunities to extend special service are available to the front desk staff. The staff should be trained to offer general information about hotel services and the local area. Since many older guests are interested in exercise, the staff's knowledge of walking or jogging routes and other exercise facilities can make a favorable impression.

Information is so important to mature travelers that Quality Inns has produced a 40-page booklet, *Tips for Travelers Over 60*, as part of its Prime Time program. This publication lists brief descriptions of hotel types (luxury, all-suite, etc.) and their price ranges, and gives addresses and telephone numbers for major travel associations and senior citizens' organizations. It also gives tips on how to select and work with a travel agent; how to travel by car, airplane, boat, bus, and train; and how to find a property that can meet the needs of older travelers. Such a publication can prove invaluable to mature travelers when they are making travel decisions.

Finding Mature Travelers. As with family leisure travelers, it is difficult to solicit individual mature travelers. Hotels can reach seniors through mailing list brokers, membership lists of senior citizens' organizations (see Exhibit 16.4), and referrals, direct mail questionnaires, and previous guest registrations.

It may be more cost-effective for a property to target mature travelers through in-house promotion of the property's senior citizen program. Mature travelers are not always aware of these programs, and a point-of-purchase display may lead mature travelers to sign up immediately to take advantage of discounts. Their pleasurable stay at substantial savings may lead to favorable word-of-mouth advertising.

Reaching Mature Travelers. Besides in-house promotions, properties might consider promoting to mature travelers through religious groups and private associations such as local community centers where seniors gather for recreation and friendship. Many of these organizations are delighted to work with hotels to help arrange low-cost vacations for their members.

Print advertising to reach this market may be placed in local and feeder city newspapers and in various magazines. While such organizations as the AARP, the National Council of Senior Citizens, and the Catholic Golden Age will not release the names of their members, they do offer publications that accept travel advertising.

Properties can also advertise to mature travelers in travel guides. In addition to the AAA and Mobil guides, mature travelers also turn to publications available at most local libraries such as *OAG TRAVEL PLANNER Hotel & Motel RedBook* and *Hotel & Travel Index*.

Collateral materials that promote special packages for mature travelers can be distributed through direct mail campaigns, travel agents, senior citizens' clubs, Chambers of Commerce, and so on.

Exhibit 16.4   Senior Citizens' Organizations

The American Association of Retired
Persons & The National Retired
Teachers Association
1909 K St., NW
Washington, DC 20049
(202) 872–4700

Mature Outlook
P.O. Box 1205
Glenview, IL 60025
(800) 336–6330

The National Council of Senior
Citizens
925 15th St., NW
Washington, DC 20005
(202) 347–8800

Catholic Golden Age
1012 14th Street NW
Suite 1003
Washington, DC 20005
(202) 737–0231

National Association for Mature
People
P.O. Box 26792
Oklahoma City, OK 73118
(405) 523–5060

These are some of the major organizations serving America's senior citizens. While many of these organizations will not provide the names and addresses of their members, they will offer advice to properties who wish to serve senior citizens, and some produce publications that accept travel advertising.

Others

Other individual leisure travelers include business travelers on extended business/leisure trips and single travelers who may be traveling alone or with a group of other singles.

Business/Leisure Travelers. Many businesspeople who extend their stays are looking for more than relaxation; they may be interested in improving in some way. A property that offers special programs—from tennis clinics and fitness weekends to language classes and financial seminars—may attract this type of traveler.

There are a number of ways to reach business/leisure travelers. Convention attendees, for example, can be asked to stay after the convention, either indirectly by providing the meeting planner with information about local attractions and special hotel packages, or directly by talking to the delegates as they arrive or at appropriate times during the convention. Delegates, especially association delegates who are attending on a voluntary basis, will often respond to a personal invitation.

Hotels can also reach business/leisure travelers by direct mail. If a businessperson makes a Thursday reservation, for example, the property can send with the confirmation notice a brochure or flier that invites the traveler to extend the stay through the weekend. Or the property may place ads in the business pages of local and feeder-city newspapers (see Exhibit 16.5). Radio spots on all-news stations are excellent ways to advertise weekend promotions to business travelers who are looking for worthwhile mini-vacations.

Selling to Leisure Travelers **415**

Exhibit 16.5   Discount Weekend Rates

Stay a whole weekend. Get half off.

For a limited time only, you can stay at the Watergate Hotel for a weekend getaway and get away with a great price. Our half-price Watergate Weekend includes Continental Breakfast for two and parking. Reserve your room or suite for Friday, Saturday or Sunday night. Call right now. Availability is limited.

The Watergate Hotel

CUNARD

A Family of Distinctive Hotels

2650 Virginia Ave. NW
Washington DC 20037
For reservations, call (800) 424-2736
or (202) 965-2300.

Many properties that cater to the business traveler during the week face low occupancies over the weekend. To help fill rooms, many properties offer special rates for guests staying over the weekend.

Single Leisure Travelers. Many single leisure travelers look for personal enrichment while on vacation, and, like the business traveler on an extended stay, may enjoy hotel-sponsored activities such as unique food events or personal enrichment seminars. Such activities provide the opportunity to meet other singles, as do recreational facilities and the "Friendship Table" concept discussed in Chapter 7.

Hotels can reach single travelers with print ads. A getaway package, for example, can be offered in the entertainment or business section of a key feeder-city newspaper. Many single travelers are attracted to sophisticated consumer magazines, which make excellent vehicles for promoting packages or programs for the single traveler. Broadcast media advertising can also be effective.

A number of single travelers join travel groups. The formation of a singles program within a chain or at an individual property could attract this market segment, as could offering singles' packages through travel agents or direct mailings.

Group Leisure Travelers

Group leisure travel business can be very beneficial to a property. First and foremost, groups can be scheduled during soft business periods, generating much-needed room occupancies and revenues. In addition, a group is easier to plan for than individual guests, since the property knows exactly when the group will arrive, how many people are in it, what services it will require (meal functions, baggage handling, and so on), and the duration of the stay.

Although group leisure travelers may be thought of as simply groups of travelers on pre-arranged vacations, they are actually part of a complex travel and tour system that has numerous dimensions. Group tour packages range from transportation, accommodations, and baggage handling to more extensive packages that include such add-ons as meals, sight-seeing, entertainment, and admission to attractions. Group tour packages are usually arranged by a travel intermediary; therefore, it is important to understand the various types of intermediaries involved.

Tour Intermediaries

Travel professionals who arrange tours include tour brokers, tour wholesalers, and retail travel agents.

Tour brokers, also known as motorcoach brokers or tour operators, are licensed by the Federal Interstate Commerce Commission to put together package motorcoach tours in the United States and, in some cases, Canada. While tour brokers do not actually provide the transportation, they contract with certified carriers such as Greyhound or Continental Trailways for the buses required, and with hospitality properties for accommodations and/or meals. Many tour brokers operate travel agencies through which tours are sold. Motorcoach tours can also be sold by motorcoach companies, tour operators, or travel companies. Tours include motorcoach transportation, room and tax, baggage handling, and tickets to attractions (when applicable).

The tour broker assumes responsibility for the success of the tour. He or she does not work on a commission basis. If seats are not sold, the tour broker must take a loss on the deposits paid out to properties, attractions, etc.

Tour wholesalers, like tour brokers, put tour packages together, but typically work with airlines rather than with ground transportation. Most tour wholesalers contract with hotels, airlines, and other travel and lodging suppliers months in advance, and put packages together that are sold through

Industry Profile

Chaney Ross worked as night manager in the advertising department of a local newspaper while attending the College of Journalism at Ohio State University, and later accepted a position as production manager in one of the city's largest advertising agencies. On both of his jobs, Chaney worked closely with salespeople. It didn't take him long to realize his fate and income were in their hands, since the financial future of both businesses depended on the salespeoples' talents and ability to produce revenue. He wanted to place his future in his own hands, so he embarked on a career in sales, selling everything from pots and pans, appliances, and automobiles to approximately ten million dollars' worth of real estate! When the opportunity arose to put his sales experience to work in the hotel industry—an industry which had long fascinated him—Chaney jumped at the chance. As a director of sales, he feels that selling hotel rooms and services—especially to the tour market—is one of the most exciting, challenging, and competitive occupations one can find.

Chaney Ross
*Director of Sales
Best Western
Landmark Bourbon
Street Hotel*

"The Best Western Landmark Bourbon Street Hotel is located almost in the very center of New Orleans' centuries-old French Quarter, which is one of the United States' prime destination sites for tour groups. These factors play an important part in the positioning of our hotel, and strongly confirm the old cliche: 'Location, location, location.' Our location is tailor-made for the tour market.

Having the right location for tour operators is only the beginning, however. It requires an all-out, disciplined effort over a long period of time to get a share of the tour market segment. There are many 'musts' to be followed to meet tour market goals.

Tour and motorcoach operators like to do business with hotels that provide good service to their clients, and the entire hotel staff must act in concert to establish this atmosphere. All groups must be met, all rooms must be pre-assigned, express check-in and smooth baggage handling must be a part of the service, and guests must feel they're wanted and are being attended to in a courteous and efficient manner. In addition to serving guests, the property must be flexible enough to meet the needs of tour operators. Operators have unusual problems from time to time, and they need and appreciate assistance. Sometimes bending the rules is necessary!

The property must be consistent and honest, and must take the good with the bad. A hotel sales representative can't tell tour operators that their business is wanted only on weekdays, not weekends; or their business isn't wanted during the hotel's peak season because their lower group rate adversely affects the average daily rate. The arrangement between the hotel and tour operators must be equally satisfactory and profitable to both. The hotel's promises should be 'good as gold.' Nothing destroys a relationship faster than a property's failure to keep its word.

One of the ways a property can tap into the tour market is by maintaining memberships in industry associations such as the American Hotel & Motel Association, the Hotel Sales & Marketing Association International, the National Tour Association, the American Bus Association, the Travel Industry Association of America, and local and state tourist commissions. In addition to these affiliations, clients can be met face-to-face through participation in trade shows and seminars.

No matter what sales avenue is chosen, it must be part of a property's long-range marketing plan. Market segments must be targeted and worked in depth; efforts should not be so thinly spread that they become diluted and ineffective. It's important to build lasting relationships with tour and motorcoach operators, and these relationships can only be built slowly and carefully.

The consistent theme behind the 'musts' I've been talking about is *salesmanship*. You are constantly selling yourself, your property, and your services. Hotels can do many things in an attempt to gain the public's attention. A hotel room, amenity, or service can be advertised, promoted, romanced, and hyped, but nothing really happens until some talented salesperson *sells* it!

Selling. That's where the action is; that's where the thrill is. I invite you to try it. **"**

retail travel agents, incentive travel companies (see Chapter 18), or their own travel agencies. These packages include air transportation, hotel or motel accommodations, and such extras as meals, sight-seeing, and entertainment, all at prices lower than those a traveler would pay on an itemized or individual basis.

Retail travel agents will be discussed in detail in Chapter 17. These intermediaries sell tours offered by tour brokers and wholesalers, as well as tour packages developed by properties.

Types of Tours

There are four types of tours commonly taken by group leisure travelers: motorcoach tours, airline tours, Amtrak tours, and property package tours.

Motorcoach Tours. Motorcoach or bus tours fall into two general categories: the overnight or non-destination tour and the destination tour.

Overnight tours are stops en route to another destination. These tours are an opportunity for a property to increase food and beverage revenues as well as guestroom revenues, provided the property can give the quick service motorcoach tour groups require for baggage handling and meals.

Overnight tour guests have usually been traveling for many hours and appreciate special services upon arrival. Many properties offer refreshments and an information session while guestroom keys are being distributed to the tour escort and baggage is being unloaded. Depending on departure time, brief local tours may be arranged for overnight guests, but, in any case, group travelers should be familiarized with the property and its attractions and facilities.

Overnight tour guests appreciate having a wide variety of food choices available. Buffets and cafeteria-style service are popular. Many motorcoach tours cater to mature travelers who appreciate light fare or room service. Breakfast service on the morning of departure should be handled quickly. Guests are usually made aware of the departure time the night before so they can allow adequate time for their morning meal. As a precaution, restaurant staff should be increased to handle the demands of the group on a timely basis.

Destination tour guests are those who will be staying a minimum of two nights to either take advantage of a property promotion or to use the property as a base of operations to tour local attractions. Often these travelers have also been traveling for a long period of time, and may appreciate being given a tour of the facilities upon arrival, both to get acquainted with the property and to stretch their legs.

While technically not motorcoach tours, since travel intermediaries and special packages are usually not involved, motorcoach charters are another potential source of group business for properties. Motorcoach charters are groups of people traveling together who select a destination and then contact a motorcoach company to charter or rent a bus to take them to their destination. Overnight stops and the destination property may be decided on by the group; in other cases, the group will ask for the motorcoach company's recommendations.

In order to attract groups traveling on a charter arrangement, a property should approach groups or organizations that typically arrange charters. (Charter arrangements are not limited to motorcoach companies; airplanes and trains can also be chartered.) Contact persons for this type of business are identified in Chapter 18 in both the corporate and association meeting planner categories.

Meeting the needs of motorcoach tour travelers. Most motorcoach tour groups enjoy being welcomed by a greeting on the property sign's reader board and a reception or happy hour either before or after their orientation tour. A welcoming party hosted by the property's manager or another hotel representative can make a favorable impression on guests and increase the property's chances for repeat business. Guests may also be impressed by such special features and services as a game room for cards, checkers, and chess; free coffee in guestrooms; free maps of the local area; discount coupons for local attractions; and excursions to nearby points of interest, escorted by a property staff member.

Both overnight and destination tour travelers look for clean, comfortable rooms and friendly service. Plenty of guestrooms with two double beds should be available, along with a few singles for the group's tour escort, bus driver, and tour guests desiring to room alone. All rooms should be equipped with basic amenities such as telephones, televisions, and full baths, and should be blocked together for group security and the supervision of children, if any. When blocking rooms, consider the nature of the group. For example, mature travelers, as previously mentioned, usually prefer ground floors.

Group safety is considered a prime factor in booking groups. Property hallways should be well-lit, elevators should have emergency telephones, and simple directional signs should be posted throughout the property. An attractive exterior and interior appearance is also important to both tour operators and guests.

In addition to meeting the needs of motorcoach tour guests, the property must also provide for the needs of the tour operator or escort, the bus driver, and other staff who may accompany a group, such as an interpreter or a physician. The property should provide ample parking for motorcoaches and should have all guests preregistered for the rapid check-in and distribution of room keys. It is also helpful for the property to make available one staff member to assist the tour escort in dealing with any last-minute changes or problems that might arise during the group's visit. Offering property-sponsored activities (theme weekends, movies, or other entertainment) will also ease the responsibilities of the tour escort. Making the escort's job easier can help generate repeat business, since the property's initial customer is the tour broker, not the individual guests.

Finding motorcoach tour brokers. Hotels can find the names of brokers for motorcoach tours in a number of ways (see Exhibit 16.6):

- Lists from professional associations such as the National Tour Association (NTA) and the American Society of Travel Agents (ASTA)

- Bus associations such as the Ontario Motor Coach Association and the American Bus Association

- Sources from the U.S. Travel Service and domestic airlines

- Travel trade journals such as *Travel Weekly*, *Travel Trade*, and *ASTA News*

Exhibit 16.6   Sources for Motorcoach Tour Business

American Bus Association (ABA)
1025 Connecticut Avenue, NW
Washington, DC 20036   (202) 293–5890

Hotels/motels can become travel industry members of ABA. Resources and services of this association include the *ABA Directory,* which lists nearly 600 major bus operators and key sales contacts, and an annual convention that matches bus operators with hotel/motel properties in their touring areas.

National Tour Association (NTA)
P.O. Box 3071
Lexington, KY 40596   (606) 253–1036

Hotel/motels can become allied members of NTA. Resources and services include the *NTA Directory,* which lists tour brokers and the areas they service, and an annual convention which features computerized matching of allied members with tour brokers.

Ontario Motor Coach Association (OMCA)
234 Eglinton Ave. E., Suite 604
Toronto, Ontario M5P 1K5   (416) 488–8855

Hotels/motels can become allied members of this organization, which, like ABA and NTA, publishes a directory and holds an annual trade show.

American Society of Travel Agents (ASTA)
711 Fifth Avenue
New York, NY 10022   (212) 486–0700

ASTA works closely with tour brokers, and publishes *Motorcoach Touring,* a manual that provides an excellent overview of the motorcoach industry to hotel/motel operators. This manual includes a state-by-state listing of ABA and NTA companies.

Official Domestic Tour Manual
2 West 46th Street
New York, NY 10036   (212) 575–9000

This manual, published quarterly by *Travel Agent* magazine, lists sources for motorcoach tours in the United States and Canada. Price: $15 annually.

- Incentive tour operators such as E. F. MacDonald and Maritz
- Recommendations from personal contacts and hotel representatives

Before attempting to sell to motorcoach tour brokers, however, a property should determine exactly what it has to offer—a location near an airport or major highway, proximity to a number of popular attractions, facilities for large groups, etc.—and contact those brokers who handle the types of tours that are best suited to the property.

Reaching motorcoach tour brokers. A property can reach motorcoach tour brokers directly by sending representatives to motorcoach trade association meetings to promote its group packages and rates, and by participating in motorcoach trade shows.

Direct mail is one of the most popular avenues of selling to motorcoach tour brokers, because it is a way to get answers to a number of questions efficiently and inexpensively. All correspondence with tour brokers should include the following:

1. *The property's rates.* Special group rates are often a deciding factor in booking motorcoach tour business. Some properties have developed group rate directories that detail group rates at various seasons of the year (see Exhibit 16.7). Since many tours are prepackaged, it is important for the motorcoach tour broker to know the total cost of the property's rooms and meals. Is tax included in the rate quoted? Does the property offer an inclusive group rate for meals? Are the rates commissionable? This last question is very important if the motorcoach tour will be sold through travel agents.

2. *Comps and discounts.* Properties should advise tour brokers about the availability of complimentary rooms and/or meals to the tour escort and driver, or of special commercial rates available to tour bus drivers.

3. *Services.* The property should list preregistration services (putting keys in envelopes with guests' names and room numbers on them, for example), baggage handling services (very important to tour brokers), and special features such as a welcoming party or a departure gift.

4. *Facilities.* The property's ability to handle group business must be emphasized. The property should "sell" its large banquet facilities or restaurants, its extra-large swimming pool or numerous recreational amenities, and its other group facilities—lounges, meeting rooms for card games or conversation, and so on.

5. *Location.* The property's location may be a deciding factor for a motorcoach tour broker. Roadside properties are ideal sites for overnight tours or meal stops, especially if the property is near the entrance or exit of an interstate or major state highway, while hotels in downtown areas or areas near a number of attractions are ideal for destination tours.

Direct mail letters can be accompanied by brochures detailing what the property has to offer. These brochures should feature photographs of groups being served at the property. A brochure should be developed for each group package offered and should speak directly to the needs of motorcoach tour brokers. A brochure that features a locator map of the property and a toll-free number will often get more attention than one that simply describes the property.

Properties can also acquaint motorcoach tour brokers with the property by offering familiarization tours (familiarization tours will be discussed in Chapter 17). These complimentary tours, which can be scheduled for slow business times, allow brokers to experience the property firsthand. The Radisson Hotel High Point in High Point, North Carolina, recently offered a Motorcoach Month promotion that offered two room nights, a complimentary breakfast, and a packet of informational materials to motorcoach tour brokers. The program generated a favorable response from the participants and increased the hotel's tour business.

Exhibit 16.7 Sample Group Rate Manual

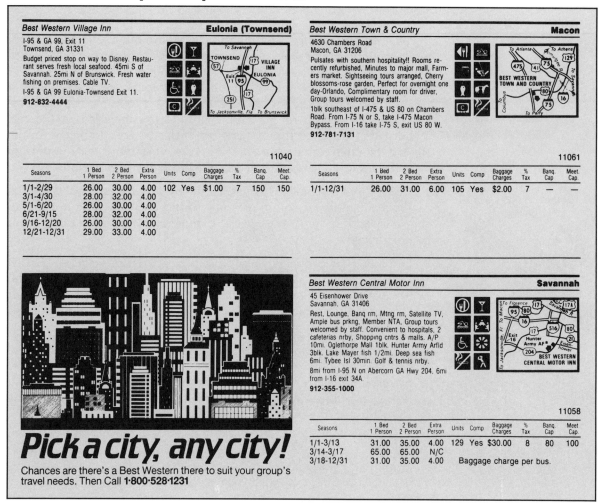

Best Western Village Inn — **Eulonia (Townsend)**

I-95 & GA 99, Exit 11
Townsend, GA 31331
Budget priced stop on way to Disney. Restaurant serves fresh local seafood. 45mi S of Savannah. 25mi N of Brunswick. Fresh water fishing on premises. Cable TV.
I-95 & GA 99 Eulonia-Townsend Exit 11.
912-832-4444

11040

Seasons	1 Bed 1 Person	2 Bed 2 Person	Extra Person	Units	Comp	Baggage Charges	% Tax	Banq. Cap.	Meet. Cap.
1/1-2/29	26.00	30.00	4.00	102	Yes	$1.00	7	150	150
3/1-4/30	28.00	32.00	4.00						
5/1-6/20	26.00	30.00	4.00						
6/21-9/15	28.00	32.00	4.00						
9/16-12/20	26.00	30.00	4.00						
12/21-12/31	29.00	33.00	4.00						

Best Western Town & Country — **Macon**

4630 Chambers Road
Macon, GA 31206
Pulsates with southern hospitality!! Rooms recently refurbished. Minutes to major mall, Farmers market. Sightseeing tours arranged, Cherry blossoms-rose garden. Perfect for overnight one day-Orlando, Complimentary room for driver, Group tours welcomed by staff.
1blk southeast of I-475 & US 80 on Chambers Road. From I-75 N or S, take I-475 Macon Bypass. From I-16 take I-75 S, exit US 80 W.
912-781-7131

11061

Seasons	1 Bed 1 Person	2 Bed 2 Person	Extra Person	Units	Comp	Baggage Charges	% Tax	Banq. Cap.	Meet. Cap.
1/1-12/31	26.00	31.00	6.00	105	Yes	$2.00	7	—	—

Pick a city, any city!

Chances are there's a Best Western there to suit your group's travel needs. Then Call **1·800·528·1231**

Best Western Central Motor Inn — **Savannah**

45 Eisenhower Drive
Savannah, GA 31406
Rest, Lounge, Banq. rm, Mtng rm, Satellite TV, Ample bus prkng, Member NTA, Group tours welcomed by staff. Convenient to hospitals, 2 cafeterias nrby, Shopping cntrs & malls. A/P 10mi. Oglethorpe Mall 1blk. Hunter Army Arfld 3blk. Lake Mayer fish 1/2mi. Deep sea fish 6mi. Tybee Isl 30min. Golf & tennis nrby.
8mi from I-95 N on Abercorn GA Hwy 204, 6mi from I-16 exit 34A.
912-355-1000

11058

Seasons	1 Bed 1 Person	2 Bed 2 Person	Extra Person	Units	Comp	Baggage Charges	% Tax	Banq. Cap.	Meet. Cap.
1/1-3/13	31.00	35.00	4.00	129	Yes	$30.00	8	80	100
3/14-3/17	65.00	65.00	N/C						
3/18-12/31	31.00	35.00	4.00			Baggage charge per bus.			

Most hotel chains produce group tour manuals that list group rates (usually 10% to 30% off) and special weekend rates for tour groups. Group rate manuals are distributed annually to bus companies, tour brokers, and tour wholesalers through direct mail efforts or at travel trade shows.

Courtesy of Best Western International, Inc.

Motorcoach tour brokers can also be reached through print advertising in travel guides and trade publications. Tour brokers often use *OAG TRAVEL PLANNER Hotel & Motel RedBook* and *Hotel & Travel Index* to obtain information about properties in a specific area, although the information within these publications is usually not geared to motorcoach tour brokers. To provide the information most important to motorcoach tour brokers, a property may also wish to advertise in trade publications such as *Bus Tours Magazine, Bus World,* and *National Bus Trader,* with ads that give the property's contact person for bus tours, deposit requirements, cancellation policies, and other information.

Properties can also generate repeat business and word-of-mouth referrals by offering special services. Some properties clean the windows of the bus and/or the interior, while other properties offer welcome gifts such as fruit baskets or a local product to the tour escort and bus driver. These gestures demonstrate that the property cares enough about the tour operators and guests to warrant repeat business.

Airline Tours. Airline tours are another excellent source of group business. Airline tours are usually arranged by airline tour wholesalers, who not only contract with properties and attractions, but also promote the tours they develop. This takes a good deal of responsibility for advertising away from the property.

Like motorcoach tour brokers, airline tour wholesalers seek to provide a vacation experience for their clients. Properties that are located in or near popular destination cities or in close proximity to a number of attractions (Disneyland, Knott's Berry Farm, and Universal Studios in southern California, for example) are attractive to airline tour wholesalers, but a property that can offer an extensive recreational package may also be able to sell to this market.

If a property is not located close to an airport, an intermodal tour can often be arranged by an airline tour wholesaler. An intermodal tour makes use of more than one form of transportation (air-motorcoach, air-sea, air-car, and so on), and is often used to promote golf vacations, honeymoon trips, and extended group trips such as fall "color" tours. Intermodal tours may include air transportation to the tour's departure city, motorcoach transportation to several points of interest, and even a ferry or boat trip.

Airline tour wholesalers also package group tours that may include cruise ship travel. Air transportation to the port of departure, hotel accommodations and meals while in port, and the cruise can be included in one package price. Properties located in popular ports or near international air terminals have an excellent opportunity to take advantage of this year-round business, especially if they can handle the demands of group travelers.

Amtrak Tours. Other opportunities to capture a portion of the group leisure traveler market can be found through contacts with Amtrak. Amtrak develops and promotes a variety of rail tours each year. Once a group has booked a reservation on Amtrak, an Amtrak representative can book hotel reservations at the destination. Groups booking through Amtrak receive lower rates than they would if they had made their own reservations independently. Properties wishing to book groups traveling by train can contact Amtrak directly through its local or regional offices.

Property Package Tours. In addition to selling special group rates and services to tour brokers and tour wholesalers who develop tour packages, a property can also develop its own tour package (see Exhibit 16.8). Before a property takes such a step, however, it must first familiarize itself with the tour industry and determine what type of tour (either an independent package or a package in conjunction with other travel suppliers) would work best for the property. An aid in learning about the tour market is the *Discover America Package Tour Handbook*, published by the Travel Industry Association of America. This handbook, first published in 1973, gives an overall view of the extensive package tour market, and provides the names of contacts for assistance or sales leads.

There are several reasons why a property should consider developing its own package tour. Property packages can:

Exhibit 16.8 Property Package Tours at a Glance

What: Property package tours are group tour packages put together by an individual property or by a chain. Property package tours offer several travel elements for one price. These elements can include lodging, meals, baggage transfers, recreational facilities, local guided tours, attractions, and entertainment. Properties that opt to include other travel suppliers—airlines, rental car companies, bus lines, etc.—can also offer transportation as part of the package.

Why: Property package tours are popular with travel agents and consumers because they can be purchased for one inclusive price. For consumers, this makes it easier to budget. For travel agents, property package tours mean guaranteed availability and lower booking costs—the agent does not have to book the individual components separately.

When: Property package tours can be developed for those times when business is most needed. They can also be developed to coincide with local events such as rodeos, food festivals, and county fairs.

How: Property package tours can be developed in a number of ways. The property can package its own services (rooms, meals, entertainment, recreational facilities, etc.) and promote the package through advertising to travel agents and directly to consumers. Many properties, however, have found that developing a package in conjunction with another attraction or travel supplier offers the benefit of the experience of the other package participant(s)—and generates a wider customer base. Selling the package to tour brokers after it has been developed is also an excellent way for the property's package to reach a wide base of potential guests.

- Increase sales by offering consumers convenience and value

- Bring in business when the property needs it most, such as off-season or shoulder periods

- Encourage property recognition, especially if the package is innovative or a real bargain

Packages can be as simple or as complicated as needed. One property may opt for a simple package of one or two room nights with a complimentary continental breakfast, while another property may put together a package that includes recreational amenities (golf, tennis, swimming), meals, discounts in the gift shop or discount coupons to nearby attractions, and turn-down and valet service. Properties that wish to provide complete vacation packages or weekend getaways can include other travel suppliers (airlines, rental cars, local bus operators, or limousine services) and attractions (amusement parks, historic sites, etc.) in their tour packages.

While developing a tour package can be profitable, it also requires knowledge. A property first has to determine which market it will target. Tour packages developed for mature travelers will differ greatly from those designed for skiers, for example. Since the needs of each market segment will be different, the property has to determine which segments it can best serve.

Once a package is developed, the next step is to promote it. A property can sell its package to tour wholesalers, travel agents, or the public. If sold through tour wholesalers or travel agents, the package should be made commissionable.

In addition to direct contact with tour wholesalers and travel agents, property packages can be promoted to them through direct mail and print advertising. Advertising in trade journals will reach many of these travel professionals. Ads should be designed to promote the benefits of the property's tour package to the wholesaler or agent as well as to guests. The property can also advertise in the *Consolidated Tour Manual*, a publication sponsored and published by participating U.S. airlines. The manual, which is distributed free to member airline sales offices and certain travel agent locations, offers hotels a full-page listing in the manual for a fee.

Properties that choose to include other travel suppliers in a tour package may enjoy the benefits of cooperative advertising and the consumer bases of these suppliers. Packages can be promoted through print advertising and by direct sales efforts on the part of not only the property but also the other travel suppliers involved. Air-ground-rooms packages, for example, may be promoted at airline ticket terminals, at the offices of bus lines involved, and at the property's front desk through colorful brochures. Or, the participants in the package could sell the entire package through tour wholesalers, saving on advertising costs.

Whatever option the property chooses, it often takes time for a property's tour package to reach consumers. It may take more than one season for a package to consistently fill rooms. The property must give a package time to work, and must make sure that a sparsely attended package has been properly promoted before it decides the package is unsuccessful. Group leisure travelers often book their reservations on a long lead time (up to two years in some cases), and may not be able to take advantage of a particular package when it is first offered. Before dropping a package, a property should measure the effectiveness of its promotional campaign and talk to tour wholesalers about the response to the package.

Conclusion

The leisure traveler market is a very large, complex market that is a valuable source of business for lodging properties. Growth in this market is expected to continue into the 1990s due to extended holidays, four-day workweeks for some employees, the increase in the number of dual-career families, longer life expectancies, and increased discretionary income.

Leisure travelers look for ease and convenience in travel and find special packages like the ones discussed in this chapter particularly attractive. Many packages designed for leisure travelers are sold through travel intermediaries. Properties should be aware of opportunities to build good working relationships with such travel intermediaries as tour brokers, tour wholesalers, and travel agents. In the next chapter, we will take a closer look at how properties can work with travel agents not only to build leisure traveler business, but also to increase bookings in all of the market segments targeted by the property.

Notes

1. From *The U.S. Resort Travel Market: A Perspective on Trends and Forecasts for U.S. Resort Travel.* Prepared as an industry service for the Resort Committee of the American Hotel & Motel Association by *Hotel & Travel Index*, 1986.
2. *The U.S. Resort Travel Market.*
3. These facts and others cited in this section were taken from Marcia Schnedler, "Senior Citizens' Travel: A Special Report," *Tour and Travel News*, 11 May 1987, p. 20.

Discussion Questions

1. Individual leisure travelers can be divided into which three general categories?

2. How are properties meeting the needs of family leisure travelers?

3. What are some of the ways families can be reached?

4. Senior citizens control how much of the nation's discretionary income?

5. How are properties meeting the needs of mature travelers?

6. What is a tour broker?

7. What are four types of tours commonly taken by group leisure travelers?

8. How are properties meeting the needs of motorcoach tour travelers?

9. What are some resources for finding motorcoach tour brokers?

10. What should correspondence with motorcoach tour brokers include?

11. What is an intermodal tour?

12. Why should a property consider developing its own package tour?

Chapter Outline

17 Selling to Travel Agents

Not too long ago, the relationship between hotels and travel agents was shaky at best. Many properties had a careless attitude toward serving travel agents, and travel agents had many complaints about the way they were treated: long waiting times on the telephone, properties failing to honor their reservations, and properties negligent about paying them promptly, to name a few. Today, however, this relationship is changing. Travel has become more complex. More and more, business and leisure travelers are turning to travel agents for help in making travel plans and reservations, and properties are recognizing that travel agents and hotels make an ideal sales team. In this chapter we will take a look at today's travel agents and the types of travelers they serve. We will also learn what properties are doing to meet the needs of travel agents.

Travel Agencies

The concept of an individual assisting other individuals with travel plans can be traced to 1841, when a British Baptist minister named Thomas Cook signed up 570 people to accompany him to a temperance meeting. Cook got the group a rate of a shilling per person for the 22-mile round trip from Leicester to Loughborough, and included a picnic lunch and entertainment as part of the "package." His tour proved so popular that by 1856 the enterprising Cook was advertising a "Grand Circular Tour of the Continent." In 1869, Cook introduced his "middle class conducted crusades" to the Holy Land.

Most American travel agencies began as "mom and pop" establishments which operated on the same principles as Thomas Cook's original tours. Tours were often "guided" by the owners of the travel agencies, based on personal experiences at the destinations. These early operations are a far cry from the travel agencies and travel agents of today.

There are over 30,000 travel agencies in the United States, staffed by over 200,000 travel agents. Travel agents book more than 70% of all U.S. airline tickets, nearly half of all car rentals, and about one-quarter of U.S. hotel reservations.[1] The complexity of the travel market has led to the modernization and computerization of travel agencies, and travel agents have become highly trained and sophisticated travel professionals.

Industry Profile

Jim Tierney's first job in the hotel industry was as Convention Coordinator for the Boca Raton Hotel and Club. He has progressed through a number of other sales management positions in his 17 years in the industry. In 1981 Tierney joined South Seas Plantation Resort and Yacht Harbour, a 330-acre luxury destination resort in Captiva Island, Florida, as Vice President of Sales and Marketing. He is a long-time supporter of Hotel Sales &

Jim Tierney, CHSE
Vice President of Sales and Marketing
South Seas Plantation Resort and Yacht Harbour

Marketing Association International, and founded the Southwest Florida chapter (where he served as president for 2½ years) in 1983. Tierney was on the Executive Committee of HSMAI from 1985 through 1987, and was elected vice president of the organization in November 1987. He is also chairman of the HSMAI Resort Committee and serves as a liaison between HSMAI and the American Hotel & Motel Association's Resort Committee.

"South Seas Plantation attracts a market that's dramatically different from any other large Florida resort. While other properties are almost totally dependent on conference or convention business, our mix is 70% individual leisure travel and only 30% group business. Of the leisure travel business that we enjoy, 35% comes through travel agents. At certain times of the year, their contribution to this market approaches 50%! Therefore, we spend a good deal of time and effort in encouraging travel agents to recommend our resort to their clients.

Being a travel agent has to be a unique and sometimes frustrating experience. Travel agents are required to work hard to make less money! Clients look for the least expensive airfare, the most economical tour package, and the best possible room rate. In finding these 'deals,' the agent makes less commission. And the agent is held personally responsible if anything goes wrong with the client's vacation or travel arrangements.

In order to make the travel agent's job easier and to increase our share of leisure traveler business, South Seas Plantation launched a major travel agency marketing program in 1982. This program included travel trade advertising, a public relations program, attending travel trade shows, a direct mail program, a toll-free number for travel agents, agency familiarization trips, and the initiation of our King's Crown Club promotion. Our weekend familiarization packages included tours of the resort, meetings to update agency owners and managers about the facilities we had to offer, food and beverage functions, and plenty of time for recreation. In 1982 more than 400 travel agents toured the property, with another 250 to 300 following in 1983. The results were almost immediate. Our leisure travel business jumped substantially in each of those years and has steadily increased ever since.

Our King's Crown Club is an important factor in our success. This incentive program is designed to reward top-producing travel agencies. In order to get into the club, agencies in 1982 were required to produce a minimum of $10,000 in rooms revenue from individual leisure travelers. If the agency also produced group business, the membership minimum was $20,000. Agency bookings were tracked on an annual basis, and once an agency reached the target, we increased its commission from 10% to 30% for additional revenue produced through the balance of the year. While only one agency qualified for the club in 1982, we had 47 agencies qualify in 1987—even though we had raised the minimum requirements to $12,500 for leisure business and $25,000 for group business.

Part of the reason that membership in The King's Crown Club is so desirable is the Annual Celebration Weekend. This is held from Thursday to Sunday in the spring, and everything's on us. The Weekend includes a recognition breakfast at which plaques are presented, photographs are taken, and information about new things going on at the property is provided to the agents. Receptions, first-class dinner functions put together by our food and beverage department, and lots of recreation time are also included.

As long as our travel agency production continues to increase, we'll continue the program. And, incidentally, that one travel agency that qualified back in 1982 is still a member today—having qualified every single year since our program was put in place.**"**

The changing face of travel agencies has not escaped the notice of the lodging industry. Hotel operators are aware that travel agents are, in effect, sales representatives for a host of travel suppliers, including hotels. Hotels are increasingly depending on travel agents to serve as a part of their sales force—salespeople who work at no overhead costs to a property.

Types of Travel Agents

Travel agents can be grouped in three basic categories:

1. Retail travel agents

2. Wholesale travel agents

3. Agents who work for consortiums or chains

Retail travel agents act as agents for airlines, steamship lines, bus lines, railroads, hotels, car rental firms, and, sometimes, wholesale travel agencies. Retail travel agents work directly with clients, supplying information on a wide array of travel services and making reservations or bookings as required.

Wholesale travel agents differ from the wholesale tour operators discussed in the previous chapter in that wholesale tour operators work almost exclusively with group leisure travelers. A wholesale travel agent specializes in putting tour packages together for individual business and leisure travelers. These tours are marketed to the public through retail travel agents or the airlines. Wholesale travel agents do not deal directly with clients unless the wholesale travel agency has a retail department, as do many of the large wholesale travel agencies.

Agents who work for consortiums or chains can be retail travel agents or wholesale travel agents. Consortiums and chain travel agencies are associations or networks of travel agencies that have banded together to share information and take advantage of bulk purchasing and cooperative marketing. The travel industry has become more complex, and there is a greater need for sophisticated technology, technology that is often too costly for individual agencies. A consortium allows agencies to pool their resources.

No matter what category a travel agent represents, he or she has one basic product: information. With today's unprecedented competition in the airline and lodging industries, the average traveler is faced with a bewildering array of services and facilities. Today's travel agent must sell more than just travel. He or she must sell information—and back that information with service.

Travelers Served

Generally speaking, travel agents serve three types of travelers:

1. Business travelers

2. Leisure travelers

3. International travelers

Business travelers now represent over one-half of all business generated by travel agents. In 1986, 25% of all business travelers and 44% of frequent business travelers used the services of a travel agent. Each month over four million business travelers book rooms through travel agents or through corporate travel planners who use travel agents.[2]

In addition to individual business travelers, more travel agencies are also serving business groups. In 1986, over 70% of the nation's travel agencies booked business group travel, 51% booked conventions, and 41% were involved in planning and directing incentive trips for their clients. This trend has led to the development of agents or separate departments within travel agencies that specialize in business meetings and groups.

The fastest growing segment of the business group market is the small meetings segment (meetings for 25 or fewer people). Over 43% of travel agents surveyed felt that small meetings would eventually become the backbone of business-travel revenue for most travel agencies, especially since many large corporations are consolidating travel purchasing. IBM, for example, recently consolidated the number of travel agencies it does business with from 1,200 travel agencies to three! And IBM is not an isolated case. In 1986, the needs of the Fortune 500 companies were handled by 8,800 travel agencies; today, there are fewer than 500 agencies handling these travel needs. This consolidation has led more and more travel agencies to focus on the small meetings market and individual business and leisure travelers.

Leisure travelers often need more assistance in planning their travel than business travelers. While business travelers usually have a predetermined destination—and may be restricted in their choice of hotels—less than half of all leisure clients know precisely where they want to go. Eighty percent of all individual visitors to resort destinations such as Hawaii, Las Vegas, the Bahamas, and Bermuda use a travel agent to help in planning or booking their vacations. Over 70% of all leisure travelers ask for an agent's help in selecting a hotel.[3]

To increase their leisure traveler business, many hotels are teaming up with travel agents by creating commissionable weekend packages. Travel agents are big sellers of weekend packages, especially in markets such as New York, Boston, New Orleans, and Washington, D.C. Travel agents are attracted to the inclusive-price feature and ease of booking inherent in many packages (see Exhibit 17.1).

International travelers can be business travelers, leisure travelers, or both. This market segment will be discussed in detail in Chapter 19, but it is important to note here that the number of foreigners traveling to the United States is increasing substantially. To promote a property to international travelers, travel agents must have adequate information. Special services, such as the availability of on-property translators, can help attract international travelers to a property.

Meeting the Needs of Travel Agents

Since travel agents deal with such a wide range of clients, it is important that properties understand what a travel agent needs in order to successfully promote a property. These needs can be broken down into two general areas: (1) information about the property, and (2) good service, to travel agents as well as their clients.

Property Information

Airline reservations systems, listings and ads in hotel directories, information packages, and familiarization tours are some of the ways properties meet travel agents' need for property information.

Exhibit 17.1   All-Inclusive Pricing

One of today's most popular trends is the offering of travel packages for an all-inclusive price which includes meals, tips, recreational amenities, and special entertainment. All-inclusive pricing is attractive to travel agents because it allows them to offer a complete vacation to clients without the hassle of having to negotiate for the various components offered.

Airline Reservations Systems. Hotels can provide basic reservation and rate information to travel agents through computerized airline reservations systems. Travel agents can access these systems through the use of computers in travel agency offices. The five major airline reservations systems are:

System Name	Airline
Apollo	United
DATAS II	Delta
PARS	Transworld & Northwest
Sabre	American
System One	Texas Air/Eastern

While 95% of the nation's travel agencies are equipped with computer terminals, over 40% of travel agents surveyed said they did not use them for booking hotel reservations.[4] The reluctance to use airline reservations systems

stems from the fact that hotel bookings are much more complicated than bookings of airline seats or rental cars. Besides price and availability, a number of other factors figure into hotel bookings, including location, hotel features, guestroom size, amenities, restaurants, special rates, and credit card policies. Airline reservations systems do not supply this type of information, and they are not programmed to answer questions or make alternative suggestions.

Hotel Directories. Hotel directories provide the detailed information that travel agents need to properly service clients. An agent can compare one property with another on costs, location, amenities, facilities, and activities, and make a recommendation to clients based on information that is much more extensive than that found in airline reservations systems.

Three of the most widely used guides are the *Hotel & Travel Index*, the *Official Hotel & Resort Guide*, and the *OAG TRAVEL PLANNER Hotel & Motel RedBook*. Each of these directories lists over 30,000 properties worldwide and provides information on hotel locations, accommodations, number of rooms, size of property, rates (including special packages), amenities, and number of restaurants. All three directories include property ads as well as a formatted listing of properties.

A survey of travel agents found that 4% use the formatted listings in hotel directories to select a property, 6% use a hotel's ad, and 90% use both to select a hotel.[5] It would be wise, then, for a property to purchase a directory ad if possible. To attract attention and get its message across, a property should choose the largest ad it can afford. Some chain properties are eligible for a special discount rate.

When polled about which elements of an ad they use, travel agents rated a toll-free number the highest (96%), information on the hotel's location second (92%), and a map of the property's location third (88%).[6] These elements make it easier for an agent to select and book a property.

There are a number of hotel directories available. It is important for a property to choose a directory that will reach a large number of readers. The cost of a directory may be an indication of its popularity.

Information Packages. In addition to providing information through hotel directories, many properties also offer information packages to travel agents. These packages may include a property fact sheet, photographs of the property, a description of property amenities, and information about booking procedures, commission payments, and special travel agent programs. While some properties include rate sheets in their information packages, as a rule travel agents do not use them. Most agents call a property directly to obtain current rate information.

A property can also include a large quantity of brochures for agency clients in its information package. These brochures should be consumer-oriented and have a blank space for the travel agent's stamp. Other collateral materials, such as colorful posters, can also be sent to travel agents. Agents should be provided with order forms, especially for brochures. Order forms can be included in the information package or mailed with the agent's commission check.

Familiarization Tours. Many properties offer familiarization or "fam" tours to travel agents. These tours can be conducted during slack periods and are an effective way to promote the property.

For fam tours to be successful, a property must first look at its objectives. What percentage of travel agents are expected to send business to the property following a fam tour? How many room nights does the property expect to pick up? If measurable objectives are not set, there will be no way to determine what type of fam tour should be offered and no way to determine a tour's success.

Planning a fam tour includes determining the ideal size of the tour group. Hosting too large a group will not allow the property to show itself off to best advantage. The property must also determine exactly what it has to sell and the best way to showcase its products and facilities. If a property is noted for its recreational facilities, for example, it will want to allow plenty of opportunity for the travel agents to experience them.

Once a fam tour has been planned, the property needs to invite travel agents to participate. Travel agents differ in the types of clients they serve, and a property that caters primarily to leisure travelers will not benefit from inviting travel agents who specialize in business travel. The best prospects for fam tours are agents who have recommended clients to the property in the past, and those who serve clients in key feeder cities. Travel agents can be solicited by direct mail or by telephone and should be given a reasonable amount of advance notice (usually from four to six weeks). The property should let agents know exactly what the tour involves: the duration of the tour, what is included (meals, transportation, and so on), whether the event is open to spouses or guests, and other pertinent information.

When the travel agents arrive for the fam tour, each should be greeted personally and given a schedule of events. Most properties assign staff members to handle the on-site details of the tour. A well-planned, well-executed tour will usually result in increased business from the travel agents involved.

While the travel agents' initial reactions to the tour may serve as a general barometer of the tour's success, it is also helpful to obtain an evaluation of the property's efforts a week or two after the tour. Questionnaires can be sent to participants to determine their perceptions of the strengths and weaknesses of the tour and the property. Of course, the real success of the tour will be measured in the number of bookings it generates.

Service   The kind of service an agent receives from a property is an important factor in whether he or she will recommend that property again. Service to travel agents includes service to their clients also. Travel agents are often blamed for bungled reservations, specific requests that are not met, and any number of details not handled to the guest's satisfaction at the property. It stands to reason that agents will be far more likely to recommend a property that has treated them and their clients well than a property that has been lax in its dealings with them and their clients. Toll-free numbers, travel agent clubs, commission payment plans, and good service to clients are just some of the ways properties can provide good service to travel agents.

Toll-Free Numbers. Most travel agents prefer to book hotel space over the telephone, and providing a toll-free number continues to reign as the most effective way to ensure travel agent bookings. A toll-free number encourages travel agents to call if they have questions. Agents can explore various options and rates, find out about special events that may be of interest to clients, ask about special services, and receive immediate confirmation of reservations.

A toll-free number serves the property as well as the agent. Property representatives are given an opportunity to sell extra services. In addition, these calls are an excellent way to bring travel agents up to date on property information. The property also has a better chance of controlling its room inventories; rooms can be pushed during slow periods and alternate dates can be suggested for business that cannot be booked due to a full house.

Since travel agents generate so many bookings, some hotels go a step further than offering a toll-free number; they dedicate a special toll-free number for the exclusive use of travel agents. This number is not available to the public and is promoted only through press releases to travel agents or through direct mail and other advertising directed to the travel trade.

Travel Agent Clubs. Another effective way properties can provide service and build rapport with travel agents is through travel agent clubs. Club members are informed of property events and special programs and discounts through direct mail or a club newsletter. Some clubs give prizes to travel agents who book a certain number of room nights at the property. An agent with 125 room nights or "room credits" may earn a watch, for example. Most clubs offer travel agents such travel-oriented promotional items as tote bags, travel alarm clocks, and baggage tags imprinted with the property's logo and the telephone number of the travel agent. Travel agents can use these items to stimulate business for themselves and the property.

Commission Payment Plans. A very important way that properties are serving travel agents is through commission payment plans. In the past, getting paid was difficult for many travel agents. Their number one complaint was that the check that was "in the mail" never arrived. But properties have taken giant strides to ensure that travel agents receive commission checks on a more regular basis.

One of the reasons for the sporadic payment of commission checks was that individual properties were responsible for generating the checks. In many cases, a property did not have the technical capabilities to track bookings, and chains that did have these capabilities charged travel agents a fee.

In 1981, the Holiday Corporation changed all that with the introduction of a centralized commission payment plan. Instead of receiving checks from each property in the chain, travel agents now receive one monthly check issued automatically through a computer in the chain's corporate office. Travel agents are no longer charged a fee. The program is subsidized through fees charged to individual properties, but properties still save money since they no longer incur the administrative, stationery, and postage costs involved in paying travel agents.

Many chains have followed this lead with similar systems. Hyatt, for example, guarantees commission payments within a week of the client's departure. Hilton's policy is to pay commissions within three weeks of check-out. In any case, with a centralized commission payment plan, checks are mailed out on a weekly or monthly basis, and the agent can deal directly with the corporate office if checks are not received. Many chains take advantage of this opportunity to contact travel agents by including with commission checks a statement of guest histories for the month, any changes made in the reservation after it was booked by the travel agent, and information relating to new hotel facilities, policy changes, and so on.

Some properties are doing more to encourage travel agent business than sending information. The Napili Kai Beach Club, a small 10-acre resort in Maui, Hawaii, for example, not only cuts commission checks within three days of a guest's departure, but also searches its records on walk-in guests. If a guest visits the property again within two years of being referred to the property by a travel agent, the travel agent receives a commission check! If the guest intends to rebook the following year, a card is sent to the travel agent to advise him or her that the commission will be protected.

Many properties offer special bonuses or incentives to agents who book clients during off-season periods or during the promotion of certain special packages (see Exhibit 17.2). Properties can also offer increased commissions or free accommodations or trips when an agent has exceeded a quota of room nights in a given period (see Exhibit 17.3).

Serving Clients. Last but not least, providing good service to travel agents means providing good service to their clients as well. It is very important to travel agents that their clients be well treated, since a client's experience at a property will likely affect the client/agent relationship. If the client has an enjoyable stay, he or she will be more likely to use the services of the travel agent again. If, on the other hand, the stay does not meet the client's expectations, the agent will lose credibility—and possibly a client.

Guests booked into the property by a travel agent should be greeted by a friendly staff, and their stay should be made as pleasant as possible. Some properties pamper their travel-agent-booked guests with complimentary wine, fruit baskets, or local specialties delivered to the guestroom with a welcoming note and a card that gives the travel agent credit for the gift.

It is easy for a property to offer special treatment to guests booked by travel agents if these guests can be readily identified. Guest registrations should be checked to determine which guests are commissionable to travel agents, and a phone call can be made to agents sending clients to the property for the first time. This action delivers a powerful message that the agent's clients will be well cared for, and may encourage the agent to recommend the property to other clients.

Checking guest registrations can also reveal travel agents who come to the property, unannounced, to see what the guest experience is really like. These agents are usually the owners or managers of top-producing agencies. When these travel agent guests are identified, a welcoming phone call can let them know that the property stays on top of travel-agent-related bookings and is tuned to the needs of the travel agency market.

Finding Travel Agents

There are five resources that can help a property identify travel agents and agencies it may want to do business with:

1. The *Official Airline Guide (OAG)*
2. The *World Travel Directory*
3. In-house records

Exhibit 17.2   Travel Agent Bonuses

The Boca Raton Hotel and Club has always been the perfect resort for your most discriminating clients. With a stunning beach, glorious golf, sensational tennis and seven magnificent restaurants. But now we've found a way to improve on perfection.

We'll pay you a 15% commission on all individual guest bookings made for the period of January 3rd through April 30th. And we're also offering a limited number of rooms at a very special rate – only $95 per person, per night.* For reservations, call toll free 1-800-327-0101. Treat your clients to perfection, while the percentages are even more in your favor than usual.

The Boca Raton Hotel and Club QUITE SIMPLY THE BEST*

*Per person, per night, double occupancy. Limited availability in The Cloister. Taxes and service charges not included. Not available to groups. From January 22nd through April 7th, stay will include M.A.P. at an additional $35 per person, per night. Boca Raton, Florida 33429

Many properties offer bonuses to make it more profitable for travel agents to book business during off-season or slow periods. Properties may also award bonuses to agents for booking a certain number of room nights or for maintaining a certain level of bookings.

4.   American Society of Travel Agents (ASTA) mailing lists

5.   Travel industry trade shows

The *OAG* lists all of the airline activity between domestic and international cities, and provides invaluable information on the flow of airline traffic into the property's locale. While this guide does not specifically list travel agents or agencies, it is beneficial in targeting the key cities from which air traffic originates. A property can then determine the names of agencies in those cities.

The *World Travel Directory* can be purchased for under $100 and lists the names of travel agencies and agents, the size of agencies, what type of business each agency specializes in, and where agencies are located. A listing of wholesale tour operators is also included. This book can be an excellent source for travel agent leads.

In-house records provide a history of commission payments to travel agents and can assist the property in targeting agents who have recommended the property in the past. In-house records can also help identify an agent's specific needs. For example, has the agent most often booked individual business or leisure travelers, or does the agent primarily serve the small meetings market?

In-house records can be used to develop a travel agent mailing list. This mailing list can be expanded through the purchase of outside lists. ASTA

Exhibit 17.3   Travel Agent Incentives

REWARD!

WANTED: America's hard working Travel Agents.

Take a well deserved break...and come stay

FREE in December!

Happy Holidays! You've been busy all year booking the finest accommodations in
Las Vegas for your clients – and now it's your turn to receive that same royal treatment
at the fabulous Flamingo Hilton. All complimentary, as our special guest.
Your exclusive Travel Agent Vacation Package includes a deluxe room for up to three
nights (single or double occupancy), plus dazzling main showroom entertainment
featuring "City Lites," including two cocktails.
For reservations, call or write the Flamingo Hilton Sales Department:
800-544-4111 or 702-733-3211; Telex 684455

Offer open to currently employed Travel Agents only.
*Nov. 22-Dec. 28, 1987, subject to space availability. (Sorry, Dec. 4, 5, 11 & 12 are sold out.)

Flamingo
HILTON
LAS VEGAS
3555 Las Vegas Blvd. So., Las Vegas, NV 89109

*In addition to bonuses, many properties offer a variety of other incentives to travel agents who have
produced business for the property. Some properties and chains offer free room nights and special
complimentary travel agent packages. This flier from the Flamingo Hilton and Tower promotes a
special vacation package.*

Courtesy of Flamingo Hilton and Tower, Las Vegas, Nevada.

mailing lists are some of the most beneficial of these outside lists. ASTA provides national, regional, and state lists on a cost-per-thousand basis.

Some properties use industry trade shows as opportunities to meet travel agents. These shows (which will be discussed later in the chapter) allow properties to communicate with individual agents and determine specific travel agent needs. Information on these shows can be obtained from ASTA or from trade publications.

Reaching Travel Agents

Travel agents can be reached through hotel directories, trade magazines, direct mail, trade shows, personal sales, and public relations.

Hotel
Directories

Perhaps the most effective way to reach travel agents is through advertising in hotel directories. Hotel directories are used by travel agents to book eight out of ten leisure traveler bookings and six out of ten business traveler bookings. Hotel directories are used extensively even when a computerized system is available: 67% of all travel agents said they consulted a hotel directory as well as a computerized system.[7]

Since travel agents receive an average of 80 to 100 directories each year, a property's directory ad must capture attention. The headline should include the property's chief benefit, and the ad itself must get the hotel's name and image across. Ads should appeal to an *agent*, not a potential guest.

Trade
Magazines

In addition to directory advertising, many properties also advertise in travel trade magazines such as *ASTA Travel News* and *Travel Agent*. Unlike consumer ads, trade ads are often lengthy, since information is so important to travel professionals. Copy should include:

1. *Pertinent location information*. Include proximity to major highways and airports or other transportation terminals, distances to popular attractions, mileage to nearby industrial complexes or downtown business areas, and availability of complimentary transportation (airport limousine, hotel courtesy van for trips to shopping malls, attractions, and so on).

2. *Rate information*. Regular rates, group rates, and special rates such as "children free" should be listed, along with special packages (rates, availability, what is included) and special discounts available for off-season bookings.

3. *Booking information*. Toll-free reservation numbers, credit card policies, and other pertinent booking information (travel agent guarantees, etc.) should be included.

4. *Commission information*. Commission information should cover payment policies and special incentives.

Photographs can be used in addition to copy to grab attention and introduce the property to travel agents. Exterior shots, lobby photographs, and photographs of guestrooms or function areas should be used as space permits.

Direct Mail   Another way to reach travel agents is through direct mail. Direct mail includes sales letters, collateral materials, promotional giveaways, and newsletters (see Exhibit 17.4). Collateral materials can be used to introduce new facilities or packages; they can be as simple as printed fliers or as elaborate as full-color folders and special advertising gimmicks. Newsletters are an excellent way to keep in touch with travel agents and inform them of price fluctuations, new promotions, and efforts to better serve the travel professional. Since travel agents receive so much mail, direct mail pieces must be attractive to avoid being thrown away unread.

Trade Shows   Another, more personal, way to reach travel agents is through attendance at industry trade shows. As mentioned previously, trade shows provide the opportunity to talk directly to travel agents and learn their individual needs. Trade shows fall into two categories: major international shows, which are organized and coordinated corporately, and traveling "marketplace type" shows, which run for several days in selected cities. The most well-known trade shows are the International Tourism Bourse (ITB) in Germany, ASTA conventions, the Travel Industry Association of America's semi-annual conference, Travel Age West, the Henry Davis Travel Show, and the Foremost trade show.

Travel agents visiting trade shows can be reached through sales presentations and the use of visual aids, including video brochures. Video brochures can be almost as effective as a personal tour of the property. When a video brochure is not available, presenters can use printed brochures and attractive posters—both travel-agent-oriented and consumer-oriented—to help the sales presentation.

Personal Sales   A property may wish to contact local, potentially high-volume agents through personal sales calls (see Exhibit 17.5). Many travel agencies are staffed by agents who have specialized areas or client followings, so it may be necessary to deal with a number of agents at each agency. Since travel agents are usually busy, it is best to call ahead for an appointment. Avoid calls on Mondays and Fridays, when business volume is heaviest.

Presentations should be brief. Travel agents offer a complex array of properties to clients; therefore, the presentation should clearly differentiate the property from competing properties. A familiarization tour or invitation to view the property's video can be offered. Getting to know travel agents and letting them get to know the property and its management is the key to success.

Public Relations   Good public relations may do more to reach travel agents than all the advertising in the world. Public relations efforts include inviting travel agents to the property to learn the inner workings of the property's reservations system. Extending invitations to travel writers to visit the property may lead to travel trade articles that are read by travel agents. Properties can also provide news releases to trade publications that appeal to travel agents.

Another public relations activity is hosting a "travel agent day," featuring educational seminars and a reception or dinner, and honoring exceptional travel agency partners through recognition in the local and trade press.

Exhibit 17.4 Direct Mail for Travel Agents

ISSUE NO. 1

N E W S

**A SAMPLER FOR CITY GUESTS.
PLUS MORE FREE OFFERS FOR
PREFERRED TRAVEL AGENTS.**

Published by Le Parker Meridien New York

DOUBLE YOUR ROOM NIGHTS—WITHOUT DOING ANYTHING EXTRA.

To help you reach the room nights you need for the gift you want, we'll give you double credit for your rack-rate bookings at Le Parker Meridien—a special offer valid January through April 30, 1987.

You won't find a better time to beef up your bookings while you enjoy the preferential treatment our Preferred Travel Agents receive.

a special
GIFT!
It's a space-age idea that could become a collector's item. Don't miss our unusual free offer described inside. An exclusive—for Preferred Travel Agents only.

MUSIC! MUSIC! MUSIC!

If you could tune out the city sounds, you just might hear snatches of melody coming from Lincoln Center. The world-famous complex is only a few blocks north of Le Parker Meridien—at West 65th Street and Broadway...

Avery Fisher Hall, home of the New York Philharmonic Orchestra; the Metropolitan Opera House; the New York State Theater, where the New York City Opera and the New York City Ballet perform; the Juilliard Building, where the Juilliard's own students perform chamber music.

THE CRITICS RAVE ABOUT OUR *MAURICE.*

Craig Claiborne calls *Maurice* one of "New York's top ten restaurants." Says Forbes Magazine: "Four Stars. For the first time a hotel restaurant makes it to the top." And Bryan Miller in The New York Times calls *Maurice* one of the preeminent luxury restaurants in New York.

But that's not all. Check the new Zagat Restaurant Survey. It talks about "sumptuous setting and impressive 'French nouvelle cuisine with American portions' " and "the kitchen hasn't missed a beat."

THE LIGHTS OF BROADWAY.

Turn down Broadway and you'll find the theater district shining brighter than ever. Among the favorites—the long-running hit *A Chorus Line*; the dazzle-packed London musical *Cats*; *42nd Street* (the production and cast are rated "pure gold"); *The Mystery of Edwin Drood*, where the audience does the solving author Charles Dickens was unable to do.

SUPERSIZE DISCOUNTS FOR THEATER BUFFS

Be sure to tip off your New York travelers to the Tkts booth where, for half price, they can pick up any unsold or otherwise available seats for performances on the same day or night for Broadway, Off-Broadway and Off-Off-Broadway shows. The booth is on Duffy Square, the narrow area of West 47th Street between Broadway and Seventh Avenue. (212) 354-5800.

Properties can use a number of types of direct mail to keep travel agents informed of new services. Le Parker Meridien, for example, offers a free newsletter to members of its La Préférence travel agent club. The newsletter is just one of the many direct mailings sent to the club's "Preferred Travel Agents."

Courtesy of Le Parker Meridien, New York, New York.

Exhibit 17.5   Guidelines for Working with Travel Agents

1. Let agents know you want and value their business. Help them sell your property by providing a checklist of what you want them to know. This checklist should include facts about your location, reservation system, accommodations, facilities, rates, packages, meeting and convention facilities, commission policies, and local attractions. If possible, list specific sales points, using actual quotes from a third party to add credibility.

2. Make the hotel easy to book. Advertise the toll-free 800 reservations number. For additional convenience, provide agents with another number to call for information they are unable to obtain from the reservationist. Above all, keep reservationists informed about your property.

3. Honor agents' reservations and avoid overbooking. Lost reservations and overbooked hotels are two of the most frequent agent complaints. If possible, guarantee the reservation with the client's credit card or an agency check.

4. Have the client's room ready when he or she arrives and add a special touch such as a welcoming note.

5. Pay commissions promptly. Brightly colored checks and promotion gimmicks aren't necessary, only the money.

6. Provide familiarization trips or special rate discounts so that agents can get a firsthand view of the hotel.

7. Make personal contact with agents whenever possible by attending trade shows or making calls and visits.

8. Educate the hotel staff so that it recognizes and knows what to do with agent reservations and vouchers.

9. In advertising the hotel, remember that agents receive 400 or more pieces of mail a week and they discard 90% of it. Fliers, brochures, and other advertising pieces are more trouble than they're worth, agents say. They rely instead on the listings and advertisements in hotel indexes.

10. When promoting the hotel, for best results include not only pictures of the hotel but also of the immediate area. Aerial shots of the hotel and the surrounding landscape are especially desirable. Include details which will help the agent sell the property to a first-time client.

11. Consider giving agents incentives such as special commissions for booking business during slow periods.

12. Above all, be consistent. Continue to build the property's reputation for good service and your reputation for dealing with agents in a manner that is deserving of their continued efforts.

Source: Adapted from *Texas and Southwest Hotel-Motel Review*, April 1980.

Conclusion

The growing variety of transportation and lodging choices makes travel decisions more complicated than ever before. Because of this, travel agents can be expected to handle even more business and leisure travel in the future. Meeting the needs of travel agents and having a positive attitude toward travel agencies can mean increased bookings and revenues for a property—at a fraction of the cost of in-house sales efforts.

Properties should explore all viable ways of developing an excellent working relationship with travel agents. Travel agents have come to appreciate the value of hotel bookings, and hotels have begun to view travel agents as an extension of their sales staff—salespeople who do not ask for payment until they have produced business.

Notes

1. "The U.S. Travel Agent Usage Study: An Analysis of the Characteristics and Hotel Bookings of U.S. Travel Agencies," a study conducted by Market Probe International for *Hotel & Travel Index*, January 1987.
2. Information in this and the following paragraphs in this section was found in "Hotels, Travel Agents and the Business Traveler," a special industry report prepared by *Hotel & Travel Index* in the spring of 1987 based on three studies: the U.S. Travel Data Center Survey of Business Travelers (1985/86), sponsored by Murdoch Magazines; the 1987 "U.S. Travel Agent Usage Study," conducted by Market Probe International; and the Harvey Communication Measurement Study, Summer 1986, conducted by the Harvey Research Organization, Inc.
3. "The U.S. Travel Agent Usage Study," *Hotel & Travel Index*.
4. "Travel Agency Automation and the Hotel Booking Process," a special industry report prepared by *Hotel & Travel Index*, Fall 1986.
5. "An Analysis of the Hotel Selection Process for Business Travelers," an article based on personal interviews conducted with travel agents by the Harvey Research Organization, Inc. for *Hotel & Travel Index*.
6. "An Analysis of the Hotel Selection Process," *Hotel & Travel Index*.
7. "The U.S. Travel Agent Usage Study," *Hotel & Travel Index*.

Discussion Questions

1. How many travel agencies are there in the United States?
2. What is the difference between a retail travel agent and a wholesale travel agent?
3. What are some of the ways properties are meeting travel agents' need for property information?
4. Why are travel agents reluctant to use airline reservations systems for booking hotel rooms?
5. Who are the best prospects for a property's fam tour for travel agents?
6. What are some of the ways in which properties can provide good service to travel agents?
7. What are the advantages of a centralized commission payment plan?
8. What are five resources that can help a property identify travel agents and agencies?
9. What is perhaps the most effective way to reach travel agents?
10. Trade magazine ad copy should include what types of information?
11. What public relations efforts might be used to develop travel agent business?

Chapter Outline

I. The Group Meetings Market
    A. Associations
        1. Types of Associations
        2. Types of Association Meetings
        3. Planning Factors for Association Meetings
           a. Timing
           b. Lead time
           c. Geographic pattern
           d. Geographic restrictions
           e. Attendance
           f. Site selection
        4. Whom to Contact
    B. Corporations
        1. Types of Corporations
        2. Types of Corporate Meetings
        3. Planning Factors for Corporate Meetings
           a. Timing
           b. Lead time
           c. Geographic pattern
           d. Geographic restrictions
           e. Attendance
           f. Site selection
        4. Whom to Contact

II. Finding Association and Corporate Group Business

III. Reaching Association and Corporate Meeting Planners
    A. Personal Sales Calls
    B. Sales Blitzes
    C. Trade Shows
    D. Print Advertising
    E. Other Sales Tools

IV. Conclusion

18 Selling to Meeting Planners

The group meetings market is only one part of a hotel's total guest mix, but it is perhaps the healthiest and most growth-oriented one.[1] Jet transportation, generally rising incomes, and increased leisure time all contribute to the growth of the group meetings market.

Group meetings business can benefit a property in a number of ways:

1. *Additional revenue.* Because group meeting guests are more or less a captive audience, they not only provide guestroom revenue, they also spend more in the hotel's other revenue centers and on hospitality suites and food and beverage functions than do other guests. Spouses are accompanying meeting and convention attendees more than ever before. This typically increases business in gift shops, health clubs, and other revenue centers.

2. *Ease in filling slow periods.* Group meetings are an excellent way to generate business during the property's slow periods.

3. *Ease in employee scheduling.* With groups, the length of each guest's stay is usually predetermined. Employees can be scheduled more efficiently and labor costs reduced.

4. *Repeat business.* Group meetings can result in repeat business from the group organizing the meeting and from individual attendees who are exposed to the property during the meeting. Individuals may later visit the property as business or leisure travelers, and can serve as word-of-mouth advertisers to friends and business associates.

There is yet another benefit to targeting the group meetings market. Group meetings business frequently increases during periods when leisure travel is on the decline due to a struggling economy. A poor economy actually stimulates group meetings business by creating the need for more direct contact among business associates.

The group meetings market can be a consistent revenue-producer for properties large and small. In this chapter we will take a close look at this market and learn how to meet the needs of the men and women who plan group meetings for associations and corporations. We will explore each segment of the group meetings market in terms of size, the types of meetings held and the requirements for these meetings, the cycle and pattern of

Industry Profile

Michael Hausman graduated from Temple University in 1966 and began his career in the hospitality industry that same year. His first position was with the Philadelphia Convention and Visitors Bureau. He worked for a number of hotel companies before his current seven-year stint with Marriott Hotels and Resorts. Hausman is a past vice president of Meeting Planners International and a current vice president of the Hotel Sales & Marketing Association International. He has received numerous honors during his career. He was inducted into the New York chapter of Meeting Planners International Hall of Fame, named Associate Member of the Year by the New York Society of Association Executives, and selected as Supplier of the Year by the International Association of Meeting Planners International.

Michael K. Hausman
Director of National Accounts—Associations Marriott Hotels and Resorts

"Of all market segments, the association market is most apt to book more than several years out. Some associations book 15 or more years out because they use virtually all of a city's hotel rooms and convention facilities. When doing long-term room rate and financial projections, knowing that several associations have made commitments with the property can be quite reassuring for the lenders, the property's owners, and corporate headquarters.

The association market covers a myriad of associations. Not only are you soliciting large, citywide associations, which are generally coordinated through a city's convention and visitors' bureau, you're also soliciting association meeting business of under 500 rooms. This includes regional, state, board of directors, and a variety of other types of association meetings. This means that virtually any hotel can solicit some part of this important market segment.

Association decision-makers may vary, but in most cases the executive secretary or executive director has a great deal of control. Very often, particularly in the case of large annual meetings, there is a board of directors or a site committee that must stamp its approval on the executive director's recommendation. It's helpful if members of the board of directors or site committee can be solicited for their support. If there is a local chapter of an association in your area, the chapter president often becomes an important contact.

As mentioned, most city convention and visitors' bureaus are in the business of soliciting major associations, and an effort should be made to coordinate your property's interests with their efforts. Often, the property can tie together an attractive package with the convention and visitors' bureau, but if there are associations that the property wants to target on its own, a number of techniques can be used.

Various encyclopedias and directories list vital information on the size and type of association meetings and the names of key executives. A phone call or letter to a decision-maker should elicit a response, but nothing is more effective than meeting with association executives. Trips to major association cities such as Washington, D.C., Chicago, and New York can be most rewarding—if planned in advance with set appointments. Other avenues include attendance at various trade shows, including the American Society of Association Executives, the National Association of Exposition Executives, Professional Conventions Managers Association, and a whole alphabet of other organizations. Many of these organizations have city and state associations which let you target markets in close proximity.

While the association market is exciting because of its vast size and the dollar value it represents to a hotel, a coordinated effort that involves selling to a number of market segments is vital to the success of a hotel. A property's percentage of association market business can vary from year to year, making soliciting other market segments a necessary addition to association selling. **"**

meetings, and the duration of meetings. We will also learn how to obtain leads, work with decision-makers to generate business, and utilize sales and advertising techniques to build group business for a property.

The Group Meetings Market

Laventhol & Horwath, an accounting firm specializing in lodging industry research, lists the proportion of U.S. hotel guests who are meeting attendees at nearly 15%.[2] Of course, for major convention hotels, this figure is significantly higher. Complexes such as the Opryland Hotel in Nashville (1,068 rooms), the New York Marriott Marquis (1,876 rooms), and the Las Vegas Hilton (3,100 rooms) attribute as much as 80% of their total sales volume to convention business.[3]

A common misconception is that all group business meetings and conventions are large gatherings of thousands of people. In reality, there are many more small meetings than large ones. Research conducted by industry trade publications shows that 75% of all corporate meetings have fewer than 100 people in attendance.[4] This means that group meetings are a potential source of business for lodging properties of all sizes.

The group meetings market can be divided into two segments: associations and corporations. While the needs of these two segments may be the same in some areas, needs are far different in others. And the many organizations within each segment have needs that vary greatly. In fact, it is rare that a single firm or organization has needs that are the same from one meeting or convention to the next! For this reason, each of these segments—and the organizations within each segment—must be looked at separately.

Associations
An association is an organization of persons having a common interest or purpose. There are many associations throughout the country and throughout the world, and the size, nature, and purpose of associations vary greatly. The Council on Education for Public Health has a membership of two; the National Association of Realtors has a membership of 720,000. There are associations for doctors, bankers, and lawyers. There are also associations for magicians, beekeepers, hospital purchasing agents, fruit growers, horseshoe pitchers, and urethane foam contractors. The American Hotel & Motel Association is an example of an association in the lodging industry.[5]

Types of Associations. Associations can be divided into at least seven general categories:

1. Trade associations

2. Professional and scientific associations

3. Educational associations

4. Fraternal and service groups

5. Ethnic associations

6. Religious associations

7. Labor unions

Trade associations are made up of individuals, companies, or corporations which have similar business needs or concerns. These associations are usually considered the most lucrative source of group meetings business because their memberships consist largely of successful executives. Many trade associations hold conventions in conjunction with trade shows, such as the trade show staged by the National Restaurant Association. Restaurant and kitchen equipment suppliers exhibit at this convention, which draws more than 100,000 delegates to Chicago annually.

Professional and scientific associations are closely related to trade associations, but differ in regard to meeting frequency. Most professional and scientific associations have regular meeting schedules, but it is not unusual for special meetings to be called if a major discovery will affect a particular association. Many of these associations are affiliated with national and international associations, and these groups are typically very large. Examples of professional and scientific associations include the American Bar Association, the International Association of Dental Students, and the American Statistical Association.

Educational associations are groups of teachers or other education professionals and supporters. Although expenses are generally paid by the educational institutions involved, these groups tend to be very cost-conscious. Examples of educational associations include the National Education Association, the Modern Language Association, and the Council of Hotel Restaurant and Institutional Educators.

Fraternal and service groups are made up of individuals who have a similar area of interest, whether it be of a scholastic, philanthropic, or social nature. Members who take part in fraternal or service group meetings typically pay their own expenses. Meetings usually include family participation. Examples of fraternal and service groups include the Benevolent Protective Order of Elks, the Fraternal Order of Eagles, and Soroptimist International.

Ethnic associations provide a common denominator based on race or national origin. Like fraternal associations, ethnic associations are family-oriented, and meeting attendees pay their own expenses. Examples of ethnic associations include the National Association for the Advancement of Colored People, the German-American Club, and the National Association of Latin Americans.

Religious associations can be divided into two groups: vocational and avocational. Vocational groups include associations of ministers or other clergy; avocational groups include educational and charitable religious groups. Religious associations as a whole are very budget-conscious. Examples of religious associations include the National Conference of Christians and Jews, and Gideons International.

Labor unions meet only at hotels that are unionized, and typically generate high food and beverage revenues because several social functions are usually included in the convention program. Examples of labor unions include the International Brotherhood of Electrical Workers, the Teamsters Union, and the United Steel Workers of America.

Types of Association Meetings. With this wide diversity of associations, it is evident that association meetings will vary. Associations generate several types of group meetings business:

- Annual conventions
- Regional conventions
- Conferences

- Seminars and workshops
- Board and committee meetings

Annual conventions are held by associations of all types. Some conventions are huge affairs attracting between 20,000 and 30,000 people, while others may have an attendance of fewer than 100. The average convention has 400 attendees.[6] Most annual conventions have a main session for all delegates supplemented by a number of smaller meetings sometimes called "breakout" meetings. Almost half of all annual conventions are held in conjunction with a trade show or with exhibits.[7] In some cases, trade shows may be held without a convention program; these functions are called exhibitions or expositions, and may be sponsored by an association or by individual entrepreneurs or companies for the benefit of the association.

Since annual conventions vary widely, it is necessary to look at the convention needs of the different categories of associations.

Trade associations usually have complex convention programs that include many meetings and social activities. These associations usually make extensive use of sophisticated audiovisual equipment.

Professional and scientific associations also make use of sophisticated audiovisual equipment. Scientific and medical associations typically hold several breakout meetings, and the availability of a number of meeting rooms is more important than provision for social events.

Educational associations also maximize meetings and minimize social functions at their annual conventions. Meetings are usually scheduled at night as well as during the day. Most educational association conventions are organized around a large general session (often featuring a political speaker), but a number of breakout rooms are usually needed as well.

Fraternal and service groups usually have annual conventions built around large general sessions. Attendees often combine vacations with convention attendance, so properties should offer recreational activities. There should also be sight-seeing areas and entertainment facilities nearby.

Ethnic associations typically prefer annual conventions with elaborate social programs. Since most of their annual conventions are family-oriented, there is a high percentage of multiple occupancy in this group, and recreational and sight-seeing opportunities are important.

Religious associations require varied facilities, depending on the nature of the religion. Conservative religions tend to look for fewer but larger meeting halls, while liberal religions are more interested in a sufficient number of breakout rooms.

Labor unions require the use of large properties, especially when the general session is the focal point of the convention. Labor union conventions usually last longer than most other association conventions and feature a great many social and food and beverage functions. These conventions often take on a political atmosphere. Prominent political speakers, signs, banners, and buttons are usually part of the program.

Regional conventions are smaller in scope than annual conventions, and are further limited by geographic restrictions. Although some members elect to fly, most members attending regional conventions drive to the convention site. Therefore, airport properties do not necessarily have an advantage when soliciting regional conventions.

Conferences are usually staged to supplement a convention program. A conference supplies information related to new developments of interest to the association's members. Conferences are more common in professional, scientific, and educational associations, although other associations may book conferences following breakthroughs in their fields, changes in tax or corporate law, and other events that would affect the association's members.

Seminars and workshops are similar to conferences but smaller in scope. They are generally used to train and educate association members. Many seminars are developed by independent seminar consultants who travel around the country presenting special programs of interest to association members, while other seminars may be developed by the association's paid staff.

Board and committee meetings are the smallest type of association group meeting in terms of attendance. They are often set in beautiful locales as a way of attracting outstanding people to serve, or as a reward for unpaid association officials. These meetings, which may range in size from ten or fewer to up to 100 or more persons, are ideal for almost any size property. Even a very small property can usually handle a meeting of ten or fewer. A large property may use the success it has with board and committee meetings to generate support for its selection as a convention site.

Planning Factors for Association Meetings. Since there is such a wide variety of associations and types of association meetings, a property must identify the needs of an individual association and determine ways to meet those needs if it wants to be selected as that association's meeting or convention site. However, there are some factors that all associations must consider when planning a convention or group meeting that properties should be aware of. These factors include the timing of meetings, lead time, geographic patterns, geographic restrictions, attendance, and site selection.

Timing. Most association conventions, whether national, state, or regional, are held at the same time each year. Some associations, in fact, insist on holding their annual convention during the same week of the same month each year.

Lead time. Most associations plan conventions well in advance. The average lead time is two years, although this may vary from as little as one to as many as 15 or more years depending on the size of the convention. This lead time, while frustrating to hoteliers, is necessary for associations to select a site and plan their convention.

Geographic pattern. Many association conventions follow a definite geographic pattern. Often a convention is rotated among three or four cities. Some associations alternate between the East and the West in site selection, but a popular variation of this pattern is to select a Midwestern city every third year.

The time of year a convention is scheduled may influence which area of the country is chosen. If a Midwestern location is chosen for a winter convention, for example, attendance could suffer in the event of a blizzard, an ice storm, or other inclement weather. Most meeting planners try to avoid weather problems through prudent scheduling. It is for this reason that the most popular months for conventions are October, May, April, June, and September, in that order.

Geographic restrictions. Some associations are limited to a site selection in their own states or within a specified mile limit. This is especially true of small or regional associations. However, there is a growing trend to bend these restrictions and choose a site that appeals to the majority of association members no matter where it is located.

Attendance. Attendance at most association meetings is voluntary. Since the option to attend is the member's, an association meeting planner must *attract* members to the meeting—and may try to do so with an appealing price, an interesting location, or special programs or events.

Site selection. While the primary needs for conventions and group meetings are adequate meeting space, an adequate number of guestrooms, and the services of an experienced staff, there are other factors that associations consider when selecting a specific site or property for a convention or group meeting.

Transportation is an important factor in selecting a site. If the membership must fly to the convention or meeting site, an airport property is most convenient; if members usually drive to the convention, a location near an interstate highway is a good choice.

Another factor in site selection is price. Most association conventions average two to four days, and since many delegates pay their own expenses, guestroom rates must be within the reach of association members. In some cases, an association meeting planner will select a property which offers the lowest cost accommodations; in other cases, the finest accommodations are necessary, and resort or upscale properties will be the meeting planner's first choice. In other words, there is no one right price level. The price an association is willing to pay for guestrooms will depend on the nature of the association and the ability of its members to pay.

Whom to Contact. Because of the many factors involved in planning a convention or group meeting and selecting a site for it, the planning and selection process an association goes through is a lengthy and often complex one. It is important for a property to become involved in this process as soon as possible. That means getting to know the decision-maker. Who is the decision-maker for an association? Depending on the type of association and/or the type of meeting, he or she may be one of the following:

- Professional meeting planner
- Association executive
- Site committee chairperson
- Board of directors chairperson or member
- Local association member

Some associations employ a *professional meeting planner* who is responsible for recommending meeting sites. Many employ an *association executive* who may be given a title such as president, executive vice president, or executive director. No matter what the title, the association executive is usually the key to property sales efforts. He or she is ordinarily involved in the initial screening and final selection of a convention or meeting site. The association executive may either visit prospective sites in person or delegate this responsibility to others. He or she may have an administrative staff that assists with convention planning.

Small associations often cannot afford the services of a full-time association executive, and may elect to use a multiple association management firm. These firms serve an association as needed—including selecting a site and planning a convention at costs the association can afford.

A *site committee chairperson* may be involved in screening convention sites and/or deciding on the final site, depending on the size and structure of the association. Chairpersons of other association committees may also be involved with the selection of sites for seminars, especially if the seminar will deal with matters important to their particular committees.

A *board of directors* is not usually involved in the decision-making process until the time for the final site selection. Many boards immediately accept the recommendation of the association executive. The acceptance of other boards may be less immediate, but in the end most boards of directors agree with the association executive's recommendation.

In many associations, especially professional and scientific ones, local chapters bid for the honor of hosting the national group. In these cases, a *local association member* can be approached by a property and offered full assistance in planning a convention or meeting if it will be held at the property. When taking this approach, however, the property must demonstrate its expertise in the convention and meetings area.

Once the key decision-maker has been identified, the job of selling begins. Techniques for selling to association meeting planners will be discussed in detail later in the chapter.

Corporations

Corporations can be a highly lucrative source of group meetings business for properties. Most corporate meeting planners average 14 meetings or conventions in a single year.[8] The short lead time required for most corporate meetings makes it easier for a property to book corporate meetings during slack periods. Corporate groups can be an important source of revenue to small properties as well as large since, as mentioned previously, 75% of corporate meetings average an attendance of fewer than 100 persons.

Types of Corporations. Corporations vary greatly in size and purpose. There are local, state, national, and international corporations which sell products, services, or both. Whatever their size and type, most corporations hold group meetings at one time or another which require lodging facilities.

Types of Corporate Meetings. There are many types of meetings held by corporations. They include:

1. National or international sales meetings

2. Regional or district sales meetings

3. Training and development meetings

4. Distributor and dealer meetings

5. Executive conferences

Industry Profile

Robert Mackey, an Ohio native, received his B.A. in psychology from Ohio University in 1972 and worked in the insurance industry from 1972 to 1977. In 1977, he began his career in the hotel industry as a room clerk at the Waldorf-Astoria. Mackey progressed through the ranks to Convention Manager and Sales Manager before leaving the property in 1979 to join the pre-opening office for Vista International New York as a sales manager. He was named Assistant Director of Sales when the property opened in 1981, and became Director of Sales in February 1982. Mackey was promoted to Director of Marketing in May, 1986, and became a Certified Hotel Sales Executive the following year. He is a past president of the New York chapter of the Hotel Sales & Marketing Association International, and currently serves as Northeast Regional Director. Mackey has been a guest lecturer at the New York City Technical College and has contributed an article to Marketing Review.

Robert C. Mackey, CHSE
Director of Marketing Vista International Hotel

66The company meetings market is a significant portion of our business here at Vista International New York. Nearly 14% of our rooms business is from the company meetings segment. Because company meetings generally take place during weekdays and non-holiday periods, the average rate this segment delivers is generally one of the highest among our market segments. The company meetings segment is also responsible for producing about 50% of our banquet food and beverage business and significant portions of the revenues from our restaurants and laundry and valet services.

The types of meetings held are as varied as the companies that hold them. Training meetings of all types are popular, as are board meetings, stockholders' meetings, new product introductions, branch managers meetings, and so on. Often, we'll get a large room block from a corporation holding a meeting at their own facilities and using the hotel for overnight accommodations. This is becoming more and more popular as companies design state-of-the-art meeting complexes into their office facilities.

It can be very difficult to identify and reach decision-makers in the company meetings segment. According to *Successful Meetings Magazine*, 80% of the company meetings planned each year are planned by non-professionals. A non-professional meeting planner is someone who devotes less than 50% of his or her time to planning meetings. An example of this could be a senior vice president of the human resources department who takes on the responsibility of planning a meeting for all the personnel managers in the company. Anyone at a company can become a meeting planner, and thus a potential client. All that's required is that the person be assigned to organize a meeting.

The best way to reach non-professional meeting planners is through the judicious use of your own in-house mailing list. Although it's often impossible to predict who within a company will become a meeting planner, it's certainly reasonable to assume that someone who's contacted you in the past might become a client in the future. Contacts within a company can also be helpful. For example, the travel manager who you work with for individual corporate business travel may be aware of employees in other departments who have been—or will be—involved in planning meetings. Another, but more expensive, method of reaching meeting planners is through consumer advertising in local newspapers and magazines. A potential meeting planner within a company may see your ad and recall your hotel when assigned to arrange a meeting.

Like all kinds of selling, selling to the corporate meetings market involves identifying a client's needs and communicating what your product or service will do to meet them. The ideal salesperson in the company meetings segment isn't a salesperson in the traditional sense, but rather a problem-solver. With non-professional meeting planners, that's often exactly the kind of salesperson they need!**99**

6. Product presentations or launchings

7. Stockholders' meetings

    8.   Board meetings

    9.   Management development seminars

  10.   Incentive travel meetings

National or international sales meetings are the oldest type of corporate meeting. Attendance is usually restricted to senior salespeople and supervisory executives. Spouses normally are not invited to this type of meeting. Average attendance is 183 persons; meetings last an average of 3.6 days.[9] Meeting requirements and site selections are varied. If a national sales meeting is scheduled to introduce new products, for example, it is important that the meeting be held at a site that can provide easy access for product delivery. If a sales meeting has been called to develop a new advertising campaign, usually the site is chosen based on ease of access by the participants. The average per-person expenditure is generally above the usual meeting average. Participants tend to stay close to the property and make extensive use of room service or dine in the property's restaurants.

Regional or district sales meetings are usually smaller than national meetings, averaging 54 persons. Ordinarily these meetings are shorter than a national or an international sales meeting, although the program is often of the same type. With lower budgets, smaller attendance, and geographic restrictions, the per-person expenditure at regional or district sales meetings drops to the medium level.

Training and development meetings average an attendance of 30 persons, and may last from one to seven days. This is a no-nonsense type of meeting—there is a high level of double occupancy of rooms and meetings are often set up schoolroom-style. Since the budget is a prime consideration for this type of meeting, especially when training entry-level employees, the per-person expenditure drops to the low-to-medium level. Training and development meetings are well-suited to small properties regardless of location, especially when a "conference center" atmosphere can be provided.

Distributor and dealer meetings are conducted to show new products or motivate dealers. These meetings are usually open to spouses and vary in length from one to three days. Top executives are often in attendance, and meeting attendees are given the best in accommodations, cuisine, and entertainment. Elaborate food and beverage functions and entertainment events make these meetings the cream of the corporate meetings market.

Executive conferences, too, can yield high per-person expenditures, since this type of meeting requires the finest accommodations available. While these meetings are usually arranged on a short lead time and attendance may vary, spouses are often invited. Additional revenue can be generated through programs for spouses and the sale of first-quality food and beverage products.

Product presentations or launchings average from two to five days and may be public or private functions. A private or trade event will have the same general requirements as those for a distributor and dealer meeting. Product presentations or launchings usually require a large ballroom or exhibit area, elaborate staging or setup, and labor and time for the dismantling of exhibits. This type of meeting may inconvenience other guests at the property.

Stockholders' meetings are the lowest income-producers of all corporate meetings, since the purpose of the meeting is to get business conducted as quickly as possible. The length of a stockholders' meeting is almost always one day, and there are no planned food or beverage functions. A property's revenues will come strictly from the rental of a large ballroom or meeting room, room accommodations for a few executives, and meals for some of those coming from out of town.

Board meetings average under 20 in attendance, but the top executives and corporate officers who attend these meetings generate a high per-person expenditure for guestrooms and food and beverages. Board meetings are usually conducted at city properties or resorts.

Management development seminars are similar to regular training and development meetings except that the per-person budget is higher. These meetings vary in attendance and length.

Incentive travel meetings generally run from five to eight days in length. Spouses are usually invited. Since incentive meetings are rewards to salespeople or other businesspeople for jobs well done, the destination is an important consideration. Almost all trips are to exotic locations (see Exhibit 18.1). Incentive meetings are best suited to resorts or properties in popular getaway spots, although for other properties there is potential for overnight stays at the point of departure and the point of return if the incentive travel program includes cruise ship or overseas travel.

There are many details that must be attended to before an incentive meeting gets off the ground. Many large corporations that sponsor incentive travel have their own travel managers who make all travel and hotel arrangements for the group. Smaller companies that do not employ a travel specialist often call on outside incentive travel companies, sometimes referred to as "motivational houses," to coordinate their incentive meetings. Incentive travel companies include E. F. MacDonald, S & H. Travel Awards, Maritz, and Top Value Enterprises. These companies assist corporate meeting planners with all stages of the travel incentive program, including negotiating with hotels; packaging transportation, lodging, and meeting accommodations; and arranging for meals, tours, and entertainment.

Planning Factors for Corporate Meetings. As with associations, there are several planning factors common to all corporate group meetings that properties should be aware of.

Timing. Unlike many association conventions or meetings, there is no particular "time cycle" for business meetings. Most meetings are scheduled as needed and may occur at any time throughout the year.

Lead time. Lead time is far more flexible for corporate meetings than for association meetings. While annual conventions or sales meetings are usually planned a year or more in advance, training meetings and seminars may be set three to six months in advance, or with even less lead time if the meeting is called to deal with a crisis. Executive conferences and board meetings also may be called on short notice.

Geographic pattern. Corporate meetings are held where they are most needed—close to corporate headquarters; near the field office; or, in the case of an incentive travel meeting, at an attractive location. Training and development meetings, executive conferences, board meetings, seminars, and so on are not rotated among a few locations, as are some association

Exhibit 18.1   Sample Incentive Ad

Properties located in exotic locations or popular destination cities have special appeal for the lucrative incentive travel market.

conventions. This lack of a geographic pattern opens the door for almost any property to land corporate meetings business, no matter what its location or size.

Geographic restrictions. Geographic restrictions usually come into play only with incentive travel meetings. As mentioned, an incentive travel meeting must offer a desirable destination—Hawaii is a popular choice, as are resort destinations such as Las Vegas, San Diego, Miami, and the Caribbean. Some companies may offer trips to exciting cities such as New York or San Francisco.

Attendance. Although there are some exceptions, attendance at business meetings is usually mandatory. Therefore, corporate meeting planners do not have to work as hard as association meeting planners to attract meeting attendees.

Site selection. The specific site or property for a business meeting is usually selected because of its meeting facilities and services. Recreational amenities are a secondary consideration.

A resort is an obvious choice for incentive meetings, but may also be chosen for a training and development meeting by a corporate meeting planner who wants meeting attendees to be free of city distractions. An airport location is ideal when convenience and speed are important. A suburban hotel may be best for attendees arriving by automobile or because of its proximity to the home or field office. Budget or mid-price downtown hotels may be the choice of a meeting planner who wishes to save money; luxury downtown hotels may be chosen by a meeting planner who wishes to house visiting executives in a posh first-class hotel.

Transportation is also an important factor in site selection, especially for annual conventions. For this reason, cities that are transportation hubs are often selected for annual conventions. Many companies return to such locations as Chicago and Dallas year after year because of the convenience factor.

A property that wants to be selected for a convention or group business meeting must provide adequate meeting space, guestrooms, security, and service—including convention or meeting planning services if necessary. In many cases, exhibit space will be needed, especially for meetings that launch new product lines. In other cases, a combination of exhibit or large meeting space and breakout rooms will be needed. Many companies prefer to have breakout rooms conveniently located near the large hall or ballroom used for the general session or group meeting.

Whom to Contact. Since corporate meetings are so varied, it is important for the property's sales staff to determine whom to contact for each type of meeting and each type of company. Whether the meeting will be for the company as a whole, a division, or a single department is also a factor in whom to contact. As with associations, decision-makers for corporate group meetings vary, and can include:

- A full-time meeting planner

- Key executives, such as a president or vice president

- Division or department heads

- A secretary or associate

Many large corporations employ a *full-time meeting planner* to oversee the organization and implementation of company meetings and conventions. This is ideal for a property because full-time meeting planners are experienced, usually know what they want, and know how to go about getting exactly what they need for each type of meeting.

There are many companies, however, that rely on *key executives* (a president or vice president, the chairperson of the board, etc.) to plan meetings and conventions. These executives will never be listed in meeting planner directories, and they do not think of themselves as meeting planners. But since they call meetings, decide where they will take place, and sometimes plan them, these executives are important to the hotel sales staff. Key executives may or may not have meeting planning experience.

Division or department heads such as training directors, personnel directors, and advertising managers may also make decisions regarding meetings, seminars, or conferences. Like higher-level company executives, these staff members may or may not have much experience at planning meetings, but still are important contacts for the property's sales staff.

Other companies may have *secretaries or associates* plan meetings. Again, it is important to remember that they may not be experienced meeting planners. Although meeting planning may be part of their job descriptions, many secretaries or associates do not know what is required for a successful meeting. They tend to worry about small details while sometimes missing the big picture (see Exhibit 18.2). In these situations a property's meeting planning experience can be a deciding factor. A property that is willing to help the secretary or associate plan a successful meeting is more likely to book the meeting than a property that just sells meeting space (see Exhibit 18.3).

Finding Association and Corporate Group Business

Group meetings business for associations and corporations may be pursued locally (at a very small cost) and nationally. A local effort can start at the property. Account files of previous group meetings business can be checked for opportunities to serve associations or corporations again. At the front desk, agents can be trained to search local newspapers for news of associations and corporate groups. In addition, property salespeople can check the yellow pages of the local phone book and the phone book of the state's capital city (many associations have headquarters in state capitals). Salespeople may also obtain leads from the reader boards of competitors or through word-of-mouth referrals.

Other opportunities can be found at the property level. Suppliers of products or services such as the local dairy operator or insurance agent are potential sources of group meetings business. Even if a property's suppliers do not require meeting space for themselves, many belong to trade, professional, civic, social, or religious organizations. The property's suppliers could recommend the property as a meeting site for these organizations.

Employees of a property may also be good sources of meetings business. Many employees belong to organizations that meet regularly or need meeting space for special occasions. Property employees could influence an organization to choose "their" property.

Local and state chambers of commerce, convention and visitors' bureaus, and industrial commissions can provide leads for local group meetings business. For national and international associations and corporations, the sales staff can consult trade periodicals and directories for leads and the names of key decision-makers.

Another good way to develop leads is to visit and exhibit at trade shows; make contacts at annual conventions; and join professional associations, especially those that are users of hospitality industry products. If the property is part of a chain, the regional or corporate office may be able to provide leads.

Reaching Association and Corporate Meeting Planners

Many properties try to reach association and corporate meeting planners haphazardly. They buy a mailing list of meeting planners and send direct mail pieces to everyone on the list, for example. While this technique may produce some results, it is far better to do thorough research and aim selling efforts at a small group of 30 to 40 "hot prospects."

Exhibit 18.2   Solving Problems for Meeting Planners

A "No Excuses"® guarantee for your next meeting.

Have You Ever Had A Projector Bulb Burn Out In The Middle Of A Big Presentation?

We can't promise that you'll never have another bulb burn out.

But we can promise that we'll have spare bulbs on hand. And that your audio-visual and sound equipment will be set up per your specifications and in good working order.

The same is true for the way we set-up your meeting space and the timing and manner in which we serve your coffee breaks. If any of these individual requirements are not the way we agreed in our meeting contract, we'll either make it right or charges for that item will be deleted from your bill.

That's the whole point of our "NO EXCUSES"® Meeting Guarantee. We have to have a lot of confidence in our ability to handle your meeting needs or we wouldn't make this promise.

You'll be dealing with professionals who know how to solve problems before they happen. And once you check-in, you'll have someone to handle your needs 24 hours a day.

They'll also be on hand to review the charges with you before you check-out. And you will be billed per the agreed format and with appropriate back-up documentation.

For more information about our "NO EXCUSES" Meeting Guarantee contact the Director of Sales at any of the participating hotels, or fill out and return our coupon, or call 1-800-MEETING.

Holiday Inn®

Many meeting planners worry about small details. This ad featuring Holiday Inns' "NO EXCUSES" Meeting Guarantee assures meeting planners that their meeting or convention will proceed as planned and that a Holiday Inn can handle any problems that may arise.

This is not to say that a property cannot make use of a mailing list or place ads in trade periodicals. But most properties find it more effective to know something about whom they are trying to sell to. If a property opts to use a mailing list, it should send out a questionnaire to research the needs of those listed before sending an expensive, full-color convention brochure to meeting planners whose requirements the property may not meet (see Exhibit 18.4).

Exhibit 18.3   Assured Meeting Agreement

Assured Meeting Agreement

TO: _____   REPRESENTATIVE OF: _____

For Meeting To Take Place At _____   On: _____
(Hotel)   (Date)

This is to certify that the management and staff of the above named Radisson Hotel are dedicated to providing the finest in facilities and services to assure the quality and success of your meeting. We attest that the Radisson Assured Meeting™ Program, including our unique 54-point checklist, is a comprehensive program designed to meet your most demanding requirements for a quality meeting. Further, it is pledged that if any items specified below should not be fulfilled properly, you will be promptly compensated or credited as indicated.

• Meeting rooms will be ready on time	OR your master account will be credited $50	• Guaranteed banquet menu prices six months in advance	The price increase will be absorbed by the hotel and not passed onto you
• Refreshment break will be served promptly	OR the refreshment break will be complimentary	• Room rates will be guaranteed one year in advance	You will pay no more than the quoted rate in the signed contract even if rates do increase
• Meal functions will be served as scheduled	OR your master account will be credited 5% of the meal cost	• No preassigned meeting room outlined on signed event orders will be changed without your approval	OR the hotel will credit your master account $50
• Meeting rooms will be refreshed during refreshment and luncheon breaks. (Does not include exhibit halls).	OR your master account will be credited $50	• The hotel will honor all guaranteed payment reservations	OR we will place the room at the closest, comparable, available hotel and pay for transportation to those accommodations and back to the hotel the next morning. We will pay for your first night's lodging at the alternative hotel and pay for the first 3 minutes of a phone call home.
• Meeting and banquet rooms will be set up according to your written specifications	OR your master account will be credited $100		
• The convention service manager or management representative will respond to any problems you may have within 15 minutes of notification	OR you will be provided with a complimentary room night		

Thus stipulated and warranted this _____ day of _____, 198 _____

_____   _____
For Radisson Hotels   General Manager

Acknowledged and Affirmed by:

_____ Front Office Manager   _____ Sales Director

_____ Banquet Manager   _____ Food and Beverage Director

The Radisson Hotels

This certificate is part of Radisson Hotel Corporation's program to put meeting planners at ease. It demonstrates the corporation's awareness of the concerns and needs of meeting planners and is an excellent way to build client confidence—and repeat business.

Courtesy of Radisson Hotel Corporation.

Hotels can also do research on a local level. The property's staff can be trained to gather marketing information by speaking to guests about their businesses or professions. It is estimated that one out of every ten guests has the potential to generate group business. It is far less costly for a hotel to pursue leads right under its roof than to spend considerable time and money on mailing lists, out-of-town trips, advertisements, and sales blitzes.

The most effective way to sell to association or corporate meeting planners is face-to-face. As we have noted, some meeting planners are not trained professionals. A face-to-face presentation provides the opportunity for the salesperson to answer any questions the meeting planner might have and reassure the meeting planner that the property is experienced at staging successful meetings (see Exhibit 18.5).

Face-to-face selling can be accomplished in three ways: personal sales calls, sales blitzes, and attendance at trade shows. The first method, personal sales calls, focuses on selling to individuals, while a sales blitz and attendance at trade shows involve prospecting and selling to a larger number of people over a short period of time.

Exhibit 18.4 Sample Questionnaire

ALADDIN
HOTEL

CONVENTION QUESTIONNAIRE

Name _____ Title _____

Firm or Association Name _____

Street Address _____ City _____

State _____ Zip _____ Phone _____

Meeting sites are selected by:

      ☐ Me   ☐ Board of Directors

      ☐ Committee   ☐ General Membership

      ☐ Other (Please specify): _____

Has your organization ever met in Las Vegas?   ☐ Yes   ☐ No

How do you classify your Las Vegas meeting?

      ☐ National/Annual Convention   ☐ Regional Convention

      ☐ Sales Meeting   ☐ State Convention   ☐ Board Meeting

      ☐ Incentive Trip   ☐ Pre- or Post-Convention

Estimated Attendance: _____ Rooms Required: _____

May we send you a written proposal for your consideration? ☐ Yes   ☐ No

Are you planning a Las Vegas visit this year?   ☐ Yes ☐ No

If so, what month? _____

Questionnaires similar to this one are often included with direct mail pieces. The information provided by respondents helps qualify them and lays the groundwork for personal sales calls.

Courtesy of Aladdin Hotel, Las Vegas, Nevada.

Personal Sales Calls

Personal sales calls are the best way to sell to meeting planners. A salesperson can schedule an appointment call to meet the meeting planner and learn his or her needs. After determining the meeting planner's needs, the salesperson can develop a presentation tailored to meet those needs and set up a presentation sales call. The techniques involved in a presentation sales call were discussed in detail in Chapter 4.

Exhibit 18.5 Sample Checklist for Meeting Planners

Marriott
HOTELS•RESORTS

Meeting Room Checklist

Determine the best setup for each of your functions.

_____

_____

_____

Are the available room sizes appropriate for your group size and proposed setups? _____

What obstructions must you plan for? _____

What are your requirements for podiums, platforms, audiovisual equipment, and other special equipment? _____

_____

What special arrangements must be made for signs/decorations? _____

_____

Determine the availability, source and cost of each of the following. If a price list is available, get it.

Microphones _____	*Overhead Projectors* _____
16-mm Film Projector _____	*Slide Projector and Carousel* _____
Remote Control _____	*Videotape Playback Equipment* _____
Computer/High Tech Equipment _____	*Tape Recorders* _____
Lectern _____	*Screen* _____
Flip Chart _____	*Blackboard* _____
Electric Pointer _____	*Chairs* _____
Tables and Skirting _____	*Risers* _____

Supplies* (pads, pencils, ashtrays, matches, water, glasses, telephones) _____

_____

Wastebaskets _____	*Lighting* _____
Outlets _____	*Temperature Controls* _____
Coat Rack _____	*Floral Arrangements* _____

Handicap Considerations _____

* *Marriott Hotels provide assorted candies and mints and pads and pencils in all meeting rooms.*

This checklist is one of a series created to assist inexperienced meeting planners in organizing successful meetings.

Courtesy of Marriott Hotels and Resorts.

Sales Blitzes   A sales blitz is essentially an intensive survey of a given geographic area over a specified time period. This time period is usually very short—one to three days is typical. Although the purpose of a sales blitz is largely to gather information, immediate business may be generated.

Planning is the key to a successful sales blitz. Most properties begin planning at least 30 days before the effort. If a blitz is new to a property, a one-day blitz may be planned as a learning experience before a more extensive blitz is undertaken.

A city directory is essential for planning a sales blitz, since sales routes should be carefully planned for the most effective use of time. Once sales routes have been mapped out, the names and addresses of individuals or companies to contact can be written on index cards and given to blitz participants along with a street map. In most cases, each person is assigned around 30 calls per day and makes approximately 90 to 100 calls over a three-day blitz period.

It is essential that blitz participants have an adequate supply of blitz survey sheets (see Exhibit 18.6) and such collateral materials as convention brochures and key chains or other low-cost specialty items. All specialty items should be imprinted with the property's name and telephone number.

Property salespeople, other members of the property's staff, or outsiders can take part in a sales blitz. A recently rediscovered and increasingly popular approach is to use hotel or marketing students to blitz an area. Nervous students can often get through doors that experienced salespeople cannot. Students should be given an indoctrination session and incentives for making calls. Incentives can range from reimbursement for out-of-pocket expenses (gas, parking, meals, etc.) to prizes or cash awards. Using students to blitz an area frees the property's sales staff to pursue other business or follow up on leads generated during the blitz.

Trade Shows   Just as a sales blitz may be an effective prospecting and selling tool for properties large and small, attendance at trade shows can help build a client base for all types of properties.

There are generally two types of trade shows. An exhibit show features booths that enable exhibitors to distribute materials and talk to buyers. A marketplace show offers a structured environment of scheduled appointments between buyers and sellers. Some of these shows are sponsored or attended by local convention and visitors' bureaus, and it may be possible for a property to share booth space and expenses with its local bureau.

At trade shows, a property's booth and personnel must accurately reflect the property's image and professionalism. Personnel should always be courteous, friendly, and informative, and the booth should be arranged to involve prospects. Many exhibitors make the mistake of setting tables across the front of their booth; it is usually more effective to place tables at the sides and back of the booth to draw people into the property's display. In addition, many exhibitors give too many items away. Since most buyers want to travel light, it may be better to show a video brochure or other audiovisual presentation and only give prospects a business card or small brochure.

A property's trade show representatives should make the best use of the time and money spent on the property's exhibit. In other words, the

Exhibit 18.6   Sample Sales Blitz Survey Sheet

Sales Blitz Survey Sheet

Organization_____

Address_____

_____Zip_____ Phone #_____

Contact_____ Title_____

Contact_____ Title_____

1. How many meetings do you have a year?_____ When?_____
   Size?_____ Who plans them?

Contact_____ Title_____

When is your next meeting?_____

Where are meetings usually held?_____

2. Do you have incoming visitors that require sleeping accommodations?
   Yes_____ No_____ How many per month? _____

   If yes, where are they housed?_____

   Do you reserve the room? Yes_____ No_____ (If not, who does?)

Contact_____ Title_____

3. Does your organization plan such things as:
   —Christmas Parties?   —Retirement Dinners?
   —Award Dinners?   —Other Social Events?

   Are you the organizer, or is there a social chairman?
   Yes___ No___ Contact_____

4. Are you, or any of your associates, affiliated with any other organizations or associations that might have need for meeting or banquet space?Yes___ No___

Name_____ Contact_____

Comments:

Taken by:_____ Date Taken_____

Survey sheets like this one are used to obtain information that will be used at a later date for personal sales calls if the prospect warrants a follow-up. An experienced sales blitz participant can complete approximately 30 of these forms a day, generating a wealth of information that may result in future business for the property.

Source: Howard Feiertag, "Blitzes and Sales Calls: Indispensible Selling Tools," HSMAI Marketing Review, Winter 1987, p. 24.

representatives should greet all prospects who walk into the property's booth, but quickly *qualify* them. Qualifying prospects ensures that a property representative doesn't spend too much time on someone just looking.

A representative can begin the qualifying process by asking "What types of meetings do you normally hold throughout the year?" or "Has your company ever booked a meeting at our hotel?" These questions can lead into other questions that will help the representative determine the prospect's needs and the prospect's influence over a meeting site decision. These additional questions can include: "How many people usually attend your meetings?" "What types of facilities are needed for your meetings?" "How do you decide where to hold meetings?" and "Who determines the location of your meetings?"

If the prospect's needs are compatible with the products and services the property offers, and if the prospect has some influence over the decision-making process, the representative should pursue the conversation further or invite the prospect to fill out a questionnaire. If the prospect is just looking, however, the representative may want to terminate the conversation as politely as possible and move on to another prospect.

Trade show booths and presentations should be directed to meeting planners rather than consumers. Meeting planners, like travel agents, need information. Guestroom sizes, types of accommodations, group rates, and convention services are the types of information important to association and corporate meeting planners.

Print Advertising

In addition to personal selling, properties also use print advertising to reach meeting planners. Properties can place ads in trade journals or magazines, or in the business or social sections of newspapers in key association and corporation feeder cities. In some instances, a property may be able to participate in advertising planned by its local convention and visitors' bureau. An entire destination area is usually featured in this type of advertising. Properties may increase their exposure by placing their own ads near the bureau's ad.

Other Sales Tools

The information theme should be carried through in direct mail and collateral materials. Meeting planners are not looking for romantic photographs; convention brochures and other direct mail pieces should feature room layouts and capacities, special services, and reservations information.

Since personal experience is a major factor in site selection, familiarization tours and public relations activities can also be effective sales tools. Public relations activities may include meeting planning seminars and social functions staged for various types of associations. "Ethnic days" or food festivals may draw local association members and meeting planners.

Conclusion

Although meeting planners can bring much-needed group meetings business to a property, dealing with meeting planners can sometimes be challenging. There are many professional meeting planners who are relatively easy to work with because they know the requirements of a business group and what it takes to put on a successful meeting. Other meeting planners are inexperienced, and some individuals, ranging from key executives to secretaries or associates, are called on to plan a meeting with no experience at all.

Almost all meeting planners, whether experienced or not, tend to be anxious about the meeting or convention they are responsible for. With their professional reputations at stake, it is understandable that most meeting planners are very concerned about a property's ability to stage a meeting and respond successfully to problems that may come up (many veteran meeting planners would change this to "problems that *will* come up"). That is why properties that sell their meeting planning experience and expertise, rather than just their meeting space, will be the most successful at selling to meeting planners.

Notes

1. Conventions and group business is discussed in depth in Leonard H. Hoyle, David C. Dorf, and Thomas J. A. Jones, *Managing Conventions and Group Business* (East Lansing, Mich.: Educational Institute of the American Hotel & Motel Association, 1989).
2. Laventhol & Horwath, *U.S. Lodging Industry—1988* (Philadelphia: Laventhol & Horwath, 1988).
3. Milton T. Astroff and James R. Abbey, *Convention Sales and Services*, 2nd ed. (Cranbury, New Jersey: Waterbury Press, 1988).
4. "The Meetings Market '85," *Meetings & Conventions*, 31 March 1986.
5. Associations and facts cited in this paragraph were found in Karin E. Koek and Susan Boyles Martin, editors, *Encyclopedia of Associations*, 22nd ed., vol. 1 (Detroit, Mich.: Gale Research Company, 1988).
6. "The Meetings Market '85."
7. "The Meetings Market '85."
8. "The Meetings Market '85."
9. This statement and many of the other facts cited in this section are from "The Meetings Market '85."

Discussion Questions

1. The group meetings market can benefit a property in what ways?

2. The group meetings market can be divided into which two segments?

3. Associations can be divided into what seven general categories?

4. What types of meetings business do associations generate?

5. What are some planning factors common to all association group meetings?

6. What is the average lead time for an association's annual convention?

Discussion Questions *(continued)*

7. Who are possible decision-makers for an association?

8. What are ten types of meetings corporations hold?

9. Who are possible decision-makers for corporate group meetings?

10. What are some ways hotels can pursue local group meetings business?

11. Who can participate in a sales blitz?

Chapter Outline

I.   International Travelers
     A.   The Decision-Maker
     B.   Meeting the Needs of International Travelers
     C.   Finding International Travelers
     D.   Reaching International Travelers
II. Honeymooners
     A.   The Decision-Maker
     B.   Meeting the Needs of Honeymooners
     C.   Finding Honeymooners
     D.   Reaching Honeymooners
III. Sports Teams
     A.   Football Teams
     B.   Baseball Teams
     C.   Basketball Teams
     D.   Other Teams
IV. Government Travelers
V.   Handicapped Travelers
VI. Other Specialty Markets
VII. Conclusion

19 Selling to Specialty Markets

While individual and group business and leisure travel are still the backbone of the hospitality industry, more and more properties are finding that they must solicit additional or specialty markets to ensure consistent occupancy. A property's ability to appeal to these sources of business will vary depending on the property's product and services, the property's location, and the specific needs of the property (the need for additional business on weekends or during the off-season, for example). There are a number of specialty markets that can be tapped. In this chapter, we will take a look at some of these markets, markets that can prove financially lucrative to a property willing to spend the time and money to research them and modify its products or services to meet their needs.

International Travelers

One of the fastest growing and most profitable specialty markets is the international traveler market. International travelers can be defined as travelers originating from points outside the United States, and are usually divided into three basic categories: North American travelers, European travelers, and other international travelers (Asian, Australian, African, and so on). According to a 1987 U.S. Lodging Industry report by Laventhol & Horwath, international travelers accounted for approximately 12% of total travel in the United States in 1986, and the market is continuing to expand.[1]

It is difficult to give a general profile of the international traveler. Visitors from different countries are interested in different attractions and have varying needs. But it is possible to define several patterns in this market:

1. *Point of origin.* Approximately 65% of international travelers visiting the United States come from Canada or Mexico, but this influx of North American travelers is on the decline, and the market may soon be dominated by Asian and European travelers. The most significant increases will be from the United Kingdom and Japan.

2. *Reasons for travel to the United States.* In recent years, the United States has been the most popular destination for British, French, and West Germans who planned to leave the European continent for vacation.[2] These travelers cited the quality of nightlife, shopping,

Industry Profile

Paddy Fitzpatrick
*Owner and Managing
Director
Fitzpatrick Hotel
Group, Dublin,
Ireland*

Paddy Fitzpatrick began his hotel career at the age of 18, when he took a practical hotel management course at the Gresham Hotel (where he subsequently became assistant manager). He later served as General Manager of the Old Ground Hotel in Ennis, Ireland, and the Managing Director of the Talbot Hotel in Wexford. Before opening his own hotel in Killiney in 1971, Fitzpatrick also worked as General Manager of the Doyle Group of Hotels. He is currently owner and Managing Director of Fitzpatrick Castle Hotel, Fitzpatrick Shannon Shamrock, Timesharing Ireland Limited, and Castle Transport & Marketing Services—the general sales agent for TWA in Ireland. His time-share complex was recently given the prestigious "Resort of International Distinction Award." Fitzpatrick has a worldwide reputation as Ireland's number one hotel ambassador. He is currently International Director of the Hotel Sales & Marketing Association International.

"I t is only when you study the trends of American marketing and sales that you realize the significant difference between the American and European approach. European hotels must look for business from the rest of the Continent and the world. Dealing with different languages and customs is a significant part of planning.

It's my impression that until recently the average American marketing and sales manager showed interest only in travelers originating from neighboring states. But with the development of air transport, and with the increasing number of international travelers coming to American shores, it's extremely necessary for American hotel salespeople to focus more attention on the international market.

What do international travelers look for in European hotels? The American visitor loves the mystique of history, and is fascinated by castles and the tracing of his or her ancestry. The English and Germans want outdoor sports and scenery; the French want luxury as well as scenery, fishing, and gourmet food. The Japanese come with their cameras, but thousands of them are also interested in playing golf and gambling.

Serving the international market requires a knowledge of the needs and expectations of many different types of visitors. The ability to attract this lucrative market is limited only by the salesperson's interest and imagination. **"**

and accommodations as reasons for visiting the United States. The devalued dollar also played a part in bringing Europeans and Asian travelers (mostly Japanese) to the United States, although the United States is considered a travel bargain regardless of the dollar's strength. Most international travelers cite the lower costs of U.S. goods and services as an important factor in vacationing in this country.

3. *Destinations.* European and Asian travelers have preferences in destinations. The Japanese tend to prefer large cities and like to stay in one spot rather than visit a number of cities. The French also tend to stay put, but favor cities that offer cultural events (theater, opera, etc.) and nightlife; California, Florida, New York City, and New Orleans are favorite destination spots for the French. Most other Europeans prefer smaller cities or vacation destinations featuring a number of attractions. The British favor destinations like the Grand Canyon and the Rocky Mountains. The Germans tend to tour a great deal or take beach vacations; Hawaii, Florida, and New York are among the destinations selected by these Europeans.[3]

4. *Length of stay.* The length of stay will depend on the type of international traveler.

Stays for individual leisure travelers usually range from three days to two weeks.

Individual business travelers are typically male and often travel on expense accounts, generating high expenditures per person. They usually stay from one to seven days. They often take vacation time at the conclusion of the business portion of the trip.

Group leisure travelers may account for short trips or long stays. First-time international visitors often travel in groups and usually prefer a two- to three-day stay. Seasoned international group travelers typically stay longer—up to two weeks or more.

Group business travelers generally stay from five to seven days and may bring spouses along if the purpose of the trip is a trade show or convention. Group business travelers may also include delegations touring factories or farms, groups traveling to international seminars, and groups stopping over en route home.[4]

The Decision-Maker

Since the international traveler market is so diverse, a property must appeal to a number of different decision-makers, including:

1. Individual guests
2. Local or foreign companies
3. Tour operators
4. Travel agents

Individual guests usually make travel decisions based on the purpose of the trip. If the trip is for business, the destination is predetermined, and only a property must be chosen. International business travelers tend to choose the familiar. They are likely to choose a chain property that operates in their home country over an unaffiliated resort or an independent property. Individual leisure travelers, on the other hand, are more likely to choose a property in close proximity to attractions of interest. Price is often of lesser importance to them. These travelers are willing to pay higher rates for special amenities or services or for a location close to attractions.

Local or foreign companies are often the decision-makers for individual or group business travelers. Local companies frequently make their decisions on the basis of credit arrangements; they will house foreign visitors in properties at which they have charge accounts. Foreign companies prefer to do business with familiar properties. They book into chain properties that operate in their home country, or contact the American company with whom they are doing business for a recommendation.

Tour operators usually make the lodging decisions for group leisure travelers. Tour operators look for a convenient location and good service. Locations easily accessible from main highways (for motorcoach tours) or airports (for air/ground packages) and areas that offer a number of attractions within a day's driving distance are favorite choices. Tour operators also want good service, and usually will return to a property that serves group meals promptly, blocks off rooms for the group, and offers discounts or all-inclusive rates (rooms, meals, taxes, tips, and so on, for one price).

Travel agents are influential in making lodging decisions for individual and group business and leisure travelers. Travel agents also look for a good location, but price plays a lesser part in selection. Since most travel agents work on a commission basis, they won't necessarily seek out the absolute lowest price, but their clients must feel they are getting value for their money. Travel agents insist on good service, and can serve as excellent sources of repeat business if previous clients have been treated well.

Tour operators and travel agents look for U.S. properties with amenities such as swimming pools and saunas (features not common in European hotels). Security may also play a part in their decision to book with a property. Operators and agents who cater to the Japanese market, especially, look for security. The Japanese are very concerned about their personal safety, and properties that offer safety deposit boxes or safes, well-lit grounds, and other security measures are attractive to them (see Exhibit 19.1).

Meeting the Needs of International Travelers

The needs of international travelers vary due to the great diversity of this market. But there are several areas of common concern:

- *Making reservations.* Whether reservations are made by an individual traveler or by a tour operator or travel agent, ease in booking is important. Properties can meet this need in a variety of ways: establish field offices in key feeder cities (Tokyo, London, Paris, Mexico City, etc.) that offer worldwide reservations services, use Telex machines and toll-free numbers, and create tie-ins with foreign air services.

- *Language barriers.* Many international travelers have difficulty communicating in English. While some international guests speak English quite well (Japanese businesspeople, for example, are usually fluent in English), others, including English-speaking guests from Britain and Australia, have trouble with our language, especially with slang. Hotels that cater to international guests can ease this problem by hiring a multilingual staff and providing multilingual menus and in-house signs. Another useful and appreciated solution is the printing of a "survival guide" in several languages. These booklets or brochures can serve as a directory of hotel services; give instructions on the operation of the phone system, television set, and air-conditioning unit; and give additional information which may make the visitor feel welcome.

- *Transportation to the hotel.* First-time international guests traveling by air often have difficulties with ground transportation to the property. Many properties offer complimentary limousine service or arrange with taxi companies to pick up international guests.

- *Methods of payment.* Many international visitors are unfamiliar with the American policy of prepayment for rooms. If possible, properties should explain payment policies before the trip.

    The property should willingly accept foreign traveler's checks or currency. Properties that accept foreign currency or provide currency exchange services, either in-house or through an agreement with a local bank, can realize a 6% to 10% profit as well as offer a much-needed service to their guests. Hotels can either employ an

Exhibit 19.1 Japanese Traveler Profile

- Typical Japanese travelers have a family income of over $50,000 per year. Thirty percent are first-time visitors to the United States; 87% book air transportation and lodging through travel agents; 87% use travel agents as information sources.

- Their visits are characterized by a short stay, with 79% returning to Japan within 10 days.

- They are probably the highest spenders per day of all international visitors. Japanese travelers spent $92 per person per day in the United States in 1986. The typical per-person budget for a 10-day trip to the United States is $4,000.

- The average adult visitor is around 31 years of age; 56% are between the ages of 18 and 44, with the largest percentage (35%) in the 25 to 34 age bracket.

- Japanese travelers are very security conscious and many cite their fear of crime and violence in the United States as a deterrent to selecting the United States as a travel destination.

- Fear of AIDS is fast becoming a major deterrent to the Japanese in selecting the United States as a country to visit, especially among parents of student travelers.

- The largest number of Japanese visitors arrive in August (some 11% of the annual total), followed by July, December, and September, with April recording the lowest number.

- The highest percentage (62.7%) visit only one state, followed by 21.4% visiting more than three states and 15.9% two states.

- The majority of Japanese outbound travel originates from the metropolitan Tokyo/Kanto areas (46%), with the Osaka/Kansai region producing some 17% and the Nagyo/Chubu district 11%.

Source: Laurence Price, "Selling and Serving the Japanese Traveler," *Lodging*, July/August 1987, p. 53.

exchange specialist who daily determines the value of foreign currency or arrange for this service through local banks. Foreign currency usually is sent to a bank each day and a check is returned to the property the following day.

- *Special appliances.* International travelers who bring such small appliances as electric shavers, hair dryers, and travel irons on their trips often have a problem with the U.S. voltage. Hotels can solve this problem by offering adapters in the room (or offering them for sale or rent in the gift shop) or by providing small appliances in the rooms.

Above all, hotels should make international guests feel at home. While some international travelers want a taste of adventure, others feel more comfortable with the familiar. They appreciate ethnic menu items and staff members who speak their language.

The Hilton Hotels Corporation is the leader in catering to Japanese travelers. The chain offers special amenities such as green tea for its Japanese visitors. The chain realizes the importance of staying in touch with Japanese guests after their stay, and sends cards or letters to Japanese visitors to further build guest loyalty.

The Sheraton Carlton Hotel in Washington, D.C., caters to a wide variety of international travelers. Located just two blocks from the White House,

Industry Profile

Jim McAllister
*Corporate Sales
Manager
Sage Hotels & Lodges*

After 13 years as a broadcast news director, Jim McAllister returned to college for a career change—and a degree in hotel management. As Corporate Sales Manager for Sage Hotels & Lodges in Boston, he is responsible for all the corporate accounts of four Boston-area properties: an airport property, a small meetings facility, a property in the heart of the medical community, and a fourth property adjacent to a large convention center. All are part of a rejuvenated city (one of the fastest growing markets in the country), and all appeal to a number of market segments.

"To reach and service the international market, sales and operations personnel alike must be of the same mind-set. As the Japanese and most Europeans have done already, we must learn a worldview. Only with the proper attitude will we be able to effectively attract and host the growing numbers of foreign visitors. This means learning new cultures, attempting new languages, and trying to understand the way these guests think.

The international market, most notably the Japanese segment, is still an underdeveloped market. A recently released report by the United States Travel and Tourism Administration says Japan, West Germany, the United Kingdom, and France are generating upwards of 14 million foreign travelers, and the numbers will only increase as we move into the 1990s.

Knowing what attracts—and repulses—this huge market, and determining similarities and differences among the various segments, will largely determine what percentage of the international market hoteliers can attract. To be effective hosts, we need to know and care about our guests. Abroad, we have the reputation of being ugly Americans; it's time to dispel this image at home. **"**

the property is situated in a popular destination area for travelers worldwide. The property's international flavor is enhanced by international time clocks which are prominently displayed. Foreign language newspapers, multilingual information brochures, and multilingual menus help travelers feel comfortable. The hotel also offers concierge service, a service prevalent in Europe, and provides on-call multilingual limousine drivers for its international guests.

Another property that depends on international visitors is the Registry Hotel in Minneapolis, Minnesota. Minneapolis is home to several large international companies (3M, Pillsbury, Control Data, etc.), and attracts a number of individual and group business guests from abroad. Employees must be fluent in at least one foreign language to work at the Registry. International travelers are further served by multilingual signs, the availability of electrical adapters, and a staff that is sympathetic to the international traveler's needs (see Exhibit 19.2).

Finding International Travelers

As we have mentioned, the familiar is important to many international travelers, so sometimes these travelers do not need to be solicited—they contact a U.S. hotel chain property after exposure to the chain's product overseas. Chains such as Holiday Inns, Quality Inns, and Sheraton are well-known abroad, and their worldwide reservations systems make it easy for international travelers to book into U.S. properties. Other properties have joined such consortiums as Preferred Hotels Worldwide to reap the benefits of worldwide recognition.

Exhibit 19.2   The International Traveler Market at a Glance

Location: Preferred property locations include gateway cities; locations near a number of attractions (cultural, recreational, geographic); proximity to hub airports (for air tours) or main highways (for motorcoach tours); near "natural wonders"—the Grand Canyon, Niagara Falls, etc.

Facilities: Preferred facilities include swimming pools, health clubs, Jacuzzis. Other desirable amenities include multilingual directional signs, gift shops that stock foreign cigarettes and other special items, multilingual menus, and security features—safety deposit boxes or safes, well-lit grounds, electronic door locks.

Price: Will depend on source of business. Tour operators look for low or discounted prices; travel agents want value but not necessarily the lowest price; individual and group demands vary—some international travelers look for budget accommodations, others want upscale accommodations.

Services: Preferred services include multilingual staff, bus parking, transportation from airport, group meals (for tour groups), currency exchange, "survival kits" printed in native languages, ethnic selections on restaurant menus, electrical adapters, concierge services, worldwide reservation services.

Decision-Makers: Individual guests, local or foreign companies, tour operators, travel agents.

Best Ways to Reach Market: Goodwill trips, personal contact, direct mail efforts, travel directory ads, ads in major international magazines and newspapers.

Most independent or small properties cannot boast this advantage, however, and must seek out international travelers. Sources of international business can sometimes be found right in a property's local community. Many schools and colleges or universities bring foreign exchange students or special study groups into the country. These institutions can also assist a property by providing translators and information about foreign customs.

Other local sources of prospects include service and fraternal clubs that may bring in international guests. The local chamber of commerce can provide information on local companies that do business with foreign firms. Many cities have "Sister City" programs that involve international visitors. Other cities may invite international guests for information exchanges, political symposiums, and so on. Properties can contact local ethnic groups to request the names of potential visitors such as students on scholarships or guest speakers from abroad.

On the state level, a property can often obtain information and potential contacts from state tourist agencies or from convention and visitors' bureaus. On the national level, a property has a number of resources: the United States Travel and Tourism Administration (USTTA), the Travel Industry Association of America (TIA), the American Hotel & Motel Association's International Travel Committee, and a number of industry associations. The names of other organizations that are involved in international travel are available in the public library in such references as *Encyclopedia of Associations* and *National Trade & Professional Associations*.

Reaching International Travelers

Since the international traveler market is so far-flung, an individual effort may be far too costly for a small to midsize property. Even larger properties may want to consider a cooperative effort when targeting international travelers. Cooperative efforts may involve affiliating the property with either a travel supplier (airline, tour group, etc.) or with an entire destination area's effort to reach overseas visitors.

Affiliation with a travel supplier may involve a number of options—from joint advertising to cooperatively offering complete package vacations or business trips. Some properties can offset the price of this type of promotion by supplying space or services to the travel supplier (convention rooms for a company convention, discounted rooms to airline crews, and so on).

Destination area efforts may be local in scope or part of a state or national campaign to attract international visitors. USTTA maintains regional marketing offices overseas. Properties can often promote their facilities through these outlets at a cost that is far less than an individual effort. State tourist agencies may also have programs to attract foreign visitors to a state or area; properties can advise these organizations of their interest in reaching the international market. Destination area efforts to reach international travelers may also include goodwill tours to "Sister Cities" overseas by municipal governments, convention and visitors' bureaus, or chambers of commerce.

Individual property efforts to reach international travelers typically involve many of the methods used to reach other markets: personal selling, participation in trade shows, advertising, direct mail, and public relations.

Personal selling often involves a hotel representative or "rep" who specializes in international sales. This rep may maintain a field office overseas, or may make goodwill tours to foreign travel agencies, corporations, and trade shows to promote the property. A property must be well-versed in national customs before choosing a rep to send to certain countries. In parts of the Middle East, for example, a property should always send a male representative.

Face-to-face contacts with foreign potential guests differ greatly from the face-to-face presentations common in our country. Whenever possible, presentations and written materials should be in the language of the country in which the presentation is taking place; business cards should show titles and other pertinent information in the prospect's native tongue. This is particularly important to the Japanese. Appointments are a must in many countries, especially with tour wholesalers and travel agents. In France, for example, the entire country "goes on vacation" in August, so drop-in calls at that time would be a waste of time and money.

There are other factors to consider when selling in person to international travelers. Spaniards and Italians, for example, tend to linger over negotiations, so it is unwise to schedule short appointments with them. The Japanese are masters at negotiation, and have the patience to wait long periods of time in order to have their demands met. In many cases, it is wiser to make personal contact with foreign potential guests through referral services or professional travel agents rather than directly contacting them.

Another way to reach international travelers is through *participation in trade shows* such as the Discover America International Pow Wow (sponsored by TIA) and the National Tour Association Marketplace. The latter show offers opportunities to reach tour brokers who arrange trips for international travelers. Travel agents can be reached through world congresses of the American Society of Travel Agents or through the International Tourism Exchange held annually in West Berlin. TIA and USTTA attend the

International Tourism Exchange. The names and locations of other shows can be obtained from USTTA or trade publications such as *Meetings & Conventions* and *Travel Weekly*.

Advertising in international markets can be extremely costly. Large hotel chains do most of the consumer advertising overseas. Small properties may find it feasible to advertise overseas if they advertise to the travel trade. Specialized "Visit USA" publications are targeted toward travel agents and tour brokers in a number of areas: *El Travel Agent Internacional* reaches travel professionals in Mexico, Central America, and South America; *Visit USA Guide* reaches travel professionals in Western Europe, Japan, Australia, South America, Mexico, and Canada.

Hotels can also reach overseas travel professionals through directory advertising in such publications as *OAG TRAVEL PLANNER Hotel & Motel RedBook* and *Hotel & Travel Index*. European travel agents seeking information about lodging facilities use hotel directories more than any other information source. A property's listing or ad should include specific information such as the proximity of an international airport or gateway city (a city with an airport that handles direct flights from other countries) and interesting facts about the local area. Such information makes it easier for the agent to make a recommendation.

If the property has a large enough advertising budget to target individual international travelers, there is the option of advertising in foreign newspapers. The names of these newspapers are usually available in the local library. It is often best to have advertising for international travelers developed by an advertising agency in the targeted country or countries.

Like advertising, *direct mail* efforts are more cost-effective when directed toward groups or travel professionals. Direct mail material should always be in the language of the recipients, preferably translated by a native of the country to which the letter will be sent.

Public relations can be an effective way to acquaint overseas travel professionals and individual travelers with a property. A property may send press releases to trade and consumer publications, or it may offer familiarization trips to international travel writers. Another avenue for publicity is the promotion of specialized services for international travelers. One hotel chain received extensive press coverage when it introduced an international traveler program which included a 24-hour translation service, currency exchange, multilingual directory, multilingual telephone information, multilingual staff, and 24-hour Telex service. Or a property can hold educational seminars or "international days" to promote the property's facilities and services and build foreign guest goodwill.

Creating goodwill seems to be the key to ensuring repeat business from international travelers. If a property can succeed at making international visitors feel at home, it may receive one of the most valuable forms of advertising available: word-of-mouth recommendations from satisfied guests.

Honeymooners

The number of people getting married is on the rise again, and since 98% of all newlyweds plan a honeymoon, this specialty market can prove to be an extremely profitable one for the hospitality industry.[5]

Honeymooners are often loyal guests. Many return to their honeymoon property for anniversary visits or recommend the property to friends. Favorite honeymoon destinations include Florida, Hawaii, California, Pennsylvania, and New York. Properties in other areas can appeal to this lucrative market if they can offer facilities that will help to create shared memories—the chief purpose of a honeymoon (see Exhibit 19.3).

Today's newlyweds are older (the average age of the bride is 24 years, while bridegrooms are usually 26 years of age), more sophisticated (many have traveled together before and are looking for "something different"), more affluent (many couples have been earning two paychecks for several years), and interested in activity as well as privacy. The fact that many couples are earning two incomes also means that honeymoons tend to be shorter, a trend that lends itself to special honeymoon weekend packages.

The Decision-Maker

The decision-maker for the honeymoon market is almost always someone in the wedding party itself—the bride and bridegroom play the most significant role, but they listen to suggestions from their parents and families as well as other members of the wedding party.

According to a recent survey, almost 70% of honeymooners now use the services of a travel agent—a figure that increased 45% in a four-year period! Of the couples surveyed, 51% had an exact destination in mind and 34% had a general idea of their destination, but 14% had no preference and were willing to rely on the recommendations of a travel agent when making a honeymoon decision.[6]

Meeting the Needs of Honeymooners

The average length of a honeymoon trip is one to two weeks. Some honeymoons last more than two weeks; some are as short as a weekend. But no matter what the length of stay, the typical honeymoon couple is looking for a romantic atmosphere, privacy, and a lot of activities at an affordable price.

Special packages are appealing to many honeymoon couples on a budget. An all-inclusive package—meals, accommodations, entertainment, sporting equipment, tips, and so on included in one price—is attractive to newlyweds who do not want to be bothered with details. Properties should keep in mind that honeymoon reservations are usually booked months in advance; honeymoon packages should be planned on a yearly schedule so that they may be promoted in plenty of time for honeymooners to consider them.

"Adventure" honeymoons have become more popular. More couples are taking art tours of Europe, archeological trips to Mexico, and safaris to Africa. U.S. properties still have the opportunity to capture business from these couples if the properties are located in a gateway city or in the city or town in which the wedding takes place. An overnight package with breakfast, complimentary champagne, and transportation to the airport or cruise ship can attract couples who will be honeymooning out of the country.

The honeymoon market has long been a mainstay in such places as the Pocono Mountains and Niagara Falls. In the lavish, four-season resorts of the Poconos, couples are treated to breathtaking scenery and rooms which feature plush carpeting, round or heart-shaped beds and bathtubs, and even in-room Jacuzzis in the shape of champagne glasses. Most of the honeymoons offered in the Poconos are available for a package price.

Exhibit 19.3 The Honeymoon Market at a Glance

Location: Preferred locations include getaway locations, gateway cities (for overseas or cruise ship travel), adventure locations.

Facilities: Preferred facilities include upgraded guestrooms or suites, special in-room amenities (Jacuzzis, round or heart-shaped beds, and so on), meaningful giveaways such as complimentary champagne in "take-home" glasses, recreational amenities.

Price: Honeymooners may prefer anywhere from economy to upscale accommodations, although most couples will spend in the medium to high ranges. Inclusive-price packages are popular with this specialty market.

Services: Preferred services include free continental breakfasts in bed, limousine service.

Decision-Makers: Traditionally the bride and bridegroom and their immediate families. Today, couples are more apt to seek advice from couples who have traveled or from travel agents.

Best Ways to Reach Market: Tie-ins with department stores or bridal boutiques, bridal fairs at the property, personal contacts, ads in consumer magazines.

Finding Honeymooners

Watching for engagement announcements in local newspapers is an excellent way to develop honeymoon market leads. Hotels can also find honeymooners by participating in the bridal promotions of local department stores or specialty boutiques. These sources can provide names of prospective brides and may also accept property advertising or participation in a bridal fair. If bridal fairs are not held in the local area, a property can stage its own event.

Since so many couples are now using travel agents for their honeymoon arrangements, it is essential that hotels not overlook these important travel intermediaries. It is especially effective to invite travel agents to tour the property during a bridal fair. In that way, the agents would have an opportunity to experience the facilities and dining offered as part of a honeymoon package.

Reaching Honeymooners

The two most effective means of reaching the honeymoon market are direct mail and advertising. Direct mail includes letters of congratulation to couples whose engagement announcements have appeared in newspapers, and invitations to special events at the property. Properties can also send direct mail pieces to travel agents; these pieces are more effective if they include all-inclusive honeymoon packages.

Advertising in newspapers and magazines can build a property's honeymoon business (see Exhibit 19.4). If the property is located in a popular destination spot, ads can be placed in newspapers in key feeder cities. Special interest magazines such as *Modern Bride* are excellent for attracting this market.

Other ways to reach this lucrative market include such public relations efforts as letting the couple experience the property for themselves during a "Champagne Brunch" or a personal tour of the property. Inviting the society writers of local newspapers to property functions encourages good coverage of the property and may lead to personal recommendations. Creating a unique honeymoon package or offering a special honeymoon package as a

Exhibit 19.4   Sample Honeymoon Ad

prize in local or national contests or on game shows may also generate publicity for the property.

Sports Teams

Another way to meet the challenge of filling guestrooms is to target sports teams. Professional, college, or local sports teams can provide a year-round opportunity to properties that can meet the needs of these groups (see Exhibit 19.5).

Football Teams   Football teams business can be generated by visiting high school teams in town for one night, college players in league games or tournaments, and professional teams in regular season games or the Super Bowl. The most important factor in attracting any of these teams is *location*. If a property can

Exhibit 19.5   The Sports Team Market at a Glance

Location: Preferred locations are within a 20- to 30-minute drive of the sports arena; close proximity to airport or major highway.

Facilities: Preferred facilities provide guestroom blocks; group function rooms; small meeting rooms; 24-hour room service or late-night restaurants; extra amenities such as game room, sauna, or swimming pool; secure storage facilities for equipment.

Price: Non-professional teams usually look for low rates; professional teams will pay higher rates. Professional and amateur sports teams look for group rates and complimentary rooms for the head coach and business manager.

Services: Preferred services include discount clubs; preregistration; late check-out; maps of shortest route to playing site; complimentary newspapers; ability to meet dietary requirements and to serve group meals on time; availability of box lunches for teams traveling by road; team welcome, including signs or banners (with permission of head coach); bus parking if needed; wake-up service; bill ready at time of departure; after-stay follow-up.

Decision-Makers: Coaches, athletic directors, athletic business managers.

Best Ways to Reach Market: Personal contacts, direct mail, advertisements in college magazines, consumer newspaper advertising to attract fans.

offer a location within 20 to 30 minutes of where the game will be played, it has a good chance to sell to this market. After this need has been met, other needs of football teams can be addressed. For most professional teams, this means service, food, and rates, in that order.

Professional football teams expect the best in service. Properties that serve this market (Marriott, Holiday Inns, and Ramada lead the field) have identified several key needs:

1. *Personal greeting.* Most properties assign someone to meet the team and attend to any special needs. This service not only makes the team feel welcome; it also makes a good impression on the head coach (who doesn't need additional hassles).

2. *Efficient registration.* Most properties receive a rooming list within five days of the team's arrival. The team is usually housed in one wing or in a quiet area away from other groups. Guestroom keys are made available to the head coach or someone else on the coaching staff for distribution to the players.

3. *Team functions.* Most professional football teams require an arrival dinner and several other meals (pre-game meal, post-game meal, breakfast, and so on). Arrangements for these meals should be made well in advance to allow for special dietary requirements. In addition to following instructions for menus, the property should serve ample portions and allow extra space at tables because of the large size of the players.

4. *Meeting rooms.* Most professional football teams require at least three meeting rooms and a room for taping the players before the game. There is usually a meeting of the whole team at which a film of the competition is shown. This may be followed by two smaller

meetings (usually groups of 35 to 50 people) of the offensive and defensive squads.

The taping room can be set up the morning of the game, and should be equipped with two eight-foot tables approximately 12 inches off the floor. This can be accomplished by placing wooden blocks under the tables (table legs are left folded up). This arrangement eases the strain on the trainers, and is a gesture that will usually be appreciated and remembered.

5. *Other services.* Many properties welcome the team with an outside sign or a sign on the lobby function board, but this must be approved by the head coach. It is also wise to check with the head coach to determine if players may have phone calls or visitors, and if there are any food restrictions (no food after 10:00 p.m., and so on). Many properties also offer a complimentary room to the head coach, provide daily newspapers to coaches and players, and offer box lunches to teams that are traveling by bus or car.

College football teams have similar requirements, although they do not expect the VIP treatment extended to professional players. Rates may be more important to these teams than service, since many college football teams operate on a limited budget. But college football teams can generate good business, especially when the property offers special fan packages to supporters traveling to cheer their team on.

Football teams can be a good source of revenue, but it is important to contact the decision-makers well in advance of the season. Most collegiate schedules are available in January. Properties can contact coaches, athletic directors, or athletic business managers by either obtaining names from the College Directory of Athletics or by making contacts at the College Athletic Business Managers' Association convention which meets in January. Properties must be a member of the association to exhibit at this meeting. Professional teams can be directly contacted by phone or direct mail, or through inquiries to the respective leagues.

Baseball Teams

While professional football teams only play approximately 20 games each year, American League and National League baseball teams play 162 regular season games each year. Baseball teams stay in hotels an average of two to four nights at a time,[7] as opposed to the one- or two-night stays of football teams. The professional baseball leagues are actively involved in hotel negotiations and recommend certain hotels after a bidding process has been completed. Although baseball teams make their own lodging decisions, most teams follow the recommendations of their league. There is also an opportunity for properties to tap into the business generated by minor league teams.

The needs of professional baseball teams differ from those of professional football teams. While most football teams focus on group functions and meals, group functions for baseball players are rare, and most of the time players are on their own when it comes to meals. Properties that offer 24-hour room service and a number of restaurants are popular with baseball teams, as are properties that are close to other restaurants and attractions.

College baseball teams, in contrast, often request group meal functions, which vary depending on the time of arrival and the game schedule. As with football teams, there may be dietary restrictions before a game, and it is best to have pre-arranged menus when serving this group.

Baseball teams may be solicited through minor and major league offices and through the athletic departments of colleges and universities. Package deals for fans may be advertised through travel agents or in newspapers in the locale of the visiting team.

Basketball Teams

While basketball teams typically use fewer rooms than football or baseball teams, they still offer the potential for increased room occupancies, especially when tournament play is involved. Tournaments are held on the professional, collegiate, and high school levels, and typically involve extended team stays as well as rooms and food and beverage business from fans.

When targeting basketball teams, it is important to remember that the average basketball player is well over six feet tall and may require an oversize bed, high ceilings, and additional leg room when meetings are a part of the team's stay.

Basketball teams can be solicited through league offices (schedules are available in June) or through collegiate athletic departments.

Other Teams

Major universities and colleges participate in a number of other sports—hockey, soccer, tennis, cross country, and track. There are professional teams in a number of these sports as well. Most of these sports teams require guestrooms when visiting other cities. Properties wishing to sell to these teams can make contacts through the appropriate professional leagues or through college athletic offices.

Still other opportunities to tap into America's fascination with sports include servicing tournaments—both amateur and professional—in such sports as bowling, tennis, boxing, and swimming. Information on events and dates can be obtained by writing to sports associations such as the United States Tennis Association and U.S. Swimming Inc.

Many properties are finding the sports teams market so lucrative that they are developing special clubs that offer discount rates to teams and fans alike (see Exhibit 19.6). Days Inns, for example, offers a Sports Plus Club that includes team discounts, rental car discounts, free local phone calls, late checkout, and room blocks, and has recently invited athletic administrators and coaches to join its sports advisory board. Winegardner & Hammons, Inc., a hotel management company, promotes a "We Promise" Sports program available at such properties as Holiday Inns, Quality Suites, Radisson hotels, and Comfort Inns.

Government Travelers

Federal, state, and local governments provide numerous opportunities for properties to increase room occupancies throughout the year. There are thousands of government agencies that require out-of-town travel to conduct business.

One of the factors that has held many properties back in the government traveler market is the complexity of soliciting government business. Another factor is the assumption of many properties that every piece of government

Exhibit 19.6   Discount Rates for Sports Teams

Some hotel chains offer discount rates for sports teams, coaches, recruiters, and fans. This flier for Holiday Inns' Sports Rate program details the benefits of the program and provides an application form.

Courtesy of Holiday Inns, Inc.

business automatically goes to the lowest bidder. By law the federal government must give every potential supplier a hearing, but the final decision is not made on the basis of cost alone. The final decision is also based on the property's ability to contribute to the efficiency and effectiveness of government operations. In other words, government officials are not necessarily looking for the lowest rates; they want value, but they are also looking for quality accommodations and service.

In order to compete for the opportunity to bid for government business, a property should be aware of the requirements involved in establishing a business relationship with the government. A property should also be aware of how expense money is allocated to government travelers.

Straight per diem is a dollar figure allocated to cover lodging, meals, local transportation, and gratuities when government employees travel on official business. This is the most common type of per diem. The amount of money allocated is based on the Consumer Price Index of the city or area the government employee is traveling to. This amount will vary from year to year.

Actual and necessary per diem is a maximum amount that can be spent regardless of location, and is usually equal to or higher than the straight per diem rate. This rate is usually given to upper-level government employees.

Contract per diem is the most complex of the pricing arrangements, and incorporates the total cost of accommodations, meals, gratuities, travel expenses, etc. For example, a government agency might want to use a hotel to stage a training program. The agency would put out the program requirements for bid. Private companies or consultants would analyze the requirements and submit a bid for the entire estimated costs, including lodging fees.

Per diems offered to state and local government employees often fall short of those offered to federal government employees. State and local employees often incur more non-reimbursable expenses, and will be more likely to choose a property that offers low rates.

If a property is interested in selling to this specialty market, it has several options. The first, of course, is direct mail contact with various government agencies and officials (names and addresses may be located in government directories available in local libraries). A direct mail package should contain a special government rate sheet or brochure or offer an opportunity for a member of the agency to visit the property.

Advertising can also be used to reach government agencies and officials (see Exhibit 19.7). The Sheraton chain, for example, launched a successful ad campaign in *The Government Executive* magazine, but only after more than three years of research.

Handicapped Travelers

It is estimated that slightly more than 15% of the U.S. population can be defined as handicapped.[8] There are three main divisions of this group: the mobility impaired (confined to a wheelchair), the hearing impaired, and the visually impaired. These physical impairments do not prevent the handicapped from traveling. In 1984, over half of the handicapped population traveled on vacation.[9] That number is expected to increase as the hospitality industry becomes more aware of the needs of this specialty market (see Exhibit 19.8).

The special needs of handicapped travelers will vary, of course, depending on the type of handicap. But there are two basic ways in which

Exhibit 19.7   Sample Ad for the Government Market

FROM PARIS TO PEORIA...
FOR GOVERNMENT RATES, WORLDWIDE,

CALL 1-800-HOLIDAY.

One easy toll-free number, 1-800-HOLIDAY, is all it takes for Government Rates information and reservations. We have over 1200 participating Holiday Inn® hotels in 32 countries. And you can guarantee your reservations and Government Rates with the same call!

Worldwide Government Rates, 1-800-HOLIDAY, and convenient locations are just some of the

reasons why more Government travelers choose Holiday Inn hotels than any other hotel chain in the world!

Government Rates rooms are limited and subject to availability, so make your travel plans early!

hospitality operations can meet the special needs of all handicapped travelers: removing physical barriers and improving the training of employees.

The removal of physical barriers does not necessarily mean just adding ramps and widening doors. While these improvements will help the mobility impaired, they mean little to hearing impaired or visually impaired guests. Visually impaired guests can be better served through directories and menus

Exhibit 19.8   The Handicapped Traveler Market at a Glance

Location: Preferred locations depend on reason for traveling.

Facilities: Preferred facilities may depend on the type of handicap:

- *Mobility impaired travelers* prefer nearby parking spaces, ramps into property, self-opening doors into lobby, grab bars in hallways and in restrooms, wider doors to rooms, swimming pools adapted for the handicapped.
- *Hearing impaired travelers* prefer special telecommunications systems; amplified phones; Visual Alert Systems (VAS) to signal telephones ringing, visitors at door, or emergencies.
- *Visually impaired travelers* prefer braille labels on elevators, menus, and directories printed in braille; property information available on audiocassette.

Price: Like other guests, the price handicapped travelers are willing to pay for accommodations will vary depending on the reason for travel and other personal factors.

Services: The most important service properties can offer is a staff sensitive to the needs of handicapped guests but not solicitous.

Decision-Makers: Individual guests, corporate meeting planners, tour operators, travel agents.

Best Ways to Reach Market: Typical avenues used to reach any guest. Consumer or trade advertising may mention special facilities for handicapped guests. Public relations efforts may include tie-ins with organizations that assist the handicapped, such as Easter Seals and the Muscular Dystrophy Association.

printed in braille, raised room numbers, and braille labels in elevators. Visually impaired guests will also appreciate having the housekeeping staff clean around items that they have left in the room.

Properties are meeting the needs of hearing impaired guests by offering amplified phones, special telecommunications services, and Visual Alert Systems (VAS). VAS includes sound-sensitive lights that let hearing impaired guests know when someone is at the door, or that the telephone is ringing, or that there is an emergency such as a fire.

Handicapped travelers can also be attracted by a courteous and thoughtful staff. Employees should be sensitive but not solicitous when dealing with the handicapped. Chains such as Holiday Inns, Sheraton, Hilton, Best Western, Ramada, and Hyatt have implemented employee training programs, but a property does not have to be a member of a chain to train employees in the proper way to serve handicapped guests. Information is available from organizations such as the Society for the Advancement of Travel for the Handicapped, or from local organizations for handicapped people.

There are several ways a property can reach handicapped travelers. The property can indicate its ability to serve handicapped travelers in its consumer ads to business and leisure travelers and its trade ads to tour operators and travel agents. Other options include direct mail (names can be obtained from directories of associations for the handicapped in key feeder cities or from referral sources) and public relations and publicity. Many properties find it rewarding to affiliate themselves with such organizations as Easter

Seals, United Cerebral Palsy, and the United Way. Properties that sponsor events (fund-raisers, Special Olympics, and so on) with these organizations may receive favorable publicity. A property can also contribute a lump sum to these organizations or donate a contribution based on a special sales promotion.

Other Specialty Markets

In this section we will take a quick look at other specialty markets which can increase occupancies and revenues:

- Travel crews
- Movie crews
- Military personnel
- Sequestered juries

Travel crews include airline personnel, train crews, and bus drivers. Travel crews often have layovers or waiting time between trips. Stays usually range from one to three days. This market can be reached by contacting local or national corporate offices or by offering a discount to travel crew members who recommend the property to their counterparts.

Movie crews typically stay on location from six to ten weeks, generating rooms and food and beverage business—and publicity for the property if a movie star is involved in the production. Movie crews usually require 40 to 70 guestrooms and 4 to 6 rooms for office facilities. Rooms for the crew should be similar (usually with one double bed), while special accommodations must be provided for the movie stars and the producer, director, and executive secretary. Room rates are usually discounted somewhat in consideration for the amount of business the production brings to the property; office space is ordinarily offered free of charge. In addition, such special amenities as flowers for the cast and free newspapers are often included.

In order to reach this market, a property can contact its state movie commission or convention and visitors' bureau as well as make personal contact with movie production offices. Familiarization tours are an excellent way to showcase the property to producers. Producers usually are the decision-makers regarding shooting locations and hotel accommodations.

Military personnel stationed at nearby military bases offer the potential for increased weekend room occupancies. A property can offer a weekend package at discounted rates to military personnel as well as their out-of-town guests. Properties can promote these packages in base newspapers or newsletters, property fliers, and direct mail.

Properties located near courthouses have the option of serving *sequestered juries*. The needs of this specialty market will be determined in part by the sheriff of the county involved or by an appointed court official. In most cases, the jurors, officer of the court, and other court personnel must be housed on one floor for security reasons, and telephones, television sets, and newspapers must be removed from rooms. Sequestered juries must have no contact with hotel employees. All arrangements for meals and transportation are made through the officer of the court.

Conclusion

Most hotels have many markets to which they can sell. Obviously, a hotel cannot precisely fit the needs of every possible market, so hotels focus on satisfying the needs of their principal markets. Frequently, however, demand from these principal markets does not keep hotel occupancies at an acceptable level year-round, and a strong effort must be made to seek out new guests.

International travelers, honeymooners, sports teams and their fans, government travelers, handicapped travelers, and other specialty markets offer an excellent opportunity for increased room occupancies—and profits—to properties that have the time and budgets to research and sell to these markets. As today's hospitality industry becomes increasingly competitive, specialty markets will become even more important. Properties that have taken the initiative in targeting these markets will be in a position to capture their share of the billions of dollars in revenues that specialty markets generate.

Notes

1. Laventhol & Horwath, *U.S. Lodging Industry—1987* (Philadelphia: Laventhol & Horwath, 1987).
2. Bob Gatty, "U.S. Top Euro Tourist Spot," *Hotel and Motel Management*, March 1985, p. 1.
3. Laurence Price, "Selling and Serving the Japanese Traveler," *Lodging*, July/August 1987, p. 52.
4. Some of the facts and figures in this section were taken from two publications by the American Hotel & Motel Association: *The Care and Feeding of Guests from Abroad*, and *The World is Your Market*.
5. Barbara Koeth, "More Marriages Spur Record Honeymoon Spending," *Tour & Travel News*, December 1987. Figures based on *Modern Bride's* 1986/1987 survey of 4,000 prospective brides. Over 632,000 couples traveled within the United States on honeymoons in 1986/87, spending an average of $1,200 per couple.
6. Coleman Lollar, "How to Book Clients Happily Ever After," *ASTA Travel News*, vol. 50, 15 December 1981, p. 63.
7. Thomas S. Yorke, "Sports Groups, Teams and Tournaments," *HSMAI Marketing Review*, Summer 1982, p. 13.
8. "Accommodating the Handicapped Traveler," Information Kit 280, compiled by the American Hotel & Motel Association's Information Center.
9. "Accommodating the Handicapped Traveler."

Discussion Questions

1. The majority of international travelers to the United States come from what two countries?

2. Why is the United States a popular destination for international travelers?

3. What are some typical lodging needs of international travelers? How are lodging properties meeting these needs?

Discussion Questions *(continued)*

4. What are some ways to find potential international travelers?

5. What percentage of honeymooners use the services of a travel agent?

6. What are some ways to find honeymoon business?

7. What are several key needs of professional football teams?

8. What is a straight per diem?

9. What are three main divisions of handicapped travelers?

10. How are properties attempting to meet the special needs of handicapped travelers?

Appendix
Sample Sales Presentation

The following is a simplified example of a sales presentation. Keep in mind the information you learned in Chapter 4 as you evaluate the salesperson's presentation and answer the questions at the end of the presentation.

Sales Situation

The Regency Hotel is attempting to book the annual meeting of the Business and Professional Women's Association. A member of the association is planning the meeting and investigating possible meeting sites; a committee will make the final selection decision. The annual meeting will be over a three-day period: a Friday through Sunday in May of next year.

Profile of the Hotel

The Regency Hotel is a high-rise, mid-priced, full-service hotel. Guest accommodations are divided into 300 standard guestrooms and 40 suites, all opening onto a central atrium. The hotel is situated on land which borders the largest river in the state. The location is halfway between the airport and the downtown business district, conveniently near a freeway exit.

Food and beverage facilities include a gourmet steak and seafood restaurant, a coffee shop, an atrium lounge, banquet service for up to 500 people, and 24-hour room service. Security features include electronic door locks for guestrooms and an attached parking garage with continuous video monitoring on each level.

All guestrooms have desks, areas suitable for dining, and separate sitting areas. There are phones on the desks as well as next to the beds. Bathrooms feature hair dryers, vanities, makeup mirrors, large towels, and a package of name-brand personal amenities (soap, shampoo, and so on). Every room has skirt hangers, a mini-bar, and a coffee machine. A free local newspaper is left at the door every morning. Suites have the same features as the guestrooms in addition to kitchenettes and separate bedrooms.

The hotel's primary market on weekdays is the business traveler, with families the primary market on weekends. Average occupancy runs 75% on weekdays and 52% on weekends. Average guestroom rate is $78.

Profile of the Prospect

The meeting planner is Ms. Penny Planner. She has been with the association for three years and has handled this meeting for the last two. Initial knowledge of the group came from Ms. Carol Law, the hotel's consulting lawyer and a member of the subject association. During a break in a recent hotel staff meeting, Ms. Law mentioned the upcoming annual meeting of this association to the hotel's marketing director. The marketing director asked a salesperson on the staff, Mr. Sam Salesperson, to investigate the possibilities.

Mr. Salesperson obtained background information about the association and asked Ms. Law about the location of previous meetings, the key personnel involved, and specific problems encountered in previous meetings. His prospect research revealed the following.

Locations of last two annual meetings:

1. Last year—upstate mountain resort. Time of year—April. Major problems: (1) poor weather limited use of outside recreational facilities—few alternative activities available due to remote location; (2) difficult to understand speakers due to noise and poor acoustics; and (3) slow management response to problems.

2. Two years ago—downtown hotel in the same city as the Regency. Time of year—May. Major problems: (1) mediocre service by employees; and (2) noisy guestrooms (airport nearby) and meeting/banquet rooms (noise from kitchen).

Size of meetings—approximately 200 attendees.

Pre-Presentation Planning

Mr. Salesperson sent a letter and a hotel brochure to Ms. Planner, requesting a meeting to discuss the possibility of using the Regency for the association's annual meeting. He followed up the letter with a phone call to set the date and time for Ms. Planner to visit the property.

He did the following before Ms. Planner's tour of the property:

1. Had his secretary call Ms. Planner's secretary to ask about Ms. Planner's travel schedule and what other properties she might be considering.

2. Sent a memo to all department heads explaining that Ms. Planner would be doing a walk-through on Thursday afternoon and requesting that the word be passed on.

3. Prepared a worksheet which listed the property's features and how they could benefit the prospect.

4. Studied the rooms forecast and budget for May and discussed negotiation limits on price concessions with the marketing director.

5. Contacted the convention service manager, Ms. Sally Service, and asked her to:

    a. Be available for the tour and presentation

    b. Schedule the sales interview in her office and have refreshments on hand

    c. Set up a typical schoolroom configuration for 50 people in one of the meeting rooms

    d. Set up audiovisual equipment in the banquet room with a videotape showing various table arrangements and decorations used in the banquet room by past groups

6. Familiarized himself with what was currently in-house in terms of functions so he would know what rooms were available to show.

7. Had the front desk hold keys to specific guest-rooms and suites.

8. Set up a signboard in the lobby to welcome Ms. Planner.

9. Had the hotel limousine pick up Ms. Planner at the airport.

Sales Call Objective

To obtain a commitment from Ms. Planner to recommend the Regency Hotel to the association's selection committee.

Sales Presentation

SALESPERSON: [Meets Planner in the lobby, extends hand and smiles.] Good afternoon, Ms. Planner. I'm Sam Salesperson, the sales manager for the Regency Hotel.

PLANNER: [Accepts handshake with a solemn look on her face.] Hello. Nice to meet you.

SALESPERSON: If you'll come with me, I'd like to show you our Convention Service office. [Escorts Planner to the service manager's office.] Ms. Planner, I'd like you to meet Sally Service. She's the convention service manager who would coordinate the activities for your meeting. Sally, this is Ms. Penny Planner. [Planner and Service shake hands and smile.]

PLANNER: How do you do?

SERVICE: Pleased to meet you. May I offer you something to drink? [Indicates the refreshment table.]

PLANNER: No, thank you.

SERVICE: Then please have a seat. [Gestures to the appropriate chair. Planner and Service are seated in easy chairs next to each other, with Salesperson seated facing them. In the middle is a small, low table to provide a platform for drinks and the presentation notebook.]

SALESPERSON: Ms. Planner, I'd like to begin by briefly explaining the concept of a service manager as we use it at the Regency Hotel. When we book an important meeting such as yours, we always assign one of our service managers to be the primary contact for the meeting planner and key meeting members. Sally will be available to you for coordination and problem-solving from the time we sign the contract until the meeting is satisfactorily concluded. We've been quite responsive to groups such as yours in the past with this system, and I'm sure you'd be pleased with us. [Confident smile.] If I may, I'd like to ask you a few questions about your meeting to be sure we understand your requirements.

PLANNER: Okay.

SALESPERSON: First, what are the exact dates for your meeting?

PLANNER:	May 2nd through the 4th, next year. [Service begins taking notes.]
SALESPERSON:	And what are the primary services you'll require?
PLANNER:	We'll need a banquet hall capable of handling 200 persons comfortably for a sit-down dinner. And we'll need a podium and excellent audio capability for our guest speaker. We'll need at least four smaller meeting rooms big enough for 30 to 75 people, with audiovisual capabilities in each room. In addition to the sit-down dinner, we'd like to have a buffet arrangement two or three times during our stay.
SALESPERSON:	[Thinks, "So far, so good."] We can meet those requirements easily. In addition to our excellent guestrooms, we have many suites available. How many of those would you want us to block?
PLANNER:	We'll need anywhere from 5 to 20 suites, depending on the response from our more prominent members. Can you handle that many?
SALESPERSON:	[Smiles.] Definitely. We have 40 suites.
PLANNER:	[Smiles—finally.] I don't think we'll need that many.
SALESPERSON:	Would you mind telling us if your group has had any problems with meetings in the past?
PLANNER:	Not at all. We had a few problems come up last year, and I found it difficult to get the hotel's management to respond quickly to them. I was also quite disappointed with the acoustics in the meeting rooms. Another problem in recent years has been the weather. Our attendees like to relax, swim, and sun during their free time, but it seems to always rain on the dates of our meetings. Obviously that's not the hotel's fault; but you asked about our past problems.
SALESPERSON:	I'm sure you'll find that none of those problems will arise this year in our hotel. If I may, I'd like to give you a tour and show you some of our guestrooms and meeting facilities. Shall we? [Rises from his chair and starts towards the door, with a gesture for Planner and Service to follow.]
PLANNER:	[Rises to join Salesperson.] I'd like that. [Tour begins with a walk through the atrium area, past the restaurant entrances.]
SALESPERSON:	We're very proud of our atrium. It brings an outdoors feeling into the hotel, even on days when the weather doesn't allow full use of our beautiful grounds. The atrium lounge always provides a bright and friendly atmosphere. We have two excellent restaurants to choose from. This is the Gourmet Room, which can accommodate over 100 people. And here is our coffee shop, which can handle up to 185 guests. [Opens the banquet room door for Planner to enter.] This is our banquet room. We can comfortably serve as many as 500 people for a dinner such as you will have. For smaller groups, we have movable walls to make the room fit the size of the group more comfortably. Does this room meet the needs of your group?
PLANNER:	I think so, but it's hard to picture how it would look all set up.
SALESPERSON:	If you'll follow me, I think I can give you a better idea of the different arrangements we've used in the past. We have a demonstration videotape for just that purpose. [Walks over to audiovisual equipment and plays videotape.] Did that help you picture your group in this room?
PLANNER:	Yes, it helped considerably.
SALESPERSON:	[Walks to the podium.] Let me demonstrate the room's sound characteristics. [Gestures for Planner to join him.] We have controls on the podium for all the lighting and audiovisual functions in the room. And, as you can see, they are clearly marked for identification.

	Sally will gladly provide instruction for their use to everyone who'll use the podium. [Gestures toward the center of the room.] If you'll move to the center of the room, I'll turn on the audio system. [Turns on the system and speaks into the microphone.] The sound quality is excellent. Don't you agree?
PLANNER:	Yes, it's fine.
SALESPERSON:	[Turns off the sound system.] Our kitchen is behind those barriers. [Points.] The barriers eliminate the noise from that area. And these walls are all designed to keep out noise from outside the room. Our most recent meeting was by Clingaman Corporation last week. Their CEO commended us on the acoustical quality of the room. [Walks toward the exit.] Do you think it will satisfy your group?
PLANNER:	[Writes on her notepad.] It seems to be adequate. [The tour continues to a meeting room.]
SALESPERSON:	[Enters.] This is one of four meeting rooms which can be adjusted with portable walls to accommodate up to 100 persons. We are the only hotel in the city with this capability. This room is set up for a group of 50, which we estimated you would require. We have a rear-projection room behind each meeting room that's capable of handling all types of projection equipment. [Gestures.] Would you like a demonstration?
PLANNER:	That won't be necessary.
SALESPERSON:	This meets your requirements also?
PLANNER:	Yes.
SALESPERSON:	[Exits the room.] Then let's take a look at our guestrooms and suites. [They make their way to a standard guestroom. Salesperson unlocks the door with an electronic key card.] As you can see, we utilize electronic locks which are encoded at the front desk when guests check in. Are you familiar with this security feature? [Planner nods her head.] All our rooms have desks, dining areas, and separate sitting areas for after-meeting work sessions or discussions. [Gestures into the bathroom.] Our bathrooms are luxurious and well-lit, with lots of mirrors for ease in making up. Did you notice that we list free personal amenities in the brochure I sent you?
PLANNER:	Yes.
SALESPERSON:	We feel this helps our guests plan their packing so they can leave the items they won't need at home and travel lighter. I'm sure your members would value that, aren't you?
PLANNER:	Yes. [They exit the room.]
SALESPERSON:	[Enters a suite.] Our suites have the same features as the guestrooms, but they also have kitchenettes and separate bedrooms. [Gestures.] All our sleeping rooms are quiet because of good insulation and the fact that we're out of the airport traffic pattern, in spite of our proximity to the airport itself. Do you think this suite would be satisfactory for your VIP members?
PLANNER:	I think so.
SALESPERSON:	[Exits the suite.] Great! Then let's go back to Sally's office and talk over any questions or concerns you might have. [Salesperson thinks, "This is a piece of cake!"]
SERVICE:	[Salesperson, Planner, and Service enter the office.] What do you think of our hotel?
PLANNER:	[Noncommittally:] It's very nice.
SERVICE:	Are you ready for something to drink yet?
PLANNER:	Yes, please. I'd like a caffeine-free Diet Coke if you have one. [Salesperson thinks, "I hope we have that!"]

SERVICE:	Of course. Please sit down.
SALESPERSON:	[Reviews the notes Service passed to him and allows time for Planner to sip her drink.] Let's review what we have agreed on so far. Our banquet room, meeting rooms, and guestroom accommodations all meet with your approval. So let me briefly tell you about other features of the Regency which I think will also please you. Since most of your members will probably arrive by car, they'll appreciate our location next to the freeway—and our parking garage. The garage is well-lit and is continuously monitored by video cameras on each level. [Short pause.] You mentioned earlier that poor service has been a problem for this group in the past, didn't you?
PLANNER:	Yes.
SALESPERSON:	I hope I can reassure you on that matter as well. We have an extensive employee training program and continually stress the importance of caring for the needs of our guests. I know that sounds like a standard sales pitch, but we really believe in service at the Regency. If I may again refer to our last group meeting, Mr. Clingaman himself praised our service as the best in the state.
PLANNER:	[Writes on her pad.]
SALESPERSON:	We have 24-hour room service. We offer savings with our free telephone and message service. In addition, we're prepared to offer your group free shuttle service between the airport and the hotel, for those who need it. And we'll provide free transportation for your members who want to visit the many attractions in town. Sally informs me that the local symphony will be performing during your stay with us, and our baseball team will be hosting the Tigers that weekend. [Pauses to let Planner take notes, then begins flipping through the pages in the presentation notebook, showing Planner 5- by 8-inch color pictures of the hotel's facilities.] We have excellent fitness facilities, including a heated pool, an exercise room, and tennis courts, and there's a jogging trail in the park next to us. Would you like to see some of our banquet menus?
PLANNER:	[Shows signs of being overwhelmed—or is it fatigue?] No, I'm familiar with your food service.
SALESPERSON:	Can I assume then that you've dined with us and have been pleased?
PLANNER:	[Smiles—thank heaven!] Yes.
SALESPERSON:	Excellent! It sounds like we meet all your requirements. Shall we discuss price then?
PLANNER:	Yes, please.
SALESPERSON:	Good. [Displays a rate schedule in the presentation notebook.] The rate for our standard rooms is $70 per night. Our suites are $150. To cover overhead costs, we charge $200 per session for the banquet room and $50 for each of the meeting rooms. And, as you are aware, our food prices are quite reasonable. I might add that the Regency is the only hotel in the city that actually charges less than dining room menu prices for the same dinners provided at banquets. Is there any additional information you'd like?
PLANNER:	I'm convinced your facilities would meet the association's needs. And your reputation for service is quite good. Frankly, that's the main reason I considered your hotel. But your guestroom prices are considerably higher than hotels I've contacted elsewhere in the state, and they don't charge for their function space. I don't think I can sell the total cost involved to the selection committee.
SALESPERSON:	[Knowing the answer:] Do you feel our competitors offer the kind of quality in service and function rooms that we do?

PLANNER:	No, you have a clear advantage there. And I'm sure my job would be less stressful if we meet here. But cost is an important factor to the association because of its limited budget.
SALESPERSON:	I'm afraid our room rates are firm; I just can't adjust that area. If we forfeited the charge for the function space, would you commit to us?
PLANNER:	That would help. But isn't there something else you could do as a show of good faith to help me sell the Regency to the committee? [Pause.] How about providing a free cocktail hour on the opening day? I think that would convince them.
SALESPERSON:	Fine, if you will commit to us that the Regency will be your only recommendation to the committee.
PLANNER:	Agreed. [Smiles and extends her hand to consummate the deal.]
SALESPERSON:	[Accepts the handshake and smiles in return.] Great! I'll send you a letter tomorrow summarizing what we've agreed to today.

Discussion Questions

1. What did the salesperson do correctly? Was anything done incorrectly?

2. Do you think it was a good idea to have the convention service manager sit in on the presentation?

3. Can you point out in the presentation examples of the following?

   a. Open- and close-ended questions

   b. Fact- and feeling-finding questions

   c. Test closes

   d. Objections

   e. Third-party endorsements

   f. Major close

4. Would you make any changes in the presentation? If so, what changes would you make?

Glossary

A

ADVANCE DEPOSIT

A deposit the guest furnishes for a room reservation that the hotel is holding.

ADVERTISING AGENCY

A company that furnishes advertising and marketing services to clients. Ad agencies may be paid by a commission from the media or a predetermined fee from the client.

AFFILIATED HOTEL

One of a chain, franchise, or referral system, membership in which provides special advantages, particularly a national reservation system.

AGENCY COMMISSION

A commission the media pays to an advertising agency. It is expressed as a percentage (usually 15%) of the gross advertising rate.

AGENCY FEE

A dollar amount agreed upon, in advance, by the agency and client which compensates the agency for all services in lieu of commission.

AIDA

An acronym for *attention, interest, desire,* and *action,* which is a formula designed to catch customers' attention, get them interested, create a desire to buy, and generate action.

AIRPORT HOTEL

A hotel located near a public airport. Airport hotels vary widely in size and service level.

A LA CARTE

A term that describes meal items priced separately on the menu.

ALL-EXPENSE TOUR

A tour offering all or most services—transportation, lodging, meals, sight-seeing, and so on—for a pre-established price. The terms "all-expense" and "all-inclusive" are much misused. Virtually no tour rate covers everything. The terms and conditions of a tour contract should specify exactly what is covered.

AMERICAN HOTEL & MOTEL ASSOCIATION (AH&MA)

A federation of state and regional hotel associations which offers benefits and services to hospitality properties and suppliers. AH&MA reviews proposed legislation affecting hotels, sponsors seminars and group study programs, conducts research, and publishes *Lodging* magazine. The Educational Institute of AH&MA is the world's largest developer of hospitality industry training materials, including textbooks, videotapes, seminars, courses, and software.

AMERICAN PLAN

A room rate that includes three meals.

AMERICAN SOCIETY OF TRAVEL AGENTS (ASTA)

A trade association of travel agents, tour operators, and suppliers to the industry with worldwide membership exceeding 13,000. ASTA's purpose is to promote and advance the interests of the travel agency industry and safeguard the traveling public against unethical practices.

AMTRAK

The name under which the National Railroad Passenger Corporation operates almost all U.S. intercity passenger trains. The intercity trains are usually operated under contract with individual railroads.

ATTRACTION

A natural or synthetic facility, location, or activity which offers items of specific interest, such as a natural or scenic wonder, a theme park, a cultural or historic exhibition, or a wildlife/ecological park.

AUDIENCE

A group of households or individuals who listen to, view, or read a communications medium.

AUDIENCE PROFILE

A description of the characteristics (sex, age, income, etc.) of individuals or households exposed to a medium. May also refer to the minute-by-minute viewing pattern of a television or radio program.

AUDIMETER

An electronic device attached to TV or radio sets in the sample households of A.C. Nielsen. It records set usage and channel information on a minute-by-minute basis, 24 hours a day.

B

BACK OF THE HOUSE

The functional areas of a hotel in which personnel have little or no direct guest contact, such as engineering and accounting.

BANQUET

A formal dinner for a select group.

BANQUET CONTRACT

The form used between hotel and client to confirm banquet arrangements.

BILLBOARD

A large panel designed to carry outdoor advertising.

BOOK

To sell hotel space, either to an individual or to a group needing a block of rooms.

BREAKOUT MEETING

A meeting that supplements a convention or larger meeting.

BROCHURE

A printed folder containing descriptive or advertising material.

BUFFET

An assortment of foods offered on a table in self-service fashion.

BUS

In the travel industry the word *bus* is reserved for a vehicle that provides scheduled service for an individually ticketed passenger. When used to perform any group tour service, the same vehicle is called a motorcoach.

C

CANCELLATION

A reservation voided at the guest's request.

CASH BAR

A private room bar setup where guests pay for their drinks. Sometimes called a COD bar or an à la carte bar.

CASINO HOTEL

A hotel with gambling facilities.

CENTRAL RESERVATIONS OFFICE

Part of an affiliate reservation network. A central reservations office typically deals directly with the public, advertises a central (usually toll-free) telephone number, provides participating properties with necessary communications equipment, and bills properties for handling reservations.

CHANNELS OF DISTRIBUTION

The methods by which sellers reach potential buyers. Travel agents, tour operators, and tour wholesalers are part of this system within the tourism industry.

CHARTER

To hire the exclusive use of any aircraft, vessel, or other vehicle.

CIRCULATION

Broadcast advertising: The number of set-owning homes within the station's coverage area. *Outdoor advertising*: The number of people passing an advertisement with an opportunity to view it. *Print advertising*: The number of copies sold or distributed by the publication.

COMMERCIAL HOTEL

A property, usually located in a downtown or business district, that caters primarily to business clients. Also called a transient hotel.

COMMERCIAL RATE

A special room rate, lower than rack rate, agreed upon by a hotel and a company. Also called a corporate rate.

COMMISSIONABLE RATE

The special rate a hotel or other facility quotes, from which travel agents may deduct a commission or upon which the hotel or facility will pay a commission.

COMPLIMENTARY ROOM

A complimentary or "comp" room is a room that is occupied, but the guest is not charged for its use. A hotel may offer comp rooms to a group in ratio to the total number of rooms the group occupies. One comp room may be offered for each fifty rooms occupied, for example.

COMPETITION ANALYSIS

An evaluation of a business's competition to identify opportunities and unique selling points. Part of a marketing audit.

CONCIERGE

An employee whose task is to serve as the guest's liaison with hotel and non-hotel attractions, facilities, services, and activities.

CONDUCTED TOUR

(1) A pre-arranged travel program, usually for a group, which includes escort service; (2) a sight-seeing program conducted by a guide, such as a city tour. Also called an escorted tour.

CONFERENCE CENTER

A property specifically designed to handle group meetings. Conference centers are often located outside metropolitan areas and may provide extensive leisure facilities. Most offer overnight accommodations.

CONFIRMED RESERVATION

An oral or written statement by a supplier (a carrier, hotel, car rental company, etc.) that he or she has received and will honor a reservation. Oral confirmations have virtually no legal worth. Even written or telegraphed confirmations have specified or implied limitations. For example, a hotel is not obligated to honor a confirmed reservation if the guest arrives after 6 p.m., unless late arrival is specified.

CONTINENTAL BREAKFAST

A small morning meal which usually includes a beverage, rolls, butter, and jam or marmalade.

CONTINENTAL PLAN

A room rate that includes continental breakfast.

COOPERATIVE ADVERTISING

A pooling of marketing dollars by several businesses for promotional purposes in order to increase market impact or reduce marketing costs.

COVERAGE

The homes which a broadcast station's signal can reach. Also refers to the number of individuals or groups exposed to a specific medium or advertisement within a specific period of time.

COVERS

The actual number of meals served at a food function.

CROSS-SELLING

In internal merchandising, cross-selling is using media in one area of the property to promote a different area. Employees can also cross-sell: employees working at one facility can suggest that guests take advantage of other facilities and services offered at the property.

CRT (CATHODE RAY TUBE)

An output device of a computer system which is usually capable of displaying both text and graphics. Also called a monitor, a display screen, or simply a screen.

D

DESTINATION

In the travel industry, any city, area, or country that can be marketed as a single entity to tourists.

DIFFERENTIATION

A marketing strategy designed to emphasize the unique selling points of a business and the differences between that business and its competitors.

DIRECT FLIGHT

A journey on which the passenger does not have to change planes. Not necessarily non-stop.

DIRECT MAIL ADVERTISING

Advertising mailed to the consumer's residence, containing copy that tries to motivate the reader to purchase a product or utilize a service. May contain a response mechanism for ordering by return mail.

DISCOUNTING

Marking down the normal room rates by some percentage or dollar amount. Discounts are usually directed toward particular markets or are instituted during a particular time or season.

DOUBLE OCCUPANCY RATE

A rate used for tours where the per-person charge is based on two to a room.

E

ESCORT

A person, usually employed by a tour operator, who accompanies a tour from departure to return and serves as guide, trouble-shooter, etc.

EXECUTIVE FLOOR

A floor of a hotel which offers exceptional service to business and other travelers. Also called a business floor or the tower concept.

EUROPEAN PLAN

A room rate that does not include any meals.

F

FAMILIARIZATION TOUR

A complimentary or reduced-rate travel program. A familiarization or "fam" tour is designed to acquaint travel agents, meeting planners, travel writers, and others with a specific destination or destinations and stimulate sales.

FAMILY RATE

A special room rate for parents and children in the same guestroom.

FEEDER CITY

A city other than the property's city from which guests arrive.

FLAT RATE

A specific room rate for a group, agreed upon by the hotel and the group in advance. Also called "run-of-the-house rate."

FLIER

A printed advertisement intended for distribution to potential clients or guests, usually by mail.

FOLIO

A statement of all transactions affecting the balance of a single account.

FORECAST

A future projection of estimated business volume.

FRONT DESK

The focal point of activity within the hotel, usually prominently located in the hotel lobby. Guests are registered, assigned rooms, and checked out at the front desk.

FRONT DESK AGENT

A hotel employee whose responsibilities center on the registration process, but also typically include preregistration activities, room status coordination, and mail, message, and information requests.

FRONT OF THE HOUSE

The functional areas of the hotel in which employees have extensive guest contact, such as food and beverage facilities and the front office.

FUNCTION BOOK

The master control of all banquet space, broken down on each page by banquet rooms and restaurants, with a page for each day of the year.

G

GATEWAY CITY

A city with an airport that handles direct flights from other countries.

GOVERNMENT RATE

A special room rate made available at some properties for government employees.

GROUND OPERATOR

A company or individual providing such services as hotel accommodations, sight-seeing, transfers, and other related services, exclusive of transportation to and from a given destination. Sometimes called a purveyor.

GROUP RATE

A special room rate for a number of affiliated guests.

GUARANTEE

The figure which a function or meeting planner gives to the hotel at least 24 hours before the function for the number of persons to be served. Most hotels are prepared to serve 5% to 10% over the guaranteed figure. Payment is made on the basis of the guaranteed number of covers or the total number served, whichever is greater.

GUARANTEED RESERVATION

A reservation which assures the guest that a room will be held until check-out time of the day following the day of arrival. The guest guarantees payment for the room, even if it is not used, unless the reservation is properly canceled. Types of guaranteed reservations include prepayment, credit card, advance deposit, travel agent, and corporate.

GUEST HISTORY CARD

A record of the guest's visits including rooms assigned, rates, special needs, and credit rating.

GUEST MIX

The variety and percentage distribution of hotel guests: individual, group, business, leisure, etc.

GUESTROOM CONTROL BOOK

A book used to monitor the number of guestrooms committed to groups.

H

HOST BAR

A private room bar setup with drinks prepaid by the host or sponsor. Sometimes called a sponsored bar.

HOTEL REPRESENTATIVE

An individual who offers hotel reservations to wholesalers, travel agents, and the public. A hotel representative or "rep" may be paid by the hotels he or she represents on a fee basis or by commission. Many hotel reps also offer marketing and other services.

HOTEL SALES & MARKETING ASSOCIATION INTERNATIONAL (HSMAI)

A professional society of hotel salespeople, managers, owners, and other sales-minded hotel executives, dedicated to the further education of its members. HSMAI conducts seminars, clinics, workshops, an annual convention, and publishes a quarterly magazine, *HSMAI Marketing Review*, as well as books and pamphlets on hospitality sales.

I

INCENTIVE TRAVEL

Travel financed by a business as an employee incentive.

INCLUSIVE TOUR

A tour in which specific elements—air fare, hotels, transfers, etc.—are included for a flat rate. An inclusive tour rate does not necessarily cover all costs.

INDEPENDENT HOTEL

A hotel with no chain or franchise affiliation, although one proprietor might own several such properties.

L

LETTER OF AGREEMENT

A document listing services, space, and products that becomes binding when signed by both parties.

LOCAL RATE

A rate the media offer to local advertisers which is lower than the national rate.

LOGO

The name of a company or product in a special design used as a trademark.

M

MAILING LIST

A list of the names, addresses, and, in some cases, titles of persons to be reached by direct mail. It can be a commercial, general, or house list.

MARKET

A geographic area defined by media coverage or sales patterns. Also refers to a population group that has purchasing power and is a prime prospect for an advertiser's product or service.

MARKETING

A system of interacting activities formulated to plan, price, promote, and make available services or products to potential customers or guests in a particular target market.

MARKETING MIX

The combination of the four "Ps" of marketing—product, price, place, and promotion—that is used to achieve marketing objectives for a target market.

MARKETPLACE ANALYSIS

An evaluation of the environmental trends and forces affecting a business, such as changes in lifestyles and societal values, economic conditions, and technology. Part of a situation analysis.

MARKET RESEARCH

The use of various techniques to obtain data on past and potential customers or guests. Used by a business to improve its marketing effectiveness.

MARKET SEGMENTATION

Dividing the market into groups of consumers with similar needs, wants, backgrounds, incomes, buying habits, and so on.

MARKET SHARE

The amount of a market a business captures relative to the total market.

MASTER ACCOUNT

One folio prepared for a group on which all group charges are accumulated. Also called a master folio.

MASTER CARD

An index card that contains a summary of everything needed for a sales effort, including the organization's name, the decision-maker(s), key contacts, addresses, telephone numbers, and so on.

MODIFIED AMERICAN PLAN

A room rate that includes two meals—typically breakfast and dinner.

MOTORCOACH

A large highway passenger vehicle used to perform any travel service other than scheduled transportation for individually ticketed passengers. Contains such passenger comfort items as climate control, carpeting, reclining seats, pillow service, etc.

N

NATIONAL TOUR ASSOCIATION

A trade association of U.S. motorcoach operators federally licensed and bonded by the Interstate Commerce Commission with the purpose of promoting member professionalism and motorcoach tour development.

NO-SHOW

(1) A passenger or guest who fails either to use or cancel his or her reservation. (2) A reservation neither canceled nor fulfilled.

O

OCCUPANCY AND ACTIVITY ANALYSIS

An analysis of a property's past, present, and potential operating statistics. Part of a situation analysis.

OPTION DATE

The pre-arranged date by which a tentative agreement between a buyer and seller must become a definite agreement or become void.

OVERBOOKING

Committing more rooms than are actually available to possible guest occupancy.

OVERSTAY

A guest who stays after his or her stated departure date.

P

PACKAGE

A special offering of products and services created by a hotel to increase sales. There are weekend packages, honeymoon packages, sports packages, and so on. A typical package might include the guestroom, meals, and the use of the property's recreational facilities for a special price.

PACKAGER

An individual or organization coordinating and promoting the development of a package tour and establishing operating procedures and guidelines for the tour.

PACKAGE TOUR

A salable travel product which offers, at an inclusive price, several travel elements which a traveler would otherwise purchase separately. A package tour can include, in varying degrees, any or all of the following elements: lodging; sight-seeing; attractions; meals; entertainment; car rental; and transportation by air, motorcoach, rail, or even private vehicle. A package tour may include more than one destination.

PAINTED DISPLAY

An outdoor advertisement painted on a billboard or wall which is usually illuminated.

PEAK PERIOD

Also known as "in-season," this is the period when demand for a property and its services is highest. Maximum rates may be charged at this time.

PERSONAL SELLING

A method of securing business through direct personal contact with potential clients or guests.

POINT-OF-PURCHASE MATERIALS

Tent cards, posters, displays, and other materials placed in prominent areas of the hotel to influence buying decisions.

POSITIONING

A marketing term used to describe how consumers perceive the products and services offered by a particular hotel in relation to similar products and services offered by competitors. Positioning strategies attempt to establish in the minds of consumers a particular image of a hotel's products and services.

PREREGISTRATION

A process by which sections of a registration card or its equivalent are completed for guests arriving with reservations. Room and rate assignment, creation of a guest folio, and other functions may also be part of preregistration activity.

PROPERTY ANALYSIS

An evaluation of a business's facilities, services, and programs to determine its strengths and weaknesses. Part of a marketing audit.

PUBLICITY

The gratuitous mention in the media of an organization's people, products, or services.

PUBLIC RELATIONS

A systematic effort by a business to communicate favorable information about itself to the public in order to create a positive impression.

Q

QUALIFY

The act of determining if a prospect has a need for or can afford the products and services offered by a property.

R

RACK RATE

The standard rate established by a property for a particular category of rooms.

RATE CARD

A printed statement of advertising rates and general information about a medium.

REACH

In print, the number of individuals or households estimated to be in the readership of a given publication or group of publications. In broadcast, the number or percent of an audience exposed to one or more announcements or programs.

RECIPROCAL ADVERTISING

The exchange of an advertiser's products or services to pay for all or part of the medium's time or space. Also called due bill advertising.

REGISTRATION CARD

A printed form the guest completes upon arrival, giving name, address, and other information.

RESERVATION

An agreement between a hotel and a guest that the hotel will hold a specific type of room for a particular date and length of stay.

RESERVATIONS AGENT

An employee, either in the front office or in a separate department, who is responsible for all aspects of reservations processing.

RESORT HOTEL

A hotel which provides scenery and activities unavailable at most other properties, and whose guests are typically vacationers.

RETAIL TRAVEL AGENT

An individual qualified to arrange and sell transportation and other travel services and products directly to the public.

RIFLE APPROACH

To concentrate sales or marketing efforts on narrowly defined targets.

ROOM BLOCK

An agreed-upon number of rooms set aside for members of a group planning to stay at a hotel.

ROOMING LIST

A list of guests who will occupy reserved accommodations, submitted by the buyer in advance.

ROOM RATE

The price a hotel charges for overnight accommodations.

ROP COLOR

In newspaper advertising, this is color used in regular sections of the paper and printed on standard newsprint.

S

SALES PROMOTIONS

Promotional activities that are neither personal selling nor media advertising. Sales promotions include offering free samples or discount coupons; staging contests, exhibits, or displays; and attending trade shows.

SALES SUPPORT MATERIALS

Materials used to assist in selling, such as printed brochures, endorsement letters, charts, video brochures, and posters.

SELF-MAILER

Direct mail literature that folds up to make its own envelope.

SERVICE CHARGE

A percentage of the bill (usually 10% to 20%) added for distribution to service employees in lieu of direct tipping.

SHOTGUN APPROACH

To spread sales or marketing efforts broadly over the market.

SHOULDER PERIOD

This is a period when the level of business for a property falls somewhere between its peak and valley periods.

SITUATION ANALYSIS

A comprehensive evaluation of a business's current position in the marketplace. Part of a marketing audit.

STANDARD ADVERTISING UNIT (SAU)

A measurement one column wide by one inch deep. National newspaper and magazine advertising is often quoted in terms of SAUs.

STAYOVER

A room status term indicating that the guest is not checking out and will remain at least one more night.

STORYBOARD

A series of drawings illustrating the characters, action, and dialogue of a proposed television commercial.

SUGGESTIVE SELLING

The practice of influencing a guest's purchase decision through the use of sales phrases.

SUITE HOTEL

A hotel whose sleeping rooms have separate bedroom and living room or parlor areas, and perhaps a kitchenette.

T

TABLOID

A newspaper smaller than a standard newspaper.

TARGET MARKETS

Market segments that a property identifies as having the greatest potential, and toward which marketing activities are aimed.

TEST MARKETING

(1) The testing of a marketing or media concept in a selected market or markets; (2) an advertising campaign conducted in conjunction with research tools to determine the advisability of extending a marketing program to a broader area of the country.

TOUR

Any pre-arranged (but not necessarily prepaid) journey to one or more places and back to the point of origin.

TOUR BROKER

An individual licensed and bonded by the Interstate Commerce Commission to operate motorcoach tours in the United States and, in some cases, Canada, as permitted by the scope of his or her license. Also known as a motorcoach broker or tour operator.

TOUR VOUCHER

A document issued by tour brokers to be exchanged for accommodations, meals, sight-seeing, and other services. Sometimes called coupons.

TOUR WHOLESALER

An individual who puts tour packages together, usually involving air transportation.

TRACE CARD

A 3- by 5-inch index card used as a reminder to call a client or check a cut-off date, filed by call-back date.

TRAFFIC COUNT

In outdoor advertising, the tabulation of pedestrians and vehicles passing an outdoor display during a specific time period.

TRANSFER

Local transportation and/or porterage from one carrier terminal to another, from a terminal to a hotel, or from a hotel to a theater. The conditions of a tour contract should specify whether transfers are by private car, taxi, or motorcoach, and whether escort service and/or porterage is provided.

TRAVEL AGENT COMMISSION

The varying amount a travel agent receives from a supplier for selling transportation, accommodations, or other services.

U

UNIQUE SELLING POINT

A competitive advantage that a business has over other businesses serving the same target markets.

UNITED STATES TRAVEL DATA CENTER

A non-profit organization devoted to the development and standardization of travel research. It publishes statistical compendiums and provides indices to measure travel, recreation, and tourism development.

UNITED STATES TRAVEL AND TOURISM ASSOCIATION (USTTA)

The official U.S. agency for the promotion of travel to and within the United States and its possessions. USTTA is an agency of the U.S. Department of Commerce.

UPGRADE

To move to a better accommodation or class of service.

V

VALLEY PERIOD

Also known as "off-season," valleys are times when demand for a property and its services is lowest. Reduced room rates are often offered during valley periods to attract business.

W

WHOLESALE TRAVEL AGENT

An individual who specializes in putting tour packages together for individual business and leisure travelers. These tours are usually marketed to the public through retail travel agents or the airlines.

Index

Educational Institute Fellows

Respected industry experts who serve as advisors to the Board of Trustees

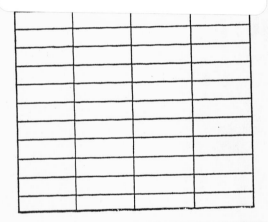